Gift of
Mrs. Grayce Cuddy
1966

# LINCOLN
# THE PRESIDENT

*MIDSTREAM*

\* \* \*

BY

## J. G. Randall

**PROFESSOR OF HISTORY
IN THE UNIVERSITY OF ILLINOIS**

*ILLUSTRATED*

DODD, MEAD & COMPANY
NEW YORK · · 1953

*To Ruth Painter Randall*
*biographer of Mrs. Lincoln*

# PREFACE

THIS study of President Lincoln finds the nation's Chief in the midst of his crucial administration. In a great complexity of public affairs attention is focused on the man and his work. Biography is an interplay of character and incident, of the person and the world about him. Lincoln's world was a vast stage. It was not merely the United States—certainly not merely "the North" or Washington—but the larger world in terms of that fundamental democracy envisaged at Gettysburg. To Lincoln the American ideal was based on no narrow concept. In speeches and writings before and during the presidency he repeatedly interpreted the American experiment in its bearing upon the cause of free government in the world.

Two questions, reciprocal in nature, arise as to Lincoln. What effect did the war, the appalling crisis, and the challenge of many problems have upon his personality? And in what respects were the developments of that troubled era different because it was Lincoln, and not another man, in the presidential chair? There are, of course, other questions. In biography there is always the factor of an impression, or portrait, of the man. How near we can come to a recovery of the real Lincoln it is not easy to say; for these pages the effort at recovery has been a matter of primary record, contemporary portrayal, and direct evidence. Such portrayal is not easy for the inner man—perhaps that is why Mark Twain considered biography to be little more than "clothes and buttons"—but for Lincoln there is more revelation of his deepest thought than is usually realized. It is desirable to seek historical appraisal in terms of large perspective, but that is not the whole task. There remains the close-up view—the mobile face, gesture, playful quip, laugh or sigh, small talk and off-duty jest. Both the broad picture and the complete limning of the immediate portrait may be unattainable in the full sense. Inadequate presentation of Lincoln is all too common. The subject has been voluminously treated without being "exhausted." Yet a new delineation may have value without aspiring to finality.

The theme is not one for hasty conclusions. One could easily emphasize the many contradictions that pervade the inquiry, yet such is the nature of historical investigation. A distinction is not worthless because it breaks down at the border, and a showing of unlike factors does not invalidate essential truth. The multiplicity of claims for Lincoln, or the numerous appropriations of his name for sponsorship of this or that view or faction, should not lead to the assumption that Lincoln himself was inconclusive or incapable of being associated with particular movements or ideals. The very intensity of opposition to him within his own party is evidence that he was taking a stand and asserting his position.

If, therefore, one discovers opposites in Lincoln research, if a generalization is worked up only to be followed by the finding of counteracting evidence, that should be taken as indicating that the subject itself is many-sided. A seeming inconsistency should not greatly disturb the mature student. Some would have said that Lincoln "saw everybody"; yet often he was inaccessible. He had a dignity and appropriateness, yet an "irresistibly ludicrous" informality. He dripped with sadness, yet exploded with laughter and anecdote. Among all our Presidents he was one of the most resourceful and eloquent in his use of the English language, yet he often slipped back into the cruder dialect of untutored folk. One could quote him for high eloquence but also for frivolity. He was denounced as a dictator; yet he was the very opposite of the militarist and the supposition that he trampled on civil rights needs to be reëxamined. There were those who from lack of understanding assailed him as a war maker; yet in his inaugural of 1861 he spoke with pathetic earnestness for peace, and in the interview with Mrs. Gurney he said that if he had had his way the war would never have begun. Some writers picture Lincoln as a great strategist or a supreme military genius; others point to incompetence and lack of effective control in military administration as directed from Washington. Instead of being upset by such contradictory elements one learns to reserve judgment, to give the second look, to keep in mind that history is not always reducible to easy generalization, and to remember that, for Lincoln as for every President, the adoption of a "general policy" did not preclude the necessity for many an individual adjustment.

For the most part the bibliography for the first two volumes serves for the present work. Other titles, however, original and secondary, are given in the annotations. Perhaps in general, footnotes should be held guilty unless proved innocent, but in these pages it is hoped they will not obtrude. They indicate sources, and for a treatment that continually calls for the showing of credentials such verification can hardly be ignored. It is believed also that they serve other purposes, but enough! The intent here is not to unloose a disquisition on historical evidence.

It has been considered desirable, in fact indispensable, to give some account of the Lincoln papers opened to investigators in July 1947; this topic has been set off to itself in an appendix. It is not claimed that the importance of that vast collection has been adequately indicated or its unique flavor conveyed; only an extended account of the many thousands of items could serve that purpose. While writing this volume the author has been, as it were, caught between two editions of Lincoln's writings. Previously it has been necessary to rely upon the so-called *Complete Works* of Lincoln edited by Nicolay and Hay (in two large volumes, later in twelve small ones); but as the present book "goes to press" (with all the finality of that dread phrase) the important new edition known as *The Collected Works of Abraham Lincoln,* in preparation for many years under the editorship of the Abraham Lincoln Association, is nearing its day of publication. Because of imperfect editing and great incompleteness, the Nicolay-Hay edition is plainly outmoded, yet the new set is still awaited. In this situation, though some references to Nicolay and Hay are kept, the actual words of Lincoln have been collated with photostats (of originals) in the files of the Abraham Lincoln Association.

Of necessity the author's many acknowledgments must be briefly and inadequately expressed. The University of Illinois has supplied the services of an assistant and has acquired extensive bodies of microfilms and photostats. The rich holdings of its library on the Lincoln theme, built up over many years, have been in constant use. These resources have been greatly enhanced by the generous donation of one of the greatest private Lincoln collections, that of Harlan Hoyt

Horner of Albany, New York.

To the noble profession of librarians a great debt is due. This is especially true of that important national institution, the Library of Congress, not only for the notable Robert Todd Lincoln Collection long kept in faithful custody and opened in 1947, but for a vast amount of other original material on Lincoln and his time. The resources of the National Archives, a voluminous treasure for which guidance and skilled access is essential, have yielded significant results; this has been made possible by the aid, counsel, and serviceableness of its willing staff. The author is also grateful to the Harvard Library, the Massachusetts Historical Society, the Boston Public Library, the New York Public Library, the New York Historical Society, Brown University, the Detroit Public Library, the University of Wisconsin Historical Society. Institutional service, of course, is always human service, as shown by the personal and scholarly contribution of Robert Gerald McMurtry of Harrogate, Tennessee, editor of the *Lincoln Herald* and director of the department of Lincolniana at Lincoln Memorial University. Of special value has been the Lincoln National Life Foundation at Fort Wayne, where elaborate files have been opened and interpreted by the friendly helpfulness of Dr. Louis A. Warren. Closer home, access has been given to the manuscripts of the Chicago Historical Society (including new-found Lincoln letters), the Illinois State Historical Library, and the Abraham Lincoln Association. Only by using that Association's full set of sources (in photostat), the Historical Library's rich collection of Lincoln originals, and similar depositories over the country, can one appreciate how largely Lincoln's own handwritten form for the great bulk of his writing is now available. The competent help of Dr. Roy P. Basler, secretary of the Abraham Lincoln Association and editor of the forthcoming set of Lincoln's works, is sincerely acknowledged while it cannot be fully recorded.

The Pratts—Harry E. Pratt of the Illinois State Historical Library and Mrs. Marion Bonzi Pratt of the Abraham Lincoln Association—stand high among the author's distinguished benefactors by reason of their incomparable knowledge, able guidance, and unstinting service. All who use the Illinois State Historical Library are familiar with the superior service of Miss Margaret Flint; to her a special recognition is due. In the Far West the Lincoln theme has been a matter of active interest and rewarding fellowship. The University of California at Berkeley has given helpful service through its Bancroft Collection, while at San Marino in the Los Angeles area the superb Henry E. Huntington Library seems to have been made for the combination of hard work with thrilling enjoyment. On both of these counts the author has profited by the assistance and understanding advice of the Huntington staff. To mention one member of that staff, Miss Norma Cuthbert, is to call to mind a scholar who has combined a high standard of librarianship with Lincoln authorship in her own right.

Carl Sandburg—that eloquent voice, eminent Lincoln writer, and beloved interpreter of the American spirit—has given encouragement and specific assistance. Indeed, in looking over the pages of this volume the author sees the footprints of friends in every chapter. He wishes herewith to record his indebtedness to Paul M. Angle, Lincoln authority and director of the Chicago Historical Society; to Theodore L. Agnew, Jr. of Stillwater, Oklahoma, for material on that redoubtable but elusive Peter Cartwright; to Miss Margaret C. Norton of the department of archives of the State of Illinois for search in original state documents; to David Rankin Barbee of Washington for the friendly sharing of material; and to that well known figure in the Lincoln fraternity, Ralph G. Newman of the Abraham Lincoln Book Shop in Chicago, whose establishment is a mecca for Lincoln devotees and who has been especially thoughtful in offering material and giving suggestions from his skilled experience. Writers often depend on collectors and in this sense as well as in friendship the author makes special acknowledgment to Alfred W. Stern, Foreman M. Lebold, and the late Oliver R. Barrett of Chicago. The important Barrett Collection, recently sold at auction in New York, is fortunately not lost to students; institutions have much of it and private collectors are usually generous with photostats. The Lincoln field is fortunately not a closed corporation.

For further response and assistance the author is grateful to S. L. M. Barlow of New York City; to Allan Nevins, editor of the series, *American Political Leaders;* to Frank Freidel of the University of Illinois, authority on Lieber; to Miss Marie K. Hochmuth of the department of speech of the University of Illinois for her penetrating study of Lincoln's 1861 inaugural; to George Winston Smith of the University of New Mexico, author of highly useful articles; and to that friend of Lincoln students in search of pictures, Frederick H. Meserve. South-

erners also have helped, and the assistance of Mr. William H. Town-
send of Lexington, Kentucky, has been a source of real delight. David
Donald of Columbia University, in critically reading many galleys of
proof, performed an invaluable service of friendship and of scholar-
ship.

In preparing the typed manuscript Miss Lida E. Voight has given
excellent service. Several graduate students of the University of Illinois have assisted in the heavy duty of research and checking. The
vigorous work of some of these young colleagues has been cited in
earlier volumes; more recently the author has been greatly benefited
by the indispensable support of Maurice G. Baxter now of Indiana
University, Lavern M. Hamand of Arkansas Polytechnic College
(Russellville), and Wayne C. Temple, now pursuing his work for the
doctor's degree at the University of Illinois. Each of these men, on
his own, has made significant contributions in the Lincoln field. For
example, the colorful personality and career of Noah Brooks is being
ably studied for a doctoral dissertation by Mr. Temple. The author
is especially grateful to Mrs. Helen Metz of Elmwood, Illinois, for the
superior quality of her assistance in preparing the index.

The author's wife, Ruth Painter Randall, after years of research
and with newly used material, has completed a life of Mrs. Lincoln
which is soon to be published. Since it is the history of a marriage—
a double biography—it is valuable for an understanding of the man
as well as of the wife. Her book deals fully with the personal life of
Lincoln. The writing of this competent biography during the period
when the present third volume has been in preparation, has been of
great advantage.

J. G. R.

Urbana, Illinois
May 31, 1952

# CONTENTS

CHAPTER | PAGE

I PRESIDENTIAL DAYS . . . . . . . . . . . . . . 1

II LONELY WHITE HOUSE PAIR . . . . . . . . . 20

III ATTENTION OF THE PRESIDENT . . . . . . . . . 42

IV THE GIFT OF LAUGHTER . . . . . . . . . . 59

V CAPITOL HILL . . . . . . . . . . . . . . 83

VI PRESIDENT AND CONGRESS . . . . . . . . . . 113

VII DEMOCRACY AND THE WAR POWER . . . . . . . 149

VIII "COPPERHEADS" AND PRISONERS OF STATE . . . . . 184

IX THE VALLANDIGHAM CASE . . . . . . . . . 212

X POLITICS IN 1863 . . . . . . . . . . . . 239

XI VALLANDIGHAM FOR GOVERNOR: FURTHER PHASES OF POLITICS, 1863 . . . . . . . . . . . . . . . 263

XII LINCOLN AND SEYMOUR . . . . . . . . . . 292

XIII NATIONS UNDER STRESS: UNITED STATES AND BRITAIN . . . 315

XIV FRIENDSHIP OF NATIONS . . . . . . . . . . 339

XV THE CHATTANOOGA FRONT: DEATH OF HELM . . . . . 363

XVI GRANT VERSUS BRAGG: MISSIONARY RIDGE: END OF 1863 . . 375

XVII "THIS STRANGE, QUAINT, GREAT MAN" . . . . . . 393

APPENDIX: THE OPENING OF THE LINCOLN PAPERS . . . 429

INDEX . . . . . . . . . . . . . . . 447

# CHAPTER I

# PRESIDENTIAL DAYS

THE year 1863 was a tremendous period for Lincoln. That was the year of the emancipation proclamation, of the first nation-wide draft, of draft riots, of Missouri troubles, of Copperhead turbulence, of Vallandigham agitation, of important international dealings, and of hard military campaigns in which the nation's fate was wavering. One needs only to mention Chancellorsville, Gettysburg, Vicksburg, Chattanooga, Chickamauga, and Missionary Ridge to realize how desperate was the growing contest on the war fronts, while mention of the Laird rams, of Napoleon III, and of Maximilian will serve to suggest the complications that arose in foreign fields.

At home it was, to an intense degree, a year of "politics." Politics was never adjourned during the whole war—though the loyal-opposition policy of Douglas would have been a factor toward such adjournment—and the year 1863 witnessed sharp and bitter contests in state and congressional elections which were of vital concern to the Lincoln administration. Finally, as the turbulent middle year drew to a close, the statesmanship of Lincoln rose vigorously to the greatest challenge of his age as he delivered his immortal Gettysburg address and turned from that, amid illness and critical fighting, to one of the most famous of his messages—the annual message to Congress of December 1863. In that message and in a simultaneous proclamation to the people, the President gave the outline of his formula for restoration. With more foresight than that of Congress he put forth a program of peace and genuine union without which the "honored dead" would have "died in vain" and the fearful conflict would have been meaningless. The whole crowded year could have been epitomized in Lincoln's phrase "environed with difficulties."

1

Fully to recover the inner story and over-all significance of the Lincoln administration is impossible, since the upheavals and emotions of that age, with their complexities and simultaneous manifestations, are beyond recall. To understand any one of Lincoln's major problems in its intensity and entirety was not even within the reach of his contemporaries. To get a merely approximate view of such things now is a large order. It may be for this reason that Lincoln is often cast in less than his full mold. It is not that the task of historical restoration can be completely performed, yet the effort for some restoration must be made.

It is in that sense that we shall try to see Lincoln struggling with his problems, adjusting his difficulties, reaching for solutions, watching a number of fronts at one time, and always keeping his eye on the main goal. The present volume will be concerned with this midstream phase, though with the necessity of omitting many factors in so complex a story. It may be well to begin with some of the things close at hand, to note the routine of presidential days, and to catch a glimpse of duties which the President could not evade.

I

Among the stories that have come down to us is that of Lincoln's remark when a friend from back home asked him "How does it feel to be President of the United States?" In reply, so the story goes, he referred to a man who was tarred and feathered and ridden out of town on a rail. When some one in the crowd asked how he enjoyed it, the tarred-and-feathered one answered: "If it were not for the honor of the thing, I'd much rather walk." The story might be apocryphal, but the point of the yarn is our present concern. There is hardly any country in which the highest office has such a dazzling preeminence as that of President of the United States. To those who seek the honor it is the supreme goal. What of those who attain it? It is not of record that Washington enjoyed the position, which brought him a world of grief and kept him away from his beloved Mount Vernon.

What of Lincoln? Was he exalted and elated by the fame and prestige of his great office? There is little record of any such feeling. He suffered unmerciful and unending abuse, much of it from his own party. At one time, as already noted, he said while President that he was more distressed than at any time in his life.[1] He is reported to have looked forward happily to the day when the burdens of office could be laid down. At times he might actually have wished to relinquish the position before his term expired, except for one factor: no man of character wants to be a quitter when he has a great task to perform. The realization that he must not fall short, must not fail the country or shirk responsibility, was always more of a motive with Lincoln than any personal pleasure in the holding of high office.

When he went to Gettysburg in November 1863 he was put on the program as an afterthought. The initial idea had been to emphasize the states, not the nation. There was little of presidential fanfare; indeed there was actual insult to Lincoln on the part of a heckler in a street audience. The orator of the day was the polished Everett. The President was invited after Everett. His convenience was but incidental, if it was considered at all. It was as if he were playing second fiddle, and it was unforeseen that his presence and his distinguished words would have great significance.[2] In making the trip to Gettysburg he had inadequate secretarial assistance, even in the scheduling of the journey. Stanton proposed that the President leave Washington at six o'clock of the day of dedication, travel laboriously via Baltimore, reach Gettysburg at noon, leave Gettysburg at six in the evening, and arrive at Washington at midnight, "thus doing all in one day."

Lincoln objected. He wrote: "I do not wish to so go that by the slightest accident we fail entirely, and, at the best, the whole to be a mere breathless running of the gauntlet."[3] The plan was accordingly changed and the presidential party arrived at Gettysburg the day before the ceremony. He gave his famous dedicatory speech to an audience tired by much standing and prolonged oratory. There was something in the occasion, or in his own sense of inadequacy, that gave him a feeling of depression and disappointment, as if he had not risen to the demands of the hour.

---

[1] *Lincoln the President*, II, 243.

[2] In the first annual report of the organization which promoted the Gettysburg dedication, signed by David Wills, Governor Curtin is emphasized and Everett featured as the orator, but Lincoln is not even mentioned.

[3] Lincoln's endorsement on note of Stanton, Nov. 17, 1863, Nicolay and Hay, *Works*, IX, 208.

Not long after returning from Gettysburg to Washington he became ill. The disease was reported as varioloid, a mild form of smallpox. The illness came at the Thanksgiving season, and at a time when the President was heavily engaged in preparing his important annual message to Congress with its accompanying proclamation.[4] People wondered about the disease, about which they were not well informed, and whether the President could die of it. There had been, as Stoddard later explained, slight thought of the President's health. Assassination fears were so familiar as to be "worn out," but another possible cause of death had hardly been contemplated. The White House was under a kind of half-quarantine, resulting not only in an unwonted loneliness, but in public apprehension. It was feared that Hamlin "could not step into Mr. Lincoln's shoes, and something of inestimable value would be lost to the country, even if Mr. Hamlin were twice as large a man as he is believed to be." It was characteristic of the clamor for office and public favors that "something like engineering" was required to protect the sick President from intruders. One of them, thought Stoddard, may have been thinking that "Lincoln could appoint him to-day and die to-morrow." The President continued to attend to official business in spite of his irritating illness. He even made it a subject of jest, suggesting the advantage of scaring office seekers by the statement that he had the smallpox, and wishing that his office might be in one of the smallpox hospitals, then reflecting on further thought that this would give him no relief. "They'd all go and get vaccinated, and they'd come buzzing back . . . ."[5]

---

[4] There are numerous records of Lincoln's illness. He explained to a governor why a response had been delayed, and reassured Mrs. Lincoln by daily telegrams while she was in New York (*Works*, IX, 216–217, 254). Various diarists mentioned the illness: "The President quite unwell" (Hay, Nov. 26); "The President has been sick ever since thursday" (Bates, Monday, Nov. 30); "The President returned ill [from Gettysburg], and . . . it was ascertained he had the varioloid" (Welles, Dec., 1863, otherwise undated). Account is taken of the sickness in the Lincoln Papers (R. T. L. Coll., 28719) and in newspapers of the day (*Nat. Repub'n*, Nov. 28; Cincinnati *Daily Gazette*, Nov. 30; N.Y. *Daily Tribune*, Dec. 2 and 10). Dr. Milton H. Shutes writes: "Lincoln became ill on the train leaving Gettysburg, so it is known that he was sick from the very day of the ceremony, November 19, until about the middle of December. . . . Varioloid is a mild form of smallpox acquired by the partially immune, . . . ." *Lincoln and the Doctors*, 85.

[5] Stoddard, *Inside the White House*, 190–192.

## II

Any day's run at the White House was crowded, tiring, and strenuous. According to Ben: Perley Poore,[1] the President was an early riser. In the morning he would devote two or three hours to correspondence, with a glance at the newspapers. He would have breakfast about nine, then walk over to the war department building, a few steps from the White House. Returning to the White House, he would go through the morning's mail with his private secretaries.[2] The preliminary screening of the mail, and the discarding of crank missives, was the function of W. O. Stoddard.[3] Some of the letters would be endorsed and sent to the appropriate department. Others were entrusted to a secretary who would make a note of Lincoln's suggestions for a reply. Still others would be retained by the President to be answered by himself. Nicolay and Hay were important and efficient helpers, but it is no disparagement of their valuable assistance to say, what is not fully realized, that Lincoln gave close and careful attention to his correspondence. He often wrote a letter twice (the first draft and the final copy) in his own hand, and was even known to draft entirely in his handwriting a letter to be issued over Hay's name.[4] "Every letter," wrote Poore, "receives attention"; he added that all that were "entitled to a reply" received one, "no matter . . . how inelegant the chirography might be."[5]

Letter writing over, the rest of the day would be taken up with manifold activities—social, official, ceremonial, often trivial, and al-

---

1 Poore's account is in Cincinnati *Daily Gazette*, Dec. 12, 1863, p. 1, c. 4.

2 For Nicolay's duties as secretary, see Helen Nicolay, *Lincoln's Secretary*, esp. chap. 7.

3 "There was a river of documents . . . . The larger number of the epistles belonged in one or another of the two tall wastebaskets which sat on either side of me . . . . It did seem to me as if the foulest blackguards on earth had made up their minds that they could abuse the President through the mails . . . . Added to these were the lunatics." "Face to Face With Lincoln," by his secretary, William O. Stoddard, ed. by William O. Stoddard, Jr., 135 *Atl. Mo.*, 333 (Mar., 1925).

4 A letter signed by John Hay and directed to J. C. Welling (July 25, 1864) was written by Lincoln himself. A draft of the letter in full is found in the Lincoln Papers, entirely in the President's handwriting. *Works*, X, 173–174; R. T. L. Coll., 34756. The matter in hand pertained to the hostile attitude of a certain Mr. Gibson. It was a difficult personal situation in which the President watched closely the wording of the letter that went out from the executive office, though he preferred that it be sent as a communication from his secretary. This is almost like ghost writing in reverse.

5 Cincinnati *Daily Gazette*, Dec. 12, 1863, p. 1, c. 4.

ways time consuming. About four o'clock the President would decline seeing any more callers. He and Mrs. Lincoln would then go
for a drive, or sometimes he would ride horseback. Dining at six, he
was usually joined by personal friends. His visits to the war office
were for a variety of purposes: chatting with a general (often Halleck), reading the military telegrams as they came over the wires
(though of course these messages could have been brought to him),
hearing what was new so that he could tell it, exchanging funny
stories, enjoying the peculiar argot of the telegraph office, holding
informal conferences, escaping White House crowds, and seeking
a retreat to avoid interruption when composing an important state
paper. The vivid account by David Homer Bates indicates that
Lincoln found enjoyment in these war department intervals. "His
tall, homely form," wrote Bates, "could be seen crossing the well-
shaded lawn between the White House and the War Department day
after day with unvaried regularity. . . . He seldom failed to come
over late in the evening before retiring, and sometimes would stay
all night in the War Department." [6] "Three or four times daily,"
wrote Gideon Welles, "the President goes to the War Department
and into the telegraph office to look over communications." [7] It was
natural for Welles to feel that he had less of a share in the President's daily attention than was due to a member of the cabinet and
the head of the navy department.

The war-department retreat was even referred to by Lincoln as
his "office." In a telegram on an October day in 1864 he wired former Secretary of War Cameron: "Am leaving office to go home." The
telegram was dated: "War Department, October 11, 1864." It implied
a distinction between the "office" in the war and navy building and
"home," which meant the White House. [8]

Lincoln's self-forgetfulness and his informal intimacy with private
secretaries sometimes made an amusing picture. In his diary of April
30, 1864, Hay noted: "A little after midnight . . . the President
came into the office laughing, with a volume of Hood's works in his
hand, to show Nico[lay] and me the little caricature 'An unfortunate
Bee-ing,' seemingly utterly unconscious that he with his short shirt

---

[6] David Homer Bates, *Lincoln in the Telegraph Office*, 7.
[7] Welles, *Diary*, II, 16.
[8] Lincoln to Cameron, Oct. 11, 1864, photograph, A. Lincoln Assoc.

hanging above his long legs & setting out behind like the tail feathers of an enormous ostrich was infinitely funnier than anything in the book he was laughing at. What a man it is! Occupied all day with matters of vast moment, deeply anxious about the fate of the greatest army in the world, with his own fame & future hanging on the events of the passing hour, he has such a wealth of simple bonhommie & good fellowship that he gets out of bed & perambulates the house in his shirt to find us that we may share with him the fun of one of poor Hood's queer little conceits." [9]

A glimpse of a harassed Executive unable to escape interruption even after going to bed appears in the following diary entry by Hay (November 2, 1863): "Tonight Schenck sent for copies of the correspondence between the President and Bradford. The Tycoon came into his room with the despatch in his hands, clad in an overcoat pure & simple reaching to his knees, & sleepily fumbled for the papers in his desk till he found them & travelled back to bed. I took the letters to the telegraph office & sent them off about midnight." [10]

## III

When the President went about he did not want body guards to accompany him, and there was in that day no regular force of secret service men comparable to that of a later day. Once he wrote to Secretary Stanton: "On reflection I think it will not do as a rule for the Adjutant General to attend me wherever I go: not that I have any objection to his presence, but that it would be an uncompensating incumbrance both to him and me. When it shall occur to me to go anywhere, I wish to be free to go at once, and not to have to notify the Adjutant General, and wait till he can get ready." Lincoln added: "It is better too, for the public service, that he shall give his time to the business of his office, and not to personal attendance on me." The correspondence indicates that the suggestion had come

---

9 Tyler Dennett, ed., *Lincoln and the Civil War in the Diaries and Letters of John Hay*, 179 (Apr. 30, 1864). Hereafter cited: Dennett, ed., . . . *Diaries* . . . *of John Hay*.

10 *Ibid.*, 115. The correspondence with A. W. Bradford, governor of Maryland, concerned the state-and-Federal problem of giving protection to loyal men at the polls when voting for state officers. Major General Robert C. Schenck was in command in Maryland. *Works*, IX, 196–198 (Nov. 2, 1863).

from the secretary of war; one wonders, not at the proposal for guarding the President, but at Stanton's impractical suggestion that the adjutant general should be the official assigned to that duty.[1]

It is not to be supposed that Lincoln was altogether unprotected or that the problem of his bodily safety was ignored. It was rather that the guarding of the President was irregular, haphazard, and inefficient, and that perhaps he preferred it so. This caused considerable worry, as shown by the advice of an anxious soul, who wrote: "You are accustomed in riding out, to be escorted by a Body guard, and you invariably take a distance ahead; and generally any number of persons follow you, either in Vehicles, or Horseback, and your habit is, to frequently ride out to your Summer retreat Soldiers Home . . . . I cannot help, but warn you. If you value your life! *do* I entreat of you discontinue your visits out of the City. Unless, less conspicuously." [2]

If this anonymous writer was concerned about the President's safety, what about his wife? It was a constant and painful worry to Mrs. Lincoln. She would insist that he have some protection—a cavalry guard, for example—as he went back and forth to or from the Soldiers' Home. (It appears that such protection was occasional rather than regular or invariable.) He would brush her off, though far from relieving her fears. "All imagination," he was quoted as saying. "What does any one want to harm me for? Don't worry about me, mother, as if I were a little child, . . . ." [3]

Along with his strong distaste for being escorted or guarded, Lincoln paid little attention to fears of assassination. Since there were "a thousand ways" of getting at him, he believed that guards could not effectively ward off the danger; if anyone wanted to kill him, he would do it. (Not a comforting principle for those genuinely concerned for his safety.) Early in the administration General Charles P. Stone, by his own report, took careful, though unostentatious, measures for the guarding of the Executive Mansion and grounds.

---

[1] Lincoln to Sec. of War, Jan. 22, 1862, copy, photostat, A. Lincoln Assoc. This questionable suggestion was one of the very first acts of Stanton on assuming the headship of the war department.

[2] The name of this writer, who was otherwise anonymous, was signed "Lizzie." Robert Todd Lincoln Collection, Lib. of Cong., 34900-01 (July 1864). This great collection of the papers of Lincoln will hereafter be given the short citation: R. T. L. Coll.

[3] Elizabeth Keckley, *Behind the Scenes,* 119.

He placed sentries in the shrubbery, put an armed guard in the basement, and put this guard in touch with Captain Lockwood Todd, cousin of Mrs. Lincoln. In addition to these precautions, service in guarding the President was done by a considerable number of alert volunteers, among whom were Cassius M. Clay and Jim (General James H.) Lane. These men, for a brief time, did nightly guard in the East Room. Part of the earlier arrangements included a cavalry guard at the White House gates, but Lincoln got rid of it. Sometimes he rode to and from the Soldiers' Home with a mounted escort. Frequently, however, he went about, even at night, "unguarded, and often alone, in his open carriage." [4]

There were incidents when the danger to the President's life was shown to be real enough. In April 1862, on his return from the Navy Yard, there was a minor accident in which horses drawing the President's carriage became unmanageable, creating alarm and compelling a change of carriage. Lincoln was unhurt. One August night, as the record has come down to us, a shot was fired as the President, riding horseback alone, approached the Soldiers' Home. A startled horse, we are told, tore into the grounds bearing a hatless President. A guard, on investigation, found the Chief's tall silk hat with a *"bullet-hole* through the crown." [5]

According to the recollection of Ward Lamon, this incident was told by Lincoln himself, but with an air of playful levity and without any apprehension that it involved danger to himself. He made it an amusing joke as he told how his horse, "Old Abe," his "erratic namesake," made a reckless bound and, as he put it, "separated me from my eight-dollar plug-hat, with which I parted company without . . . assent . . . ." The President seemed unwilling to attach any importance to the affair. He concluded that the shot "was the result of an accident." Dismissing that aspect of the matter, he went on to compare Old Abe's performance with the "historic ride of John Gilpin, and [Senator] Henry Wilson's . . . equestrianship on the stray army mule from the . . . battle of Bull Run." In the delayed Lamon version we have Lincoln's further comment: "I can truthfully say that one of the Abes was frightened on this occasion, but modesty forbids my mentioning which of us is entitled to that

---

[4] Francis F. Browne, *Every-Day Life of Abraham Lincoln,* 310.

[5] *Ibid.,* quoting a body-guard, John W. Nichols, 541–542.

distinguished honor." The President went on to make it clear that he wanted no publicity given to the event. It seemed to Lamon that the Chief Executive sometimes "acted an unnatural part" in order to forget the agonizing loss of his son Willie.[6]

When in February 1865 certain Union officers were captured by a guerrilla band at Cumberland, Maryland, Thomas Ewing wrote to Stanton: "I am surprised that it was not the President and yourself [that were captured] in Washington. The President could be seized any reception evening, in the midst of the masses assembled round him, and carried off by fifty determined men armed with bowie knives and revolvers, and once out could be put into a market wagon guarded by a dozen horsemen, and borne off at will,—the conspirators having first set a dozen or twenty hacks in motion to distract attention —look out for some such dash soon." [7]

It is known that at about this time the Booth plan to kidnap Lincoln was actually being plotted and the date set, though not so elaborately as the Ewing letter would suggest. Another expression of uneasiness, very close to the time of the assassination, came from a correspondent of Ward H. Lamon. On April 4, 1865, W. H. Hanna of Bloomington, Illinois, wrote: "I hope the President will keep out of danger, . . . Mr. Lincoln's personal safety is of such vast importance to the country . . . that his friends feel more or less solicitous when they read of his 'going to the front.' But he has made a glorious trip this time." [8]

## IV

In what would now be called "off the cuff" speaking Lincoln showed restraint and reluctance. He disliked commonplace utterance in public; if he spoke at all, he wanted his words to be effective and

---

[6] Dorothy Lamon Teillard, ed., *Recollections of Abraham Lincoln, 1847–1865, by Ward Hill Lamon,* 266–269. In the Lamon account the date of this startling incident seems to be August 1862; in the Browne-Nichols account (see preceding note) it is given as August 1864. Lamon had a special responsibility for guarding the President, but he was not present at the Soldiers' Home. In addition to the difference as to date, the Lamon account makes no mention of the bullet hole in the hat. Yet there is similarity in the two accounts.

[7] Thomas Ewing to Stanton, Feb. 22, 1865, Ewing MSS., Lib. of Cong.

[8] W. H. Hanna to Ward H. Lamon, Bloomington, Ill., April 4, 1865, Lamon MSS., Huntington Lib.

not too repetitious. On one occasion, being taken by surprise at a serenade, he asked Fenton of New York to precede him and give him "a peg to hang on." Achieving a "peculiarly quaint" remark which "raised a good laugh," he considered it a happy exit line and withdrew.[1]

When in May 1862 he spoke to the soldiers of the Twelfth Indiana Regiment, he began by saying, "It has not been customary heretofore, nor will it be hereafter, for me to say something to every regiment passing in review. It occurs too frequently for me to have speeches ready on all occasions." After thanking the men for their satisfaction as to his own performance "in the difficulties which have surrounded the nation," he added that it was the soldiers who were more to be thanked. The nation, he said, "is more indebted to you, and such as you, than to me. It is upon the brave hearts and strong arms of the people of the country that our reliance has been placed in support of free government and free institutions." [2]

The speech just mentioned included all fighting men while showing special recognition to those who faced him; for the boys who thus heard and saw their President it was an incident to remember, a high spot in their war experience. Again in late October 1864 Lincoln favored a regiment with a speech. Addressing the 189th New York, and not forgetting that he was speaking just prior to a presidential election, he praised the soldiers for sustaining his administration, recognizing that they had "not only fought right," but "voted right." [3]

There could be no neglecting, or dodging, of serenades. They could happen when least expected, but they could certainly be expected because of an outstanding or notable event. When told that a serenade "was coming" just after the emancipation proclamation of September 1862, and asked if he "would make any remarks,"

---

1 "It was just when General Sherman was *en route* from Atlanta to the sea, and we had no definite news as to his safety or whereabouts. After one or two sentences, rather commonplace, the President . . . said he had no war news other than was known to all . . . ; that 'we all knew where Sherman went in, but none of us knew where he would come out.' This last remark was in the peculiarly quaint, happy manner of Mr. Lincoln, and created great applause." (In print the remark seems quite ordinary; there must have been something in the President's look or manner that produced the audience response.) R. E. Fenton, in Rice, *Reminiscences of Abraham Lincoln*, 71.

2 Speech to Twelfth Indiana Regiment, New York *Evening Post*, May 15, 1862.

3 New York *Times*, Oct. 25, 1864, p. 1, c. 5.

Lincoln said "No"; yet he did say a few words. Referring to himself as "environed with difficulties," and avoiding any comment in support of his proclamation, he shifted the emphasis, and the glory, from himself and his administration to "those who, upon the battle field, are endeavoring to purchase with their blood and their lives the future happiness and prosperity of this country." Speaking at a time of military deliverance (just after South Mountain and Antietam), he mentioned "battles bravely, skillfully and successfully fought" and called for three cheers for the "brave officers and men who fought those successful battles." [4]

This call for cheers, seemingly a little thing, gave the President a graceful cue to bow out. It fitted perfectly the mood of the crowd, which was in "glorious humor" [5] that night, serenading and demanding speeches not only from Lincoln, but also from Secretary Chase, Cassius M. Clay, and Attorney General Bates.

On the whole Lincoln did not perform badly in response to serenades. "The speeches of the President at the last two serenades," wrote Hay in November 1864, "are very highly spoken of." [6] There were times when some of his most quotable and epigrammatic phrases were delivered in such offhand speeches, though they presented unusual difficulties, not only as to preparation and delivery, but also as to reporting in the papers. A serenade response by Seward was "horribly butchered" in the *Chronicle,* and in order to avert a similar fate Hay wrote out one of Lincoln's night speeches "after the fact" (it was Lincoln's; Hay watched the reporting of it), while for the next serenade the President carefully wrote his words in advance and read them from manuscript.[7]

## V

How did the lanky President look on horseback? Very well, according to Nicolay; awkward and careless, according to others. When a "grand review" of the army was held near Washington on Novem-

---

[4] Reply to serenade, Sep. 24, 1862, New York *Tribune,* Sep. 25, 1862.

[5] On this occasion of the post-Antietam serenade, Hay thought the President's "half a dozen words" were said "with great grace and dignity." Dennett, ed., . . . *Diaries . . . of John Hay,* 50.

[6] *Ibid,* 239.

[7] *Ibid.,* 238–239; Nicolay and Hay, *Works,* X, 261–265 (Nov. 9 and Nov. 10, 1864).

ber 20, 1861, with fifty thousand men in line, the President rode
out in his carriage, then mounted his horse. "Seward I think," wrote
Nicolay, "remained in his carriage." The occasion was something
of an endurance test, Cameron giving out and dismounting midway
in the performance, "while the President went through the whole
without the least symptom of fatigue." He rode up and down before
the standing troops; then he and the officers took their stand on an
acclivity while the soldiers marched past. "Hay and I," wrote Nicolay,
"started home near sundown and the columns had not yet finished
passing." "The President," he noted, "rode erect and firm in his saddle as a practised trooper—he is more graceful in his saddle than
anywhere else I have seen him." [1]

In contradiction of this—a minor example of the contradictions
that run all through the Lincoln subject—we have a critical and
ludicrous (indirect) account of Lincoln's technique when reviewing
troops. A gentleman wrote from Wall Street, New York, to admonish
the President as to "the receiving of military citizens (as all the volunteers are)." He thought it was a serious matter whether the Chief Executive pleased them or not; "soldiers write home to their friends
in this town with reference to their disappointment in your bearing
and manners when reviewing them—"

They say [he continued] when you are on horseback, and platoons of
men marching by you, that you lean about and turn your head to talk with
people behind you, when they claim that you should sit erect & talk to
nobody and look straight at the saluting soldiers—that you ought to assume some dignity for the occasion even though your breeding has not
been military— It makes but little difference whether the demand is reasonable or not—it dont require half so much sacrifice on your part, to
rectify it as it does of the men to go from their homes for the hardship
they undertake—

And when you are passing lines of soldiers, reviewing them, afoot, they
say you take your boys along, and straddle off as if you were cutting across
lots, to get somewhere in the quickest time you can, and pay a good deal
more attention to your own getting along, than to the soldiers whom you
start out to review—

These things dont sound well at all— The influence is bad here— The
complaint may be frivolous and based on a mistake: but such things are
written home here and fortify Raymond in his position of advertising for

[1] MS., Ill. State Hist. Lib., published in Pratt, *Concerning Mr. Lincoln*, 89–90. See also
Nicolay and Hay, *Lincoln*, IV, 469.

a "Leader"— He has got over that, rather, but there is no need of your being so infernally awkward, if these things are true— For God's sake consult somebody, some military man, as to what you ought to do on these occasions in military presence— Nobody will volunteer advice, probably, and if you are arbitrary and conceited on these little things, as Webster used to be, you will alienate your friends and go where he went and John Tyler too, towit where a man has no party—I dont mean a political party, but a great and universal body guard of men who speak well of you and will do anything to bear aloft and above reproach your administration—

The gentleman informed the President that the people cared "a mighty sight" about their soldiers. Even an autocrat would have to give attention to army evolutions and to let the soldiers know that, in reviewing them, he appreciated the business in hand. He would have the President know that his manner was as important as his talk. A lawyer in his office could rest his feet on a table, but not the Commander in Chief of the Armies of the United States. He must "pretend" to be a soldier even if his knowledge was deficient. The letter continued:

You had better let some officer put you through a few dress parades in your leisure moments, if you can get any, and get some military habit on you so you shall feel natural among military men— Dont let people call you a goose on these *very, very* important relations to the Army—
Mrs Lincoln is growing popular all the while, because people say she is mistress of her situation— She aptly fits herself to the times— The dinner service she bought at Houghout's makes people think she is "in town"— they like to talk about her and say she has a good deal of sense and womanly wit about her—she is coming into excellent reputation in this naturally prejudiced city against you and her both—
My impression is that you will do well by paying more attention to your manners and make less effort at wit and story telling— All well enough in private but publicly it is a nuisance— Your talent is conceded—be a gentleman and courtly in your manners when you ought to be— Now I dont care whether you take this well or ill— I voted for you and have a desire to be proud of your administration and I dont wish to see you over slaughed by these damaging stories when you could prevent it so easily— [2]

Walt Whitman, who saw Lincoln frequently in Washington days, thought that the President and his cavalry guard, with sabres drawn, made "no great show in uniforms or horses." Whitman lived on the

2 Robert Colby to Lincoln, 47 Wall Street, New York, May 18, 1861, R. T. L. Coll., 9943–9949.

route the President took to and from the Soldiers' Home. "Mr. Lincoln," he wrote, "on the saddle, generally rides a good-sized, easy-going gray horse, is dressed in plain black, somewhat rusty and dusty; wears a black stiff hat, and looks about as ordinary . . . as the commonest man. . . . Sometimes one of his sons, a boy of ten or twelve [Tad was ten in 1863], accompanies him, riding at his right on a pony." [3]

## VI

Combining his function as ceremonial head of state with that of responsibly active Chief Executive, Lincoln found increasingly heavy demands on his time. Visiting the Navy Yard, he "personally and minutely inspected" its foundries and workshops where six hundred men were employed.[1] One night at the observatory he "took a look at the moon & Arcturus." [2] Pausing at the Capitol on one of his rides, he viewed the newly placed statuary of the east pediment. This evoked a bit of presidential art criticism; he "objected to Powers's statue of the Woodchopper, as he did not make a sufficiently clean cut." [3] Fairs sought him out for a speech, a personal visit, a gift, or a written statement. The president of the Sanitary Commission, returning from California, brought and personally handed him "a present of great beauty and value from a few citizens of that state"—a gold box bearing the letters "A L" and containing "a number of singularly beautiful golden crystals . . . embedded in fine velvet." [4]

Another "interesting ceremony . . . at the White House" was the "presentation to President Lincoln of a truly beautiful and superb vase of skeleton leaves, gathered from the battlefield of Gettysburg." They had been gathered by the ladies of the Philadelphia Sanitary Fair, at which over a million dollars had been raised for soldier welfare. Gettysburg was an exalted theme; tribute to the nation's defenders at Bloody Angle had already been paid. The speaker of the Gettysburg address was now called upon to sound the same note; and that, shortly after the death of Edward Everett. It was one more among countless demands upon the President's time and energy, but

3 Rice, *Reminiscences*, 469–470.
1 Washington *Daily Chronicle*, Apr. 7, 1861, p. 3, c. 6.
2 Dennett, ed., . . . *Diaries . . . of John Hay*, 82.
3 *Ibid.*, 79.
4 Washington *Daily Chronicle*, Oct. 29, 1864, p. 2, c. 6.

the occasion could not be passed off lightly. Though the event was reported as "wholly unexpected," Lincoln responded with a speech. It was like being asked to paint the lily. "So much," wrote Lincoln, "has been said about Gettysburg, and so well said, that for me to attempt to say more may, perhaps, only serve to weaken the force of that which has already been said." Lincoln did not paint the lily. He acknowledged the gift "with emotions of profoundest gratitude," referred handsomely to the departed Everett, paid appropriate tribute to the women of America, and gave assurance that the "kind wishes" extended to him were sincerely reciprocated.[5]

Personal tragedies of the war were repeatedly brought home to the President in the funerals at which his attendance was required. A service for Col. Elmer E. Ellsworth, shot down in Alexandria early in the war, was held in the White House, May 26, 1861. Known to the nation as the dashing commander of a volunteer regiment of zouaves, and as the first striking example of a martyr to the Union cause, he was further known to Lincoln as a youth of zest and gusto who had studied law in the Springfield office, had participated in the 1860 presidential campaign, and had accompanied the President Elect on his trip to Washington. Lincoln was present at the rites for General Amiel W. Whipple who fell in battle at Chancellorsville, in May 1863, and at the ceremony for fifteen victims of an accident at the arsenal grounds in June 1864. On the latter occasion it was estimated that 25,000 people attended, coming by boat and every type of conveyance. When it was found in January 1864 that Lincoln could not attend the funeral of John Hughes, Catholic archbishop of New York, a letter was sent in the President's behalf by Secretary Seward in which the distinguished prelate's national service was acknowledged and tribute was paid to his loyalty, fidelity, and practical wisdom.[6]

At times the President would honor an occasion by being part of

---

[5] Reply to a committee, Washington *Daily Chronicle,* Jan. 25, 1865. Everett had died on January 15; Lincoln's reply was on January 24.

[6] A letter was sent by Seward on Lincoln's behalf. After expressing regret for inability to attend the funeral of the archbisnop, Seward continued: "The President formed the acquaintance of the Archbishop in the earlier period of our national troubles, and highly appreciated his counsels and advice. At a conjunction of deep interest the Archbishop went abroad and did the nation a service there, with all the loyalty, fidelity, and practical wisdom which, on so many other occasions, illustrated his great ability for administration." Washington *Daily Morning Chronicle,* Jan. 21, 1864, p. 2, c. 2.

an audience. He attended the lecture on the battle of Gettysburg delivered by Dr. J. R. Warner in May 1864 in the hall of the House of Representatives,[7] and was present in the same hall when Anna E. Dickinson, abolitionist girl orator, spoke for the benefit of the Freedmen's Aid Association.[8] His attendance was duly announced to stimulate the sale of tickets. He also attended when Bayard Taylor, in December 1863, delivered his lecture on "the geographical, social, political and economic history of Russia." [9] On the numerous occasions when the President's attendance was requested but had to be declined, the declination required a letter from himself or a secretary; at times such a communication took on the nature of a state paper.

Despite constant demands in Washington Lincoln was to a considerable extent a traveling President. Besides the well known speaking occasions at Gettysburg and Baltimore, the record of his presidential travels, if compiled, would include an expedition to Norfolk and Fort Monroe (May 1862), where he actually took a hand in directing operations,[10] various trips through Hampton Roads and up the James, the famous conference at Hampton Roads, a hurried visit to West Point to consult General Winfield Scott, a visit by boat to Mount Vernon, excursions on the Potomac, a trip to Point Lookout, many visits to soldier camps and to the headquarters of McDowell, McClellan, Hooker, Meade, and Grant, and notable visits late in the war to City Point and Richmond. Sometimes he would take Tad with him, sometimes Mrs. Lincoln, or one of his private secretaries, or Ward Lamon, or Noah Brooks. Where a cabinet secretary accompanied the President, it would usually be Seward or Stanton, or less frequently Bates or Chase.

Of his visits to the army one of the most extended and noteworthy was that of April 4–10, 1863, when he combined recreation and duty by spending six whole days at Hooker's headquarters for the Army of the Potomac at Falmouth, Virginia. In the party were the President, Mrs. Lincoln, their beloved Tad, Dr. A. G. Henry, Noah

---

[7] Rev. J. R. Warner of Gettysburg delivered his lecture on the battle of Gettysburg in the hall of the House of Representatives on May 18, 1864. "President Lincoln and many other distinguished gentlemen . . . were present." *Nat. Intelligencer*, May 21, 1864, p. 3, c. 4.

[8] James Harvey Young, *Anna Elizabeth Dickinson and the Civil War* (abstract of doctoral dissertation, Univ. of Illinois, 1941), 6.

[9] Washington *Daily Chronicle*, Dec. 19, 1863.

[10] *Lincoln the President*, II, 78–80.

Brooks, a Mr. Crawford, and Attorney General Bates. There were several reviews, in grand style, of what was considered the finest and biggest army in the world. Henry was very sure that the nation had the right man (Hooker) and that he would promptly "take his army into Richmond" and "to New Orleans if necessary." It was reported that 15,000 well mounted cavalry, 300 pieces of field artillery, and "about 150,000 of the finest looking, & best disciplined Infantry . . . ever seen in one Army" passed before the reviewing President, whose visit would "add intensity to their zeal and confidence." [11]

Noah Brooks's pen added color to the spectacle. The President wore a high hat and rode "like a veteran." Tad rode with the cavalry in charge of a mounted orderly, "his gray cloak flying in the gusty wind like the plume of Henry of Navarre." "It was a grand sight to look upon, this immense body of cavalry, with banners waving, music crashing, horses prancing, as the vast column came winding like a huge serpent over the hills past the reviewing party, and then stretching far away out of sight." After the review the President insisted on going through the hospital tents, "Stopping and speaking to nearly every man . . . and leaving a kind word as he moved from cot to cot." When the party rode from camp to headquarters, "tremendous cheers rent the air from the soldiers, who stood in groups, eager to see the good President." [12]

Welles thought the President traveled too much. In his "intense anxiety" concerning the military situation in June 1864 the President visited Grant at his headquarters. Welles disapproved of "these Presidential excursions" and tried to discourage them, though Stanton and Chase, he said, favored them. "He can do no good," thought Welles. "It can hardly be otherwise than harmful, even if no accident befalls him. Better for him and the country that he should remain at his post here. It would be advantageous if he remained away from the War Department and required his Cabinet to come to him." [13]

Travel was arduous and a good deal of time was thus consumed, but business was attended to on some of these trips, and they may have afforded variety, diversion, and much needed recreation to a cruelly burdened President. They gave him direct contacts outside Washing-

---

11 A. G. Henry to his wife, Washington, Apr. 12, 1863, MS., Ill. State Hist. Lib.
12 Noah Brooks, *Washington in Lincoln's Time*, 48-49.
13 Welles. *Diary*, II, 55 (June 20, 1864).

ton (contacts inside the capital being rather uninspiring); at times they would enable him to skip a cabinet meeting. At an early stage in the war the New York *Times* informed its readers that the President was "given to unannounced journeying." "His trip from Harrisburg about fifteen months since took the nation by surprise [the secret night ride through Baltimore to Washington in February 1861]; his recent visit to the army and navy yard at Fortress Monroe and Norfolk was as unexpected as it was significant; and the last excursion, taking the whole North by storm, is but one of a similar series." [14]

---

[14] New York *Times*, June 26, 1862. "In the latter part of June [1862] the President . . . had made . . . a visit to General Scott in his retirement [the general was then at West Point] to ask his counsel. It is probable that at this . . . interview the appointment of Halleck as general-in-chief was . . . suggested by General Scott." Nicolay and Hay, *Lincoln*, VI, 2.

# CHAPTER II

# LONELY WHITE HOUSE PAIR

THROUGHOUT his life as President, though this has not been sufficiently understood, one should think not alone of Lincoln, but always of the Lincolns. They were a close-knit couple—not that all their tastes were similar; it was rather that they were united; their concerns were mutual. Their children meant everything to them. The welfare of each was inseparable from that of the other. Mrs. Lincoln wrote: ". . . my husband told me that I was the only one he had ever thought of, or cared for." [1] (Referring as a young man to his feeling for Mary Owens, whom he knew before he met Mary Todd, Lincoln had written that he was "a little in love with her.") As to the Lincolns being a loving and thoroughly de-voted couple there can be no doubt on the part of those who know their story.

## I

Mrs. Lincoln, not being of a blasé temperament, was elated by her high position, enjoyed it (at first), and plunged into the dazzling new life with buoyancy and enthusiasm. One of her sisters even referred to her "court." Her first duty as she saw it was to make a suitable and properly furnished abode out of the sadly unpresentable White House. No informed person could deny the need for such a transformation. There was a congressional appropriation of $20,000 for fitting out the President's mansion and when she undertook the expenditure of this seemingly large amount she had her first lesson in the intricate economics of officialdom.

In her love of beautiful things and her honest wish to perform her task suitably, she was flattered by merchants, carried away by her

---

[1] Mrs. Lincoln to Mrs. Gideon Welles, Dec. 6, 1865, Welles MSS.

own quick approval of the purchases she wanted, and victimized by the rather general tendency to gouge that impersonal entity known as "the Government." Mrs. Lincoln did not perform badly in what she bought, but in the lack of a proper check on her ordering she did exceed the appropriation. At the moment of purchase the problem of budgeting was not her main thought. (There was more to it than that; it seemed beyond Mary Lincoln's power to think straight about money matters.) She was in tears when she realized what she had done: tears of penitence and also of distress when she saw that she was creating a difficulty for her overworked husband.

To Lincoln the need for all this refurbishing did not register as with her, and when the matter was brought up by the commissioner of public buildings—B. B. French—the President was indignantly disgusted. He stood ready to pay the excess—about $7,000 over the appropriated amount—but the matter was adjusted by Congress with deficiency appropriations.[2] Of course this business of exceeding an appropriation and appealing to Congress to make it up, while undesirable in terms of finance, was a familiar procedure. It is a procedure which has not yet been outmoded.

This episode of the expenditures was but one of many which brought heartaches for Mary Lincoln. The White House, with humanity crowding its doors, was becoming a lonely and a hostile place. As the months passed the bitter extent and depth of that hostility became a sore trial to this lady of unstable health. Her physical strength was never adequate to these demands of public life. She was shaken by chills and fever, had devastating migraine headaches, and suffered a severe head injury in a carriage accident. Emotional instability and (beginning with the presidency) a species of irrationality, were parts, though minor parts, of her constitution, along with an unsteadiness of nerves. Was she to blame for this? A fully explanatory answer to this question cannot be easily given. All the conditions involved, and all the balancing factors including fine attributes, would have to be considered. To give the answer has not been within the reach of superficial writers—certainly not of Herndon. It would take a physician and a well informed and understanding one at that. A sudden noise—the slamming of a door—would send her nerves quiv-

---

[2] For the details, see Harry E. Pratt and Ernest E. East, "Mrs. Lincoln Refurbishes the White House," *Lincoln Herald*, Feb., 1945.

ering. Calmness had not been her forte. She had always had a timidity, a tendency toward panic in a storm, and a sense of insecurity. These qualities did not make for the fullest self control in an emergency. Yet speaking generally as to her public conduct she did show poise, mastery, and control; her social deportment was excellent.[3]

## II

Social occasions in the President's mansion were elaborate and stately, though often overcrowded. Shortly after the 1861 inauguration the Lincolns held their first "levee or reception." Among those attending was William H. L. Wallace, an attorney of Ottawa, Illinois, on an office-seeking visit to Washington. He wrote to his wife: "The throng was immense. Ladies crinoline suffered mercilessly. The crowded [White House] was thickly sprinkled with the gay uniforms of the army & navy & the diplomatic corps. Mr. Lincoln wore white kid gloves & worked away at shaking hands with the multitude, with much the same air & movement as if he were mauling rails. Mrs. Lincoln seemed from the happy glance I had of her, to be doing her part of the honors with becoming grace." [1]

For her at least, since she was not well during the White House years, something was done to ease the strain on these exacting occasions. William O. Stoddard, whose post of duty was by Mrs. Lincoln's side, relates that she stood some steps to the right of the President and farther back; much of the procession would sweep past without shaking the hand of the First Lady. "Her hand," wrote Stoddard, "is not so hard as his, and could not endure so much grasping and shaking. Even his iron fingers weary sometimes." [2]

The general party in March 1863, at the close of the winter social season, was typical. People formed in line awaiting entrance. Long before 8:30, the hour set for the opening, it was reported that "crowds of ladies and gentlemen" filled the approaches to the entrance of the mansion. In an effort to keep the crowd under some control a file of

---

[3] There was one sad exception which would be greatly misunderstood if taken as typical. It came near the end of Lincoln's life and involved an unfortunate scene created by Mrs. Lincoln (at City Point in March 1865) who was angered by a general's wife (Mrs. Ord) riding horseback beside the President.

[1] Pratt, *Concerning Mr. Lincoln*, 70–71.

[2] Stoddard, *Inside the White House in War Times*, 92.

soldiers was stationed at the doors. "Mr. Lincoln stood in the reception room, with Mrs. Lincoln on his right, and after the ladies and gentlemen were presented to the President and his lady they passed on and entered the East room, where the promenading took place." So wrote the reporter, first person plural, for the Washington *Chronicle*. He continued: "In the latter room we noticed several distinguished officers, both of the civil and military departments of the Government, accompanied by their wives, daughters, and friends. . . . The ladies endeavored to rival each other in the brilliancy of dress, and it would take a *Jenkins* to decide which was the belle of the evening . . . ." [3]

Next year another of the huge levees was described as surpassing all its predecessors. "The reception last evening, being the last of the season, attracted an overflowing attendance; indeed, the 'oldest inhabitant' would be at a loss to name one in the history of Washington so densely crowded. It is within bounds to state that thousands, on account of the immense throng, were unable to pay their respects to the President and Mrs. Lincoln, the latter of whom was exquisitely attired, and excited general admiration."

"The President," wrote the reporter, "was, as usual, affable and urbane to every one who approached him, bestowing upon all a friendly smile and cordial grasp of the hand, and to his official and social intimates a warm salutation and a pleasant word." The "distinguished personages" who were present in "large number" included members of the cabinet, senators, representatives, officers of army and navy, and foreign ministers. [4]

New Year's Day was regularly the occasion of a general public reception. For this event in 1862 the newspaper accounts glittered with journalistic superlatives. The affair was "very brilliant." The people who attended in large numbers were "of the first order of Society." "The President never appeared in finer spirits, and Mrs. Lincoln, supported by a bevy of the fairest of the metropolis, received with grace and elegance." Then came a mention of the man with whom Lincoln almost fought a duel in 1842. "General Shields [James Shields of Illinois, former senator, brigadier general of volunteers] made his appearance at the levee, and being originally from Illinois, and an

---

3 Washington *Daily Morning Chronicle*, Mar. 3, 1863, p. 3, c. 1.
4 *Ibid.*, Apr. 20, 1864, p. 2, c. 8.

acquaintance of the President and his family, was the special object of attention by Mr. and Mrs. Lincoln." After this levee was over, "a choice party was invited to listen to several patriotic songs from the Hutchinson Family in the red room." [5]

The first day of 1863 is remembered in history for the definitive proclamation of emancipation, but for Lincoln the hours and moments as they passed were harassing and exhausting. In addition to the public handshaking (or jerking) the President had a distressing interview with Burnside (who was getting nowhere in Virginia) and was confronted with the resignations of the highest ranking army leaders: Halleck, general in chief, and Burnside, commander of the Army of the Potomac. The trouble was temporarily patched up and the two resignations withdrawn (which did not solve the Burnside problem, or the Halleck one either), but on the historic day when they were proffered, those resignations were ugly facts.[6] One of the features of the New Year's Day reception of 1864 was the attendance of the diplomatic body with "felicitations . . . as cordial as they were demonstrative." The entire corps were present with the exception of the minister from Nicaragua; detained by illness, he sent his "most friendly apology." [7]

After officers, diplomats, and special groups had been received in the morning, a kind of free-for-all party followed. About noon, "the doors were thrown open, and the crowd surged in, trampling on one another's heels and toes, and doing some considerable damage to hats, bonnets and fine dresses." Entering at the front (the north door) of the White House, and moving first to the right, the sweeping mass of humanity pushed "through the Green, Blue and Reception rooms; and near the west door of the latter stood President Lincoln, and with a smile for all, [he] shook hands with his visitors of high and low degree." Ward Hill Lamon, marshal of the District of Columbia, made the presentations to the President; B. B. French, commissioner of public buildings, the introductions to Mrs. Lincoln. In the meantime the Marine Band "discoursed excellent music." Visitors passed into the great East Room, and "thence out by a substantial platform through one of the windows onto the pavement." "Coverings were

[5] New York *Herald*, Jan. 8, 1862, p. 10, c. 2.
[6] *Lincoln the President*, II, 252–253.
[7] Cincinnati *Daily Gazette*, Jan. 4, 1864, p. 3, c. 5.

placed over the elegant carpets in all the rooms, in order to prevent them being soiled by the mud." The throng of army officers, estimated at "between five and seven hundred," had assembled in the lower hall of the war department building, "completely jamming its entire space." In orderly formation "they proceeded at 11¼ A. M. to the Executive Mansion on their errand of courtesy, headed by the distinguished General-in-Chief [Halleck]." [8]

For Gideon Welles, ever ready to see that his diary was informed on such matters, the undignified wedging and squeezing at these functions reflected no credit on the Chief's household organization. Describing one of the large parties, he wrote: "It was a jam, not creditable in its arrangements to the authorities." Observing that the "multitude were not misbehaved, farther than crowding together in disorder and confusion," he added: "Had there been a small guard, or even a few police officers, present, there might have been regulations which would have been readily acquiesced in and observed. There has always been a want of order and proper management at these levees or receptions, which I hope may soon be corrected." [9] The big reception to open the year 1865, however, showed the same lack of order. It was held on Monday, January 2, and the people enjoyed it, but Welles thought a "little more system at the President's would improve matters." [10]

So it went: dinners, receptions, matinees, concerts, perhaps a picnic for Negroes on the White House lawn, serenades, introductions, parades, reviews, generals to greet, foreign dignitaries to receive, crowds shaking the President's hand, studio pictures to be posed for, delegations or committees to be heard and answered, Sanitary Fairs to be attended or addressed by letter, speeches to be made, soldiers to be visited in camp or hospital, presentations, openings, dedications, inspections—no end to the continual round, while through it all the nation's existence and fate depended on the manner in which the gravest and most serious problems were faced and handled by the President.

A casual or random glance would find Lincoln speaking to a regiment, reading a prepared address of welcome to a diplomat, attending a funeral, visiting an observatory, testing a new gun, attending

---

[8] *Ibid.*, Jan. 7, 1864, p. 2, c. 2.          [9] Welles, *Diary*, II, 15 (Apr. 20, 1864).
[10] *Ibid.*, II, 219.

a lecture, or visiting the Capitol to observe progress on the construction of the unfinished dome.

Unusual interest in Washington society attached to the wedding
of the famous belle, Kate Chase, daughter of the secretary of the
treasury, to Senator (former Governor) William Sprague of Rhode
Island. On this occasion "a large and brilliant concourse of guests
thronged the hospitable mansion of Secretary Chase . . . . The
President of the United States, members of the Cabinet, the diplomatic corps, eminent officers of the army and navy, with citizens of
Washington and friends invited from a distance, lent distinction to
the scene, as their wives and daughters shed grace and beauty on the
gay assemblage." [11]

These incidental and miscellaneous duties collected their toll of
energy, time, and thought. To be constantly called upon to say and
do the appropriate thing on innumerable occasions, giving attention
to each small duty without revealing boredom, is one of the exacting
trials of a public man. Yet the people wanted to see their President.
They pressed their attentions upon him. It was out of the question,
nor was it desired by Lincoln, to deny them access. For thousands it
was precisely these small occasions for which Lincoln in person was
remembered.

An impressive lady reformer has left a unique first-hand account
of President and Mrs. Lincoln. Mrs. Jane Grey Swisshelm was a journalist, an aggressive abolitionist, vigorous newspaper editor, and lec-
turer. For a time she conducted at Pittsburgh the antislavery paper,
the *Saturday Visiter;* at times she contributed to Greeley's *Tribune;*
later at St. Cloud, Minnesota, she published the St. Cloud *Democrat.*
Coming to Washington in January 1863, and in spite of being a Republican, she did not wish to meet President and Mrs. Lincoln, regarding Lincoln as an "Obstructionist" to the cause of abolition. She
resisted various opportunities to meet the Lincolns, but at last she
was persuaded to attend a levee at the White House (April 2, 1863).
The notable alteration of her impressions of the Lincolns when she
met them face to face was recorded in her words as follows:

"I watched the President and Mrs. Lincoln receive. His sad, earnest,
honest face was irresistible in its plea for confidence, and Mrs. Lin-

---

[11] Cincinnati *Daily Gazette,* Nov. 20, 1863, p. 1, c. 4.

coln's manner was so simple and motherly, so unlike that of all Southern women I had seen, that I doubted the tales I had heard. Her head was not that of a conspirator. She would be incapable of a successful deceit, and whatever her purposes were, they must be known to all who knew her.

"Mr. Lincoln stood going through one of those dreadful ordeals of hand-shaking, working like a man pumping for life on a sinking vessel, and I was filled with indignation for the selfish people who made this useless drain on his nervous force. I wanted to stand between him and them, and say, 'stand back, and let him live and do his work.' But I could not resist going to him with the rest of the crowd . . . ." [12]

Later Mrs. Swisshelm attended a Union meeting (March 31, 1863) attended by the President and his cabinet. She gave her record of the scene as follows: "He is very tall, and very pale. He walked quickly forward, bowed and took his seat. He was dressed in a plain suit of black which had a worn look; and I could see no sign of watch chain, white bosom or color. But all men have some vanity, and during the evening I noticed he wore on his breast, an immense jewel, the value of which I can form no estimate. This was the head of a little fellow ["Tad" Lincoln], about seven years old, who came with him and for a while sat quietly beside him in one of the great chairs, but who soon grew restless and weary under the long drawn out speeches . . . , and who would wonder [wander] from one Member of the Cabinet to another, leaning on him and whispering to him, no doubt asking when that man was going to quit and let them go home; and then would come back to father, come around, whisper in his ear, then climb on his knee and nestle his head down on his bosom."

Mrs. Swisshelm was impressed by the simplicity of the President forming one of the audience and by the picture of the father with his boy. She wrote: "As the long, bony hand spread out over the dark hair, and the thin face above rested the sharp chin upon it, it was a pleasant sight. The head of a great and powerful nation, without a badge of distinction, sitting quietly in the audience getting bored or applauding like the rest of us; soothing with loving care the little

---

12 Jane Grey Swisshelm, *Half a Century*, 236.

restless creature so much dearer than all the power he wields—a power greater than that exercised by any other human being on earth." [13]

## III

When a dinner was given, or some other party which was invitational, the Lincolns, like all presidential couples, were sure to encounter grief on the question as to whom to invite. In this respect one of the White House functions was described in the New York *Herald* as a "blunder." To the one who used this phrase it meant that the "wrong people" had been invited, the "right" ones neglected. Later, however, S. P. Hanscom of the *Herald* was able to inform his illustrious editor, James Gordon Bennett, that "corrections" had since been made. "Some of the first families in the country have been invited who were before neglected, while it is a fact that parties were invited who would not be admitted to the first circles in New York, Boston, or Philadelphia. The whole programme has changed in regard to the lines drawn with reference to the Diplomatic *Corps*, Brigadier Generals, and some Colonels, such as Mr. Astor &c., who were ruled out." [1]

As topics of general discussion, White House affairs were comparable to crises in foreign relations. "Next to the British question," wrote one of the journalists, "the forthcoming party at the White House is the principal subject of comment. The limitation of the number of invitations to only five hundred and fifty occasions many disappointments and heart burnings." The "general expression of disapprobation," he added, "makes it very questionable whether the gratification afforded to the five hundred and fifty favored guests will compensate for the sore disappointment and chagrin occasioned to five thousand five hundred who believe themselves equally entitled to the distinction of an invitation. The whole affair is regarded as a social blunder much to be regretted." [2]

This dispatch was written on February 2, 1862, but soon the correspondent had come to see things in a different light. Next day he wrote:

---

[13] St. Cloud (Minn.) *Democrat,* April 9, 1863.

[1] S. P. Hanscom to James Gordon Bennett, "private," Wash., D.C., Feb. 4, 1862, Bennett MSS.

[2] New York *Herald,* Feb. 3, 1862, p. 1, c. 2.

"The wise course which is being pursued by Mrs. Lincoln, in returning to the customs of the early days of the republic, in her manner of receiving visitors, is applauded by all excepting some few envious individuals who are unable to procure invitations. It is fully time that festivities at the residence of the President of the United States should cease to be infested by crowds of individuals, neither whose manners, habits, nor antecedents entitle them to a place in respectable society. It cannot be expected, crowded as Washington is, that every candidate for office, every petty placemonger, every contract seeker, every quidnunc, whose time hangs heavily on his hands of an evening, should feel entitled as one of the 'great unterrified,' to while away his hours in companionship with the ladies who compose the refined circle of the accomplished lady of our excellent President. It was not so in the days of Washington and Adams . . . . The party [here he referred to the large reception to be held on February 5, 1862] . . . is the uppermost topic of conversation. Over eight hundred invitations have already been issued. The preparations are upon a scale of the greatest magnificence." [3]

It is unimportant to speculate on the reason for the change of tone in the *Herald* correspondent's dispatches of the second and third of February. Perhaps by the latter date he had received his invitation. When he presented his lavish report of the party as held, he marshaled his best adjectives to describe "a truly brilliant array of fashion, beauty and manliness." He went on: "Such a display of elegance and taste and loveliness has perhaps never before been witnessed within the walls of the White House. . . . The President . . . greeted the guests with courteous warmth, and chatted familiarly with many whom he recognized as old friends. He was attired in a plain suit of black." Mrs. Lincoln, the reporter added, was "in half mourning for Prince Albert." [4] To take this newspaper account of this fifth-of-February party in 1862 would be most inadequate. As will be seen later, the occasion was to become a ghastly memory for the Lincolns.

William O. Stoddard of the President's secretarial staff had a *bon mot* for that type of formidable occasion that was called a "ball." When, because of the crowding masses of people, there was no dancing, he thought the affairs could have been so called only by those

---

[3] *Ibid.,* Feb. 4, 1862, p. 1, c. 3.          [4] *Ibid.,* Feb. 6, 1862, p. 5, cc. 4–5.

who were "thinking of cannon balls." After considering all the cabinet members, judges, diplomats, admirals, generals, and governors, with their wives, he measured the floors with a tape line to estimate "standing-room." Custom, he said, required for each President a "routine of official dinners, dull, stately, costly affairs, . . . in a wearisome string through the season." In addition to the usual worries attending such affairs there was, in the case of the Lincolns, "the perpetual peril of having some official jollification set down beforehand for the evening after the arrival of stunning news from the army." [5]

It was not a matter of Washington people only. Over the country, "great society people," together with "the would-be great," wrote in for invitations. Many "applications" had to be rejected, which swelled "the storm of absurd disapprobation . . . aroused by this unfortunate 'reception with refreshments.' " [6]

Not merely admission, but recognition of personal importance, was demanded. The desire was not merely to be accommodated but received as specially favored gentlemen, with cards of invitation second to none. This business of inviting people "as gentlemen," or in such manner as to recognize degrees of personal prestige, could not fail to be serious in a democracy where human worth and equality was emphasized in principle. It was evident that in social invitations equality was not wanted in practice. Men could be invited as officials; that was not always easy, but at least it was a recognized principle. Where, however, cards of invitation were given to officials, others—e. g., reporters—might "be admitted," though without cards. The trouble was that this would not satisfy certain "proudly indignant" individuals. If they could not attend "as gentlemen" they would not attend at all. They had to be told that everyone who had a card of invitation received it by reason of official character, not because of "social position." The reporter of a leading paper would, of course, not be excluded, but he was to understand that he "had no more right to an invitation [by official card] than . . . any hod-carrier on Pennsylvania Avenue." As a precedent (not precisely an analogous one), Stoddard mentioned the prideful conduct of Charles Dickens,

---

[5] Stoddard, *Inside the White House in War Times*, 193–194.
[6] *Ibid.*, 195.

who "refused to perform his theatricals before the Queen, at her command, because he was not a gentleman of England, and could not be received at court." Such situations bring to mind the fact that to the exclusive minded the word "gentleman" connotes superiority, and that many who theoretically praise democratic "equality" do not at all object to exclusiveness so long as they are within the chosen circle.

The presence or absence, also the manner and facial expression, of diplomats was a matter of special observation. In a period of strained relations between the United States and Britain it was noted that no difficulty could have been guessed from the deportment of Lord Lyons, British minister. "No American," it was noted, "has shaken hands more heartily than he with the President . . . ." On the same occasion Stoddard observed: "France is not here, and it is understood that he will not come to-night; but if his absence has any ominous diplomatic meaning the hint is utterly lost upon Mr. Lincoln." The White House was "not a good workroom for intrigue." [7]

## IV

Of the three living Lincoln sons—Robert, Willie, and Tad—only two were part of the daily White House scene; for Robert, who came of age in the summer of 1864, was attending college at Harvard. It was Willie and Tad, with their exuberance and pranks, who gladdened, while they also complicated, home life in the presidential household, if home life it could be called. Abraham and Mary Lincoln loved their little sons with a love that was ardently reciprocated. Yet with official business conducted in the mansion—endless conferences, visitings, and interviews—there was little chance to enjoy family life.

Willie, their third son, was ten years old when his father became President. Well endowed, good looking, and lovable, he was the center of animated boy life, which included parties in which his mother took a special interest. "Willie Lincoln," wrote his playmate Julia Taft Bayne, "was the most lovable boy I ever knew, bright, sensible, sweet-tempered and gentle-mannered." Willie and Tad, she wrote, "were two healthy, rollicking Western boys, never accustomed to

[7] *Ibid.*, 94–95. (For Stoddard's reference to Dickens, see p. 197.)

restraint, and the notice which their father's station drew upon them was very distasteful. Willie would complain, 'I wish they wouldn't stare at us so. Wasn't there ever a President who had children?' " [1]

In the wretched unhealthiness of Washington, with its shocking lack of adequate sanitation, Willie caught a serious illness, and it was announced on February 8, 1862, that "the usual Saturday reception at the White House and the levee on Tuesday would be omitted, on account of the illness of the second son [he was really the third son] of the President, an interesting lad of about eight years of age [another error], who has been lying dangerously ill of bilious fever [at another time reported as typhoid] for the last three days. Mrs. Lincoln has not left his bedside since Wednesday night [February 5], and fears are entertained for her health." [2]

Days passed while the Lincoln household was plunged in anxious gloom. It was reported on February 11 that the lad had been "very ill," but was "much improved." [3] Next day it was stated that the "little son" was "reported out of danger." In the altered tempo of life at the White House not only the levee, but the "usual Cabinet meeting" was dispensed with, while the President was often at the bedside. On February 18 Attorney General Bates noted in his diary: "The Prest.'s 2d. son, Willie, has lingered on for a week or 10 day[s], and is now thought to be in extremis[.] The Prest. is nearly worn out, with grief and watching." [4]

As the grieving President and his wife continued their agonized vigil it was announced that the boy was "pronounced past all hope of recovery." [5] Next came the report: "The White House is still overspread with the gloom of the expected death of the President's second son, who is reported more easy to-day, but no hope of his recovery is entertained. The President and Mrs. Lincoln are overwhelmed with grief." [6] In the midst of all this it was noted that Tad was "now threatened with a similar sickness." [7] In his unceasing solicitude for his sons

---

[1] Julia Taft Bayne, *Tad Lincoln's Father*, 8–9.

[2] "News from Washington," New York *Herald*, Feb. 10, 1862, p. 5, c. 3.

[3] *Ibid.* (news dated Feb. 11), Feb. 12, 1862, p. 5, c. 4.

[4] Bates made the common error of referring to Willie as the Lincolns' second, instead of their third-born son.

[5] New York *Herald*, Feb. 19, 1862, p. 1, c. 3.

[6] *Ibid.*, Feb. 20, 1862, p. 1, c. 4.

[7] Helen Nicolay, *Lincoln's Secretary: A Biography of John G. Nicolay*, 132. (Quoted from a letter by Nicolay to Therena Bates, his future wife.)

Lincoln "gave them their medicines and spent as much time as possible in the sickroom." [8]

## V

In a letter written at the time it was reported of Mrs. Lincoln: "She is . . . just now sadly affected both of her little boys are down with fever, and one is very dangerously sick. She & the president have been watching for ten days, & she looks haggard enough." [1]

On February 20 there was the "same routine," with the President "very much worn and exhausted." As Nicolay wrote: "At about five o'clock this afternoon [February 20] I was lying half asleep on the sofa in my office when his entrance roused me. 'Well, Nicolay,' said he, choking with emotion, 'my boy is gone—he is actually gone!' and, bursting into tears, turned and went into his own office." [2]

"Me and father" had been pals or companions in frolic, travel, and adventure, as well as at home. When he was but eight years old, in June 1859, Willie had written to a friend from Chicago: "This town is a very beautiful place. . . . Me and father have a nice little room to ourselves. We have two little pitcher[s] on a washstand. The smallest one for me the largest one for father. We have two little towels on a top of both pitchers. . . . [etc.]" [3]

To those who have a feeling for the Lincolns as a family there has come the thought—if Willie had lived. He was thus described by Mrs. Elizabeth Todd Grimsley: "Willie, a noble, beautiful boy of nine years, of great mental activity, unusual intelligence, wonderful memory, methodical, frank and loving, a counterpart of his father, save that he was handsome. He was entirely devoted to Taddie who was a gay, gladsome, merry, spontaneous fellow, bubbling over with innocent fun, whose laugh rang through the house, when not moved to tears. Quick in mind, and impulse, like his mother, with her naturally sunny temperament, he was the life, as also the worry of the household. There could be no greater contrast between children."

---

8 *Ibid.*

1 Unidentified letter, signed James, to "My dearest Mary," Washington, Feb. 16, 1862, photostat of ms., Abr. Lincoln Assoc.

2 Nicolay, *Lincoln's Secretary*, 132–133.

3 Willie Lincoln to "Dear Henry" [Remann], Chicago, June 6 [?], 1859, MS., Univ. of Chicago Lib. The name Remann is verified by Mrs. Mary Edwards Brown of Springfield, who formerly owned the letter.

Mrs. Grimsley continued: "Our first Sunday in the White House, we all went to the New York Avenue Presbyterian Church, Dr. Phineas D. Gurley's, which had been decided upon as the church home, and ever after, the boys attended the Sabbath School, Willie conscientiously, and because he loved it, Tad as a recreation, and to be with Willie." [4]

Tad recovered, though his illness was no slight matter. He was now the one boy living in the White House. It is impossible to put on paper the depth and intensity of Lincoln's grief, of Mary Lincoln's, and of Tad's. On March 2 Mrs. Ninian W. Edwards, Mary's sister, visiting the White House, wrote in a letter to her daughter: "It is enough to feel . . . that my presence here, has tended very much to soothe, the excessive grief, that natures such as your Aunt's experience. And moreover to aid in nursing the little sick Tad, who is very prostrated with his illness and subdued with the loss he evidently suffers from, yet permits no allusion to. His mother has been but little with him, being utterly unable to control her feelings." On March 12 Mrs. Edwards wrote again: "Your Aunt Mary still confines herself to her room . . . and at times, gives way to violent grief. . . . Tad is still feeble, can barely walk a few steps at a time. He deeply feels the loss of his loving brother." [5]

Another touching record of Tad's grief remains. In the series of home letters just mentioned, Mrs. Edwards referred to a trunk she was sending home to Springfield. In it Tad was sending two toy railroad cars to a little cousin. Mrs. Edwards wrote "It [the trunk] contained *two cars* that belonged to Willie. Tad insisted upon sending them to Lewis [Edward Lewis Baker, grandson of Mrs. Edwards], saying he could not play with them again." [6]

## VI

It was in this month of February 1862 that a favorable turning point was reached in the bitter war, with the important western vic-

---

[4] Elizabeth Todd Grimsley, in *Journal*, Ill. State Hist. Soc., XIX, nos. 3–4, 48–49 (1926–27).

[5] For the use of these original letters of Mrs. Ninian W. Edwards the author is indebted to the kindness of one of her descendants.

[6] This letter, though undated, was evidently written to her daughter, Mrs. Edward Lewis Baker, by Mrs. Edwards from the White House in April 1862. See previous note.

tories at Fort Henry and Fort Donelson. It was stated in the papers that the "rebellion . . . [was] receiving fatal blows" under Lincoln's administration. Much was to be made of Washington's Birthday that year. Meetings for public celebration all over the country had been planned. "As a patriot and as President of the United States," wrote one of the journalists, "Mr. Lincoln has occasion to feel the proudest satisfaction in the success of our arms on land and sea; while, as a father, he is called to endure the severest domestic calamity. There is an indescribable gloom in the White House. The muffled bell, and the profound silence in those noble rooms . . . produce a strange effect upon the visitor who goes there to look upon the lifeless form of the pretty boy, . . . the sprightly, sweet tempered and mild mannered child, . . . . To-day the obsequies of little Willie took place. . . . Mrs. Lincoln . . . was too ill . . . to be present at the funeral ceremonies. . . . Here [in the East Room] were seated in a circle President Lincoln and his oldest son Robert, and the members of his Cabinet. . . . Mr. Lincoln was bowed down with grief and anxiety, and looked as if nearly worn out with watching." [1]

In New Hampshire a former President, who would not ordinarily have been moved to write to Lincoln, broke silence to send a touching letter of sympathy and condolence. On the eve of taking office in 1853, Franklin Pierce had suffered a devastating bereavement when his eleven-year-old son, Benny, had been killed before his eyes in a railway accident. On matters concerned with the spiritual life he had been reticent. Now came the following letter in Pierce's hand:

Concord N. H.<br>
March 4, 1862

My dear Sir,

The impulse to write you, the moment I heard of your great domestic affliction was very strong, but it brought back the crushing sorrow which befel me just before I went to Washington in 1853, with such power that I felt your grief to be too sacred for intrusion.

Even in this hour, so full of danger to our Country, and of trial and

---

1 New York *Herald*, Feb. 26, 1862, p. 10, cc. 3–4. News in this dispatch was reported as of February 24, the day of the funeral. The minister who conducted the service was Dr. Phineas D. Gurley, pastor of the New York Avenue Presbyterian church in Washington. Departments were closed; both houses of Congress adjourned as a token of respect; government buildings were not illuminated on Washington's Birthday.

anxiety to all good men, your thoughts will be, of your cherished boy, who will nestle at your heart, until you meet him in that new life, when tears and toils and conflict will be unknown.

I realize fully how vain it would be, to suggest sources of consolation.

There can be but one refuge in such an hour,—but one remedy for smitten hearts, which, is to trust in Him "who doeth all things well", and leave the rest to—

"Time comforter & only healer
  When the heart hath bled"

With Mrs Pierce's and my own best wishes—and truest sympathy for Mrs Lincoln and yourself

                    I am, very truly,
                    yr. friend
                    Franklin Pierce [2]

His Excy—
        A. Lincoln
            Presdt  &c
      &c  &c

## VII

For Mary Lincoln the death of Willie came as a crushing and shattering blow. Social functions were sharply curtailed. Never again would the life of the First Lady have the glamor of its first brief phase. When a lady nurse, quickly summoned to attend the broken woman, arrived, she found the President where one could have expected to find him, by the bedside of his sick wife.

It was his habit to be constantly solicitous of her, sending daily telegrams when she or he was away, keeping her informed of military movements (knowing her deep interest in the progress of national events), and constantly striving to have some sister or cousin on hand to assist and keep her company. For her part she found numerous ways of helping him: contriving to overcome his moods of depression, suppressing her own complaints to avoid worrying him with them, offering relaxation, watching out for his meals (which he neglected), and instituting the practice of a daily carriage ride. Thought for his safety amid the lurking dangers and cruel burdens of his position was with her a constant anxiety.

Deprived of any element of joy by the death of her beloved son, the White House became for Mrs. Lincoln a storm center and a kind of dismal trap. Whatever she did or omitted to do, she was sure to

---

[2] R. T. L. Coll., 14792.

be criticized. An example was the expensive and elaborate party (on February 5th) at the White House within the period when Willie lay ill. It had been planned well in advance and when Mrs. Lincoln considered canceling it, which would have been her wish, she was assured of her son's recovery while of course she could not forget her function as hostess. She was in an agony of suspense while the party was on as she realized that the boy was not improving; afterward she had to endure the stabbing injustice of a devastating set of verses, misnamed a poem, on the "Lady President's Ball," a savage piece of misplaced sarcasm put in the supposed mouth of a dying soldier and scoring her thoughtless extravagance and gaiety while men of the army were writhing and dying in neglect. The false implication that she did not care as to the welfare of soldiers—anyone who knew her realized that she cared very deeply—was of a piece with the incredible campaign of abuse of which she was the victim. Yet if she omitted social functions, she was equally denounced for that. Parties and dinners were not in general omitted in Washington in war time, and when she cut down on them in those months of '62 following Willie's death, she had to bear the accusation that she was denying her people that to which they were entitled. She was even accused of being a "rebel" at heart and a Confederate spy in the White House. No one in the nation was a more firm and earnest Unionist than she. It should be added that she showed notable friendliness and understanding toward the colored people. The enduring tradition among those people of worshipful friendliness to her has vastly more validity than the fabrication of some—alas, too many—among the whites.

There were two things that somewhat sustained her in her prostrating grief: first, her realization that Lincoln suffered too and that it was her duty to hearten him; and in addition her service in soldier hospitals. It was an impressive sight to see her ministrations as she visited the sickbeds of the wounded, brought them delicacies from the White House kitchen, and by her presence and conversation reanimated the spirits of the men who on their part—so different from the alleged soldier in the poem—gave her a sincere and grateful response. In her sensitiveness to suffering she was deeply affected by the painful scenes she encountered, but this, together with the constant danger of contagion to herself, she heeded not. It was W. O. Stoddard's view that she missed a chance in public relations by not deliberately publicizing this hospital service. That was not her nature. In her own person she did not seek the limelight. Her feeling about the matter, in addition to the impulse to help, was that without these humane employments her heart would have been broken by the loss of her child.

Unscrupulous men wormed their way into the mansion, gained access to the lady of the house, and made her an unsuspecting victim of their low intrigues. Such a man was one John Watt, the White House gardener whose extracurricular activities and juggling as to payrolls revealed him to be a disloyal cheat. Another impostor was the fabulous Henry Wikoff, an unprincipled adventurer who had been dismissed from Yale and had seen the inside of prison. He was a traveler extraordinary, wealthy idler, courtier, amateur diplomat, frequenter of foreign courts, supposed authority on Napoleon III, and purveyor-in-chief of various kinds of fancy gossip. The name "Chevalier Wikoff" became attached to him because of an unimportant decoration he had received in Spain. This disreputable but socially attractive man ingratiated himself in Mrs. Lincoln's favor for the furthering of his own intrigues, one of which had to do with the smuggling of unauthorized information to James Gordon Bennett's *Herald*. (That Bennett denied the connection with Wikoff was to have been expected both of Bennett and his type of journalism.) The story of Wikoff's machinations need not be given in detail here; the time came, none too soon, when he was told by the President to leave the White House and never return.

## VIII

It did not help matters in Mary Lincoln's "furnace of affliction" (to use her own phrase) that Lincoln's secretaries, Nicolay and Hay, could exchange letters belittling her—Hay going so far with his overclever pen as to call her a "Hell-cat." To say the least, a greater respect should have been shown by the secretaries for the President's own wishes and attitudes; he was not ignorant of her imperfections, but he dealt with her in kindness and understanding. A private secretary, to serve adequately, should be an aide to the President. Mrs. Lincoln had her difficulties with these secretarial youths on matters of the household payroll and of social invitations.

To know this side of the story from the standpoint of the Lincolns will enable one better to realize why it was that the President planned differently for 1865. These young men were slated to be provided for by appointments abroad and it was arranged that Noah Brooks should be private secretary for the second presidential term. One of the ablest men in Washington, Brooks was the correspondent of the Sacramento *Union*. He has importance in the Lincoln story for his reportorial records and for his specially intimate relation with the President; he was one of the few spirits of whom Lincoln was genuinely fond and with whom he felt comfortably at ease. It is Brooks who has given us one of the most striking comments on the vicious weapons aimed against Mrs. Lincoln. He knew and indignantly resented the abusive slanders of the Washington rumor-factory; he knew better, for he knew Mrs. Lincoln as she was. Brooks wrote:

"The wife of the President has been so frequently and cruelly misrepresented and slandered that, though hesitating to approach so delicate a subject, your correspondent cannot refrain from saying a word in strict justice to this distinguished and accomplished woman. When the present administration came into power, the National Capital was infested as well as besieged by rebels, and every conceivable means was adopted to render the members of the new Administration unpopular. To this end slanders innumerable were circulated concerning the habits of the President and his family; and it is not many months since when candid and loyal men were to be found believing that our temperate President drank to excess, and that Mrs. Lincoln was a vulgar, ill-bred woman. Such stories are scandalous, and though time has done justice to the President, who is seen and read of all men, Mrs. Lincoln is denied the privilege of defense, and in the privacy of a household clad in mourning has not yet had justice done her by the public."

To Brooks's mind the inexcusable outrage was that "loyal people, more shame to them, without knowing the truth of what they repeat, still allow themselves to become the media for the dispersion of scandals as base as they are baseless." Feeling most keenly that a correction was long overdue, he continued:

"It is not a gracious task to refute these things, but the tales that are told of Mrs. Lincoln's vanity, pride, vulgarity and meanness ought to put any decent man or woman to the blush, when they remember they do not *know* one particle of that which they repeat, and that they would resent as an insult to their wives, sisters or mothers that which they so glibly repeat concerning the first lady in the land. Shame upon these he-gossips and envious retailers of small slanders. Mrs. Lincoln, I am glad to be able to say from personal knowledge, is a true American woman, and when we have said that we have said enough in praise of the best and truest lady in our beloved land."

This comment was part of a long article giving at some length a first-hand description of life as it was lived in the White House, a subject on which Brooks could speak with assurance. He was letting his far-off Pacific coast readers share with him the inside view of the mansion: its ante-room for those seeking the President, its parlors, upholstery and fittings, satin and damask, "profusion of ormulu work," vases and the like bought or presented during the administrations of Madison and Monroe, its grand piano, its full length portrait of Washington, its richly colored hangings. Most people, he said, admired the blue room, "formed in the graceful curves of a perfect ellipse," its windows commanding "a lovely view of the grounds in the rear of the house and of the Potomac."

No part of the mansion seems to have escaped him. He wrote of the family apartments, dining room, conservatory, servants' rooms, kitchen, and basement. There was no "Kitchen Cabinet," he noted, "but the present presiding lady of the White House has caused a terrible scattering of ancient abuses . . . below stairs." There had been "suckers" who stole from kitchen and conservatory, "spies in every room in the house." When they were dispersed, they "circulated innumerable revengeful yarns . . . and there were . . . credulous people who believed them." He noted how vandals had snipped off bits of lace, drapery and carpet as relics; he wondered how they could have the "cheek" to exhibit these objects to friends at home with accounts as to how they were stolen.

After all this elaborate description and this indignant refutation of fabricated yarns, the observant Brooks concluded: "Republican simplicity and Republican virtues [upper case in the newspaper] reign at the home of the American President; thousands of private citizens in our prosperous country are more luxuriously lodged, and more daintily fed; but, search the wide nation over and you will not find a more united household or a more noble and loving family than that which to-day dwells in all of the anxious cares of the White House." [1]

What was said by Noah Brooks was made evident by another close and competent observer, Ben Perley Poore, who wrote: "The President's wife . . . ought not to be left unmentioned, although there is little of interest to chronicle in her daily round of serving, reading and visiting hospitals, which occupies the time of Mrs. Lincoln. She may have made mistakes—who does not? in her invitations, and thereby have provoked envious criticisms. Neither do those of the Democratic [party] era admit there can be any courtesy displayed here now-a-days. But I am sure that since the time that Mrs. Madison presided at the White House, it has not been graced by a lady so well fitted by nature and by education to dispense its hospitalities as is Mrs. Lincoln. Her hospitality is only equaled by her charity, and her graceful deportment by her goodness of heart." [2] Not all the mud slinging and shameful abuse can rob Mrs. Lincoln of that which was admitted by contemporary writers not governed by prejudice: her performance as hostess and First Lady. She served with dignity in all the exacting social world of the presidency. [3]

---

[1] Letter from Washington, signed "Castine," Nov. 7, 1863, in Sacramento *Union*, Dec. 4, 1863. The excellent reporting in this article was typical of the work of Noah Brooks.

[2] "From Our Regular Correspondent," Washington, Nov. 30, Boston *Journal*, Dec. 1, 1863, signed "Perley."

[3] The author has been greatly assisted by studying in manuscript the biography of Mary Lincoln by his wife, Ruth Painter Randall. Many points in the life and personality of Mrs. Lincoln, used in this chapter, are to be amplified and fully documented in Mrs. Randall's book which is scheduled for early publication.

# ATTENTION OF THE PRESIDENT

## I

FEW men of his time understood the extent of Lincoln's presidential burden. Patronage, dealings with Congress, public relations, civil and military duties, and an appalling amount of detailed business pertaining to the army, crowded upon his waking hours and robbed him of sleep. The unceasing demands upon him as the court of high appeal in numerous personal cases took heavy toll of his time and energy, of his patience and emotional endurance.

On hundreds of private requests the President had to give or refuse permission. What about the case of "Sue and Charlie"—Mr. and Mrs. Charles Craig, cousins of John Todd Stuart? Dislodged from their home by war's desolation, they wanted to go back and cultivate their farm near Helena, Arkansas. They needed a pass through the lines and assurance of non-molestation by the military authorities. Accompanied by Henry T. Blow of St. Louis ("old friend" of Lincoln, successful business man, and leading Republican), Sue called at night at the White House, saw Lincoln, and presented her request. Writing on a Sunday, Stuart informed his wife that "Mr. Lincoln . . . granted all Sue's wishes and promised to have the papers made out for her by tomorrow." This bit of personal business involved "influence" of prominent men, use of the President as errand boy, the writing of an official "A D S" (autograph document signed) by the President, the making out of various papers, and due attention to the details by the proper authorities. The matter was mentioned along with the problem of "a permit for *Cousin Ann* [Mrs. Ann Todd Campbell of Boonville, Missouri, cousin of Mrs. Lincoln] to trade in Cotton down the Mississippi." Stuart thought the affairs of sun-

42

dry cousins were going well. "How *we apples swim!*" he remarked.[1]

An "old lady of genteel appearance" called with a "piteous appeal." Having fitted up portions of the old Duff Green building in order to take in boarders, and having engaged members of Congress to board there, she was given an eviction notice with a quick deadline; aside from the "ruin" occasioned by the loss of her financial outlay, she could find no other shelter for her head. Her appeal was given personal consideration by the President, resulting in his "A L S" (autograph letter signed) to Secretary Stanton in the lady's behalf.[2]

Were these trivial matters? Of course they were matters that should never have been brought up to the President, but if one is studying Lincoln's presidential days and how they were spent, the accumulated weight of such things cannot be ignored; Lincoln's time was continually devoted to precisely such appeals. A loyal Mississippi lady had taken the Federal oath of allegiance and had leased her plantation "to parties of unquestioned loyalty." By military sanction it had been leased to other parties. So Lincoln had to write to Adjutant General Thomas to have the matter, about which he knew nothing, straightened out.[3] Could something be done about the request of Dr. William Fithian, friend of Lincoln and substantial citizen of Danville, Illinois, who wished to recover the remains of a stepson in Missouri? Lincoln did what he could, wiring to General Samuel R. Curtis, asking that the necessary facilities be extended.[4] Was there a Confederate prisoner named Joseph J. Williams confined at Camp Chase, Ohio? Or was he at Camp Douglas near Chicago? Would the officer in charge "tell him his wife is here, and allow him to Telegraph her."[5]

Sometimes the request was for a recommendation. Though he had "but slight personal acquaintance" with Mrs. Lotty Hough, Lincoln knew of her by reputation and had "never heard ought against her." She was struggling to support herself and little boy. The President hoped that opportunities to succeed would be afforded her.[6]

---

[1] John T. Stuart to his wife, Dec. 29, 1863, MS., Ill. State Hist. Soc.; Pratt, *Concerning Mr. Lincoln*, 105–106.

[2] Lincoln to Stanton, Jan. 1, 1863, photostat, A. Lincoln Assoc.

[3] Case of Mrs. Eugenia P. Bass. Lincoln to Lorenzo Thomas, Jan. 15, 1864. Lincoln MSS., Lib. of Cong.

[4] Nicolay and Hay, *Works*, VIII, 144.

[5] *Ibid.*, VII, 10.

[6] *Ibid.*, X, 238 (corrected by photostat, A. Lincoln Assoc.).

In unnumbered personal cases the President sought to relieve distressed human beings of the harassments of war. In a generalized letter of instruction to commanding officers in West Tennessee he wrote: "It is my wish for you to relieve the people from all burdens, harassments, and oppressions, so far as is possible, consistently with your military necessities;  . . .  the object of the war being to restore and maintain the blessings of peace and good government, I desire you to help, and not hinder, every advance in that direction." [7]

It is remarkable that so many hardship cases and personal appeals came up to Lincoln himself. A Unionist-minded lady was reported to be seeking separation from her husband who was in the Confederate army. The President would not offer her, or any wife, "a temptation to a permanent separation from her husband," but if her mind was "independently and fully made up to such separation," he wished certain "property . . . to be delivered to her, upon her taking the oath" of loyalty. A lady with her six daughters wished to go to her father in Richmond, Kentucky; Lincoln directed the officer in command at Knoxville, Tennessee, to allow the trip. A poor widow had a son in the army, who for some offense had been sentenced "to serve a long time without pay, or at most, with very little pay." Lincoln wrote to his secretary of war: "I do not like this punishment of withholding pay—it falls so very hard upon poor families." [8]

Sometimes an individual appeal would involve a broad public policy. Frequently the problem would be an excessive use of military authority in matters appropriate for the courts. A provost marshal, for example, seized a building, with premises and furniture, belonging to a lady whose husband "went off in the rebellion," though she was the owner of the property, independently of her husband. The basis of the seizure was vague, and the property was not taken for any military object. "The true rule for the Military," wrote the President, "is to seize such property as is needed for Military uses and reasons and let the rest alone." The case involved complicated and serious legal questions—whether either husband or wife was a traitor, which one owned the property, and whether the wife's prop-

---

[7] To commanding officers in West Tennessee, Feb. 13, 1865, photostat, A. Lincoln Assoc.

[8] For these cases see Nicolay and Hay, *Works*, X, 27–29, 72–73 (photostats, A. Lincoln Assoc.).

erty was confiscable for the treason of her husband—"all which," wrote Lincoln, "it is ridiculous for a provost-marshal to assume to decide." He directed that the case be adjusted and revised on these principles.[9]

## II

Often the thing desired of Lincoln was his signature. One jovial visitor stated that he would prefer it "at the foot of a commission."[1] A lady wrote a "complimentary poem" to the President and asked for his autograph. Lincoln wrote: "I thank you for it, and cheerfully comply with your request."[2] A bride-to-be, signing her name as Polly Peachblossom, asked the busy President for an autograph on an enclosed piece of silk, to be placed in her wedding quilt. "All the other Peachblossoms," she wrote, "had a silk quilt ready for their wedding and why should not I?"[3] These little requests were satisfied with a sense of form suited to the occasion. When a wish for his autograph was expressed by Lady Villiers, Lincoln wrote: "I beg that her Ladyship will accept the assurance of my sincere gratification at this opportunity of subscribing myself Very truly Her Ladyship's obedient servant A. Lincoln."[4]

There were numerous pleas for notes of introduction. And there was the case of "a fair, plump lady" of Dubuque. Just before a cabinet meeting she pressed forward, saying she "was passing East and came from Baltimore expressly to have a look" at the President.[5] Among other questions he was asked to approve a benefit raffle. So a presidential telegram went to Mother Mary Gonyeag of Keokuk: "The

---

[9] Lincoln to Gen. Joseph J. Reynolds, Jan. 20, 1865, photostat, A. Lincoln Assoc. (Erroneously given in Nicolay and Hay, *Works*, IX, 287–288, as Jan. 20, 1864.)

[1] Rice, *Reminiscences of Abraham Lincoln* . . . , 229–230.

[2] *Works*, X, 253 (Oct. 26, 1864).

[3] R. T. L. Coll., 32804 (Apr. 4, 1864). The lady who presented this "modest request" put it up to the President: there could be no wedding without the quilt, and no quilt without the autograph. She enclosed a poem, "The Maul," depicting Lincoln as a rail-splitting young hero who rose under his "Star of Fame" till his pen became "the heaviest maul" of all. This Victorian effusion is printed in Moore, *Rebellion Record* ("Poetry and Incidents"), IX, 13–14, under the name Mary E. Nealy. See also Ruth Painter Randall, "Little Stories from the Lincoln Papers," *Lincoln Herald*, vol. 50, 26–27 (Feb. 1948).

[4] Photostat, A. Lincoln Assoc. (May 20, 1862).

[5] Welles, *Diary*, I, 528.

President has no authority as to whether you may raffle for the benevolent object you mention. If there is no objection in the Iowa laws, there is none here." [6] Sometimes in this endless round there would be a flash of homely kindness and human sympathy. Toward laboring people especially the President showed particular consideration. He held an interview with a committee of Philadelphia working women to hear their complaints. In the sewing that these women did they had a poor pittance which was "reduced one-half to gratify and enrich a class of grasping contractors." In the Forney press of Washington and Philadelphia we find the comment: "It is rather a unique spectacle to find the chief of a great Republic . . . quietly and patiently hearing the complaints of a committee of plain and humble women, . . . . This, however, is one of the most beautiful examples of a republican Government. The voice of the poor is not often heard by the politician, and particularly the voice of poor women, who have no votes and no influence in primary conventions. . . . These persecuted women go to the President with their grievances, and tell him their story with the simple, homely way of the housewife. And the result is precisely what was anticipated by all who know Abraham Lincoln and his great, good heart. . . . The sewing women will hereafter receive justice. . . . The poor men and women will find that their greatest friend is the President, and that when their errand is justice, no one will be more patient, and sincere, and prompt than the laboring man of Illinois who sits in the Executive chair at Washington." [7]

It might be a new invention that the President would be asked to pass upon. Often it was a personal request for employment. Perhaps it was the disunionists of Maryland or the Unionists of Eastern Tennessee who required attention. A congressman would offer his services. A governor would demand an explanation. Serious Indian troubles in Minnesota in the summer of 1862, "involving official frauds on the one hand and Indian depredations on the other," required an arduous trip by John G. Nicolay to the scene of turmoil, so that Lincoln might have at that distant point "an unprejudiced observer"

---

[6] *Works*, IX, 259 (Dec. 15, 1863).

[7] Washington *Daily Morning Chronicle*, Jan. 28, 1865, p. 2, c. 2 (reprinting from the Philadelphia *Press* of Jan. 27).

who could be, if not an *alter ego,* at least a kind of domestic presidential envoy. In performing this duty—meeting with United States officials and conferring with Chippewa chief Hole-in-the-Day—Nicolay was absent for an extended period during which he wondered whether his scalp was safe. Next summer there was a flare-up of Indian trouble in Colorado, and again Lincoln sent Nicolay, this time "to accompany the Governor of Colorado Territory down to Connejos in the San Juan Valley and to conclude a treaty with the Utes." The secretary "looked upon that visit to Colorado as one of the rare experiences of his life." "A little black notebook that he carried in his pocket fairly explodes with adjectives praising the beauty of the scenery, the fantastic grades at which alleged roads climbed steeple-like peaks, only to drop again into valleys in a way to make a traveler's head swim." [8]

Such things can be voluminously listed—it is like going over a file of government papers—but when that is done it is still difficult to recover an adequate picture of the executive job as it existed under Lincoln. To enumerate his diverse "problems" is not enough. One problem alone might be supercharged with vexation and annoyance; yet to analyze the intricacies of his tasks, or explore their limits and boundaries, is impracticable. In his routine of duties Lincoln had to have eyes and ears for all parts of the country and for matters within every department. Decisions had to be made as to the Almedan mine in California. [9] Attention had to be directed to the breaking of ground for the Union Pacific Railroad, the restoration of Virginia, espionage in the Confederate capital, American participation in the London "exhibition of the products of industry of all nations" (1862), the bringing of produce through the military lines, "the subject of a Reciprocity Treaty with the Sandwich [Hawaiian] Islands," [10] and to the request that Brigham Young be authorized to raise a force to protect the property of the telegraph and overland mail companies in Utah Territory.

8 Helen Nicolay, *Lincoln's Secretary,* 151–155, 172–174.

9 Bates, *Diary,* 303, 338; Welles, *Diary,* I, 397, and II, 338; Leonard Ascher, "Lincoln's Administration and the New Almaden Scandal," *Pacific Hist. Rev.,* V, 38–51 (1936); Milton H. Shutes, "Abraham Lincoln and the New Almaden Mine," *Calif. Hist. Soc. Quar.,* XV, 3–20 (1936).

10 Lincoln to the Senate of the United States, Feb. 5, 1864, photostat, A. Lincoln Assoc.

The President's time, as he himself wrote, was subject to "constant and unexpected requisitions." [11] At another time he referred to "the multitude of cares" claiming his "constant attention" because of which he had been "unable to examine and determine the exact treaty relations between the United States and the Cherokee Nation." [12] One becomes accustomed to the unusual, and inmates of the White House, as Stoddard called them, became familiar with "this strange, unnatural, wartime atmosphere." "Mr. Lincoln," he wrote, "bears it better than could another man in his place, perhaps, but it is telling upon him perceptibly. . . . All kinds of people come on all kinds of errands, and most of them, nowadays, besiege the Capitol and the Departments, but there is a long list of persistent visitors who hang around the White House and wait for chances to see the President, even after they are assured that he cannot and will not see them." [13]

## III

In the face of all these demands the accessibility of the President and his willingness to meet people was a source of wonder, even though by many it was taken for granted. If, however, some found him "hard to see," that was but another evidence of the extent of his burdens. The White House staff sought as far as possible to protect him. There were "guards or footmen" whose duty it was to divert the many who called from curiosity or without sufficient business.[1] Sometimes, because of this, those who had serious business could not see him. Charles D. Drake, chairman of a delegation from Missouri, having submitted documents "of great length," waited for three days seeking a conference in order to get the President's answer to some very serious and vexing questions pertaining to the muddled situation in Missouri. He remained in Washington for that purpose alone. Failing to see Lincoln, he left; then it turned out that this was a matter requiring such detailed and extended study that Lincoln wrote a long and involved answer, over two thousand words, in

[11] Lincoln to J. R. Fry, Apr. 30, 1864, R. T. L. Coll., 32709–10.
[12] Lincoln to John Ross, Chief of the Cherokee Nation, Sep. 25, 1862, photostat, A. Lincoln Assoc.; R. T. L. Coll., 18626.
[13] Stoddard, *Inside the White House in War Times*, 37.
[1] R. T. L. Coll., 25610.

the nature of a substantial state paper.[2] So much concentration was required by Lincoln when he got round to this task that others who sought audience with him had to be disappointed. "The President," it was reported, "excluded all visitors to-day. The Missouri delegation think he is at work on a reply to them."[3]

Another caller wrote: "I called for a personal interview, & have done so many times since, but found you engaged with some Major General, cabinet officer, member of the Senate or House: or the throngs pressing upon you, their varied claims or propositions; & so . . . retired for a more favorable opportunity."[4]

Often it required a good deal of endurance to succeed in meeting the nation's Chief, but the main point is that Lincoln wanted to see people, disapproved of anything that kept them away from him, submitted to constant annoyance, and actually did see an amazing number. Of course he had assistance and time-saving devices. Secretaries were at hand, ready for the immediate sending of telegraphic messages, a bell at his touch for summoning needed help, a clerk to sign land warrants [W. O. Stoddard], and authorities on many subjects ready to respond with specialized advice, as when George Bancroft was asked for historical information, or the storehouse of official lore was tapped for points as to procedures of earlier Presidents reaching back to Jefferson and even to Washington. The march of data into and out of Lincoln's mind would make an impressive procession. He was not as unmethodical as is sometimes supposed, was aware of the importance of files, and in tricky or serious matters was prudently careful to keep records of what he said and of the precise extent of his commitments.

None of his manifold problems came singly. They were tossed into the President's lap in heaps, with nagging persistence and exhausting repetition, bursting at times, or threatening to burst, into acute crises. Easier things—those for which a ready answer could be found— could be handled as department matters, or dealt with by subordinates. It was the bothersome, baffling, or painfully difficult aspects of a case, or questions involving larger trends of governmental ac-

---

[2] Lincoln to Charles D. Drake and Others, Oct. 5, 1863, *Works*, IX, 155–164.
[3] Cincinnati *Daily Gazette*, Oct. 5, 1863, p. 3, c. 3.
[4] A. F. Williams (seeking the non-existent office of commissioner of emancipation) to Lincoln, Mar. 7, 1864, R. T. L. Coll., 31364.

tion, that would reach the President. Broad trends, however, or what was called general policy, could never suffice for all the decisions Lincoln had to make. The very concept of "general policy" was somewhat illusory. The particular case, the human aspects of a situation brought before his eyes, had always to be considered.

To "see" Lincoln and shake hands with him was not the same as knowing him or having contact with his mind. The outward Lincoln, when people met him socially, might be playful, friendly, or seemingly relaxed. Finding him so, people would, in the fuller sense, not meet Lincoln at all. Leaving his presence they could have said something of his face and figure, his clothes, his smile, his manner of bowing and greeting; but they would not have known the burdens and perplexities of the Chief Executive within those clothes, nor would they have glimpsed the feelings and emotional stresses of the inner man.

It was fortunate that strength and patience were given to Lincoln beyond the usual measure. His rugged features were furrowed with anxiety. When Grant's army was hacking its way through the Wilderness there was a week when it was said that "he scarcely slept at all." Carpenter the artist met him in the "main hall of the domestic apartment on one of these days, . . . clad in a long morning wrapper, pacing back and forth a narrow passage leading to one of the windows, his hands behind him, great black rings under his eyes, his head bent forward upon his breast,—altogether such a picture of . . . sorrow, care, and anxiety as would have melted the hearts of . . . adversaries, who so mistakenly applied to him the epithets of tyrant and usurper." [5] There was an irregularity about his eating habits; trays would be carried upstairs, but left untouched for long intervals. The "weary air . . . became habitual during his last years . . . and no rest and recreation . . . could relieve it." As he expressed it, the remedy "seemed never to reach the *tired* spot." [6] The significant thing about all this strain and anxiety is that Lincoln endured it. It did not break him. His was not one of those "high-wrought nervous organizations" as has been said of Jefferson Davis.[7] His nerves were under balance and control, and unlike Davis he had a great American sense of humor.

[5] Carpenter, *Inner Life*, 30–31.         [6] *Ibid.,* 217.
[7] Gamaliel Bradford, *Lee the American*, 51.

The whole nation, with constant attention to its great future, occupied his thought. Problems were not timed to suit his convenience; matters of peaceful development crowded in with the wretched tasks of war. Lincoln had to be mindful, not only of preserving the nation, but of the kind of nation he was preserving. A war was on, but affairs could not be static for that reason. Industrial growth, foreign relations, and westward advance required as much thought certainly as they had under Buchanan. Even the non-war activities under Lincoln were not "ordinary." Things that were formative, and would be effective for decades to come, aside from the battles and campaigns, took shape in Lincoln's four years.

## IV

It is known of Arthur Hugh Clough that he wrote distinguished poetry. It is also known that he spent many hours wrapping and mailing brown paper parcels for Florence Nightingale.[1] If biography is a story of how a man's life was spent, everyday things cannot well be omitted. In August 1862 Abraham Lincoln was watching for his chance—i. e., a victory—so that he might issue the emancipation proclamation. In that month, on August 9, he also gave his attention to a snuff-box presented by the son of Henry Clay.[2] Perhaps the snuff-box, a memento of him who spoke "for the Union, the Constitution, and the freedom of mankind," was not such a small object to Lincoln, nor the service for Florence Nightingale a trivial thing for Clough. If an incident *seemed* small, it may have had real meaning. It could not be considered altogether insignificant that on May 30, 1864, Lincoln handed a little boy a note: "This little gentleman has seen me, and now carries my respects back to his good father, Gov. Hicks."[3]

That was Lincoln's side of the correspondence on this small matter. The incident is of sufficient interest to justify us in noticing the circumstances on the Hicks side. The governor of Maryland had well served the Union cause in the severe crisis of secession, for which

---

[1] Lytton Strachey, *Eminent Victorians*, 174.
[2] Lincoln to John M. Clay, Aug. 9, 1862. The President, as in numerous other cases, wrote this letter twice: in a worksheet (R. T. L. Coll., 17537), and in final smooth form (photostat, A. Lincoln Assoc.).
[3] MS., Ill. State Hist. Lib.

Lincoln had a lasting gratitude; after that he served usefully in the
United States Senate. There is a quality of respect and dignity in the
letters he wrote to Lincoln which one finds, in legible handwriting,
in the Lincoln papers. In 1863 his ankle was so severely injured that
the foot had to be amputated. He therefore paid his personal respects
to the President through the assistance of his son. On the day of Lincoln's note just quoted, Hicks wrote to the President, concluding
with the words: "I sit at yr door in carriage until I hear your determination. Wish I could climb the stair way as formerly, and see
yr Honor myself. yr obt. Servant, Tho. H. Hicks." [4]

Nor was it an unimportant detail when President Lincoln wrote
to John H. Bryant of Princeton, Illinois (brother of William Cullen
Bryant), concerning a monument to the memory of Owen Lovejoy,
whose brother (Elijah P.) had fallen a martyr to the antislavery cause.
In the late fifties the managers of the Republican party (notably
David Davis) had worked hard, largely behind the scenes, to counter-
act the influence of such as Owen Lovejoy, who was an upstanding
and fearless leader against slavery.[5] Now, in May 1864, Lincoln wrote
beautifully of his "increasing respect and esteem" for the man who
"bravely endured the obscurity which the unpopularity of his principles imposed." It would indeed have taken a man of the highest
principles and character to have earned the carefully phrased tribute
which Lincoln paid. The President continued: "Throughout my
heavy, and perplexing responsibilities here, to the day of his death,
it would scarcely wrong any other to say, he was my most generous
friend. Let him have the Marble Monument, along with the well-

---

[4] R. T. L. Coll., 33420.

[5] As revealed in the R. T. Lincoln Collection, Republican leaders in the prewar
period were animated by drives for party success and not by antislavery zeal. The result
was that those who were moved by strong abolitionist sentiment and who wished to
use the party for that purpose were deliberately repelled. Whig support was courted, also
that of "Americans"—those who were moved by prejudice against men of foreign birth.
(W. H. Gray to Lincoln, Carlyle, Ill., May 31, 1858, R. T. L. Coll., 816.) "Less of the
[slavery] discussion," wrote W. M. Chambers from Charleston, Illinois (July 22, 1858),
"and less of the favoring of negro equality" (ibid., 1009). David Davis wrote on ". . . in
Bureau and Lasalle [counties] success will enure to you if conservative men are nominated. If out & out abolitionists . . . are nominated, then I should fear trouble" (ibid.,
1118). Again, August 3, 1858, David Davis wrote, "All the [Republican] orators should
distinctly & emphatically disavow negro suffrage—negro[es] holding office, serving on
juries & the like. . . . For God's sake dont let [Owen] Lovejoy go into Tazewell" (ibid.,
1130).

assured and more enduring one in the hearts of those who love liberty, unselfishly, for all men." [6]

When the ladies in charge of the Northwestern Fair for the Sanitary Commission asked the President to donate the original draft of the emancipation proclamation, Lincoln sent it, thus parting with a manuscript which he valued highly. He wrote: "I had some desire to retain the paper; but if it shall contribute to the relief or comfort of the soldiers, that will be better." [7] The paper was "offered for sale [as stated by Isaac Arnold] at the Sanitary Fair held at Chicago, in the autumn of 1863. It was purchased by Thomas B. Bryan, Esq., and by him presented to the Chicago Historical Society . . . ." [8] In the great Chicago fire of 1871 this valuable Lincoln original was burned; had Lincoln kept the document, it would presumably have remained with his papers, which are now safely kept in the Library of Congress. [9]

The personal attention of the President was also required in connection with the children's petition that he "would free all slave children," sponsored by Mrs. Horace Mann and handed to Lincoln by Senator Sumner. [10] The thought that went into the writing of this letter to one of the notable Peabody sisters was Lincoln's own; the petition was preserved in his papers.

In addition to broad national causes—soldier relief, emancipation, and the like—requests kept piling up for merely local or personal favors. One such was mentioned by Secretary Welles: "The

---

6 Lincoln to John H. Bryant, May 30, 1864, photostat, A. Lincoln Assoc. One of Lincoln's carefully written letters. Where Lincoln wrote "Throughout my heavy . . . responsibilities," etc., Nicolay and Hay (*Works*, X, 111) erroneously give "very" instead of "my."

7 Lincoln to Ladies having charge of the North Western Fair, Oct. 26, 1863, photostat, A. Lincoln Assoc.

8 Isaac N. Arnold, *Life of Abraham Lincoln*, 266 n.

9 Bryan was a "Chicago philanthropist and business man," active in promoting the fair. Having paid $3000 for the document, he gave it to the Soldiers' Home. It was securely kept there for several years, placed temporarily in a bank vault, and then moved to the new building of the Chicago Historical Society, where it was so firmly framed and fastened to the wall that it could not be rescued from the 1871 fire. Either at the Soldiers' Home or at the bank it would have escaped. Owing to Mr. Bryan's thoughtfulness, however, a number of lithograph copies were made. For these and other interesting details, with illustrations, see Paul M. Angle, "How Emancipation Manuscript Was Lost," *Chicago Sunday Tribune Grafic Magazine*, Feb. 8, 1948.

10 Lincoln to Mrs. Horace Mann, Apr. 5, 1864, photostat, A. Lincoln Assoc.

President sends me a strange letter from [Vice President] Hamlin, asking as a *personal* favor that prizes may be sent to Portland [Maine] for adjudication." The Secretary of the Navy did not like this. Such a matter "was not to be disposed of on personal grounds or local favoritism"; other New England ports would have equal claims; additional prize courts would be expensive; Portland had no navy yard or station, nor did it have facilities for examining captured vessels, or for confining prisoners. But, said Welles, Hamlin was not moved by such considerations; he wanted all this extra paraphernalia to be set up at Portland "and solicited them of the President, as special to himself personally." [11]

Perhaps this language was a bit strong, though Welles was correct in principle. Nor can it be forgotten that Lincoln himself had played the politician, promoting merely local interests by way of log rolling, while in the legislature of Illinois. Where great advantage was attainable in wartime expenditures, facilities, and appointments, it was natural for many localities to seek their shares of that advantage, but it was essential that the nation's effort be not dissipated by such demands. Here was a case where Lincoln, under constant pressure from such appeals, was careful to refer the matter to the appropriate minister even in a request that was hard to deny because of the personal influence of the Vice President.

## V

After one considers the seemingly small matters that had real significance, there remain hundreds that were small only, having no other meaning than to show how Lincoln was harassed, badgered, and importuned in innumerable requests that, to say the least, fell short of the national or patriotic motive. People continually tried to exploit him. He was asked to recommend cotton traders to the military authorities—i. e., to advise that particular men seeking profit in cotton trading be given military facilities. The answer came that the President could not write "that class of letters." [1] Yet in some cases, where trading in enemy territory was represented to him in the best light, he did give permission.[2] Lobbyists for special interests crowded

---

[11] Welles, *Diary*, I, 366–367.　　　　　[1] *Works*, X, 71 (Apr. 7, 1864).
[2] *Ibid.*, XI, 48–50 (Mar. 8, 1865). For a scheme of Orville H. Browning, James Hughes,

the hotel bars and could by no means be kept out of the White House. One of these is portrayed by W. O. Stoddard as coming out of Lincoln's room, propelled by a large foot. Some of those who sought to use Lincoln, wrote Stoddard, were "thieves, counterfeiters, black-legs—the scum and curse of the earth." [3] Toward such men Lincoln was not kindly. He was decidedly blunt.

As to the vast unceasing flow of these miscellaneous requests the reader must be spared, though Lincoln was not. A few instances will indicate the type. There came a request for the use of block-ade vessels to bring out a "lady-relative" of a Chicago friend; [4] for permission to a Mrs. Keenan for "her and her little nephew to pass our lines and go to her father in Rockingham, Virginia"; [5] for cadets by the hundred to be appointed to West Point.[6] So tormented was Lincoln "by visitors seeking interviews for every sort of frivolous and impertinent matter [wrote Francis F. Browne], that he resorted some-times, in desperation, to curious . . . inventions to rid himself of the intolerable nuisance." One of "these bores" was scared off by the pointed statement that the President's varioloid was "very con-tagious." " 'Some people,' said the President, 'said they could not take very well my proclamation; but now, I am happy to say, I have *something that everybody can take.*' " [7] When an editor of a small weekly called at the White House claiming to have been the first to suggest Lincoln's nomination for the office of President, the busy

---

and James W. Singleton, for bringing Southern produce through the lines with prospects of some private profit, see Browning, *Diary*, II, 1–3, 7, 14, 15, 17. Arrangements were completed by Charles H. Ray of Chicago and others, late in the war, to "give the rebels whiskey for cotton" and in general to exchange a variety of Northern goods for South-ern products to be obtained from the interior of Mississippi and Alabama. It was stated that the articles taken down could be disposed of (exchanged for cotton) at four times their New Orleans value. C. H. Ray to Lincoln, Vicksburg, April 11, 1865, Ray MSS., Huntington Lib. Other letters in this collection in the Huntington Library give addi-tional details concerning this venture, which was approved by military authorities, by C. A. Dana (assistant secretary of war), and by the President. If fully treated, this North-ern trading within Southern lines would be a vast subject.

3 Stoddard, *Inside the White House in War Times*, 58.

4 Lincoln to the Secretary of the Navy, May 28, 1861, Naval Records, National Archives, photostat, A. Lincoln Assoc.

5 *Works*, X, 73.

6 West Point records in the National Archives at Washington contain numerous brief notes and endorsements by President Lincoln, showing his careful and minute attention to cadetships at the United States Military Academy. Photostats are in the files of the Abraham Lincoln Association.

7 Browne, *Every-Day Life of Abraham Lincoln*, 459–460.

Chief sought to escape him by saying he was going over to the war department to see Stanton. The editor then offered to walk over with him and Lincoln said "Come along." "When they reached the door of the Secretary's office, Mr. Lincoln turned to his visitor and said, 'I shall have to see Mr. Stanton alone, and you must excuse me,' and taking him by the hand he continued, 'Good-bye. I hope you will feel perfectly easy about having nominated me; don't be troubled about it; *I forgive you.*' " [8]

## VI

That the presidency under Lincoln was not limited to legally official acts was shown by his leadership in the observance of Thanksgiving. It was through him that the day became for the first time a matter of regular annual proclamation by the President. By so using his position he was widening the reach of the presidency itself, making it an institution touching the hearts and expressing the emotions of the American people.

The religious ceremony of giving thanks for the harvest and for other blessings was, of course, an old American custom, as old as the early days of the Plymouth colony. Down the years the custom had become established with special importance in New England, yet before Lincoln's administration there was no regularly recurring annual proclamation by the President. Washington, John Adams, and Madison had called upon the people for specified days of public thanks or prayer, but these earlier presidential calls were not annual and were not associated with the harvest festival, nor with any particular time of the year. The days set aside ranged through January, February, April, May, August, September, and November. The occasions had to do with such matters as the establishment of the Constitution in 1789, the suppression of the whiskey insurrection in 1795, and the making of peace with Britain in 1815.

While the Thanksgiving custom was becoming more firmly established and was spreading to the South, it was the governors who issued the proclamations and indicated the days to be observed in their states. This was not fully satisfactory and in the 1840's a prominent and tireless editress, Sarah Josepha Hale ("Madonna in Bustles") began a campaign of persistent appeals year by year in *Godey's*

---

[8] *Ibid.*, 461.

*Lady's Book* urging that the governors concur in proclaiming a uniform date, the last Thursday in November. This idea took hold, though not completely; then in 1863 she had another plan. Would not a proclamation by the President, unvarying as to date from year to year, be the best device to establish Thanksgiving Day along with Washington's Birthday and the Fourth of July in the calendar of holidays? The President, she proposed, would proclaim a day of national thanksgiving for the District of Columbia, the territories, the army and navy, and American citizens abroad. Also she hoped he would "appeal" to the state governors to unite with him in proclaiming the same date so that the nationwide festival would become not only a common event for all, but also a great force for the Union. She continued this agitation through the fifties, though in the unenlightened politics of that decade the Union emphasis became inaudible in the noise and clamor of sectional agitation.

Mrs. Hale's letter to Lincoln, embodying her idea that the President should proclaim Thanksgiving, was written on September 28, 1863. Five days later Lincoln issued his eloquent proclamation. In the midst of "a civil war of unequaled magnitude" he noted that peace with other nations had prevailed and that the year had been "filled with the blessings of fruitful fields and healthful skies." Noting the continuance of peaceful industry amid war, he declared: "No human counsel hath devised, nor hath any mortal hand worked out these great things. They are the gifts of the . . . most high God . . . . I do, therefore, invite my fellow-citizens in every part of the United States, and also those who are at sea and those who are sojourning in foreign lands, to set apart and observe the last Thursday of November next as a day of thanksgiving and praise." The editress's appeal was repeated in 1864, and on October 20 of that year Lincoln issued the second regular annual presidential proclamation of Thanksgiving. He recommended "fervent prayers" to God for "inestimable blessings." (On July 15, 1863, Lincoln had issued a proclamation for national thanksgiving, setting August 6 as the date, but this was for notable recent victories; it was a special proclamation, not to be confused with the annual autumn custom.)

Lincoln had done it in his own way. Mrs. Hale's idea had been that the President should proclaim the event for those under national (as distinct from state) jurisdiction and should appeal to the governors for concurrence as to date. Instead of that procedure—which seemed confined to a pattern of jurisdiction, legal authority, and official right—Lincoln simply invited all his "fellow-citizens" to join in the common observance. So far as the President's proclamation was concerned the governors were not brought into the picture. The state executives, of course, also issued their own proclamations and it is of interest to note in the Lincoln Papers the handsome crop of gubernatorial proclamations of Thanksgiving in 1863 and 1864. The newer and more sparse the state or territory, the more elaborate was the printed proclamation. It was a matter in which the governors took pride.

It was fitting that the nationalizing of Thanksgiving should be associated with the man who led the country through what Allan Nevins has called the "Ordeal of the Union." The custom has been continuously followed by all subsequent Presidents,[1] but in the case of its originator it had special significance. In making the proclamation Lincoln was acting not in terms of legal duty or appointed function, but rather as a focus of national thought, as the man to whom the people turned, the spokesman of the nation. The President does various things which cannot be encompassed if one has in mind only his official duties assigned by law. There is an irreducible core of presidential tasks, but beyond that there is a wider field of presidential spokesmanship, and it is worth while to remember how Lincoln performed, how he initiated certain manifestations of leadership, in this broader dimension. We are dealing here with a matter of public relations, with emotional and intangible elements of the national Union, with the virtue and merits of unity itself, and with the President as the embodiment of that unity.[2]

---

[1] From the time of Lincoln the fixing of the holiday was a matter of annual presidential proclamation until 1941. In that year Congress for the first time enacted that Thanksgiving Day should thereafter be "a legal public holiday," and that the date should be "the fourth [not the last] Thursday of November." Though Congress has fixed the date, the President continues the customary proclamation which Lincoln originated. *U.S. Stat. at Large,* vol. 55, pt. 1, 862 (Dec. 26, 1941).

[2] The subject of Lincoln and Thanksgiving has been treated by the author in *Lincoln Herald,* October 1947. Annotations of that article are not repeated here.

# CHAPTER IV

# THE GIFT OF LAUGHTER

## I

A MAN might recall Lincoln only partially, yet remember his laugh. An old-timer in Springfield wrote to Robert Todd Lincoln: "I remember only the general form of your father as I saw him in the office of Bledsoe and Baker, his height, his length of limb, the cheery laugh in response to a salutation seems to sound in my ears yet." His laugh has also been described as "boisterous," "ringing," "happy," "joyous," and "the President's life preserver." Henry Villard wrote: "A high-pitched laughter lighted up his otherwise melancholy countenance with thorough merriment. His body shook all over . . . and when he felt particularly good over his performance, he followed his habit of drawing his knees, with his arms around them, up to his very face . . . ." Though a laugh is curative and wholesome, there is an even warmer quality in a smile. A newspaper comment in 1860 was: "when he smiles heartily it is something good to see." [1]

Without smile and laughter it would not have been Lincoln. He was born to a sense of humor. As a lad in the Pigeon Creek neighborhood of southern Indiana he had amused his friends, on the sly, with those salty verses, the "Chronicles of Reuben." Forney recalled that

[1] For these descriptive touches the citations are scattered: Samuel Willard, quoted in *Chicago History*, II, 205 ("cheery"); Hay, in *Century Mag.*, Nov. 1890, p. 37 ("boisterous"); Carpenter, *Inner Life*, 150 ("ringing"); Keckley, *Behind the Scenes*, 168 ("happy"); Mrs. Lincoln to David Davis, Chicago, Mar. 4, 1867, MS., Ill. State Hist. Lib. ("joyous"); Carpenter, 161 ("life preserver"); Villard, *Memoirs*, I, 143 ("high pitched," etc.); Helen Nicolay, *Lincoln's Secretary*, 44 ("something good to see"). The quotation from Mary Lincoln, just cited, deserves a further word. Commenting on the "malignity" of Herndon's playing up of the Ann Rutledge romance, Mrs. Lincoln wrote: "Nor did his [Lincoln's] life or his joyous laugh, lead one to suppose that his heart, was in any unfortunate woman's grave."

he "liked the short farce." [2] He was conversant with the humorists of his day. He could anticipate a joke in the making and see how it would be played by such a man as Orpheus C. Kerr. (This pseudonym, a play on "office seeker," was the trade mark of Robert H. Newell.) When General Meigs once inquired who this individual was, Lincoln remarked that his papers were in two volumes and that any one who had not read them "must be a heathen." He enjoyed them best when they poked fun at Welles or Chase. Some of those aimed at himself "rather disgusted him." [3] A sufficient reason for this would have been the dull or misfit quality of some of the anti-Lincoln thrusts.

Lincoln knew also the works of Petroleum V. Nasby (David R. Locke). The humorist himself wrote: "The 'Nasby Letters' . . . attracted his attention . . . . He read them regularly. He kept a series in a drawer in his table, and it was his wont to read them on all occasions to his visitors, no matter who they might be, or what their business was. He seriously offended many of the Republican Party in this way." [4]

He particularly enjoyed a piece in which Nasby ridiculed the opposition of men in the border states to the use of Negro soldiers, and the quick change of opinion on this subject when they realized the advantage of having colored men serve as substitutes for unwilling whites. (It would not have been necessary to associate this attitude with the border region. The same sentiment appeared in New England and elsewhere.) On one occasion, when Noah Brooks spent a night at the Soldiers' Home, the "President, standing before the fireplace, recited the whole of Nasby's letter" which most people had forgotten.

Part of it ran: "Arowse to wunst! . . . Rally agin the porter at the Reed House! Rally agin the cook at the Crook House! . . . Rally agin Missis Umstid! Rally agin Missis Umstid's childern by her first husband! Rally agin Missis Umstid's childern by her sekkund husband! . . . Rally agin the saddle-kulurd gal that yoost 2 be hear! Ameriky fer white men!" [5] If such a passage does not seem very funny now, it may be because one cannot recapture its flavor when written. Satire must have a target, and in this passage the target, now largely

---

[2] John W. Forney, *Anecdotes of Public Men*, I, 38.
[3] Welles, *Diary*, I, 333 (June 17, 1863).   [4] Rice, *Reminiscences*, 447–448.
[5] Noah Brooks, *Washington in Lincoln's Time*, 108–110.

forgotten, was the inconsistency of contemporary anti-Negro attitudes.

A great favorite with Lincoln, of course, was Artemus Ward (Charles Farrar Browne), the foremost professional humorist of his day. It was Ward's "High Handed Outrage in Utica" that Lincoln chose for reading to his impatient cabinet on the day when he presented his emancipation proclamation to them.[6] Ward's humor, like Nasby's, was thoroughly dated. Much of its flavor has evaporated. The droll spectacle of Ward in action could be enjoyed only by the immediate audience as they watched him exhibit his wax works or hold forth with bland irrelevance on "The Babes in the Wood."

Lincoln never met Ward, whose highly advertised contacts with the President were fictitious, but he did meet Jeems Pipes of Pipesville, who instructed his hearers on "Eating Roast Pig with the King of the Cannibal Islands." Pipes was the guest of Lincoln in the White House, and an account has come down to us of the President suggesting a bit of stage business for an act imitating a stammering man. Suiting the action to the stammer, Lincoln showed how "irresistibly ludicrous" it would be if Pipes would punctuate his limping speech with an occasional whistle. There is complete lack of dignity in the sound-picture that comes before us: the President turned comedian, the humorist catching on and rehearsing a trick of his trade, their hilarious laughter at this bit of burlesque ringing through the corridors of the Executive Mansion.[7]

## II

There is no need to box the compass as to Lincoln's stories. Some of them were reminiscent of boyhood days in Indiana, a state famous for fun and humor. Others, told with equal nostalgic relish, brought back the Illinois prairie days. Amusing incidents that he knew of personally would be stored in his retentive memory and brought to the front of conversation when needed. When some senators demanded a wholesale shake-up of the cabinet because one change had been made, the President was reminded of the farmer who went after seven skunks with a shotgun. "I took aim," said the farmer (as Lincoln retold

[6] Diary of S. P. Chase (Annual Report, Am. Hist. Assoc., 1902, II), 87.

[7] Ruth Painter Randall, in Lincoln Herald, 50, 27–28 (Feb. 1948); R. T. L. Coll., 33567–9.

it), "blazed away, killed one, and he raised such a fearful smell that I concluded it was best to let the other six go." [1]

Of course Lincoln did not invent all, or most, of the stories he told. Some of them were old acquaintances, and many of the tales or quips attributed to him were not his at all, but were merely pinned on him. The story about Grant's whiskey drinking (Lincoln wanted some of the "same brand" for his other generals) is one of the most familiar, but it was disclaimed by Lincoln, who probably wished he had told some of the good ones for which he was credited. It has been suggested that one should thank a New York *Herald* writer, not the President, for this Lincoln story,[2] and David Homer Bates mentions the Grant-and-whiskey remark as belonging to the category of stories that were current in former times, saying: "Lincoln disclaimed the story in my hearing . . . ." [3] A similar remark in a slightly different form has been attributed to King George II. When some one mentioned that General Wolfe was mad, the King's reported comment was: "Mad, is he? Then I wish he would bite some of my other generals." [4]

It was the view of W. O. Stoddard that Lincoln had "never so much as heard" the vast number of "so-called jokes" attributed to him. When a bit of foul humor was accredited (or debited) to him, the President's face would "flush and darken." [5] In that sense there was hazard in the President's fame as a "funny man." Altogether unjustly, his humor was associated with thoughtless indifference or even with vulgarity. Not all the yarns gratuitously given him were harmless and the general reputation of being a joker was used against him. There were stories which he indignantly denied because they were forgeries made up by his enemies,[6] and others which he disowned simply because they were not his.

There is, however, an ample supply remaining after one has winnowed out the chaff and rejected the spurious. The story about being

---

[1] Rice, *Reminiscences*, 236.

[2] F. L. Paxson, in *Amer. Hist. Rev.*, XLIII, 168 (Oct. 1937).

[3] Bates, *Lincoln in the Telegraph Office*, 197.

[4] C. R. L. Fletcher, *An Introductory History of England from the Restoration to the Beginning of the Great War* [1660–1792], 214. (A similar remark has been attributed to more than one king.)

[5] W. O. Stoddard, *Inside the White House in War Times*, 55.

[6] As to a certain story told against him in 1860, Lincoln wrote: "it is a forgery out and out." Lincoln to H. J. Raymond, Dec. 18, 1860 ("Confidential"), photostat, A. Lincoln Assoc.

"within one mile of Hell" [7] (that far from the Capitol) can be con-
temporaneously traced, and the one about Negro Joe's dilemma between two roads is found in the Welles diary. This story was an example of a Lincoln anecdote which "clicked" perfectly because of its
appositeness to the problem in hand. Deliberation in cabinet had
turned upon the Dominican problem as of early 1864, in which Lincoln wisely chose to avoid the blundering policy which Grant un-
successfully attempted a few years later, and which "almost wrecked"
the Republican party.[8] In a milieu of local tyranny, civil war, and
military action by Spain to recover control over the Dominican republic, the question arose as to whether the United States should intervene and perhaps annex this island domain. To seize control or
intervene would have angered Spain; to make a point of refusing to
do so would have created resentment among Negroes and their sympathizers.

Having decided to keep clear of this explosive and dangerous en-
tanglement, Lincoln, in cabinet meeting, told of an interview between two Negroes. One of them, a preacher, admonished his friend:
"There are two roads for you, Joe. . . . One . . . leads straight to
hell, de odder go right to damnation." Joe answered: "I go troo de
wood." The Welles diary continues: " 'I am not disposed to take any
new trouble,' said the President, 'just at this time, and shall neither
go for Spain nor the Negro, but shall take to the woods.' " [9]

Welles is also authority for an uncomplimentary but humorous remark of Lincoln's concerning Greeley, another of those Lincoln sayings that have the reminiscent western flavor. Lincoln recalled that
in early Illinois, with few mechanics and small means, it was customary to make a pair of shoes wear as long as possible with much mend-
ing, but the time would come when the leather was so rotten that "the
stitches would not hold." He thought Greeley was like an old shoe;
"the stitches all tear out." [10] It would be a mistake, however, to evolve
a broad conclusion from a casual remark of this nature; Lincoln gave
repeated expression of a high regard for Greeley.[11]

Sometimes the origin of a Lincoln story is clouded while at the same
time the clouding does not indicate that the story was necessarily un-

---

[7] See below, p. 132.　　　　　　　[8] Allan Nevins, *Hamilton Fish*, 250.
[9] Welles, *Diary*, I, 520 (Feb. 2, 1864).　　[10] *Ibid.*, II, 112.
[11] Archer H. Shaw, ed., *Lincoln Encyclopedia*, 142–143.

true. So it was with the President's oft-quoted remark that he "hadn't much influence with this administration." [12] This famous quip is supported by reminiscences of contemporaries, yet Noah Brooks doubted that Lincoln ever said it as usually reported—i. e., with special reference to Secretary Stanton and the war department.[13] It was a familiar item of Washington chit-chat, the more so because of its frequent and pointed applicability. It sounds so much like Lincoln that if he did not originate it he probably wished he had.

Yet, as would naturally be true with such a many sided subject, the applicability of this remark was only partial and should not be taken as giving the whole tone of Lincoln's administration. When, for instance, it was suggested that Lincoln should dismiss the postmaster general from his cabinet, he stated clearly that he himself would be "the judge as to when a member of the Cabinet shall be dismissed." [14]

Other Lincolnian items, of varying quality, are substantiated by contemporary record. There was the President's pun at the time when a young captain was arraigned by court martial as a Peeping Tom; Lincoln remarked that he should have been elevated "to the peerage." There was also the devastatingly sarcastic remark apropos of the political principle that you should "be always on the side of your country in a war." The President said: "Butterfield of Illinois was asked at the beginning of the Mexican War if he were not opposed to it; he said, 'No, I opposed one war. That was enough for me. I am now perpetually in favor of war, pestilence and famine.' " To hear such items is like participating in Lincoln's informal and unpremeditated conversation, listening in, as it were, on his table talk, and catching his unrehearsed or spontaneous witticisms, as when he said that troops "dwindled on the march like a shovelful of fleas pitched from one place to another." Once in a rather atrocious pun, Lincoln was quoted as saying that he was "thin as a shad (yea, worse —as thin as a shadder.)" Pun making was a habit, or disease, of the age, and that remark was not so bad as some atrocities that appeared, for instance, in *Punch*.

Sometimes a story would be associated with Lincoln by context, his own words being quoted along with those of other men. There

---

[12] J. P. Usher, in Rice, *Reminiscences*, 100; John N. Kasson, *ibid.*, 379.
[13] Brooks, *Washington in Lincoln's Time*, 29.
[14] Lincoln to Stanton, July 14, 1864, photostat, A. Lincoln Assoc.

was, for instance, in a string of random jottings on Lincoln, a recording by Hay of Ben Wade's remark that in praying for the prolongation of Taney's life (to outlast Buchanan's administration) he was afraid he had "overdone the matter." Similarly there was a well pointed story—one that Lincoln probably enjoyed—attributed to General Spinner at the time when Richmond papers were going so far as to call Morgan's raid a "success." "Genl Spinner: 'They remind me of a little fellow whom I saw once badly whipped by a bigger man, who was on top of him & jamming his head on the floor. The little cuss, still full of conceit & pluck, kept saying, 'Now, damn you, will you behave yourself?' " Lincoln, his generals, his intimates, and some at least of his people, were going through the tragic war, certainly with no thought of flippancy, but with jests on their lips.[15]

Noah Brooks, later to become a friend of Mark Twain and Bret Harte, was a skilled raconteur, and when he told a Lincoln anecdote it usually had point and flavor as well as closeness to the original. Brooks was considerably amused at the President's brand of diplomacy when dealing with one of the White House "corps of attaches of Hibernian descent." "One morning the President happened to meet his Irish coachman at the door, and asked him to go out and get the morning paper. The Jehu departed, but, like the unfilial party of whom we read in Scripture, he said, 'I go,' but went not, and the anxious President went out himself and invested five cents in a *Morning Chronicle*. It afterwards transpired that the coachman did not consider it his business to run errands, which coming to the President's ears he ordered up the carriage the next morning at six o'clock . . . ." This summons at an uncomfortably early hour, presumably for an important presidential purpose, could not be ignored. Instead of using the carriage himself, however, the President "sent a member of his household in the equipage to the Avenue, where he bought a paper and rode back, with the mortified coachee on the box."

Another anecdote via "Castine" (Brooks's pen name) pertained to a gentleman who had "been waiting around Washington for three months" in order to obtain a pass to Richmond. Finally he applied "as a *dernier resort*, to the President for aid." "I would be most happy

---

15 For random witticisms in this and the preceding paragraph, see Dennett, ed., . . . *Diaries* . . . *of John Hay*, 53, 79–80.

[said Lincoln] to oblige you if my passes were respected; but the fact is I have within the last two years given passes to more than two hundred and fifty thousand men to go to Richmond, and not one of them has got there yet in any legitimate way." [16]

## III

Of all the humorous recordings the best are to be found in Lincoln's own works. This goes far to explain the endless fascination of his writings, even down to the commonest jottings or incidental endorsements. It might be the humor of a sharp dig, homely simile, clownish fun, or play acting. It might be nonsense, to which the best humorists have descended, or rather risen; for if we were to omit delightful nonsense we should have to discard the gems of Gellett Burgess, of Edward Lear, and of Lewis Carroll. That Lincoln shared the joyousness of nonsense was shown in 1848 when he was speaking in Congress on internal improvements. Favoring such improvements and supporting huge governmental expenditures for the purpose, he was refuting the objection that they should be financed, not by the Federal government, but by "tonnage duties, under state authority, with the consent of the General Government." He continued: "How could we make any entirely new improvement by means of tonnage duties? How make a road, a canal, or clear a greatly obstructed river? The idea that we could, involves the same absurdity as the Irish bull about the new boots. 'I shall niver git em on,' says Patrick 'till I wear em a day or two, and stretch em a little.' We shall never make a canal by tonnage duties until it shall already have been made awhile, so the tonnage can get into it." [1] Similarly, applying the idea of absurdity, Lincoln said of Douglas that he was using the horsechestnut style of argument. By this Lincoln meant "a specious and fantastic

---

[16] "A Pair of Lincoln Anecdotes," Sacramento *Daily Union*, May 27, 1863, p. 1, c. 5. In the Castine letters that appeared in the Sacramento *Union* one finds a rich storehouse of authentic source material on Lincoln. Inadequate attention has been paid to Brooks. A careful historical study is given in Wayne C. Temple, "Noah Brooks—Friend of Lincoln," master's dissertation, Univ. of Ill., 1951.

[1] Speech on internal improvements, House of Rep., June 20, 1848, photostat of Lincoln's autograph MS., A. Lincoln Assoc. (Nicolay and Hay, *Works*, II, 41-42.) Lincoln's logic may not have been quite up to his humor if he implied that a bridge or road ought never to be financed on the basis of anticipatory tolls. Such a basis has been proved sound. His whole speech, however, on internal improvements (of which this passage was a small part) was an effective and logically constructed argument.

arrangement of words, by which a man can prove a horse-chestnut to be a chestnut horse." [2]

The continual interweaving of **good** fun in his writings and speeches shows that humor was no mere technique, but a habit of his mind. When, as he thought, Polk was mistakenly appealing to a declaration by Thomas Jefferson, Lincoln showed that Jefferson's true position was against that of Polk. Then he added: "this opinion of Mr. Jefferson, in one branch at least, is, in the hands of Mr. Polk, like McFingal's gun: 'Bears wide, and kicks the owner over.'" [3] Using exaggerated ridicule to destroy Douglas's position on slavery in the territories (a position which Lincoln considered a "sort of do-nothing sovereignty . . . that is exercised by doing nothing at all"), he considered it "as thin as the homeopathic soup that was made by boiling the shadow of a pigeon that had starved to death." [4] And when thinking of courts—how they should be set up—Lincoln dreaded a "Puppy Court"—i. e., petty local judges, too many of them, and with "salaries so low as to exclude all respectable talent." [5]

Politics aside, one should note Lincoln's whimsical twist in asking a renewal of a railroad pass. "Says Tom to John 'Heres your old rotten wheelbarrow.' 'I've broke it, usin on it' 'I wish you would mend it, case I shall want to borrow it this arter-noon.' Acting on this as a precedent, I say 'Heres your old "chalked hat." I wish you would take it, and send me a new one, case I shall want to use it the first of March.'" [6]

At times a Lincolnian figure of speech would be chosen for its universality and homely appeal: Buchanan after the election of Pierce in 1856, was, said Lincoln, like "a rejected lover making merry at the wedding of his rival." [7] Or the Lincoln phrase would be one that every farmer would understand—e. g., his self-depreciating comment that his speech at Gettysburg would "not scour," [8] or that under John

---

[2] Nicolay and Hay, *Works*, III, 229 (Aug. 21, 1858); see also *ibid.*, IV, 212.

[3] Speech, June 20, 1848, photostat, A. Lincoln Assoc. (Nicolay and Hay, *Works*, II, 38–39).

[4] *Ibid.*, IV, 379–380 (Oct. 13, 1858).

[5] Tracy, *Uncollected Letters*, 23 (June 24, 1847).

[6] Lincoln to R. P. Morgan, Feb. 13, 1856, photostat of facsimile, A. Lincoln Assoc.

[7] Speech at Republican banquet, Chicago, Dec. 10, 1856, *Ill. State Jour.*, Dec. 16, 1856.

[8] "He said to me on the stand, immediately after concluding the speech [at Gettysburg]: 'Lamon, that speech won't *scour*.'" Lamon, *Recollections*, ed. by Dorothy Lamon Teillard, 173. (In colloquial farmer language a good plough "scours" when it cuts cleanly through the soil.)

Quincy Adams the post office service "cut its own fodder." He could use current patter (Burnside's "mud march"), or classical mythology ("Procrustean bed"), or Shakespearean metaphor ("a shelled peascod," referring to Pierce).[9]

On the question whether Lincoln's jokes were sometimes risqué, reports and reminiscences differ. One finds diametrically opposite statements, but on the whole the answer would be that Lincoln's humor was sometimes as exquisite as the tooled binding of a volume de luxe, while at other times he fell into expressions that were none too choice and anecdotes that were not intended for the parlor. Such robust yarns occurred off duty, on occasions for which they were not, or their hearers thought they were not, unsuited. After meeting informally with Lincoln in Springfield, Donn Piatt reported Lincoln's manner of talking with "those good honest citizens, who fairly worshiped their distinguished neighbor." Giving way to his natural bent for fun, Mr. Lincoln, reported Piatt, "told very amusing stories, always in quaint illustration of the subject under discussion, no one of which will bear printing." [10]

Some people like risqué stories; some do not; some like them without admitting it. There are degrees, moods, and tenses of unparlorable humor, and a story may be amusingly risqué without being offensively vulgar. It is known that Lincoln's thoughts and conduct were clean. Most of his humorous chit-chat has evaporated and is impossible to recover. Much of it was off the record. What then? If we had all of it barring none, and if parts here and there would need expurgating, one would still ask, to whom should the task of expurgation be assigned? And after all the purification had been accomplished there would remain for undignified sinners a lively demand for the unexpurgated edition.

## IV

Lincoln's humorous diversions were not always appreciated or well received. There were contrasting attitudes in American folkways. American wit was irreverent, and religion itself, if too unbending, "provoked the irreverence of professional jokers." [1] There remained

---

[9] Speech at Republican banquet, cited above.
[10] Donn Piatt, in Rice, *Reminiscences*, 485.  [1] Sandburg, *War Years*, III, 301.

in America something of a holdover from the days, even of Shakespeare, when Puritans made war upon the theater and other forms of amusement. Religion was unimaginative, somber, and rigidly repressive. "The Devil was as real as the Red Indian." [2] To minds under such a killjoy spell, Lincoln's quips seemed almost sinful—or at best profitless frivolity. In his cabinet, when he read some tomfoolery by Artemus Ward, the heavy burden of the occasion—discussion of the emancipation proclamation—was to Lincoln all the more reason for a bit of preliminary playfulness, while to Chase's Puritan mind such levity on a serious occasion was incomprehensible. As a young man Chase had continually chided himself on his unworthiness, had suffered miserably from religious self distrust, had repeated psalms when bathing or dressing, and had considered it a sin to waste time. There was a charming young lady with whom, as he wrote in his diary, he would have fallen in love if she had not been "fond of the gay world" and "disinclined to religion," which he valued "more than any earthly possession." [3]

Much of the contrast between Lincoln and Stanton is revealed by the comment that if Lincoln would be telling a rich story and Stanton would enter, the story and the laughter would die. [4] If the President got along better personally with Seward than with others of his cabinet, it may have been partly because Seward had a sense of humor, as when he said: "Did you ever hear Webster's recipe for cooking cod? 'Denude your cod of his scales, cut him open carefully, put him in a pot of cold water, heat it until your fork can pass easily through the fish, spread good fresh butter over him liberally, sprinkle salt on the butter, pepper on the salt, and—send for George Ashmun and me.' " [5]

Among those who had no ear for Lincoln's humor was Henry Wilson, Republican senator from Massachusetts. When Wilson and Goldwin Smith, with several English friends, were conferring with the President, conversation turned on the subject of battle losses, which the distinguished Englishman illustrated by reciting statistics of killed, wounded, and missing. No one was more emotionally moved

---

2 *Ibid.*
3 Robert B. Warden, *Private Life and Public Services of Salmon Portland Chase,* 190.
4 Stoddard, *Inside the White House,* 165.
5 Dennett, ed., . . . *Diaries . . . of John Hay,* 196.

by these human tragedies than Lincoln; but, crossing his long legs, he solemnly observed that as to such matters one should apply darky arithmetic. The visitor did not know of two systems of arithmetic, upon which the President offered to illustrate the point by a "little story," much to the embarrassment of the senator; "had he [Wilson] known a thousand stories he would not have told one of them to Prof. Smith and his grave-looking British friends; and he was mortified that the President, who in all things had few superiors in easy dignity of manner [this is the comment of W. D. Kelley], should so inopportunely indulge in such frivolity."

Lincoln went on with the story. Darky Jim wanted to know "what is 'rithmetic?" It's when you add up things, explained the other. " 'When you have one and one, and you put them together, they makes two. And when you subtracts things. When if you have two things, and you takes one away, only one remains.' 'Is dat 'rithmetic?' 'Yes.' 'Well, 'tain't true den; it's no good.' Here a dispute arose, when Jim said: 'Now, you s'pose three pigeons sit on that fence, and somebody shoot one of dem, do t'other two stay dar? I guess not, dey flies away quicker'n odder feller falls.' " The trifling story seemed to the President to illustrate the arithmetic to be used in estimating the actual losses resulting from great battles. "The statements you refer to [he said, turning to the Professor] give the killed, wounded and missing at the first roll-call after the battle, which always exhibits a greatly exaggerated total, especially in the column of missing." [6]

Petroleum V. Nasby wrote: "Grave and reverend Senators who came charged to the brim with important business—business on which the fate of the nation depended—took it ill that the President should postpone the consideration thereof while he read them a letter from 'Saint's Rest, wich is in the state of Noo Jersey,' especially as grave statesmen, as a rule, do not understand humor, or comprehend its meaning or effect." [7]

There were those, such as Adam Gurowski, who simply could not understand Lincoln's language. The ferocious old Count considered Lincoln a "brat" and worse: "he is no fit for be President." [8] Even

---

[6] William D. Kelley in Rice, *Reminiscences*, 286–288.

[7] David R. Locke, *ibid.*, 448.

[8] Dennett, ed., . . . *Diaries* . . . *of John Hay*, 177; see also LeRoy H. Fischer, "Lincoln's Gadfly—Adam Gurowski," *Miss. Vall. Hist. Rev.*, XXXVI, 415–434 (Dec. 1949).

old-time associates, who comprehended Lincolnian humor readily enough, found occasionally (though not often) that it grated on them. When O. M. Hatch and Jesse K. Dubois asked for a certain appointment, Lincoln wired in 1863: "What nation do you desire Gen. [Robert] Allen to be made quarter-master-general of? This nation already has a Quarter-Master-General." [9] Hatch and Dubois then wrote to Lincoln explaining their request. Allen had notified Governor Yates that there was to be "a new Quarter Master General" and had asked "will you go for me," asking also that he wire the President and get other state officers to do the same. Yates was absent, and, "supposing that General Allen *knew what he said,* . . . and believing him competent," these men (Hatch was secretary of state for Illinois; Dubois was state auditor) had telegraphed Lincoln urging the appointment. They added: "We profess to be your friends and have no desire to embarrass you, . . . We trust the same spirit governs you —though we confess your despatch read harshly to us." [10]

Lincoln's humor had misfired, and he was quick to correct the first impression. On receiving the Hatch-Dubois letter he at once telegraphed: "The particular form of my despatch was jocular, which I supposed you gentlemen knew me well enough to understand. Gen. Allen is considered here as a very faithful and capable officer; and one who would be at least thought of for Quarter-Master-general if that office were vacant." [11]

## V

It was a sad thing that Lincoln's fondness for stories and his enjoyment of humor were so inscrutable. His biographer, William H. Herndon, had it all physiologically accounted for. We have a remarkable Herndonian passage in which the humorless partner-biographer mounted his unbridled steed and dashed off on an analytical gallop to clarify the profound subject of Lincoln's laughter. The passage illustrates a curious combination of qualities—a ridiculous approach which has no importance for a serious biographer, combined with a curious readability.

---

9 Lincoln to J. K. Dubois and O. M. Hatch, telegram in cipher, Sep. 15, 1863, photostat, A. Lincoln Assoc.

10 O. M. Hatch and Jessie K. Dubois to Lincoln, Springfield, Ill., Sept. 16, 1863; R. T. L. Coll., 26310-1.

11 Lincoln to O. M. Hatch and J. K. Dubois, Sep. 22, 1863, photostat, A. Lincoln Assoc.

Lincoln, explained Herndon, had a low and feeble circulation. His "whole organism moved slowly to the influences of all kinds of stimuli." His body and mind "needed oiling." He had spells of gloom and melancholy. "This state of Mr. Lincoln made him . . . unconscious of his surroundings and to arouse that somewhat dormant consciousness he needed a stimulant and that was found in a story and tell it he would."

There follows a readable passage in which Herndon vividly pictures Lincoln in a typical story-telling scene with an unappreciative secretary. It comes out as a lifelike portrayal of such a situation (though at second hand, because Herndon knew practically nothing directly about Lincoln as President), but it is all mixed up with one of Herndon's own inventions—a theory of Lincoln's laughter which is something of a howler.

"This story telling [continued Herndon]—this stimulant, sending more blood to the brain, aroused the whole man to an active consciousness . . . . Grave men in grave times, sometimes his ministers, would approach him in order to state the urgency of some matter that needed his immediate attention. Mr. Lincoln would look up to his minister half sleepily—dreamily, saying—'Mr Secretary take a chair': he would, in a moment or two, after the secretary had stated his errand, tell some story much to the disgust of his minister, who would censuringly say—'Mr President, this is no time for story telling—the times are grave and full of war, and the country is fast drifting to ruin.' Mr. Lincoln would good naturedly reply—'Come Mr Secretary, sit down—sit down—I have a perfect and profound respect for you and were it not for these stories I should die; they are rents through which my sadness—gloom and melancholy escape.' Mr. Lincoln would thus arouse his half dormant consciousness into activity . . . ; and after he had been thus aroused he would listen to what the . . . minister eagerly told him, like a philosopher and in a short moment he would make his answer . . . so wisely and earnestly as to convince the man that that point . . . had been . . . maturely considered before, long, long before this moment of meeting."

In this immediate passage, describing Lincoln's manner with a humorless cabinet member, Herndon gives something like a reasonable treatment of Lincoln's joking, but what follows indicates the peculiar kind of hash that he was so apt to dish up. "This state of Mr Lincoln [he wrote], particularly so if it was accompanied by a mental & nervous exhaustion, produced by long and intense study, caused him to have delusions—saw apparitions—specters & the like." Lincoln's laughter was thus associated with something supposedly abnormal, as if he was not himself when in good humor. Lincoln, wrote his partner, was usually "a gloomy & melancholy man, but at exceptional times a momentarily happy one." To follow this line of reasoning would be to identify Lincoln's humor with a kind of illusion, as if the laughter-loving Lincoln were seeing things.

Poor Lincoln! He was so beset, or so physiologically sluggish, that he had to whip up these jokes and stories. We ought to understand it and not be too hard on the man. The passage continues: "Let no man blame Mr Lincoln for being sad or seeing apparitions: his sadness and his gloom came naturally out of his organism and his apparitions from the same source somewhat and from nervous & mental exhaustion. Let no man rudely censure Mr Lincoln for his story telling . . . ."[1] And so on.

It is fair to add that we are dealing here with one of Herndon's numerous and voluminous letters to his literary collaborator, Jesse Weik. In these letters, frankly given as something very different from a finished product, Herndon simply poured out his thoughts and ruminations as they rushed through his mind. He didn't try to check them. Sometimes he would admit that they were to be taken only in part, and only for what they might be worth, and that Weik was to be the judge. "Draw on your imagination and fill up [he once wrote]: it will please the people . . . . Pick out what you like and cast away the balance. I have no time to elaborate—amplify &c &c nor correct."[2]

This quality of Lincoln, thought Herndon, was good for the country. Had Lincoln been ardent, "with swift and strong volumes of blood pouring through his brain," had he been impulsive and rash, the national cause would have failed. "This feeble low circulation —this slow irritability which slowly responded to stimuli—this organism . . . [etc.] saved the nation from disunion and consequent ruin." Herndon knew that his collaborator disliked "such stuff ter-

---

[1] "Lincolns nature—one side," Herndon to Weik, Dec. 22, 1888, Herndon Weik MSS.
[2] Herndon to Weik, Nov. 13, 1885, *ibid*.

ribly, and yet some persons may like it." [2] He now had Lincoln's humor vivisected. It was explainable. He had cleared up what might have remained a permanent mystery. The great man's story telling actually had its good side! Herndon could reconcile it. It was about like saying that sunshine should not be too much regretted and if a man had his happier moments his friends should do their best to endure it.

Herndon, who was bored by Lincoln's story telling, was explaining Lincoln's humor, as on other occasions, unbeliever that he was, he "explained" Lincoln's religion. This was the biographer who had so much to do in setting Lincoln, and Mary Lincoln, before the world in a manner which the world has too largely accepted. In the whole passage, which has to be read carefully to be believed, the emphasis is on two things: in elucidating his hero's humor Herndon stresses, above all, his utter gloom, sadness, and melancholy; and, physiologically speaking, he puts the stress on the man's sluggish circulation of blood. It did not seem to occur to him that there must have been something other than gloom in a man who could brighten a conversation as Lincoln did, and that the quickening of circulation could just as well have been a cause as a result of mirth.

## VI

When one thinks of Lincoln as a man of humor (perhaps a better term than "humorist" which suggests a calling or occupation), one thinks also of Mark Twain. As one develops the comparison—which has already been drawn and need not be repeated here [1]—the life and personality of the man Lincoln, set against the man Clemens, becomes a theme of major import. Starting with Pigeon Creek and Holliday (Cardiff) Hill, the subject unfolds till it embraces the human race and touches the mysteries of life. One can show how Lincoln and Clemens were alike and how they differed. Both were of Southern origin, both knew the border between North and South, and both lived their formative years in a pioneer, or near-pioneer society. They shared the same type of native background, folkways,

[2] Herndon to Weik, Dec. 22, 1888, *ibid.*

[1] Dixon Wecter, "Lincoln, Mark Twain, and the Human Race," *Abr. Lincoln Quar.,* II, 157–175 (Dec., 1942); Bernard DeVoto, *The Portable Mark Twain* (intro.), 5.

and dialect. Both had a minimum of conventional education and formed their characters and intellects in the school of experience. Both had the advantage—for them—of growing up as poor boys. Both knew the rude horseplay, the side-splitting jest, the practical joke, and the preposterous tall tale of the West. Both were close to nature, with a tenderness for animals, though that was hardly a backwoods characteristic.

The same fascination, spell, and adventurous lure of the river stirred in their hearts. Clemens became a licensed river pilot and produced masterpieces of river literature. Lincoln's love of the river produced no literary results, but his biography would be incomplete without his river experiences. Coming down the Sangamon River in a large canoe was "the manner of A's [Abraham's] first entrance into Sangamon County." [2] His early introduction to the majesty of a local court was related to a boyhood river incident, his specialization in river navigation was of early political importance, and his inventive genius turned to the problem of easing a steamboat over shoals.

Each was to become, in a supreme sense, the very embodiment of that combination of qualities that we call "American." Both were "stamped unforgetably with the American brand." [3] Both had a sympathy for the Negro, and both gave poignant expression (Twain with devastating satire) to a sense of outrage at the mistreatment of the colored race. Both felt a kind of collective guilt on this subject and a long overdue debt which the white race owed to the colored. And of all the traits which they had in common, the most dominant and deeply felt was an overwhelming sense of protest against social abuse and human injustice.

There were, of course, contrasts between them. Lincoln's soul endured the fiery ordeal, and in the heat of war's crisis his leadership was shaped and his character forged. Clemens sat out the war, so to speak, or escaped it in a part of the far West that was, as Lincoln said, "undisturbed by the civil war." [4] They had a similar lack of enthusiasm for military "glory." Both Sam and Abraham recalled their brief army experiences as matters of burlesque and comedy. There was the obvious fact that Clemens was not a political leader and Lincoln

---

[2] Autobiography, June 1860, R. T. L. Coll., 3219.
[3] Wecter, in *Abr. Lincoln Quar.*, II, 157.
[4] *Works*, VIII, 99 (annual message to Congress, Dec. 1, 1862).

not (in the professional sense) a man of literature; but that did not mean that Twain ignored matters of statesmanship in his thinking, or that the President lacked the gift of expression. Mark could have written something like Lincoln's contribution to the Rebecca "Lost Township" letters or some of his less serious speeches, and Lincoln could have done some of the paragraphs of the *Gilded Age*. Mark Twain's comments on political life in Washington, on the party spirit (which he characterized with sharp bitterness), and on the meaning of patriotism, showed how much his mind was occupied with fundamentals of political and social democracy. One of their strongest traits in common was a deep-seated conviction of the need for self criticism in a democracy. For each the intolerable thing was imprisonment of the human mind. One of the faults which they both despised was a smug and unrealistic complacency in the face of crying abuses, North and South.

Lincoln's contrast to Clemens can be extended, both as to environment and as to personality. Clemens's association with men of wealth, his impracticality, his Sellers-like speculative dreams, restless travel, theatrical poses, boyish display, extravagance, craving for applause, and fastidiousness of dress set him apart from the homely lawyer and unpretentious President. And, as Dixon Wecter has pointed out, the ultimate philosophical outlook of Twain was, or seemed, the opposite of Lincoln's.

That is to say, Lincoln developed a serenity of optimism and democratic faith to which he gave classic expression, while Clemens seemed (or professed) to have a low opinion of the "damned human race," and, as his writings would indicate, became in the darkened evening of life bogged and tangled in a jungle of fatalism and despair. To each, of course, had come great personal tragedy—to Lincoln in the death of mother, sister, father, and two boys; to Clemens in a whole series of family casualties, including the terrible death of his brother Henry, the loss of children, and the passing of his beloved Olivia. It was Lincoln whose spirit was better able to recover from, though never to forget these sorrows; and, though both had disgust for conventional creeds and dogmas, it was Lincoln who was better able to grasp for his own personal uplift the eternal assurances of Christianity.

Looking over the whole subject, one realizes that Lincoln and Clemens would have understood each other if they had met and

conversed, which they never did. It has been remarked that they
would have enjoyed the same jokes, which was true; but that is a small
part of the subject. Each had a spirit sensitized to the tragedies of
Adam's breed. The bonds of personality that would have united
them were their Americanism, their humor, and their understanding of the human heart.

## VII

There are factors in life which need not so much to be explained
as to be appreciated and accepted. It is those who have relish for
Lincoln's humor who come nearest to understanding Lincoln the
man.

There is little profit, however, in disquisitions on the cause and
purpose of Lincoln's humor. The best place to seek his humor is
not in a cheap collection such as *Old Abe's Jokes, Fresh from Abraham's Bosom . . . .*[1] Humor is like caviar or *hors d'oeuvres*. One
should not make a meal of it. The passing moment has much to do
with the matter. The success of a joke is not always predictable. The
mood must be right, also the delivery, timing, and congeniality with
the listener. Humor in action or in running discourse is better than
humor in bottles with labels, or piled up in joke books. By contemporary accounts Lincoln's humor was successful. It was not of the
labored, limping variety which makes the inveterate jokester something of a nuisance.

It was in fact notably successful. People enjoyed Lincoln the better, and had more of a fellow feeling for him, as they repeated tales
of how he rode a galloping thunderstruck cow, or how he outwitted a
judge in a horse trade by swapping a saw-horse for the judge's sorry-
looking nag. His playfulness, in the western tradition, became in
his own lifetime at once a mark of popularity and a factor in American folklore.

It was true, of course, that sometimes his humor was turned against
him in denunciation or ridicule. For the campaign of 1864 there
appeared the following: "Only Authentic Life of Abraham Lincoln,
Alias 'Old Abe.' A Son of the West. With an account of his birth and

---

[1] Monaghan, *Lincoln Bibliography*, no. 335. This collection, published in 1864, was
the first of a considerable category. The subtitle ran on: "Containing all his Issues, Excepting the 'Greenbacks,' to call in some of which, this work is issued."

education, his rail-splitting and flat-boating, his joke-cutting and soldiering, with some allusions to his journeys from Springfield to Washington and BACK again. Sold by all Newsdealers in the Country." [2]

The journey *back to Springfield* was to have its unspeakable pathos after April 15, 1865, but in this 1864 leaflet the suggestion was only that Lincoln would be defeated in the coming election. As to making fun of his soldiering, one would need only to quote Lincoln himself. "By the way, Mr. Speaker [said Lincoln in Congress, in his rollicking speech in ridicule of Cass in the campaign of '48], did you know I am a military hero? Yes, sir; in the days of the Black Hawk War I fought, bled, and came away. Speaking of Gen. Cass' career, reminds me of my own. I was not at Stillman's defeat, but I was about as near it, as Cass was to Hulls surrender; and, like him, I saw the place very soon afterwards. It is quite certain that I did not break my sword, for I had none to break; but I bent a musket pretty badly on one occasion. . . . If Gen Cass went in advance of me in picking huckleberries, I guess I surpassed him in charges upon the wild onions. If he saw any live, fighting indians, it was more than I did; but I had a good many bloody struggles with the musquitoes . . . ." [3]

One should not bother too much to settle the questions as to how Lincoln "used" his mirth and pleasantry. One may think of it as part of him, indeed as part of his greatness. Tyrants and dictators do not laugh, nor do they induce genuine laughter. Popular jokes become associated with them, but the dictator is the butt or target, not the participant or raconteur, of the jest. Lincoln's anecdotes were human, close to the soil, and drawn from life. A famous example was his parable-like reference in 1858 to Stephen, James, Franklin, and Roger producing timbers which fitted together so perfectly as to convince the ordinary man that they had worked in collusion. [4] He knew that this type of illustration would make his point against Douglas and others memorable. It is always a question how many statements people will preserve in memory from a speech which they hear, but it is a

---

[2] *Ibid.*, no. 336.

[3] Speech in House of Representatives, July 27, 1848, photostat of Lincoln's autograph MS., A. Lincoln Assoc. (Nicolay and Hay, *Works*, II, 75–76.)

[4] *Works*, III, 10 (house divided speech, June 16, 1858). This simile was subject to criticism, since no such conspiracy between Douglas, Buchanan, Pierce, and Taney existed: see *Lincoln the President*, I, 108.

rather safe bet that they will recall the homely example or the concrete instance.

Chauncey M. Depew wrote: "His power of managing men, of deciding and avoiding difficult questions, surpassed that of any man I
ever met. A keen insight of human nature had been cultivated by the
trials and struggles of his early life. He knew the people and how to
reach them better than any man of his time. I heard him tell a great
many stories, many of which would not do exactly for the drawing-
room; but for the person he wished to reach, and the object he desired to accomplish with the individual, the story did more than any
argument could have done.

"He said to me once, in reference to some sharp criticisms which
had been made upon his story-telling: 'They say I tell a great many
stories; I reckon I do, but I have found in the course of a long experience that common people'—and repeating it—'common people, take
them as they run, are more easily influenced and informed through
the medium of a broad illustration than in any other way, and as to
what the hypercritical few may think I don't care.' "

". . . He said that, 'riding the circuit for many years and stopping
at country taverns where were gathered lawyers, jurymen, witnesses
and clients, they would sit up all night narrating to each other their
life adventures; and that the things which happened to an original
people, in a new country, surrounded by novel conditions, and told
with the descriptive power and exaggeration which characterized such
men, supplied him with an exhaustless fund of anecdotes which could
be made applicable for enforcing or refuting an argument better than
all the invented stories of the world.' " [5]

It was characteristic of Lincoln's joking while President that the
very darkest and stormiest of times would set off an explosion of
humor. "A frontiersman," he was quoted as saying, "lost his way in
an uninhabited region on a dark and tempestuous night. The rain
fell in torrents, accompanied by terrible thunder and more terrific
lightning. To increase his trouble his horse halted, being exhausted
with fatigue and fright. Presently a bolt of lightning struck a neigh-
boring tree, and the crash brought the man to his knees. He was not
an expert in prayer, but his appeal was short and to the point: 'Oh,

---

[5] Chauncey M. Depew, in Rice, *Reminiscences*, 427-428.

good Lord, if it is all the same with you, give us a little more light, and a little less noise!' " [6]

An appeal was once made to the President on behalf of a lieutenant who was accused of embezzling government money. It was charged that the officer had corruptly received while on duty the sum of forty dollars. "Why, Mr. Lincoln," exclaimed the officer, "it wa'n't but thirty dollars." This reminded Lincoln of an Indianian who got into a quarrel with a neighbor. "One charged that the other's daughter had three illegitimate children. 'Now,' said the man whose family was so outrageously scandalized, 'that's a lie, and I can prove it, for she only has two.' This case is no better [said Lincoln]. Whether the amount was thirty dollars or thirty thousand dollars, the culpability is the same. Then, after reading a little further, he said: 'I believe I will leave this case where it was left by the officers who tried it.' " [7]

A good story that has come down pertained to Lincoln's droll remark about one of his generals. As remembered by Ward Lamon, the President, arousing himself from meditation, remarked: " 'Do you know that I think General —— is a philosopher? He has proved himself a really great man. He has grappled with and mastered that ancient and wise admonition, 'Know thyself;' he has formed an intimate acquaintance with himself, knows as well for what he is fitted and unfitted as any man living. Without doubt he is a remarkable man. This war has not produced another like him.' "

" 'Why is it, Mr. President' asked his friend, 'that you are now so highly pleased with General ——? Has your mind not undergone a change?'

" 'Because,' replied Mr. Lincoln, with a merry twinkle of his eye, 'greatly to my relief, and to the interests of the country, *he has resigned*. And now I hope some other dress-parade commanders will study the good old admonition, "Know thyself," and follow his example.' " [8]

## VIII

By easing into a story Lincoln could change the climate of an interview. He could carry the ball, shape the trend, and control the

---

[6] Rufus Rockwell Wilson, *Intimate Memories of Abraham Lincoln*, 423.
[7] Lamon, *Recollections of Abraham Lincoln*, ed. by Dorothy Lamon Teillard, 83.
[8] *Ibid.*, 125–126.

direction of a conference. Conversation may be partly a matter of holding the floor. Lincoln would do this by bland good nature, his partner or opponent in discussion hardly realizing just how or why the breeze was shifting; then the President would conclude the conference with a smiling face without actually agreeing; or, in a crowd or reception, would slip away behind a barrage of merriment.

Lincoln's joking usually had pertinence to the subject in hand, but to think of every bit of his humor as serving a purpose or carrying a point would be a mistake. His laughter was a kind of release. It was Seward's impression that he "had no notion of recreation as such; enjoyed none; went thro' levees &c purely as a duty—found his only recreation in telling or hearing stories in the ordinary way of business—often stopped a cabinet council at a grave juncture, to jest a half-hour with the members before going to work; joked with every body, on light & on grave occasions. This was what saved him." [1]

Lincoln's humor was not "put on"; it was never artificial. A glimpse of the manner in which his fun making belonged to the daily, or hourly, Lincoln is seen in a newspaper item pertaining to Mrs. Lincoln who was visiting an ocean resort in the summer of '61. When she left for Washington a *Herald* reporter wrote that it was largely because she thought Lincoln was lonely. He needed some one to listen to his fun making. She said that he always joked and jested at the supper table "no matter what the labors and fatigues of the day"; he was always "[l]ively, sociable, and agreeable." [2]

The by-play of laughter was part of Lincoln's knack of being good company. It was an attribute of his magnetism. He was the man around whom fellow lawyers and courthouse loungers would cluster. Though his published works were usually serious, dignified, and well polished, humor served him as a kind of popular language. More than that, it was an actual resource in thought and deliberation; for the man of humor is superior in mental tools. He does not stop with the obvious stereotype or the conventional stock phrase. He takes another look at a problem, turns it over, gives it a new relevance. He frees himself from uninspired literalness. Characterizing a well known

---

[1] Henry W. Bellows to his wife (reporting a conversation with Seward), Apr. 23, 1863, Bellows MSS., Mass. Hist. Soc.

[2] New York *Herald*, Aug. 25, 1861, p. 2, c. 4; article dated at Long Branch, N.J., Aug. 23, 1861.

type, Robert Louis Stevenson remarked that "Some people swallow the universe like a pill." [3] These are the folk who take what is ladled out to them, who "fall for" partisan ballyhoo, who accept the politician at face value (which is more than politicians themselves do), and who believe what they see in print. But in a democracy the type of opinion that is vitally needed is of the sort that sees behind the demagogue's façade, or punctures the pompous orator's dignity. Such an attitude, stimulated by Lincolnian humor, is thus actually an element in the formation, or conditioning, of opinion.

To say that playfulness for Lincoln was a life-saver was no exaggeration. It was therapy of the spirit. Turning from dark worry to laughter was not, as Herndon ponderously supposed, a kind of deliberate or laborious setting-up exercise to induce circulation of the blood. Often it was an easing down, a relaxation, a healthy release from mental imprisonment. It is the man who can find such release who has the free intellect. To understand this fully is to attempt to realize, or perceive, pretty much the whole of Lincoln's wartime task, with all of its care, anxiety, immense responsibility, and unending pressure. Remembering this from direct observation of Lincoln, Depew wrote: "He knew the whole situation better than any man in the administration, and virtually carried on in his own mind not only the civic side of the government, but all the campaigns. And I knew when he threw himself (as he did once when I was there) on a lounge, and rattled off story after story, that it was his method of relief, without which he might have gone out of his mind, and certainly would not have been able to have accomplished anything like the amount of work which he did." [4]

For the rest, his lighter moods were a means of disarming (or winning over) an antagonist, of getting a hearing, of assuring popularity, of keeping the common touch, of enriching and enlivening the day's work. Even had there been no more to the subject—and there was vastly more—it would be enough to remember that anecdotes and jests were for Lincoln a source of enjoyment.

---

[3] R. L. Stevenson, "Crabbed Age and Youth," *Virginibus Puerisque and Other Papers,* 102.

[4] Rice, 428–429.

# CHAPTER V

# CAPITOL HILL

## I

IN 1833 an English observer penned a description of the American Congress. The principal object of the members, he said, was to impress constituents by long, meaningless speeches to be printed and sent home. Debate, rambling on from one topic to another, was confusing to listeners. There was, he thought, a certain difference between the two houses, with the Senate gaining, but only slightly, by the comparison. In the upper chamber, though there were some outstanding men such as "Livingstone [sic], . . . , Webster, . . . Hayne, . . . [etc.]," he found "the same loose, desultory, and inconclusive mode of discussion . . . but . . . less talking for the mere purpose of display, and less of that tawdry emptiness and vehement imbecility which prevails in the Representatives." [1]

Thirty years later Gideon Welles, recalling his visit to the Senate in the year 1829, contrasted his old-time memories with what he knew of the upper house in 1863. "There is [he said] an impotent and ridiculous attempt at self-sufficient and presuming airs, an exhibition of lame and insolent arrogance, on the part of many Senators towards men who are, to say the least, their equals in every good quality." "If the present room is larger [than thirty-four years earlier]," he wrote, "the Senators seem smaller." At another time he observed: "The demagogues in Congress disgrace the body and the country. Noisy . . . professions, with no useful policy or end, exhibit themselves daily." [2]

---

[1] *Annual Register* [London], 1833, 467–470. Allowing for the unescapable truth in these observations, one is nevertheless reminded of Lowell's essay "On a Certain Condescension in Foreigners," *Atl. Mo.*, XXIII, 82–94 (1869).
[2] Welles, *Diary*, I, 224, 244, 206.

This was a familiar *motif*—the theme that the quality of Congress had deteriorated. Another observer who recorded the same impression was Carl Schurz, writing of the time when Charles Sumner entered the Senate. It was a new era (about the end of 1851); the voices of Calhoun, Clay, and Webster were no longer to be heard in that famous body. Schurz wrote: "What was left of the old generation of public men was mediocrity and commonplace—country lawyers grown up in the politics of their localities and had [*sic*] a slight smattering of general knowledge gathered from the reading of some of the standard histories—tobacco-chewing statesmen with dull and heavy minds, uncouth manners and pompous airs." [3]

On this matter, of course, opinions differed, and encomiums on Congress in Lincoln's day were not lacking. One of the members, A. G. Riddle, remarked on the Thirty-Seventh Congress (1861–63) that history does not "show any large body of men surprised by a great emergency, which ever met it more unitedly or with a more determined spirit." The Congress of those days, he wrote, was "a huge committee of ways and means, where should work the brain, and the controlling will, and whence should issue the law, the mandates, the sinews, which together should accomplish the real purpose to be wrought out by the war itself." He thought the President and the armies were on a less important level. "In this view the President merely executed the expressed will of Congress. The great armies, with their generals, . . . were the mere mechanics of the struggle." [4]

On another page Riddle left a different set of impressions. In casting his eye over members of the House, his first thought was "wonder as to how half the men ever got there." "One is next impressed," said Riddle, "by the audacity, or serene stupidity, which enables so many men to be willing to occupy these seats." He wondered whether there was anywhere in the world "so melancholy a book as *The Political Register and Congressional Directory* . . . by Ben: Perley Poore?" [5]

---

[3] Arthur Reed Hogue, ed., *Charles Sumner: An Essay by Carl Schurz*, 8 (intro.). This is from Schurz's first draft; the passage was considerably weakened when redrafted.
[4] Albert G. Riddle, *Recollections of War Times*, 36, 42.
[5] *Ibid.*, 222.

## II

It was in 1861, Lincoln's first year as President, that the Republican party had for the first time in American history a majority in the Congress. It was called, however, a "rump Congress." Of the thirty-four commonwealths in the United States it included members from only twenty-three that adhered to the Union. (In addition, what was called "restored Virginia" was represented, and Senator Andrew Johnson of Tennessee retained his seat for some months after his state seceded. Later in the war West Virginia and Nevada were admitted.) If the Congress had been fully national—i. e., if the eleven seceded states had been represented—the Republicans would not have had a majority.[1]

Under these circumstances it was but natural that the 1861 Congress consisted chiefly of new men. "From Maine every representative was a new man; of the thirty-three members from New York, only eight had held seats in the last Congress; of the five representatives from New Jersey, three were new men. Two thirds of the entire delegation in the House consisted of men who had never before held seats in Congress."[2]

A glance at the roster of members in the period 1861 to 1865 proves puzzling now; so many of the names strike no chord. Who was Socrates N. Sherman of New York? Or Ambrose W. Clark or Burt Van Horn from the same state? Few would be able to identify such men as Portus Baxter of Vermont, George T. Cobb or John L. N. Stratton of New Jersey, Sydenham E. Ancona or John P. Verree of Pennsylvania or Robert H. Nugen of Ohio.[3]

This newness, inexperience, and obscurity on the part of many members tended toward submissiveness, giving expanded influence

---

[1] Coöperationists in the South in the crisis of 1860–61, noting that Lincoln was not an abolitionist and "not in harmony with the extremists of his party," argued further that "even if he wished to encroach upon the South, he would be unable to do so, because majorities in both branches of Congress would be against him." In the Senate, supposing all the states represented, the opposition to Lincoln was estimated to have a majority of eight; in the House, a majority of twenty-one. Dwight L. Dumond, *The Secession Movement, 1860–1861*, 130–131.

[2] *Harper's Pictorial History of the Civil War*, I, 184.

[3] *Biographical Directory of the American Congress* (House Doc. No. 783, 69 Cong., 2 sess.), 266–274.

to a few leaders or managers. That these managers were anti-Lincoln is constantly to be borne in mind in any study of the wartime situation. It was the leading managers who stayed on; otherwise there was a considerable turnover of congressional membership. The Republicans did not fare well by the election of 1862,[4] and the consequence was described as follows by one of the members: "Seldom has the personnel of a House been so completely changed without a change of parties."[5]

As times changed it might have been said that America had passed from the period of senatorial grandeur—the era of Webster, Calhoun, Clay, and Benton—but had not outlived the age of grandiloquence. In the sixties the spreadeagle style, often in decadent form, was still in vogue. Much was mere oratory, designed not so much to promote legislation as to offer a sounding board for particular members. The attention of those who (presumably) would read the speeches when mailed to them, and the approval of the galleries, were seldom disregarded. The floor of Congress was more the scene of exhibitionist performance than of serious business.

It was said of President Lincoln's first Congress, as well as of himself and his cabinet, that they were chosen "to do anything, everything, except what fell to them to do—fight the greatest civil war of history, one of the enormous wars of modern times."[6] This task "came upon them as an utter surprise. . . . The great contest passed . . . through all stages—moral, political, legislative, judicial—and no man of the North (and perhaps few of the South) was at first in the least aware of the tendency, until, armed, they stood confronting each other, neither believing the other intended very war."[7]

The House of Representatives, thought Riddle, was "unquestionably the worst place in America for a man to speak in." What with members sauntering in and out, loafing, telling stories, and creating a general air of confusion and inattention, it became necessary for the member who (in a manner of speaking) had "the floor" to raise his voice to so high a volume (for the reporters) "as to preclude all free mental action."[8] Sometimes the Congress was enveloped with the

---

[4] *Lincoln the President*, II, 232–234.    [5] Riddle, 249.    [6] *Ibid.*, 37.
[7] *Ibid.*, 37–38. That Lincoln did not intend war is brought out by Riddle (38–39).
[8] *Ibid.*, 223.

"lurid atmosphere" of battle, with artillery actually shaking the walls of the Capitol. Whether that battle setting was literally present or not, the national legislature "was an arena in which men could not win distinction or secure the attention of the press or public." [9] "During the entire war [wrote Riddle] the American people knew little, saw little of the men in Congress, and cared only that they should create and supply the needed money, and back Mr. Lincoln and the Secretary of War." [10] The point of all this is that, while men spoke for display, and while full galleries indicated popular curiosity, the people neither cared much for Congress nor were conversant with its proceedings.

Riddle found it hard to understand "the attachment that men form for Congressional life." It seemed strange to him that some members were so "bitten of it" that after ceasing to be members they would work hard to be appointed sergeant-at-arms, doorkeeper, or postmaster "where once they were masters." This Ohio member spoke with loathing of the title "Honorable" prefixed to members' names. His comment brings to mind Congressman Lincoln's request in 1848 that his wife avoid the title in her letters to him. As for the volumes of the *Globe,* they aroused in Riddle no more enthusiasm than a retiring congressman's "scrapbook filled with newspaper laudations and criticisms." Taking satisfaction in the fact that he had at least escaped personal injury, Riddle remarked: "No man has ever served through three congresses and returned healthfully to take up his old . . . pursuits." As for the upper house, he thought, "nobody cares much for the Senate save to get into it." [11]

The very building, its passageways and odors, had become offensive to Riddle, and in the years following his brief congressional service, if he visited the Capitol—he was then practising law in Washington —he found that "the old dismaying flavor assails me, bringing momentary heart failure." His friendships had not been confined to men of his own party. He remarked: "Indeed, I have always found disinterested friends [he also called them "assured" friends] among the Democrats, and have observed among politicians that the warmest personal ties are usually across party lines." [12]

---

9 *Ibid.,* 32.　　10 *Ibid.,* 40.　　11 *Ibid.,* 40, 224-225.　　12 *Ibid.,* 226-227.

## III

Of one thing there was no doubt: members of Congress in Lincoln's day were picturesque individuals. Their habits, clothes, visages, posturings, and verbal displays offered many a theme for the artist and the reporter. Curiosity as to seeing public men in person and watching them perform has long been an American trait, as shown by the visitors who regularly crowded the galleries of House and Senate. In the upper chamber on a typical day there were about forty or less in attendance. Total membership was forty-eight, including two from Virginia (the "restored" government set up at Wheeling). Some of the senators—such as Lafayette S. Foster of Connecticut, Richard S. Field of New Jersey, Anthony Kennedy of Maryland, and Robert Wilson of Missouri—made only a slight impression. Those who were "well known" numbered hardly more than a dozen. Leaders who were largely effective in actually shaping public affairs were still fewer.

One of "the few men whom visitors to the Senate galleries first asked to have pointed out" was Charles Sumner of Massachusetts. Conscious of his superiority, meticulously careful in pose and dress, this successor of Webster was the very model of an important senator. "His favorite costume was a brown coat and light waistcoat, lavender-colored or checked trousers, and shoes with English gaiters," otherwise known as spats. It has been reported from his own lips that "he never allowed himself, even in the privacy of his own chamber, to fall into a position which he would not take in his chair in the Senate." In that seat and on the floor he was "studiously dignified." Preparation for his speeches was made weeks in advance, and prying youngsters, with no respect for his privacy, could see him in his rooms, "before a pier-glass . . . , studying the effect of his gestures by the light of lamps placed at each side of the mirror." [1]

Though his manner was pedantic, he was assisted by a "magnificent voice" and genuine learning. Lincoln is said to have remarked that Sumner was his idea of a bishop.[2] The senator "regarded his position

---

[1] Noah Brooks, *Washington in Lincoln's Time*, 24-25.

[2] Frank Maloy Anderson, ed., *The Mystery of "A Public Man": A Historical Detective Story*, 216. Lincoln may or may not have made the remark, but it describes Sumner and it has a Lincolnian flavor.

as Chairman of the Committee on Foreign Relations as superior to all others in Congress, while he was unquestionably the leader of the Abolition wing of the Republican party." [3]

In the camps of leading generals the feeling toward Sumner and men of his kind was not always favorable. From Meade's headquarters Colonel Theodore Lyman wrote as follows on March 5, 1864: "I find that politicians, like Sumner and company, have a way of saying of officers who have had their very clothes shot off their back and have everywhere displayed the utmost skill and courage, that 'their hearts are not in the cause,' or 'they are not fully with us'; meaning that these officers do not happen to fully agree with every political dogma the party may choose to enunciate." He added: "it would appear that Washington people often think the best test of faithfulness is to stay away from the fighting and make a good many speeches to people who entirely agree with your sentiments." [4]

Some of Sumner's associates considered him dictatorial and insufferable. His speaking perfection was carried to an extreme; it was like an overindulgence in "fine writing." He was too scholarly and precise; his rehearsed performance and self-conscious emphasis smacked of the oracular, while his "fastidiousness," even in matters of ordinary routine, "provoked injurious comments." [5]

All told, however, Sumner was a man worth noting; there were times (notably in the *Trent* affair) when the country would have been poorer without his public service and achievement. Fully to appraise him, one must remember that the principles in which he ardently believed—international peace, antislavery, rights for Negroes—were, for him, burning and compelling impulses; he was not animated, as many were, by the commoner motives of the politician. Into the advocacy of these principles he put tremendous—albeit pompous and self-righteous—effort. He felt and believed, deeply and sincerely, in what he was working for. Though rhetorical to excess, he was by no means a mere orator. One cannot study his life fully without realizing that he was fearless, disdainful of upper-class petting or praise, outspoken in dealing with matters on which others were timid (e. g., the shocking denial of civil rights in the fugitive slave act of 1850), and earnestly

---

[3] Poore, *Perley's Reminiscences*, II, 98.    [4] Agassiz, ed., *Meade's Headquarters*, 78–79.
[5] Brooks, 23–24.

conscious of moral imperatives. The regret is that he was difficult—some would have said impossible—to get along with. In his "Crime against Kansas" he was terribly at fault in his abuse of Southerners; that his message was clothed in a superior garb of ostentatious learning and misplaced similes made the abuse no easier to bear. (Preston Brooks was vastly more at fault in thinking that the answer to Sumner was to assault him with a cane and give him a severe beating. Nor did Brooks's answer gain true validity by its guise of "honorable" conduct.) [6]

Sumner and his partner from Massachusetts were sometimes mentioned in the same breath,[7] but in personal characteristics they were of different mold. Henry Wilson had none of Sumner's elegance. As described by Noah Brooks he was "rather loose and ramshackle in his manner of speech; his enunciation was not distinct, his delivery was slipshod, and he was neither precise nor fortunate in his choice of words . . . ." He was not handsome or prepossessing, but "stout, florid, dark-haired, and of a portly figure." [8]

Wilson was, however, one of the key men in the Senate. He was more concerned with congressional business and formulative labor than with oratory or showmanship. As chairman of the committee on military affairs, with a background as brigadier general of Massachusetts state militia, he had an active part in devising, explaining, and promoting legislative measures touching the raising and organizing of the army. This is not to say, however, that his measures were always well chosen.

No study of the wartime Senate, especially in the latter part of Lincoln's administration, is adequate without frequent reminders of the prominence of Benjamin F. Wade of Ohio and Zachariah Chandler of Michigan.[9] Wade was described as of the "Cromwellian type," a man "of rugged, fierce, and vindictive feeling." [10] Noah Brooks al-

---

[6] See the work by E. L. Pierce (4 vols.), and the briefer account by Moorfield Storey. Sumner's voluminous papers are in the Harvard library. David Donald, author of *Lincoln's Herndon*, is preparing a full-length biography. Carl Schurz's eloquent essay on Sumner, unfinished at Schurz's death, remained buried for many years. It has been brought to light and edited by Arthur Reed Hogue (Univ. of Ill. Press, 1951).

[7] For Gurowski's withering comment on Sumner and Wilson, see *Lincoln the President*, II, 209.

[8] Brooks, 23.

[9] *Lincoln the President*, II, 209–210.

[10] Cox, *Three Decades of Federal Legislation*, 88.

lowed that the Ohio senator was "tender-hearted" and "lovable," "the embodiment of the high qualities that he possessed—manliness, courage, vehemence, and . . . bulldog obduracy . . . ." Having said this, Brooks noted further that his "impatience" with the Lincoln administration "betrayed him into frequent exhibitions of bad temper, . . . and his intense radicalism too often hurried him into complications with the more conservative Union politicians . . . ." Brooks thought that "he did not always extricate himself from these entanglements with credit to himself." [11] In one of his thumbnail portraits Ben: Perley Poore wrote: "Then there was bluff Ben Wade, of Ohio, whose honesty was strongly tinged by ambition, and who looked at the contest with the merciless eyes of a gladiator about to close in a death-grip." [12]

Much the same mixture of eulogy and denunciation is to be found in accounts of Zach Chandler. George F. Hoar of Massachusetts found him "strong as a rock, true as steel, fearless and brave, honest and incorruptible." In a glowing passage, too long to repeat here, Hoar went on to speak of the senator's plain spoken simplicity, scorn for elegant phrases, and disregard "for fine sentiment or the delicacies of a refined literature." Without such men as Chandler, Hoar believed that "the Union never would have been saved, or slavery abolished, or the faith kept." [13]

Such a comment indicated, what is well known, that Chandler had his partisans. If one thinks, however, of Lincoln and of his chances for success with Congress, the quality for which Chandler became most conspicuous, and in which he was most influential, was his "distrust," [14] or rather his acrimonious hostility, to presidential policies, and toward the President himself as a leader. The senator's vindictive aggressiveness on domestic problems was matched, as is often the case, with startling jingoism in international outlook. The partisanship of the man, directed toward the utter dominance of a faction within a party, was to appear in later years. His success as a politician rested

11 Brooks, 26.

12 *Perley's Reminiscences,* II, 100. A. G. Riddle, Wade's eulogist and biographer, called him "the first man in the Senate." Riddle, *Recollections,* 40.

13 Hoar, *Autobiography of Seventy Years,* II, 75 ff. Hoar, however, admitted that Chandler had "great faults" (p. 77), and wrote, as did others, of his vigorous control of patronage.

14 McClure, *Men of War-Times,* 62.

on questionable use of patronage to build up his political control in Michigan.

## IV

In judging of the House of Representatives one needs to distinguish between the façade, or showcase, and the unpublicized situation behind the scenes. In terms of later standards one might have regarded the office of speaker as of great importance, but during the Lincoln administration that office lacked the dominance that it was to acquire in the days of Thomas B. Reed or Joseph G. Cannon. Yet some of the most exciting episodes in the House wing were connected with the election of the speaker. In the last prewar Congress it had taken eight long weeks of wrangling and balloting to elect to the speakership William Pennington of New Jersey, a man of little distinction.[1] The Republican choice for the Thirty-Seventh Congress (1861–1863), Galusha A. Grow of Pennsylvania, was known for pioneer vigor, physical impressiveness, combativeness toward Southerners, and earnest agitation for free homesteads, but he was not destined to become outstanding in the history of the speakership.

Of Schuyler Colfax it might be said that he was the stuff of which vice presidents are made.[2] Not that he should be written off as altogether a minor figure; indeed he was one of the best known men of his time. He was described as "neat, nimble, shiny, on his face a constant smile which might easily have been called a smirk." [3] This smile was a trademark; he was known as "Smiler Colfax." It was observed that in presiding over the House his manner "left something to be desired." He performed "like an auctioneer." [4]

James A. Garfield of Ohio belonged to the small group of men—

---

[1] In this Congress the first vote for speaker was taken on the first day, December 5, 1859, the eventual winner (Pennington) receiving one vote, that of John Sherman of Ohio. *Cong. Globe*, 36 Cong., 1 sess., 2. On the forty-fourth and last ballot, Feb. 1, 1860, Pennington received 117 votes, the minimum necessary to a choice. *Ibid.*, 655. He could not have been chosen but for Knownothing votes, and should not be regarded as a leading contender for the speakership; that designation should be applied to McClernand on the Democratic side and Sherman on the Republican.

[2] In 1868 Schuyler Colfax was nominated as Republican candidate for Vice President after five ballots in the national convention. He was elected and served during Grant's first administration, but for the second term he was rejected in favor of Henry Wilson. Edward Stanwood, *History of the Presidency*, I, 321, 328, 348.

[3] D. B. Chidsey, *The Gentleman from New York: A Life of Roscoe Conkling*, 64.

[4] Brooks, 21.

including Edward D. Baker, Frank P. Blair, Jr., and Robert Schenck —who alternated between a military and a congressional career. Such men, though something of a problem for Lincoln, attracted particular attention, as when Garfield entered upon his service in the House (December, 1863) in the uniform of a brigadier general, soon to be exchanged for civilian clothes. In 1861, with no previous military experience, he had left the principalship of the institute that later became Hiram College in Ohio to form a regiment, of which he became colonel and in which a large portion of his student body enlisted. Brigadier general at the age of thirty, and shortly thereafter major general and congressman, he was well started, though that was hardly suspected at the time, on the road to the presidency.[5]

Henry Winter Davis of Maryland, Republican radical, is chiefly remembered for his sharp hostility toward Lincoln's policy for restoration of the South. This was bitter enough, but his opposition to the existing administration did not end there. He extended his activity to other fields, including the international. In 1864 he introduced a resolution intended as a rebuke and check upon Secretary Seward, and designed to give the lower house control of foreign policy. His resolution asserted that Congress "has a constitutional right to an authoritative voice in declaring and prescribing the foreign policy of the United States" and "it is the constitutional duty of the President to respect that policy . . . in diplomatic negotiations." When a matter was pending in Congress, his resolution continued, it was "not a fit topic of diplomatic explanation with any foreign Power."[6] Incidentally, remembering the declaration of the House in 1861 in approving the unauthorized act of Wilkes, the Davis principle would have made it impossible for Lincoln to have adjusted the *Trent* affair, thus seriously endangering the nation, besides robbing the Lincoln government of a significant diplomatic success.

"Having turned Radical, for a purpose," wrote Edward Bates, "he [Davis] seems to ignore all former doctrines, and stakes his all on the struggle for leadership of his faction." Bates noted how "peremptory,"

---

5 Robert Granville Caldwell, *James A. Garfield: Party Chieftain.*

6 Davis's resolution died with the session. It was offered on June 27, 1864; the session ended on July 2. To have voted on the resolution in the existing parliamentary situation would have required a suspension of the rules. How far Davis expected a vote is doubtful; he supposed "the House will probably be too impatient to give it much consideration." *Cong. Globe*, 38 Cong., 1 sess., 3309 (June 27, 1864).

yet how "conveniently vague," Davis's resolution was. He predicted
that the Marylander would "kill himself off." "The original radicals
will not trust him—His knavery is of a different sort from theirs." [7]

Gideon Welles looked upon Davis's drive for power as part of a
"disposition to make the legislative . . . the controlling power of
the government." "Davis," he said, "never has been, and never will
be, a useful Member of Congress. Although possessing talents, he is
factious, uneasy, and unprincipled." Welles bracketed Davis with "a
clique of malcontents" which he also characterized as an "embryo
party." [8]

Davis was a member of the Thirty-Eighth Congress (1863–65), but
not of the Thirty-Seventh (1861–63). We have the following description by Noah Brooks: "At that time he was about forty-five years of
age [forty-seven in 1864], . . . with a round, boyish head, sandy
hair and mustache. He had a high, clear, ringing voice, and a manner of speaking which was peculiar in its sharpness and firmness. He
was a brilliant speaker, but not a ready debater . . . . Garfield once
said of him that his eloquence was 'clear and cold, like starlight.' " In
summing up his appraisal of Davis, Brooks observed that he had "not
left any lasting trace of his public career" except for one thing—"his
record as a persistent and violent critic of Lincoln's reconstruction
policy." [9]

Conspicuous among the "politicos" was Roscoe Conkling of New
York. Handsome and well endowed, he was superb in masculine
beauty, with well modeled head, full beard, and pendant curl atop
his forehead. Like Garfield, John Sherman, and Blaine, his chief
prominence was to be reached in garish postwar decades. With his
striking appearance, unbounded confidence, oratory, and talent for
politician-like management, he was to ride the crest of triumphant
Republicanism almost to the presidency, while he was also to contribute to the intraparty factionalism so evident in the eighties. "Possibly like Pooh Bah," writes his biographer, "he was *born* sneering."
"He was touchy, temperamental . . . , incalculably conceited."
Though he became a boss, he was not the friendly "mixer" type.
Rather he was "haughty, supercilious, aloof." As for crowds, he

---

[7] Bates, *Diary*, 380 (June 28, 1864).          [8] Welles, *Diary*, II, 202 (Dec. 19, 1864).
[9] Brooks, 18.

wanted them "in front of him and a little below, respectfully listening." He was a Beau Brummell "in the exact sense that while he did
not originate fashions he sported them incomparably." [10] Known as
a successful lawyer, in which capacity he was famous for "bullying
witnesses," [11] the gentleman from upstate New York was a formidable
fighter in controversial, even hateful, episodes. In certain obvious
matters he and the President were in apparent or alleged agreement.

When Lincoln wrote in 1864 that "no one could be more satisfactory" [12] to him than Conkling, he may have had in mind the congressman's vigorous support of emancipation and of measures friendly
to the Negro race. Also it should be remembered that the choice was
limited to men who were actually available, and that the Republican
faction opposed to Conkling was unfriendly to the President.

Conkling, in fact, developed a reputation as a "staunch supporter"
of Lincoln, also as being the "legatee of Seward." [13] This was misleading. His attitude toward Southern reconstruction was the opposite of Seward's, while his support for Lincoln was belied by his
friendliness toward Thad Stevens, his similarity to Henry Winter
Davis, his prominence in the formation of the committee on the
conduct of the war, his severe denunciation of General Charles P.
Stone, his vindictiveness, and his full assortment of "radical" [14] tendencies. It is hard to see how in the full accounting he should have
been deemed an upholder of Lincolnian policies. Here was something
of a paradox. The successful invoking of Lincoln's name (where convenient) by a man such as Conkling was one of the misleading signs
of the times. Both Henry Winter Davis and Roscoe Conkling were

---

10 Chidsey, *Roscoe Conkling*, 1–2, 4–5.

11 *Ibid.*, 11.

12 If Lincoln praised Conkling here it was indeed faint praise. He added: "I do not
mean to say there [are] not others as good as he in the district; but I think I know him
to be at least good enough." Lincoln to Ward Hunt, Aug. 16, 1864, photostat, A. Lincoln Assoc.

13 Alfred R. Conkling, *The Life and Letters of Roscoe Conkling, Orator, Statesman,
Advocate*, 188, 204. This is a worshipful eulogy by a nephew. For a colorful, modern,
and highly readable treatment, see the biography by Donald Barr Chidsey, cited above.

14 The reader, of course, will not be misled by the term "radical" applied to Conkling.
While belonging to the group specifically known as "radicals" (Thaddeus Stevens, Henry
Winter Davis, and their kind), he was conservative on economic and social questions,
undemocratic, supporter of Grant against "Liberal Republicans," and in later life "a
prosperous corporation lawyer with some unsavory but rich clients." Chidsey, *Roscoe
Conkling*, 364.

considered good Republicans; yet the Marylander was famous for assailing Lincoln, while it was said of the New Yorker that "the mantle of the late Winter Davis" had fallen upon him.[15]

## V

Of the "peace Democrats" in the House, the most conspicuous, not to say notorious, were Clement L. Vallandigham of Ohio and Fernando Wood of New York. The Ohioan came to be shunned and scorned by men of his own party.[1] His attitude was complex and not susceptible of easy definition. He denied the allegation that he was anti-Union. What can be said with assurance is that, from the standpoint of the Union cause promoted as a war movement against the Southern Confederacy, he was regarded as disloyal (this again being a charge that he would have stoutly denied). His opposition to the Lincoln administration was made abundantly clear, as was also his belief that the war was wicked, atrocious, and futile.

Vallandigham was dangerous in that he used the time-honored traditions of civil rights as weapons against the existing government. He was "altogether a personable man," with regular features, complexion "fresh and fair," manner "agreeable and prepossessing." Though he spoke with great excitement and convulsive gestures, he was described as "a good speaker—smooth, plausible, and polished, . . . well versed in literature, history, and politics." He had high nuisance value in "filibustering" tactics. At a "wave of his hand" the Vallandigham faction in the House would "scud into the  . . .  cloakrooms"; at another signal they would rush back to their seats when needed."[2] (This is not to imply that they accomplished much on the floor of the House.) Sometimes a movement with which a man

---

[15] Conkling's sarcastic personal enemy, James G. Blaine, could not endure this comparison. "The resemblance is striking," he said. "Hyperion to a satyr, . . . mud to marble, . . . a singed cat to a Bengal tiger, a whining puppy to a roaring lion. Shade of the mighty Davis, forgive the almost profanation of that jocose satire!" *Cong. Globe*, 39 Cong., 1 sess., 2299 (Apr. 30, 1866).

[1] The Vallandigham element proved a serious embarrassment to McClellan in 1864, and when Democrats and moderate Republicans were promoting the Philadelphia convention of August 1866, designed to develop sentiment for non-vindictive reconstruction, Democratic leaders made it clear that they did not want Vallandigham to be associated with the movement.

[2] Brooks, 18–19.

is indelibly associated embraces more than the man himself, and that was true of Vallandigham. As will be noted in another chapter, the whole subject of Lincoln's "arbitrary" rule on the one side, and wartime civil rights on the other, was dramatized and focused in the Vallandigham case.[3] In the long run he probably increased the number of pro-Lincoln votes.

Fernando Wood of New York was for good reason regarded as an ally of Vallandigham, but the two men were very different in personality. The Ohioan was nervous and fiery, the New Yorker polished, restrained, and calculating. Adept in Manhattan "politics," Wood had achieved influence in Tammany Hall, but he became much more prominent by organizing "Mozart Hall," a vigorous rival of the Tammany Society.[4] Much of his life was involved in the roaring factionalism of metropolitan politics in the days of "Dead Rabbits," "Bowery Boys," and other riotous gangs.[5] He was a "democrat" with the small letter, battling against Whig conservatism, opposing nativist intolerance, and favoring free trade in opposition to the protective tariff. In several terms as mayor of New York City he promoted movements for a better and more efficient city administration. In the secession crisis of 1860–61, having naturally opposed the election of Lincoln, Wood took the view that Southern withdrawal was inevitable, remembered that New York City was joined by many business links with the South, and declared that the metropolis ought to secede from the United States and set itself up as a "free city." This novel idea produced a flurry of discussion but went no further.

For a time, just after the Sumter outbreak, Wood spoke for vigorous and non-partisan support of the Union, but in a few months he was bitterly denouncing the Lincoln administration, opposing conscription, favoring peace negotiation with Southern leaders, and, by the admission of his friendly biographer, coming "dangerously close to treason." [6] As congressman in the years 1863 to 1865 he continued

---

[3] See below, chap. ix.

[4] For a thorough and detailed study, revealing the intricacies of metropolitan, state, and national Democratic politics, see *Fernando Wood of New York*, by Samuel A. Pleasants (1948). Though admitting Wood's defects, including conduct that "approached the line of disloyalty during the Civil War," this biographer urges (p. 201) that "a comprehensive estimate of the man should note more creditable features as well."

[5] Pleasants, *Fernando Wood*, 80, 81.

[6] *Ibid.*, 120.

the agitation of Vallandigham, who was not in Congress during that period.

Described as a "born politician," Wood is said to have "depended far more upon . . . the sharing of drinks and the manifestations of a warm personal interest in the ordinary voter, than upon the more orthodox methods." [7] It was said that he "knew every longshoreman in his district by name." [8] As portrayed by Brooks, he "was always calm, cool, and collected. His hair and mustache were dyed black, and his thin, spare face, elegant manners, and precise method of speech, gave him the appearance of a refined and scholarly man. He never lost his temper, was always agreeable, polite and even courtly." [9]

The full story of these two stinging gadflies—Vallandigham and Wood—cannot be told in a paragraph. It is true that Wood worked with Vallandigham and that the pair were thought of as a team of "peace Democrats." It is also true, however, that Wood "did not like Vallandigham, and on more than one occasion he held long conversations with President Lincoln in regard to the notorious Ohio Copperhead. He was especially anxious that Lincoln should not make a martyr of Vallandigham . . . ." [10] On the question of peace, and of the return of the Southern states to the Union, he wrote challenging letters to Lincoln, worrying the President with nagging demands that the President's own letters, meant to be confidential, should be published.[11]

Also prominent among the outspoken anti-Lincoln Democrats was the "Tall Sycamore of the Wabash," Daniel W. Voorhees, representative from Indiana. His virulent speaking was the more effective because of his striking appearance, natural talent for eloquence, and mastery of invective. In his strong dislike of abolitionists and of the Republican party he was sometimes bracketed with Vallandigham and Wood, but his career was not always negative and obstructionist. He was vigorous in denouncing arbitrary arrests and was described by an admirer and colleague as "an eloquent tribune of the people." [12]

A vivid personality among the House Democrats was S. S. ("Sunset") [13] Cox of Ohio. He was not a man to be overlooked, being often

[7] *Ibid.*, 27.　　　[8] *Ibid.*, 202.　　　[9] Brooks, 19-20.　　　[10] *Ibid.*, 20.
[11] To be treated in a later volume, in connection with peace discussions of 1864.
[12] Cox, *Three Decades*, 224.
[13] So called because of his vivid passage describing a sunset.

on the floor, and was known for witty, facetious, and emphatic speeches. Though personally friendly toward Vallandigham, his general attitude was that of a loyal Democrat supporting measures to uphold the Union cause, and coming forward with constructive proposals for the adjustment of the *Trent* affair, the abandonment of privateering, and the honorable treatment of crews and officers on captured Confederate ships. It was he, according to his own statement, who "nominated [William T.] Sherman to President Lincoln as the first choice of Ohio for a brigadier general." [14] Cox's long career was remarkable not only in politics. He was a distinguished lawyer and was interested in western development. With his flair for writing, he was known also for achievement in journalism and literature.

## VI

Thaddeus Stevens of Pennsylvania was well understood to be the Republican leader in the House of Representatives. It is true that he disclaimed the role of party spokesman, saying rather that he was "ahead of the party" and that he did "not speak the sentiments of this [Republican] side of the House." When Maynard of Tennessee pointed out that the Pennsylvanian's remarks would be taken as "those of a representative of his party," Stevens replied: "I speak for myself only." Maynard's rejoinder was: "it will not be so understood." [1] From this colloquy it will appear (1) that Stevens's power in the House was so widely known that he was recognized as the spokesman of the Republican party; and (2) that this spokesmanship was so ill defined, vague, and unauthorized that all responsibility could be easily brushed aside. The House could not control Stevens; yet (not always, but as a regular thing) Stevens went far toward controlling the House. It was not a matter of leadership duly organized and officially determined, but rather of a forceful man imposing his will by methods of his own upon a working majority of the House.

Stevens's official status was that of chairman of the committee on ways and means, whose duty it was to study what would now be called the budget (a word not much used then) and to prepare tax legisla-

---

14 Cox, *Three Decades*, 208.
1 *Cong. Globe*, 37 Cong., 3 sess., 240 (Jan. 8, 1863).

tion, but he got tangled up on tax questions [2] and his activities could not be described in terms of committee functions. In what sense, then, was Stevens a "leader"? Who made him a leader? He was not speaker of the House, nor was he majority leader in the fully recognized sense. If it suited him he would speak for the House; otherwise he would claim to speak only for himself. Yet people came to look to him as more of a spokesman of the party than Lincoln. Since it was the party in control, his word passed as that of the most numerous branch of the national Congress.

What was called Stevens's leadership was strongly flavored with boss rule. On one side of the coin one sees Stevens with his forceful scowl and domineering personality. The reverse of the coin was a kind of weakness or follow-the-leader habit on the part of large droves of Republicans in the House. Power was exerted by the making of "deals," by party caucus, by informal agreements, and by striking the fear of the Lord into the hearts of any who might stand up against him. In July 1861 Stevens maneuvered it so that Galusha A. Grow, whom he could manage, was chosen speaker instead of Frank Blair, Jr., whom he hated. Blair, besides being friendly to Lincoln, was by far the more forceful man; Stevens's hand in the affair made all the difference.[3] In December 1863, at the opening of the Thirty-Eighth Congress, a visitor to the House would have noted that Washburne of Illinois nominated his rival, Colfax of Indiana, for speaker, and that with the smoothness of a well oiled machine Colfax was easily chosen. What was not evident on the surface was that this was by Stevens's design. It had all been worked out by backstage combinations and bargains among House Republican members.

Stevens's coarse manner and rough bluster were among his means of control. On one occasion, when debate was to end at a certain time, a Republican member, Ashley of Ohio, yielded to permit a further half-hour of Democratic discussion. With a big gallery, everyone excited, and nerves on edge, a large group of angry Republicans including Stevens gathered round Ashley's seat. As a journalist recorded it: "There was Thad. Stevens, got up in full fighting trim . . . , shaking his finger at Mr. Ashley for giving way and reading him a

---

[2] *Ibid.*, 238–240.
[3] William E. Smith, *The Francis Preston Blair Family in Politics*, II, 118.

lecture. Stevens's face looked fire, while Ashley's was as red as a fresh cut of beef." It was not as if Ashley was the kind of man to stand up to Stevens. The significance of the incident lay in the fact that he was controllable by Stevens's steam-roller tactics.[4]

Stevens's technique was manifest in his relations with the House committee on military affairs. It might have been supposed that that committee, of which Frank Blair, Jr., was chairman, would work up plans for military legislation, as was true of the corresponding committee of the Senate headed by Wilson of Massachusetts. Stevens, however, ignoring Blair's committee, presented his own military bill to the House in 1861. When asked by Mallory of Kentucky why the military committee was not allowed to perform its proper functions, Stevens had the rudeness to reply that if Blair reported a different bill it should be rejected at once. Though Blair was regarded as a friend and supporter of the President, the bill of Stevens was railroaded through.[5]

On another occasion, when Republicans in the House were faltering and threatening to revolt on a measure which Stevens was determined to have passed, A. K. McClure sat by him and watched his methods during the moments before the session formally opened. ". . . I heard a leading Pennsylvania Republican approach him," wrote McClure, "to protest against committing the party to that policy." Stevens did not plead, argue, or seek to persuade. He simply commanded the "trembling suppliant" to do as he was told and vote for the measure. The dissenting member obeyed. Had he not done so, said McClure, he "would have been proclaimed to his constituents, over the name of Stevens, as a coward, and that would have doomed him to defeat."[6]

Toleration and caution, important with Lincoln, were not in the "Commoner's" vocabulary. It stands to his credit that he used his power for such liberal causes as Negro suffrage in the District of Columbia and abolition of slavery by constitutional amendment, but it was also used for measures associated with hatred and war hysteria, proscription of Southerners, sweeping confiscation of their

---

4 Richard Nelson Current, *Old Thad Stevens: A Story of Ambition,* 206; New York *Herald,* Feb. 2, 1865. See also A. K. McClure, *Abraham Lincoln and Men of War-Times,* 277 ff.
5 *Cong. Globe,* 37 Cong., 1 sess., 72 (July 11, 1861); Smith, *Blair Family,* II, 121.
6 McClure, 280–281.

property, denial of civil rights, reconstruction on a pattern opposed to Lincoln's, and (at a later time) for irregular and unfair procedure in the impeachment of Andrew Johnson.[7]

In addition to his terrifying manner and ruthlessness of party control, Stevens had supporting qualities. His parliamentary competence was of a high order. When he spoke, members listened to him as to a manipulator who was pulling the ropes and an oracle who knew how the pending matter of business was going to turn out. Contrary debate was merely tolerated if permitted at all. Where others were bewildered, Stevens's mind was made up. At all times he knew the status of legislative proposals as they wended their way through the intricate parliamentary maze, which could have been said of very few members. He was sarcastic to the point of insolence, but this very coarseness made him formidable. He was "a born dictator in politics."[8] In his unrefined way he was a capable speaker, though his persuasiveness, some thought, was that of the highwayman. When schemes for special interests arose, he would block some and promote others as he wished. He opposed and defeated a canal project in which Washburne of Illinois was interested, but was watchful of interests close to his own Caledonian Iron Works. The linking of the Republican party with capitalistic interests, one of the chief economic features of the time and of later decades, was a central factor of Stevens's policy. Party control of the government, and business support of the party, constituted the Stevens pattern as interlocking factors of a neatly working scheme. "With such a champion as Stevens," writes Richard N. Current, "Northern industrialists were

[7] After the 1867 "investigation," or testimony hunting in which perjured testimony was sought and used, the resolution to impeach President Johnson was decisively voted down in the House. The 1868 impeachment proceeding began, not with an investigation, nor even with the presentation of charges, but with the Covode resolution which declared that Johnson "be impeached of high crimes and misdemeanors," without naming even one instance of such a crime or misdemeanor. This resolution was referred, not to the committee on the judiciary, but to Stevens's committee on reconstruction. It was quickly passed; then a committee (loaded against Johnson) was appointed, not to investigate, but to "report articles of impeachment" against the President. This was *after* he had already been "impeached" without consideration of the reasons therefor. The committee was interested, not in justice to Johnson, but in the value of each article for producing conviction in the Senate. This 1868 matter is pertinent here for its bearing upon the spirit and method of the anti-Lincoln Stevens when attacking the President who sought to fulfill Lincoln's restoration program. It was the same Stevens. Randall, *Civil War and Reconstruction,* chap. xxxiv.

[8] McClure, 280.

steadily intrenching themselves in the favor of a generous government . . . . And he was interesting himself in policies . . . which,
by keeping Republican politicians and their allies in power, would
assure to them . . . the fruits of peace." [9]

The relations between this most powerful man in the House and
Abraham Lincoln were, wrote McClure, "seldom cordial," though
"always friendly." Stevens did not prefer Lincoln for President in
1860 or 1864, was not "enthusiastic in Lincoln's cause," "believed
him weak," and "never saw Lincoln during the war except when
necessity required it." He "often grieved" the President, and, to the
recollection of McClure, spoke only once in "positive and enthusiastic commendation of Lincoln, and that was when he issued his Emancipation Proclamation in 1862." The two men, said McClure, a
competent observer, were "seldom in actual harmony." [10]

These remarks by McClure, though clearly showing the lack of
cordiality between Stevens and Lincoln, may be set down as under-
statements. The full extent of the radical leader's enmity to the President is not easy to measure. It has been suggested that under certain
circumstances Stevens would not have withheld the weapon of impeachment against Lincoln. [11] Ward Hill Lamon, who knew Lincoln
well, believed that Stevens's "demand for the head of 'that man at
the other end of the Avenue,' would not have been a whit less ferocious" against Lincoln than in fact it turned out to be against Johnson. Believing that Lincoln could not have been made "a tool and an
instrument" of the radicals, Lamon wrote: "Mr. Thaddeus Stephens
[*sic*] was to the best of my knowledge the only leading man in the
[Republican] party shameless and impudent enough to avow his
hostility to the Union. He was not the exponent of our views and he
represented not even a fractional part of the honest millions who cast
their votes, spent their money and shed their blood to bring back the
Government of their fathers." [12]

It is perhaps unnecessary to probe Lamon's meaning as to Stevens's
hostility to the Union. It is obvious that Old Thad did not favor restoring the Union on the prewar basis, with slavery preserved and

9 Current, *Old Thad Stevens*, 197.      10 McClure, 281, 284.
11 Current, *Old Thad Stevens*, 305 n.
12 Ward H. Lamon to Andrew Johnson, Wash., Feb. 26, 1866, Johnson MSS., 9550–
9555.

with the rights of Southern states remaining as before. In this attitude Stevens was sincere. What needs to be borne in mind in these pages is the incompatibility between the Lincoln program and that of the Pennsylvanian. Where he was to blame from the Lincolnian standpoint, it was not for being antislavery, but for the unfairness, intolerance, and hatefulness of his manner and method. He was spoiling a good cause. On the famous Crittenden resolution in the House, July 22, 1861, declaring that restoration of the old Union was the purpose of the war, Stevens did not vote. That resolution, regarded as law and gospel by Lamon, expressed the very opposite of the Pennsylvanian's policy.

## VII

The way of a senator towards another senator was one of the quaint things under the Washington sun. The most devastating statements could be uttered if they were given in formal or superficially respectful phrasing. It would not do for Wilson of Massachusetts, a Republican, to say of Cowan of Pennsylvania, another Republican, that he was a liar or didn't know what he was talking about. He would not even use the name Cowan. He would put it thus: "I desire to say a . . . word to the Senator from Pennsylvania before I sit down. I was sorry to hear him say . . . what is said so often without . . . being sustained by the facts . . . ." [1] When Wade of Ohio had a colloquy with this same Cowan, he did not blurt out that Cowan was a traitor, doing all in his power to aid and abet the enemy of his country. The Ohioan merely suggested that Jefferson Davis would pray "for just such an advocate" as the senator from Pennsylvania.[2] Cowan replied that Davis would pray "for just such a statesman as the honorable Senator from Ohio, the most effective ally he ever had or could have."

Hale of New Hampshire did not say that Cowan was absurd, mentally fogged, and the victim of delusions. He gave his colleague a qualified compliment, then followed it with language of polite debate. Once the meaning of his language was apprehended, however, it had all the sting of a verbal blackjack. He said: "My friend from Pennsylvania is a man, whatever may be said of his politics, of re-

---

[1] *Cong. Globe,* 38 Cong., 1 sess., 3307 (June 27, 1864).
[2] *Ibid.,* appendix, 136 (June 27, 1864).

markably clear intellect; and where he has not suffered his intellect to be led away by the absurdities of black-letter English law, I have no doubt is a good lawyer . . . ." [3]

No one could have said that Reverdy Johnson was disrespectful toward Charles Sumner. He did not say that this scholar in politics was a learned fool. He pointed out that "the honorable member" from Massachusetts "reads everything that comes out that is worth reading." Then he added: "he will pardon me for saying he sometimes reads what is not worth reading." [4]

It was not always easy to tell when a member passed the bounds of parliamentary etiquette. Clever members managed well enough within those bounds. Riddle of Ohio referred to an opponent's utterances as "slobbering balderdash." When Holman of Indiana quoted from an Ohio journal, Riddle was indignant that the Hoosier member "flaunted a soiled rag of a newspaper in our faces." "Ohio," he remarked, "will select her own organs, and we will answer . . . without the officious aid of any meddler from outside." [5]

Sometimes this backbiting would take the form of a legislative resolution. With near unanimity (105 to 1) the House passed a resolution of Morrill of Vermont, declaring that it was "the duty of all loyal American citizens . . . [and] of every department of the Government—the legislative branch included—as a unit, to . . . unitedly strike down the assassins . . . who have conspired to destroy our Constitution, our nationality . . . [etc.]." [6] Cox, Ohio Democrat, then offered an "explanatory" resolution. He would have the House resolve that "the word 'assassins,' used in the resolution this day offered by the member from Vermont . . . is intended . . . to include all men, whether from the North or the South, who have been instrumental in producing the present war, and especially those in and out of Congress who have been guilty of flagrant breaches of the Constitution, and who are not in favor of the establishment of the Union as it was and the Constitution as it is." Cox's resolution, aimed at Republicans, was tabled, 85 to 41. [7]

A great deal of forensic heat was engendered in proceedings look-

---

3 *Ibid.*, 3308 (June 27, 1864).    4 *Ibid.*, 2900 (June 13, 1864).
5 Riddle, *Recollections*, 212.
6 *Cong. Globe*, 37 Cong., 3 sess., 14–15 (Dec. 5, 1862).
7 *Ibid.*, 15 (Dec. 5, 1862).

ing to the expulsion or censuring of individual members. One target of such an attack was Alexander Long, an Ohio congressman to whom little attention had been previously attracted. His offense was that he had favored recognizing the Confederacy. No bare account of the "proceedings" could convey an idea of the dramatic intensity of this incident. As described by Noah Brooks it was one of several "field-days in Congress," with Garfield comparing Long to Benedict Arnold, while Speaker Colfax's voice "trembled with emotion" as he urged a resolution of expulsion. In the midst of the excitement a Maryland "Peace Democrat," Benjamin G. Harris, got up and endorsed the views of Long, believing his proposal to be the only method of obtaining peace. The House was now "in the wildest confusion, and a score of members were on their feet shouting to the Speaker and endeavoring to be recognized." In a "stentorian voice" which rose above the tumult, Washburne of Illinois moved to expel Harris, as Colfax had moved in the case of Long, whereupon Fernando Wood "tried to slide in a little speech" to the effect that he, too, agreed with Long and was alike deserving of expulsion.

The debate raged on. Washburne shouted that Wood should also be put out, Long delivered an impressive speech of defense, and Thad Stevens, having come from a sick bed, "arose like a column of iron" to vindicate his Union-saving attitude against aspersions that had been cast during his absence. When an opponent tried to offer some words in reply, "the stern old Pennsylvanian waved him down by a motion of his hand." [8] After long drawn out and excited discussion the motions to expel Long and Harris failed for want of the necessary two-thirds vote. Instead of expulsion, both men were then stigmatized by severe votes of censure.[9]

Where members actually entered Confederate military service they were naturally dropped from Congress at Washington. In the House this was true of John W. Reid and John B. Clark, both of Missouri; in the Senate, Waldo P. Johnson and Trusten Polk of Missouri and John C. Breckinridge of Kentucky.[10] For a different

---

[8] Brooks, *Washington in Lincoln's Time*, 98 ff.

[9] For the prolonged and elaborate debate, see *Cong. Globe*, 38 Cong., 1 sess., 1505–1635 (Apr. 9 to 14, 1864).

[10] On Clark, see *Cong. Globe*, 37 Cong., 1 sess., 116–117 (July 13, 1861); on Johnson and Polk, *ibid.*, 37 Cong., 2 sess., 263–264 (Jan. 10, 1862); on Breckinridge, *ibid.*, 37 Cong., 2 sess., 9–10 (Dec. 4, 1861); on Reid, *Biog. Cong. Direc.*, 1452. Reid's case is almost that

reason Senator Jesse D. Bright of Indiana was expelled after an elaborate debate of nearly three weeks. His offense was that before the war (March 1, 1861) he had written a minor letter of recommendation to Jefferson Davis. It was remarked that the expulsion vote in the case of Bright "was based perhaps as much on personal and political opposition as on the charge of treason." [11] Having expelled him for treason against the United States, very few senators would have seriously expected him to be tried and convicted in the courts for that offense on the basis of the accusation and evidence concerning the unimportant letter to Davis.

## VIII

The formula "be it enacted" implies a determined and collective will. It is a legislative imperative and may be regarded as the essence of a legislative "act." If, however, one goes behind the record, in diaries and correspondence, he begins to wonder what is the actual significance of legislative "intent" as embodied in completed legislation. Much the same is true if he takes the open record itself and seeks to correlate discussion with final enactment. One cannot very well enact a stump speech. When varying purposes simmer down to a legislative act, the end result may indeed evoke a majority of affirmative votes, but such affirmation may often fall short of genuine concurrence of thought. A resolution may be a kind of catch-all, so that partial consent as to sections may be misleading if interpreted as total consent for the whole measure. With disorder prevailing and attention lacking, with management in the hands of a few party leaders, and with the attitude of members largely predetermined, the content of unremembered debates would seem a minor factor.

In any parliamentary situation, of course, as in a popular election, composite concurrence of a majority may be difficult to break down in terms of individual approval of specific provisions and interpretations. Compromise and adjustment of differing views are normally expected as regular aspects of democratic procedure. Yet in some cases individual doubts or imperfections of understanding may be so

---

of a vanishing congressman; it is stated that he "withdrew" from the House on August 3, 1861, and joined the Confederate army.

11 *Dic. of Amer. Biog.*, III, 46.

serious that one may consider the "intent" of Congress as little more than an abstraction. After a bill was passed in the upper house, one senator remarked that a colleague had "entirely misapprehended" what it was all about.[1] When the habeas corpus law was passed, March 3, 1863, it was claimed that incorrect procedure had been used in forcing the vote, while the language of the act was so ambiguous as to admit of diametrically opposite meanings.[2] Matters would get into such a jam at the end of a short session that important bills would be lost for no good reason while others would be passed in sheer exhaustion. Secretary Welles noted that a bill affecting the navy department (concerning an "advisory board") was passed without the secretary of the navy having even seen it. When asked about the matter Senator Grimes reported that "the bill had never been discussed; he did not approve of it; . . . he had expected it would be killed in the House." Another bill, wrote Welles, "must have been got through surreptitiously." [3]

On the subject of the American Constitution in its relation to the existing emergency congressional minds differed widely. The idea of adhering strictly to constitutional provisions was emphatically urged by anti-Lincoln Democrats who were shocked at what they called the President's disregard of the nation's fundamental charter. When men spoke of adhering to the Constitution, of course, they meant such adherence to be understood in terms of their own interpretation. There were those, however, who believed that the Constitution should be ignored or evaded. Sometimes this would amount to a deliberate and conscious violation of plain constitutional provisions. There were times when the men of Congress found their constitutional problem too much of a task, and at such times there was a tendency to enact or repeat the words of the Constitution and let the Supreme Court figure out what they meant. Pure reasoning or deduction, or detached legal exposition, of the Constitution was rare. Comments on the meaning of the great document were usually colored by the motive back of each man's attitude. This situation was brought out by a Massachusetts member when he declared that

---

[1] Senator Ira Harris of New York made this statement concerning Senator Trumbull's understanding of the confiscation bill. *Cong. Globe*, 37 Cong., 2 sess., 3381 (July 16, 1862).

[2] Randall, *Constitutional Problems Under Lincoln*, 130–131.

[3] Welles, *Diary*, I, 245.

"not a man will oppose this bill [making paper money legal tender] . . . upon constitutional grounds, unless he is opposed to it for other and satisfactory reasons." [4]

To some the idea was that they were voting and acting *in extremis.* The classical smartness of the phrase lent dignity to this type of reasoning. If it had a Latin name it could not be wholly bad; at least it could be labeled, recognized, and related to ancient precedent. Some, however, objected to applying this principle except where dire extremity actually required it. In 1862 Wright of Pennsylvania said: ". . . I voted, during the extra session of Congress [July–August 1861], to affirm the act of the President . . . in the suspension of the writ of *habeas corpus.* I voted also to approve his act by which he declared . . . seaports in a state of blockade. I also voted to approve his act declaring the establishment of military law. I did it for the sole reason that . . . the exigency had arisen which justified us and the President . . . in violating a constitutional provision. It was a vote *in extremis.* . . . [He also approved presidential seizure of the railroads because that was an extreme case.] And now we are called upon . . . to . . . declare it to be . . . legal to make paper itself money." This, he felt, was going too far. "I call upon gentlemen to show me how, when, and where, in what particular, we have power, under the Constitution, to make anything, except gold and silver, a legal tender?" To do this, he felt, would be to set "all . . . precedents at defiance." [5]

There were some who favored changing the Constitution. Such a change, however, presented practical difficulties, especially in a period of civil war, and the tendency was to attempt the process of amendment only as a kind of compulsion when the constitutional obstacle was insurmountable for a measure which was plainly a necessity. It was realized, of course, that a time of unbalance and emotional tension did not offer the best atmosphere for the task of revising a nation's enduring constitutional instrument. It was also considered questionable to make such alterations at a time when a large Southern area was outside the Union.

Where constitutional thinking seemed to smack of casuistry there were cautious minds that objected to the idea of constitutionalism be-

---

[4] *Cong. Globe,* 37 Cong., 2 sess., 659 (Feb. 5, 1862).
[5] *Ibid.,* 37 Cong., 2 sess., 662–663 (Feb. 5, 1862).

coming whatever the members chose to make it. The aged Crittenden of Kentucky, whose years of prime belonged to the period of
Monroe and John Quincy Adams, deeply regretted the legislative
"doctrine which makes the end justify the means." "The argument
here," he said, "is exactly the argument of the Jesuit—fix your mind
and attention upon one object which you think a lawful one, and
then all the means are lawful." [6]

In the face of these constitutional discussions Thaddeus Stevens
showed a blunt impatience, both against those who held back because of negative constitutional scruples and those who went to
great lengths to square their affirmative votes with the Constitution.
He wanted neither objections nor constitutional justifications. He
declared: "I say that you cannot justify nine out of ten of the acts
of the Government, or of our own acts here, if you consider the
Constitution a valid and binding instrument with reference to those
in arms in the rebellious States." On that theory, said Thomas of
Massachusetts, "we are every day passing unconstitutional acts, we
are every day violating our oaths recorded in heaven to support the
Constitution of the United States." To Olin of New York, however,
it seemed that nothing but obedience to the Constitution could justify
the prosecution of the war. It was his view that if there remained
"but a single man . . . loyal to the Constitution in any one of the
seceded States, he . . . [was] entitled to all the rights, . . . privileges, and . . . immunities granted to any citizen in any loyal
State." [7]

Stevens would not allow to the people of the South any constitutional rights. He would tax them though they were not in the Union;
at the same time he would take from them "every particle of property,
real and personal." [8] Then he would "sell" that property for the
benefit of the nation. To carry out Stevens's scheme and confiscate
all the property of the people in "these conquered provinces" and sell
it, would have been a gigantic affair. Uncle Sam would have been going into the real estate business, not to mention personal property,
on a colossal scale.

[6] *Ibid.*, 37 Cong., 3 sess., 1290 (Feb. 25, 1863).

[7] For references in this paragraph, see *Cong. Globe*, 37 Cong., 3 sess., 240–242 (Jan. 8, 1863).

[8] *Ibid.*, 37 Cong., 3 sess., 240 (Jan. 8, 1863).

## IX

To contemplate a large representative assembly, and study the manner in which measures take shape in such an assembly, is a primary problem of political scientists and a necessary task for all who would understand the actual workings of democracy. Congress may be considered collectively, as a "branch" of the government. At any particular time, however, the nation's legislature consists of human beings, of politicians—or, it may be hoped, of statesmen. Sometimes men of no more than ordinary capacity may be brought to high achievement by able leadership. If the nation has a vigorous and competent President, the matter of his leadership as to Congress will necessarily arise. One may ask: If the President does not lead, who does? One may also ask: Who among our capable Presidents has felt that his function as leader in legislative matters could be neglected? As issues were drawn in Lincoln's day, the need to turn to Congress, and to wait upon measures passed by Congress, was a continuing factor. This being so, the peculiarities of its members, suggested only in part in this chapter, had to be kept in mind, for these were the men with whom Lincoln had to deal. In such dealing he had often to conceal his exasperation and muster up a tact and skill in which many of the honorable gentlemen were deficient.

The relation of Congress and the President to the American "two-party system" also comes into view. If one speaks of party leadership he must of course recognize the President as a leader. The following comment, though recent, has a general significance: "The history of American politics has been that when the President lost control of his party we had no effective government." [1] It has been pointed out, however, that at times the two-party system, as to Congress, seems rather meaningless. [2] What was called Republican policy, 1861 to

---

[1] Philip Willkie, in New York *Times*, editorial page, Oct. 26, 1949.

[2] In discussing recent aspects of party organization in Congress, Clarence A. Berdahl has pointed to the lack of clear-cut party responsibility, the "coalition" of a few Democrats with a major portion of the Republicans, and the fact that "party organizations in Congress are almost completely independent of the national party organizations." He mentions the "extraordinary looseness in party performance" that coexists with "passionate attachment to party labels." As to the situation in 1948 it is shown that "Governor Dewey, as the Republican Presidential candidate, felt obliged to urge strongly the election of Republican candidates for the Senate and House, even though those men were opposed to the Dewey policies and would presumably so vote in Con-

1865, in the congressional sense was not Lincoln's policy, though Lincoln was a Republican President. These are but a few of the difficulties and complexities of a subject that cannot be fully discussed in this book, but which will receive further treatment in some of its phases in the next chapter.

---

gress." Thus Dewey was campaigning "for men who were actually his political opponents." One can readily see the analogy of this situation to that existing under Lincoln, when many Republicans in Congress, a majority of them, were voting against Lincoln's views and measures. For Berdahl's illuminating analysis, see *Amer. Pol. Sci. Rev.*, XLIII, especially pp. 309, 732, 733.

# CHAPTER VI

# PRESIDENT AND CONGRESS

## I

THE difficulty of using war as an instrument of policy, and of controlling a particular war in order to adhere to a solemn declaration made at the outset, was illustrated whenever Congress got round to discussing the purpose and meaning of the growing struggle. In the passing of the Crittenden resolution that the war was not waged for any other purpose than restoring the Union (mentioned in a previous volume),[1] we find only the first phase of congressional attitude concerning war aims. That was in the summer of 1861 (July 22), but by the summer of 1862 a marked change had come about. Crittenden's resolution, passed just after the defeat at first Bull Run, was soon abandoned, and the policy of confiscation and punitive emancipation was adopted.[2] As the war unfolded far beyond its foreseen outline, earlier declarations of purpose receded into the unrecoverable past. It was obvious that institutions would be shaken and that slavery would be treated with no gentle hand. This was not surprising. Perhaps the surprising thing was that, with the "radical" spirit on the march, more was not done by way of dispossessing Southerners and punishing "traitors."

Time and again some member, in one form or another, would propose a reaffirmation of the Crittenden declaration, but always without success. An example was in December 1863, when Finck of Ohio offered a resolution that the war was not being carried on in any spirit of oppression, but to defend the Constitution. When finally this resolution was disposed of (April 11, 1864), it was laid on the

---

[1] *Lincoln the President*, II, 127-128.
[2] *Cong. Globe*, 37 Cong., 2 sess., Appendix, 412-413 (July 17, 1862).

table in the House by vote of 81 to 64. A similar resolution was defeated, 88 to 66, under the leadership of Thaddeus Stevens.[3] On this question of the purpose of the war, border-state members, Democrats generally, and the less vindictive Republicans were voted down by the radical Republican majority. As these tendencies increased there were those who felt that the party in power was multiplying the enemies of the Union cause and that serious wedges of factional difference were dividing the North.

What were called "war aims" were, of course, in reality peace aims. The purpose of war itself is to kill, maim, destroy, break down morale, annihilate enemy fighting power, and produce victory by force. What that victory shall signify, and what a nation is "fighting for," can never be achieved except by peace, and by conditions and attitudes as they persist during years of peace. There were honest souls who felt, as did Lincoln, that it would be most unfortunate for the country to continue to be divided by sectionalism and partisanship after the conclusion of a war whose avowed purpose was the reuniting of the nation.

This matter of purpose that looked beyond war to long eras of peace was properly a function of both Congress and the President. If there could be harmony between executive and legislative minds, and if that harmony could be kept on a high level, something constructive might be accomplished. If not, there would be a sorry sequel to Lincoln's high resolve that the nation's dead should not have died in vain.

The whole issue of so-called "war aims" involved a serious clash of ideologies. Divisions on this subject were stubborn and obstinate; tempers were hateful and intense. Those who honestly differed with the radicals and desired a moderate policy were branded as traitors or as sympathizers with treason who "prate learnedly about the Constitution."[4] In a war against disunion the gulf was widening within the Union itself. Vindictiveness was growing. It had been supposed, early in the war, that there was room for agreement by which men at Washington would stand together with loyal men at the South. Instead of that, as Cowan of Pennsylvania remarked in the Senate,

---

[3] *Ibid.*, 38 Cong., 1 sess., 1532 (Apr. 11, 1864); 22 (Dec. 14, 1863).

[4] Thaddeus Stevens in House of Representatives, *ibid.*, 37 Cong., 2 sess., 440 (Jan. 22, 1862).

hardly a day passed that some bill was not introduced that increased the animosity and added to the irritation.[5] How far and how deep would the fury extend? Said Thomas of Massachusetts: "You cannot . . . carry on a war with a fierceness and severity that would destroy life as rapidly as it germinates." Whoever talked of "a war of extermination," he said, was "mad." [6]

Those who favored a reasonable vision as to aims agreed with Lincoln; but, as the war seemed to be failing of its pacifying purpose as stated by the President, the words of Lincoln were thrown back at him. Strongly partisan anti-Lincoln speeches were made by way of denouncing a vindictive war for which Lincoln was blamed, though in all conscience he of all men wished an end to vindictiveness. This meant that Lincoln was assailed for opposite reasons. Some attacked him on the ground that harsh measures were being used which amounted to a violation of civil rights. Such denunciation ignored the fact that, for a war President, Lincoln was in practice lenient. Others attacked him for that very leniency and for a broad policy that was considered too generous toward "rebels" and too trustful of Southerners' good intentions.

Loyal border-state men, vigorously favoring the Union which was so important for Kentucky, West Virginia, and their neighbors, were saying that there had been no sufficient provocation in terms of Northern aggression, that the South had suffered no serious grievance. Senator Waitman T. Willey of Virginia [7] declared in December 1861: "Mr. President, how utterly absurd are all the pretexts of the insurgents for their rebellion. . . . If the South had remained loyal to their Government, . . . what could your President or your party have accomplished prejudicial or objectionable to the South." He compressed his views into a resolution (not passed) which declared that the war had been "forced upon the country by the States in rebellion, without justifiable cause or provocation . . . ." [8]

With congressional oratory, however, becoming ever more heated,

<hr/>

[5] *Ibid.*, 37 Cong., 2 sess., 2993 (June 28, 1862).
[6] *Ibid.*, 37 Cong., 3 sess., 651 (Jan. 31, 1863).
[7] Willey was United States senator from "restored Virginia." He was chosen by the "reorganized" legislature (claiming to act for the yet unbroken state) in its special session at Wheeling in July 1861.
[8] For Willey's resolution and his long, formidable speech in its support, see *Cong. Globe*, 37 Cong., 2 sess., appendix, 32 ff.

it appeared that grievances, which men such as Willey considered lacking in the prewar sense, were being offered in increasing supply. Part of the trouble was the continual tendency of some Northern members to identify Southernism with slavery, so that a denunciation of the peculiar institution was likely to take the form of a tirade against what was broadly called "the South."

But could one ignore antislavery voices? Could there be such a thing as guaranteeing slavery absolute immunity from the war? Should the antebellum past be kept upon the throne? Was slavery worth saving? Was it not slavery that had "caused" the war? Was the opportunity for extinguishing the evil of human bondage to be neglected? What if the war did become a crusade? [9] Some thought the conflict unjustified unless it were exactly that. Was not freedom a lofty cause?

These were potent considerations, though it should not be forgotten that moderate policy to a large extent allowed for abolition, not by one stroke or immediately, but by progressive steps. The main problem was whether other freedoms were to be kept while freedom from slavery was established. The issue to be decided was whether policy against slavery should be constructive rather than vindictive, corrective rather than punitive. Should not the hand of reform be laid upon slavery as an institution, not upon Southerners as persons? Should not enlightened Southern coöperation be welcomed? It was not contemplated by the best moderates that an unchanging "Old South" was to be projected into an indefinite future, but that liberation when it should come, as come it would, should not be marred by partisanship or frustrated by narrow sectionalism. Moderates believed that a postwar regime could be better launched by men who would coöperate with well disposed Southerners than by those who would perpetuate the war mind, crystallize sectionalism in party terms, and make resentment permanent. As early as 1861, and continuously throughout the war, Lincoln showed deep concern that the

---

[9] When he voted against the Crittenden resolution in July 1861, A. G. Riddle of Ohio was angrily assailed and urged to change his vote. In "white heat," as reported by himself, he retorted: "Not a man of you believes that slavery is eternal. . . . You all believe that it is to go out, when it does go, through convulsion, fire, and blood. That convulsion is upon us. The man is a delirious ass who does not see and realize this." Riddle, *Recollections*, 43.

nation's purpose should "not degenerate into a violent and remorseless . . . struggle." [10]

## II

This basic question of policy and method, of broad plans for
future years, of clarifying the issue as to what the war was about, was
distressingly illustrated in connection with the problem of the confiscation of Southern property. In the records of the time, entombed
in the *Congressional Globe*, one finds an excessive flow of language
on this vexatious subject. Every member, it seemed, had a confiscation speech in his pocket. It was, however, the kind of unenlightened
and rambling debate that leaves the reader (if any) in doubt as to the
design and purpose of congressional oratory. With discussion remaining so long at a tentative stage and with members sometimes
betraying ignorance of the bill or the motion on which they were
presumably speaking, it can hardly be said that the cause of legislation was notably promoted by what was said on the floor or what was
spread forth in the appendix of the *Globe* with "leave to print."

The bill for confiscation was started in the Senate by Trumbull
of Illinois, but the measure as passed, though he voted for it, was not
Trumbull's. The roving debate, or congressional maneuvering, extended all the way across the long session of the Thirty-Seventh Congress, from the opening day, December 2, 1861, when the question
was first presented, to the last day, July 17, 1862, when final action
was taken. Some of that final action was mere patchwork. Trumbull's
bill provided for "absolute and complete forfeiture forever to the
United States of every species of property . . . belonging to persons beyond the jurisdiction of the United States" who should "take
up arms against the United States, or . . . aid or abet the rebellion." [1] What happened from the point where Trumbull presented
his bill was a long-drawn-out story. Weeks passed; then the Senate
committee on the judiciary, of which Trumbull was chairman, reported its bill, which resembled Trumbull's. Liability to confiscation
under this bill derived from participation in the "rebellion," but
Trumbull had a limited idea as to reaching the offender's property.

---

10 Nicolay and Hay, *Works*, VII, 51.
1 *Cong. Globe*, 37 Cong., 2 sess., 18 (Dec. 5, 1861).

"Where the rebel can be reached by judicial process," said he, "the punishment for his crimes can be visited upon him personally, and this bill does not propose to interfere with his property at all." [2] It was explained that this manner of approach was for the purpose of avoiding constitutional difficulties concerning the punishment for treason. The method of his bill—directed against those who could not be reached by the Federal courts—was punitive in a non-judicial sense; the property of offenders was simply to be seized by the military authorities without any judicial process whatever.

As the Trumbull bill, with its substitutes and amendments, wended its tortuous way through the congressional jungle, it encountered unexpected obstacles. Inherently the problem of confiscation was bad enough with all its ramifications, but the trouble was enhanced by inconsistencies in the bill itself and by discordant arguments put forth by its sponsor as against the declarations of the many who participated in the debate. Forfeiture was intended as punishment for crime—the crime of "rebellion." Yet the punishment, according to Trumbull, was to be inflicted by the military authorities without judicial hearing to determine the individual's guilt. Moreover, as he proceeded, Trumbull seemed to forget the principle of domestic insurrection (or rebellion) for which forfeiture was to be decreed as a penalty. Warming to his theme, he put the bill in the category of strictly military or belligerent measures, as if it were merely a matter of invoking a rule of war. If confiscation had been an established and unquestioned rule of war, and if the existing conflict was a regular war between recognized belligerents, no special law of Congress would have been necessary. Trumbull was supposed to be an authority on constitutional matters, as his position at the head of the judiciary committee would imply, but as the months passed his analysis of perplexing constitutional problems was neither accurate nor conclusive. At one time he spoke as though he intended the punitive forfeiture of *all* property of offenders. At another time he referred to the property of Southerners as "prize of war," as if the situation were analogous to maritime capture, for which the law is international with personal guilt of the owners left out of the picture.

---

[2] *Ibid.*, 942 (Feb. 25, 1862).

On both sides of the debate there was great diversity of motive and intent. Some arose to oppose the measure with friendliness toward the Lincoln administration. These were among the most reasonable men in Congress. Others opposed it with the bitterest feeling of antagonism to Lincoln. Affirmative speakers were really in favor, not so much of the particular confiscation bill, as of a confiscation policy. Wide ranging speeches on confiscation in the broad sense were more often a kind of exhibition than a specific contribution to the difficult legislative process. Some favored the measure because of its bearing upon treason, some because of the (ineffective) emancipating feature, others because of the colonization clause, still others because of confiscation itself.

To assume that confiscation as enacted was a clear matter of legislative purpose would be to imply that the majority voted for the bill in knowledge of its content, visualizing its practical effect when administered, favoring it as an act necessitated by the existing emergency, and justifying it as a constitutional measure. It would be very questionable to assert that any such genuine majority existed. Some of the members admitted that they did not like certain features of the bill, but cast their votes for it because their Republican brothers were voting that way and they felt it expedient to follow the party line. There were motions to substitute radically different measures for the bill in hand, motions to refer, to amend the bill, to amend the amendment, to lay on the table, and to force the previous question. Finally, as noted in a previous volume,[3] Lincoln wrote out a veto message stating his objections to the confiscation bill which very obviously he disliked.

Then an extraordinary thing happened. Determined that a forfeiture bill be passed, the leaders of Congress, instead of altering the text of the bill which the President, so to speak, was in the act of vetoing, hastily prepared what was called an "explanatory joint resolution" to the effect that the bill was not intended to work forfeiture of real estate beyond the natural life of the offender. This did not by any means correct all, or the most important, of the features of the bill to which Lincoln objected. In particular there was no correction

---

[3] *Lincoln the President,* II, 228–229.

of the provision which required the condemnation of property with out allowing a personal hearing to the "supposed criminal." That presidential objection was left unanswered.

At this point Lincoln himself did a most unusual thing—something without precedent and with no later matching instance in executive procedure. He approved the distasteful measure to which he had so convincingly objected, and signed the bill and the explanatory resolution as "substantially one." Then he transmitted to Congress the veto message expressing disapproval of the bill he had signed. Thus he put on record his statement of presidential judgment, and sought to clinch the point that any parts of the bill inconsistent with the resolution—which, by the way, was not an amending measure—were of no force. It appears that he never intended a vigorous enforcement of the act. Certainly the attorney general, Edward Bates, had no stomach for such enforcement, even if the ill drafted measure had been capable of practical execution.[4]

### III

In January 1864 there was a curious sequel to the 1862 proceedings in Congress concerning confiscation. James F. Wilson, representative from Iowa, offered a resolution (January 13) to "amend" the last part of the explanatory joint resolution, the part that had been added to avoid forfeiture beyond the offender's life. In place of the words of the explanatory resolution, Wilson moved to substitute the words of the Constitution itself, as follows: "The Congress shall have Power to declare the Punishment of Treason, but no Attainder of Treason shall work Corruption of Blood or Forfeiture, except during the Life of the Person attainted."[1] Just why an act of Congress should reënact a provision of the Constitution was not clear, nor why a congressional measure should contain the words "The Congress shall have Power," etc. Congressman Wilson explained: "We do not propose by resolution to determine the question of the legislative construction of the Constitution, whether we may provide

---

[4] The tangled and amazing history of the second confiscation act of July 17, 1862, is treated in Randall, *Constitutional Problems Under Lincoln*, 276–280. In addition the author has drawn upon his own unpublished MS., "Confiscation of Property during the Civil War," doctoral dissertation, University of Chicago, 1911.

[1] *U.S. Constitution*, art. III, sec. 3.

for forfeiture of fee or confiscation of the real estate during life. The pending resolution leaves the whole matter to the court. In other words, we simply submit the section of the Constitution relating to the forfeiture of real estate to the courts . . . to determine whether forfeiture may be in fee or only for life." [2] This bit of proposed legislation—a joint resolution to amend a joint resolution explanatory of an act—was submitted by Wilson as coming from the House committee on the judiciary. It was thus the work of that committee of the House whose duty it was to interpret and apply the Constitution in legislative matters.

As questions piled up, it was evident that the members were facing complexities with which they could not cope. Would not the Wilson proposal render the whole meaning of the confiscation act doubtful? Would it not show that Congress did not even profess to know the meaning of its own law and was for that reason leaving the matter to the courts? Every law, of course, has to be interpreted and applied by the courts, but it is an odd proceeding for Congress in the very act of legislating to dodge the meaning and intended effect of what it was doing. What about persons buying an estate under confiscation proceedings? How could they know what they were buying, and how avoid the possible loss of the value they were paying?

What, after all, was meant by the words of the Constitution: "except during the Life of the Person attainted"? Did this phrase mean that confiscation should be only temporary, terminating with the condemned person's death, or (which would be rather doubtful) that a lasting forfeiture was to be effected, so long as the court decree of forfeiture was completed and issued during the offender's life? Part of the difficulty was that some members were assuming a double punishment of both confiscation and death being visited upon the same victim, and of an interpretation which would absurdly allow confiscation to apply only during the interval between the imposing of the sentence and the day of execution.[3] This would become even

2 *Cong. Globe*, 38 Cong., 1 sess., 185 (Jan. 13, 1864).
3 This point was threshed out in the House by Godlove S. Orth of Indiana who asked: "Did our Constitution, else so redolent with wisdom . . . , intend . . . such a farce as that the property of the traitor should be forfeited . . . only for that brief . . . time . . . between the day of the sentence and the day of execution?" *Cong. Globe*, 38 Cong., 1 sess., 187–188 (Jan. 13, 1864).

more absurd if the sale of the real estate would require forty days while the unfortunate defendant would be executed thirty days after sentence.[4]

In brave efforts to master such problems the deliberation got bogged down in a semantic morass, and "Sunset Cox" of Ohio rose in the House of Representatives to dispute what he called a point of "technical logomachy." Mustering the authorities ("Worcester, Webster, and all other dictionaries"), descanting upon "progressive philology," citing Justice Story, and tracing the word "except" to the Latin *ex* and *capio,* he led up through an elaborate passage to what was expected to be a clinching pronouncement. Then he said: "There are some clauses which interpret themselves. Discussion only obscures and does not elucidate their meaning. This clause is one of them." [5]

Discussion ran on and one wonders how a visitor could have understood the ponderous language emitted on a typical afternoon of confiscation discussion—on January 14, 1864, for instance, the legalistic and lexicographical field day on which the points of "technical logomachy" were elucidated by Cox. After protracted debate the House of Representatives resolved to change the wording of the explanatory joint resolution of July 17, 1862, striking out the words which were intended to limit the forfeiture to the offender's life and putting in a solemn provision that there should be no forfeiture "contrary to the Constitution of the United States." This resolution, which dodged the question as to what the Constitution meant (the very ques-

---

[4] This question of the duration of the forfeiture—whether the property should fully be taken in fee, leaving the heirs no rights, or whether the offender surrendered only a life interest—was one of the many problems with which the Supreme Court struggled in its elaborate interpretations of the confiscations acts. As to the act of 1861, directed only against the property, it was held by the Court (as in cases of smuggling) that the whole title was surrendered, so that nothing could be recovered by the heirs. Kirk *vs.* Lynd, 106 U.S. 315. On the other hand, in forfeitures under the act of 1862, based on the guilt of the owner and directed against him as a punishment, the Court decided that a decree of condemnation and order of sale conveyed only a "right . . . terminating with the life of the person for whose act it had been seized." Bigelow *vs.* Forrest, 9 Wall. 339. (All of this implied, of course, that confiscation should be imposed, but not confiscation and death.) The effect of the Court's ruling was that heirs of the offender would, even during his life, have a future interest in the property, and that they could fully inherit the estate when the offender died. Such considerations, however, only faintly suggest the Court's perplexities in applying confiscation. Randall, *Constitutional Problems Under Lincoln,* 275–341 (as to the duration of the forfeiture, 286 ff.).

[5] *Cong. Globe,* 38 Cong., 1 sess., 211 (Jan. 14, 1864).

tion on which the whole tedious debate had hinged), was passed by the House by a vote of 83 to 74.[6]

The parliamentary situation at this point was as follows. Congress had passed the confiscation bill of July 17, 1862. Lincoln had objected to it, partly because he considered it unconstitutional. Thinking to repair that defect, Congress had hastily enacted an explanatory resolution in order to make the law conform to the Constitution. This was done to avert a presidential veto, for which an able veto message had been prepared by Lincoln. Now, in 1864, Congress in a lengthy debate was floundering and stumbling as to the meaning of the explanatory resolution which it had enacted. Then, instead of explaining what was meant, the House resolved that nothing was intended that was contrary to the Constitution.

After all this, when the matter came up in the Senate, Trumbull moved that the explanatory resolution of July 17, 1862, on which Lincoln's reluctant signature of the confiscation bill had hinged, be *repealed,* offering his motion as an irrelevant "rider" on the bill to establish the freedmen's bureau.[7] This trick would have caught the President in a position where he could not have vetoed the repeal without vetoing the whole measure concerning the care of freedmen. The Senate was then off to another wordy debate on confiscation, in which grave constitutional doubts were raised and Trumbull subjected to embarrassing questions. Carlile of Virginia [8] said:

. . . it was made known to Congress that that bill [the confiscation bill] could not receive the approval of the President, and could only become a law by the passage of this very joint resolution, a portion of which is now proposed to be repealed, and that portion, too, which the President required should be adopted before he would approve it. . . . Well may the Senator from Massachusetts [Sumner] . . . ask the Senator from Illinois [Trumbull] not to load his [freedmen's bureau] bill with this proposition. Unless the President has reread his constitutional duties, . . . he never can sign this bill with this proposition in it.[9]

Senate discussion now became still more complicated, involving not merely the question of the advisability of Trumbull's "rider,"

6 *Ibid.*, 38 Cong., 1 sess., 501, 519 (Feb. 4–5, 1864).

7 *Ibid.*, 38 Cong., 1 sess., 3304 (June 27, 1864).

8 John S. Carlile was one of the senators from "restored Virginia" (not the new state of West Virginia). *Biog. Cong., Direc.,* 273.

9 *Cong. Globe,* 38 Cong., 1 sess., 3306 (June 27, 1864).

but also the basic problem as to whether confiscation was a wise policy, whether it was approved under international law as a belligerent right, and whether Congress was justified in "adding a new provision to the laws of nations and of war." After proceedings which Cowan of Pennsylvania thought were "enough to drive a sane man mad," [10] the Senate passed, as a rider to the freedmen's bureau bill, the Trumbull amendment to repeal the joint resolution "amendatory" of the confiscation act. The amendment failed of enactment because of postponement in the House; later the House passed its own repealing section. That repealing provision, however, was not actually enacted, despite each house going on record in favor of it; this was because the two chambers did not agree on an identical wording of the measures which they severally voted.

In the final analysis the amount of property actually confiscated in the Federal courts in accordance with the act of July 17, 1862, was so small as to make those members seem ridiculous who had glibly predicted that confiscation would serve as a means of financing the war.[11] As to the features of the bill which pertained to emancipation, that part of the act was poorly drawn. It was lacking as to procedure to make freedom legally effective; the result was that in actual practice the enforcement of this antislavery portion, which certain voting members considered its main feature, was utterly negligible. Emancipation arrived nowhere by the confiscation route.[12] Taking it all in all, it can hardly be said that in the field of confiscation the men of Congress presented a very efficient performance. Showing scant regard

[10] *Ibid.*, appendix, 137 (June 27, 1864).

[11] It was reported by the solicitor of the treasury in 1867 that proceeds of confiscation under the act of July 17, 1862, had been deposited in the United States treasury in the amount of $129,680.67. (*Sen. Doc. No. 58*, 40 Cong., 2 sess.) This report omits proceeds under the confiscation act of 1861, which were small, and does not include confiscations in Virginia, Kansas, and elsewhere. There were defaults and irregularities, and the full total is a somewhat obscure matter, but it has been estimated that if allowance is made for these factors, the total proceeds from confiscation sales would probably not exceed $300,000. This amount, roughly speaking, was comparable to the value of two estates such as Lee's Arlington. Arlington itself, however, was seized, not under the confiscation acts, but under the Federal direct tax in the South. Ultimately the United States government paid $150,000 to the Lee heirs, and it is upon this basis (i. e., purchase) that title to Arlington has rested. Randall, *Constitutional Problems Under Lincoln*, 288–292, 320–322.

[12] Commenting on the ineffectiveness of the second confiscation act of July 17, 1862, Lincoln wrote: ". . . I cannot learn that that law has caused a single slave to come over to us." Reply to a committee, Sep. 13, 1862, *Nat'l Intelligencer*, Sep. 26, 1862 (Nicolay and Hay, *Works*, VIII, 30).

for the President's well considered but modestly presented advice, the law makers made something of a muddle of their own measure.

## IV

The manner of congressional deliberation was further revealed in connection with the subject of Negro troops. None of these debates can be fully summarized, but it may be worth while to glance at some of the ideas expressed.

*Crittenden of Kentucky:* ". . . shall we, sir, stigmatize . . . our brothers, the white free-born men of this land, as being so degenerate as to shrink from this contest, and compel you to appeal to your own black men to defend the liberties of the white men? . . . You stigmatize them, while you invite them into the field. . . . You employ them as soldiers to fight your battle, but give them only one half pay, and exclude them from command . . . ." [1]

*Cox of Ohio:* "Now, the present pending law . . . is intended to place the African soldier upon a perfect equality in every regard with the white soldier . . . ." [2]

*Stevens of Pennsylvania:* "I have not said so. I said the object was to put them upon an equality as to the protection which the President could afford them. I do not mean to say that they are to be put upon a social and political equality." [3]

This unwillingness to give genuine equality to Negroes even when using them as troops was indicated by the House of Representatives when it passed, July 16, 1862, a measure providing that the pay for Negro troops should not be above $10 a month, while the pay of the white private was $13 a month.[4] One would have expected those who opposed the use of Negro troops to show an unwillingness to extend equal treatment. The surprising thing is to note the ungracious arguments put forth by those who favored their use. In presenting to the House a resolution for a more vigorous policy to enlist persons of African descent "at an early day and in larger numbers," Josiah B. Grinnell of Iowa made the point that the more extended employment of colored persons would be "a relief to our northern

---

1 *Cong. Globe*, 37 Cong., 3 sess., appendix, 73 (Jan. 29, 1863).
2 *Ibid.*, 599 (Jan. 29, 1863).        3 *Ibid.*
4 *Ibid.*, 37 Cong., 2 sess., 3398 (July 16, 1862).

soldiers, unacclimated and unused to manual labor" and that it would "lessen the number [of white men] to be taken from their homes and from the industrial pursuits . . . where there is now an unusual demand for labor." [5]

Speaking of the manner in which the conscription act served to "elevate the sentiment of this nation," Senator Wilson of Massachusetts pointed out that when the act was passed there was "a wild, unreasoning prejudice against using a black man to fight the battles of our country." Then he added: "But when people who were filled with these prejudices saw they must go themselves, and bare their bosoms to the shot and shell of the enemy, they learned that the black man's blood was no more sacred than their own, and that they would as soon have a black man stand up and fight the battles of the country as to do it themselves. The most popular thing to-day is to crowd black men into our armies." [6] Again Senator Wilson said: ". . . if there be anything in the prosecution of this war that the people are in favor of, it is the raising of black troops to fight the battles . . . . Everybody now demands it." [7]

Senator Grimes of Iowa agreed with him. Get more colored men into the army, was Grimes's policy. If that had been done, he said in 1864, "we need not have required a single new white soldier to enter the army." [8] This motive for obtaining colored troops was confirmed by Senator Fessenden of Maine. Asking for "what purpose" they were procured, he said: "Is it not to relieve . . . the country of the necessity of furnishing white men?" [9]

One aspect of this movement in Congress to promote the further enlistment of colored men was to give "credit" to certain Northern states in such a way as to reduce their liability to conscription. A military curiosity of the time—one of many—was the practice by which men of color, recruited in the South, were credited to Northern states. There were recruiting agents of these Northern states operating in the South for this purpose, a doubtful state activity in connection with a nationally enacted and administered program of conscription. Senator Doolittle of Wisconsin offered an amendment providing that colored troops mustered into the service of the United States should

5 *Ibid.*, 38 Cong., 1 sess., 427 (Feb. 1, 1864).
6 *Ibid.*, 80 (Dec. 22, 1863).          7 *Ibid.*, 160 (Jan. 12, 1864).
8 *Ibid.*, 162.                         9 *Ibid.*, 240 (Jan. 16, 1864).

"be credited upon the quota of the State within which they are enlisted, and not upon the quota of any other State." [10] The measure
passed the Senate,[11] but it is significant to note that among those voting against it were Senators Dixon of Connecticut, Fessenden of
Maine, Harris of New York, Howard of Michigan, Sprague of Rhode
Island, and both Sumner and Wilson of Massachusetts.[12]

## V

Recruitment and conscription were frequent subjects of discussion.
In a remarkable debate in the upper house on January 8, 1864, the
point of deliberation was a sensible amendment, brought up from
Senator Wilson's committee on military affairs, that so much of
the conscription (or enrollment) act of 1863 as authorized the exemption of drafted men on payment of $300 "be, and the same is hereby,
repealed." [1]

So it began, but before the deliberation concluded or halted, Sumner moved to amend the amendment. This was after a good deal of
discussion. More discussion ensued; then Sumner modified his amendment to the amendment to the statute.[2] Days passed, and the Massachusetts senator came up with yet another modification.[3] After thousands of words had poured forth, Sumner's proposal (his altered
modification of his amendment) was voted down.[4] This having been
done, the question was now upon the committee's original amendment for repeal of the $300 exemption or commutation clause.

The idea of Sumner's much battered amendment was that, instead of a flat sum of $300 as the price of exemption from the draft,
the amount should be ratable according to a man's income. Sumner
felt that a wealthy man, being well able to do so, should pay at a
higher rate "as a commutation for the service which the country
has a right to expect from him." [5] He mentioned twenty per cent (of

---

10 *Ibid.*, 38 Cong., 1 sess., 246 (Jan. 16, 1864).

11 As it went into the statute book the law provided that "men of color . . . , while
they shall be credited upon the several states, or subdivisions of states, wherein they
are . . . drafted, enlisted, or shall volunteer, shall not be assigned as state troops, but
shall be mustered . . . as United States colored troops." *U.S. State at Large,* XIII,
11; act of Feb. 24, 1864, sec. 24.

12 *Cong. Globe,* 38 Cong., 1 sess., 247 (Jan. 16, 1864).

1 *Cong. Globe,* 38 Cong., 1 sess., 139 (Jan. 8, 1864).

2 *Ibid.*, 141 (Jan. 8, 1864).                    3 *Ibid.*, 154 (Jan. 12, 1864).

4 *Ibid.*, 159 (Jan. 12, 1864).                   5 *Ibid.*, 140 (Jan. 8, 1864).

a year's income), pointing out that this would be a small contribution, considering the immense benefit of relief from military service. He emphasized that the Senate must vote whether the rich man who was drafted should pay more than the poor man. Sherman, however, dashed cold water on the proposal by showing that Sumner's amendment would amount to "a new income tax, to be imposed only upon those who are drafted." If the scheme amounted to a tax, thought Sherman, it ought to be imposed "upon all wealthy citizens." Every man, he said, held his property subject to the nation's taxing power, and every able-bodied man was also subject to whatever military service was required by law, but he did not favor mixing the two systems.

Proceeding further in his argument, Sherman showed the dilemma of the conscription policy in terms of avoiding the draft by a money payment. Retain the commutation clause, he showed, and you may exhaust the basis of future drafts and reënforcements. (It was generally agreed in the discussion that volunteering was insufficient.) On the other hand, said Sherman, "if you make your draft arbitrary and require every one to render military service, you will incite resistance to the draft." Nothing, he added, could justify resistance, but it might nevertheless "excite it." [6]

In addition to the basic misconception of putting a money price on exemption from military service—making it a kind of sales arrangement between the government and the conscript and constantly emphasizing procedures by which service could be avoided—the unwisdom of the enrollment act was shown also in connection with the question of substitutes. Clark of New Hampshire reminded the Senate that the conscription act had been passed so that the government could get men. Then came the idea, said Clark, "that a man should either go himself or furnish a substitute, or give the Government money enough to obtain a substitute for him." Clark was speaking of this aspect of the system favorably; he referred to the fact that in his state "we furnished more men under the draft than any other State in the Union; we furnished fifty per cent. of the call." [7]

[6] Ibid., 154 (Jan. 12, 1864).

[7] Ibid., 140 (Jan. 8, 1864). According to the army report the number called for in New Hampshire in the draft of July 1863 was 8002. To meet this call 181 were "personally held" (drafted), and 2240 substitutes were furnished. Thus the total for the state brought into the army by the draft amounted to 2421. (In addition there were 571 who

Here was an odd type of thinking. If men were drafted and "could not well go themselves" (these were Clark's words, as if going into the army were a kind of convenience), the curious supposition was that they would be doing approximately the equivalent if they "furnished" substitutes to serve for them. If a man went into the military service, exposing himself to the hazard of being killed or wounded, and if he added effectiveness to the army, his service was the significant thing, not the fact that so-and-so had "furnished" him. It is hard to see the merit that attaches to army "service" by proxy.

And what type of thinking was it to suppose that the *buying* of soldiers as "substitutes" could be done by the government itself, if a drafted individual but furnished the money! If the conscripted person could get a substitute and pay for him, he could *select* him. This meant bargaining, for often the amount paid for a substitute was a good deal more than $300. The next step, as it worked out, was that a "substitute broker" would do the actual bargaining, buying, and selecting. But if all these methods failed (though quite a few men actually preferred furnishing substitutes to paying commutation money, feeling somehow they were making more of a contribution), the drafted man might pay $300. In that case, such was the reasoning of certain congressional minds, the government, coming in as a kind of last resort, might select and buy the substitute.

By that time, the idea that a soldier so procured could be considered a "substitute" at all, was absurd. In any case the government must take a man if he goes into the service; if the government takes him, he should be regarded as serving in his own right. But according to the procedure of exempting for money and bargaining for "substitutes," the government would be excusing the originally drafted able-bodied man for a period of three years, and thus reducing by so much the basis for future drafts. This gem of congressional thinking was indeed a far cry from modern concepts of military duty and selective service.

At last the unsatisfactory $300 provision was repealed, but in the Senate the repealing motion barely carried by a close vote of 18 to 17, with such influential men as Henderson, Hendricks, Sherman,

---

paid commutation money; in army statistics they were included when figuring the "total accepted.") These records do not seem to harmonize with Senator Clark's statement as to furnishing fifty per cent of the call, but they do emphasize the large number of "substitutes" obtained by the system of conscription used in 1863. *Offic. Rec.*, 3 ser. V, 730–732.

and Trumbull voting in the negative, and fourteen senators absent.[8] In the lower house, where the repeal was carried by 65 to 53, it was opposed by such men as J. G. Blaine and Thaddeus Stevens.[9] Among other things, this showed the manner in which comparatively few men did the effective voting; sixty-five men in the House amounted to little more than a third of the membership from the Union states.

## VI

How did Lincoln feel about the Congress which the people—or the politicians—had given him? He once said concerning a maneuver of Republican senators: "They wish to get rid of me, and I am sometimes half disposed to gratify them." On hearing of the proceedings of this group he added: "I have been more distressed than by any event of my life." [1] "I am to be bullied by Congress, am I?" he once asked.[2] Again, referring to appeals for clemency, he said: "Congress has . . . left the women to howl about me." [3] Ward Lamon recalled that he once found the President in the private room of the White House lying on a sofa, "greatly disturbed and . . . excited." Jumping up, according to Lamon, Lincoln said: "I am President of one part of this divided country . . . ; but look at me! I wish I had never been born! . . . With a fire in my front and rear; having to contend with the jealousies of the military commanders, and not receiving that cordial co-operation and support from Congress which could reasonably be expected; with an active and formidable enemy in the field threatening the very life-blood of the government,—my position is anything but a bed of roses." [4]

There were occasions—just a few—on which Lincoln was asked to take a hand in intraparty contests for nominating a representative in Congress. In 1864 a particularly hot campaign was waged within Republican ranks to prevent the renomination of Isaac N. Arnold of Chicago, who was serving as congressman and desired another term. It was represented to the President that John L. Scripps, known for his connection with the Chicago *Tribune* and his authorship of a

[8] *Cong. Globe*, 38 Cong., 1 sess., 3491 (July 2, 1864).
[9] *Ibid.*, 3525 (July 2, 1864).   [1] Browning, *Diary*, I, 600-601.
[2] Rice, 93.   [3] *Ibid.*, 489.
[4] Lamon, *Recollections*, 182-183.

campaign biography of Lincoln in 1860, was using his position as postmaster in Chicago "to defeat Mr. Arnold's nomination to Congress." Lincoln thereupon wrote to Scripps, saying that he was "well satisfied" with Arnold, and asking Scripps not to constrain any of his subordinates in the exercise of his vote for congressman. The matter developed into a considerable row in the period when Lincoln's prospects for his own reëlection were at the lowest ebb. Scripps, himself a candidate for the congressional nomination, denied using post-office control for his own ends, but went on in a complaining letter to denounce Arnold, accusing him of seeking support among Federal office-holders, boosting Frémont, and taking measures that would lead to the choice of John Wentworth, whom Scripps deemed undesirable. After a considerable flow of denunciatory statements, Scripps asked Lincoln to oppose the selection of Arnold. Meanwhile Arnold was hurt and offended by the episode and freely expressed his feelings in letters to the overworked President. According to Arnold's account he had hoped for a "friendly understanding" by personal interview in Chicago but was met by a "storm of rage and passion" on the part of Scripps.

The upshot of this bickering within the party was that Arnold withdrew, pointing out that both the *Tribune* and the post office were against him. As a result John Wentworth was nominated and elected as a Republican to the Thirty-Ninth Congress.[5] In terms of the purposes of President Lincoln it was no small matter to lose the support of such a man as Arnold.[6]

Commenting on the radical attitude, with emphasis upon Wade, Joshua Giddings wrote of the manner in which senators were de-

---

[5] John Wentworth ("Long John") was a vigorous and colorful Chicago leader, Democratic in former background, antislavery in sentiment but not bitterly vindictive. He had a distinguished career as editor, civic leader, early promoter, picturesque character, and mayor of Chicago. In an excellent short biography (*Dic. of Amer. Biog.*, XIX, 657–659) Carl Sandburg wrote that he "had striven with the generations who found Chicago a swamp mudhole and saw it made into an audacious metropolis." In the 1864 congressional race, Wentworth, on the Union (Republican) ticket, defeated the Democratic candidate, Cyrus H. McCormick, noted inventor and producer of the reaper. The Congress chosen in 1864 did not, of course, meet until after Lincoln's death.

[6] On the Scripps-Arnold controversy, see Nicolay and Hay, *Works*, X, 141–142 and 168 (two letters of Lincoln to Scripps, deploring the use of official power in the post office "to defeat Mr. Arnold's nomination to Congress"); R. T. L. Coll., 34223, 34498, 34544, 35854. For similar rows concerning Roscoe Conkling in New York, and William D. Kelley in Philadelphia, see Nicolay and Hay, *Lincoln*, X, 362–363.

nouncing Lincoln; then he generalized: "The truth is that from that day [early in 1861] to the present [January of 1862] Congress has been the theatre for making Presidents and not to carry on the war." [7] One of the milder comments, typical of the radicals, was that of Senator Chandler: "The President is a weak man." [8] Lying "in wait" [9] against the President, these men opposed him on confiscation, on war aims, on methods and pacing as to slavery, on Southern rights, on cabinet composition, on amnesty, on the election of 1864 (in which they would have preferred another man), and on reconstruction.

According to an incident reported in Washington in 1862, a senator once called at the White House and vehemently denounced the President for his "calm and moderate views," ending with the words: "Sir you are within one mile of Hell!" To this Lincoln offered no dissent, but with a gentle nod of his head as if talking to himself, replied: "Yes, yes it is just one mile to the Capitol!" [10]

## VII

Some concept of Lincoln's difficulties with Congress may be obtained by studying that organization known as the joint committee on the conduct of the war.[1] This congressional group collected and caused to be printed a huge mass of testimony, six volumes of it exceeding 4000 pages, about two million words. Yet only a few of the military episodes were investigated; attention was focused chiefly on the Army of the Potomac, and, as to that army, the 1862 campaign on the Peninsula. Much less interest was shown in the Maryland campaign.

The effort of the committee was not to get a well rounded account of military events or to hear both sides of a given controversy equally.

---

7 Giddings to G. W. Julian, Montreal, Canada, Jan. 28, 1862, Giddings-Julian MSS.

8 Zachariah Chandler to his wife, Dec. 18, 1862, Chandler MSS., Lib. of Cong.

9 Bates, *Diary*, 241.

10 The remark about "one mile from Hell" became a topic of familiar chitchat and has been often quoted. See, for instance, Browne, *Everyday Life*, 503. The above form of the joke is found in a letter from A. J. Bleeker to B. Galbraith of New York, July 14, 1862, James Gordon Bennett MSS. This manuscript reference to the incident in mid-July of 1862 has special significance; this was a period of special stress and of serious difficulty between President and Congress, especially on the subject of confiscation.

1 For the formation of the committee, its character, membership and activity, see *Lincoln the President*, II, 20 n., 62–64 (with bibl.), 80–83, 87–88.

In the committee's activities there was always a slant, a preconceived notion of who was to blame, an effort to shape the proceedings so as to fasten blame upon particular scapegoats, these being especially Democratic generals. The harrying of victims was not confined to actual committee proceedings which were relentless enough; there was also an accompaniment of wild rumor and irresponsible publicity. The group served the purposes of a faction—the radicals—and the nature of its maneuvers may be illustrated by its atrocious handling of the case of General Charles P. Stone. That officer, a Democrat, was blamed for the minor Union disaster at Ball's Bluff (October 21, 1861) at which Colonel Edward D. Baker was killed. Stone's special duty was guarding the city of Washington and vicinity; he was a man of admirable record; reliable observers resented the drive to put the blame for Ball's Bluff upon him. In its long drawn out "investigation" the committee gave ear to worthless stories of the man's alleged disloyalty, caused him to be arrested (through Stanton), refused to inform him as to charges and witnesses, denied him the right to be heard, and subjected him to a continued ordeal of vague defamation. It was not until February 1863, a year after his arrest, that the committee gave Stone a copy of the charges against him; his answer was so convincing that he was restored to command, but the vindication never caught up with the defamatory campaign. Sick and broken in spirit, with an entirely undeserved blot upon his character, Stone resigned from the army in September 1864; after the war he served for a time in the Egyptian army. It was the conclusion of J. G. Blaine that the testimony regarding Stone was not sifted by the committee, that the case was "prejudiced," and that the drive against the general was conducted in an atmosphere of rumor and "victim-hunting mania." [2]

The committee with its publicized reputation for vigilant watchfulness to prevent or expose military mistakes, had certain targets, such as McClellan, Stone, Fitz-John Porter, and Franklin, and it had also its favored pets such as Frémont and Butler. It showed by no means a uniform record of severity toward military incompetence. As to the investigation of the operation at Fort Fisher (December

---

[2] Blaine, *Twenty Years of Congress*, I, 381–395. "Rumors and exaggerations filled the newspapers; and the public, in that state of credulity which is an incident of victim-hunting mania, accepted everything as true" (*ibid.*, 382).

1864), one of Butler's failures, the following observation has been made: "The inquisitors had already prejudged the case, and their only purpose was to assemble evidence which would help the general. . . . Butler was given the widest latitude in his answers, and his testimony consisted of a series of long prepared statements. There was no cross-examination." [3]

If one asks how the officious maneuvers of this committee affected the President, the first observation is that the prominently active members were anti-Lincoln men such as Wade, Chandler, and Julian. The committee was strongly favored by Stevens and, from a different party angle, Vallandigham.[4] There is no doubt that the group was a pain to Lincoln. In a conversation with Ward Hill Lamon the President is reported to have said: "I have never faltered in my faith of being ultimately able to suppress this rebellion and of reuniting this divided country; but this improvised vigilant committee to watch my movements and keep me straight, appointed by Congress and called the 'committee on the conduct of the war,' is a marplot, and its greatest purpose seems to be to hamper my action and obstruct the military operations." [5]

The attitude of committeemen toward the President may be judged by the remark of Chandler to his wife: "Folly, folly folly reigns supreme. The President is a weak man . . . & these fool or traitor Generals rule wasting precious time & yet more precious blood in indecisive battles and in avoidable delays." Again he wrote: "The Cabinet is weak & Lincoln weaker . . . ." [6] One might ask what did the committee accomplish? It recommended no legislation and the generals that it favored were by no means the efficient ones. The committee's air of omniscience in military matters was matched only by the lack of military experience on the part of its members. It dealt in partisanship and in the kind of "flagrant wrong" of which, as Blaine has written,[7] General Stone was the victim.

---

[3] T. Harry Williams, *Lincoln and the Radicals*, 366–367.

[4] In supporting the resolution to set up the committee Vallandigham congratulated the country that "gentlemen of the majority" were falling back upon his own (Vallandigham's) principles. *Ann. Cyc.*, 1862, 304.

[5] Lamon, *Recollections*, 183.

[6] Zachariah Chandler to his wife, Dec. 18, 1862, and Feb. 10, 1863, Chandler MSS., Lib. of Cong.

[7] Blaine, *Twenty Years of Congress*, I, 395.

## VIII

Students of the American government will find in the Lincoln administration no such coöperation between President and Congress, and no such presidential leadership in legislation as existed under Wilson [1] or under Franklin D. Roosevelt in the earlier New Deal years. Lincoln's chief effort to promote a specific project of legislation —i. e., to obtain Federal approval and practical financial help to support state emancipation—fell flat despite the President's earnest appeals, conferences with legislators, formal messages, and presidential drafting of a sample bill. In military leadership, in the blockade, in international dealings, and in such matters as the presidential proclamation of emancipation, treatment of disloyal persons, reconstruction, and other important measures, the President either went his way regardless of Senate and House, or was actually checked and angrily challenged by Congress.

As a matter of regular procedure (legitimate, and proper enough if not abused) President Lincoln was questioned by one or the other house of Congress, or requests were sent to him for information. The President usually transmitted the desired documents,[2] almost as a matter of routine, but there were times when requests were refused. He explained the refusal on the ground, traditional in such cases reaching back to the time of Washington, that response to the congressional request would be "incompatible with the public interest." [3] The withholding of information under such circumstances was done with full respect to Congress and no issue was made of it; in-

---

[1] In the general picture Woodrow Wilson's leadership was notably effective in Congress, both in domestic and foreign matters. The great exception—a deeply unfortunate one for the United States and the world—was the defeat, by a minority of the Senate, of Wilson's program for adherence to the League of Nations. For a summary, see *Lincoln the Liberal Statesman,* chap. vii ("Lincoln's Peace and Wilson's").

[2] *Works,* VI, 334.

[3] *Ibid.,* VI, 335; VIII, 188–191. In Lincoln's assertion of his right to choose whether or not to submit certain information to Congress, there was a close analogy to the withholding of information by Washington on the pending Jay treaty with Great Britain. Washington declared that he would not withhold information which "the public good shall require to be disclosed," but under the circumstances he considered that a concession of the right then demanded by the House of Representatives "as a matter of course" would constitute a "dangerous precedent." He justified his interpretation by the intention of the Constitution framers. Washington to the House of Representatives, Mar. 30, 1796, Richardson, *Messages and Papers of the Presidents,* I, 194–196.

deed, members were sometimes careful to point out that questioning the President was not to be construed as a vote of censure.[4]

At times, however (aside from requests for information), the Congress came near to censuring the President, and there were frequent occasions when lack of confidence in the Executive was the dominant sentiment. The fact that censure or want of confidence was not formally voted seems to have been chiefly for the reason that such votes are not a parliamentary custom in the United States. Such lack of formal censure, however, was small comfort to a President having to deal with an uncoöperative body whose members gave out frequent censure in their own statements. A few examples of such statements must suffice:

*Julian of Indiana,* House of Representatives, December 11, 1861: "I . . . infer that the general policy of the Administration . . . renders necessary some action on the part of Congress, looking to a change of that policy." [5]

*Thaddeus Stevens of Pennsylvania,* House of Representatives, December 16, 1861: "I do not understand where the President gets his facts which he states in this respect [on conditions in Kentucky]. I believe he has been misled. I believe he is laboring under a hallucination of mind upon this subject, as fatal as that of Samson under the manipulation of Delilah." [6]

*Hale of New Hampshire,* Senate, December 16, 1861: ". . . I venture to predict . . . that if the American people . . . shall find in the future that they have been trifled with . . . there will be such a storm come upon your heads as history has never yet recorded; and it does not want a very great degree of faith to hear the distant rumblings of that thunder-storm that will overwhelm the Administration and the party in power if they do not see the things that belong to the day and the hour before they are hidden from their eyes." [7]

These criticisms, however, were mild when compared to such a document as the "Wade-Davis Manifesto" (August 5, 1864), a scorching denunciation of the President in the midst of the campaign for

---

[4] Trumbull was an example. *Cong. Globe,* 37 Cong., 2 sess., 95 (Dec. 16, 1861).
[5] *Ibid.,* 37 Cong., 2 sess., 59.          [6] *Ibid.,* 103.
[7] *Ibid.,* 93.

his reëlection. This hostile declaration, issued by men of importance in congressional leadership, had a bearing chiefly upon the subject of reconstruction and will be discussed in that connection.

## IX

It might have clarified the situation if those who were so vigorously denouncing Lincoln had faced up to the necessity of going on record in an actual vote of censure. The consequences of such a vote would have been serious, but that very fact might have had a sobering effect upon some of those who were hounding the nation's leader. Absence of formal censure should not obscure the fact that, as George W. Julian said concerning one occasion, "the action of the President [as to confiscation] was inexpressibly provoking to a large majority of Congress." [1]

Though there were ups and downs in his popularity, Lincoln stood continually in need of support. People who could not see the whole picture, and could not appreciate the Executive's paramount emphasis upon the Union, would express their impatience with the President. Intemperance of language seemed characteristic of this type of person. At the time of Lincoln's first regular annual message to Congress in December 1861 an Illinois radical wrote: "Not *one single manly, bold, dignified* position taken . . . . No response to the popular feeling . . . but . . . a timid, timeserving, commonplace sort of an abortion of a message, cold enough with one breath, to *freeze* h—ll over." [2] He thought Lincoln must have looked southward when he wrote it.

On those rare occasions when the Chief Magistrate was commended in Congress he would, like as not, be praised in an unfortunate sense. It was like getting applause in the wrong places. Early in the war, when Lincoln's arrests were being discussed in the Senate, Wilson of Massachusetts remarked that "the loyal people of this country were electrified; they felt that they had a government that was ready to exert its power to save the country." Wilson's next remark gave the whole passage a dubious twist: ". . . they rejoiced [at the

---

[1] Rice, *Reminiscences*, 58.
[2] S. York to Lyman Trumbull, Paris, Ill., Dec. 5, 1861, Trumbull MSS.

arrests] as they did when Mason and Slidell were clutched from the deck of a British vessel, and imprisoned at Fort Warren . . . ." [3] Since the Lincoln administration was finding the seizure of Mason and Slidell most unfortunate, and was doing its best to work out a solution which ultimately involved the release of the envoys, this sort of senatorial approval gave no comfort. Wilson's declaration (December 16, 1861) came while the vexing problem of what to do with Mason and Slidell was pending; so far as the troubled administration was concerned, it struck the wrong note.

Referring to the attitude of "the leading men of the two Houses," A. G. Riddle wrote: "he [Lincoln] . . . became the theme of criticism . . . [and] reproach on the part of these gentlemen. The New York *Tribune* was largely the organ of these congressional critics, and . . . Mr. Greeley . . . was diligently searching . . . for a man to succeed him [i. e., to succeed Lincoln]. To such extent did this condemnation reach, that, at the end of the Thirty-seventh Congress [March 1863], there were in the House but two men, capable of being heard, who openly and everywhere defended him—Mr. Arnold of Illinois, and Mr. Riddle of Ohio." [4]

This astounding statement—that the President had only two unwavering defenders (if indeed the two mentioned could be so described)—need not be taken too literally, but Riddle was a keen observer. His statement has significance as indicating the general attitude of the House, which was that of opposition to, or divergence from, the views of Lincoln. If one goes so far as to assume that Riddle and Arnold were the only men in the House of Representatives who were really friendly to Lincoln, it should be remembered that neither of these men was reëlected in 1864. Riddle did not seek reëlection, and Arnold, despite his appeal to Lincoln to help him in seeking another term, was stopped in his efforts to remain in Congress. The situation becomes the more remarkable when one remembers Riddle's eulogistic friendliness toward Senator Wade, a bitter and powerfully active opponent of the President.

To document his statement that he was a supporter of the President, Riddle referred to a speech he had made in the House on Feb-

---

[3] *Cong. Globe*, 37 Cong., 2 sess., 94 (Dec. 16, 1861).
[4] Riddle, *Recollections*, 218 n.

ruary 28, 1863, concerning the bill to indemnify the President—i. e.,
to afford protection for those who had made irregular arrests and
seizures in accordance with presidential orders. In that speech Mr.
Riddle had declared:

. . . How easy it is to abuse, traduce, and denounce. That it requires
neither wit, grace, or truth, is illustrated by the assaults of those gentlemen
on the President. . . .

Sir, the Executive is the arm of the people under our Constitution, and
with it only can we deal a blow upon the rebellion. . . . Whoever
strengthens this arm, strengthens the national cause; whoever weakens it
strengthens the enemy. . . . You cannot separate the Executive from the
*personale* of the President; and whatever detracts from him personally
weakens the Executive force . . . .

The President, without the people, and all of them, can no more conduct this war to a successful issue than can the people without him.
. . . With a united people he is irresistible, spite of mistakes and acci-
dents. A united people and President can control fate and compel success.
They must stand together; and woe unutterable to the wretches whose
words or deeds shall separate them. . . . They [i. e., millions of the peo-
ple] will discuss the events and management of the war. . . . But I submit if the just limit of criticism and manly debate has not been brutally
outraged in the fierce denunciation of the President by gentlemen on this
floor, and which have been caught up and reëchoed by their partisan
press?

. . . . . . . . . . . . . .

. . . If any man here distrusts the President, let him speak forth here,
. . . and no longer offend the streets and nauseate places of common resort with their . . . clamor. . . . He [the President] may not have in
excess that ecstatic fire that makes poets and prophets and madmen; he
may not possess much of what we call heroic blood, that drives men to
stake priceless destinies on desperate ventures, and lose them; he may not
in an eminent degree possess that indefinable something that school-boys
call genius, that enables its possessor through new and unheard-of combinations to grasp at wonderful results, and that usually ends in failure . . . . He is an unimpassioned, cool, shrewd, sagacious, far-seeing
man, with a capacity to form his own judgments, and a will to execute
them; and he possesses an integrity pure and simple as the white rays of
light that play about the Throne. It is this that has so tied the hearts and
love of the people to him, that will not unloose in the breath of all the
demagogues in the land. It is idle to compare him with Washington or
Jackson. Like all extraordinary men, he is an original, and must stand in
his own niche.

. . . contemplate, if you can, . . . the fearful responsibilities imposed upon this man. Is it not a marvel . . . that he sustains them so well? [5]

It is not surprising that Lincoln welcomed the days and months when there was no assembled Congress. When, after a long session, the Senate adjourned in July 1862, the New York *Herald* remarked that this would relieve the President of embarrassment; he could carry on without senatorial annoyance and hindrance.[6] Some of the solons, however, wanted Congress to remain in permanent session. It is significant that many of Lincoln's principal executive measures were taken when Congress was not sitting. This was true of the initial call for troops in April 1861, the blockade, the enlargement of the regular army, the overruling of Frémont, the suspension of the habeas corpus privilege, the preliminary proclamation of emancipation, and the important speech of April 11, 1865, on postwar policy. If Lincoln had had a coöperative Congress, most if not all of these measures ought to have been the combined product of the legislative and executive branches.

At one of those periods when Lincoln was having particular difficulty with an uncoöperative Congress, his friend Orville Browning of Illinois called on him at the White House. The day was July 15, 1862. The President was trying to check the course that leaders of Congress were taking on the question of confiscation. At the same time he was shaping up his emancipation policy and was struggling with a military situation that led to the elevation of Halleck and Pope over McClellan. As if this were not enough, the international situation and the coming congressional election were on his mind.

The President, as Browning wrote in his diary, "was in his Library writing, with directions to deny him to every body. I went in a moment. He looked weary, care-worn and troubled. I shook hands with him, and asked how he was. He said 'tolerably well' I remarked that I felt concerned about him—regretted that troubles crowded so heavily upon him, and feared his health was suffering. He held me by the hand, pressed it, and said in a very tender and touching tone —'Browning I must die sometime', I replied 'your fortunes Mr President are bound up with those of the Country, and disaster to one

---

[5] *Cong. Globe*, 37 Cong., 3 sess., 1400 (Feb. 28, 1863). Though the speech is reproduced in Riddle's book, the text as here given is based on the *Globe*.

[6] New York *Herald*, July 13, 1862, p. 4, c. 6; p. 5, c. 1.

would be disaster to the other, and I hope you will do all you can to preserve your health and life.' He looked very sad, and there was a cadence of deep sadness in his voice. We parted I believe both of us with tears in our eyes." [7]

It is not argued here that Lincoln's depression was altogether attributable to the difficulties he was having with Congress. It is rather that, when tribulations from many a quarter were piling up their accumulated weight, Congress added its bit by rebuffing his suggestions and pursuing policies of which he strongly disapproved. As the second session of the Thirty-Seventh Congress neared its close, Senator Fessenden of Maine, conversing with Browning of Illinois, indicated doubts as to the wisdom of his colleagues. "During recess met Fessenden [wrote Browning on July 16, 1862], and in a conversation about the confiscation bill he said very emphatically that he thought with me it would have been better not to have legislated upon the subject . . . at all." [8]

We are dealing here, of course, with the disharmony between Lincoln and the radicals, which has been pointed out earlier as a pervasive dualism running throughout the Lincoln administration,[9] and which was a primary factor in the President's unsatisfactory dealings with Congress. In this respect the two factors were that Republican radicals came increasingly into control of Congress; and that, in the minds of these radicals, opposition to Lincoln rose steadily in an embittering crescendo. These were "the men to whom the nation . . . turned as the great representative men of the new political power." They "did not conceal their distrust of Lincoln, and he had little support from them at any time during his administration." Except for some of the younger leaders, declared A. K. McClure, "he would have been a President without a party." McClure added that the "one man who rendered him [Lincoln] the greatest service of all at the beginning of the war was Stephen A. Douglas, his old competitor of Illinois." Speaking of the manner in which Republican leaders "were hesitating and criticising their President," McClure remarked upon "the general distrust and demoralization that existed among men who should have been a solid phalanx of leadership in the crisis that confronted them." [10]

[7] Browning, *Diary*, I, 559-560.    [8] *Ibid.*, I, 560.
[9] *Lincoln the President*, II, 1-2.    [10] McClure, 62.

Since Congress and the President were not traveling the same path, Lincoln simply took over certain powers without regard to Congress. "The President was . . . compelled to decide for himself in the multitude of conflicting counsels what policy the administration should adopt, and even a less . . . conservative man than Lincoln would have been compelled . . . to move with the utmost caution." [11] When, in addition to all this, it is remembered that the President got little comfort and much interference from his cabinet, that his generals were often a trial to him, and that few of the state governors were genuinely enthusiastic for him, one can understand Lincoln's loneliness in his lofty office.

## X

The question arises: Were there constructive and hopeful factors at work in Congress? The answer, of course, is in the affirmative. The very fact that Congress existed—that it was not abolished, intimidated, prorogued, or suppressed—was evidence that the nation was not under a dictatorship and that the principle of representative government still endured. The whole government, including the armed forces and the civil establishment, depended upon Congress. Bureaus and departments, courts, military systems—all such things existed by congressional enactment. Vital matters of finance, the raising of the army, specific appropriations for a thousand purposes, rested with the men on Capitol Hill. (Such a thing as executive expenditures from the Federal treasury without congressional appropriation, though it did occur,[1] was highly exceptional.) Since Congress possessed the power of the purse, together with the broad function of determining what branches should or should not exist, it was central in the whole governmental structure. It is true, of course, that Congress could administer virtually nothing. Practical management of the nation's business, execution of the laws, administrative tasks, belonged to the executive branch; but in any comprehensive view it would be a great mistake to underestimate the legislative role.

It is the judgment of J. F. Rhodes that "the senators and representatives labored with zeal, sagacity, and effect." Referring to the

---

11 *Ibid.,* 63.                                    1 *Lincoln the President,* I, 375.

long session of the Thirty-Seventh Congress (December to July, 1861–1862), he wrote: "The laws of this session show how much an able and honest Congress may accomplish when possessed of an earnestness and singleness of purpose that will prevail against the cumbrous rules which hedge about the action of a democracy's legislative body, unfitting it for the management of a war." [2]

A noteworthy aspect of the war period was the continuing concept of the nation's greatness and permanence which animated both President and Congress. War measures were perforce the chief preoccupation of the law makers. Through all this, however, and beyond it, there was the thought of an enduring nation whose peaceful growth and prosperity was, in the long run, the government's main concern. As a relief from the many episodes that showed the excesses of the war mind, it is well to note those moments of deliberation which envisaged a nation that would survive its internal struggle, promote the vital task of restoration, and go on from there to normal peaceful advance and improvement.

It is true that such deliberation left much to be desired, so that the "Gilded Age" was to be a time of extravagance and coarseness, but no history of Lincoln's day is complete without noticing lasting accomplishments that pertained to non-war pursuits and developments. For the first time in the nation's history a department was created in the United States government for the promotion of agriculture. In his annual message of December 1861 Lincoln called attention to this need. "Agriculture," he said, "confessedly the largest interest of the nation, has not a department, nor a bureau, but a clerkship only, assigned to it in the government." Congress acted to create the department of agriculture on May 15, 1862, and President Lincoln appointed as its head one of the nation's most devoted and competent public servants, Isaac Newton. A personal friend of Lincoln, Newton was serving in the agricultural division of the patent office of the department of the interior. With a department of his own he now went ahead to organize a highly serviceable agency, so that in December 1862 Lincoln reported the establishment of "an extensive system of correspondence and exchanges, both at home and abroad, which promises to effect highly beneficial results in the development of a correct knowledge of recent improvements in agri-

---

2 J. F. Rhodes, *History of the United States*, IV, 57–58.

culture . . . ." [3] He went on to comment on specific services of the new department, such as the collection of agricultural statistics, the introduction of new products, and the distribution of seeds, plants, and cuttings.

Lincoln's interest in agriculture is an extensive subject in itself. He had spoken prominently before the Wisconsin Agricultural Society at Milwaukee on September 30, 1859, this being one of his major addresses. As in the case of Jefferson, he associated agricultural activity with democracy, and in this spirit, in 1864, he referred to Newton's department as "peculiarly the people's department, in which they feel more directly concerned than in any other." [4]

There was more in this than agriculture, great as that was. In such matters the Lincoln administration was treating the function of government broadly, as involving more than the restricted sphere of keeping order and suppressing crime. Rather, the instruments of government were to be devoted in a broad sense to serving the people's needs, developing the resources of the country, promoting general prosperity, improving the means of livelihood, stamping out pests, and performing those functions that are beyond the reach of individual or merely local effort.

This purposeful, rather than negative, use of government was illustrated in other fields. Realizing a scheme projected by Jonathan B. Turner, earnest and public spirited professor at Illinois College at Jacksonville, Illinois, Congress enacted and Lincoln signed a far reaching law in 1862. It is one of the landmarks in American education. Known as the Morrill land-grant-college act, this statute set up a plan for the establishment of colleges to promote agriculture and the mechanic arts with the aid of public lands donated by the Federal government. The act took its name from one of its legislative sponsors, Senator Justin S. Morrill of Vermont. While it was passed in the midst of war, this law had more than wartime importance. Its significance as a national project to be projected far into the future was illustrated after the war when its benefits were extended to those states which, in Lincoln's day, were in the Confederacy, as well as

---

[3] Annual message to Congress, Dec. 1, 1862, MS. in clerk's hand, Nat. Archives; photostat, A. Lincoln Assoc. (Nicolay and Hay, *Works*, VIII, 109).

[4] Annual message to Congress, Dec. 6, 1864, photostat, A. Lincoln Assoc. (Nicolay and Hay, *Works*, X, 302).

to commonwealths still to enter the Union. Liberal donations of public lands and other forms of government aid were also employed by Congress in the launching of ambitious railroad projects designed to reach the Pacific and complete the span of transportation across the continent.

The notable homestead act of 1862 belonged in this category of welfare measures enacted during the Lincoln administration. In the campaign of 1860 a great deal of Republican emphasis was placed upon the theme that every man should "possess the means of gaining a fair living and bringing up his family respectably." For that reason it was urged that *"A homestead should be granted . . . to every poor man who needs it, desires it, and will cultivate it."* Arguments were raised against the undemocratic regime that results "whenever an excessive share of land has been accumulated in the hands of any person or class of persons." [5]

The homestead act, signed by the President on May 20, 1862, was one of the most significant of all the non-war measures enacted during the Lincoln administration. It provided that one hundred sixty acres, a quarter-section, of land was to be given out of the public domain to a bona fide homesteader on payment of a nominal fee after five years of actual residence. The effect of the law on American social and economic development, though it needs to be rejudged by the fuller findings of recent writers,[6] was far reaching. As a measure frankly devoted to welfare, and not to the more restricted functions of government, it is an early landmark.

These developments would have been enough to cause the Lincoln administration to be remembered for its permanent contributions, altogether apart from the war and the nobly great question of emancipation, but the constructive story does not end here.[7] Industry was promoted in numerous ways. Prejudice against "aliens" was avoided. Immigration was encouraged. Foreign laborers were brought in under the contract system, whose later exploitive aspects were at

---

[5] Hartford *Evening Press* (pro-Lincoln), Oct. 25-26, 1860, reprinted in Howard C. Perkins, ed., *Northern Editorials on Secession*, I, 63.

[6] Paul Gates, "The Homestead Law in an Incongruous Land System"; Fred A. Shannon, "The Homestead Act and the Labor Surplus." For these two papers, see *Amer. Hist. Rev.*, XLI, 637–681 (1936).

[7] J. Duane Squires, "Some Enduring Achievements of the Lincoln Administration, 1861–1865," *Abr. Lincoln Quar.*, V, 191–211 (1948).

variance with the original intent of the law. Sympathy toward men of other countries was stimulated. Valuable progress was made in surgery, medicine and nursing. New devices were used in public finance and in the much needed national regulation of banking. The National Academy of Sciences was set up by Congress (March 3, 1863), such distinguished scientists as Joseph Henry and Asa Gray being original members. The Capitol at Washington was completed under Lincoln. In the relation of the President to the governors, in state and Federal coöperation, and in the general emphasis upon the human importance of government, the period 1861 to 1865 still stands out as an era of great significance. It amounted, in fact, to a new orientation. Never again would the relation of the people to the government be so detached, so restricted and undeveloped, as in the age that ended with Buchanan.

Part of this congressional activity was trial and error; in certain aspects the result was frustration; permanent effectiveness did not always attach to the legislation of the time. Some of the "resolutions" of Congress fell flat. Confiscation accomplished almost nothing at all —certainly nothing that was constructive. Generals were pilloried by the committee on the conduct of the war. Attacks upon the cabinet led to no beneficial result. Republican "reconstruction" was abandoned by its own sponsors in 1877. The optimism that greeted the homestead act—the assumption that free land in the West would relieve the congestion and distress of a labor surplus in the East— proved illusory. The fine purposes of the homestead law met with disappointment in later decades because of fraud and shameful exploitation by profit seeking interests.[8] Despite these factors, which belong to sordid postwar years, it is nevertheless true that in those moments when Congress was at its best, measures were launched which, though attracting minor attention in contemporary history and memoirs, were planned on lines of a progressive design and were indicative of a hopeful and forward looking outlook even in the nation's darkest hours.

It is in this sense that one should read Lincoln's messages to Con-

---

8 Paul W. Gates, "The Homestead Law in an Incongruous Land System," *Amer. Hist. Rev.*, XLI, 652–681 (1936). For the later situation which "made a mockery of the presumed intention of the Homestead Act," see Fred A. Shannon, *America's Economic Growth* (3rd ed., 1951), 376 ff.

gress. They reveal a sense of time, an unwavering concept of a nation with a future. Matters just treated—agriculture, the homestead system, aid to education, railroads to the Pacific, immigration, scientific improvement, and so on—were called to the attention of Congress by Lincoln.

Naturally a great deal of space in his messages to Congress was devoted to the Union cause, to the distress and challenge of war making, to undoing (partially) of the effects of the war, to slavery and emancipation, and to the high ideal of "freedom disenthralled." [9] These were affairs of immediate urgency. Yet it is remarkable to observe how often and how confidently he spoke of matters that were natural and peaceful. At times he became so inspired with visions of the country's growth that his predictions turned out to be overstatements. There were men then living, he thought, who would live to see the United States contain a population of 250 millions.[10] He did not, however, think merely of numbers. He drew attention to America's health and harvests, its abundant resources, and, as the war progressed, to "the improved condition of our national affairs." [11] In the western territories he saw regions untouched by war, areas of hope, with prospects for new States in the Union.[12] In a significant passage he described and extolled the Middle West, which he called "the great body of the republic." He recognized in "this great interior region" natural advantages which made it "one of the most important in the world." He could not bear the idea that so vast and centrally located an area should be "cut off," as it would be if there should be a separation of "our common country into two nations." [13]

In terms of lasting adjustment he wrote eloquently of labor and capital, with marked emotional emphasis on the dignity of labor.[14] Public works, public lands, postal and telegraphic arrangements, internal improvements, Indian affairs, participation in "the exhibition of the industry of all nations to be holden at London in the year 1862" —all such topics were treated by Lincoln on more than a perfunctory

[9] Last sentence, message of Dec. 8, 1863, photostat, A. Lincoln Assoc.
[10] Last paragraph, message of Dec. 3, 1861.
[11] First paragraph, message of Dec. 8, 1863, photostat.
[12] Message of Dec. 1, 1862, photostat.
[13] Message, Dec. 1, 1862 (Nicolay and Hay, Works, VIII, 113–115).
[14] On various occasions Lincoln dealt at some length with labor's indispensable contribution and its relation to capital. Examples are his agricultural address at Milwaukee, Sep. 30, 1859, and his annual message of Dec. 3, 1861.

level. Above the ruin and abnormality of war the President was look-ing forward to the time when the nation's concern would be with healing, making whole, restoration, and healthy growth. It was in this sense that he viewed the function of government, of the Union itself. Referring in December 1861 to the growth of the nation's population since 1790, he declared that the "increase of those other things which men deem desirable has been even greater." He con-sidered this an argument for democracy, showing "at one view, what the popular principle applied to government, through the machinery of the States and the Union, has produced in a given time; and also what, if firmly maintained, it promises for the future." "The strug-gle of today," he concluded, "is not altogether for today . . . ." [15]

[15] Concluding paragraph, message of Dec. 3, 1861, photostat, A. Lincoln Assoc.

# DEMOCRACY AND THE WAR POWER

WARTIME procedures under Lincoln offer many a text in politics and philosophy. When the government of a democratic nation chooses harsh methods as an alternative to extinction there will be sincere protest and criticism, and there will be slurs upon democracy itself. This criticism will come if the nation survives, but suppose it does not survive. Suppose it goes down by reason of division, dissension, or treason within the walls? In that case there will be worse criticism stressing the weakness and inadequacy alleged to be characteristic of a democratic nation in an emergency.

In facing this situation Lincoln was in a position where he would be condemned either way. If he did not preserve all the niceties of the Constitution he would be assailed not only by those who genuinely valued civil liberty, but also by enemies and opponents whose motive was criticism itself and whose animus was partisanship. Far heavier would have been the denunciation if the whole experiment of the democratic American Union had fallen as it seemed possible that it might fall. If such a disaster had come, where would have been the use of the Constitution whose procedures had been adhered to?

Such in part was Lincoln's problem, but to state the case in this way does not exhaust the subject. Suppression is a matter of degree. To use a discreet amount of it does not imply the utmost of brutality, severity, and despotism. Things regarded as severe in Lincoln's time would have seemed soft and "decadent" to a Hitler, a Heydrich, or a Himmler. It becomes, therefore, a matter of importance to examine the Lincoln procedures, to perceive them for what they were, to study them against the background of those threatening times, and to note the qualifications, concessions, compromises, and ameliorations that appeared in the human application of measures that looked harsh on the books.

To speak of the government as Lincoln's is in part true and in part a matter of rhetoric. Everything pertaining to the United States was Lincoln's in the language of the secessionist press: it was Lincoln's government, Lincoln's army, Lincoln's navy, his hirelings, Hessians, raw head and bloody bones. One cannot of course identify everything in the United States of 1861–65 with Lincoln. One may, however, speak of what happened "under Lincoln" as denoting in point of time the period of Lincoln's rule. Much that happened was indeed shaped by the personality, discretion, and executive procedure of the President. Yet things were done, by Congress and by military leaders, of which Lincoln disapproved.

In managing the government Lincoln acted. He took authority; he was out in front; he did not depend upon Congress; he did not take his cues from the courts; he made the presidency, to a large extent though not completely, the dominant power, certainly more so than it had normally been. He came to a major clash with Congress because he attempted to exert his leadership in the shaping of postwar policy. In this sense, and in others in which the radicals opposed him, his will did not prevail. The intent, pattern, and method of that administration in its emergency aspects must now be examined.

# I

It is a traditional Anglo-Saxon principle that rulers must not be arbitrary. A citizen is entitled to redress. He may appeal to the courts. If they find that officials have wronged him in person or property by measures beyond the bounds of legitimate government, not only is reparation due, but rulers and administrators may themselves be brought to book.[1] No American official is above the law. Military power is by no means unlimited.[2] Down through the decades the curtailing of army authority has had repeated emphasis, from the Virginia Declaration of Rights (1776) on down to the Milligan decision (1866) and beyond. It is not merely that, until recent years, a large standing army in time of peace has been considered undesirable and

---

[1] *Constitutional Problems Under Lincoln,* esp. chaps. ii, vii, viii, xx.
[2] *Ibid.* (foreword to revised ed., 1951), xvii–xx.

has not been the American policy.[3] It is also true that with their dislike of military excess Americans have had definite concepts of the
limits beyond which army power must not go.

Time of war is different, but even then it is a mistake to suppose
that all the basic safeguards are to be shattered. We are familiar with
the idea "necessity knows no law," the maxim "inter arma silent
leges," and the oft-repeated phrase "military necessity." But it would
be a great mistake to argue, by using such phrases, that anything and
everything can be justified by the demands of war. "Necessity knows
no law" is a dangerous half-truth. If it has a kernel of genuine meaning, being applicable to a situation of utmost extremity, it should
always be watched as to how it is applied. If a commander appeals to
"military necessity," which he would not do except for something
wrongful or irregular, he should be ready to show that the main
object is justified. (Beginning an aggressive war, as in the attack upon
Belgium in 1914, would not be such an object.) He should also show
that the case is desperate, that the public urgency is imperative, that
the means used are not excessive, and that these means are conducive
to order. No reputable commander even in war will do a deeply
dishonorable thing. Proper military rule leaves some space for civilian
rights. One can understand the characterization that war is crime,
yet wanton criminality has no place in the procedures of a reputable
government drawn into war. What has been called phony currency
is not to be tolerated. Mass killings, genocide, brutal collective re-
prisals, the rounding up of hostages, slaughter of refugees, torture
chambers, camps of horror, labor enslavement, annihilation of whole
villages—such procedures are not to be justified because war is on.
The kind of government to use such practices would be the kind to
start a war.[4]

Martial law is a kind of by-passing of law. It is the commander's
will in a situation so unusual that ordinary rules do not and cannot

[3] As late as 1910 the regular army of the United States numbered only 80,718, with
the national guard (119,660) as an imperfect reserve. Peacetime conscription, well established in Europe, was not used in the United States until 1940, a time of world upheaval. At the mid-century (1950) compulsory universal military training had not been
adopted as a permanent peacetime program, while the postwar draft and huge defense
program (from 1945 on) have been obviously related to the abnormal stress of a wretched
world crisis.

[4] Randall, "Civil and Military Relationships Under Lincoln," *Pa. Mag. of Hist. and
Biog.*, vol. 69, 201–202 (July 1945); *Constitutional Problems Under Lincoln* (revised
ed., 1951), foreword, xxix–xxxi.

apply.[5] Yet one should note how seldom such measures have actually been found "necessary" by the American national government. Up to Lincoln's day there was very little Federal use of martial law. Up to March 1863 Congress never approved the general suspension of the habeas corpus privilege. It did so then with reluctance and ambiguity. No such suspension was declared under Woodrow Wilson or Franklin Roosevelt.[6]

When one considers the kind of man Lincoln was—considerate, tolerant, and regardful of civil liberty—one realizes forcibly the dilemma he faced in assuming war power. He to whom democracy was fundamental and precious became the target for attack by those who called him a despot. He became the wielder of such expanded executive authority that he was referred to as a "dictator." He was compared to Nero or Caligula. It has been noted in an earlier volume how, in the eighty days between the April call for troops and the meeting of Congress on July 4, 1861, Lincoln performed a whole series of important acts by pure assumption of presidential power.[7] He proclaimed, not "civil war" in those words, but the existence of "combinations too powerful to be suppressed by the ordinary course of judicial proceedings." He called forth the militia to "suppress said combinations" which he commanded "to disperse and retire peacefully" to their homes. Congress has the constitutional power to declare war, but suppression of rebellion has been recognized as an executive function, for which the power of setting aside civil pro-

---

[5] British and American citations on martial law are given at length in *Constitutional Problems Under Lincoln*, 144 n. For a short selection of American authorities one may cite: G. B. Davis, *Military Law of the U.S.;* W. S. Holdsworth and H. Earle Richards, in *Law Quar. Rev.*, XVIII; H. W. Ballantine, in *Yale Law Rev.*, XXIV and *Columbia Law Rev.*, XII; *Ex parte* Milligan, 71 U. S. 2.

[6] Under Franklin Roosevelt there were instances when military executions were not overruled by invoking the right of habeas corpus, but that right itself was not set aside. An example is the Yamashita case (327 U. S. 1). The courts were available for inquiring into military procedures, trials, and punishments. If one goes farther back he finds that civil procedures were retained and martial law avoided under Washington in the Whiskey Insurrection, under John Adams in the Fries Rebellion, and under Jefferson in the Burr Conspiracy. Jackson's use of martial law in Louisiana during the War of 1812—his actual imprisoning of a judge and a district attorney who tried to stop him—was disapproved in the regular courts and the famous general subjected to a fine. The remission of the fine many years later by Congress was a personal tribute to Jackson when on the eve of the grave, not a justification of his act as a sound precedent. All of these factors point up the exceptional nature of the procedure under Lincoln, but of course the Civil War happened only once.

[7] *Lincoln the President*, I, chap. xiii.

cedures has been placed in the President's hands. In this initial phase Lincoln also proclaimed a blockade, suspended the habeas corpus privilege, increased the size of the regular army, and authorized the expenditure of government money without congressional appropriation. He made far reaching decisions and commitments while Congress was not in session.

The irregularity, or at least the unusual character, of these measures, was indicated by Senator John Sherman's statement, "I never met any one who claimed that the President could, by a proclamation, increase the regular army." [8] Sherman's statement referred, not to the April call for 75,000 militia to serve for three months, but to a further call (May 3, 1861) directing "that the regular army of the United States be increased . . . , making . . . a maximum aggregate increase of twenty-two thousand seven hundred and fourteen officers and enlisted men . . . ." [9]

Lincoln did not deny that he had stretched his constitutional power. "These measures," he declared, "whether strictly legal or not, were ventured upon, under what appeared to be a popular demand, and a public necessity; trusting then, as now, that Congress would readily ratify them." [10] Lincoln thus confronted Congress with a *fait accompli*. It was a case of a President deliberately exercising legislative power, and then seeking congressional approval or legalization after the event. There were those who believed that in doing so he had carried his authority too far.

## II

These constitutional questions—the validity of initial war measures, the legal nature of the conflict, Lincoln's assumption of war power—came up to the Supreme Court in one of the most fundamental cases ever heard by that tribunal. The decision, in the *Prize Cases*,[1] came in March 1863, though the specific executive acts had been performed in 1861. The particular question before the Court pertained to the seizure of vessels for violating the blockade, whose

8 New York *Tribune*, Aug. 23, 1861, p. 7, c. 6.
9 Call for 42,034 volunteers, May 3, 1861, photograph of original, A. Lincoln Assoc.
10 Message of July 4, 1861, *Sen. Exec. Doc. No. 1*, 37 Cong., 1 sess., p. 9.
1 67 U. S. 635.

legality had been challenged since it was set up by presidential proc-lamation without congressional declaration of war. The problem, however, had much broader aspects, since the blockade was only one of the emergency measures taken by Lincoln in the "eighty days" by his own authority.

It was argued in the *Prize Cases* (in which proceedings for a number of captured ships were joined) that Congress alone has power to de-clare war, that the President has no right to institute a blockade until after such a declaration, that war did not lawfully exist when the seizures were made, and that judgments against the ships in lower Federal courts were invalid. Had the high court in 1863 decided ac-cording to such arguments, it would have been declaring invalid the basic governmental acts by which the war was prosecuted in its early months, as well as the whole procedure (in terms of law and authority) by which the government at Washington had met the 1861 emergency. In some minds the matter went further and it was supposed that a decision adverse to the President's power would have overthrown, or cast into doubt, the legality of the whole war.

Pondering such an embarrassment to the Lincoln administration, the distinguished lawyer Richard Henry Dana, Jr. wrote to Charles Francis Adams: "Contemplate, my dear sir, the possibility of a Su-preme Court deciding that this blockade is illegal! What a position it would put us in before the world . . . ! It would end the war, and how it would leave us with neutral powers, it is fearful to contem-plate!" [2]

Under these circumstances it was a great relief to the Lincoln ad-ministration when the Court sustained the acts of the President, including the blockade. A civil war, the Court held, does not legally originate because it is declared by Congress. It simply occurs. The "party in rebellion" breaks its allegiance, organizes armies, and com-mences hostilities. In such a case it is the duty of the President to resist force by force, to meet the war as he finds it "without waiting for Congress to baptize it with a name." As to the weighty question whether the struggle was an insurrection, or a "war" in the full sense (as if between independent nations), the Court decided (here and elsewhere) that it was both. Justice Grier, who delivered the opinion,

[2] R. H. Dana, Jr. to Charles Francis Adams, Mar. 9, 1863, quoted in Adams, *Richard Henry Dana*, II, 267.

showed a dislike of legal refinements on this point, as he had earlier shown an impatience (1861) with legalistic efforts to justify the treatment of Confederate privateersmen as "pirates." [3] He refused to approve any "such anomalous doctrine" as that "a war levied on the Government . . . to dismember and destroy it, is not a *war* because it is an *insurrection*."

Lincoln's acts were thus held valid, the blockade upheld, the convenient double-nature theory of the war announced, and the condemnation of the ships sustained. But all this was by a narrow escape. The decision, which was handed down on March 10, 1863, was five to four, the Chief Justice (Taney) being among the dissenters. The five constituting the majority were Grier of Pennsylvania, Wayne of Georgia, Swayne of Ohio, Miller of Iowa, and Davis of Illinois. The minority included Taney of Maryland, Nelson of New York, Catron of Tennessee, and Clifford of Maine. This was weighty dissent, all the more so when one remembers the traditional policy of the Court to avoid smashing pronouncements on "political" questions, as well as the urgency of sustaining a government in time of desperate war. On analyzing the situation further it is found that three of the five justices who sustained Lincoln's acts, where every one of the five was essential to a majority, were men of his own appointing (Swayne, Miller, and Davis), while another (Wayne) was of the deep South.

This situation gives particular importance to James Moore Wayne of Georgia and to the special service which he performed in terms of his sincere adherence to the Union. He had remained on the Court despite the secession of his state, unlike Campbell of Alabama, also a man of great sincerity, who, though not himself a secessionist, resigned from the Supreme Court when his state seceded. Wayne's career was that of "legislator, mayor of Savannah, judge of the Eastern Circuit of Georgia, congressman during the Jackson era, president of two constitutional conventions in his State, [and] associate justice of the Supreme Court of the United States for thirty-two years . . . ." [4] Appointed by President Jackson in 1835, he remained on the Court until his death in 1867, his service falling within the period of eleven Presidents. Of the justices who served with John Marshall he was the last to survive. Wayne's strong Unionism is

---

3 Randall, *Civil War and Reconstruction*, 586–587.
4 Alexander A. Lawrence, *James Moore Wayne: Southern Unionist*, vii.

clearly shown by his biographer, who writes: "On the night that his State seceded Benjamin H. Hill shut out the light of the bonfires from his room and grieved in darkness for the shattered Union. Herschel V. Johnson left Milledgeville sick at heart. But none was more heartbroken than Mr. Justice Wayne. And none saw more clearly the disaster which lay ahead." [5]

In recognizing, however, the full seriousness of the governmental situation touching the *Prize Cases* in their bearing upon the legality of Lincoln's war measures, it is important to avoid exaggeration. The idea that the war policy would have broken down and the war have ended if the decision had gone the other way, is not merely an over-dramatization; it is an erroneous supposition as to the substance of the decision. The matter in legal doubt was the validity of presidential war measures prior to July 13, 1861; [6] it was then that Congress, in the words of dissenting Justice Nelson, "recognized a state of civil war." [7] After this July date there was no serious question. The whole Court agreed that after the congressional authorization the President was properly invested with the war power. They divided, with the venerable Chief Justice in the minority, on the validity of Lincoln's measures before that time.

### III

It was not, however, the enemy in arms, but rather the condition of internal agitation and dissension, that caused the most heated and serious constitutional disputes under Lincoln.[1] Confronted with a startling threat to law and order at home—a threat to the very existence of the national government—Lincoln chose to set aside civil guarantees. In a series of proclamations and orders he suspended the privilege of the habeas corpus writ, that ancient and respected procedure by which the civilian is protected against arbitrary arrest.

The first act of Lincoln for such suspension was his communication to General Scott:

---

[5] *Ibid.*, 179.
[6] The act of July 13, 1861, for collection of duties "and for other Purposes," authorized the President to declare a state of insurrection. *U.S. Stat. at Large*, XII, 255–258.
[7] 67 U. S. 696.
[1] For "Copperhead" disloyalty and the like, see below, chap. viii.

The Commanding General    Army of the United States:

You are engaged in repressing an insurrection against the laws of the United States. If at any point on or in the vicinity of any military line which is now or which shall be used between the city of Philadelphia and the city of Washington you find resistance which renders it necessary to suspend the writ of habeas corpus for the public safety, you personally or through the officer in command at the point where resistance occurs are authorized to suspend that writ.[2]

The date of this early proclamation was April 27, 1861; the purpose was to deal with the isolation of the nation's capital, the severing of communications, the serious situation growing out of the mob attack upon Federal troops in Baltimore (April 19), and the widespread confusion and fear of violence occasioned by anti-government leaders and agitators. Born of a startling emergency, this Lincoln policy was at first experimental, tentative, and undeveloped. As explained in a later official pronouncement of Secretary of War Stanton "By order of the President," defection and treason pervaded the very government itself. "Treason was flagrant,"—thus read Stanton's order. "The capital was besieged, and its connection with all the States cut off." It was further stated that secret societies were forming, passions were highly excited, arms and war supplies were assembled, army and naval officers were deserting their posts, and garrisons were being betrayed or abandoned. Congress was not in session. In its previous session (before the war, to be sure) the national legislature had not anticipated or provided for the emergency.[3]

Aside from Washington itself, this sharp emergency at the outset of the war was most startling in the state of Maryland. It was there that the earliest incidents occurred in the suspension of civil guarantees by the Lincoln administration. If control of Maryland had been seized by the secessionists as an "inside job," the nation's capital city would have been surrounded by the enemy. Short of this, which was a real threat, there was also great danger that powerful activities of a disloyal nature would be continually conducted in Maryland, partly as an underground movement, but also as open defiance and resistance. It would be a faulty method to treat the subject in the ab-

---

2 *Offic. Rec.,* 2 ser. II, 19; 1 ser. LI, pt. 1, 337; Nicolay and Hay, *Works,* VI, 258.

3 Nicolay and Hay, *Works,* VII, 100–104 (Feb. 14, 1862).

stract, or in its merely legal aspects, without an awareness of these difficult facts.

There was, of course, genuine Southern sympathy in the state and especially in Baltimore. The mayor and chief of police of that city were pro-Confederate and anti-Lincoln. The failure to prevent the murderous and disorderly mob attack upon Federal troops as they passed through the city in April of 1861 showed both an inadequacy and a lack of diligence on the part of the city authorities. It was not that Maryland in general was "disloyal." Confederate trouble makers, however, were numerous, inflammatory, destructive, and sufficiently active (and local officials sufficiently inactive) so that Union authorities, as they viewed the situation with no chance for long-drawn-out deliberation, decided that they had to resort to arrests, seizures, and emergency measures. One can hardly visualize the turbulent situation: a "thousand conflicting stories and rumors," [4] bridges destroyed for the deliberate purpose of obstructing the passage of troops, such destruction justified by local officials, anti-administration newspapers whipping up disunion sentiment, and, most threatening of all, the legislature about to meet with an active element of that body planning to have the state secede from the Union, thus seeking by political action to extend the boundaries of the Confederacy northward, deep within Union lines. It is not to be intelligently supposed that Maryland could have been "neutral" if it had seceded. A seceded government of Maryland would have been a pro-Confederate government, in all probability proclaimed as a part of the Confederacy. Perhaps a rival pro-Union government might also have been formed, but the existence of two conflicting governments in the state would have been most embarrassing and confusing.

On the Union side Lincoln watched the government's step, being determined to avert an explosion, avoid undue severity, and yet, above all, to save the national cause. Governor Thomas H. Hicks, loyal and pro-Union, was nevertheless apprehensive lest suppressive measures should misfire. Others in the Maryland drama were Secretary Seward, directing the arrests (until early in 1862); Cameron, secretary of war, not a very prominent figure; and such generals (in one capacity or another) as Scott, McClellan, Butler, Cadwalader, Banks, and Dix.

---

4 *Offic. Rec.*, 2 ser. I, 571.

Also in the picture were R. B. Marcy, Lafayette C. Baker, Frederick Seward, and a secretive person who signed his name as E. J. Allen, better known as Allan Pinkerton. Scott was the aged general in chief. McClellan was given chief command of the armies in July 1861 and succeeded Scott in November. Butler, Cadwalader, Banks, and Dix, in that order, were Union commanders in the Baltimore area.[5] Lafayette C. Baker, later a vigorous secret agent of Stanton's war department, was acting in that general capacity for Seward, watching to see what secessionists—for instance, in Canada—should be arrested. Pinkerton and Marcy were on McClellan's staff.

Out of this situation there grew a number of prominent Maryland arrests. There was, for example, the case of the mayor of Baltimore, George William Brown, which loomed large in the voluminous record and correspondence. Though General Dix considered Mayor Brown an amiable person, "the dupe rather than the willing accomplice"[6] of trouble makers, the mayor was arrested in mid-September 1861, held in various Federal forts including Fort Warren at Boston, released for thirty days, recommitted, transferred from the state to the war department, and set free after the Maryland storm had subsided. At the time of the April excitement (April 21, 1861) Lincoln had conferred with Brown in Washington, along with General Scott and the cabinet, as to the best way to move troops through Maryland and yet avoid a collision.[7]

George P. Kane, Baltimore chief (marshal) of police, described as "notoriously in deep sympathy with the rebels,"[8] was arrested as "a measure of military precaution" on June 27, 1861. Four days later other members of the Baltimore board of police commissioners were also arrested on suspicion of disloyalty and collusion with the enemy.

Even more spectacular was the arrest of members of the Maryland legislature. On September 11, 1861, Secretary Cameron wrote General Banks: "The passage of any act of secession by the Legislature of

---

[5] This command, known for early months as the Department of Annapolis, covered "a vital corridor from the free states to the Union capital." F. H. Harrington, *Fighting Politician: Major General N. P. Banks,* 56. With headquarters at Baltimore, it was commanded successively by B. F. Butler, George Cadwalader, and N. P. Banks. By early August 1861 John A. Dix was commanding at Baltimore over a larger area known as the Department of Pennsylvania. *Offic. Rec.,* 2 ser. I, 567–589.

[6] *Offic. Rec.,* 2 ser. I, 645. For a summary on Brown, see *ibid.,* 619.

[7] Nicolay and Hay, *Lincoln,* IV, 130–131.

[8] *Offic. Rec.,* 2 ser. I, 620.

Maryland must be prevented. If necessary all or any part of the members must be arrested. Exercise your own judgment as to the time and manner, but do the work effectively." ⁹ It was believed at this time that "at the coming session" some effort would be made "on the part of the 'Tory' majority to convulse the State and force it into an attitude of hostility to the Government." ¹⁰

Even if such belief was unfounded, it was felt that a grave risk existed, that prevention was what the loyal citizens of the state desired, and that arrests were a justifiable safeguard. Directing that "any meeting of this Legislature at any place or time" was to be prevented, General Banks ordered the arrests, indicating how it should be done, and how those taken should be conveyed by special train to Annapolis, and thence by steamer to the place of detention. Banks reported that nine legislators were arrested on September 17, these being "all the members of the Maryland Legislature assembled at Frederick City on the 17th instant known or suspected to be disloyal." ¹¹ In addition, the chief clerk of the senate was arrested. It was explained that "the opening of the session was attended chiefly by Union men and . . . but nine secession members were found in the city." ¹²

There have been conflicting opinions as to whether this arrest of legislators was a wise move. If it is not certain that this is what turned the trick, at least the trick was turned. Governor Hicks, a man who greatly respected the fundamentals of law and order, concurred in what was done. He wrote to Banks: "We see the good fruit . . . produced by the arrests. We can no longer mince matters with these desperate people." ¹³ Men of the time felt that a hands-off policy of gentleness and of full freedom as in peace time for dangerous plotters was not among the methods practically open to them. Use of stern measures, they felt, was their only choice. Secessionists themselves were none too scrupulous about full democracy. Perhaps Maryland could have been saved without these arrests; that seems probable. If so, the error was a misjudgment as to facts and probabilities. Such misjudgment may have been unfortunate, but the arrests were not made with evil intent. Severity in the Maryland case is to

---

⁹ *Ibid.*, 678–679.          ¹⁰ *Ibid.*, 679.          ¹¹ *Ibid.*, 684.
¹² Dix made one or two other arrests. Some of the prisoners were promptly released. Hicks referred (Sep. 20, 1861) to the arrest of "some eight or ten" legislators. *Ibid.*, 685.
¹³ *Ibid.*. 685.

be appraised as part of the whole picture which included, after all, more leniency than brutality.

## IV

In this urgent situation in Maryland, at a time when it was felt that a desperate and violent minority at the very door of the capital city was aiming a pistol at the heart of the government, there had arisen a famous arbitrary arrest and a notable judicial pronouncement in the case of one John Merryman. This otherwise unimportant individual was arrested by military authority on May 25, 1861, near Cockeysville, Maryland (north of Baltimore), "charged with various acts of treason and with . . . holding a commission as lieutenant in a company having in their possession arms belonging to the United States and avowing his purpose of armed hostility against the Government." [1] It was asserted that his readiness to coöperate with the enemy could be clearly established. The prisoner was confined in Fort McHenry and came under the custody of General George Cadwalader commanding at Baltimore, though that general did not order, nor was he responsible for, the original arrest.

Roger B. Taney, Chief Justice of the United States, now came into the picture. Taney being on circuit duty, General Cadwalader was commanded to appear before him. This was done by writ of habeas corpus which Taney issued. In the language of the writ the command was: ". . . that you have with you the body of John Merryman . . . and make known the day and cause of the capture and detention . . . , and that you then and there do submit to . . . whatsoever the . . . court shall determine . . . [etc.]." [2]

The fact that the judicial writ was issued, that it was the Chief Justice who issued it, that the general was commanded to hold himself subject to the court, and that in reality the high authority of the President was being challenged, gave the case unusual, indeed sensational, importance. Merryman was one among hundreds, but, thus singled out, his became a test case. Failure to sustain the executive (military) power would have caused the whole system of "political arrests" to break down.

---

[1] *Ibid.*, 2 ser. I, 576.
[2] *Offic. Rec.*, 2 ser. I, 575; *Ex parte* Merryman, 17 Fed. Cas. 144.

It was not, however, a case before the Supreme Court. It was a proceeding before one justice, Taney, who heard and granted the petition for the habeas corpus writ while on duty in the United States circuit court at Baltimore. (It was not that a whole court was in session; the proceeding was before Taney alone.) Cadwalader was under instructions from Washington to decline to produce prisoners in answer to all such writs. He answered that he was "duly authorized by the President . . . in such cases to suspend the writ . . . ." [3]

It was a clash of authority, but actual physical clash was out of the question. Orders of a court may be enforced by a marshal, if need be with the aid of a *posse comitatus;* but such a *posse* is seldom used, [4] and this type of procedure presupposes a broad and peaceful regime of law and order. To deal with widespread violence or disturbance is an executive function. It was not seriously proposed that Taney should have ordered his marshal to call out the citizenry in opposition to the President and army of the United States.

That, however, to his mind, did not mean that he could ignore his duty in the matter of civil rights. He could announce the law. Accordingly he put on file a long and impressive opinion, replete with historical and constitutional argument, emphasizing that the power to suspend the writ, which should only be done with "extreme caution," belonged only to Congress, and not to the President.

## V

Taney was dealing here with one of the most controversial questions in American constitutional history. [1] The Constitution of the United

---

[3] *Offic. Rec.,* 2 ser. I, 576.

[4] The question how far a marshal of a United States court may go in using a *posse* of citizens as a large force to maintain order arose in Kansas in 1858–59. W. P. Fain, marshal of the territory of Kansas, being confronted with serious violence on the part of lawless desperadoes, took the unusual course of keeping a standing *posse* continuously in the field for months in order to arrest the lawbreakers or drive them out. Several hundred men were assembled; they carried on until disbanded on orders from Washington. It was made clear in this case that a marshal is a ministerial officer for executing judicial writs or orders, and is not authorized to maintain a quasi-military force or keep a large body of men in the field for an indefinite period in order to break up an insurrection. Documents on this subject (Attorney General's papers, now in the National Archives) are cited in *Constitutional Problems Under Lincoln,* 160 and n.

[1] *Constitutional Problems Under Lincoln,* chap. vi.

States contains the following provision: "The Privilege of the Writ of Habeas Corpus shall not be suspended, unless when in Cases of Rebellion or Invasion the public Safety may require it." This statement has produced volumes of discussion. The privilege may be suspended—that is clear enough—in the specified emergency and for the indicated purpose: to guard the public safety in cases of rebellion or invasion. The prohibitory emphasis of the Constitution, with the monitory tone of the clause, shows that such suspension was considered highly exceptional. But if suspension should occur, who was to judge of the occasion or necessity? Was the power exclusive with Congress, exclusive with the Executive, or concurrent between them? Could the authority be delegated to subordinates? Would rebellion in one part of the country justify suspension in a remote and loyal part? Even if suspension were provided by Congress, did not the President have considerable importance in the ordering and controlling of arrests? Suspension would be a legal condition. What about the acts performed under that condition? If a summary regime were instituted, there would have to be executive discretion as to how, when, and where arrests should be made, what should be done with prisoners, when the regime should be terminated, and so on. But if the President could do nothing at all in setting aside the privilege, that would be a significant limitation on presidential and military power. To many it would have seemed a beneficial limitation.

Having developed his constitutional argument that the power of suspension belonged only with Congress, and never with the President, Taney went considerably further. He wrote:

. . . And even if the privilege of the writ of habeas corpus was suspended by act of Congress and a party not subject to the rules and articles of war was afterwards arrested and imprisoned by regular judicial process he could not be detained in prison or brought to trial before a military tribunal, . . . . [This was because of the sixth amendment requiring jury trial and various other safeguards in criminal prosecutions.]

And the only power therefore which the President possesses where the "life, liberty or property" of a private citizen is concerned is the power and duty . . . which requires "that he shall take care that the laws be faithfully executed." He is not authorized to execute them himself or through agents or officers civil or military appointed by himself, but he is to take care that they be faithfully carried into execution as they are expounded and adjudged by the coördinate branch of the Government to which that duty is assigned by the Constitution. It is thus made his duty to come in aid of the judicial authority if it shall be resisted by a force too strong to be overcome without the assistance of the executive arm. But in exercising this power he acts in subordination to the judicial authority, . . . .

Taney therefore declared: ". . . I can see no ground whatever for supposing that the President in any emergency or in any state of things can authorize the suspension of the privilege of the writ of habeas corpus or arrest a citizen except in aid of the judicial power." To suppose such a thing, thought Taney, was to suppose that the Constitution "conferred upon him [the President] more regal and absolute power over the liberty of the citizen than the people of England have thought it safe to intrust to the Crown—a power which the Queen of England cannot exercise at this day and which could not have been lawfully exercised by the sovereign even in the reign of Charles the First."

Such in brief was Taney's reasoning in this celebrated case. In his conclusion he noted that if the President had the power in question "the people of the United States are no longer living under a government of laws, but every citizen holds life, liberty and property at the will and pleasure of the army officer in whose military district he may happen to be found."

What, then, was the duty of the nation's highest judicial official, and what was his disposition of the case? His duty, wrote Taney, "was too plain to be mistaken." He had done all he could, but his power had "been resisted by a force too strong" for him to overcome. Taney therefore caused the record and opinion in the case to be filed in the Federal circuit court, and a copy to be transmitted under seal to the President of the United States. "It will then remain [he wrote] for that high officer, in fulfillment of his constitutional obligation to 'take care that the laws be faithfully executed,' to determine what measures he will take to cause the civil process of the United States to be respected and enforced." [2]

Beyond the case books in law, and the famous Taney opinion, Merryman is a forgotten man. All students of American constitutional law know of the Merryman "case," but very few could tell what happened to him. (It is often so with celebrated cases. The

_____
[2] *Offic. Rec.,* 2 ser. I, 585; 17 Fed. Cas. 153.

Supreme Court's pronouncement is the accepted climax; beyond that the "follow-up" is lost.) As a matter of fact, Citizen Merryman did not suffer for long. Secretary of War Cameron, visiting Fort McHenry on July 4, promised the prisoner a "parole," and on July 12 Cameron sent a letter to General N. P. Banks, who commanded the Department of Annapolis, directing him to cause Merryman to be delivered to the marshal of the district court when that should be demanded on lawful warrant. Actual release of the prisoner from military custody to civil authority occurred on July 13, forty-nine days after his arrest.[3] Merryman was now under the control of the district court of the United States at Baltimore, as Chief Justice Taney said he ought to have been from the beginning. He was under a wordy indictment for treason; it was charged that "he did intend to levy war and carry on war, insurrection, and rebellion against the United States of America." He was not held in confinement, however, being released (July 13, 1861) upon entering into a recognizance in the sum of $20,000 for his appearance in the United States Circuit Court at Baltimore, to which the case was handed over. It went no further. The recognizance was "respited"; the case was continued by order of the court; there was no prosecution; the matter faded from the record as Merryman had already faded from notice as a person.[4]

Thus, so far as Merryman was concerned, though historical and legal treatises usually ignore this aspect of the affair, the processes of judicial protection and civil procedure were actually complied with —not immediately nor by honoring the Chief Justice's writ, but within a fairly short time after the prisoner was seized. There was nothing done judicially to punish him, and this fact gives some point to the contention of the Lincoln administration that the courts were too slow and clumsy for handling the dangerous situation. It could also be said, however, that Lincoln was not going all the way with the "usurpation" which Taney charged. Arbitrary punishment for treason was not the main executive purpose. Military detention,

---

[3] E. G. Campbell (assisted by Elizabeth B. Drewry), War Records Section, National Archives, Wash., D. C., to the author (citing specific documents in the Archives), Jan. 16, 1950.

[4] For these obscure details of the case, after Merryman's military release, information was kindly supplied by Arthur L. Spamer, clerk of the U. S. district court at Baltimore, in a letter to the author, Feb. 6, 1924. *Constitutional Problems Under Lincoln*, 162 n.

though arbitrary—and serious enough, to be sure—was only temporary. For the acute and brief emergency at Baltimore for which it was used, such detention, so it could be argued, served the presidential purpose.

## VI

For many months, while sharp controversy raged, Congress made no declaration of legislative will on the disputed question as to the authority for suspension. In the short special session of July–August 1861 certain emergency orders of the President were ratified, but the habeas corpus privilege was not specifically mentioned in this connection (though the matter had been debated), and the ratifying provision was inconspicuously and irrelevantly tucked away as a "rider" in an act to increase the pay of privates in the army.[1] What is more remarkable is that in the long session from December to July, 1861–62, no law was enacted on this much discussed subject. The issue dragged on while lawyers and agitators poured out elaborate discussions. Then, in the closing hours of the short session which ended on March 3, 1863, the "habeas corpus act" was passed.

This act was railroaded through, said its opponents. What happened was that in each chamber there was a lively filibuster against the measure. In the House, for instance, obstruction took the form of numerous excuses for absence on the ground of being "unwell" and the like, in the course of which Colfax of Indiana, rising to a point of order, was told that he was "absent." Despite the filibuster the bill passed the House on March 2, by vote of 99 to 44.[2]

The following night produced a prolonged and confused session in the Senate. Powell of Kentucky, Bayard of Delaware, and others ·—men of genuine purpose, not mere obstructionists—struggled to keep the floor, occupy time, and prevent a vote, holding forth with lengthy speeches, which rang the changes on Magna Carta, Shakespeare, Cowper, Molière, Marshall, Webster, and other authorities and poets. Meanwhile Trumbull and other friends of the bill used all their strength to keep awake, maintain a quorum, prevent adjournment, and seize the floor for a motion to concur in a conference re-

---

[1] U. S. Stat. at Large, XII, 326 (act of Aug. 6, 1861).
[2] Cong. Globe, 37 Cong., 3 sess., 1479 (Mar. 2, 1863).

port and thus get the bill enacted into law. During these maneuvers the yeas and nays were taken on the question of adjournment five times.

Finally, at about five o'clock in the morning of March 3, 1863, the presiding officer (Senator Pomeroy) unexpectedly put a *viva voce* vote amid great confusion. He then announced that the bill had passed, denied the floor to senators who insisted it had not passed, and, against the vociferous protests of filibusterers (who shortly before had been demanding adjournment), declared the Senate adjourned.[3]

The measure so enacted declared in oracular phrase that "during the present rebellion, the President of the United States, whenever, in his judgment, the public safety may require it, is authorized to suspend the privilege of the writ of habeas corpus in any case throughout the United States, or any part thereof." [4]

Did this settle it? Who, then, had the power to suspend? Diametrically opposite interpretations were given as to the essence and meaning of this action. The measure passed was in fact a masterpiece of legislative ambiguity. The oracular statement—"the President . . . is authorized to suspend"—might be interpreted to mean that this was a power which Congress was *recognizing* as rightly belonging to the President; or on the other hand it could mean that the power to suspend, as Taney said, was purely legislative, and that this function of legislative suspension was then being exercised by *conferring* upon the President, for the emergency, authority which otherwise he did not have.

Congress had spoken; so had the Chief Justice of the United States. Yet neither the Taney opinion in the Merryman case nor the habeas corpus act of 1863 controlled the government. The Lincoln administration did not regard the Taney opinion in the Merryman case as a binding or final declaration of the law. This is evident from statements of cabinet members after the decision was issued. On January 31, 1863, Attorney General Bates, in an unpublished and confidential communication to Stanton, showed not only that he considered the basic question undecided, but also that he did not want the matter pushed to a conclusion. There had been a Wisconsin decision

---

[3] *Ibid.*, 1477.                         [4] *U. S. Stat. at Large*, XII, 755.

challenging the President's power to suspend,[5] and word had come to Bates that Stanton was intending to have the case brought up for review before the Supreme Court of the United States. In an emphatic statement Bates advised against it. A decision of the highest court pronouncing arbitrary arrests to be illegal, he said, would "do more to paralyze the Executive . . . than the worst defeat our armies have yet sustained." He also considered that such an adverse opinion was not unlikely, in view of the "antecedents and present proclivities" of a majority of the Court, taken in connection with the expressed opinion of some of the justices.[6]

Throughout the war two things were evident as to the executive attitude in this matter: (1) the Chief Executive intended to assert and exercise the presidential power of suspension; (2) there was an uneasy apprehension that the administration would be seriously embarrassed if the matter came up for final decision by the Supreme Court. As to the first of these points, it is to be noted that Lincoln, on September 15, 1863, six months after the passage of the habeas corpus act, issued a proclamation that "the privilege of the Writ of Habeas Corpus is suspended throughout the United States," and that "this suspension will continue throughout the duration of the . . . rebellion, or until . . . modified or revoked."[7] A similar proclamation had been issued on September 24, 1862; this confirmation of executive policy made the matter more emphatic.

Cabinet uneasiness as to a possible Supreme Court decision was shown late in the war by a statement of Gideon Welles concerning a consultation between Lincoln and his attorney general, James Speed. They were conferring over "an apprehended decision of Chief Justice Chase, whenever he could reach the question of the suspension of the writ of *habeas corpus*."[8] Speed, noted Welles, "is apprehensive Chase will fail the Administration" on this question.[9] Whether Chase "would have" decided against the administration and

---

[5] A state judge in Wisconsin held that the Federal Constitution "knows no 'political' . . . cause of imprisonment," that there "must be a 'process of law,'" that the President did not have the "political powers" which had been claimed for him, and that Lincoln had acted illegally in suspending the privilege. *In re* Kemp, 16 Wis. 396.

[6] Bates to Stanton ("Confidential"), Jan. 31, 1863, Stanton MSS., 52223.

[7] Proclamation suspending writ of habeas corpus, Sep. 15, 1863, photostat, A. Lincoln Assoc.

[8] Welles, *Diary*, II, 242 (Feb. 21, 1865).

[9] *Ibid.*, II, 245.

whether that would have been the decision of the Court, is not clear,[10] but at least the statements of Bates and Welles indicate that at the end of the war the question of the President's suspending power was still a matter on which the Supreme Court had not given a pronouncement. It was also abundantly clear that the ponderous habeas corpus act of 1863, passed after so much ado in Congress, was not regarded as having settled the matter of the exclusive power of Congress to suspend, or of the alleged illegality of Lincoln's course.

But this was not the only matter that lawmakers had failed to settle. It was supposedly the intention of Congress, in the habeas corpus act of 1863, to grasp and deal with the administrative matter of arbitrary arrests. The law set up a kind of compromise between camp and bench. The President's power to suspend was recognized (or, some would have said, conferred); military officers were relieved of the obligation to answer the writ; and (as an important feature of what came to be called the "indemnity act" as well as the "habeas corpus act") officers who might be prosecuted for searches, seizures, arrests, or imprisonments in compliance with an order of the President or "under his authority," were to be indemnified and given the benefit of Federal court protection. To military officers and administrators high and low this was important. Damages or imprisonment or fines for false arrests would have ruined them. Under such prosecutions "Stanton said he would be imprisoned a thousand years at least." [11]

On the other hand, as concessions to the bench, lists of political prisoners were to be furnished to the Federal courts; then, where grand juries found no indictments against them, they were to be discharged from military custody *by judicial order* upon taking the oath of allegiance. If such lists were not furnished (a congressional confession of doubt as to their law being obeyed), it was provided that a Federal justice might discharge a prisoner on habeas corpus petition.

---

[10] Even with Taney on the Court, there had been a five-to-four decision in support of the President's war power in the *Prize Cases*. Those five justices were still on the Court at the end of the war, and there is reason to suppose (though the opposite result was apprehended) that, if the matter had come up at any time during the war, the Court would have sustained Lincoln on the question of arrests, as it had on the extraordinary use of the war power between April and July of 1861. Substitution of Chase for Taney obviously did not make for greater Court opposition to the President's war powers.

[11] Welles, *Diary*, II, 206.

Only a superficial reading of history, however, would leave the matter here, for on careful search it is found that, like other congressional measures of the time, the habeas corpus law was largely a dead letter. When Stanton directed that lists of prisoners of state be sent to district and circuit justices, Judge Advocate General Holt reported that the lists had "not been furnished within the twenty days specified in the act." Such lists as were furnished were incomplete, omitting important facts—e. g., "what the offense was or charge." Holt then went on to criticize the law itself. "The act [he wrote] does not appear to have been carefully framed and has been found to be extremely difficult of construction." Holt therefore did his own construing; he did not believe the act was intended "to invite attention to cases of persons charged with purely military offenses or . . . suffering under sentences of military tribunals." [12] In the Milligan decision the Supreme Court was to hold that the act should properly have applied to citizens under such sentence, which was declared illegal in non-military areas, but this decision did not come until after the war; it was the Holt interpretation (later discredited) which fixed the pattern during the war.

The truth was that the executive, not the legislative or judicial, branch determined policy as to arrests and imprisonments, both before and after the passage of the habeas corpus act in which Congress presumably fixed the pattern. It does not appear that things were changed by this law. Numerous arrests—including the most famous of all, that of Vallandigham—were made after the act was passed. Moreover, where prisoners were released after that act, it was done not by Federal judges but by authority of the war department. Since the act confirmed the President's power to suspend and provided legal immunity for those acting under his orders, the policy as to political prisoners was understood to have a stronger sanction and legal force than before. A clerk of one of the district courts after examining the record reported that he could find no instance of a list of prisoners having been turned over to the court by the war department, and no record of any order of judicial release.[13] It should be

---

[12] *Offic. Rec.*, 2 ser. V, 765–766.

[13] Clerks of the United States district courts at Indianapolis and Cleveland reported to the present writer that they found no wartime cases of lists being supplied or of prisoners judicially released, thus signifying that the act was not observed. Similar re-

added that civil procedures during this period were not fully destroyed. They were rather dormant. The military itself showed some restraint (Lincoln saw to that), but so long as the war continued the army was the dominant power.

## VII

The extent of that dominant power of the President appears more fully when some of the half-forgotten procedures of the period are recalled. Such was the expansion of the executive power under Lincoln that, in addition to other wartime increases of authority within the executive branch, there were considerable instances when the legislative function was controlled by the President, and also when judicial duties were taken over by the executive.

In important respects the President got along without Congress, though this was perhaps overbalanced by the extent to which Congress thwarted him on the issue of reconstruction. So far did he take over legislative functions that one could speak of some of his acts as "presidential legislation." [1] It is obvious that the two emancipation proclamations trenched upon the legislative sphere. As another example, Lincoln issued a set of "regulations" for the enforcement of the militia act of July 17, 1862. Actual conscription was not specifically provided in the law as passed by Congress, yet conscription was used to raise troops. It was done simply under executive regulations. The matter went even further, for under these regulations governors of the states could set up their own systems of compulsory service as an alternative to following the President's orders. There has been considerable discussion of Lincoln's exercise of legislative power when, beginning in December 1863, he promulgated and later developed his presidential system of reconstruction.

It could also be said that a function belonging to Congress was performed by Lincoln when he issued a whole elaborate code for the governing of the armies in the field. This important code had

---

sults appeared in other courts, and a special search in the war department failed to reveal any measures taken in compliance with the act, other than Judge Advocate General Holt's letter to Stanton, June 9, 1863 (above cited), in which it was indicated that the law was given a strict war-department construction and that compliance was slight. *Constitutional Problems Under Lincoln,* 163–168, especially 166 n.

[1] *Ibid.,* 37.

a significant history. Two men were especially active in its preparation—Henry W. Halleck, general in chief of the Union armies, and Francis Lieber, noted German-American expert in political science. Born in Germany, Lieber had served at Waterloo, lying all night on that battlefield (a fact he often recalled in later life), had been wounded at Namur (1815), had previously dreamed of assassinating Napoleon, had studied and traveled in Europe, and had come to the United States in 1827. He wrote elaborate treatises and became a distinguished authority on public law. After productive literary work at Boston and Philadelphia he served for twenty-one years as professor in South Carolina College at Columbia. His important works included his *Manual of Political Ethics* and his famous work *On Civil Liberty and Self Government*. From 1857 he served on the faculty of Columbia College in New York.[2]

With a friendliness toward radical Republicans, a hatred of slavery, and a strong ethical sense, Lieber had a comprehensive understanding of law and government throughout the world and down the ages. Having three sons in the army (one in Confederate service), Lieber knew the agony of scanning casualty lists and the personal tragedy of learning that one of his sons was killed in the war and another severely wounded. His interest in military practices was not merely academic as he observed the lack of adequate system concerning the usages of war. A variety and multiplicity of questions called for clarification: the distinction between soldiers and guerrillas or bushwhackers, the problem of runaway slaves (whose return by McClellan aroused Lieber's indignation), pillage, espionage, the proper penalty for spies (should it be death?), retaliation, flags of truce, treatment of prisoners of war, exchange of prisoners, stealing, burning of homes, attitude toward non-combatants, seizure and destruction of private property, compensation for such destruction, occupation of enemy territory, and—as a subject of special interest—the wartime problem of Negro emancipation.

Coming up through Lieber's elaborate study and his voluminous correspondence with Halleck, the military code took shape with the assistance of a special board of army officers headed by General E. A. Hitchcock, and was issued in May 1863. It appeared as "General Or-

---

[2] Frank Freidel, *Francis Lieber: Nineteenth Century Liberal.*

ders No. 100: Instructions for the Government of the Armies of the United States in the Field." [3]

One may speak of this as an instance of presidential legislation. It is difficult to trace Lincoln's personal attention to the actual codification, but here was an essentially legislative duty performed entirely within the executive domain. The Lieber code could have been adopted by Congress and if so adopted it would have been considered a proper exercise of the congressional power, under the Constitution, to "make Rules for the Government and Regulation of the land and naval Forces." Congress, however, despite all its elaborate attention to the "conduct" of the war, did not perform the task, or even undertake it. It was through the executive branch that the great talents of Lieber were utilized, and thus one of the most important legal tasks of the war was accomplished by expert skill under presidential authority. Through the decades since the Civil War the code has undergone modification and development as regulations for the armies and manuals for service schools. Its basic principles have reappeared in Hague conventions. The fact that military practices in "World War I" and "World War II" have departed from the declared standards of these conventions (though they have not been formally revoked) is no disparagement of the work of Lieber. [4]

After considering presidential legislation (sketched here only in part) one may turn to the subject of presidential justice. It was under the executive, not the judiciary, that wartime judicial functions were performed in occupied portions of the South. It required years for normal business of Federal courts to be reëstablished in regions recovered from enemy control. State courts carried on in part during the occupation, but their duties were limited. [5] It was felt at times that

---

[3] *Offic. Rec.*, 3 ser. III, 148–164; 2 ser. V, 671–682.

[4] The author has studied, in original manuscript, the elaborate two-sided correspondence between Francis Lieber and General Halleck (Lieber MSS., Henry E. Huntington Library); he has also had access to the highly useful notes of Professor Frank Freidel of the University of Illinois. The authoritative account is Frank Freidel, *Francis Lieber: Nineteenth Century Liberal*, chap. xiv. For General Orders No. 100, see *Offic. Rec.*, 3 ser. III, 148 ff. See also Brainerd Dyer, "Francis Lieber and the American Civil War," *Huntington Libr. Quar.*, II, 449–467 (1939); Frank Freidel, "General Order 100 and Military Government," *Miss. Vall. Hist. Rev.*, XXXII, 541–556 (1946).

[5] It was held that a soldier of the United States who committed murder in Tennessee while that state was under Federal occupation was not subject to prosecution by a Tennessee court. Coleman *vs.* Tenn., 97 U.S. 509. Yet it was also held that insurrection and war do not loosen the bonds of society, and on this principle the Supreme Court treated

provost-marshal justice, or military-governor justice, was carried too far. There was resentment when General Butler exercised his military power at Norfolk in a manner which infringed upon the judicial authority of the Unionist state government under Pierpoint. On this point Attorney General Bates wrote: "I have heretofore forborne too much, to avoid a conflict of jurisdiction, but it only makes the military usurpers more bold and insolent." [6] It was, of course, a general situation which Bates resented, not merely a matter of concern at Norfolk. In North and South the executive power of courts martial controlled the process of justice as to men in the armed services (which was normal), while the military commissions, also purely executive, claimed and exercised unusual powers not only over civilians guilty of military offenses (such as destroying bridges), but also (though this power was seldom used in the North) over civilian deeds coming broadly under the category of disloyal acts. Aside from these military tribunals, whose sentences were reviewable by the President and whose operation was under the executive rather than the judicial branch, it should be added that "special war courts" were set up—e. g., in Louisiana—by presidential authority. One such was the "provisional court of Louisiana" which was created by President Lincoln in December 1862. It had almost unlimited jurisdiction, its powers being confined only "by the limits of human acts and transactions capable of becoming subjects of judicial investigation." It exercised both Federal and state functions.[7] In addition, judicial powers were grasped by administrative bureaus or executive agencies. The treasury department had much to do with matters of trade and land tenure in Southern regions, and local judicial activity on an extensive scale was assigned to the freedmen's bureau under the war department. (The bureau hardly got under way until after Lincoln's death, but the bill creating the agency was passed in March 1865 and was signed by Lincoln.)

These are but examples. The full situation would amply justify the generalization that the Civil War President, for what he deemed

---

the ordinary acts of states within the Confederacy (for maintaining police regulations, punishing crime, protecting property, etc.) as valid and binding. *Constitutional Problems Under Lincoln*, 237–238.

[6] Bates, *Diary*, 401 (Aug. 20, 1864).

[7] Judge Charles A. Peabody, "United States Provisional Court for . . . Louisiana, 1862–1865." *Annual Report.* Amer. Hist. Assoc., 1892, 199–210; *Ann. Cyc.*, 1864, 480 ff.

necessary and unavoidable reasons, extended his sphere of activity throughout the whole government—civil and military, state and Federal, legislative and judicial as well as executive. In the economic field, of course, the scale of governmental activities under Lincoln was in no sense comparable to that under Wilson or Franklin Roosevelt. The principle, however, of expanded national economic power was illustrated in such affairs as the national banking system, the deep penetration of taxation, the support of economic enterprise by United States bonds, army efforts to control working conditions, new regulations as to bringing laborers in from abroad, and governmental seizure of railroads and telegraph lines.

## VIII

The general question as to where the war power resided arose in Congress (June 25, 1862) and was debated in the Senate by Browning of Illinois and Sumner of Massachusetts. Sumner argued that the war powers of Congress were virtually without limit. "There is not one of the rights of war," he said, "which Congress may not invoke. There is not a single weapon in its terrible arsenal which Congress may not grasp." [1] Browning, on the other hand, contended that rights of war were by their very nature matters of emergency and military necessity; for that reason he urged that they belonged to the executive arm. Browning went so far as to "defy . . . any man to point to one single word . . . in the Constitution which confers upon Congress any power to do any act in the exigency of war which it cannot do in times of peace." [2]

Whatever may have been the merits of the senatorial arguments, the result was that both Congress and the President exercised war powers. The President did it first at the outset of the struggle and repeatedly throughout the contest. Lincoln believed that he had powers in time of war that Congress did not have. In July 1864 (in a state paper concerning the Wade-Davis bill [3] which he killed by a pocket veto) he proclaimed that he was "unprepared . . . to de-

---

[1] *Cong. Globe*, 37 Cong., 2 sess., 2919.     [2] *Ibid.*, 2923.
[3] Sponsored by Benjamin F. Wade in the Senate and Henry Winter Davis in the House, this bill provided for reconstruction in terms very different from those favored by Lincoln.

clare a constitutional competency in Congress to abolish slavery in States . . . ." [4] Yet his own definitive emancipation proclamation had been issued a year and a half earlier.

Initiative, decision, and important action was chiefly executive; yet a listing of the war powers exercised by Congress would cover a considerable range—confiscation, conscription, dealing with crimes (rebellion, conspiracy, obstructing the draft), creating the state of West Virginia, legalizing privateering, authorizing (or recognizing) the suspension of habeas corpus, levying a direct tax against Southerners, extending the jurisdiction of Federal courts, giving the President the authority (already mentioned) to take possession of railroad and telegraph lines, and, in the military field, setting up the busily active, officious committee on the conduct of the war. As to reconstruction, it was there, perhaps, that we find the most far-reaching powers that any Congress ever assumed, including the creation of a military regime in the South by which the functions of state governments were superseded.

It was not as if Lincoln had been eager to seize arbitrary power. So far as the President's purpose was concerned, if it was a matter of circumspectly watching to avoid abuse, he did not stand in need of Taney's admonition in the Merryman case. (Even so, Taney's strong conviction that a government of laws should be preserved is a worthy part of American constitutional history. Lincoln was no despot, but neither could it be said that the Chief Justice in advising against military despotism, was asserting a vain principle.)

The matter is so important that one should notice how and why Lincoln acted. His suspension of civil guarantees was announced with great reluctance. Only a qualified suspension was ordered in 1861 when the emergency was undeniably alarming. Military authorities were enjoined to use the power sparingly. The President's action was taken during a recess of Congress, and at its first convening the matter was laid before that body in Lincoln's message of July 4, 1861. In one of the passages of that important message he gave what may be called his answer to Taney.

It is instructive to note the workings of Lincoln's mind as he thought through the preparation of that message. This becomes more

---

[4] "A Proclamation," July 8, 1864, photograph, A. Lincoln Assoc.

striking as we compare the original handwritten draft of the document with the finished product as finally submitted. The two forms are given below in parallel columns.[5]

| *Original Autograph Draft* | *Published Form* |
| --- | --- |
| Soon after the first call for militia, I felt it my duty to authorize the Commanding General, in proper cases . . . to suspend the privilege of the writ of habeas corpus. . . . At my verbal request, as well as by the Generals own inclination, this authority has been exercised but very sparingly. Nevertheless, . . . I have been reminded from a high quarter that one who is sworn to "take care that the laws be faithfully executed" should not himself be one to violate them. Of course I gave some consideration to the questions of power, and propriety, before I acted in this matter. The whole of the laws which I was sworn to . . . [execute] were being resisted, . . . in nearly one third of the states. Must I have allowed them to finally fail of execution . . . ? To state the question more directly, are all the laws, *but one,* to go unexecuted, and the government itself go to pieces, lest that one be violated? . . . But, . . . I was not, in my own judgment, driven to this ground. In my opinion I violated no law. The provision of the Constitution . . . is equivalent to a provision . . . that [the] privilege may be suspended when, in cases of rebellion, or invasion, the public safety *does* require it. I decided that we have a case of rebellion . . . . | it was considered a duty<br><br><br><br><br>This authority has purposely been exercised . . . sparingly.<br><br><br><br>the attention of the country has been called to the proposition, [etc.]<br>. . . some consideration was given . . . before this matter was acted upon.<br>The whole of the laws which were required to be . . . executed.<br>Must they be allowed to finally fail of execution . . . ?<br><br><br><br><br><br>But it was not believed that this question was presented. It was not believed that any law was violated.<br><br>It was decided, [etc.] |

---

[5] The autograph draft has been checked with the original in the Lincoln Papers (R.T.L. Coll., 10503-42); the official printed form with *Sen. Exec. Doc. No. 1*, 37 Cong., 1 sess., pp. 1-17.

The working draft shows the questioning and struggling that went on in Lincoln's mind. The decision as to arbitrary power troubled him. Any suggestion or appearance of dictatorship caused him concern and pain. When the matter was presented to Congress the wording was impersonal: "Some consideration was given"; "the attention of the country has been called . . ."; "the laws . . . were required to be executed" and so on. But as he first thought it out, these problems were his own; they touched him closely: "I gave some consideration to the question . . ."; "I have been reminded from a high quarter . . . [the reference was to Chief Justice Taney]"; "the laws which I was sworn to [execute]." The finished form was, as Nicolay and Hay have pointed out, a "state paper"; [6] the early working draft reflected the mind of the man in the White House meeting and coping with the duty of his office.

## IX

The preciousness of civil rights even in time of war has produced a great deal of emphasis upon the guarding of those rights in the courts. It is a healthy sign in a democracy to have such emphasis. Yet in treating the Lincoln administration it would be an error to put all the stress on presidential power in terms of harshness or unjustifiable cruelty. Lincoln's regime was no juggernaut. Restraints were applied. The war was actually conducted *in vinculis,* which is not only democratically necessary but is preferable to a militarized state. (The opposite tendency would lead at its worst extreme to a Dachau or a Buchenwald.) Throughout the struggle in Lincoln's day there was a constant tempering of severe rules. Deserters were sometimes executed, but by far most of them were spared. Killing in battle was done by duly organized forces in military operations. (Predatory or criminal activities of guerrilla warfare, as in Missouri, were among the irregular by-products of the war. They were unauthorized and completely lawless.) Where men were put to death in the exercise of military discipline, this was done by court-martial trial under competent control. Seizure of property by the armies was done *as a rule* in an orderly and non-predatory manner. (Plundering by Sherman's

---

[6] Nicolay and Hay, *Lincoln,* IV, 177–178.

"bummers" in his "march" through Georgia and the Carolinas was exceptional. It was an unfortunate example of soldier conduct getting out of hand.) Prisoners of war were treated under the rules of war. Death for treason, much talked of, was not applied.[1] Discretion was exercised in carrying out orders against disloyal persons; escape from penalties was made possible by taking the oath of loyalty; first offenses were passed over; excuses were considered; the shooting of sentries was disapproved; [2] even spies were released on acceptance of stipulated terms.

By comparison with other regimes, political prisoners were mildly treated. Vallandigham, arrested contrary to the President's judgment, was not the brutally persecuted victim he was represented to be. Many thousands who sympathized with Vallandigham were not molested at all. Crews of Confederate ships were called "pirates," and the penalty for piracy was death; but this was a matter of language, not of action. It is true that Lincoln issued a proclamation (April 19, 1861) declaring that any person acting under "pretended authority," who should "molest a vessel of the United States" (e. g., resist the blockade) would be held "amenable to the laws of the United States for the prevention and punishment of piracy." [3] This policy, however, of punishing Confederate crewmen for piracy was not carried out, either by the courts or by the executive branch. The main purpose seems to have been to uphold the theory that the Confederate States could not be "recognized," that their naval vessels were not legitimate warships, that their letters of marque and reprisal were invalid, and that theirs was only a "pretended" government with no rightful standing.

Judicial embarrassment over this problem arose in the case of the *Petrel*, a privately owned schooner (formerly a U. S. revenue cutter) commissioned as a Confederate privateer. This vessel was sunk in a fight with a U. S. warship and its crew became Federal prisoners.[4]

---

[1] The case of William B. Mumford, executed by sentence of a military commission in New Orleans in 1862 for having torn down the United States flag, was an exceptional and isolated case, being altogether out of keeping with presidential and judicial policy. It was an episode in the eccentric rule of Benjamin F. Butler, who was removed from his New Orleans command by Lincoln in December 1862 and replaced by N. P. Banks.

[2] For denunciation of the practice of shooting sentries—"insignificant atoms of armies" —see *Harper's Weekly*, V, 407 (June 29, 1861).

[3] Proclamation of blockade, Apr. 19, 1861, photograph of original, A. Lincoln Assoc.

[4] William M. Robinson, Jr., *The Confederate Privateers*, 125–127.

They were taken to Philadelphia and were indicted—thirty-five in number—in the United States circuit court for treason, their offense being also denoted as "piracy," the equivalent of treason. There was immense popular excitement as the case, along with other cases of "treason," was brought up, but the justices who had to deal with the problem, not as theory but as human facts, were disgusted. Justice Grier of the United States Supreme Court, on circuit duty at Philadelphia, blurted out that he did not "intend to try any more of these cases." "I have other business to attend to," he said, "and do not mean to be delayed . . . from day to day in trying charges against a few unfortunate individual men here out of half a million that are in arms against the government." The "laws of war [he added] must be observed, or you will lay it open to the most horrid reactions that can possibly be thought of; hundreds of thousands of men will be sacrificed upon mere brutal rage. . . . I will not sit on another case." [5] In general neither treason nor piracy cases were pursued to completion in the United States courts. There were indictments, but the cases were simply continued on the dockets and eventually dropped. In the few cases where convictions for treason resulted, they were considered an embarrassment. Judgment was suspended and the men were ultimately released.

As with the courts, so with the executive. A study of the Lincoln Papers shows that the purpose of the government was not to convict and punish any individuals for treason because of service for, or aid to, the Confederacy. The purpose of arrests was to uphold respect for the law and give protection against disloyalty in its effect upon the war effort. The object of the administration was precautionary, not punitive. Seizure and temporary detention of dangerous characters —rather than pursuing the whole course of indictment, trial, conviction, sentence, possible appeal, and eventual execution—was the administration's view of the appropriate and practical method.

If Confederate privateersmen and naval men had actually been punished for piracy—i. e., executed as traitors—, retaliation would have resulted. Union captives were in fact held as hostages by Confederate authorities, and if the utmost penalty had been used as had

---

[5] J. Hubley Ashton, assistant district attorney for eastern Pennsylvania, to Attorney General Bates, Nov. 4, 1861 (enclosure), Attorney General's papers, MSS., National Archives.

been announced *on paper*, the conduct of the war would have degenerated into a kind of savage orgy below the "civilized" level. This was one of many problems making necessary the codification of the usages of war (above treated) by Francis Lieber. In the case of captured Confederate officers and crewmen of privateering vessels the solution adopted was to treat them as merchant marine personnel. Trials, as in the case of the *Petrel* crew, were accordingly dropped, the crews being released and sent South.[6] The war was grim, but regard for civilized opinion was always a factor with Lincoln.

Part of the confusion on this and other subjects was due to an aspect of governmental policy which was essentially abstract. There was a constant and stubborn refusal to "recognize" the Confederacy. Technically, diplomatically, and formally that government was never given recognition by the United States. (Nor, except as a belligerent, was it ever recognized by any foreign power.) Language of the department of state and formal procedures of the government at Washington were carefully watched to avoid such recognition. Yet, when this subject is analyzed realistically in terms of actualities, it will be found that this denial of recognition was hardly more than a stickling for theory. It was precisely the theory that was deemed important. Language had to be correct; etiquette and procedure had to be watched; protocol had to be observed. Deeds were another matter. In practical affairs pertaining to the conduct of armies the usages in the main were the same as would have prevailed if the conflict had been waged between two fully recognized independent nations. The Union government *treated* the Confederates as regular belligerents though it did not *recognize* them as such.

The attitude of the Washington government toward that at Richmond, as generally applied and fully matured, was about as follows. To the Confederate army belligerent rights were "conceded, in the interest of humanity." These rights, by the statement of the Supreme Court, were "such . . . as belonged, under the laws of nations, to the armies of independent governments engaged in war against each other." The Court also stated that "The Confederate States were belligerents in the sense attached to that word by the law of nations [international law]." [7] The subject is to be understood, not in terms

---

6 Robinson, *Confederate Privateers*, 150–151.

7 Ford *vs.* Surget, 97 U. S., 605, 612.

of consistency, but of variance between language and deed, between form and substance, between diplomatic punctilio and essential conduct. In the view of the Washington government secession was a nullity and the whole Southern nation illegal. Those who took part in the Confederacy were insurgents warring against their rightful government. They were technically traitors and were theoretically amenable to the municipal power in the same sense that the Whiskey insurgents during Washington's administration were amenable. In addition, they were "enemies" in the sense used in international war. The area declared by the constituted authorities to be in insurrection was "enemies' territory" and all persons residing in the designated area were liable to be treated as "enemies."[8] Both belligerent and sovereign powers could be brought into play in dealing with such areas —e. g., the belligerent power of blockade and the sovereign power of punishing for treason. Yet to avoid cruelties and inhuman practices, soldiers and officers of the "rebel" army were accorded all rights connected with the mode of prosecuting "lawful war." Confederate officers and privates were not held to individual responsibility. Confederate authority might be considered a mere usurpation and Confederate acts invalid, but those in military service who proceeded under such authority were not in fact held to account. Nor, ultimately, were those in civil authority held personally to account. Jefferson Davis after the war was held in military custody for two years and (after military release) was indicted in the United States circuit court at Richmond for treason under the law of 1790, where the penalty was death; but no other Confederate official was given anything like so long a military detention, most of them being allowed to go free, and Davis's case in court was allowed to drag on without trial till finally the prosecution was dropped.[9] In general the postwar "flight into oblivion" of certain Confederate leaders was unnecessary if regarded as an escape from severe treatment.

Throughout all these complex problems of war power the historian must constantly recognize that pronouncements of law, which can be cited on both sides of every issue, were lacking in finality. Though a lawyer of great shrewdness, capable of supporting a cause by impres-

---

[8] *House Report No. 262*, 43 Cong., 1 sess., 6 ff.

[9] Roy F. Nichols, "The United States *vs.* Jefferson Davis," *Amer. Hist. Rev.*, XXXI, 266–284; Randall, *Constitutional Problems Under Lincoln*, chap. v.

sive legal reasoning, Lincoln, after all, made his decisions in terms of what he thought was needed to support and maintain the government. On a point of governmental relations he could uphold a principle— for instance, refusing recognition to the Confederacy—without the embarrassment of getting out on a legalistic limb. When he had made up his mind on a matter of presidential conduct whose legal aspects he had canvassed, he was neither disrespectful toward legal opposition nor upset by it. Taney differed with him fundamentally on questions of war power; yet the difference consisted only of dignified assertion of opposite views. The President and the Chief Justice never came to an unseemly open break or personal clash. The Supreme Court in general, partly by a kind of avoidance, gave support to the President.

# "COPPERHEADS" AND PRISONERS OF STATE

## I

DISCUSSION of suppressive measures leads unavoidably into the subject of so-called "Copperhead" activity.[1] Throughout the war years (especially in 1863 and 1864) the Lincoln administration constantly faced the perplexing problem of disunity, underground activity, and violence, always considerably mingled with politics and amounting at times—so it was claimed—to disloyalty or treason. The remedy was not simple. A complicated problem was posed which required administrative resourcefulness and demanded something other than the crude method of seizure and incarceration for matters of opinion.

As one seeks reliable generalizations on this subject he notes an inexactness in the use of terms. Dissent was to be expected. There were sincere differences of judgment and opinion. Disagreement was rife, and desertion was startlingly extensive in the army. Disaffection behind the lines was widespread. In using the terms "disloyalty," "conspiracy," "rebellion," and "treason" people were employing a familiar vocabulary without stopping to put into these terms a definite content

---

[1] On the "Copperheads" and related activities, see: Wood Gray, *The Hidden Civil War: The Story of the Copperheads;* George Fort Milton, *Abraham Lincoln and the Fifth Column;* J. F. Rhodes, *Hist. of the U.S.,* V, 317 ff.; *War of the Rebellion: Official Records,* esp. 2 ser. II, and 2 ser. VII; *Report of the Judge Advocate General on "The Order of American Knights," Alias "The Sons of Liberty,"* . . . (Wash., Chronicle Print., 1864 [same report in *Offic. Rec.,* 2 ser., VII, 930–953]); Nicolay and Hay, *Lincoln,* VIII, chap. 1; Paul B. Smith, "First Use of the Term 'Copperhead,' " *Amer. Hist. Rev.,* XXXII, 799–800; Ollinger Crenshaw, "Knights of the Golden Circle: The Career of George Bickley," *ibid.,* XLVII, 23–50.

with reference to solid acts, or even as to general attitudes. The difficult subject becomes no easier when ethics, philosophy, and ultimate values are brought into consideration.

Was it treasonable to be for peace? Or, to turn the phrase around (from the standpoint of a man such as Joseph Holt or Burnside), were not "peace men" the promoters and abettors of treason? Certainly the "anti-war" rallies and the "peace agitation" of the period were at the opposite pole from the "Union rallies," the Union League meetings, and the voluminous literature of the Loyal Publication Society. According to their own claim, these "Union Leagues" held in a kind of partisan monopoly the standard of loyalty and patriotism.

Could the national effort be so easily reduced to a party label? To take one example among hundreds, was John Scott Harrison of Ohio, son of one President and father of another, disloyal because he accepted in 1861 the Democratic nomination for lieutenant-governor of his state? The question is absurd, but precisely such absurdity—i. e., the tendency to pin the label of disloyalty upon members of one of the major parties—was shockingly prevalent in that period. First causes and ultimate objectives were a matter of some confusion. Motives were mixed and finality was not so certain a factor as leaders and publicists would imply. Opinion for or against the Lincoln administration, or the Republican party, or "the cause" in the sense of war against the South, was a matter of contributing factors, of antecedents and sympathies, of party preference, and of ups and downs when elections impended, as they did in every year of the war, or when military fortunes shifted.

There were broad regions—as in southern Ohio, Indiana, and Illinois—where disaffection prevailed at least in the sense of opposition to Republicanism, and to the Lincoln government.[2] One need not go back into the remote past of glaciers to explain it, but scientists would no doubt find a correlation between geological backgrounds, with their resulting soil conditions, and those human elements which became manifest in party affiliation. In the Middle West, as Wood Gray has pointed out, the "people of the less favored southern third tended to be envious of their more fortunate neighbors to the north."[3] Variations in agricultural wealth bore a demonstrable relation to

---

[2] Well treated in H. C. Hubbart, *The Older Middle West,* 1840–1880.

[3] Wood Gray, *The Hidden Civil War: The Story of the Copperheads,* 17.

differences in political attitudes. Immigration into these middle states had left a marked pattern: people of the more southerly counties were both geographically close to the South and humanly akin as descend- ants of Southerners if not Southerners themselves by birth.

There was a constant tendency to oversimplify, and this was espe- cially true as to the position of parties, in which oversimplification became falsehood or misrepresentation. Not all Republicans were genuinely pro-Lincoln. Certainly the "anti-war" attitude in the sense of being anti-Union was emphatically repudiated by the Democratic party. The difficulty was to come to grips with reality. The peace group —those who agitated for an immediate cease-fire order looking to "negotiation" with the Confederacy—would be represented as anti- Union and as supporting the enemy; but they would deny these im- putations and would maintain that war could never succeed in restor- ing the Union, but that negotiation could do so. Southerners, it was said, could not work with Republicans, but could coöperate with Northern friends.

When, however, such men took the next step, they posed a serious question; they stoutly maintained what the administration considered a fallacy, that Confederate leaders would end the war by negotiation on the basis of reunion. This was supposing that Southern leaders would voluntarily liquidate their own Confederacy. This was made to sound plausible, but there was an element of unreality in such a policy. There were, of course, Southerners who were ready to accept reunion, but armistice and negotiation required an official Southern instrument. The Confederate government, fully committed to dis- union and separation, was the agency that ruled the South and the only agency with which the United States government could negotiate, since it controlled the armies. Obviously it was not a suitable mouth- piece for those Southerners who were ready to call off the war without victory and rebuild the United States as a reunited nation.

## II

The matter of labels only added to the confusion. On the one hand the name "Union" was increasingly appropriated by one party at the North. On the other hand the term "Copperhead" took hold rapidly and became a common word, or byword, in the political glossary. By the summer of 1862 it was a familiar term; it had been used by the New York *Tribune* as early as July 20, 1861.[1] Spoken, written, or flashed on a cartoon, the word "Copperhead" became a devastating term of reproach, suggesting always the slimy and venomous snake. Efforts to give it a favorable connotation by linking it with the copper penny, the coin of the common people, were ineffectual, though cut-out heads of the penny were worn by some who thought to adopt the term as their own.

Like other labels of scorn and hate, the word came to be so inexactly used as to lose all genuine meaning and to become a mere trick of name-calling. So far as the word had a justifiable, specific significance it may be said to have denoted secret, subversive, pro-Confederate, or treasonable groups at the North. To put it in other words—where there were such groups it was understandable to stigmatize them with this word of burning scorn. Then came the next step: the label came to have such crushing force as a whiplash of reproach that it offered a cheap advantage to those who would use it irresponsibly to smirch political opponents. The ancient legend of the Trojan horse was not much used in this connection, nor the modern "fifth column," nor the term "underground" in the sense of the nineteen-forties and after. Perhaps this was because, while there were secret organizations and mysterious conclaves, much of the anti-war agitation—very much indeed—was carried on in the open. It should also be remembered that these movements were really Northern. Some few Southern spies were sent North to work with them, but that was only a minor factor. The groups that worked against prosecution of the war might be "pro-Southern," but for the most part they were under Northern organization, leaders, and agitators, rather than under Confederate agents. There were, it is true, a few such agents,[2] and Confederate spies were daringly active in the North, but subversive activities did not on any large scale take on the nature of a Trojan horse.

Though groups actually subversive could properly have been called

---

[1] After mentioning this use of the term in the *Tribune*, Wood Gray points out that "it had in fact been used as a general term of opprobrium long before the war." He adds: "Since it was purely an epithet, it never had any definite range of application, being sometimes used to refer only to those believed to be actively in sympathy with the Confederates but on other occasions fixed on the Democratic party as a whole." *Ibid.*, 140–141.

[2] For Confederate agents—e. g., Thomas H. Hines—working with Northern plotters, see *ibid.*, 167 ff., 181 ff., and *passim*.

"Copperheads," the term came soon to be applied to "peace Democrats." Then with shameless disregard of obvious truth the serpent label was attached to Democrats in general; this became a kind of Republican trick to disseminate the idea that to be a Democrat was to be disloyal! After the war the meaningless use of the term was part of the "bloody shirt" tradition characteristic of the vituperative politics of a whole generation. A careful scholar has written: "The disloyalty, real or unreal, of . . . Southern sympathizers at the North created a detestation for Democrats which lasted, like an incurable cancer, long years after the war ended—often terminating only with the death of the haters and the hated." [3]

When speaking of organizations deemed subversive one thinks first of the Knights of the Golden Circle. Taking the full story of its origin and history, it is amazing how small was the sum-total of its proved accomplishments. Ollinger Crenshaw has elaborately shown how the organization began before the Civil War as an ambitious yet abortive Southern filibustering venture to promote ideas of "young America" and "manifest destiny" in the proslavery sense. The order was founded by G. W. L. Bickley, a versatile Southerner who intended it as a scheme to colonize, "Texasize," or annex Mexico, and thus extend powerfully the cause of proslavery domination over the United States. If this annexation could have been accomplished, it was hoped that "fifty new slave state senators would one day appear in Washington and sixty or more new members of the House of Representatives." (Or perhaps this wholesale annexation could be effected by a "Southern Confederacy.")

The esoteric and aggressive order which Bickley founded was strongly militaristic, being conceived and organized as a kind of private "army." (That fact alone, as to the private army, would stamp the group as essentially un-American, however much it flaunted the phrases of Americanism. In this sense it was like the Ku Klux Klan and other similar groups whose professional patrioteering have masked ulterior and sinister motives. Private armies, with ambitious leaders seeking control of affairs, have no place in the American polity.) With its high-sounding ritual, codes, secrets, and flamboyant titles, its castles and lodges, its appeal to "chivalry" combined with expansive promises

---

[8] William A. Russ, Jr., in *Pa. Hist.*, V, 245 (1938).

of Mexican land (640 acres for a private), and its affiliation with shipping and financial agencies, the prewar K. G. C. was calculated to have
an alluring attraction for human ambition, swaggering vanity, misapplied "patriotism," and cupidity.[4] In its fraternal aspect it could
exploit the joining urge so characteristic of Americans. Like other
similar organizations it was double-faced, having an impressive front
and sonorous declarations of purpose which half-concealed its undemocratic and conspiratorial activity.

### III

In describing these secret orders it would not be hard to paint a
lurid picture. One could tell of their hide-outs, their guarded meetings, their grapevine intelligence, warning signals, hailing signs,
countersigns, inner-door passwords, and cryptic markings on houses.
Members were armed and under impressive oaths with terrible penalties for violation. "In all correspondence by the members," so it was
reported, a device would be used which "reverses the whole matter;
so they write one thing when they mean another." To write: "You
are not in 33" would mean: "You are in danger." It was testified by
a former member of the K. G. C. that their object was "to oppose everything the Administration may do toward putting down the rebellion;
oppose all war measures whatever, such as preventing enlistments,
encouraging desertions, &c." He added: "The promulgation of treason
against the Government is the business of every member." He added:
"I have heard leading men say at their meetings that Jeff. Davis had
violated no rights that they claim in this Government; that he was
a better man than Lincoln, and that John Morgan [Confederate
cavalry leader] was as good." None but the "leading members," it was
pointed out, understood "the true meaning and intentions of the
K. G. C.s." In Missouri, where lodges were numerous, it was reported
that a prominent leader, "thoroughly disloyal," was "in constant communication with Price's [Confederate] army." [1]
    In the local scene the activities of these secret societies took the form
of recruiting for the enemy, discouraging Union enlistment, aiding
desertion, distributing disloyal literature, resisting the draft, destroy-

---

4 Ollinger Crenshaw, in *Amer. Hist. Rev.*, XLVII, 23 ff.
1 *Offic. Rec.*, 2 ser. VII, 741 ff., esp. 742–744, 747, 753.

ing enrollment lists, and demolishing government property. On the larger scale there were reports of ambitious and far reaching plots to assist "rebel" raids from the rear, to form a great "Northwest Confederacy" that would unite with the South, to liberate Confederate prisoners, and to split the North in such a way as to facilitate Confederate victory. There were schemes to assassinate Union officers, there was talk of hanging Lincoln,[2] and there were conspiracies for using Canadian soil as hatching ground and base for pro-Confederate raids into the United States.

Testimony as to these Copperhead plottings is voluminously available, but the story becomes anti-climactic when the grandest and darkest of these schemes are reduced to completed accomplishment or even fair prospects of accomplishment. These orders were a menace, but the assessment of their importance should be approached as a matter of realistic history. Their strength should be neither exaggerated nor underestimated. Statements on the subject are not always exact or specific. Deponent for the government would often use such phrases as "I have heard," "they say," "some claim," "My own belief is . . . ," or "I think . . . but am not certain."[3]

On closer inspection the ineffectiveness of these gentry is revealed. Many of the knights were ignorant of the intentions of the lodges and it was believed that a large number "would leave the order if they were not deceived by the officers and leading men."[4] Such a condition hardly gave the basis for a determined fighting force of daring rebels with the will to win. One man who joined the K. G. C. swore under oath: "I claim to be a Douglas Democrat, but my Democracy has ever taught me to be always on the side of my country, willing to aid in putting down conspiracies instead of sustaining them."[5] Investigators on the hunt for members of these groups, though aided by spies and informers, would sometimes report that in certain supposedly disaffected localities they found few or none. As to their military organization, there were companies for drill and military "districts" with "district commanders," but squad organization was emphasized, and it was said to be understood that if a "general war" should take place

---

[2] A Chicago commission merchant "said [as reported] they intended to go down and hang Abe Lincoln, his Cabinet, and all the abolitionists." (What "they" would have done after that was not stated.) *Ibid.*, 2 ser. VII, 747.

[3] *Ibid.*, 746–747.    [4] *Ibid.*, 744.    [5] *Ibid.*

the squads would "act separately, the guerrilla mode of warfare being adopted." That does not sound like much of a plan for a "general war," whatever that might mean. Civil war experience showed that warfare in guerrilla fashion could be a cursed annoyance, but it never became a major menace.

As for a rising to help a Confederate raid into the North, the facts did not bear out the supposed menace. When Morgan swept into southern Indiana and Ohio in the summer of 1863 the expectation that men of these secret societies would help the enemy was doomed to utter disappointment. A captain who rode with Morgan wrote: "The Copperheads turned out and fought by the side of their loyal neighbors and no aid in any shape was afforded the raiders." [6] The historian of that raid, Basil W. Duke, writes: "the 'Copperheads' and 'Vallandighammers' fought [on the Union side] harder than the others." [7] The "Democrats were disgusted with Morgan," writes J. F. Rhodes. When he plundered shops or took food he did not stop to inquire whether he was robbing Republicans or Democrats. "Whatever they might do it was almost certain that they [members of the K. G. C.] would not rise with arms in their hands to give assistance to the invading enemy in his work of ravaging the Northern States." [8]

A fact to be remembered is that there were government spies within the order—men operating in the cause of Lincoln, or agents of a governor such as Morton—and this considerably nullified the value of an elaborately studied secrecy that often proved deceptive. One hears much of plans for a general "rising" in the North or Northwest (perhaps that was what their term "general war" signified), but it is only a matter of conjecture to suppose that large numbers of knights who enjoyed their local out-of-the-way meetings in the woods would actually have "risen" in force. It is also mere conjecture to say that, if they had done so, they would have had any chance of success. If Copperheads had risen, nothing was more certain than that Union-minded citizens would also have done so, having the home guard, militia, army, and authority of constituted government on their side, which would have been an enormous advantage. When the knights talked of rising they had in mind, as motive, something political or partisan,

---

6 *The Southern Bivouac*, Dec. 1886, 442; quoted in Rhodes, *Hist. of the U. S.*, V, 316 n.
7 Basil W. Duke, *History of Morgan's Cavalry*, 439.
8 Rhodes, *Hist. of the U. S.*, V, 317.

which is what they had chiefly in mind on the whole accounting. They would, or thought they would "rise" if this or that thing should happen—for example, if another attempt (say in 1864) should have been made to arrest Vallandigham, or if Lincoln should have forcibly interfered in the elections.[9]

These plots, of course, could not be ignored. The point is that since the Union intelligence system, never of course perfect, was operating, the government knew about these orders. That being so, the avoidance of what might be called all-out suppressive measures against them was a calculated avoidance. It was not due to ignorance or inadvertence. The Lincoln government, with its shrewdness in recognizing realities, would have done much more to "crack down" on these groups than it did, if that had been deemed necessary. On the whole it was considered wiser to let a horrendous, colossal plot fizzle out than to create trouble by taking it too seriously.

With continued war, mounting radicalism, shocking casualties, profiteering, conscription, arrests, and doubtful prospects for a military decision, more was heard of these conspiratorial groups, but the Knights of the Golden Circle, under that name, faded into the background. By 1863 a new fraternity, the Order of American Knights, was carrying on the work. That it largely absorbed the K. G. C. was due to its compactness, centralized organization, and "new militancy."[10] Then in February 1864 "a so-called national meeting of its moving spirits took place in New York in which the name was changed to the Sons of Liberty, thus claiming spiritual kinship with the patriotic society of the Revolutionary period."[11] It was this organization of which Clement L. Vallandigham was chosen supreme grand commander. The over-all number of the organization has been given as 500,000, or even one million, but J. F. Rhodes shows that even the halfway figure was "an obvious exaggeration."[12] In the three states where it was strongest in numbers—Ohio, Indiana, and Illinois—"it may have counted 175,000." If one adds two other states—Kentucky and Missouri—the total would hardly have exceeded a quarter of a million. Outside of the five states named the number of "Knights" or "Sons" was "inconsiderable."[13]

[9] Offic. Rec., 2 ser. VII, 747.    [10] Gray, Hidden Civil War, 164.    [11] Ibid., 166.
[12] Report of judge advocate general, in Offic. Rec., 2 ser. VII, 935; Rhodes, V, 318.
[13] Rhodes, V, 318.

An explanation of the purpose and nature of the order in other than disloyal terms was given in a long letter to Lincoln in 1865. The writer, a high official of the Sons of Liberty in Illinois, attributed most of the accusations of wrongful acts leveled against the society to "the suppositions . . . understandings . . . guesses, and loose generalizations of a portion of the witnesses." The organization, he wrote, was not intended to aid rebellion but to serve as an auxiliary to the Democratic party, as an "offset to the secret organization called the 'Union League,' and as a safeguard of the personal . . . rights of Democrats." [14]

This partisan motive must constantly be kept in mind in order to understand these orders. The brothers all had their instructions how to vote—as did the Union Leagues—and any history that would ignore this aspect would be most imperfect. In Indiana, where the knights or their successors were especially notorious, it has been said that Governor Morton "was undoubtedly more afraid that his Democratic opponent, Joseph E. McDonald, would defeat him for Governor in the October election of 1864 than that the Sons of Liberty would rise and depose him from power." [15] If one looks at the subject somewhat obliquely, Morton might have thanked these "Sons." Though bitterly and savagely anti-Republican, such *sub rosa* groups actually helped the dominant party. Republicans could denounce treason, point to these "treasonable" groups, and show, which was true, that the efforts of these societies were directed toward Democratic success. In this they would conveniently omit to show that in the whole broad picture Democrats were overwhelmingly loyal, patriotic, and firm for the Union. Copperheads—if one uses this inexact term to apply to men who were obstructing the existing national effort—were not really helping the Democratic party. If Copperheads were Democrats, that did not mean that all Democrats were Copperheads. Yet many people lacked the elementary intelligence to detect the obvious fallacy of this kind of reasoning.

---

[14] S. Corning Judd to Lincoln, Washington, Mar. 3, 1865 (endorsed on envelope in Lincoln's hand), Nicolay and Hay MSS. (VIII: 1), Ill. State Hist. Lib. Judd, a lawyer of Lewistown, Fulton County, Illinois, was active in Democratic politics. During the war "he was a determined opponent of the war policy of the Government." Bateman and Selby, *Hist. Encyc. of Ill.*, I, 310.

[15] Rhodes, V, 319–320.

## IV

It has been seen how the executive policy of arbitrary arrests under Lincoln began at the very outset of the war, how the alarming situation in Maryland claimed chief attention at first, and how a major legal controversy—one of the most famous in American history—developed over the presidential power of suspension, with the Chief Justice officially denying the validity of that power, while Congress delayed for years and then dodged the main issue. It becomes necessary now to look further into the activities of the government with regard to prisoners of state.

In the first year of the war the problem was handled, not by considered planning, but by improvisation. The attorney general's tiny staff was unable to cope with the situation, while the secretary of state, though his office pertained to international affairs, was ready to assume executive responsibilities and was conveniently available as a kind of factotum for a variety of duties on the domestic front. Thus it came about that William Henry Seward, through most of the first year of the war, had the responsibility for the detection, arrest, examination (if any), and confinement of "political prisoners"—an unusual term in American vocabulary.

Seward threw himself into this "arbitrary, largely secret, and altogether unusual" business with a good deal of vigor, and the activities of his department were on a wide scale as he set up a "personal blockade," required passports for those who departed the country, directed the disposition of prisoners, determined punishment, and where he thought proper, ordered releases.[1] Arrests were sometimes effected by Seward's confidential agents, sometimes by local police on direct order of Seward, or at other times by military authorities or marshals of Federal courts.

Those taken were not told why they were seized. It was not a matter of clearly formulating, much less substantiating, the charges prior to arrest. The state department, as Frederic Bancroft shows, "never made up its case." [2] "If Seward," writes Bancroft, "had carried on his system in time of peace, he would have been the most despicable tyrant of the

---

[1] Bancroft, *Life of Seward*, II, 259 ff.; see also 254–280.
[2] *Ibid.*, II, 276.

century. Its sole moral justification must rest upon its necessity." [3] The victim would often be "seized at night, searched, borne off to the nearest fort, deprived of his valuables, and locked up in a casemate, or in a battery generally crowded with men that had had similar experiences." [4] To get a hearing by the secretary was difficult; to obtain a release was often a matter of "political and personal pressure." [5]

The general hue and cry against "traitors" and spies gave the occasion for irresponsible accusation and abuse. One of the most flagrant instances of this was the case of ex-President Franklin Pierce of New Hampshire, who was the victim of an anonymous letter and of the thoughtless manner in which the affair was handled by Seward and his staff. The writer, embellishing his letter with meaningless cryptic symbols, wrote: "President P—— in his passage has drawn many brave and influential men to the league." (This was supposed to refer to the Knights of the Golden Circle; the man was assumed to be Pierce.) The letter came into the hands of Federal officials, and as a result Seward wrote to the ex-President suggesting the need for an "explanation."

Furiously indignant, Pierce wrote to Seward expressing surprise that, on such a flimsy basis, this incoherent and meaningless "extract from the vagaries of an anonymous correspondent . . . should have been sent for explanation to one who during his whole life has never belonged to any secret league, society, or association." Pierce added: "Nothing but the gravity of the insinuation, the high official source whence it emanates, and the distracted condition of our recently united, prosperous, and happy country could possibly lift this matter above ridicule and contempt."

This drew from Seward a clumsy apology in which the secretary expressed regret and explained that he had devolved upon a department clerk the duty of preparing a note to Pierce. (The note had been signed by Seward.) In this he supposed that he was rendering the ex-President a "service." Pierce answered with a cold but dignified letter showing that he could not pass over the matter as blithely as Seward suggested. "You will excuse me," he wrote, "if I regard even a suggestion from a source so eminent that I am 'a member of a secret league, the object of which is to overthrow this Government,' as rather too grave to have been sent off with as little consideration as a note of

---

3 *Ibid.*, II, 259.                4 *Ibid.*, II, 261.                5 *Ibid.*, II, 279.

rebuke might have been addressed to a delinquent clerk of one of the departments." Pierce's name had not appeared in the anonymous extract (only "President P——"); yet Seward had referred to it as an "injurious aspersion on your fair fame and loyalty." Pointing to a serious defect in procedure, Pierce wrote: "I think you will . . . arrive at the conclusion that the whole ground upon which the allegation is repeated should, as a simple act of justice, have been placed before me."

This slanderous bit of trash did not merit an explanation, but, since the correspondence would become a part of the government files, and because Pierce wanted no ambiguity in the record, he wrote: ". . . it is proper—perhaps it is my duty—to add that my loyalty will never be successfully impugned so long as I enjoy the constitutional rights which pertain to every citizen of the Republic, and especially the inestimable right to be informed of the nature and cause of accusation and to be confronted face to face with my accusers."

After this preposterous accusation of Pierce had been taken up in the Republican press, and in Congress (where Seward was asked to submit the correspondence but omitted part of it until a senator called it to his attention),[6] the whole libelous affair was shown to have been a fabrication and a hoax. The perpetrator, a certain Dr. Guy S. Hopkins of North Branch, Michigan, was accused of secessionist leanings, but this he flatly denied. To cut the long story short, he was a Democrat who had noted with disgust frequent paragraphs in Detroit papers charging Democrats with treason and referring to a pro-Confederate secret league.[7] The worst accusations were being directed against men whom he "admired as statesmen and loyal Americans." He therefore concocted the letter, with its reference to "President P——" and a good deal else, with the expectation "that it would be sent to one of the treason-shrieking presses, and when exploded would produce lots of fun." The "universal reign of suspicion" and the manner in which disgraceful stories were being used to blast the reputation of well-intentioned men had so irritated him that it entered his mind "to sell the Detroit [Republican] press by writing a letter full of dark innuen-

---

[6] *Cong. Globe,* 37 Cong., 2 sess., 1370–71 (Mar. 26, 1862).

[7] The K. G. C. was of slight importance in Michigan, especially in 1861 when the fabrication as to Pierce was perpetrated. The statement of the judge advocate general that the later order of O. A. K. had "about 20,000" members in Michigan was given as of 1864 and was an exaggerated guess. *Offic. Rec.,* 2 ser. VII, 935.

does and hints, but which in reality would mean nothing." Later he deeply regretted his trick, which he referred to as "one moment's indiscretion," "this fanciful practical joke," and "that doubly-accursed letter." With detectives on the alert and all sorts of accusations flying around, it was not remarkable that the letter should have been held for investigation, but by the time the hoax was revealed (which required no extraordinary sleuthing) the harm had been done through unfortunate publicity and Seward's bungling. Refutation could not catch up with accusation, the slander could not be easily wiped off, and the senseless injury lingered.[8]

The defects of Seward's system may have been due to the alarming emergency, the hasty improvisation, the lack of organization, and the unfamiliarity of this kind of treatment in American experience. Whatever may have been the excuses, the fact was that the use of these crude methods gave the policy of summary arrests an unfortunate turn at its earliest stage. With far less than the requisite attention to so difficult a matter, a machinery had been set up for catching the innocent with the guilty, while the methods of release were capricious and unpredictable. Frederic Bancroft mentions the current story "that Seward boasted to Lord Lyons that he could ring a little bell and cause the arrest of a citizen of Ohio or order the imprisonment of a citizen of New York, and that no one on earth except the President could release the prisoner." [9]

If a man is quoted as having made a certain remark, it may be difficult to prove that he did not make it. The point is, rather, to find proof *for* the remark; otherwise, to consider it unproved. After reporting an elaborate search in the sources, in which no evidence for this bit of Seward conversation was found, J. F. Rhodes notes that it became a stock Democratic argument, was referred to in Marshall's *American Bastile* as "undisputed historical truth," and as such was quoted by S. S. Cox in *Three Decades*.[10] On reading the record, and the summary by Bancroft, one gathers that the question of Seward's oft-quoted remark is less important than the fact of his far-reaching one-man power and the manner in which he used it. Bancroft con-

---

[8] For the Pierce episode see *Offic. Rec.*, 2 ser. II, 1244–1267 (for Hopkins's explanation of the hoax, 1250–51); Bancroft, *Seward*, II, 271–276; Roy F. Nichols, *Franklin Pierce*, 519–520. The Seward-Pierce correspondence extended from December 20, 1861, to January 7, 1862.

[9] Bancroft, *Seward*, II, 280.      [10] Rhodes, *Hist. of the U. S.*, IV, 413 n.

cludes that, while Seward was "almost as free from restraint as a dictator or a sultan," he did not act like one. He writes: ". . . in the great mass of documents on the subject of political prisoners there are no manifestations of improper motives or of extreme prejudice or of personal considerations except in the Pierce episode."

It is hard to make a final appraisal on so complex a subject. There were plots behind the lines, the military threat to Washington was startlingly serious, the very life of the nation was at stake, and the persistence of pro-enemy activity, if unchecked, would have weakened the confidence of European countries in the ability of the government to survive. On the other hand, any large program for arresting political prisoners is open to abuse, and even in the case of so easy going a secretary as Seward it has been conceded that he "sought and was given too much responsibility." [11]

## V

In the evolution of Lincoln's policy—or that of the Lincoln government—concerning arbitrary arrests, the year 1862, and especially February of that year, was marked by several important administrative steps. For one thing, control over arrests was shifted from the department of state under Seward to the war office under Stanton. In a war department order (February 14) over the signature of Stanton ("By order of the President") it was indicated that the startling aspects of the emergency were now past, that "a favorable change of public opinion" had occurred, and that the whole situation had improved. In view of these facts (so the order read) the President directed that all political prisoners held in military custody "be released on their subscribing to a parole engaging them to render no aid or comfort to the enemies in hostility to the United States." (Exceptions from this release could be made by the secretary of war at his discretion in the case of spies "or others whose release . . . may be deemed incompatible with the public safety.") It was announced in this order that presidential amnesty for past offenses was granted to those released if they kept their paroles. Also, as illustrating the increasing importance of the war department, it was declared, "Ex-

---

[11] Bancroft, *Seward*, II, 280.

traordinary arrests will hereafter be made under the direction of the
military authorities alone." [1]

All this looked like governmental relaxation as to arrests, but
against that supposition there were several factors to consider. The
February order came near the beginning of Stanton's administration
of the war department. Soon the government would have within that
tightening department, a detective bureau and a secret service. The
head of that secret police service, La Fayette C. Baker—colonel (later
brigadier general) and special provost marshal—became famous, or
rather notorious, for his snooping, his disregard of due process, his
raking-in of perjured testimony, his accumulation of a fortune for
himself, his "habitual carelessness in mixing truth and fiction," [2] and
the whole rapid pace of his melodramatic career.[3] He is best known
for his later activities in the man hunt after Lincoln's assassination,
his amazing "documents" in connection with the impeachment of
Johnson, his secretive methods of combating the hidden system of
Confederate espionage, and his trailing of deserters, Negro-stealers,
and bounty jumpers. Of this branch of the service Perley Poore
wrote: "How they watched and waited at official doors till they had
bagged the important secret of state they wanted; how they stole
military maps from the War Department; how they took copies of official documents; how they smuggled the news of the Government's
strength in the linings of honest-looking coats; and how they hid army
secrets in the meshes of unsuspected crinoline—all these became familiar facts, almost ceasing to excite remark or surprise." [4] As Seward
gave way (in the seizure and control of prisoners) to the newly appointed Stanton, a so-called "premier" who has been compared to a
dictator and whose office had done a shocking injustice to an ex-
President, was relinquishing his "dangerous machinery" [5] to an official who was prepared to use it with the resources of a much greater
and more specialized staff, but with no less severity.

1 Order issued by war department, Feb. 14, 1862, signed by Stanton, secretary of war,
Nicolay and Hay, *Works*, VII, 100–104.

2 Thomas Denton McCormick, in *Dic. of Amer. Biog.*, I, 523.

3 *Secret Service, By Gen. La Fayette C. Baker, Organizer and First Chief of the Secret
Service of the United States* (Washington, 1898). This self-important book has the cheap
paper, lurid illustrations, and racy style of a dime novel or popular thriller.

4 Ben: Perley Poore, *Perley's Reminiscences of Sixty Years in the National Metropolis*,
II, 110–111.

5 Bancroft, *Seward*, II, 278.

In applying the policy of release under Stanton a special commission was set up, consisting of Edwards Pierrepont and John A. Dix, to examine the cases of political prisoners and determine whether they should be discharged, kept in military custody, or turned over to the civil authorities for trial. Of this two-man commission, Pierrepont was a distinguished New York lawyer and judge, while Dix, in his sixty-third year when the war opened, was a soldier, lawyer, former senator, and prominent Civil War general. Both Pierrepont and Dix were Democrats and both strong Unionists.[6] The creation of the commission was evidence of the need for more system in the process of release, but the commission acted under orders from Stanton, who was still in command of this whole business, by "authority of the President."

In the first year and a half of the war suspension of the habeas corpus privilege had proceeded by specific orders of limited coverage; then came an order which in effect made of these arbitrary arrests a kind of normal wartime procedure. On September 24, 1862, two days after the preliminary edict of emancipation, President Lincoln issued a proclamation:

. . . be it ordered, first, that during the existing insurrection . . . , all Rebels and Insurgents, their aiders and abettors within the United States . . . [etc.] shall be subject to martial law and liable to trial and punishment by Courts Martial or Military Commission.

Second. That the Writ of Habeas Corpus is suspended in respect to all persons arrested, or who are now, or hereafter . . . shall be, imprisoned . . . by any military authority or by the sentence of any Court Martial or Military Commission.[7]

Here was an indication that policy as to arrests was being tightened rather than relaxed under Stanton.[8] The war secretary has

---

[6] For correspondence of the Pierrepont-Dix commission see *Offic. Rec.*, 2 ser. II *passim;* for sample list of prisoners examined and released, 277–279.

[7] Proclamation suspending writ of habeas corpus, Sep. 24, 1862, photostat, A. Lincoln Assoc.

[8] In addition to Lincoln's proclamation of September 24, 1862, which has elicited the most discussion, there were other presidential orders of a general nature covering the suspension of the famous privilege. In particular, one should note his proclamation of September 15, 1863 (suspending the privilege under the specific authority of the statute of March 3, 1863), and his instruction to military officers, September 17, 1863 (in which he presupposed that the writ should issue, and that the military officer should make "proper return thereto," but that the prisoner should not be produced). See below, p. 223.

been credited with greater caution in the invasion of personal liberty than Seward; it has been said that he traced his authority to Lincoln's suspension while feeling that such suspension "in no wise justified arrests not required by the public safety." [9] It must be remembered, however, that the number of arrests under Stanton was far greater than those under Seward, that Baker's secret service was a Stanton institution, that its methods were highly surreptitious, and that the Baker papers in the war department have been closed to investigators, so that the whole subject is considerably hidden. The vast series of volumes known as the *Official Records of the Union and Confederate Armies* contains elaborate and detailed accounts of political prisoners under Seward, [10] but no such detailed report of Baker's, or Stanton's, arrests has been issued. Furthermore, Stanton is one of those leading figures of the Lincoln period for whom we have no adequate biography.

## VI

Though the number of political prisoners under the Lincoln administration has been greatly exaggerated, the total was undoubtedly large. No definite, all-inclusive estimate seems possible to find, but the records of the commissary general of prisoners contain the names of 13,535 citizens arrested and confined in military prisons between February 1862 and the end of the war. To this one would have to add those confined before that date, being under the state department, those arrested under naval authority, and those held in prisons and penitentiaries of the several states. [1] The statement that the arrests totaled 38,000 is only an exaggerated guess. [2]

How were these thousands of prisoners treated? For an answer to this question the pages of *American Bastile*, by John A. Marshall,

---

[9] George C. Gorham, *Life . . . of Edwin M. Stanton*, I, 262–263.

[10] See esp. 2 ser. II.

[1] "Notwithstanding the many mentions of . . . political or citizen prisoners in the . . . *Official Records*, . . . I do not believe that it will ever be possible for any one to gather from any source an approximately definite estimate of the total number of such prisoners held by Federal authorities during the Civil War." Major General Robert C. Davis, Adjutant General of the United States, to the writer, June 26, 1925, quoted (with additional data) in *Constitutional Problems Under Lincoln*, 152–153 (footnote).

[2] An estimate based on this guess was given by Alexander Johnston. See the article "Habeas Corpus," in J. J. Lalor, *Cyclopaedia of Political Science . . .* [etc.]; see also Rhodes, IV, 230 ff.

published in 1869, must be considerably discounted without being fully discarded. The book reads like the bitterest anti-Lincoln wartime propaganda. Its author was the historian of the "Association of State Prisoners," chosen by that organization in convention assembled. Along with voluminous abuse of the Lincoln government the volume gives numerous case histories of particular prisoners whose tribulations are presented in the author's rhetorical phraseology, with a kind of horrifying embellishment. The uprightness of Lincoln's opponents, their heroism, their sacrifices for the cause of freedom, and their suffering are thrown in contrast to the coarse cruelty of Lincoln's agents and the black despotism of his methods. Liberty Bell, Magna Carta, and the Constitution are referred to in ironic emphasis to show how the free principles of the founding fathers had become in Lincoln's day an idle boast. The book has a kind of fractional authenticity in the sense that there were thousands of prisoners (vastly more than the cases mentioned), that they did suffer, that normal civil guarantees were in fact denied them, and that the concentrated bitterness dripping from these pages was a mental fact, being not only part of the war mind, but also an element of well-intentioned protest.

Prisoners of state, according to Marshall's mordant book, were housed in a stable, made to sleep in the open air on a "cold and dreary night upon the frozen ground," kept in rooms "not fit for . . . human beings," inhaled "fetid . . . atmosphere," were plundered "in a hundred different ways" (as by the sale of articles of poor quality at a "profit of five hundred per cent."), and were "in danger of being shot" by frenzied guards. In the case of one prisoner it was stated: "His Republican creditors bankrupted him while in prison, and left his helpless family in destitution." [3] Frederic Bancroft writes: "Month after month many of them were crowded together in gloomy and damp casemates . . . . Many had committed no overt act. There were among them editors and political leaders of character and honor, but whose freedom would be injurious to the prosecution of the war." [4]

Yet on a fair generalization it must be recognized that prisoners were not brutally treated. Comforts were allowed them and they

---

[3] Marshall, *American Bastile* (for quoted portions, see pp. 124, 133, 160–161, 329, 691).
[4] Bancroft, *Seward*, II, 277.

were permitted to receive articles sent by friends and relatives. Under inspection they could transmit and receive letters, obtain newspapers, and receive visitors. Even Marshall, with all his abuse, reveals, under careful reading, that prisoners, where in camp, sometimes had housekeeping privileges, that one of them was allowed to board himself in a nearby town, that "hospital accommodations were, with some exceptions, as good [in the Old Capitol Prison] as could be expected in a place conducted without regard to system," that prisoners were allowed some recreation, and that, after the election of November 1862, "the condition of the prison [Old Capitol] became somewhat improved." [5] Any period of being held in custody, even with some freedom of movement, is a hardship, and it is not to be denied that these imprisonments were a grievous experience.

The harsh features, however, were due rather to lack of space and to general conditions of prison management (not all of which have even yet been remedied) than to deliberate cruelty. Most of those seized were imprisoned for short periods. Prisoners were often men of proud spirit, keen upholders of right principle as they understood it—too proud, many of them, to purchase their liberty by taking an oath of allegiance which would put their previous conduct in the wrong (as they thought), and which their consciences could not approve. Personal attention was given by Seward to "the comfort of the prisoners" at Fort Lafayette, while at Fort Warren the instruction was given "That the prisoners be securely held and . . . allowed every privilege consistent with this end." [6] Though the whole system was in many respects deplorable and regrettable, a book as long as Marshall's could be made up to show moderation and a fair amount of leniency in the actual treatment of prisoners.

## VII

To give case histories of the many prisoners, or even a representative sampling, is impracticable, but a passing word as to a few of them may be appropriate. F. Key Howard, prominent lawyer and editor of the Baltimore *Exchange*, was arrested on the night of September 12–13, 1861, being "publicly known to be in deep sympathy

[5] Marshall, *Amer. Bastile*, 124, 125, 328, 331.
[6] *Offic. Rec.*, 2 ser. II, 118, 111.

with the rebels." His paper (according to the state department "Record Book") "zealously advocated their cause." [1] In his possession was found a large quantity of manuscripts, "mostly of a decided secession character." He could not see how the Union could be preserved against majority Southern opposition and said so. [2] In effecting his arrest one sees the fine hand of Allan Pinkerton, under authority of General Dix. After being confined in Forts McHenry, Monroe, Lafayette, and Warren—a rather familiar itinerary—he was released on November 27, 1862.

Henry May of Maryland, member of Congress (successful competitor against Henry Winter Davis, Republican), was arrested at the same time as Howard. May was suspected of criminal intercourse with the enemy in connection with a visit to Richmond in July 1861. The judiciary committee of the House of Representatives investigated his case but found no evidence to prove matters charged against him; the accusations or suspicions were based only on newspaper reports. He was released on December 2, 1861. [3]

William H. Winder, a citizen of Philadelphia, was arrested on September 11, 1861, charged with treasonable correspondence with the Confederates. He admitted having "condemned without stint . . . the abolition wing of the Republican party," and was shocked at what he considered the "barbarity" of Lincoln's emancipation proclamation. He stubbornly defended the rightness of his conduct, and one of the difficulties of his case was his proud refusal to take the oath of allegiance. Contending that he had done no wrong and that the whole system of arrests was unconstitutional, he looked for an "unconditional release" and a full acquittal. "To be called upon [he wrote] to take an oath to support the Constitution, &c., as a condition of my release is by my own act to indorse my arrest and imprisonment as being deserved." [4] Had it not been for such an implication, he would willingly have sworn to support the Constitution as in fact he had done in joining the Philadelphia Home Guard. Secretary Seward offered a modified oath which Winder also refused,

---

[1] *Ibid.*, 2 ser. II, 778–779.     [2] Marshall, 700.

[3] *Offic. Rec.*, 2 ser. II, 790 ff.; *Cong. Globe*, 37 Cong., 1 sess., 196 ff. (July 20, 1861).

[4] *Offic. Rec.*, 2 ser. II, 730. For the Winder case in general, see *ibid.*, 721–747; Marshall, 268–289.

as he said it would render him "tongue-tied under the grossest imputations." There was an elaborate correspondence on the case of
Winder, who was befriended by distinguished Boston lawyers, such
as Benjamin R. Curtis, Sydney Bartlett, Samuel Dexter Bradford,
and George S. Hillard. On November 27, 1862, he was given what he
had demanded—an unconditional release at Fort Warren.

Others among the thousands of prisoners—though there is no
space to treat them—included Charles J. Faulkner of Virginia, minister to France under Buchanan, arrested for supposed disloyalty, held
as a hostage, and as such released in return for Confederate release
of Alfred Ely, congressman from New York; George W. Jones of
Iowa, minister resident at Bogotá (sympathizer with Jefferson Davis);
Judge Richard Bennett Carmichael of Maryland's Eastern Shore;
Charles S. Morehead, Kentucky governor and congressman (he also
refused to take the oath of allegiance but was nevertheless released
on parole); and William M. Gwin, senator from California, Confederate sympathizer, arrested in November 1861 and released after
two weeks. The roll of state prisoners also included John S. Emerson
steamboat captain suspected of spying but soon released); Tench
ьchley, similarly suspected; and such well known women spies of
the Confederacy as Catherine Virginia Baxley, Rose O'Neal Greenhow, and Belle Boyd. It would fill hundreds of pages to tell only the
stories of these clever and daring women—their underground connections, ruses, courage, and biting hatred of Yankees in general and
Seward and Stanton in particular.

Some of the charges, such as being a "noisy secessionist," selling
Confederate "mottoes and devices," or "hurrahing for Jefferson
Davis," seem trivial and insignificant. Yet, as one reads the record, it
appears that most of those summarily arrested were seized because
they were suspected of serious offenses. It was shown or believed that
they had been acting as Confederate agents, furnishing supplies to
the enemy, encouraging desertion from the service of the United
States, committing outrages upon Unionists, stealing military stores,
destroying bridges, engaging in bushwhacking, making drawings of
fortifications, conveying "treasonable" correspondence, or otherwise
assisting the enemy. Many of them were actual spies.

If one takes the list of prisoners of state confined in the famous

Old Capitol Prison in the shadow of the Capitol at Washington (on ground now occupied by the Supreme Court building), the designations read as follows: carrying goods South, violating blockade, bushwhacker, contrabandist, guerrilla, sutler robber, sutler robber and guerrilla, blockade runner, disloyalty and stoning guards, rebel mail carrier, rebel spy, and using altered pass.

The list goes on: awaiting sentence for treason, refugee, refugee drunk, dealer in Confederate money, sending recruits to the insurgents, attempting to escape to the insurgents after taking the oath of allegiance, murdering and robbing Federal soldiers, being a spy and holding a commission in the insurgent army, persecuting Union men, attempting to go South in violation of the President's proclamation, furnishing information which led to the murder of Federal pickets, being an officer in the Confederate signal corps, "held until army moves," deserter and spy, kidnapper, following the army without pass, showing "secesh" sentiments, causing the arrest of Union men, "rabid rebel," smuggler, suspicious character, one of a party who made a raid, aiding the enemy in raid at Catlett's Station, scout for Mosby and White, and forging soldier's discharge paper.

The enumeration becomes at times repetitious, but the more surprising thing is the variety of offenses and the extent to which the sins of these men (and women) are particularized without repetition. Some of the causes in addition to those already listed are: refuses to take the oath, abusive language to Col. Drew, crazy wanderer, harboring guerrillas, damaging draw on Long Bridge (near Washington), burning commissary stores, aiding and piloting deserters, burning barges, "held for Sec. of War," "committed by Sec. of War," "Turned over to L. C. Baker," "scold for a time," kidnapping negroes, citizen of Richmond conscript, defrauding government, horse thief, notorious blockade runner, within our lines—no pass, held as witness by order of Sec of War, subject to orders from Genl L. C. Baker (a considerable number of these), "charged with passing himself for Brig Genl USA & having forged papers in his possession," committed by War Dept (many such), news boy sent out of lines, furnishing citizen clothes to soldiers, "knowingly enlisting an enlisted man," laborer with ball and chain, and so on. The term "hidden Civil War" comes to mind when one peruses this kind of list and tries to imagine the full stories of these numerous men who were caught.[5] Though one seldom reads about this type of activity in detail, it was a large part of the wartime story.

## VIII

That Lincoln would have avoided these arbitrary arrests if he could, and that, permitting them, he wished them held under curb, is evident from a careful study of his sayings and acts. Harsh things were done reluctantly; their harshness did not extend to the worst extremes; as for those measures which proved most unfortunate, they were not done by Lincoln nor in terms of his intent. In some respects—especially as to military repression—what is called the "Lincoln administration" should be called the Stanton administration, or (in 1861) the Cameron administration.

Take the question of arresting the members of the Maryland legislature. When this problem arose at the outset of the war Lincoln wrote to General Scott recognizing the danger that this legislature, about to convene at Annapolis, would act "to arm the people of that state against the United States." Should the general in view of this truly alarming situation, "arrest, or disperse the members of that body"? Lincoln answered: "I think it would *not* be justifiable; nor, efficient for the desired object." The President thought that these legislators had a legal right "to assemble." It could not be known in advance that their action would "not be lawful, and peaceful." If arrested, they would become prisoners, but not for long; when liberated, they would reassemble and proceed as if never imprisoned; if dispersed, they would reassemble somewhere else. Lincoln would, indeed, use strong measures if the legislature should "arm their people against the United States," but he disapproved of a premature and perhaps unnecessary use of such measures.[1] As seen above, a few of the legislators were arrested in September 1861; but this action was more the work of Cameron, Banks, and Dix (with the reluctant concurrence of Governor Hicks) than of Lincoln. At least the government did not rush hastily into that kind of measure; moreover,

---

5 "Prisoners of State: Old Capitol Prison, vol. 303, Dept. of Washington," MSS., War Dept., National Archives. (Even where quotation marks are omitted in the above enumeration, the wording has been taken from the archival original.)

1 Lincoln to Scott, April 25, 1861, R. T. L. Coll., 9404–06.

that episode of arrest was not only exceptional but unique. When it did occur, the views of Lincoln were in favor of great governmental caution and restraint. In a published quotation of his words the President was reported at the time as assuring the people of Maryland: "In no case has an arrest been made on mere suspicion, or through personal or partisan animosities, but in all cases the Government is in possession of tangible and unmistakable evidence, which will, when made public, be satisfactory to every loyal citizen." [2]

Another clue as to how Lincoln felt about these matters came up in the case of one of the arrested police commissioners of Baltimore. The President took the ground that this commissioner, at the time of his arrest or "at any time" later, could have obtained release "by taking a full oath of allegiance to the government of the United States." If the gentleman refused the oath, then, wrote Lincoln: "If Mr. Davis is still so hostile to the Government, and so determined to aid its enemies in destroying it, he makes his own choice." [3]

In a revealing letter (a private one) to Reverdy Johnson of Maryland in 1862, Lincoln recalled Maryland events in 1861, and showed that he had not miscalculated in counting on the strength of Union sentiment in that state. He had been warned, the day after the Baltimore riot in April, "that it would crush all Union feeling in Maryland for me to attempt bringing troops over Maryland soil to Washington." "I brought the troops notwithstanding [he added], and yet there was Union feeling enough left to elect a Legislature the next autumn which in turn elected a very excellent Union U.S. senator!" (Johnson would have no difficulty in guessing who that senator was.)

"I am a patient man," continued Lincoln, "—always willing to forgive, on the Christian terms of repentance; and also to give ample *time* for repentance. Still I must save this government if possible. What I *cannot* do, of course I *will* not do; but it may as well be understood, once for all, that I shall not surrender this game leaving any available card unplayed." [4]

---

[2] *Ann. Cyc.*, 1861, 448. This statement is not to be taken as proof that there were no ill considered arrests. It harmonizes, however, with Bancroft's conclusion that improper motives did not appear except in the Pierce instance (*Seward*, II, 280), and in any case these words show the President's wish and judgment as to how these matters should be handled.

[3] Endorsement on letter of John W. Davis, [Sep. 15?] 1861, photostat, A. Lincoln Assoc.

[4] Lincoln to Reverdy Johnson, July 26, 1862, copy in Hay's hand, photostat, A. Lincoln Assoc.

## IX

When rightly considered, loyalty is a thing that runs deep, a thing of the spirit. It is a matter, not merely of sworn fealty, but of a man's very nature. To speak of loyalty is to speak of one's soul or good name. A man without loyalty is a lost soul. There may be loyalty oaths for a governmental purpose—and Lincoln favored such oaths if kept simple and not abused—but loyalty at its best is like devotion or affection; it is not a thing of compulsion.

Horace Bushnell, distinguished Congregational minister whose place in religious thought stands high, wrote in 1863: "Loyalty then is no subject of law or legal definition. It belongs entirely to the moral department of life. It is what a man thinks and feels and contrives, not as being commanded, but of his own accord, for his country and his country's honor—his great sentiment, his deep and high devotion, the fire of his habitual or inborn homage to his country's welfare. It goes before all constitutions, . . . ." [1]

The hard thing is where two honest loyalties conflict. This was a problem—North and South reading the same Bible and praying to the same God—that Lincoln pondered with tolerant recognition of the difficulty of saying the final and all-conclusive word, though he perceived a certain rightness in devotion to the United States and to human freedom which he did not perceive in slavery and disunion.

There is, of course, such a thing as corporate loyalty, and it is there that a species of compulsion may come into view. That is to say, the compulsion of human society, of organic social life, the vital necessity of cohesion in the great body of a nation if that nation is to survive, cannot be ignored. A criminal is not to be tolerated merely because he has his code, nor left unchecked on the principle that there is "honor among thieves." If a man actually serves the enemies of his country, his alien type of adherence, which should not in this connotation be termed loyalty, may be justified in his own reasoning, but the corporate bonds of society require that the traitor be held answerable as a supreme criminal. Such corporate loyalty, however, pertains to the great enduring fundamentals; it does not pertain to a party or a faction. It presupposes unanimity of homage to the na-

---

[1] Horace Bushnell, in *New Englander*, XXII, 565 (July 1863).

tion's cause, but it allows for democratic differences of opinion as to policies, procedures, and administrations. Furthermore, it is broadly corporate in the sense of belonging to the whole body of the people. Its enforcing is not a self-appointed function of a group, a clique, a secret society, a "front," a Klan, or a partisan league.

If serious cracks or faults should develop in this fundamental adhesion, then indeed, thought Lincoln, the nation would be in danger of destruction; but, as he believed, it would be self-destruction. The mature Lincoln thought thus, but so also did the young Lincoln, who had more maturity than is usually supposed. In his lyceum address in 1838 he said: "At what point . . . is the approach of danger to be expected? I answer, if it ever reach us it must spring up amongst us. It cannot come from abroad. If destruction be our lot, we must ourselves be its author and finisher. As a nation of freemen, we must live through all time, or die by suicide." That was why Lincoln was horrified at the wild passions of his time in America— at the hanging of Negroes, the murder of white citizens, at "dead men . . . dangling from the boughs of trees," at a "mulatto man by the name of McIntosh . . . seized in the street, dragged to the suburbs of the city [St. Louis], chained to a tree, and actually burned to death." When mob law ran riot, Lincoln realized that its effects were pervasive; "the innocent [he said], those who have ever set their faces against violations of law in every shape, alike with the guilty, fall victims to the ravages of mob law; and thus it goes on, step by step, till all the walls erected for the defence of the persons and property of individuals, are trodden down, and disregarded." [2]

When Lincoln thought in war time of testing and demanding loyalty, he did not think in terms of name calling or of witch hunts. Where accusations of disloyalty were raised, he set down his idea of fairness in construing an act of Congress for that purpose: the accused, he wrote, "are not to be punished [under the treason, or confiscation, act of July 17, 1862] without regular trials in duly constituted courts under the forms and all the substantial provisions of law and of the Constitution applicable to their several cases." [3] These

---

[2] "The Perpetuation of our Political Institutions," speech before Young Men's Lyceum, Springfield, Sangamo Journal. Feb. 3, 1838. If one wonders why, in terms of current facts in 1838, Lincoln spoke thus of the wild, undemocratic disorders of his time, a certain light of disillusionment will come by reading Fettered Freedom by Russell Nye.

[3] Message, July 17, 1862.

forms of law, to be sure, were not applied in the case of those arbitrarily arrested, but as to his feeling with regard to this abnormal procedure, Lincoln expressed real distaste. He wrote: "thoroughly im-
bued with a reverence for the guaranteed rights of individuals, I was
slow to adopt the strong measures which by degrees I have been
forced to regard as being within the exceptions of the Constitution,
and as indispensable to the public safety." Part of his distaste was
due to his realization that "instances of arresting innocent persons
might occur, . . . and then a clamor could be raised . . . which
might be . . . of some service to the insurgent cause." [4]

---

[4] Lincoln to Corning and Others, June 12, 1863, Nicolay and Hay, *Works*, VIII, 302–
303.

# CHAPTER IX

# THE VALLANDIGHAM CASE

WHAT was called "Copperhead" agitation, with all its
repercussions in popular emotion and governmental
policy, was focused and personalized in the case of
Clement L. Vallandigham. It was the *cause célèbre* of the Lincoln
administration. This handsome Ohio politician, whose fiery yet plausible oratory has already been noted, was the leading spirit among
Northern antiwar Democrats. His strength—or power for mischie
—lay in his handsome appearance, eloquence, marked ability, fea
less defiance, apparent readiness to go all the way to martyrdom, an
vigorous championship of civil rights. He also had points of weakness
or of irritation. He denounced the war as a method of maintaining
the Union so vigorously that he was accused—unjustly, he insisted—
of being opposed to the Union. The effect of his agitation was to
arouse civil disturbance, promote disobedience, discourage enlistment, confuse the public mind, and spread disunity. It was alleged
that he was a conscious and deliberate instrument of the Confederacy.
He denied this, but at least his course of conduct tended toward breaking down all organized forcible opposition to Jefferson Davis and the
Confederate movement.

It has sometimes been made to appear that the whole prewar
problem of peace instead of war could be centered in Vallandigham. Vallandigham would have avoided war. So would Lincoln. But Vallandigham's accusation that Lincoln and his friends
were wholly responsible for the war, and that when the Union was
broken nothing (by way of using armies) should be done about it,
was too oversimplified, too plausible and fluent, to be taken as the
last word. The cause of possible Union-saving conciliation in the

## THE GARDNER FULL FIGURE—1863

One of several photographs taken by Alexander Gardner in his studio on Sunday, Nov. 15, 1863, a few days before the Gettysburg address.

MRS. LINCOLN

As to the Lincolns being a loving and thoroughly devoted couple there can be no doubt on the part of those who know their story.

### LINCOLN FAMILY

*Upper left:* Mrs. Lincoln. (Courtesy of Lincoln National Life Foundation.)

*Upper right:* Robert Todd Lincoln. (Brady photograph, National Archives.)

*Center:* Lincoln with Tad. (Brady photograph, National Archives.)

*Lower left:* Willie (William Wallace Lincoln). (Meserve Collection.)

*Lower right:* Tad (Thomas Lincoln). (Brady photograph, National Archives.)

FRANKLIN PIERCE

The Pierce story has relevance to the Lincoln presidency in two connections: a preposterous accusation of disloyalty which turned out to be a hoax, and a most beautiful but slightly known letter which the ex-President wrote to Lincoln after the death of Willie.

## CARL SCHURZ

Brave German revolutionary, distinguished German-American, diplomat, brilliant speaker, Union major general. In the center picture the trappings (busby, pelisse, cape, saber—complete with riding whip and cigar) are not those of any identified uniform. (Center, upper left, and lower right photographs are by courtesy of the State Historical Society of Wisconsin; lower left, of Federick H. Meserve of New York; the others, of the National Archives, Washington.)

### TWO VIEWS OF THADDEUS STEVENS

Radical, anti-Lincoln politician; master of the House of Representatives; advocate of vindictive, punitive, and avowedly partisan measures; prominent in his opposition to the policies of reconstruction which President Lincoln favored.

THOSE GUILLOTINES.—A LITTLE INCIDENT AT THE WHITE HOUSE.

SERVANT. "If ye plase, Sir, them Gilliteens has arove."
MR. LINCOLN. "All right, MICHAEL.—Now, Gentlemen, will you be kind enough to step
[ou]t in the Back Yard?"

UNIVERSAL ADVICE TO ABRAHAM.
DROP 'EM!

CARTOONIST'S VIEW OF HIGH MILITARY LEADERSHIP AFTER FREDERICKSBURG

Both cartoons appeared in *Harper's Weekly:* the one at the left on January 10, 1863; that at the right on January 3, 1863; that at the left on Janu-
ary 10, 1863. The theme is the same: after Burnside's shattering defeat in the battle of Fredericksburg, December
1862, it is suggested that top military command in Washington is hopeless and that Halleck and Stanton must
be dropped.

PRINCIPALS IN THE VALLANDIGHAM CASE

Vallandigham was an Ohio Democrat. For making a speech on May 1, 1863, he was arrested under General Burnside's command, tried by military commission, and sentenced to imprisonment during the war. Lincoln regretted the arrest, and the sentence was commuted to removal beyond Union military lines. Later in the war Vallandigham returned to Ohio and was unmolested. (Denial of freedom of speech was not the regular policy of the Lincoln administration.)

MEN OF NEW YORK

Thurlow Weed, Horatio Seymour, and John A. Dix

*Frederick H. Meserve of New York and Dr. R. Gerald McMurtry of Lincoln Memorial University*

## HARVEST OF WAR

*Upper left and right:* Col. Elmer E. Ellsworth of the 11th New York, "The First Fire Zouaves." Close friend of the Lincolns. On May 24, 1861, after tearing down a Confederate flag flying over the Marshall House in Alexandria, Virginia, he was shot dead by the hotel keeper. The President and Mrs. Lincoln were in deep grief at Ellsworth's death. *Lower left:* Ben Hardin Helm, Confederate general, killed at Chickamauga, September 20, 1863. *Lower right:* Helm and his wife. Emilie Todd Helm was a much younger half-sister of Mary Todd Lincoln. There is great poignancy in the shattering effect of Helm's death, in Emilie's visit to the White House in December 1863, and in the unbroken love, beating against the impassable barrier of war, between the Lincolns and Emilie, beloved "Little Sister."

### GEORGE H. THOMAS

A Virginian who adhered to the Union cause; "Rock of Chickamauga"; successor of Rosecrans; it was Thomas's soldiers who carried Missionary Ridge. His decisive defeat of Hood's army in December 1864 was a highly important factor in final Union strategy.

## CONCERNED WITH ANGLO-AMERICAN RELATIONS

*Upper left:* Lord Palmerston, British Prime Minister. (From his last photograph, courtesy of New York Public Library.) *Upper right:* Earl (Lord John) Russell, British Foreign Secretary. (Courtesy of New York Public Library.) *Center:* John Bright, Liberal statesman and friend of United States. (Copy in Brady Collection, National Archives.) *Lower left:* Charles Francis Adams, United States minister at London. (Photograph by courtesy of Massachusetts Historical Society.) *Lower right:* His son and secretary, Henry Adams. (Courtesy of Massachusetts Historical Society.)

## WILLIAM S. ROSECRANS

Led the Union forces against Bragg; concerned with important operations in Tennessee in 1863; after the battle of Chickamauga there were important shifts in command; Grant became supreme commander in the West, and Rosecrans was superseded by Thomas.

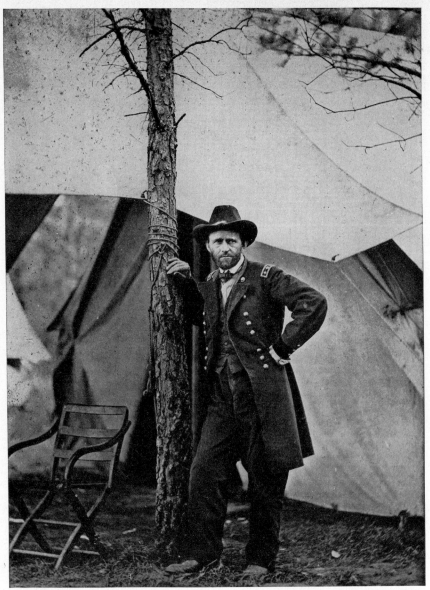

## SUPREME COMMANDER IN THE WEST, 1863

Conduct of war for Lincoln was often a matter of personal relations. There were many Union generals who, in relations with the President or with brother officers, proved difficult or impossible. Grant was a notable exception. Of prominent commanders it was he who gave the President the least personal annoyance. After his important command in the West in 1863, Congress, in addition to conferring a gold medal, revived the rank of lieutenant general to which in March 1864 Grant was elevated. As such he was supreme commander of the Union armies. Even yet there was to be hard fighting and long, disheartening delay, but Grant's leadership did not waver and the conditions of Union triumph had been achieved. Congressman Washburne said of him: "He fared like the commonest soldier in his command . . . ."

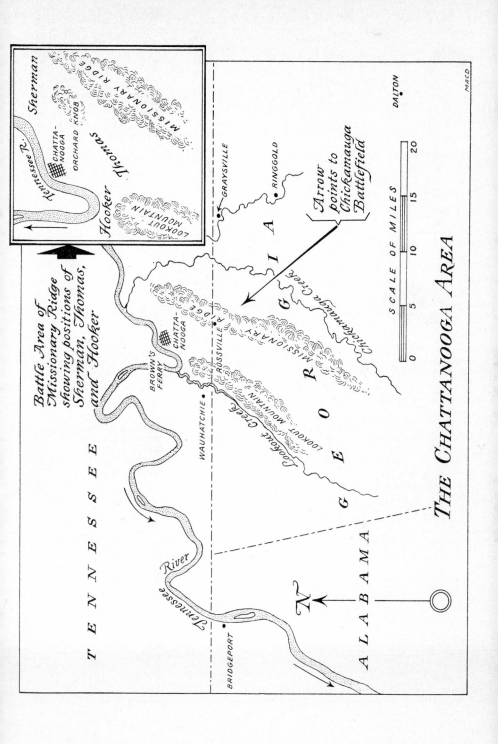

Battle Area of
Missionary Ridge
showing positions of
Sherman, Thomas,
and Hooker

Arrow points to Chickamauga Battlefield

THE CHATTANOOGA AREA

SCALE OF MILES

0   5   10   15   20

TENNESSEE

ALABAMA

GEORGIA

Tennessee River

BRIDGEPORT

WAUHATCHIE

BROWN'S FERRY

CHATTANOOGA

ROSSVILLE

Lookout Creek

LOOKOUT MOUNTAIN

MISSIONARY RIDGE

Chickamauga Creek

GRAYSVILLE

RINGGOLD

DALTON

MᵃᶜD

Inset labels:
Sherman
Tennessee R.
CHATTANOOGA
ORCHARD KNOB
MISSIONARY RIDGE
Thomas
Hooker
LOOKOUT MOUNTAIN

THE FACE

OF

LINCOLN

". . . the homeliest man I ever saw." Donn Piatt.

"None of the pictures do him the slightest justice." Utica *Morning Herald*, June 27, 1860. "His presence is commanding—his manner winning to a marked degree." *Ibid.*

"Fancy a man six foot high, and thin out of proportion; with long bony arms and legs . . . always in the way . . . . Add . . . a head . . . covered with rough, . . . uncombable hair that stands out in every direction . . . a face furrowed, wrinkled and indented . . . ; and then add to all this an air of strength, physical as well as moral, and a strange look of dignity coupled with all this grotesqueness, and you will have the impression left upon me by Abraham Lincoln." *Macmillan's Magazine*, May 1862.

". . . his expressive face . . . now seeming almost to laugh outright in its grimaces of fun, and now as . . . sorrowful as a tomb." Mrs. Amanda Poorman, daughter of Dennis Hanks, in St. Louis *Post-Dispatch*, May 26, 1901.

*Grateful acknowledgments to University of Nebraska Library (for picture, Beardstown 1858, in white coat), to Miss Charlotte Ward of Urbana, Illinois, for copy of 1860 ambrotype (upper right), and to Frederick H. Meserve.*

great sectional crisis is to be judged in terms of all its broad and complicated factors, not in terms of Vallandigham's speechmaking or wartime anti-Lincoln agitation.

## I

As of 1863 Vallandigham's career had been that of lawyer, legislator, officer in the Ohio militia, Democratic organizer, and orator. He had served in Congress before the war and during the early part of the conflict, but had not been reëlected in 1862, though the congressional election of that year had gone against the Republicans, especially in Ohio, whose delegation to the lower house of the Thirty-Eighth Congress (1863–65) was predominantly Democratic.

Putting together his statements in Congress and on the stump, in resolutions, conversations, and convention deliberations, Vallandigham's avowed views were substantially as follows. He favored, as he said, Union, peace, and harmony of the sections. Before the war he desired, not disruptive sectionalism and conflict, but friendliness toward "our brethren of the South." He considered the Democratic party the best upholder of the Union, favored it as an instrument of progress in the West, and deeply deplored the prospect, at Charleston in 1860, that the party would be split apart. As a result of such a split, if it should occur, he foresaw "one of the bloodiest civil wars on record, the magnitude of which no one can estimate." [1] He took the ground that he was not for the North nor for the South, but for the whole country, with emphasis on the hope-filled West. In the 1860 convention at Charleston Vallandigham had favored Douglas as the Democratic candidate who was most truly national. (This should not be taken as implying that his course in time of war was harmonious with the views of Douglas or of like-minded men.)

He looked to the day when Americans should hear no more of sections. He despised abolitionists because of the disintegrating effect of their agitation, and he opposed the Republicans as the Northern party of disunion. Put an end to the Republicans and abolitionists, he urged, and "the extreme Southern pro-slavery 'fire-eating' organization of the Cotton States (its offspring) will expire in three months."

---

1 James L. Vallandigham, *A Life of Clement L. Vallandigham,* 138.

(This, to say the least, was rather an underestimate of the intensity of proslavery, Yankee-hating opinion, and of its dominance in the South.) In November 1860 he declared that, as congressman, "he never would . . . vote one dollar of money whereby one drop of American blood should be shed in a civil war."[2]

When the war came, which he blamed on the Republicans and the abolitionists,[3] he declared that "the Union as it was must be restored," that the conflict must not be perverted into a war of subjugation or conquest, that extinguishing any of the states or moving "toward the declaring of a dictator" would be a "high crime."[4]

With such background and views the Ohio agitator proceeded according to form as the war progressed, denouncing the Lincoln administration for promoting an unjust war, for refusing reasonable peace, destroying the Union of the fathers, and suppressing fundamental civil liberties.

Throughout the Vallandigham subject there are two kinds of emphasis, and in the stress of these opposite contentions one can visualize much of the internal civil war in the North. Newspapers friendly to the agitator made his statements appear patriotic, pro-Union, orderly, and proper as dignified protest. On the other hand, citizens of Butler County, Ohio, who had heard him on the twelfth of October 1861, believed his speech calculated "to render aid and comfort to the traitors now in hostility against the Government of the United States." In its general tone, they reported, it "was just such a speech as might very well have been addressed to and been applauded by an audience of rebels." The arrest and "safe-keeping" of Vallandigham was therefore recommended by these protesting citizen many months before that arrest occurred.[5]

S. S. Cox, a Democratic colleague of a different type and trend from Vallandigham, said: "No man has been more thoroughly misunderstood and abused than Clement L. Vallandigham, of Ohio. There never was a man in public life who had a greater devotion to the Constitution and institutions of his country than he. His motto

---

[2] *Ibid.,* 141.

[3] The concept that Republicans were one with the abolitionists, though many earnest Americans would have wished to have it so, was quite contrary to the whole practical emphasis of Republican managers and leaders. Incoming letters in the Lincoln papers (R. T. L. Collection)—e. g., for 1858—make this abundantly clear.

[4] *Ann. Cyc.,* 1863, 234–235.          [5] *Offic. Rec.,* 2 ser. II, 128.

was to do right, to trust in God, in truth, and the people." [6] By contrast, the following was said by Roscoe Conkling of those who defended Vallandigham: "Now I am entirely of opinion . . . that we ought not . . . even to seem . . . to give one single inch to the rant and fustian and clamor of these men. . . . They would array popular passion and prejudice against this Administration, . . . . I know they are hypocrites and they know they are." [7]

## II

The Vallandigham case arose in the following manner. General Burnside, commanding the "Department of the Ohio" with headquarters at Cincinnati, issued an order, April 13, 1863, which was intended to suppress Northern disloyal agitation. In this document ("General Orders, No. 38") the commanding general announced that "all persons found within our lines who commit acts for the benefit of the enemies of our country will be tried as spies or traitors, and, if convicted, will suffer death." To this he added: "The habit of declaring sympathy for the enemy will not be allowed in this department. Persons committing such offenses will be at once arrested, with a view to being tried as above stated, or sent beyond our lines into the lines of their friends." [1]

In deliberate and open defiance of this order, Vallandigham delivered a fiery speech on May 1, 1863, at Mount Vernon, Ohio. The occasion was a rousing Democratic mass meeting with the trimmings of a popular gathering—decorated wagons in procession, hickory poles, American flags, and heads cut from copper pennies.

Four days after the speech General Burnside caused the orator to be arrested at his home in Dayton, Ohio. A military commission was then convened under Burnside's order and the prisoner was haled before that tribunal. The charge against him was that of publicly expressing sympathy for those in arms against the United States, "declaring disloyal sentiments," and violating Order No. 38. In the specification to support the charge various phrases of the Mount Vernon speech were presented.

---

[6] Cox, *Three Decades*, 80–81.
[7] Alfred R. Conkling, *Life and Letters of Roscoe Conkling*, 192–193.
[1] *Offic. Rec.*, 1 ser. XXIII, pt. 2, 237.

As a lawyer's problem the Vallandigham case involved three stages: (1) trial, conviction, and sentence by the military commission; (2) Federal court hearing on habeas corpus petition; (3) the proceeding, months later, before the Supreme Court of the United States.

At the military trial Vallandigham offered no plea, contending that such a court had no jurisdiction to try him, but a plea of "not guilty" was entered for him by direction of the commission.[2] The proceedings of the commission were not those of a drumhead court-martial; neither were they according to the standards of a court with due process of law. The accused was allowed counsel, permitted personally to cross-examine witnesses, and given the advantage of compulsory attendance of witnesses in his favor. If, however, a regular court had been trying him because of that speech, they could have found no statutory basis for indicting or convicting him. Testimony by officers in civilian clothes concerning what was said in the speech was followed by Vallandigham's own cross examination of these witnesses. It is in this testimony and the questions and answers that followed it, that we have the record, such as it is, of the famous speech. As J. F. Rhodes has written, these "are the only reports of the speech, and are of little value as historical evidence, for detached sentences and isolated remarks fail to give the tenor of a discourse." Rhodes adds that the address was sharply anti-Lincoln, and "went as near giving 'aid and comfort to the rebellion' as any talk could that proceeded from a good lawyer who knew the law."[3]

According to this testimony, Vallandigham denounced the wicked and cruel war, denied that restoration of the Union was the purpose, and asserted that the Union could have been saved without war if certain reasonable plans had been adopted or French mediation accepted. The administration, he was quoted as saying, was seeking to suppress public meetings. He expressed contempt for such power as was indicated in General Order No. 38; he trampled on it; he did not ask Tod (governor of Ohio) or Lincoln or Burnside for his right to speak. He was resolved never to submit to a military dictator prohibiting free discussion. The people, he allegedly said, should remember that this was not a war for the preservation of the Union, but "a wicked abolition war." It was "a war [he was quoted as saying] for the libera-

---

[2] Ibid., 2 ser. V, 635.     [3] Rhodes, Hist. of the U. S., IV, 247.

tion of the blacks and the enslavement of the whites." As for him, he would "never be a priest to minister upon the altar upon which his country was being sacrificed."

Other testimony or summaries of the speech exhibited further statements. The country had been told that the war would be terminated in three months, then in nine months, then again in a year, but there was still no prospect of its being ended. Richmond was not taken, nor Charleston nor Vicksburg; "the Mississippi was not opened and would not be so long as there was cotton on its banks to be stolen or . . . contractor or officers to enrich." The administration had been rebuked in the election of November 1862; "no more volunteers could be had." Such were a few of the orator's reported assertions. As to the tone of his speech, it may be judged by quoted epithets or catchwords—"King Lincoln," "Lincoln's minions" (army officers), and the like.[4]

Those who wish to follow the proceedings in detail (which cannot be done here) would be interested to read Vallandigham's examination of hostile witnesses. In that cross examination the following points were brought out by the accused, being admitted by witnesses: Vallandigham, in urging peace, did not favor disunion; he believed the military commission unconstitutional; persons if guilty of treason ought to be tried by a judicial court and a jury. It was admitted that one of the witnesses made no notes of the speech, but "made minutes" of the discourse after returning to his hotel. S. S. Cox, the well known Democratic congressman who had been a speaker at the same meeting as Vallandigham, testified that Vallandigham applied no "epithet" to Burnside, that he opposed any attempts to restore peace by a separation of the states, that he denounced applause given to Jefferson Davis, and that he "counseled no resistance except such as might be had at the ballot-box."[5]

A curious aspect of the case was that on May 6, while Vallandigham was in prison awaiting trial, Cox, according to his own statement, "was informed by General Burnside that Mr. Vallandigham would not be convicted" and was "requested to so advise Mrs. Vallandigham, who was in great distress." Another queer feature was that, by some mistake of reporting, Cox's words were given "as the words of Val-

4 *Offic. Rec.*, 2 ser. V, 633 ff., esp. 636, 641.
5 *Ibid.*, 2 ser. V, 642–644.

landigham." [6] The evidence was not clear as to what the prisoner had said about the conscription act. Cox testified that, to the best of his recollection, Vallandigham "did not say a word about the conscription." He added that reference was made to French conscription, by Cox himself, not by the accused.[7]

## III

The military commission found Vallandigham guilty—i. e., guilty "Of the charge—" [1] and sentenced him to be imprisoned during the continuance of the war. The proceedings, findings, and sentence were confirmed by General Burnside. It was evident that this was not an Ohio matter or a Burnside matter only, but a serious problem, and an embarrassing one, for President Lincoln and his administration. Embarrassment increased as the case grew more complicated, and on May 29, 1863, Burnside sent the President a despatch referring to differences between himself and the administration. Convinced, he said, that his action had been a "source of embarrassment" to Lincoln, but unchanged in his views, except that he preferred increased instead of diminished rigor, he wrote that he would "be glad to be relieved" if the public service required it.[2] To this Lincoln answered by wire: "Your despatch of to-day received. When I shall wish to supersede you I will let you know. All the cabinet regretted the necessity of arresting, for instance, Vallandigham—some perhaps, doubting, that there was a real necessity for it—but, being done, all were for seeing you through with it." [3]

Under the circumstances Lincoln felt that he could not release Vallandigham,[4] whose arrest he would not have approved. Neither

---

[6] Cox, *Three Decades*, 83.          [7] *Offic. Rec.*, 2 ser. V, 643.

[1] He was found not guilty as to certain words attributed to him in the "specification," but guilty "Of the charge." The evidence was not clear as to the words used. *Ibid.*, 2 ser. V, 646.

[2] *Offic. Rec.*, 2 ser. V, 717.

[3] Lincoln to Burnside (telegram in cipher), May 29, 1863, photostat, A. Lincoln Assoc.

[4] Certain writers have concluded that Lincoln made a mistake in not simply releasing Vallandigham, since he disapproved of the arrest and did not intend to enforce the sentence of imprisonment. Had this release been effected, the Ohioan would have had to make a contest to obtain the Democratic nomination for governor of Ohio in 1863. As it was, delegates who disagreed with him voted for him because he had become a kind of symbol or test case for important rights, and he was nominated by acclama-

did he wish the sentence of the military commission enforced. Commuting the sentence, as was his presidential function, he directed through Stanton that the orator be sent to the headquarters of Rosecrans "to be put . . . beyond our military lines." In case of his return, he was "to be arrested and kept in close custody for the term specified in his sentence." Rosecrans was notified by Stanton (by order of the President) that the prisoner was to be put beyond Union lines, "and if he returns within your command you arrest and keep him in close custody during the war or until further orders." [5]

Turning the pages of Vallandigham's voluminous biography written by his brother, we read of the exile's ride under military escort and flag of truce to the Confederate outposts, his "proposition" to General Rosecrans that he be allowed to address the Union soldiers, his prediction that by his words they would be moved to "tear Lincoln . . . to pieces," and his nomination for the governorship of Ohio on the Democratic ticket. Reading further, we learn of his escape to Canada after a dash through the blockade, his sojourn at Windsor, his addresses "to the people" in which he rebuked the "weak despots at Washington," his elaborate reply to visiting students from the University of Michigan (one wonders whether the students did not regard the affair as a lark), and his determination to "recover his liberties or perish in the attempt." Under a Falstaffian disguise, aided by a thick mustache and a large pillow, he returned to the States. Then he threw off the disguise and participated prominently in the screaming campaign of 1864.[6] After this return from Elba his speeches were as violent as before, but Lincoln's sense of humor was still in working order and he allowed Vallandigham to go unmolested. The terms of the banishment, and the specific orders in the case, called for reimprisonment in case of return, but Vallandigham in jail would have done more harm to the Lincoln government than Vallandigham free.

Since it was a matter of opinion, Lincoln made it so. Opinion was allowed to take its sway. A clear test of free opinion came in 1863 in

---

tion. G. H. Porter writes: "Much better would it have been, had Mr. Lincoln rescinded the sentence of the military commission and allowed Vallandigham to go free . . . ." *Ohio Politics during the Civil War*, 177. See also, for criticism of Lincoln, Rhodes, *Hist. of U.S.*, IV, 250–255.

[5] *Offic. Rec.*, 2 ser. V, 657.

[6] J. L. Vallandigham, *Life of Vallandigham*, 297–365.

the defeat of Vallandigham for governor of Ohio. In that election Vallandigham and his friends gave all they had in appeals to the people; the people voted; Lincoln's Union policy was sustained and Vallandigham defeated.[7] The 1864 situation still remained. That is another story, to be treated when it comes up; it too involved a sharp defeat of all that Vallandigham stood for, but it was a defeat with Vallandigham in the open, which made it all the more effective.

A curious and remarkable feature of the Vallandigham case appears when we consider the part played by Captain J. Madison Cutts, a Democrat, a brother-in-law of Stephen A. Douglas, and an officer on Burnside's staff. He, of all men, was the judge advocate at the military trial—thus becoming the chief instrument in the actual prosecution—yet he strongly disapproved of the whole proceeding. What is even more surprising is that this same Cutts—a minor figure who gains importance because of certain personal difficulties and especially because of an exquisite reprimand by Lincoln—went so far as to send the President the following telegram: "To His Excellency Abraham Lincoln President of the United States (Private & in cipher.) I advise you to relieve Major Genl A. E. Burnside from command of the Department of the Ohio *immediately,* by Telegraph. He has been plausibly pressing a policy hostile and adverse to your wishes and instructions, and those of the Secretary of War and General in Chief." Cutts added: "Order 38 has kindled the fires of hatred and contention —and Burnside is foolishly and unwisely excited and if continued in command will disgrace himself, you and the country, as he did at Fredericksburg. . . . I am absolutely right. Douglas was my preceptor." [8]

Later, on July 26, 1863, Cutts wrote to Lincoln: "In my opinion that policy of Genl. Burnside's which developed itself without your previous knowledge or consent, in the trial of Mr Vallandigham has inflicted a lasting injury upon *your administration* . . . . I do now state that the first step should be the immediate withdrawal of Ambrose E. Burnside from the command of this Department. I have always been opposed to General Burnside's policy. . . . I was forced to enforce it, but determined I would do so with as much judgment as possible, and so as to inflict as little harm as possible."

---

[7] See below, chap. xi, espec. pp. 273–274.    [8] R. T. L. Coll., 25018–19.

Cutts filled his letter with further details. Then he wrote: "Ambrose E. Burnside has refused to do that which would have remedied the *evils of his own creation.* There *was perfect quiet, peace* and good feeling among all parties before he came to this Department. He still persists in the same *bad policy.* . . . Who is the President of the United States, and what are his duties, his power, and his authority? I again advise you to send some thoroughly brave man to take his place—and I have strong reasons for recommending Hooker. I pronounce myself a determined unwavering War Democrat." [9] Just how much attention Lincoln paid to this advice of Cutts is not known. We know, however, that Burnside did not long remain in Cincinnati. He was shifted to command of combat operations in east Tennessee, and by the first week in September we find him established with headquarters at Knoxville. His unimportant successor in the command of the Department of the Ohio was General John G. Foster.

## IV

To return to the course of events in the Vallandigham case, after the famous prisoner had been found guilty and sentenced by the military commission, the next step was a civil proceeding, a hearing before Judge Humphrey H. Leavitt of the United States circuit court at Cincinnati, on an application for a writ of habeas corpus. Here was a problem: Could a Federal court review, and possibly overrule, the proceedings of a military commission? If military rule was carried to the point of arresting, trying, and sentencing a civilian for the expression of certain opinions, could the civil courts intervene?

In this habeas corpus proceeding for Vallandigham it was argued that the writ should be issued "as of right" (or as "of course") at once, and that the hearing, including the response of General Burnside, should occur "when the body of the prisoner should be brought into court." This meant that the purpose of the writ was not necessarily to release the prisoner—gruesomely referred to as the "body"—but to have a hearing to see whether he should be ordered released. Instead of this manner of handling the case, Judge Leavitt decided to "hear

---

[9] *Ibid.* (eight-page letter), 25144–48. In studying the activities of Cutts in relation to the Vallandigham affair and other matters, the author has made use of an extensive file in the National Archives.

the argument on the application"—i. e., to hold up his decision whether the writ should issue until the answer—usually considered a response to the writ itself—should be presented.[1]

Burnside submitted a lengthy answer. We were in a state of war, he pointed out. Criticisms of the government were demoralizing the army. It was his duty to prevent or stop it. An enemy delivering speeches to demoralize the troops would be "tried and hung if found guilty." Why should our public men be spared? The emergency required suppressive measures. The constituted authorities had the power "to inaugurate a war policy," and he was determined to support "their policy." Fear as to the people "losing their liberties" was but "the cry of demagogues." The army was part of the people and was educated in the love of civil liberty. It was not to be feared that our "citizen soldiery" would ever support a "military despotism." On this basis Burnside justified order No. 38 and the military proceedings concerning Vallandigham. As to the trial by the military commission, the general merely alluded to it without indicating its outcome. "The result of that trial [he stated] is now in my hands." [2]

In denying the writ of habeas corpus Judge Leavitt did not consider it necessary to "notice the charges" directed against the prisoner; nor was the court informed whether he had been condemned or acquitted on those charges. "Whether the military commission [he said] . . . was legally constituted and had jurisdiction of the case is not a question before this court." He pointed to the desperate crisis in the country and the constitutional power "to arrest persons who by their mischievous acts of disloyalty . . . endanger the military operations . . . ." "The sole question [he continued] is whether the arrest was legal, and as before remarked its legality depends on the necessity . . . for making it, and of that necessity . . . this court cannot judicially determine."

Justice Leavitt's main purpose seemed to be to indicate the things he could not decide. He considered that the situation was beyond the judiciary, and as he thought rightly so. In contrast, Taney had considered that an arbitrary arrest was beyond the judiciary not as a matter of right, but only of superior force. Habeas corpus, according to Leavitt, ought not to impede the military, even if that were

---

[1] *Offic. Rec.*, 2 ser. V, 574, 576 ff.        [2] *Ibid.*, 575–576.

possible. He could not "judicially pronounce the order . . . for the arrest of Vallandigham as a nullity." [3] He found no sufficient ground for granting the writ.

If as noted above the writ had issued as of right, that would have been similar to judicial approval of a motion to begin the hearing of a case. To institute a hearing is the purpose of the writ. In such a hearing the judge would consider the military officer's answer or "return." If that answer should prove satisfactory, no further judicial action would follow. Should the judge find no adequate basis for holding the prisoner he could order his release; if, then, the officer in charge should prove contumacious, a possible procedure would be an order holding him guilty of contempt of court. Lincoln's orders had not stated that the writ was suspended; it was rather the "privilege of the Writ," which is the wording of the United States Constitution. Presidential orders seemed to allow that the writ should issue, but that executive suspension of the privilege should constitute an adequate answer. This manner of handling the military "return" was later specifically prescribed in the President's instruction of September 17, 1863. Instead of upholding Leavitt's interpretation—i.e., that presidential suspension meant that the writ should not issue— this document by Lincoln indicated exactly the opposite. Lincoln's instruction was: "Please order each military officer of the United States, that, whenever he shall have in his custody any person, by the authority of the United States and any writ of *habeas corpus* shall be served upon him, commanding him to produce such person before any court or judge, he, the said military officer, make known to the court or judge issuing such writ, by a proper return thereto, that he holds such person by the authority of the President . . . ." This instruction also directed that the officer refuse to "produce such person according [to] said writ" and that any enforcing effort by the judge be resisted by force. [4]

If the procedure thus indicated by the President had been followed in the Vallandigham case, Burnside still could have given the answer which he did submit, but it would have been done as a "return" to the writ, which is the usual custom, instead of a military

---

[3] *Ibid.*, 576–584.
[4] The original, all in Lincoln's hand, is in the National Archives, Washington (WR RG 110: Pro. Mar. Bur., vol. II, H 319 [1863]); photostat, A. Lincoln Assoc.

statement bearing upon the application. The point is that it belongs to the judge to decide whether a judicial inquiry shall be made. The layman would hardly be aware of this point, but to a defense lawyer or a legal authority it would have more than technical significance. Lincoln's instruction showed his proper understanding of the law.

## V

It is hard to convey an idea of the immense outcry in the country occasioned by Lincoln's policy of arbitrary arrests. Editors, lawyers, agitators, politicians, generals, members of Congress, poured out a stream of protest. John M. Palmer of Illinois, referring to the administration's "letters de cachet," was shocked at the power claimed (in January 1862) by the secretary of state, which "simply converts this Constitutional Republic into a despotism." [1] There was extended discussion in Congress. Senator Bayard of Delaware asked whether sympathy was "to be the ground on which a man is to be hung." "Suppose [he said] a man believes that the restoration of the Government . . . over the revolted States cannot be effected by war; the Administration may say that is an evidence of sympathy with rebellion, and hang a man for that!" [2] (The administration, of course, was doing nothing of the sort. There were no such hangings.) Sherman of Ohio said that "we cannot afford these arrests." [3] Cox of Ohio, always vigorous in denunciation of what he considered the despotic acts of the executive branch, presented in the House of Representatives a resolution "that the House . . . do hereby condemn all such arrests . . . as a usurpation of power [etc.]." By vote of 80 to 40 his resolution was laid on the table. [4] Similar resolutions were voted down. Senator Latham of California said: "I see no necessity for trampling upon the Constitution in order to maintain it. I see no necessity for violating all law . . . in order to preserve the laws." [5]

Though arrests were military, it is not to be supposed that outstanding generals always approved of them. Seizure of persons by military authority at Shawneetown, Illinois, for example, elicited protest from U. S. Grant in 1861. [6] John Pope, who later commanded

---

[1] John M. Palmer to Lyman Trumbull (postscript), Jan. 1862, Trumbull MSS.
[2] Cong. Globe, 37 Cong., 3 sess., 19 (Dec. 8, 1862).     [3] Ibid., 30 (Dec. 9, 1862).
[4] Ibid., 2 (Dec. 1, 1862).          [5] Ibid., 37 Cong., 2 sess., 95 (Dec. 16, 1861).
[6] Protest against military arrests, signed by U. S. Grant and others, Nov. 5, 1861. Reavis MSS., Chicago Hist. Soc.

the principal Union army in the East, wrote in December 1861: "I dread to witness the rapid strides toward despotism which we have made during the past six months." [7]

Nor should it be supposed that complaints as to summary military procedures in disregard of civil guarantees came only from extreme agitators, partisans, or men of the recognizable "anti-Lincoln" type. When Lincoln had issued his suspending proclamation of September 24, 1862, Benjamin R. Curtis, former justice of the United States Supreme Court, strongly assailed the President in a pamphlet, *Executive Power*, published in 1862 in Boston.[8] Newspaper criticism on the same theme was emphatic. Historians have noted that the suspending edict was a factor in the setback to Lincoln and the Republican party in the congressional election of 1862. Lincoln's oldtime law partner at Springfield, John Todd Stuart, considered the proclamation, along with the emancipation edict, "most unfortunate." Senator Fessenden of Maine was quoted as saying that "the proclamation suspending the privilege . . . of Hab: Corp: in the loyal states where no insurrection existed was an exercise of despotic power which he [Lincoln] did not possess, and very dangerous." A similar view was held by old Thomas Ewing, who "said the Presidents emancipation and Habeas Corpus proclamations had ruined the Republican party in Ohio." [9]

Lincoln's dilemma in the Vallandigham case—his disapproval of Burnside's course weighed against the practical consequences of overruling and weakening the military power—was shown by his own statements, and by the record of cabinet discussion. When the incident came up in cabinet meeting, according to Welles, "All regretted the arrest, but, having been made, every one wished he had been sent over the lines to the Rebels . . . ." [10]

A meeting of Union-supporting Democrats was held at Albany, New York, on May 16, 1863, while the case was hot. The Democrats, so the meeting resolved, had loyally supported the war and had suffered great sacrifices as evidence of their patriotism, but liberties of the citizen must be recognized and the Constitution maintained. In

---

[7] John Pope to Lyman Trumbull, Otterville, Mo., Dec. 31, 1861 (typed), Trumbull MSS.

[8] *Lincoln the President*, II, 175–176.

[9] For the views of Stuart, Fessenden and Ewing, see Browning, *Diary*, I, 585, 588, 592 (Nov. 12, Nov. 28, Dec. 5, 1862).

[10] Welles, *Diary*, I, 306 (May 19, 1863).

view of these principles the meeting denounced "the recent assumption of a military commander to seize and try a citizen of Ohio, Clement L. Vallandigham, for no other reason than words addressed to a public meeting . . . ." [11] The document was directed to the Vallandigham case, but was in fact a protest against the whole policy of arbitrary arrests.

This Albany meeting drew from Lincoln one of those dignified, carefully worded statements addressed to a person or occasion, but intended as a kind of state paper. In a long letter (to Erastus Corning and Others, June 12, 1863) the President used the language of utmost courtesy toward those who were criticising his policy. He noted their patriotic promise to support "our common Government and country." If they differed with him, it was not as to purpose, but only as to "the choice of means." From this beginning the President launched into a defense of his policy concerning military arrests. Enemies of the government, he argued, were seeking to destroy the Constitution while relying on its guarantee to protect them. Civil courts, suited for quiet times and for trials of individuals "on charges of crimes well defined in the law" were "utterly incompetent" to deal with the problems arising out of the existing rebellion and the serious threat posed by immense numbers of insurgents and their sympathizers. The Constitution itself, permitting the setting aside of the habeas corpus privilege "in case of rebellion," attested "the understanding of those who made the Constitution that ordinary courts . . . are inadequate" to such an emergency, and that in such a crisis the regular safeguards could be suspended.

The arrests, he noted, were not for treason nor for defined crimes committed. They were "preventive" rather than "vindictive." The government had been lenient, as shown by the fact that notable leaders "now occupying the very highest places in the rebel war service" had been allowed to go free though it had been within the power of the government to arrest them. As to Vallandigham, Lincoln refused to admit that he was arrested "for no other reason than words addressed to a public meeting." He was seized, said the President, because of his hostility to the war for the Union, and because he was "laboring, with some effect, to prevent the raising of troops; to en-

---

[11] McPherson, *Rebellion*, 163.

courage desertions from the army; and to leave the rebellion without an adequate military force to suppress it."

Lincoln was dealing with the fact of war, and with the need of military force to suppress the rebellion. These ugly facts were not agreeable to him, nor was the arrest of Vallandigham. But he assumed that the Albany meeting was in favor of using the army to overcome the enemy and maintain the Union. Armies "cannot be maintained unless desertion shall be punished by the severe penalty of death." Then followed Lincoln's famous question: "Must I shoot a simple-minded soldier boy who deserts, while I must not touch a hair of a wily agitator who induces him to desert? This is none the less injurious when effected by getting a father, or brother, or friend, into a public meeting, and there working upon his feelings till he is persuaded to write the soldier boy that he is fighting in a bad cause, for a wicked Administration of a contemptible Government, too weak to arrest and punish him if he shall desert."

Lincoln believed certain things to be constitutional in cases of rebellion or invasion which are not applicable "in times of profound peace and public security." The Constitution itself made this distinction. He then added a point which showed that he was sensitive on the subject of civil rights and felt as keenly as anyone the necessity of preserving those rights in normal times. "Nor am I able," he said, "to appreciate the danger . . . that the American people will, by means of military arrests during the rebellion, lose the right of public discussion, the liberty of speech and the press, the law of evidence, trial by jury, and *habeas corpus* throughout the indefinite peaceful future which I trust lies before them, any more than I am able to believe that a man could contract so strong an appetite for emetics during temporary illness as to persist in feeding upon them during the remainder of his healthful life."

It "gave me pain," said Lincoln, "when I learned that Mr. Vallandigham had been arrested—that is, I was pained that there should have seemed to be a necessity for arresting him—and . . . it will afford me great pleasure to discharge him so soon as I can, by any means, believe the public safety will not suffer by it." As the war progressed, Lincoln believed that opinion and action, then in confusion, would "take shape and fall into more regular channels." In that case he thought that the necessity for strong dealing would decrease. He closed on a conciliatory note. "I have every reason to desire that it should cease altogether, and far from the least is my regard for the opinions and wishes of those who like the meeting at Albany, declare their purpose to sustain the Government . . . ." [12]

## VI

The Vallandigham case ultimately reached the Supreme Court of the United States on a petition (for a writ of *certiorari*) to review the sentence of the military commission.[1] The opinion (Ex parte Vallandigham) was announced on February 15, 1864.[2] In Vallandigham's behalf it was urged by his counsel, George E. Pugh, that military commissions have a limited function and that this one had exceeded its jurisdiction in trying a civilian unconnected with the armed forces. The argument against Vallandigham was presented by Judge Advocate General Holt, and this argument became the basis for the Court's decision handed down by Justice Wayne.[3] The substance of the opinion was a denial of authority in the premises. A military commission was not a "court" within the meaning of existing laws for the Federal judiciary. The Supreme Court, therefore, "cannot . . . originate a

[12] This is the reply as published at the time. McPherson, *Hist. of the Rebellion*, 163–167. The text in Nicolay and Hay, *Works*, VIII, 298–314, shows only minor differences; Lincoln's original draft (R. T. L. Coll., 23995–24071) is substantially the same as the final published version, variations being minor matters of form with one exception. In his finished letter, in the statement that the arrest of Vallandigham gave him pain, Lincoln inserted the words: "that is, I was pained that there should have seemed to be a necessity for arresting him." In adding this qualification, indeed in the whole letter, the President was attempting the most careful and precise definition of his difficult position as a man appreciative of civil rights, and at the same time as chief of state in a time of great turbulence and danger.

[1] Attorney General Bates, who had a low opinion of Vallandigham and who supported the President's power of military arrest without civil process, objected strongly to the proceedings before the Supreme Court. He considered the motion for *certiorari* "so utterly without law & so clearly against law" that he found it "hard to guess the object, . . ." "It may be only a peg on which to hang a denunciatory speech against the administration generally & the war in particular." Bates to Stanton, Attorney General's Office, Jan. 19, 1864, Stanton MSS., 54025. Lawyers continually differ, but in view of the Milligan decision of 1866 one may question Bates's air of finality in saying that the motion was "so clearly against law."

[2] 68 U. S. 243.

[3] In "The Supreme Court during the Civil War" (doctoral dissertation, Univ. of Ill., 1940) David M. Silver has shown how, in the Vallandigham opinion, Justice Wayne not only took his arguments, but also his phraseology, from Holt's brief. This is shown conclusively by parallel columns.

writ of *certiorari* to review . . . the proceedings of a military commission."

In the published report it is stated that Nelson, Grier, and Field "concurred in the result" of the opinion by Wayne and that Miller, having not been present at the argument (which occurred on January 22, 1864), took no part.[4] Of the ten justices on the Court in this period, all except Taney were present, as shown by the unpublished minute book, on February 15, 1864. These nine were Wayne, Catron, Nelson, Grier, Clifford, Swayne, Miller, Davis, Field. The statement that Nelson, Grier, and Field concurred in the result signifies that they agreed in what the Court did—i. e., in denying the petition—though not concurring in all of Wayne's wording; it should not be taken to signify that none of the other justices participated. The proper inference—so the author is reliably informed—is that all participated in the decision except Taney and Miller, and that those not mentioned as having done otherwise (Catron, Clifford, Swayne, Davis) presumably concurred with Wayne. There is no record that any justice dissented; had there been any dissent, it would have been recorded. Just what were the reasons that caused Nelson, Grier, and Field to concur only in the result remains an unanswered question. They did not, as did various justices in the Dred Scott case, submit individual concurring opinions.[5]

The effect of this action, or non-action, by the highest court of justice was that the military proceeding was sustained by the simple process of denying the right to examine into it. The merits of the case—the charges against the prisoner, his guilt under those charges, the competence of the military commission, and the appropriateness of the sentence—were not considered. Arguments against the fairness of a proceeding, though not refuted, become unavailing when a court decides that it is without authority to act.

One should notice the cumulative effect of the Wayne decision when added to the earlier Leavitt decision. Neither case recognized any judicial function to inquire into the essential issue or the substance of the question. Leavitt was not concerned whether the military

---

[4] 68 U. S. 254.

[5] In studying how the justices stood, the author has been greatly assisted by an informative letter (with a copy from the minute book) from Helen Newman, librarian of the Supreme Court of the United States, July 12, 1951.

authority had acted legally or illegally. It had acted, and nothing judicially could be done about it. Wayne's position was not that the military commission had acted rightly, but that there was no rightful
jurisdiction on the part of the Supreme Court to supply a remedy.
And all these disclaimers on the part of Federal justices, when traced
to the origin of the case, pertained to a military prosecution which
was not the action of the President and was not approved by him, but
was rather the order of one of the generals—a man, by the way, who
did not long continue to retain the confidence of the Washington administration in his command of the Department of the Ohio.

In two respects the contemporary view of the Vallandigham case
was faulty if judged by the long-range view. In the first place, the
proceeding against Vallandigham was inevitably associated with "the
Executive," despite the fact that the arrest and the trial were not correctly attributable to the President's true intention. The press of the
day did not fail to note the significance of the Vallandigham decision
as a factor upholding the arm of the President. The New York *Times,*
observing that the "Copperheads" had not hitherto abused the Court,
seeming to imagine "that it had proclivities in their favor," remarked
that there had been no warrant for this supposition. "In no single
instance," declared the *Times,* "has its opinion been at variance with
the executive action of the President." [6]

In the next place, the whole point of law which was announced in
the decision soon became outmoded. It took but two years (and especially the ending of the war) to demonstrate that the Vallandigham
decision did not set the pattern of ruling law in the United States.
The Court's position on the principle involved was reversed (1866)
in the famous Milligan case. In October 1864 Milligan and his associates were placed under arrest in Indiana, tried on the charge of
conspiracy and membership in disloyal organizations, and found
guilty. Milligan was sentenced to be hanged and the day fixed at May
19, 1865. Execution was suspended, and in 1866 the Supreme Court,
through Justice David Davis, announced a decision which was the opposite of that given in the Vallandigham case. "If there was law to
justify this military trial," said the Court, "it is not our province to
interfere; if there was not, it is our duty to declare the nullity of the

---

[6] Editorial, Feb. 16, 1864, p. 4, c. 3. (Chief Justice Taney's opinion in the Merryman
case had not been that of the Supreme Court.)

whole proceedings." "Martial law [so the opinion continued] cannot arise from a *threatened* invasion. The necessity must be actual and present; the invasion real, such as effectually closes the courts and deposes the civil administration. . . . Martial rule can never exist where the courts are open, and in the proper and unobstructed exercise of their jurisdiction." [7]

One does not need to defend the Ohio politician for all that he was doing, nor agree with him in his attacks upon Lincoln, in order to perceive and emphasize the foremost point in the whole Vallandigham case—namely, the precious principle of freedom of speech. Not that freedom of speech has no limits, but the Lincoln practice was to permit such freedom in general, even to the point of tolerating the most vociferous and bitter denunciation of the government. Lincoln had no need to place reliance upon such methods as those of General Burnside. Arrests for speech making were so far from the regular procedure under Lincoln that aside from Vallandigham there was hardly an instance of an arrest for that reason. Furthermore, in the latter part of the war, even though the reëlection of Lincoln was at stake, the speaker was unmolested. There were honest protests against arrests in the war period and of the denial of habeas corpus, but that is not to say that all the excessive complaints of Vallandigham and his followers were justified. In a dictatorship Vallandigham would have been far more severely treated. He would doubtless have been liquidated.

Going back over the decades, though opposite examples come to mind, it will be found that the curtailing of military power has had more emphasis than the stretching of army control. The time honored principle that the military power is subordinate to the civil was not forgotten by the Lincoln administration. This well known principle made all the more painful the many episodes under Lincoln which involved clashes of military with civil authority. It might be a local imbroglio or a tempest in a teapot, but at times the trouble reached great proportions, even threatening civil war behind the Union lines. A kind of *opera bouffe* conflict between Ward Lamon and General Wadsworth on the matter of slaves fleeing from Maryland into the District of Columbia, has been treated in an earlier volume.[8] Atten-

---

[7] *Ex parte* Milligan, 71 U. S. 119, 127.
[8] *Lincoln the President,* II, 134–135.

tion has also been given to the Frémont incident in Missouri in 1861, in which the general imposed such military severity upon the lives and property of civilians that his orders had to be overruled by the President, the more so because Frémont had exceeded his proper military authority, had issued orders outside his competence, and had shown a tendency to appeal for popular favor in opposition to the government at Washington. The issue was not merely the question of emancipation—a matter of high policy which the President was keeping in his own hands—but the serious implications of an order that said in effect that Frémont was the state and that the military power superseded the civil.[9] If one were to follow up this matter of the stretching of military authority even with regard to one general only—let us say Benjamin F. Butler—he could fill a book which would show the unusual character, and the un-Lincolnian tone, of some of the commanders.

## VII

As a subject of public discussion—in speeches, pamphlets, legal treatises, and editorials—the problem of arrests and of civil guarantees during Lincoln's presidency became one of the most notable controversies in American history. In the Congress the administration was defended by such men as Dixon of Connecticut, Wilson of Massachusetts, Hale of New Hampshire, and, to a certain extent, by Browning of Illinois.[1] In and out of Congress the names of Cox, Pugh, and Vallandigham of Ohio, Voorhees of Indiana, Richardson and Singleton of Illinois, Seymour and Wood of New York, and Bayard of Delaware, come readily to mind among those who assailed Lincoln, but it is not feasible to enumerate the men of this group. The President's course was defended by the Philadelphia lawyer Horace Binney in an elaborate legal and historical treatise on habeas corpus,[2] and officially by Edward Bates, the attorney general. Bates's opinion was a legal essay of more than five thousand words, of which the keynote was the statement: "The power to do these things [suspend the habeas

9 *Ibid.*, II, 16–23.

1 *Ann. Cyc.*, 1862, 285; *ibid.*, 1863, 236; Browning, *Diary*, I, 554 n.; *Cong. Globe*, 37 Cong., 2 sess., 2943–2953.

2 Horace Binney, *The Privilege of the Writ of Habeas Corpus under the Constitution* (Phila., 1862).

corpus privilege, etc.] is in the hand of the President, placed there by the Constitution and the statute law as a sacred trust to be used by him in his best discretion in the performance of his great first duty— to preserve, protect and defend the Constitution.  . . . He is the chief civil magistrate of the nation and being such *and because he is such* [author's italics] he is the constitutional Commander in Chief of the Army and Navy, and thus within the limits of the Constitution he rules in peace and commands in war and at this moment he is in the full exercise of all the functions belonging to both those characters." [3]

In the best statements in support of Lincoln's policy the militaristic type of argument was notably absent. The bearded, conservative attorney general was as unbelligerent an individual as one could find. In that very document supporting the executive policy of arrests which has just been quoted, Bates indicated that the main purpose of investing the President with the function of Commander in Chief was to uphold the supremacy of the civil over the military authority. It is not the military arm that controls the government, but the government that controls the military.

## VIII

The Vallandigham case was not Burnside's only non-Lincolnian act of military severity. From his attack on freedom of speech he proceeded to a sensational move against freedom of the press. On June 1, 1863, he issued the following order: "On account of the repeated expression of disloyal and incendiary sentiments, the publication of the newspaper known as the Chicago Times is hereby suppressed." [1] There had been sore provocation. The paper had been praising Vallandigham, assailing Burnside, and bitterly criticizing the policy of prosecuting the war. It was described as "the foul and damnable reservoir which supplied the lesser sewers with political filth, falsehood, and treason." [2] The act of seizure occurred on June 3 when a detachment of soldiers from Camp Douglas under Captain Putnam occupied the *Times* establishment, stopped publication, and put the premises under guard.

---

[3] *Offic. Rec.,* 2 ser. II, 29; *Constitutional Problems Under Lincoln,* foreword to revised ed. (1951), xix.

[1] *Offic. Rec.,* 1 ser. XXIII, pt. 2, 381.          [2] Rhodes, *Hist. of the U. S.,* IV, 253 n.

The reaction of public opinion was immediate. Some Chicagoans favored the suppression, but a public meeting was held in the court-house square on the evening of the 3rd, where "Twenty thousand loyal citizens of Illinois" resolved that law was the bulwark of liberty, that infringement of freedom of the press was a blow at the Constitution, and that "military power is and must remain subordinate to the civil power." "If the 'Times' or any other public journal has ex-ceeded the limits of lawful discussion or criticism," so read the reso-lution, "the civil tribunals, and they alone, are the competent and lawful judges of its crime." [3]

To make effective this appeal to the courts an application had been made to Judge Drummond of the United States circuit court at Chicago for an injunction to restrain Captain Putnam from inter-ference with the newspaper; that judge at once issued a restraining order while entertaining the question of a permanent injunction.[4]

This use of the judicial authority over the military power, how-ever, became unnecessary, and the Drummond proceedings went no further. President Lincoln, having had enough embarrassment from Burnside's unauthorized measures, took prompt action. On the day of Burnside's order of suppression (June 1) and two days before the actual seizure, Stanton wrote to the general: ". . . the President has been informed that you have suppressed the publication or circu-lation of the Chicago Times in your department. He directs me to say that in his judgment it would be better for you to take an early occasion to revoke that order. The irritation produced by such acts is in his opinion likely to do more harm than the publication would do. The Government approves of your motives and desires to give you . . . support. But while military movements are left to your judg-ment, upon administrative questions such as the arrest of civilians and the suppression of newspapers not requiring immediate action the President desires to be previously consulted." [5] In this, as in the arrest and trial of Vallandigham, Burnside had acted without the approval of Washington. "The President—and I think every member of the Cabinet—[wrote Gideon Welles] regrets what has been done." [6]

Final responsibility, however, was with the President. That is an

3 *Ann. Cyc.*, 1863, 424.
4 *Constitutional Problems Under Lincoln*, 493–494.
5 *Offic. Rec.*, 2 ser. V, 724.      6 Welles, *Diary*, I, 321 (June 3, 1863).

inescapable duty of the presidency: to be saddled with the effects and the blame of what is done by scores and hundreds of men who see only the smaller or more immediate aspects of a problem as it affects their headquarters or their particular departments. It is one thing to see an abuse; it is quite another to shape the remedy. It was realized at the White House that, while the *Times* was a thorn in the flesh, misusing the protection of the laws and the shielding influence of the President, yet it would be unwise to strike impatiently at the abuse, and thoughtful men could only lament, as Welles wrote, "that our military officers should, without absolute necessity, disregard those great principles on which our government and institutions rest." [7]

The fault in Burnside's procedure appears in the fact that, if he had consulted Washington first, the order of suppression would not have been issued. Nor would it have been issued if Stanton's above-quoted communication telling of Lincoln's strong disapproval had been sent by telegraph instead of by mail. The President, in his function of undoing the mistaken work of subordinates, held a cabinet meeting at which it was decided that Burnside's suppression order must be revoked. Word was flashed to Burnside at Cincinnati, and by his command the revocation was ordered (June 4) by "direction of the President." [8] Actual suppression had lasted two days, Wednesday and Thursday, June 3 and 4, 1863. [9]

Meanwhile a lesser Burnside, General Milo S. Hascall at Indianapolis, had issued "General Orders, No. 9" proclaiming suppressive action in accord with Burnside's "No. 38," against newspapers and speakers counseling resistance to conscription or bringing the war policy of the government "into disrepute." [10]

Hascall's order "No. 9" set off an explosive tempest in Indiana, as well it might in the supercharged politics of 1863. That military gentleman, practically unknown till then, got himself more and more deeply involved as he sought to follow up the original order which, as was to be expected, was openly defied. For example, from his Indianapolis headquarters of the "District of Indiana" (under Burnside) the general on May 8 sent a peremptory order to the editor of the Columbia City (Ind.) *News*. The editor was bluntly told to do one of two things: recant his resistance to order "No. 9" or discon-

7 *Ibid.*, I, 322.  
9 *Ann. Cyc.*, 1863, 424.  
8 *Offic. Rec.*, 2 ser. V, 741.  
10 *Offic. Rec.*, 2 ser. V, 485.

tinue publication "until further orders." [11]

If anything was designed to show up Burnside's policy, making it intolerably obnoxious and a bit absurd in Indiana, the Hascall treatment was so calculated. Lincoln's emphatic disapproval was made clear, though in doing so the President knew that he had to tread carefully so as not to offend the dignity of state executives. As expressed through Stanton in a despatch to Burnside, the President's answer was discreet and tactful, but firm and unmistakable: "Whatever dissatisfaction there may exist . . . within your department is liable to be increased by the presence of an indiscreet military officer, who will unnecessarily interfere with the political condition of the State and produce irritation by assuming military powers not essential to the preservation of the public peace." On recommendation from Washington, Hascall was promptly shifted to duty elsewhere and his rather useless military command at Indianapolis was terminated. His "No. 9" was revoked.[12] One of the surprising things about the Hascall episode is that his interference with newspapers began in mid-April and had reached such a crisis by May 27, 1863, that David Davis, then at Indianapolis, notified Stanton that his "immediate removal" was "demanded by the honor and interests of the Government." [13] Yet after this, and with Hascall's record before him, Burnside issued the order suppressing the Chicago *Times*. He knew this kind of conduct was not approved at Washington.

## IX

In a fair historical appraisal it is important to avoid misunderstanding the Vallandigham case. It was bound in the shallows of wartime politics, but it is not correct to treat as proved all the familiar assumptions. One should not assume that this agitator was truly representative of the main body of Northern Democrats. It was to a large extent the faulty machinery of party management (through the unsatisfactory workings of the Ohio Democratic convention), plus the reaction against his arrest, that gave him more prominence than he would otherwise have had. It is worth remembering that in the con-

---

11 *Ibid.*, 725. Similar orders were issued to other Indiana editors.

12 *Ibid.*, 752, 759; Stampp, *Indiana Politics during the Civil War*, 202.

13 *Offic. Rec.*, 1 ser. XXIII, pt. 2, 369. On the same date, May 27, Governor Morton wrote Stanton asking that Hascall be removed "at once" (*ibid.*).

gressional election of 1862, though that was overwhelmingly a Democratic year in Ohio, Vallandigham was a candidate but was defeated; certainly in that year he was not synonymous with the party; certainly also he was no asset to the party. In Ohio as elsewhere Democrats claimed always to be "devoted friends of the Constitution and the Union."[1] If this is brushed off as a party statement, then the opposite effort to make all Democrats appear as traitors should be taken no more seriously than the general run of party propaganda. Much of the fallacy was in equating two things that were not at all the same—the cause of the Union was being promoted (e. g., by the Union League) as if it were the precise equivalent of Republicanism. Democrats could hardly be blamed for resenting that theory. Yet when all is said, the Democrats were out of luck. They were inept, poorly led, and quite vulnerable to the rough and clumsy weapons used against them. To be saddled with Vallandigham was their chief wartime misfortune,[2] and it was their party managers that did the saddling.

Having noted these things, one should also avoid wrong assumptions as to Lincoln. Where he approved of irregular measures it was because in his opinion, under the terrific stress of war, he had to. To deny the ordinary course of civil justice was, for him, to play an unwelcome and unnatural role. It would seem superfluous to repeat that firm adherence to the fundamentals of civil rights was one of Abraham Lincoln's most characteristic and persistent traits. The fact that these things were done in an emergency did not mean to him that they would be perpetuated in normal times. Even where using arbitrary measures he held those measures within bounds. If the Democratic party was unlucky to have Vallandigham infixed in

---

[1] *Ann. Cyc.*, 1862, 696.

[2] For the factor of Vallandighamism in the "politics" of 1863, see below, pp. 263 ff. After the war his influence within the Democratic party was negligible. Regretting Lincoln's assassination, he wrote to Horace Greeley, April 20, 1865: "We must lay aside for a time past & future differences, & associate upon the pressing questions of the moment." (Greeley MSS., N. Y. Pub. Lib.) Even when he advocated reasonable measures —peaceful relations between the sections and return to normal civil procedures—his fellow Democrats, interested in the same measures, seemed to avoid his coöperation as the kiss of death. Thus in August 1866, when a convention was held at Philadelphia to unite Northerners and Southerners in favor of non-vindictive restoration, there was a disposition to exclude Vallandigham from the convention. A Democrat of Hamilton, Ohio, L. D. Campbell, wrote to O. H. Browning (July 31, 1866): "We must *squelch* him. He means mischief. . . . He is as full of pure cussedness as an egg is of meat." Browning, *Diary*, II, xiv–xvi, 84 n., 89.

their organization, so was the President unfortunate in being subjected to blasts of abuse for what was untypical, what he did not do, and indeed for what he particularly opposed. He had not ordered Vallandigham's arrest. He was not overrating the man's influence. He never gave an order for severe treatment of the "wily agitator" whose safe protection, while soldier-deserters were being shot, he mentioned with stinging sarcasm. As for the order suppressing the Chicago *Times,* he disapproved of the order at the very outset and promptly ordered its revocation.

# POLITICS IN 1863

ONE thinks broadly of significant elections in the United States as belonging to even numbered years—a President elected every fourth year, members of Congress every two years. There is also the tendency to regard state elections as having only minor and local importance. It may be for these reasons, or perhaps from inadvertence, that insufficient attention has been given, in general histories and Lincoln biographies, to the numerous state elections in 1863. From Massachusetts to Kentucky, and from Iowa to Pennsylvania, the Union war policy was impressively sustained. Vallandigham was defeated for governor in Ohio by the war Democrat, John Brough; Curtin was re-elected as Republican governor of Pennsylvania; an opponent of Seymour was elected secretary of state in New York; Andrew was re-elected governor of Massachusetts; in addition, the Union forces also carried Connecticut, Maryland, Delaware, Kentucky, and other states.

I

In New England the political campaigns brought Republican victory without exception as to any state, though the contests were waged with great intensity. Three New England states voted in March and April: New Hampshire, Rhode Island, and Connecticut. In Rhode Island the Republicans triumphed for governor, legislature, and the state's two members of Congress.[1] There was a peculiar

[1] *Ann. Cyc.*, 1863, 810–811. In this Rhode Island election (April 1863) the Republican candidate, James T. Smith, a cotton manufacturer, was chosen governor. In 1861 he had defeated the wealthy and handsome William Sprague. Sprague was a Democrat of the rich, conservative type that attracted Republican votes; he later became a Republican

situation in New Hampshire, where Justice Ira A. Eastman, Democratic candidate for governor, received nearly 33,000 votes as compared to 29,035 for the Republican contender, Joseph A. Gilmore; yet Gilmore was elected. This was because of an unimportant third ticket in the field, which took enough votes to leave Eastman without an overall majority; the choice of governor was consequently thrown into the legislature; that body, under Republican control, elected Gilmore.[2]

In Connecticut the 1863 contest was keen and exciting. It was, wrote Greeley, "chosen as the arena of a determined trial of strength . . . between the supporters and opponents . . . of the War for the Union."[3] William A. Buckingham, incumbent governor, contended for re-election against the popular former governor Thomas Hart Seymour, who could be described as a "peace Democrat," which implied avowed opposition, not to the Union, but to the Lincoln administration and the existing war policy. In the election, which was fairly close, and in which soldiers participated, success came to the Republicans, with 41,000 votes for Buckingham against 38,000 for Seymour. The Republicans also won control of the legislature and obtained three of the four seats in Congress.[4] It has been pointed out by W. B. Hesseltine that military intervention and presidential patronage were among the factors at work in this Connecticut election, that a wealthy gentleman vowed that he would raise $100,000 to "buy up the damned state," and that an ordnance official "put pressure on Connecticut's munitions manufacturers to force their workers to vote for Buckingham."[5]

A somewhat sensational feature of the contests in New England was the fervid stump speaking of the amazing girl orator from Philadelphia, Anna E. Dickinson. This female whirlwind, not much over twenty, stormed through New Hampshire and Connecticut especially, electrifying her audiences with rapid-fire speeches in the most approved radical style. Anna was not merely an abolitionist. Her speeches were not merely Republican. They were flaming tirades in

---

and as such served as senator, 1863–1875. He is best known as the husband of the brilliant and beautiful Kate Chase.

[2] *Ann. Cyc.*, 1863, 681.       [3] Greeley, *Amer. Conflict*, II, 486.

[4] *Ann. Cyc.*, 1863, 330.

[5] Hesseltine, *Lincoln and the War Governors*, 320.

which she gloried in bloody suppression, dished out hatred against Southerners, compared Jefferson Davis to a hyena, denounced "Democratic generals," and praised to the heavens such men as Frémont and Butler. At a time when Republicans were appealing to men of all parties to forget their differences and unite for the com- mon cause, she habitually referred to Democrats as traitors, while her Republican sentiments were always voiced with an extreme radical accent. This factional emphasis was illustrated by her emphatic de- nunciation of Seward, whom she actually represented as somewhat of a traitor, while dubbing him "Fox of the White House."

Antislavery zeal was a strong stimulus to her tempestuous oratory. She soared the more easily for not being confined by solid informa- tion or temperate judgment. This was the climax of her career (1863–64); she liked applause; audiences gave her a heady thrill; Re- publican managers knew how to use her for their purposes. They knew that popular audiences, once they recovered from the un- Victorian spectacle of a political campaigner in petticoats, would be readier to take extravagant statements from feminine than from masculine lips. To hear Anna was a dramatic experience. There was something fascinating about her youthful presence, her voice, and her forward style of calling down Almighty thunderbolts upon rebels and Democrats. In appearance she was much like a female Henry Ward Beecher.

Anna had been coached by the secretary of the New Hampshire Republican state committee, Benjamin F. Prescott, "to use the method of attack, to point out the disloyalty of the Democrats . . . , the incompetence of their generals, the folly of their slogan prating of the Constitution as it is and the Union as it was . . . ." She was warned "against expecting too much of her audiences." [6] In both Connecticut and New Hampshire the Republicans were very grate- ful to this girl who was being compared to Portia, and whose vigor- ous championship of the colored race was warmly approved by men of good intent. In New Hampshire Prescott wrote that she had done "more good than any other speaker," Gilmore told her personally that her speeches had secured his election, and she received the un-

---

[6] James Harvey Young, "Anna Elizabeth Dickinson and the Civil War" (ms. doctoral dissertation, Univ. of Ill., 1941), 87–88.

precedented honor of being invited into that lofty masculine organization, the Union League.[7] Since the leading Democratic candidate in the Granite State had received almost four thousand more votes than Gilmore, and since Gilmore lacked a clear majority by about 8,000, the thanks of these Republicans indicated, and they said as much, that without the girl's oratory they would have suffered even a worse popular repudiation and would have lost the New Hampshire election.[8] That might well have happened had there been no third ticket.

## II

Amid the agitations of politics—and with some relation to them —there occurred in the summer of 1863 an abortive effort toward negotiation between the governments of Richmond and Washington. Some writers have belittled this effort and there have been conflicting speculations as to its objectives, but since it involved an attempted mission to Washington on the part of Alexander H. Stephens, Vice President of the Confederacy, and required study by Lincoln and his cabinet, the episode should not be passed over too lightly.

After preliminary correspondence and consultation between Stephens and President Jefferson Davis, a steamer went down the James River under flag of truce bearing the Vice President together with Robert Ould, agent of the Confederate government for the exchange of prisoners.[1] These men were on their way to Washington if the Union authorities would permit the journey. Whatever broader objects may have been in mind, the stated purpose of the mission was to provide for the exchange of prisoners. This assuredly was no minor question. It proved one of the most wretched problems of the war, being hopelessly enmeshed with interrelated problems: the status of the Confederacy, Union use of Negro troops, dire threats of retaliation by the Confederacy, the proclamation of President Davis branding General ("Beast") Butler as an outlaw, the order for Butler's ex-

---

[7] *Ibid.*, 92.

[8] For an account of Miss Dickinson, see also James Harvey Young, "Anna Elizabeth Dickinson and the Civil War: For and Against Lincoln," *Miss. Vall. Hist. Rev.*, XXXI, 59–80 (1944).

[1] Moore, *Rebellion Record* (Diary), VII, 24; Stephens, *War Between the States*, II, 558–568.

ecution if caught (denying exchange), and the declaration (also by Davis) "that no commissioned officer of the United States, taken captive, shall be released on parole, before exchange, until the said Butler shall have met with due punishment for his crime." [2] (Among other things, Butler had caused a man to be put to death in New Orleans for tearing down the Union flag; it was urged that the general was disregarding the laws of war—indeed, that he was an "enemy of mankind.")

Earlier in the war a cartel for prisoner exchange had been worked out by General John A. Dix for the United States and General D. H. Hill for the Confederacy. Its object was to release all prisoners of war and to deal with an excess on one side by having surplus prisoners released on parole not to take up arms again.[3] After Davis's retaliatory proclamation—which came, by the way, after Lincoln had removed Butler from New Orleans—Secretary Stanton put an end to the Dix-Hill cartel. Union authorities were outdoing the Confederates in the number of prisoners taken, deriving an advantage all the greater in view of the over-all Union superiority in man power. With hundreds of thousands of prisoners suffering and thousands dying, and with each side accusing the other of brutal atrocity, the situation became a crying disgrace. Though need for redress was realized, nothing effective was done.

On July 4, 1863, the boat bearing Stephens and Ould was met by a Union boat under flag of truce, and Stephens conveyed the purpose of his trip to Admiral S. P. Lee, U. S. N., in Hampton Roads. Bearing a letter by Jefferson Davis to be put before Lincoln, the Vice President wished permission to go to Washington and present the communication in person. Though Ould was met by his opposite number, Colonel W. H. Ludlow (Union agent for prisoner exchange), and though the two men conferred, the mission failed on all counts, and on June 6 the Confederate steamer returned up-river with the unsuccessful Southern officials.

At Washington the problem of the Southern mission was discussed in cabinet meetings on July 5 and July 6. Welles has left a rather full account which is informative as to cabinet differences and sarcastic

---

[2] Randall, *Civil War and Reconstruction*, 438; Moore, *Rebellion Record* (Docs.), VI, 291–293.

[3] Hesseltine, *Civil War Prisons*, 32–33.

as to Seward who was disposed to manage the affair and to take it out of the hands of the navy department in which it had originated. Various alternatives were proposed for the answer to be sent to Hampton Roads, the President even suggesting at one point that "it would be well [so Welles quoted him] to send some one—perhaps go himself—to Fortress Monroe." [4]

It was decided, however, that no good could come of the proposed negotiation, upon which the only further question was the manner and phrasing to be adopted in communicating the answer to those concerned. Giving this matter his personal attention, with a combination of diplomatic caution and lawyerlike precision, Lincoln at first wrote out a draft of a statement—not a reply directed to Stephens, which would have involved what is now called "protocol" as to status, titles, and the like—but simply an order to Admiral Lee. In this autograph draft the President indicated that Stephens was not to be permitted to proceed to Washington and took occasion to reject any communication "in terms assuming the independence of the so-called Confederate States." He added that "anything will be received and carefully considered . . . when offered . . . in terms not assuming the independence of the so-called Confederate States." [5]

This earlier tentative form, which was of moderate length, was then reconsidered and the President wrote out a much briefer form (Welles to Lee) merely stating that the Stephens request was "inadmissable" and that "customary agents and channels" were "adequate for all needful communication . . . between the United States forces and the insurgents." [6]

Had Stephens been received, spokesmen for disunion (and anti-Lincoln spokesmen in the North) would have made the most of the occasion. Specifically the Confederate gentlemen were to confer as to exchange of prisoners, and no one could rightly deny the need for such a conference; but the evidence is pretty clear that larger problems were in Stephens's mind. He had written to President Davis: "While . . . a mission might be despatched on a *minor* point, the greater one could possibly . . . be opened to view . . . ." [7] All this was happening while the political campaigns of 1863 were rag-

[4] Welles, *Diary*, I, 359 (July 5, 1863).
[5] Nicolay and Hay, *Lincoln*, VII, 373; R. T. L. Coll., 24665.
[6] Nicolay and Hay, *Lincoln*, VII, 374.
[7] Stephens, *War Between the States*, II, 560.

ing in Northern states, and Confederates were counting on the Vallandigham type of partisan opposition to Lincoln as a factor working to their advantage. Stephens was one of the milder of the Confederate leaders, yet he was speaking not only of a permanently broken Union, but of the prospective defeat and overturn of the Lincoln government. (The idea that defeating Lincoln and putting a Democratic administration in its place would have meant Northern consent to disunion showed misunderstanding of Northern opinion, but misreading of public sentiment was a constant wartime factor; indeed, such misunderstanding had contributed to producing war.)

There could be no realistic discussion of the attempted negotiation on any assumption of accepting Confederate terms; [8] the mere thought, or wishful dream, of such acceptance was dashed even in Confederate minds by the coincidence of the mission with major military events. Assuming, or guessing, that the Lincoln government might have yielded to Confederate pressure if Lee had been successful and had threatened Washington, Stephens and other Confederate leaders realized how slight was any such prospect in the atmosphere of Gettysburg and Vicksburg. One need not criticize Stephens for the attempt, which had its humanitarian aspects and which President Lincoln considered carefully before rejecting it; but the Southern statesman was not bringing with him the essentials of peace. Then and thereafter Lincoln's terms for ending the war were simple and they were generous, but they included the indispensable factor of reunion and that was beyond Confederate acceptance.

### III

After a considerable interval—a momentous one that included Morgan's raid as well as the victories at Gettysburg and Vicksburg —Kentucky voted in August. The situation there presented unusual features. It was a Southern state, a shifting battleground of Confederate and Union forces. At the same time it was shaken by guerrilla ac-

---

[8] Commenting on terms to be taken for granted, the Richmond *Enquirer* of July 7, 1863, outlined in part the following: "acknowledgment of the independence of every State now in the Confederacy"; "free choice" of Maryland to join it (Kentucky and Missouri being "already members" thereof), and navigation of the Mississippi "though lost to the United States by the trial of battle." Quoted in Moore, *Rebellion Record* (Diary), VII, 26–27.

tivity and constant disorder. It was under martial law.[1] There were elements that smacked of coercion. By proclamation of Governor Robinson a loyalty oath was required of voters. They had to swear Federal
allegiance, pledge not to take up arms against the United States and
to give no aid to its enemies, and disclaim fellowship with "the so-
called Confederate States" and Confederate armies—all this under
the threat that violation of the oath might lead to death or other
punishment by judgment of a military commission.[2] It was claimed,
but denied, that the result in Kentucky was due to military interference and the intimidation of Federal bayonets.

The contest in Kentucky was between Union Democrats and Peace
Democrats. Thomas E. Bramlette, who had held a commission in
the Federal army, was the Union candidate; Charles A. Wickliffe, also
a Unionist (for he had opposed secession), headed the Peace Democratic ticket. The issue between the two candidates was not that of
union against disunion; Wickliffe, for instance, would not have favored having the state join the Confederacy. Spokesmen for the peace
party declared "this rebellion [to be] utterly unjustifiable . . . and
the dissolution of the Union the greatest of calamities." [3] The parties
differed in the fact that the Bramlette group was considered "entirely too subservient to Lincoln," while the Wickliffe group, bitter
in denouncing Lincoln, was the party for those "who were looking
for peace, and . . . who wished to register their protest against the
military régime and the various unpopular acts of the National administration." (It was said also to be the party "for those . . . who
favored secession, if any there should be," [4] but under all the circumstances the plain fact was that the secessionists had no ballot.)

Though Kentucky was predominantly Unionist (a fact which some
Kentuckians seem to have forgotten), the Republican party had virtually no existence in the state. The Negro question was highly difficult and embarrassing; the men of the Bluegrass still thought
unrealistically of conserving slavery, as of course they could do under
existing law. This commonwealth of Lincoln's birth had some of the
aspects of a region under military occupation. An *"unconditional
union man* a General Jackson Democrat" has been quoted as saying

---

[1] *Constitutional Problems Under Lincoln,* 171 ff.; E. M. Coulter, *Civil War and Re-
adjustment in Kentucky,* 177.

[2] Coulter, 177.          [3] *Ibid.,* 174.          [4] *Ibid.,* 174, 176.

that it would require tact and non-interference on the part of Federal officials to prevent a result in the state election that would be unfavorable to the Union Democrats. In the event of such an adverse result it was feared that a greatly increased Federal military force (the number 100,000 was even suggested) would be required "to hold the State." [5]

It was a light vote—a total of 85,000 as compared to 145,000 in the election of 1860—but, if the situation was not too closely analyzed, the figures looked well for the Union cause: 68,000 (round numbers) for Bramlette, 18,000 for Wickliffe.[6]

The peace party (one is using here the terminology of the time) took their defeat in bitter mood. They attributed it to flagrant military interference, but "It must . . . be remembered [writes E. M. Coulter] that many returned Confederates and Confederate sympathizers had counted on profiting by the profound discontent in the state and that precautions in the election were hence necessary." [7] Lincoln's special interest in the Kentucky outcome was shown in a letter to Mrs. Lincoln on August 8, 1863: "The election in Kentucky," he wrote, "has gone very strongly right." He added: "Old Mr. Wickliffe [well known in Kentucky in the days when Mary lived there] got ugly, as you know, ran for Governor, and is terribly beaten." Another well known Kentuckian, Brutus Clay, brother of Cassius, was, as Lincoln remarked, "largely elected" as a member of Congress.[8]

## IV

There were no state or congressional elections in Illinois or Indiana in 1863, but nowhere was politics more heated and furious. In Illinois the party wrangle led to the proroguing of the legislature. In Indiana there occurred a collapse of constitutional government, resulting in a remarkable dictatorship by Governor Morton.

From the beginning Indiana Democrats had continually declared that only a restoration of their party could preserve or restore the Union, while Hoosier Republicans, albeit with a "no party" front, sought persistently to seize a partisan monopoly of both Unionism and patriotism. In 1862 Republicanism was "repudiated" by Indi-

---

[5] *Ibid.*, 175–176.        [6] *Ibid.*, 178.        [7] *Ibid.*
[8] Lincoln to his wife, Aug. 8, 1863, R. T. L. Coll., 25444.

ana voters. By an election in October of that year the Democrats triumphed largely as to state officials, congressmen, and members of the legislature.[1]

There followed a battle royal, leading to utter deadlock between the Republican governor, Oliver P. Morton, and the Democratic legislature. Morton was both a vigorous and a party-minded executive. He labored tirelessly for the war effort and for Indiana soldiers, but Democrats, and some Republicans, were irked by his habit of appropriating to himself too exclusively the sure-fire credit of being the "soldiers' friend." In the brief 1863 session of the legislature (January to March) each party was set to outmaneuver the other, with the result that the Democrats overplayed their hand and the Republicans, though in a minority, came through with the main advantage.

Though the Democrats had a majority in both houses, the Republicans wielded a powerful weapon of obstruction, since under the state constitution the session was limited to sixty-one days, no law could be enacted without a quorum, and that quorum was defined as two-thirds of each house. Indignant at Morton, who was treating the major party as a group of traitors, the Democrats sought to push through a series of bills to set up an executive council, reorganize the militia, and otherwise reduce the governor's power. The Republicans retaliated with a party bolt, absenting themselves from the legislature and leaving the majority powerless for lack of a quorum. Under these circumstances of complete frustration the session ended in early March with no appropriations and no revenue measures passed; there would not be another legislative session until January of 1865.

Throughout the rest of 1863 and all of 1864 the state of Indiana presented the spectacle of a virtual gubernatorial dictatorship. Kenneth Stampp refers to the situation correctly as "the collapse of constitutional government." [2] Disregarding the constitution and ignoring state officials such as treasurer and auditor, Morton practically took over the government, organized a bureau of finance, borrowed money on his own assurances, obtained loans from bankers, paid in-

---

[1] Typical Democratic majorities in Indiana in 1862 were: for secretary of state, 9500; total popular votes for congressmen, over 11,000. The Democrats elected seven members of the House of Representatives, the Republicans, four. Some of the voting was close, but in certain districts the Democrats had majorities from two to four thousand.

[2] Kenneth M. Stampp, *Indiana Politics during the Civil War*, chap. viii.

terest on the state debt, and enlisted the financial support of the Federal government.[3] It happened that Congress, with no thought of subsidizing a state government, had passed a statute appropriating $2,000,000 to be spent at the President's discretion in supplying arms and other aid to citizens of states where rebellion existed or was threatened. Since there was talk, or rumor, in Indiana that rebels would seize the government,[4] the congressional statute was stretched to cover the Hoosier emergency, and an order was issued by President Lincoln advancing $250,000, one-eighth of the total appropriation, to Morton, who was made accountable for the sum; he used $160,000 of it to pay interest on the state debt—i. e., on his own borrowings. The honesty and serious public purpose of the governor were evident, but here was a case where public funds were paid out from the United States treasury, without an appropriation for the special purpose, in order to assist a state whose financial system had broken down. By these and other measures the Morton administration succeeded in tiding over the emergency until in 1865 the legality of these proceedings was established by a Republican legislature. In the long run it was Morton and the Republicans who came out ahead.

It was, of course, a situation which ought never to have occurred. Party wrangling is not government. It was not true, as the Republicans would have it believed, that Indiana Democrats were traitors. Far from it. Though there were extremists in the state, and though there was "Copperhead" activity eventuating in the Milligan case, the careful study by Kenneth Stampp reveals that Republican rumors— as to the Democratic party conspiring to seize the arsenal, free Confederate prisoners, inaugurate a revolution, et cetera—were without substantial basis. Democrats held mass meetings and jubilees, as-

---

[3] When Morton was conferring with Lincoln and Stanton in Washington, according to a story that has come down to us, Stanton was told that Lincoln knew of no law by which Federal financial aid could be extended to Indiana. To this the secretary of war is said to have replied: "By God, I will find a law." W. D. Foulke, *Life of Oliver P. Morton*, I, 261.

[4] These rumors, sedulously cultivated by Republicans, had reached Lincoln's ears. In a conversation with Senators Hale of New Hampshire and Browning of Illinois on January 9, 1863, he mentioned that the Democratic party in Illinois and Indiana "was talking of a union with the lower Mississippi states." Browning, *Diary*, I, 611. At a time when the Indianapolis *Journal* (Republican) "saw a conspiracy in every Democratic move, a rebel plot in every criticism of war policy," Morton had telegraphed Stanton (January 3, 1863) that the Indiana legislature intended to recognize the Confederacy and urge the Northwest to dissolve all constitutional relations with the New England states. Stampp, 167; *Offic. Rec.*, 1 ser., XX, pt. 2, 297.

sailed Morton and Lincoln, opposed Burnside's militarism, criticized
the extralegal Republican regime in their state, applauded Vallandigham, denounced arrests, and in times of military gloom urged
pacification and armistice. Stampp, however, shows that, though "Republicans sought to misconstrue their purpose into a disloyal desire,"
the emphasis of peace men was upon "the nation's integrity." "Most
Democrats," he writes, "never repudiated the war, but even those
who did, generally favored only peace *and* Union." [5]

Times were changing, and much of the Democratic resentment
was epitomized in the stirring personality of Daniel Voorhees who,
like other "Jacksonian agrarians," resented current movements tending to "political and economic revolution." [6] It was, of course, a shameful misrepresentation that only Republicans in Indiana were loyal
to their country. "Even in 1863," writes Stampp, "most Democrats
continued to support the war and believe that only its vigorous prosecution could restore the Union." Governor Morton admitted that
southern Indiana (overwhelmingly Democratic) was the most loyal
part of the state, and the Indianapolis *Sentinel,* Democratic to excess, "spoke often for the suppression of the rebellion by force of
arms." [7]

Indiana Democrats were not all of one faction. Some were like
Senator Jesse Bright, some like Douglas. There were many thousands of Democratic enlistments, and men such as Voorhees did not
fail to vote for supplies to sustain the army. They naturally could
not accept the idea that Indianians in service were Morton's soldiers
only. They saw real menace in the deliberate efforts to work up
party feeling among Indiana troops, who were induced to pass angry
resolutions and to threaten marching back and suppressing "treason" at home. This smacked too much of making the army the agent
of a party, and earnest men could be pardoned for real alarm at
"threats of military intervention in civil government." [8]

## V

In Lincoln's own state the year 1863, though an off-year for elections, was a period of hot and furious political agitation. Hatred of

----

5 Stampp, 162.        6 *Ibid.,* 152, 211.        7 *Ibid.,* 210–211.
8 *Ibid.,* 175–176.

Lincoln's administration flared ominously in the North, and the word "Copperhead" sprang readily to the tongue. Many factors were working together. Friendship toward Southerners, defeatism, disgust toward a war which was considered a failure—all these elements, together with motives called "political," were operating to consolidate the opposition to Lincoln into what was coming to be known as a "peace party." Illinois was no exception to the statement that the election of 1862 in the Middle West had been a sharp blow to Lincoln's administration and an encouragement to his foes.[1] Under the ordeal of war this middle area had revealed itself as two sections (at least two): the prairie and lake regions farther north constituted a division distinct from the older areas of Egypt, Cincinnati, and the Ohio River counties. One finds it hard, therefore, to generalize about the Middle West as if it presented a clear pattern. Yet, writes H. C. Hubbart, "taken as a whole it had repudiated its own greatest man, Abraham Lincoln, and his administration at the polls."[2]

On top of this came 1863, the year of the emancipation proclamation—a glorious event to many, but a divisive factor in the North. To this was added the habeas corpus controversy, conscription, Union defeat until July, intensified "Copperhead" activity, huge Vallandigham excitement, the Chicago *Times* affair, sharp controversy between Lincoln and Seymour, and peace talk focusing on Alexander H. Stephens.

While Lincoln's opponents were becoming more bold and vigorous, the administration was meeting the challenge by a lenient policy, releasing some who had been imprisoned, and thus becoming weaker by its very effort to avoid too despotic an appearance. There was somewhat of a dilemma as to releases. Where men were arbitrarily held as political prisoners, they were rallying cries for those who denounced the President as a tyrant and a denier of civil liberties. Let them be released, however (the release being a mere executive act without trial, the kind of thing the President or secretary of war could do "on his own"), and the former prisoner, now a hero, made the utmost capital of his sufferings as he traveled about, regaling large audiences with accounts of his experiences and with denunciations of "bastilles, . . . of despotism, desolation and death."[3] In either case, released

---

[1] *Lincoln the President*, II, 232–237.    [2] Hubbart, *The Older Middle West*, 190.
[3] *Ibid.*, 192.

or not, a man once arrested became an anti-Lincoln exhibit.

The overwrought wartime situation in Illinois was manifest in connection with the 1862 movement for a new state constitution. The constitutional convention elected for this purpose turned out to be fully under the control of the Democrats who made unwise use of a device of fundamental democracy which ought to have been above parties. The frame of government which the convention prepared, when submitted to popular vote, was defeated; one of the articles, however, prohibiting immigration of Negroes into the state, was overwhelmingly approved. This was at a time when Cairo witnessed the arrival of Negroes shipped by army officials from the South. As Republicans (some of them) urged farmers to employ this form of cheap labor, it became politically profitable to denounce the so-called "Africanization" of the state.[4] Lincoln might be freeing the slaves, but the people of his own state were decidedly not ready to receive free Negroes.

Lincoln was quoted as saying "that the democratic legislatures of Illinois & Indiana seemed bent upon mischief."[5] This was in January 1863. Governor Richard Yates of Illinois was like Morton of Indiana in Union loyalty, concern for soldiers, and party intensity. In Illinois the situation was constitutionally not so desperate as in Indiana, but the feuds of partisanship were equally as bitter. The bothersome anti-Yates and anti-Lincoln legislature proved so obnoxious to the Republicans that the legislators of that minority party withdrew so that a quorum was prevented. The business of legislation in the state was thus brought to a standstill, and Yates decided that he would prefer it so rather than yield to Democratic control. Finding a clause in the state constitution which had never been used before and has not been employed since, Yates declared the legislature prorogued. The two houses had disagreed on a matter of adjournment, and the governor, acting under article V, section 9, of the constitution of 1847, put an end to this session of the general assembly. Defending his action after the war, in a speech at Elgin, Illinois, on July 4, 1865, Yates explained that the enemy was fortified in the state house, that this enemy was starting "to run the government upon the . . . manner of the rebel states," and that under

[4] *Civil War and Reconstruction*, 601-602.   [5] Browning, *Diary*, I, 611 (Jan. 9, 1863).

these circumstances he called his staff into consultation and resolved to attack the enemy in his stronghold.⁶ There was thus, with
differing legal devices, a collapse of representative government both
in Indiana and Illinois. In each case it was the Republicans, with
minorities in the heat of controversy, that gained ascendancy.

On June 17, 1863, Democratic agitation reached its culmination
in a giant rally, a vast meeting held at Springfield. These great
popular meetings, or "conventions," had been a familiar device since
the days of Jackson. Those who attended this one, estimated at
40,000, had traveled long distances by a great variety of conveyances
as well as by foot. They listened to Democratic orators, such as Senator William A. Richardson of Illinois, the old veteran John Reynolds
who had been governor of Illinois in Black Hawk War days, Daniel
W. Voorhees, and S. S. Cox. The most famous action of this meeting
was the adoption of a resolution "in favor of peace upon the basis
of a restoration of the Union." For the accomplishment of this object, continued the resolution, "we propose a national convention to
settle upon the terms of peace, which shall have in view the restoration of the Union as it was, and the securing, by constitutional amendments, such rights to the several states and the people thereof as
honor and justice demand." ⁷

## VI

As a foil to all this activity the Union men of Illinois planned their
own huge demonstration. In August a call was issued to a mass assemblage to be held at Springfield on September 3, 1863. If only as
a spectacle and a diverting entertainment, such an occasion was calculated to attract immense attention, but this one was heavily
freighted with political interest. The call was for the "Unconditional
Union men of the State of Illinois, without regard to former party associations, who are in favor of a vigorous prosecution of the war
against this unholy and accursed rebellion." All such men were requested "to assemble together in a Grand Mass Meeting." Printed

⁶ This speech is quoted in Richard Yates (the younger), *Richard Yates, War Governor
of Illinois,* 24.
⁷ John Moses, *Biographical Dictionary . . . of the Representative Men of the United
States* (Illinois volume), 2d ed., II, 688; A. C. Cole, *Era of the Civil War,* 299–300; *Ill.
State Register,* June 18, 1863.

repeatedly in the *Illinois State Journal* (Republican organ), the call was underwritten by an impressive list of signers arranged by counties. The names included Governor Richard Yates, Jesse Dubois, Charles W. Matheny, Owen Lovejoy, W. H. Herndon, W. H. Bailhache, and many others. In an editorial when the call was launched the *Journal* fell easily into superlatives, remarking that it would "require no persistent drumming . . . to render it the largest and most imposing popular demonstration ever held in the State." [1] Day after day the advertisement of this monster meeting was continued. The people liked a show, they liked a state fair, which was to coincide with the great meeting, and they liked excursions. Passengers bound for the rally could obtain railroad tickets at half price.

For this occasion, planned well in advance, the President was invited to attend as the main speaker, not merely to give "a few appropriate remarks," as later at Gettysburg. The committee on arrangements was headed by Lincoln's Springfield friend, James C. Conkling, who had married Mary Todd's chum Mercy Levering. On August 14 Conkling wrote to the President, telling of the grand mass meeting of unconditional Union men and asking him to gratify, by his presence, the "many thousands" who would attend.[2] To this Lincoln replied by cipher telegram (August 20): "I think I will go, or send a letter—probably the latter." [3] Next day the *Journal* ran an article headed: "President Lincoln will Probably be Here." The paper was "happy to announce . . . that [in answer to the committee's invitation] President Lincoln has given assurances justifying a strong hope that he will be here."

It is doubtful whether the President seriously expected to attend the meeting, though his secretaries state that for a moment he "cherished the hope of going to Springfield, and once more in his life renewing the sensation, so dear to politicians, of personal contact with great and enthusiastic masses, and of making one more speech to shouting thousands . . . ." [4] Advance publicity, of course, required that the supposed probability of Lincoln's attendance should be overplayed. In this connection the *Journal* editorialized: "It is

---

[1] *Ill. State Jour.*, Aug. 17, 1863, p. 2, c. 3.
[2] R. T. L. Coll., 25601-2.
[3] Lincoln to Conkling, Aug. 20, 1863, photostat, A. Lincoln Assoc.
[4] Nicolay and Hay, *Lincoln*, VII, 379-380.

now two years and a half since Mr. Lincoln bade adieu to his friends
in Illinois to assume the vast responsibilities which attach to the office of President of the United States." There were words of eulogy
and a reference to the dark times of '61; then the editorial continued:
"Nothing could be more fitting . . . in this hour of national triumph and hope, than that he should visit his old home and receive
the greetings of his friends of the Prairie State." [5]

At about the same time the Washington correspondent of the New
York *Evening Post* wrote: "The President still resides at the Soldiers'
Home. Every evening at about six o'clock, he can be seen leaving
the Executive Mansion at the head of a mounted escort of 15 or 20
soldiers. The cares and responsibilities of his office are obviously
telling upon the health of the President. He looks thin and feeble,
and his eyes have lost their humorous expression. His friends entertain much solicitude about his health, and have endeavored to persuade him to leave Washington to recuperate, but so far the pilot
sticks to his helm, and does not seem disposed to leave it so long as
he has strength to hold it." [6] It was the hope of the editor of the
*Illinois State Journal* that these considerations of Lincoln's friends
"will be effectual in inducing him to be here on the 3d of September
next." [7]

The huge Springfield gathering was but one of the popular rallies
planned for this summer of 1863. There were small local ones, as at
Virginia, Illinois, on August 25, where the redoubtable Dr. Peter
Cartwright spoke of the "inconsistency of the Copperhead Democracy." [8] And in Indiana a big assemblage of "war Democrats" was
planned for August 20, for which such prominent speakers as Henry
S. Lane, Lewis Cass, John A. Logan, John A. McClernand, John

---

[5] *Ill. State Jour.*, Aug. 21, 1863, p. 2, c. 3.

[6] *Ibid.*, Aug. 22, 1863, p. 2, c. 1, quoting New York *Evening Post.*

[7] Editor's comment in the *Journal*, same issue.

[8] *Ill. State Jour.*, Sep. 2, 1863, p. 1, c. 2. Cartwright, Lincoln's opponent in the congressional election of 1846, took little active part in politics during the war, but there
were several instances of his making Union speeches. In 1862, in exhorting brother
preachers to sustain a church paper in St. Louis, he noted with commendation that its
editor "advocates gradual emancipation and colonization . . . till the dark, damning
sin of slavery is swept from our nation." *Central Christian Advocate* (St. Louis), May 15,
1862. The attitude of Cartwright was linked with that of Douglas. As the same editor
wrote, "we thank God for the patriotism of Mr. Douglas and Dr. Cartwright, and of all
others who are true to the Union of the United States." *Ibid.*, Jan. 8, 1863. On this matter
the author has been assisted by Theodore L. Agnew, Jr., of Stillwater, Oklahoma, who is
preparing a biography of Cartwright.

Brough, David Tod, James Guthrie, and Alvin P. Hovey, were announced as invited.

Meanwhile some of the plans of the so-called "Copperheads" had miscarried. A meeting of the grand castle of the K. G. C. was held at Chicago on August 4, attended by two delegates from each county containing as least one castle, said to be true of seventy-one counties. It leaked out, however, that "the Government had got hold of a member of the order and obtained such facts . . . as made it dangerous to transact any business." So all that was done was "to investigate the case of the supposed informer." It was reported that the knights returned to their castles "very much disappointed." [9]

The crescendo of excitement mounted as the day of the Union meeting approached. On September 2 loyal men were reported arriving in large numbers, with hotels overflowing and the people "determined to make the demonstration one which shall convince traitors abroad and sympathizers with traitors at home that the Government will be sustained and the rebellion crushed." "Partisanship," so ran the editorial of the *Journal*, "is discarded, and Democrats and Republicans will be found nobly burying their minor differences, and uniting heartily upon the platform of the Constitution and the Union." [10]

When the day arrived the editor wrote: "Thousands of loyal men will greet each other in the Capital of Illinois to-day. It is no ordinary occasion that calls them together. There is no election in immediate prospect—the interests of no particular candidate are to be urged or advanced. The object of the meeting . . . is to sustain the Government in the hour of its trial." The main issue was to defeat the effort to overthrow the government. "All minor issues should be forgotten." [11]

## VII

While the plans for the Springfield rally were proceeding Lincoln had to think of many things—serious military developments in Tennessee, difficulties in army command, draft troubles on many sides, foreign affairs, and problems of a peace drive that could neither be ignored nor trusted for a favorable result. Elections were yet to come

[9] *Ill. State Jour.*, Sep. 2, 1863.  [10] *Ibid.*, p. 2, c. 1.
[11] *Ibid.*, Thursday morning, Sep. 3, 1863. p. 2, c. 1.

in the most critical states; reconstruction efforts were afoot in the
South (especially in Louisiana and Tennessee); the President's unpublished opinion on the draft law was being carefully worked out;
the debate with Seymour of New York was growing more intense; and
the forces of Vallandighamism were working both openly and in
secret.

It was, and this was typical, a time of petty or nagging details along
with larger matters. What should be the compensation of Dr. Charles
M. Wetherill, chemist in the department of agriculture? What about
charges against (and by) John A. McClernand? How about the New
Almedan mine in California, also the California land claim of General Daniel E. Sickles? And what was to be done about the persistent
demand of Illinois that the Federal government refund to the state
"two per cent. on the sales of public lands," a claim which the President considered (at such a time) "ungracious." Nor could the President ignore the importance of notifying Mrs. Grimsley of Springfield
that he was "appointing Johnny to the Naval school." [1]

It was outrageous that the President's time had to be taken up
with all such details, but in following the daily course of the Lincoln
administration one needs constantly to bear in mind this persistent
pressure of the trivial, the personal, and the miscellaneous along
with grave and portentous problems of government.

In sending a letter to be read at the Springfield meeting,[2] Lincoln delivered by proxy what amounted to a political (though non-
partisan) address; it has been called his "last stump speech." [3] The sentences were short. The language was popular. There were applause
lines interspersed with reasoned arguments. There were in fact two
simultaneous letters to Conkling: the public letter to be read at
the grand rally, and a transmitting letter in which the President briefly
explained that he could not leave Washington, but added: "Herewith is a letter instead. You are one of the best public readers. I
have but one suggestion. Read it very slowly. And now God bless
you, and all good Union-men." [4] Lincoln wanted his absent per-

---

[1] Nicolay and Hay, *Works*, IX, *passim* (latter half of 1863).
[2] Paul Selby, "The Lincoln-Conkling Letter . . . An Explanation of Lincoln's Most
Famous Epistle," *Transactions*, Ill. State Hist. Soc., 1908, 240–250.
[3] Nicolay and Hay, *Works*, IX, 95 (footnote).
[4] Lincoln's letter to be read at the rally was dated August 26, 1863, his letter of trans-
mittal, August 27; photostats, A. Lincoln Assoc.

sonality and his message presented with due effect. He dated the letter August 26, but the matter remained in his mind, and five days later, thinking that the beneficial effect of the emancipation proclamation had not been sufficiently emphasized, he sent a third communication with an instruction for a substantial passage to be inserted.[5]

This Conkling letter belonged to presidential publicity on a national level. Lincoln was concerned not only as to the local occasion, which was no small factor; he was also interested in the wider reception in the press. It mortified him to find, on the day of the meeting, that the letter had been "botched up, in the Eastern papers." [6]

In the earlier portion of the address Lincoln was on the defensive, which shows how fully he was conscious of the criticism directed against his policy. There were those, he knew, who were dissatisfied with him. To them he put the question: You desire peace, but how can we obtain it? By three ways: (1) Suppress the rebellion by arms. That was what he was "trying to do." (2) Give up the Union. He said simply: "I am against this. Are you for it? If you are, you should say so plainly." (3) "If you are not for *force* [wrote the President], nor yet for *dissolution,* there only remains some imaginable *compromise.*" But, he said, the army was the strength of the rebellion: "no paper compromise to which the controllers of Lee's army [he meant the government at Richmond] are not agreed, can at all affect that army." He added: "In an effort at such compromise [with alleged negotiators who lacked full authority] we should waste time, which the enemy would improve to our disadvantage; and that would be all." He assured his hearers that no peace compromise had emanated "from that rebel army, or from any of the men controlling it." Insinuations to the contrary were "deceptive and groundless." He promised: "if any such proposition shall hereafter come, it shall not be rejected, and kept a secret from you." He was the servant of the people and responsible to them.

Still on the defensive, the President then passed to the controver-

---

[5] This communication giving a passage to be inserted has been preserved in several forms: Lincoln's autograph (original at Brown Univ.); office copy in R. T. L. Coll., 25933-4; and the telegram as received (original in Ill. State Hist. Lib.).

[6] Lincoln to Conkling, Sep. 3, 1863, photostat, A. Lincoln Assoc.

sial subject of the Negro; this he did with full awareness of the difficulty of that subject in Illinois and elsewhere. Here he differed with
his "dissatisfied" friends. "I certainly wish that all men could be free,"
he wrote, "while I suppose you do not." He then launched into an
argument on emancipation. He denied that his proclamation was
unconstitutional (though this had been argued by so distinguished a
man as the former justice of the Supreme Court, Benjamin R. Curtis).[7]

Then he said: "Some of you profess to think its retraction would
operate favorably for the Union. Why better *after* the retraction, than
*before* the issue? There was more than a year and a half of trial to
suppress the rebellion before the proclamation issued, the last one
hundred days of which passed under an explicit notice that it was
coming, unless averted by those in revolt, returning to their allegiance.
The war has certainly progressed as favorably for us, since the issue of
the proclamation as before."

It was at this point that Lincoln, by a subsequent telegram, inserted
a passage showing the effect of the proclamation on the progress of
the war. Some of the commanders, he said, "believe the emancipation
policy, and the use of the colored troops, constitute the heaviest blow
yet dealt to the rebellion." "Among the commanders holding these
views," he added, "are some who have never had any affinity with what
is called abolitionism, or with republican party politics; but who hold
them purely as military opinions. I submit these opinions as being entitled to some weight against the objections, often urged, that emancipation, and arming the blacks, are unwise as military measures, and
were not adopted, as such, in good faith."

"You say you will not fight to free negroes," wrote Lincoln. "Some
of them seem willing to fight for you; but, no matter." This was a
justifiable thrust. It was also a deserved tribute to the colored race,
emerging into the status of free men willing to bear the burdens that
went with their new-found dignity. "Fight you, then," wrote Lincoln,
"exclusively to save the Union. I issued the proclamation on purpose
to aid you in saving the Union. Whenever you shall have conquered
all resistance to the Union, if I shall urge you to continue fighting,

----

[7] *Lincoln the President*, II, 175–176.

it will be an apt time then for you to declare you will not fight to free negroes."

Was this a suggestion that emancipation was not one of Lincoln's war aims? Did it mean that emancipation might be dropped if the Union were made secure? Should it not rather be read in the light of the President's main argument—that, as of 1863, emancipation was vitally important for the Union and the Union for emancipation? The next passage clarified the point. Negroes, he said, "like other people, act upon motives." "Why should they do any thing for us, if we will do nothing for them? If they stake their lives for us, they must be prompted by the strongest motive—even the promise of freedom. And the promise being made, must be kept."

At this point in the Springfield letter it was as if a composer had changed the movement of a symphony. A different note was struck. After all, this was a Union meeting. It was time that an affirmative word should be said for the national cause. "The signs look better," wrote the President. "The Father of Waters again goes unvexed to the sea. Thanks to the great North West for it. Nor yet wholly to them. Three hundred miles up, they met New-England, Empire, Key Stone, and Jersey, hewing their way right and left. . . . The job was a great national one; and let none be banned who bore an honorable part in it. . . . Nor must Uncle Sam's Web-feet be forgotten. At all the watery margins they have been present. Not only on the deep sea, the broad bay, and the rapid river; but also up the narrow muddy bayou, and wherever the ground was a little damp, they have been, and made their tracks. Thanks to all. For the great republic— for the principle it lives by, and keeps alive—for man's vast future— thanks to all."

Then he closed: "Peace does not appear so distant as it did. I hope it will come soon, and come to stay; and so come as to be worth the keeping in all future time. It will then have been proved that, among free men, there can be no successful appeal from the ballot to the bullet; and that they who take such appeal are sure to lose their case, and pay the cost." Here he had a word for colored men who with steady eye and well-poised bayonet had helped mankind on to this great consummation, and white ones who had hindered it. He continued: "Let us be quite sober. Let us diligently apply the means, never doubting

that a just God, in his own good time, will give us the rightful result." [8]

On the day after the huge Springfield meeting Lincoln's friend
Conkling wrote a letter to the President. "Our Mass Meeting," he
reported, "was a magnificent success. I should judge there were
50 000 to 75 000 present, and the largest meeting by far that ever assembled together in the State. Doolittle, Lane Chandler and Oglesby
delivered splendid speeches. Seven stands were used during the day
and on the most of them speaking continued without intermission
from 11 o'clock to 5 P M. The most unbounded enthusiasm prevailed.
The speeches were of the most earnest, radical and progressive character and the people applauded most vociferously every sentiment in
favor of the vigorous prosecution of the war until the rebellion was
subdued—the Proclamation of Emancipation and the arming of negro soldiers and every allusion to yourself and your policy." [9]

Not once in his Springfield letter did Lincoln claim credit for his
party or use the language of partisanship. At the beginning he had
addressed his "old political friends" and "those other noble men whom
no partizan malice or partizan hope can make false to the nation's life."
The call for the meeting had been to Union men "without regard to
party associations." It has already been seen how the *Journal* declared
that partisanship had been "discarded" and "minor differences" (between Republicans and Democrats) buried.

Yet mass meetings of this sort, in which Democratic participation
was sought and obtained, were unhesitatingly used for Republican
advantage. It was realized that effort in prosecuting the war, as well
as ultimate victory in the war, however much it might be unpartisan
in the factors and elements contributing to it, would inure to the
benefit of the party in power. The name "Union" was appropriated
and used for Republican triumph. Such was always the purpose of
the Union League. And along with this there was the growing tendency to refer to Democrats as if they were the "peace party," the
party of disloyalty, and of "Copperheads." This is not said lightly.
It is unmistakably evident in the record of those times.

---

[8] For the letter to Conkling, Aug. 26, 1863, Lincoln's autograph draft has been followed
(R. T. L. Coll., 25846–54); comparison with the letter as sent, in copyist's hand, shows
only negligible variations (MS., Ill. State Hist. Lib.).

[9] James C. Conkling to Lincoln, Sep. 4, 1863, R. T. L. Coll., 26041.

This attitude was carried forward into later decades and became the pattern of Republican history writing. As to this very Springfield meeting, loudly advertised as including all Union men regardless of party, Nicolay and Hay wrote: "The meeting was an extraordinary one . . . ; it was addressed by the greatest orators of the Republican party; . . . . The speeches were marked by the most advanced and unflinching Republican doctrine; . . . and . . . every reference to Mr. Lincoln's name was received with thunders of applause . . . ." Having thus characterized it as a party meeting, which was the very opposite of its declared purpose, Nicolay and Hay wrote: "In this spirit the campaign [i. e., the party struggle in certain states] was fought through to its victorious close." They added: ". . . in this memorable contest the Republicans presented a united front to the common enemy . . . ." [10]

That common enemy—the Democratic party, as Nicolay and Hay understood it—was finding it hard to maintain itself as a party of opposition and at the same time promote the war for the Union. If it was a matter of party advantage—strictly that—they were as much entitled to it as the Republicans, but the wartime dilemma of the Democrats was obvious. As a writer of the time put it, "It does seem to me the most obvious folly . . . for an opposition to suppose that it can sustain the prominent measures of the party in power, without its support enuring to the benefit of that party altogether. . . . Common sense people at once say 'Will you uphold the main policy of the administration, why not let us vote for it . . . in preference to you, if we desire the spoils?' " [11] In reading this comment on a well recognized situation, one is led to the reflection that when great matters are at issue there is something essentially inadequate in the party motive. If men of differing political opinions pull together for the common cause, there is injustice in the two facts that the "ins" must gain party advantage, and the "outs" lose it, because of the common effort. If the occasion requires that partisanship be set aside in the interest of broader motives, the people and the leaders should make it so.

---

10 Nicolay and Hay, *Lincoln*, VII, 380, 386, 388. Writing in the 1880's as Republicans, Nicolay and Hay showed a partisanship that was notably lacking in Lincoln's letter.

11 James B. Walle to William Henry Hurlbut of New York, Burlington, Vt., no date (probably 1864), S. L. M. Barlow MSS.

# CHAPTER XI

# VALLANDIGHAM FOR GOVERNOR: FURTHER PHASES OF POLITICS, 1863

## I

THOUGH citizens and soldiers in many states were balloting in 1863, and though all the votes were important, the most outstanding of these contests was in Ohio, where the Democratic campaign was pointed directly against Lincoln and where Vallandigham himself was candidate for governor. It would indeed have been a sensational occurrence had he been popularly chosen to that office. All the excitement and bitter resentment concerning military rule, arbitrary arrests, the "Vallandigham case," the quarrel with Seymour, the suppression of the Chicago *Times,* and the government's war policy were concentrated in the furious Ohio campaign.

When the Democratic state convention met at Columbus on June 11 the Vallandigham excitement was at its highest, the military situation prior to Gettysburg was full of gloom and uncertainty, and the agitation against conscription was vocal and menacing. It was a time when military measures *at home* were receiving special emphasis, as it was supposed on the one side that methods of free government were being cast aside, and on the other hand that subversive secret societies were seeking to undermine the army and leave the Union without adequate defense. These factors were associated with a peace drive which, though offering nothing for Union advantage, made its appeal to war-sick millions.

In its voluminous resolutions the Ohio Democratic convention expressed itself with strong indignation. The Democratic party, they declared, was the law-abiding party, favoring guarantees of public and private liberty. Their plea was for things which the American people held fundamental: free thought, free speech, and free government by the people's will. The emancipation proclamation, they protested, was unwise, unconstitutional, and void. Powers assumed by the President under the guise of military necessity were unwarranted. The arrest of Vallandigham "for no other pretended crime than . . . uttering . . . legitimate criticism upon the . . . Administration in power" was a "palpable violation" of the Constitution. Said arrest, furthermore, was "a direct insult offered to the sovereignty of the people of Ohio." It was an "unmerited imputation upon their intelligence and loyalty." At the time of the arrest Vallandigham was "a prominent candidate" for the Democratic nomination as governor [i. e., prominently considered; he was not yet nominated]. The Democratic party was "fully competent to decide whether he was a fit man for that nomination." [1]

The nomination of Vallandigham was unanimous by acclamation. By this act the Democratic convention was asking the people of Ohio to elect as their governor the man who, besides being probably the most famous and outspoken of Lincoln's critics in the North, was under sentence of a military commission which had found him guilty of aiding and encouraging the enemy, and of inducing in his hearers "a distrust of their own Government, sympathy for those in arms against it and a disposition to resist the laws of the land." [2]

It was conceivable that this Democratic politician could have been confined in Fort Warren or some other fortress of the United States and chosen governor of Ohio while so imprisoned. Instead of that, he was named as a candidate while in exile. His dramatic absence as a Federal prisoner-of-state under banishment added greatly to his importance, so much so that the people were moved more by sympathy for him as a "case" for civil rights than by agreement with his sentiments. This situation was illustrated when George Ellis Pugh, a Democrat who had resisted the extreme proslavery element of his party at Charleston in 1860, spoke in Vallandigham's stead, accepting the nomination for him. Pugh was not fully "a Vallandigham

---

[1] The convention that nominated Vallandigham met on June 11. He had been arrested on May 5, tried on May 6–7, and sentenced on May 7. For the resolutions see McPherson, *Hist. of the Rebell.*, 167–168.

[2] See the specifications, findings, and sentence of the military commission. *Offic. Rec.*, 2 ser. V, 635, 646.

man," since he had disagreed with the agitator as to procedures in deciding upon peace. Yet he considered the civil rights issue so important that he made "a speech many times more violent than any of Vallandigham's utterances," [3] for which he was not arrested. After this he was nominated on the Vallandigham ticket as lieutenant governor.

Out of this meeting there came a formal protest to the President, submitted by a committee of the convention, consisting of M. Birchard, Alexander Long, George H. Pendleton, and other Ohio Democrats. In a letter to the President, June 26, they "most respectfully" submitted the resolutions of their convention which, they said, was "one of the most earnest and sincere, in support of the Constitution and the Union, ever held in that State." Not "as a favor" but "as a right due to an American citizen" they prayed the President for "the revocation of the order banishing Mr. Vallandigham," whose arrest, trial, and exile had "created wide-spread and alarming disaffection among the people of the State, . . . impairing . . . confidence in the fidelity of your Administration to . . . free government . . . ." Noting that the President had been distressed at Vallandigham's arrest, the committee assured him that the public safety would be "far more endangered by continuing Mr. Vallandigham in exile than by releasing him."

The Birchard committee developed their argument at great length, using for the purpose the President's own letter on the same subject to the Albany committee.[4] Admitting that Vallandigham may have differed "with the President, and even with some of his own political party," they urged that this did not prove him unfaithful as an American citizen. They reminded the President that, during the Mexican War, opponents of the administration then in power opposed and denounced the war, which they declared to be unjust and unholy. With as much reason, they thought, as in Vallandigham's case, it might have been said of these opponents of President Polk that their discussions were calculated "to discourage enlistments, . . . to induce desertions . . . and leave the Government without an adequate military force to carry on the war."

They then touched upon Lincoln's answer to Corning. The Presi-

---

[3] G. H. Porter, *Ohio Politics during the Civil War Period*, 171.
[4] See above, pp. 226–228.

dent had admitted that if making a public speech were Vallandig-ham's only crime, the arrest was wrong, but had argued that his of-fense was more than that; he was laboring to prevent the raising of troops and to leave the rebellion without any adequate military force to suppress it. "He was warring upon the military, and this gave the military constitutional jurisdiction to lay hands on him." The com-mittee argued that, if any one was discouraged from enlisting because of hearing Vallandigham's "views as to the policy of the war as a means of restoring the Union," and if Vallandigham was rightly subject to punishment on that account, then "upon the same grounds every political opponent of the Mexican war might have been convicted and banished from the country." (It was plainly implied, though not stated, that this would have included Lincoln himself.) After dis-cussing habeas corpus, arrests, and summary trials, the committee put the President in the role of an unconstitutional ruler. Banishment, they urged, was "unknown to our laws"; they could not see the Presi-dent's right to prescribe this, or torture upon the rack, or other un-usual punishments.[5]

## II

Lincoln was prompt and courteous in his reply to this Ohio com-mittee. He began by referring the protesting gentlemen to his Albany letter which, he noted, had been used by the committee itself. On the Mexican War question, though reluctant "to waste a word on a merely personal point," he denied that he had "opposed, in discus-sion before the people, the policy of the Mexican war." It was only by implication that the committee was bringing Lincoln's own at-titude of 1848 into the picture. They were pointing to the analogy between Vallandigham and the opponents of Polk's war policy. To mention the analogy was natural enough, but Lincoln, taking it as an accusation pointed at himself, answered it by denying that he had opposed the Mexican War in popular discussion. Lincoln's state-ments, of course, had been made in Congress.

Ohio opponents of the war policy of 1863 could hardly have been impressed by this argument. Lincoln in 1846–48 would have re-

---

[5] For the letter from the Birchard committee, see McPherson, *Rebellion*, 167–170; R. T. L. Coll., 24427–49.

sented it if his Whig friends—e. g., Thomas Corwin of Ohio or Daniel Webster of Massachusetts—had been imprisoned or banished for denouncing the Mexican War, whether in Congress or elsewhere. After treating the attitude and speeches of such men, the historian of the Mexican War writes: "Going far beyond the limits of reasonable criticism and helpful suggestions, and indulging in language calculated to dishearten and hamper the administration, they encouraged the enemy." [1] It must be added that many thoughtful, upright, and patriotic men in the time of Polk agreed with critics of the war against Mexico. Abolitionists did so with unanimity. It was a subject of complexities and difficulties, not a theme that lent itself to easy elaboration either for the President's purpose or otherwise. Lincoln knew that he had to touch it lightly.

The President then launched into a considerable discussion of the habeas corpus privilege under the Constitution and of the authority to suspend it. "You claim," he wrote, "that men may . . . embarrass those whose duty it is to combat a giant rebellion, and then be dealt with in turn, only as if there were no rebellion. The Constitution itself rejects this view. The military arrests . . . which have been made . . . have been for prevention, and not for punishment—as injunctions to stay injury, as proceedings to keep the peace . . . . The original sentence of imprisonment in Mr. Vallandigham's case was to prevent injury to the military service only and the modification of it was made as a less disagreeable mode to him of securing the same prevention."

The President was "unable to perceive an insult to Ohio in the case of Mr. Vallandigham," being quite sure "nothing of the sort was or is intended." He had been unaware that the gentleman was, when arrested, a candidate for the Democratic nomination for governor. He was grateful to Ohio "for many things, especially for the brave soldiers and officers she has given in the present national trial to the armies of the Union."

On the main question—Vallandigham's injury to the national cause—the President gave a convincing statement. He did not know that the orator had "by direct language advised against enlistments and in favor of desertion and resistance to drafting." But all knew,

---

[1] Justin H. Smith, *The War With Mexico*, II, 280. Since Webster has been mentioned, it may be added that Major Edward Webster, his son, died in service near Mexico City.

he said, that combinations for that purpose existed "and that quite a number of assassinations have occurred from the same animus." This maiming and murder the President solemnly declared to be due to Vallandigham's course "in greater degree than to any other cause; and . . . to him in a greater degree than to any other one man." (Vallandigham was, in fact, to become early in 1864 supreme commander of the Sons of Liberty, this being the new name of the grandiloquent Order of American Knights, an organization similar to the Knights of the Golden Circle.) The whole burden of Vallandigham's speeches was to stir up men's minds against the prosecution of the war.

This, the President pointed out, was the man nominated for governor by the Ohio Democratic convention, while in their statement they showed no awareness of an existing rebellion. Since their nominee was known to have opposed using the army to suppress the rebellion, Lincoln wrote to the committee: "Your own attitude . . . encourages desertion . . . and the like . . . ." Such an attitude, he considered "a real strength to the enemy." The position of the Ohio men being a good deal weaker as to sustaining the Union than that of the Albany men, the President sought to pin them down, or to elicit a simple pledge. Would they sign their names as endorsing three propositions? If so, he promised Vallandigham's release. In brief these propositions were: (1) that there was in existence a rebellion to destroy the Union for whose suppression the army and navy were the constitutional means; (2) that they would not hinder the increase of the army or navy or lessen their efficiency; (3) that each of them in his sphere would labor to have the officers and men of the forces paid, fed, provided for, and supported. Let them sign these statements and their banished friend would be released.[2]

These signatures were not forthcoming. The purpose of the committee was to make a party issue against the President, to put him in the wrong, not to have him set up the conditions of Vallandigham's release or state the terms by which they should put themselves in the right. So they sent another letter, expressing surprise at the President's suggestions. The people of Ohio, they wrote, were concerned not so much because of Vallandigham's safety as because they visioned

---

[2] Lincoln to M. Birchard and Others, Nicolay and Hay, *Works,* IX, 1–10 (June 29, 1863). This text differs but slightly and not significantly from Lincoln's autograph draft (R. T. L. Coll., 24494–506).

an attack upon their own rights. They wanted his release as "an abandonment of the claim to the power of such arrest and banishment." However much the committee might feel inclined to endorse the President's propositions, they had no authority to bargain as to the conditions of release. Their pro-Union views were well known, but they resented the demand for a pledge which they regarded as an imputation upon their sincerity, as a concession of the legality of this instance of arrest, trial, and banishment. They asked the revocation of the order "not as a favor, but as a right due to the people of Ohio." The President's suggestion, they thought, was "a mere evasion," the more so as his letter had ended with an intimation that the presidential acts complained of might be repeated.[3]

Thus ended, with forensic banners waving on both sides, the Lincoln-Birchard debate. Both sides had appealed to high principles and neither side had given in. Ohio friends of Vallandigham were invoking time-honored traditions as if no desperate emergency existed and as if the processes of peace were appropriate to a tremendous civil war. They had a strong talking point in their stressing of civil rights, but they were unsatisfactory in their assumption that Vallandigham was doing no injury to the nation. As to this very question of civil rights they would have been in a stronger position had it not been that in previous years Ohio Democrats, though they were not the only ones, had scornfully denied basic rights to antislavery agitators. Toward such agitators they had been far indeed from allowing freedom of speech, of the press, of petition, of academic teaching, and the like.[4]

Lincoln was convincing in his insistence that the effect of Vallandighamism was to aid the enemy, but he was greatly embarrassed by Burnside's measures of which he did not approve. He would not have ordered Vallandigham's arrest and he promptly revoked the general's order suppressing the Chicago *Times*. He was ready to release Vallandigham, realizing that the "case" had given a handle to his critics and a continuing theme for denouncing his administra-

---

[3] The President had closed his Birchard letter as follows: "Still, in regard to Mr. Vallandigham and all others, I must hereafter, as heretofore, do so much as the public safety may seem to require." Nicolay and Hay, *Works*, IX, 10. For the Ohio committee's rejoinder, see McPherson, 172–175.

[4] These startling attacks upon civil rights and free expression of opinion are treated in Russell Nye, *Fettered Freedom*.

tion; but he realized that such release, if interpreted as a weakening of the military authority, would be an added embarrassment. Weighing one factor against another, the President stood ready to agree to the release, but he wanted some compensating assurance on the part of those who were making capital of what they were denouncing. He did not, of course, honestly intend that men should be imprisoned for criticising him—that was so evident that it hardly needed assurance—but he did believe, in a desperate civil war, that military arrests were a proper and constitutional emergency measure to prevent those activities behind the lines which injured the national cause and gave substantial aid and comfort to the enemy. It was not so much that he was prosecuting these men; he was intending to take such temporary measures as would "stay injury."

There was one point in the case which Lincoln left unstated. He said in the Birchard letter that, under the conditions indicated, the "order" as to Vallandigham would be revoked. This must have referred to the President's order of banishment. The assumption was, of course, that this would have allowed Vallandigham to go free. Then what about the sentence of imprisonment imposed by the military commission? In the 1863 situation—as also in the later action (or non-action) of the Supreme Court—there was nothing in law to check the enforcement of that military sentence. The President had the authority to set aside the sentence of a military commission if he thought best, but there was another way out, and in the Birchard letter Lincoln indicated that already, nearly at the outset of the case, his mind was disposed toward what was actually allowed to happen next year—i. e., to permit the sentence to become a dead letter. The order of banishment had provided reimprisonment according to the sentence of the military commission in case of Vallandigham's unauthorized return. For the prisoner to go free, it would have been expected that this part of the order as well as the banishment would be revoked if the prescribed conditions were met. Actually to have revoked the order or the sentence, however, especially in view of the obvious fact that it was proving an embarrassment to the government rather than an effective treatment for an ugly situation, would have been distasteful, and would have produced trouble in the war department. Publicity favorable to the Albany and Columbus committees was not the only kind to consider, for there were voices equally strong on the other side. After the imbroglio had developed as it did in 1863, there was no perfect solution. Realizing this, Lincoln looked the other way when, later, the notorious prisoner escaped and reappeared in the United States. The President did nothing, thus disregarding both the presidential order and the military sentence.[5] It was as if he had said: Here is that Vallandigham again—he's back. So what? Let him talk.

For the Ohioan's exile was brief. On July 5, two months after his arrest, he was reported as arriving at Halifax, N.S. He had escaped through the blockade to the British West Indies, whence he had sailed to Nova Scotia. On July 15, 1863, from Niagara Falls on the Canadian side just across the United States border, he vigorously entered the political campaign with an address to the people of Ohio. Recounting his hazards by land and sea, he declared that he found himself first a freeman when on British soil; under the British flag he enjoyed the rights which "usurpers insolently" denied him at home. "I return," he said, "with my opinions and convictions . . . not only unchanged, but confirmed and strengthened." It was not, in its wording, an anti-Union address, but rather a lofty political battle cry for liberty, popular government, and freedom of speech. Strongly denouncing the "party of the Administration," he warned that whoever voted its ticket would "forfeit his own right to liberty, personal and political, whensoever other men and another party shall hold the power." [6] (He was talking to the theme of freedom of speech, but this threat did not sound very much like freedom of voting.)

## III

Not all the Ohio Democrats approved of Vallandigham. A small group known as "War Democrats" convened at Columbus on September 22 and took a stand declaring the nomination of Vallandigham a mistake and opposing any kind of peace except one that re-

---

[5] In a speech at Peru, Indiana, in the summer of 1864, Schuyler Colfax gave his interpretation of Lincoln's reason for not arresting Vallandigham on his return in 1864. According to Colfax, though not knowing "the details" of the movement, the President was aware of a dangerous secret conspiracy in the Northwest, and "knew the intention was to make Vallandigham's arrest a pretext for lighting the torch of civil war all over the Northwest." (This theory seems inconsistent with the fact that Lincoln never approved of the arrest at any time.) Buffalo *Morning Express*, Sep. 2, 1864, p. 2, c. 2.

[6] Frank Moore, ed., *Rebell. Rec.* (Docs.), VII, 438–439.

quired "unconditional submission to the Constitution and laws of the United States." [1] The effect of this splinter party was negligible. The Ohio Democratic banner had been appropriated by the Vallandigham forces. Managing politicians had put the party in a position which did not genuinely reflect the views of its supporters. Many Democrats resented this in 1863, just as millions of Democrats were to find bitter reason to resent the Vallandigham stigma in 1864.

Vallandigham's opponent, John Brough, "Union" candidate for governor of Ohio, was a Democrat, known not as a politician but as a business man, journalist, and orator. The campaign was spirited and angry. The Vallandigham men played their highest card—the issue of civil rights—but they overplayed their hand in announcing that in case of their hero's election a huge force of armed men would "receive their Governor-elect at the Canadian line and escort him to the State House to see that he takes the oath of office."

This bit of sensational theatrics was as badly misplayed as the statement by Daniel Voorhees of Indiana promising that such a move would be supported by the Democrats of his state. [2] These tactics enabled Brough's party to predict that Vallandigham's election would produce civil war in Ohio. Not that this was likely, any more than that Vallandigham's men, if victorious in the election, would have invited support in terms of a Confederate invasion of the state. Such things belong in the category of melodramatic predictions and are to be set down to the sometimes incredible and irresponsible intensity of political campaigning. There was enough reason for opposing Vallandigham without supposing that civil war within the state or a shift of allegiance of the whole commonwealth would have been the result if he had been chosen governor by a majority of Ohio voters. Predictions of this sort, however, did harm to the Democratic cause and probably added considerably to the vote for Brough. Just what "would have" been the result if Vallandigham had been elected can only be a matter of conjecture. As governor of a Union state, with actual responsibilities of office, he would have been less free to agitate than as a politician out of office. Perhaps he would have become simply a more vociferous Seymour. Yet with his record and personality, different from Seymour's, he would have been a menace to the cause for which Lincoln worked.

---

[1] Porter, *Ohio Politics*, 181.          [2] *Ibid.*, 182.

In commenting on the Ohio contest the *Republican* of St. Louis noted a curious fact: "neither of the candidates for Governor represents the party nominating him. Brough claims to be a Democrat, and in his speeches pretends that he has never left that party. The Democratic party of Ohio generally repudiate the doctrines of Vallandigham, so far as they relate to the war and . . . its prosecution." It was added that sympathy because of his arrest was the reason for the famous agitator's nomination.[3]

This somewhat confused situation as to candidates, labels, and organizations should not be taken as indication that party differences were being erased in Ohio. The "Union" party in that state was essentially the Republican party, while in the accounts of the time the group that nominated Vallandigham was regularly called the Democratic party. Thus the fact that many Democrats supported Brough, himself a "war Democrat," and the further fact that without such support Vallandigham would not have been defeated, never redounded to the advantage of the Democratic organization. It was quite the contrary. Democratic votes helped strongly to produce an election result which, *as interpreted in the party sense,* assisted only the Republicans.

One could, of course, speak of the Union cause, and Democrats did that; but it could not be overlooked that the word "Union" was appropriated for a party. It was not as if the Republican party had been abandoned, as if a new star had arisen in the party firmament, or as if a new political body, neutral in the party sense, had been created. One could not say that a Democratic-Republican organization, with dual party machinery working toward a strictly bipartisan effect, and with equal importance for both Democrats and Republicans under the combined name of "Union," had been brought into practical existence. The Republicans wanted Democratic votes, and they wanted the support (on election day) of those who earnestly favored the national cause but did not like Republicanism. Their managers, however, never intended that the victory for which the Union Leagues were springing into vote-getting action, should be otherwise treated than as a Republican triumph.

When the votes were counted in the Ohio election, which occurred on October 13, the result reflected the bitterness of the campaign

---

[3] St. Louis *Republican*, Oct. 13, 1863, clipping in R. T. L. Coll., 27197–8.

and the intensity of public concern. The dimensions of Brough's victory were striking. In the largest vote ever cast in the state, including about 43,000 soldier ballots, Brough was elected by a majority of 101,000. (These soldier votes were a contributing, but not a controlling, element.) It was also of significance that a legislature was elected which included large Union majorities in both houses.[4] It was generally recognized that the victories at Gettysburg and Vicksburg were important factors. It was, of course, a great advantage for the Republicans that it was their President who was in power in a desperate war where the vital cause of national survival was identified with the success of the administration. The fighting cause and the Lincoln cause could not be separated. This situation was evident in the overwhelming majority of the soldier vote that was cast for the Union candidate: 41,000 votes (round numbers) as compared to 2,000 for Vallandigham.

## IV

Special interest attached to the 1863 contest in Pennsylvania. To take only one aspect, it involved a species of popular referendum (at least it might be so interpreted) on the legality of the draft. A. G. Curtin, somewhat reluctantly, was standing for reëlection against the judge who had issued a decision declaring the national conscription law unconstitutional. This judge was George W. Woodward of the Pennsylvania superior court; the decision (*Kneedler* versus *Lane*) became a topic of Democratic propaganda; the New York *Tribune* referred to it as a "partisan harangue."[1] The tone of the Democratic campaign was sharply critical of Lincoln, with emphasis upon arrests and with extension of thanks to Ohio Democrats for their vigorous stand. In contrast, Curtin, more than certain other Republican governors, was regarded as strongly pro-Lincoln. "It was hardly possible," wrote Greeley, "to make an issue more distinctly than was here made between the supporters and the contemners of the War for the Union."[2] It was vitally important from the party standpoint to win the 1863 contest as a prestige factor for the larger

[4] Porter, *Ohio Politics*, 183.

[1] New York semi-weekly *Tribune*, Nov. 13, 1863; for the decision, see 45 Pa. 238.

[2] Greeley, *Amer. Conflict*, II, 509.

struggle in 1864.[3] At the same time it was realized that Pennsylvania was a "doubtful" state and that chances of Republican victory were by no means sure. Curtin wrote to Lincoln, on September 4, 1863, that if the election were to occur then the outcome would be extremely doubtful. It was impossible, he added, to magnify the importance of the Pennsylvania result.[4]

An incident of the Pennsylvania campaign was a letter from General McClellan endorsing Woodward; this served to increase the imprecations against both Woodward and McClellan.[5] Before this, writes his biographer, the general had "kept clear of any partizan course"; what he now did in endorsing Woodward, though "intended by him merely as a personal act," was to prove a political blunder and a serious handicap to the general in 1864. It put him "not only with the most bitter opponents of the [Lincoln] administration but also with those who were opposing the war." This was entirely against McClellan's intent. He was, in fact, in no affinity with Copperheads; on the contrary, he was "strongly in favor of a vigorous prosecution of the war." [6] Only very recently, in fact, men favoring a vigorous war had earnestly urged the reinstatement of McClellan as head of the main army.

The Pennsylvania election was fairly close, but the Republicans gained a clear victory. Curtin came through with 269,000 votes to Woodward's 254,000; [7] the Republicans also gained a slight majority in the legislature. In this election David Agnew, Republican, was elected chief justice of the state. He promptly proceeded to re-

---

[3] A correspondent of Simon Cameron wrote telling why he wished Curtin reëlected: ". . . it will enable us to elect our President [he did not say Lincoln] next year. If we are defeated in the State this year it will take the prestige of success from us next year." (As for Cameron himself, he had worked against Curtin's nomination but had to support him in the election.) James S. Chambers to Simon Cameron, Phila., Oct. 9, 1863, R. T. L. Coll., 27067.

[4] *Ibid*, 26043-4.

[5] "I understand Judge Woodward to be in favor of the prosecution of the war with all the means at the command of the loyal States, until the military power of the rebellion is destroyed. . . . Believing our opinions entirely agree upon these points [McClellan had also mentioned regard for private rights, avoidance of military excess, etc.], I would, were it in my power, give to Judge Woodward my voice and my vote." McClellan to Charles J. Biddle, Oct. 12, 1863. (The Pennsylvania election occurred on October 13.) *Ann. Cyc.*, 1863, 740.

[6] William Starr Myers, *General George Brinton McClellan*, 427-428. Myers (p. 428) considers this letter "one of the greatest mistakes of McClellan's career."

[7] *Ann. Cyc.*, 1863, 740.

verse the Woodward decision which declared the conscription act unconstitutional. That decision, wrote Agnew, had been "made in a one-sided hearing . . . in a preliminary way, during a time of high excitement, when partisan rage was furiously assailing the law." [8]

Not all Pennsylvania Republicans were pleased with the result. The long-standing feud between Curtin and Cameron flared up, and the Cameron element had worked with intense determination to defeat Curtin's nomination, preferring John Covode, Republican radical famous for the Covode investigation-and-report assailing Buchanan's Kansas policy. When Curtin was nominated, Cameron (to quote William B. Hesseltine) "fumed in frustration and his cohorts hissed in the galleries." [9] Pennsylvania soldiers, while they did not possess the vote in 1863, made their influence felt by writing home, conveying "earnest appeals" for Curtin's reëlection. It has been remarked that this Republican governor was reëlected "by the votes of Democrats . . . influenced solely by their sympathy with . . . sons and brothers in the field . . . ." [10]

## V

For its general significance in the complex, yet oversimplified, world of Republican politics, it is important to take a closer look at Governor Curtin, the victor in this hard-fought Pennsylvania contest. While Republican activity was being increasingly interpreted in terms of radical influence, the plain fact was that such Republicans as Curtin and such Union men as Brough, who carried important doubtful states in 1863, were most assuredly not of the radical type. For one thing, at least as late as June 1863, Curtin was understood to have favored McClellan for highest military command.[1] Leaving aside the controverted question as to McClellan's military leadership, this attitude of Curtin, which was shared by a great many people and soldiers at that time, shows conclusively that the governor was in the opposite camp from the radicals. The ugly antagonism

---

[8] 45 Pa. 310; *Constitutional Problems Under Lincoln* (revised ed.), 11–12, 32–33, 259.

[9] Hesseltine, *Lincoln and the War Governors*, 329.

[10] McClure, *Abraham Lincoln and Men of War-Times*, 266.

[1] "It was well known here that Govr Curtin had in June last . . . expressed himself favorable to the return of Genl McClellan to the Army of the Potomac or to the chief command in place of General Halleck . . . ." D. H. Williams to S. L. M. Barlow of New York City, Pittsburgh, Sep. 29, 1863, Barlow MSS.

of Cameron to Curtin was another evidence that such was the governor's position; this factor had importance for Lincoln, since Curtin sympathized with the President, while Cameron especially from about the end of 1861, directed his partisan activity along radical lines. It will be recalled that Cameron had caused keen embarrassment to Lincoln; few men had shown less genuine readiness to coöperate with the President in his difficult problems.

A. K. McClure, an authority on this subject, points to Curtin's "profoundly loyal" enthusiasm for the Union cause and shows the Pennsylvanian's great importance (with Lane of Indiana) in bringing about Lincoln's nomination in 1860. There "was not a . . . phase of the war," writes McClure, "at any time that did not summon Curtin to the councils of Lincoln." The governor's relations with Stanton were by no means cordial, and, when matters became difficult between these two men, Lincoln would interpose in Curtin's behalf, to the great irritation of the secretary of war.

For the 1863 story one of the most interesting episodes revealed by McClure is Curtin's willingness to retire as governor and the proposal he made in that connection. (Early in 1863 retirement from the severe burdens of his position seemed advisable because of ill health, but he improved later in the year and lived on with much active postwar service till 1894.) What Curtin proposed was the kind of thing that hardly ever happens in American politics but which in a critical situation would be of great public value. Curtin's suggestion was that he would retire as governor—i. e., not seek renomination—if the Democrats would nominate William B. Franklin, an able Pennsylvania general who had commanded a corps in the Army of the Potomac but had become the target of radical attack.

The plan was that the Republicans would also nominate Franklin, though he was a Democrat. McClure writes: "I was present when Curtin first made this suggestion to a number of his friends, and he made it with a degree of earnestness that impressed every one. He said that it was vastly more important to thus unite the whole Democratic party with the Republicans on an honest war platform than that any party or any individual should win political success." Less inspired counsels prevailed, however, and the plan fell through. The Democratic party was under the control of the "Bourbon" element; the judge who had ruled against conscription was nominated; partisanship was intensified; and Pennsylvania lost an opportunity to make the submerging of party politics not merely a matter of talk, but an actuality.[2] The career of Curtin gives evidence that devotion to the Union and loyalty to Lincoln were by no means synonymous with partisanship in the Republican sense.[3] He "sincerely sympathized with the Liberals" [4] of the party (1872) rather than the radicals and regulars; at important stages he was not in harmony with Republican leaders; furthermore, he realized in Lincoln's day the strength of the opposition to the Republicans in Pennsylvania.[5]

## VI

In New York, though it was not a national election, nor for governor, the 1863 contest had unmistakable national significance. In the large it was a question of supporting either the administration of Lincoln or that of Seymour. The people were to vote for state officials other than governor—such as secretary of state, comptroller, and attorney general—but the declarations of the two parties spoke the language of Federal affairs. The Democrats favored united support of the national government for suppressing the rebellion and restoring the Union. They declared secession a false doctrine. At the same time they denounced conscription, favored conciliation, objected to infringement of state rights, assailed what were called illegal and unconstitutional arrests, and expressed highest approval of the administration of Governor Seymour.

The New York Republicans resolved in favor of maintaining the

[2] McClure, *Abraham Lincoln and Men of War-Times*, 248 ff, esp. 251, 258, 261, 262.

[3] Curtin supported Greeley instead of the regular Republican candidate, Grant, in 1872; later he went over to the Democratic party. In the 80's he served six years as Democratic member of the House of Representatives.

[4] McClure, 275.

[5] "I traveled in company with Gov Curtin from Harrisburg to Altoona & during the entire trip he spoke freely in regard to current politics. He stated in his recent interview with Lincoln and Stanton that Penna would be carried against them. . . . The whole tenor of his conversation was that nothing but the letter of Gen McClellan in favor of Woodward, prevents his coming out on our [Democratic] side. . . . I do believe an effort of a proper character would bring him to us . . . ." Jos. C. McKibbin to S. L. M. Barlow, Oct. 1 [no year given; probably 1864], Barlow MSS. There were comments in this letter which showed dissatisfaction with the Lincoln administration. To that extent the correspondent of Barlow gave a picture of Curtin very different from that of McClure; that correspondent, of course, was an intense Democrat. It should be added that where Curtin was displeased with doings at Washington his dissatisfaction was not so much with Lincoln as with Stanton.

integrity of the Union and the supremacy of the Constitution over
the whole national domain, insisted on strengthening the armies,
condemned all who embarrassed the government, denounced misleading tenders of peace, and specifically expressed "gratitude . . .
to the administration of Mr. Lincoln" for steadfast courage, financial
ability, preservation of peace with foreign nations, and splendid victories.[1]

When the votes were counted the result was revealed as a rebuke
to Seymour and an endorsement of Lincoln. It is necessary only to
note the totals for secretary of state, which were typical: Chauncey
M. Depew of Peekskill, defender of Lincoln, received over 314,000
votes; his democratic opponent, Daniel B. St. John, less than 285,000.
The Union ticket prevailed overwhelmingly in the choice of both
houses of the legislature. In the senate the strength of this party was
21 as compared to 11 for the opposition; in the assembly the division
was 82 to 46.[2]

In Massachusetts the Democrats strongly favored the Union, but
with resolutions that slanted toward criticism of Lincoln. This was
plainly evident in their declarations as to subjugation, martial law,
and military usurpation; it appeared also in their expression of
"thanks" to Seymour of New York. At the head of their ticket, for
governor, they named a prosperous lawyer of little fame, Henry W.
Paine.[3] The Republicans, strongly endorsing the emancipation proclamation and deprecating the idea of peace by negotiation with
"rebels," renamed John A. Andrew for governor. On November
3, 1863, Andrew was "largely elected," as Lincoln would say; his vote
was 70,000, Paine's 29,000. For the legislature strong Republican
majorities were chosen.[4] Support of Andrew had the more significance

---

[1] *Ann. Cyc.*, 1863, 688.        [2] *Ibid.*, 689.

[3] Henry William Paine (1810–1893) was a successful lawyer of Maine, later of Boston,
and a teacher of law at Boston University. For a closely studied, though highly eulogistic,
account, see the article by William Mathews in *New Eng. Mag.*, X, 189–197 (Apr., 1894).
The author sets forth Paine's fine New England ancestry, learning, extraordinary
memory, benevolence, "Websterian front," keen logic, and personal integrity. He states
that "there was probably no one of his legal brethren who was engaged in so many and
so important lawsuits . . . as Mr. Paine" (p. 191). Yet this man, the 1863 Democratic
contender against Andrew, is so far forgotten that his name does not appear in the index
of the voluminous life of Andrew by H. G. Pearson. His nomination shows that Massachusetts Democrats were offering, not a politician, nor a controversial figure, but a man
of high ability and character.

[4] *Ann. Cyc.*, 1863, 626; N. Y. *Tribune Almanac*, 1864, 58; report on return of votes in

by reason of his ardent antislavery policy and his enthusiastic efforts for raising Negro regiments.

As the months passed with state election days at staggered intervals all over the country, the smaller states gained considerable publicity. The result in Maine was not quite as easily predictable as might have been supposed. The election for governor and other state officials, was held on September 14. Samuel Cony, Union candidate, was elected governor by a vote of 67,916 against 50,366 for Bion Bradbury, Democrat.[5] On the day of the election J. G. Blaine, chairman of the Union committee for the state, telegraphed to Lincoln from Augusta: "Maine sustains your Administration by a majority of 15,000." The next day he sent word that the majority was greater than first estimated.[6]

## VII

The situation in turbulent Maryland pertaining to the election of 1863 forced itself voluminously upon Lincoln's attention. The election was for members of Congress, members of the state legislature, and minor state officials (comptroller and commissioner of the land office). The state, so recently a battleground and so torn by riots in 1861, was shaken not only by the usual war agitation but by a combination of vexing factors: absconding slaves, colored soldiers, arbitrary arrests, citizens possessing arms, widespread accusations of disloyalty, and a series of suppressive military orders by General Robert C. Schenck. This officer, who commanded the "Middle Department" with headquarters at Baltimore, was of the radical type; he was not in full harmony with Lincoln, though the President had sought by careful personal approach to promote harmony.

The whole American Civil War was epitomized in Maryland as in Kentucky and Missouri. One has in mind here not so much the issue of secession, for Maryland was safely in the Union after the uncertainty of 1861, but those troublesome clashes by which brothers and neighbors were divided. It was in fact the divisions among pro-Union men that were agitating Maryland. Union Leagues, assuming

---

election of Nov. 3, 1863 (photostat from archives division, office of the secretary, Commonwealth of Mass.).

[5] *Ann. Cyc.*, 1863, 604.                [6] R. T. L. Coll., 26275, 26292.

to themselves a kind of exclusive function to organize "Union" men within the state, were pressing hard for state emancipation, for support of "the whole policy of the [national] Administration," and for having congressmen pledged to "abide by the Administration caucus for Speaker of the House of Representatives." This was plainly the language, not simply of the Union, but of the Republican radical machine. It was misleading language in the sense that people would suppose that the word "Administration" had to do with the President and his policy, while in reality the pledge to vote according to the "caucus" meant, being interpreted, to follow the dictates of Thaddeus Stevens.

After much sparring and dissension, with unsuccessful efforts to unite conflicting groups in conference, the position of affairs crystallized as a struggle between "unconditional Union men" (largely the radicals, the Union League group) and "Union men" who preferred the more moderate approach. Both groups strongly and unequivocally supported the Union and both opposed slavery. Their wordy "resolutions" and platforms need not detain us. The difference between them can, perhaps, be no better expressed than by noting that one type was personified by Henry Winter Davis; the other, less bitter, type, by Thomas Swann. Davis was driving hard for an "ultra" type of Republican control which was the opposite of Lincoln's. Though a Republican, he was an outspoken critic of the President and a close ally of Stevens and Wade. Swann, of the more moderate group, supported emancipation, having freed his numerous slaves, but favored the President's pattern for abolition and later for reconstruction. (Davis was a candidate for Congress; Swann the chairman of the Union State Central Committee.) Part of the trouble was the bitter storm raging over the head of Montgomery Blair, postmaster general, whom radicals vociferously denounced, but whom the President was retaining in his cabinet.

It was the moderate group that wanted unity. They tried to draw both groups together, but this did not appeal to the Union-League element. In seeking to eradicate "the evil of slavery" the moderates did not consider this an "excuse for violence"; they sought to avoid that "aggravation of feeling" which they believed would "have the effect of retarding rather than facilitating" the desired object.[1]

---

[1] *Ann. Cyc.*, 1863, 617.

The far-reaching repercussions of these political episodes were in evidence in connection with the activities of the Blairs. This famous family was persistent in its drive for influence, patronage, and all that went with political power. In one sense the contest was a phase of reconstruction development in a period when differences of policy as to restoration were causing savage factional disputes within the Republican party. It was ultras against conservatives, moderates against radicals, in clashes which proved to be but a foretaste of the long drawn out nation-shaking storm that was to come.

Of the principals in this struggle it could probably be said that the man who caused the greatest annoyance to the Blairs was Secretary Chase. This cabinet member with presidential ambitions was building up his influence with the radical element of the Republican party, and the tactics which he and his followers were using were intolerably distasteful to the Blairs. It was not easy to endure Chase's appointment of his partisans to treasury positions, but a far worse thing was the hawking of false charges of corruption against Frank Blair, Jr. There was also the question of the cotton trade within enemy lines, a shabby practice which Chase was promoting and the younger Frank Blair was stoutly denouncing and exposing. Being loyal to the President, the Blairs "regarded Chase as a traitor to the Chief." [2] Reading his motives and tactics, they perceived a scheme to achieve the presidency through encouraging the radicals and enabling them to control the Republican party.

It was under these circumstances that Montgomery Blair, on October 3, 1863, delivered at Rockville, Maryland, a speech in which the postmaster general, agitated by apprehensions as to radical schemes and angered by the Chase enmity, let himself go in emphatic warnings against ultras of the Republican party. The people of the country, he said, were "menaced by the ambition of the ultra-Abolitionists, which is . . . despotic in its tendencies, and which, if successful, could not fail to be . . . fatal to republican institutions." [3] The speech looked forward to the great problems of restoration and presented a dire picture of the dangers of a radical policy which would abolish state constitutions in the South and submerge that whole

---

[2] William Ernest Smith, *The Francis Preston Blair Family in Politics,* II, 235.
[3] *Ibid.,* II, 237.

broad section (under the designation of conquered territory) as a region to be governed by a radical Congress.

In his favoring non-radical reconstruction the views of Montgomery Blair were basically those of Lincoln, but that situation made it all the worse for the President, since the reaction to the Rockville speech, which was compared to a "bombshell," was highly unfavorable while at the same time it was supposed to be expressive of the President's sentiments. It was a matter of the President having an unskillful spokesman. In large part Blair's ideas did have the President's approval, but Lincoln would never have employed the Blair words nor used the Blair tone. Coming shortly before the President's launching of his main reconstruction policy (put before the country in early December of 1863) the intemperate speech was simply another of the many factors causing the vitally important question of a restored Union to be hung up and entangled in intraparty disputes.

It was the fate of the Blairs to be misunderstood. Frank Blair, Jr., for factional reasons, was actually called a "Copperhead," [4] which was false to the point of absurdity. Montgomery, for denouncing abolitionists—denouncing them because of their attitude toward the Southern people and states—was misrepresented as being friendly to slavery. The charge, of course, was slanderously false. Among the main elements of Montgomery's public service were his free-soil principle, his opposition to Buchanan, his service as counsel for Dred Scott, his prominence as an antislavery man in the Republican party in 1860, his firmness for the Union, and his readiness to uphold the antislavery standard in Maryland.[5] People were misled as to which men were supporting the administration. Readers of some of the newspapers were asked to believe that it was the radicals who were "administration men," while the Blairs were misrepresented as if they were warring against the administration.[6]

---

[4] *Ibid.*, II, 228.

[5] Among other evidences of his opposition to slavery was a letter which Montgomery Blair wrote on June 21, 1864, to William Lloyd Garrison. Addressing Garrison as a friend, he hoped that, despite differences as to method, their "one common object—emancipation" would be kept in mind. He explained that he had tried to buy an interest in the Baltimore *Clipper* in order to advocate the cause of abolition in Maryland. The letter was published in the *Liberator*. A rough draft is in the Blair MSS., Lib. of Cong. See also W. E. Smith, *Blair Family*, II, 268–269.

[6] Just after the Maryland election a Washington journalist wrote: ". . . measures have lately been taken to make General Blair [Frank P., Jr.], as well as his brother

There was also the difficulty that the Blairs were principals in a major cabinet split.[7] The savage opposition against Seward was brought into the picture, and people came to speak of the factional quarrels between the Chase-Stanton faction and the Blair-Bates-Seward faction. Seward was a special target of radical attack, while always the tendency was to include denunciations of the President in the same breath with criticism of Seward. The President was being injured by his friends. It was said that in Pennsylvania in 1863 the Rockville speech had cost the Republicans 20,000 votes.[8] Yet sincere Unionists who genuinely agreed with Lincoln and who supported his policy were friendly to Montgomery Blair. James Dixon, for instance, Republican senator from Connecticut, wrote the postmaster general expressing approval of his Rockville speech. "In the Senate I know you will find many supporters among the Republicans. It is impossible that the intelligence of that body should have sunk to so low a point as to permit the errors of the radicals to prevail there. In the House of Representatives you will also have much strength." [9]

## VIII

As election day (November 3) approached, the hills of Maryland resounded to a clamorous war of words: protests to Lincoln by Swann and Governor Bradford, military orders, proclamations, letters by the President, and fulminations by the newspapers. In "Order No. 53" dated October 27 (modified, and first published on November 2), General Schenck declared that "evil disposed" (pro-rebel) persons were threatening disturbance. In view of this he gave a three-pronged command: (1) that provost marshals and other military officers should arrest "all such persons [i. e., those described in the preamble of his order as "evil disposed persons, . . ."] found at, or hanging about, or approaching" any polling place; (2) that a prescribed oath of al-

---

[Montgomery], understand that their warfare on the Administration from within . . . , had better be stopped." Cincinnati *Daily Gazette*, Nov. 9, 1863, p. 3, c. 4.

[7] "Old Abe told me once that Fessenden & Hamlin remonstrated with him against allowing 'the Blairs' to rule everything." Montgomery Blair to S. L. M. Barlow, Montgomery Co., Md., Aug. 15, 1865, Barlow MSS.

[8] Smith, *Blair Family*, II, 241.

[9] James Dixon to M. Blair (private), Hartford, Oct. 7, 1863, R. T. L. Coll., 27009–10. As to Republican senators sharing Blair's moderate views, Dixon may have had in mind such men as Doolittle of Wisconsin, Collamer of Vermont, and Cowan of Pennsylvania.

legiance should have military support; (3) that military officers should
report to Schenck's headquarters any state judge of election refusing
to require the oath of allegiance of anyone whose vote should be
challenged on the ground of "disloyalty or hostility to the Government." [1]

On October 31 Governor Bradford protested strongly against these
measures. The right of suffrage, he thought, was being restricted,
and detachments of soldiers, not residents of Maryland, were "expected to exert some control or influence" on the election. He could
not but think that these things were being done without the President's personal knowledge.[2]

These Maryland difficulties took a distressing amount of Lincoln's
time. Answering Governor Bradford at length (November 2) he
pointed out that violence was "almost certain . . . at some of the
voting places . . . unless prevented by . . . provost guards." The
presence of troops was to make it possible to run a "Union" ticket.
The oath, which had been represented as a restriction on suffrage, was
intended, wrote Lincoln, to assure "the right of voting to all loyal
men." He did not think that "to keep the peace at the polls, and to
prevent the persistently disloyal from voting" constituted "just cause
of offence to Maryland."

The President did, however, make one concession. He revoked the
first of the three parts of Schenck's order. Where the general had
ordered military arrest of a whole class of evil persons aiding the rebellion who might embarrass the election or foist enemies of the
United States into power, Lincoln directed that the order be considerably modified: in the amended form the word arrest was not
used; the injunction was "That all Provost Marshals, and other military officers do prevent all disturbance and violence at or about the
polls, whether offered by such persons as above described or by any
other person or persons whomsoever." [3]

This assurance and concession by the President did not satisfy the
governor, who issued a lengthy proclamation on November 2, the
day before the election, vigorously denouncing Schenck's "extraordinary order." The general then issued, on the day of election, an
order strongly denouncing Bradford's "very extraordinary Proclama-

---

[1] McPherson, 309.                    [2] Ann. Cyc., 1863, 618.
[3] Lincoln to Gov. Bradford, Nov. 2, 1863, photostat, A. Lincoln Assoc.

tion." [4] Also on the day of election the governor sent the President an intolerably long letter reviewing, calling attention, insisting, solemnly protesting, informing, hardly supposing, confessing himself unable to imagine, and, after nearly two thousand words, having "the honor" to conclude. A duplicate of his letter was sent to the press.[5]

These formidable documents are too voluminous to be quoted or summarized here. On one side there was uneasy dread of a clash between citizens and the military power, together with resentment of military interference where state judges of election were, as the governor said, "exclusive judges" of voters' qualifications. On the other side there were reported activities of disloyal men presaging trouble, petitions from "respectable and loyal citizens" imploring military protection, and Schenck's affirmation that his only purpose was to prevent collisions and secure peace and order at the polls. Lincoln was supporting Schenck whom he nevertheless restrained; he was giving ear respectfully to Maryland protests while not admitting all the Federal abuses that were charged. He was keeping his temper while seeing representatives of both sides personally.

Amid these verbal explosions the people of Maryland went to the polls on November 3 for the purpose, essentially, of choosing between "conservative" Union men and "unconditional" Union men. The latter were understood to be more earnest toward emancipation than the former. Anti-Union men and what were called "peace men" had no candidate. It was the "unconditional" men who won by strong majorities. Their candidate for comptroller (Goldsborough) received 36,000 votes; his opponent a bit less than 16,000. In the choices for Congress the "unconditional" ticket was successful in four of the five districts.[6]

As a kind of post-mortem on the 1863 campaign, Governor Bradford delivered a message to the legislature in January 1864, recounting abuses perpetrated by the military authorities and deploring that a "part of the army which a generous people had supplied . . . was . . . engaged in stifling the freedom of election in a faithful State, intimidating its sworn officers, [and] violating the constitutional rights of its loyal citizens, . . . ." [7] Another sequel to the election was the series of steps that led in 1864 to abolition of slavery as a matter

---

[4] *Ann. Cyc.*, 1863, 619–621.    [5] *Ibid.*, 621–623.    [6] *Ibid.*, 623.
[7] *Ibid.*, 624.

of Maryland law. Still another effect was that in the final Congress of
the Lincoln administration—the Thirty-Eighth, which began its first
session on December 7, 1863 [8]—the President had to contend with
the forceful and unrelenting opposition of Henry Winter Davis,
chosen without any rival candidate by 6200 Maryland votes in the
third congressional district. It would be a mistake to suppose that
the Maryland election was altogether an advantage to Lincoln.[9]

It is necessary to take another glance at the election of Henry Winter Davis as congressman. His third congressional district, consisting
of thirteen wards of the city of Baltimore, contained a population of
138,040. (This included, as a minor factor, 1769 slaves, at a time when
the population ratio for the apportionment of House seats among
the states was based on the constitutional provision that two-fifths of
the slaves were to be included in the calculation.)

For the Thirty-Eighth Congress (on the basis of the census of 1860)
the formula called for one representative for 122,614 of population.[10]
There was, of course, no strict conformity of particular districts to
that overall formula; deviations among the districts were, and remain, quite common. The factor that does arouse wonder, however,
is the small vote for Davis (6200) as compared to the general ratio
(122,000). This was a remarkably small vote, made smaller, no doubt,
by the fact that Davis had no competitor. If one were to suppose
roughly that no more than one-fifth of the total population were
entitled to vote (though some would figure it at approximately one-
fourth),[11] the number of eligible voters in Davis's district would be
over 24,000. Thus, for a Congress destined to deal with large national
questions including reconstruction, this Republican opponent of

---

8 To present-day readers the practice of choosing congressmen in odd-numbered years
seems unusual, but such was the system in Maryland in this period. In November 1863
Marylanders chose congressmen for a term that legally began in the previous March,
though the actual session did not open until December. There was an obvious economy
in choosing congressmen along with the regular state election.

9 "Davis never forgave the President for choosing Blair Postmaster-General instead of
him." William Ernest Smith, *Blair Family*, II, 277. For election of Maryland congressmen
in 1863, showing Davis's total of 6200, see *Ann. Cyc.*, 1863, 623.

10 *Historical Statistics of the U. S., 1789–1945* (U. S. Bur. of the Census, 1949), 294.

11 In an offhand estimate of the number of eligible voters one would have to make a
large deduction from total population to exclude minors and then deduct about half of
the remainder to exclude women. It should also be remembered that Negroes did not
vote in Maryland in 1863. One does not need, however, to make all these calculations
exactly in order to realize how small was the vote for Davis.

Lincoln, one of the sharpest of the "radicals," was chosen by about one-fourth of the potential voters of his district and by less than one-twentieth of that district's population. A small vote for Congress was characteristic of the 1863 election in Maryland, but in the first district, where there was competition, the total vote was 12,224, about twice the total vote in the Davis (third) district. Just how far Henry Winter Davis could have been said to represent the sentiment of Maryland, or Baltimore, is a question. The support he received was hardly a measure of the strength of sentiment for the Union in the Lincolnian sense. His heavily over-weighted influence in Congress was out of proportion to the constituency whose views he reflected.

## IX

At the pitch of excitement in the 1863 campaigns President Lincoln took a step concerning one of the chief targets for his opponents —the question of arbitrary arrests. On September 15, 1863, he issued a formal proclamation, with the most careful legal wording, suspending the habeas corpus privilege "throughout the United States." [1] Why did he do this, seeing that he had already (September 24, 1862) proclaimed a general suspension of the privilege "now, or hereafter during the rebellion"? The answer would appear to be that the 1862 proclamation was on presidential authority only, resting on no statutory basis, and subject to the well known objection that the President was arbitrarily seizing power that should be exercised, if at all, by Congress. Though Lincoln did not accept the validity of this objection, which he refuted with legal chapter and verse, he recognized that the civil-rights issue was being potently used against him and that this issue was likely to be a strong factor in certain pending elections which his administration could not afford to lose. He had no intention of giving up military arrests, but if such arrests were formally placed on a statutory basis, that would be a factor of strength. This 1863 proclamation (September 15) was comprehensive and all-sufficient for any military arrests yet to come. The "privilege of the Writ of Habeas Corpus . . . throughout the United States" was suspended in all cases where officers under the President's authority were holding certain classes of persons as spies, aiders of rebellion, et cetera,

---

[1] Photostat, A. Lincoln Assoc.

or "for any other offense against the military or naval service." The suspension was to "continue throughout the duration of the . . . rebellion," or until modified or revoked by the President.

It is significant to note the preamble of this presidential document. In a series of "whereas" clauses the conditions justifying suspension and making it a matter of law, were recited: the constitutional provision, the fact that a rebellion existed, the statute of March 3, 1863, the provision of that statute which recognized (some would have said conferred) the authority for presidential suspension, and the controlling fact that, in accordance with both statute and Constitution, the "public safety" did require the setting aside of the privilege.

There was in this action of the President both a concession to legal objectors and a reënforcement of the administration's firm position. Arrests were to continue, but they were now placed squarely upon the foundation of a law of Congress. All the wording of the 1863 proclamation indicated that the President was then and thereafter to have the statute as a basis for the seizure and holding of prisoners without civil trial.

There remained, of course, several questions. Neither the executive nor the judicial branch was complying with that feature of the law of March 3, 1863, which required that lists of prisoners be furnished to the Federal district and circuit courts, and that, if grand juries brought no indictments, or if no lists were furnished and the judge was satisfied as to the allegations of the petition, prisoners were to be discharged *by judicial order*. In that respect the law was not being made effective. There was also the question of the six-months delay: a September proclamation issued in accordance with an act passed in March. One could have raised the point that the Vallandigham proceeding was not in accordance either with the congressional act or the pattern of executive conduct indicated in the President's proclamation of September 15, 1863. Nor was it in keeping with the President's above-mentioned instruction of September 17, 1863, prescribing the conduct of a military officer in giving a "return" to the judge when served with a writ of habeas corpus.[2] The method of that instruction, as we have seen, was not followed in the Vallandigham case.[3]

---

[2] See above, p. 223.

[3] Judge Leavitt in the Vallandigham case not only refused the relief sought by the

It should be noted that Lincoln issued this proclamation prior to the important October elections. This was not true, however, as to another proclamation—the call for further troops, by draft if necessary. Such a call was obviously on the agenda in September, but Lincoln "deemed it prudent to defer a fresh call for troops until after the October States had voted." [4] The elections in Ohio and Pennsylvania, favorable to Lincoln, occurred on October 13; on October 17 the President called for troops on a large scale; 300,000 men were called; the states were to raise their quotas if possible by volunteering; where enlistments were deficient, the required number was to be taken by drafting. Men so taken were "to serve for three years or the war, not however, exceeding three years." [5]

Officially the President held himself aloof from the state elections which we have been considering in this and the preceding chapter; yet no one doubted their national bearing. The Lincoln administration, the President's war policy—all this was an issue in these contests. In one sense, of course, Lincoln did take a hand in these canvasses. The political letters he wrote were not specifically addressed to the competition between parties; yet one could hardly overlook the import of his letters to Seymour, Corning, Birchard, and Conkling. If one were collecting political material pertaining to what could have been called the "campaign of 1863," Lincoln's statements would be among the most important documents to be included. People could not properly speak of these contests as if they were local. Behind the scenes the President was constantly advised as to the progress of party campaigns in the states and was influenced in the timing of executive acts for their bearing upon the elections. Whether people voted as they did because of party, or because of Lincoln's personality, or to sustain the national cause in a year of crisis, the various elections of 1863 had somewhat the same effect as Gettysburg, Vicksburg, and Chattanooga. They were victories, milestones, indicators of support for the main Union effort as directed from Washington. There were, of course, clouds soon to appear. While the Republican party, in the main, won these Northern elections, that party was not united.

---

writ; he refused the writ itself. He thus refused to inquire into the accusations and reasons for the military arrest.

[4] Rhodes, *Hist. of the U. S.,* IV, 417.

[5] Call for 300,000 volunteers, Oct. 17, 1863, photograph, A. Lincoln Assoc.

Moderates like Lincoln, examining the political scene carefully, could not but realize with growing regret that the radicals were insisting it was their party.[6]

On November 20, 1863, in a finely balanced letter to one of those radicals (Zachariah Chandler), Lincoln briefly related the 1863 elections to his own conduct. He wrote: "I am very glad the elections this autumn have gone favorably, and that I have not, by native depravity, or under evil influences, done anything bad enough to prevent the good result. [A modest statement—as if the President had been only a negative quantity in contests where his personality and policy had been vital and pivotal.] I hope to 'stand firm' enough to not go backward, and yet not go forward fast enough to wreck the country's cause." [7] This was not a mere colorless doctrine such as some noncommittal politicians would have counseled. Lincoln at this time was working out one of the most important programs of his whole career —his reconstruction plan, soon to be announced in his third regular annual message to Congress. That program was the very opposite of Chandler's. When the matter is considered not only in relation to the elections, but to basic policy at this midway stage, there were worlds of seasoned wisdom in Lincoln's statement that he would not go backward, yet not forward impulsively or too fast.

---

6 Immediately after reporting the results of the 1863 elections, with emphasis on Republican success, Lincoln's secretaries wrote that "within their own organization" the Republicans were experiencing "bitter differences." Nicolay and Hay, *Lincoln*, VII, 388. In the presence of these differences the outlook for the President's plans was not encouraging.

7 Lincoln to Chandler, Nov. 20, 1863, marked "private," photostat, A. Lincoln Assoc.

# CHAPTER XII

# LINCOLN AND SEYMOUR

IN A WAR situation in which the Federal government relied upon coöperation by the states, President Lincoln had to encounter persistent questioning in the Empire State of New York, largest of them all. In that commonwealth the Democratic governor, Horatio Seymour, boldly challenged the President's policy. This opposition was no minor episode. Seymour was Lincoln's major opponent, though not his only embarrassment, among the governors.

## I

What about Seymour? Within the orbit of his own antecedents, associations, and experience, his views and predilections were understandable. In the excellent biography by Stewart Mitchell he stands forth as a consistent personality and a man of distinction—a conservative Democrat whose service went back to the "Albany Regency" days of Van Buren, eminently respectable, believing in the Democratic party, content with the "good life," distrustful of reformers, devoted to the Burkian concept of the expedient as the guiding rule of statesmen. This, together with his temperament, explained why he had never joined the crusade against slavery.[1]

Amid the divisive tendencies of the New York Democrats—to say nothing of their opponents, the Whigs and later the Republicans—Seymour had adhered to the "Hunker" (or less democratic) wing of the party, and had served his state as assemblyman, speaker of the house, and governor in prewar years. In 1860 he had enough prominent mention in connection with the Charleston convention (which

[1] Stewart Mitchell, *Horatio Seymour of New York*, 229.

he did not attend) to enable his biographer to speculate as to the possibility that he might then have become the nominee of a united Democratic party. Though this should not be taken too seriously, it is presented as one of those fascinating "ifs": "a two-man contest between Abraham Lincoln and Horatio Seymour might have changed the course of American history." [2] In that campaign Seymour favored Douglas and in the election of that year he honestly regretted the minority-won success of a sectional party. Had his party remained united, and had it been successful in the election, he believed that war would have been averted.

In 1862 he was elected governor of New York in a hard-fought contest in which his opponent, General James S. Wadsworth, supported Lincoln and emancipation, while Seymour pointed to the danger of allowing the government at Washington to "continue unchecked by intelligent and active opposition." [3] If, in New York in 1862, it was a question of popular will expressed at the polls (though there may be error in oversimplifying this aspect of the problem), there was reason to claim that, as between Seymour and Lincoln, the mandate was in Seymour's favor. He reminded his hearers that "if northerners and southerners had taken the trouble to know each other well, the Civil War could never have occurred." [4] (To illustrate the complexities of the subject, it may be remarked that this sentiment—the need for mutual understanding, North and South—was also sincerely felt and repeatedly expressed by Lincoln.)

With all the immense and many-sided burdens of 1863, the President treated Seymour with great respect, patiently answered his complaints, and sought continually for a working adjustment of conflicting views. During these months of controversy the nation was going through severe ordeals as it watched the military news while also, in the states, the political pot was boiling in state elections spread out over a tiresome period from spring until late fall.

## II

Prominent in all this Seymour discussion was the excitement and disturbance associated with resistance to the draft. This was not all agitation and threat; at times it broke out into violence; in New York

2 *Ibid.*, 212.                    3 *Ibid.*, 249.                    4 *Ibid.*, 252.

City it came to a frightful climax in the bloody draft riots of July.

Draft disorders were not confined to any one area. Serious clashes of police with mobsters occurred in Boston,[1] and in New Hampshire there were reports of "a widespread and organized determination . . . to resist" enforcement and an unusual sale of fire-arms "significant of bad feeling and probably of bad action." [2]

The draft riot in New York City, mentioned in an earlier volume,[3] was unique as the only disturbance that reached large proportions. Raging for three days, it presented a ghastly contrast to the celebrations of July victory, but in its murderous destruction it was untypical. It was certainly not typical of New York, whose support of the war was a notable factor. It was typical of mobs, but that does not mean that mobs were typical of America. The New York episode was that of spasmodic impulse and undisciplined fury: mobs looting, killing, destroying enrollment lists, disarming soldiers in barracks, stoning a provost marshal, beating Negroes to death, burning a colored orphans' home leaving hundreds of children homeless, seizing rifles, destroying a police station, and engaging in a pitched battle with police. A summary of those days of disorder ran as follows:

Thus the days wore on, with dust and smoke, with fire and flame; with sack of private dwellings and burning of charitable institutions, armories, and draft stations; with blood and wounds, and every imaginable instance of atrocity on the part of the maddened mob, till regiments, hurriedly withdrawn from the front, came speeding back to the city, and we saw the grim batteries and weatherstained and dusty soldiers tramping into our leading streets as if into a town just taken by siege. There was some terrific fighting between the regulars and the insurgents; streets were swept again and again by grape, houses were stormed at the point of the bayonet, rioters were picked off by sharpshooters as they fired on the troops from the house-tops; men were hurled, dying or dead, into the streets by the thoroughly enraged soldiery; until at last, sullen and cowed, and thoroughly whipped and beaten, the miserable wretches gave way at every point and confessed the power of the law. It has never been known how many perished in those awful days.[4]

Such was one picture of the draft riot, and a worse one was presented by Horace Greeley.[5] On the other hand, Stewart Mitchell de-

[1] "Riots in New York, Boston, and Elsewhere," *Ann. Cyc.*, 1863, 811–818.
[2] *Offic. Rec.*, 3 ser. III, 513, 565.     [3] *Lincoln the President*, II, 294–295.
[4] Morgan Dix, *Memoirs of John Adams Dix*, II, 75.
[5] Greeley, *Amer. Conflict*, II, 501–507.

clares that the whole uprising was "magnified until it became a political myth" for the purpose of making out a case against the governor and the Democratic party.[6] Mitchell points out that much of this partisan use of the episode came out in the political campaign of 1868. Some of the atrocities—e. g., the burning of a colored orphan asylum—are admitted by Mitchell; he also admits collisions between mobs and police.[7] He points out that the disorder lasted three days—July 13, 14, and 15—not four, as sometimes stated. Mentioning a thunderstorm and downpour which scattered the crowds, he remarks that "nature did quite as much, if not more, than the forces of law . . . in restoring the city to temporary quiet." [8] As to the number who lost their lives in the riot Mitchell gives no specific answer; he finds that their "small number" cannot be exactly stated. Against the widely varying claims of anti-Seymour writers (ranging from three hundred to more than a thousand) the governor's biographer finds "no evidence that any more than seventy-four possible victims of the violence of three days died anywhere but in the columns of partisan newspapers.[9] The meaning of this is that Mitchell finds evidence of seventy-four deaths attributable to the riot—a significant conclusion, since he has done more than any other writer to sift the evidence critically. He does not, however, set up that figure, nor any figure, as the total number of those who lost their lives (such a total being impossible to ascertain), nor does he state the number of wounded. The historian must attach great value to Mitchell's careful analysis and must therefore discount the exaggerated accounts that were all too common. Even when all is said, however, the riot stands out as a serious and disgraceful episode. To associate Seymour with the riot or to insinuate (as partisan writers did) that he sympathized with the rioters—because, forsooth, he allegedly began an impromptu speech with the words "My Friends"—would be grossly unfair.

## III

Riots are usually short lived. To put down the disturbance was to handle the problem on one plane, but on another plane—the higher

---

6 Mitchell, *Seymour*, 306. Mitchell does not mean that it was promoting a "myth" to say that a riot occurred, but that extreme partisan statements as to what happened—e. g., as to the extent of bloodshed—overstepped the bounds of reality.

7 *Ibid.*, 330.                    8 *Ibid.*, 330, 335.                    9 *Ibid.*, 333.

one of state-government protest—the labor and embarrassment to Lincoln was even greater. To send troops to prevent further mob action was one thing. To deal over many weeks with the serious challenge presented by Horatio Seymour, conscientious and dignified governor of New York, was quite a different thing. In the heavy strain of 1863, in a wretchedly difficult situation, the President had to muster up all his skill, courtesy, and tact toward the governor, whose opposition, though impressively justified by his defenders, was not unmixed with anti-Lincoln politics.

Lincoln never denounced Seymour, nor can a biographer explain the complicated situation by branding the governor, in the words of Nicolay and Hay, as having a "bitterly prejudiced mind"; these writers on another page have conceded his integrity and patriotism.[1] It was a matter of divisions in a democracy, of horror at the thought of civil war, of Americans being unready for conscription, of distress at the miserable system of compulsory service then in use, and of anxiety in contemplating a growing bureaucracy in Washington taking over functions of the states. The fact that the states were not performing nationwide functions adequately was the other side of the coin.

Lincoln's first letter to Seymour (March 23, 1863) was by way of a very human approach as one who introduces himself and wishes to make friends. "You and I," wrote the President, "are substantially strangers, and I write . . . that we may become better acquainted. I, for the time being, am at the head of a nation which is in great peril, and you are at the head of the greatest State of that nation. As to maintaining the nation's life and integrity, I assume and believe there cannot be a difference of purpose between you and me. If we should differ as to the means, it is important that the difference should be as small as possible; that it should not be enhanced by unjust suspicions . . . ." The President pleaded informally for "a good understanding." He asked: "Please write me at least as long a letter as this, of course saying in it just what you think fit." [2]

If ever there was a warm, hearty letter phrasing a friendly appeal, discarding official stiffness, and asking for a rising above differences,

---

[1] Nicolay and Hay, *Lincoln*, VII, 11, 13.

[2] Lincoln to Seymour, Mar. 23, 1863, autograph draft, R. T. L. Coll., 22581 (this text differs but slightly from Nicolay and Hay, *Works*, VIII, 230–231).

this was it. Seymour waited three weeks, then answered in much less cordial fashion, giving "pressure of official duties" as the excuse for not giving his views in the manner he intended. (The governor was then dealing with a legislative session, but it is hard to believe that his duties were pressing any more heavily than those of Lincoln.) Seymour went on to disclaim political resentment and promised support on all measures adopted "within the scope of . . . constitutional powers." [3]

The governor was not completely unresponsive, though he did fundamentally differ with Lincoln on peace-and-war and on conscription. That basic difference, after all, was the explanation of the trouble—that, and politics. Lincoln was asking for coöperation in terms of national conscription; Seymour was ready to give it in terms of New York's volunteer effort. The governor may have felt that the President wanted smooth relations on his own terms; from the gubernatorial point of view the advantage of the elimination of differences would have been one sided. Because of the historical attention given to Lincoln's letter of March 23, 1863, it might be supposed that the President had made the first overture, but as far back as January of that year, at the beginning of Seymour's administration as governor, he had sent his brother, John F. Seymour, to hold a friendly and coöperative conference with the President.

In that interview, as recorded by John Seymour, we see Lincoln laying aside official formality and conversing easily on matters of common interest with an opponent. Lincoln said that they, Governor Seymour and himself, "had the same stake in the country." Both were party men, and that brought up the question of the next President; but if the country were broken up, said Lincoln, "there could be no next President." There would be no presidency (of states united).

Lincoln admitted that he himself was a party man, yet he pointed out that "he had appointed most of the officers of the army from among Democrats." As to the main issue, Lincoln said (as reported) that there were but three courses to take: fight until enemy leaders were overthrown; give up the contest altogether; or "negotiate and compromise with the leaders of the rebellion." But he thought such compromise "impossible so long as Davis had the power"; Davis and the other

_____

[3] Seymour to Lincoln, Apr. 14, 1863, Nicolay and Hay, _Lincoln_, VII, 11.

enemy leaders "would never consent to anything but separation and acknowledgment"—i. e., permanent disunion.

Seymour's brother told the President that, "while holding him [Lincoln] responsible," the governor "would sustain him against any unconstitutional attempts against his administration from any quarter." The rebellion, as the brother explained, was a great grief to the governor, though it was not his manner to indulge in loud denunciations. The benefit of the country was the governor's concern, but he was "especially vexed at some of the Republican party who claimed to have a patent right for all the patriotism." [4]

## IV

Seymour asked Lincoln to do some things that the President could not agree to. He asked the suspension of the draft in New York. On August 3, 1863, he sent the President a lengthy letter. He mentioned the mob attack "which ultimately grew into the most destructive riot known in the history of our country." Though giving credit to Federal forces, military and naval, he asserted that the disturbance was put down chiefly by the city police. The general government, he said, could not "give any substantial aid." "It could not even man its own forts." The city of New York, he insisted, showed that they were able to put down the riot "without aid from any other quarter." He then went into the matter of quotas, credits, et cetera, for New York, charging partisan inequalities in the numbers demanded by districts. He mentioned state bounties and reported optimistically as to their effect in stimulating volunteering.

Then he wrote: "I ask that the draft may be suspended in this State . . . until we shall learn the results of recruiting which is now actively going on . . . ." He added: "It is believed by at least one-half of the people of the loyal States that the conscription act . . . is . . . a violation of the supreme constitutional law." The governor placed great confidence in New York volunteering, which he labored vigorously to promote. He wrote of ruinous results that would follow an attempt "to exact obedience at the point of the bayonet." His

---

[4] For the visit of John F. Seymour and the interview, see Mitchell, *Seymour*, 276 ff.; Alexander J. Wall, *A Sketch of the Life of Horatio Seymour*, 29–31.

argument was for "peace of the public mind," winning popular acquiescence, having "subordinate laws" square "with the supreme law of the land." [1]

That was Seymour's side of it, and it was well stated; but as long as the governor's willingness to support the enrollment act remained doubtful, the whole problem of the draft throughout the nation was in abeyance. Governor Kirkwood of Iowa wrote to Stanton, July 15, 1863: "The enforcement of the draft throughout the country depends upon its enforcement in New York City. If it can be successfully resisted there, it cannot be enforced elsewhere. For God's sake let there be no . . . half-way measures." [2] With the same idea in mind a Federal enrolling official wrote: "If New York [City] is excused from the draft the rest of the State will claim the same exemption, and if New York [State] is exempt, of course other States will claim as much. In other words, if the mob conquers in New York it will at least try as much throughout the land." [3] It was of necessity Lincoln's function to look at these matters from the standpoint of the nation, not of any one state. In a mild and conciliatory way he expressed that idea to the governor of New Jersey: "It is a very delicate matter to postpone the draft in one State, because of the argument it furnishes others to have postponement also. If we could have a reason in one case which would be good if presented in all cases, we could act upon it. . . . I beg you to be assured I wish to avoid the difficulties you dread as much as yourself." [4]

On the question of constitutionality Lincoln and Seymour differed in the manner that was to be expected. As Mitchell writes: "Seymour, like many Americans before and since, rationalized his dislike of a law into a conviction that it was contrary to the Constitution. He believed the draft was inexpedient and he persuaded himself that it was illegal." [5] Lincoln, who wrote an unpublished paper explaining that the conscription act was justified under the Constitution,[6] was ready to leave the question of constitutionality to the Supreme Court, but he could not suspend the law on any anticipation that the Court's de-

---

[1] *Offic. Rec.*, 3 ser. III, 613–619.    [2] *Ibid.*, 494.

[3] *Ibid.*, 530.

[4] Lincoln to Governor Joel Parker, July 20, 1863, R. T. L. Coll., 25011; Nicolay and Hay, *Works*, IX, 36.

[5] Mitchell, *Seymour*, 345.    [6] *Lincoln the President*, II, 298–300.

cision might be unfavorable. He was an executive and as long as the law stood it was his duty to enforce it. He wrote: "I do not object to abide a decision of the United States Supreme Court, or of the judges thereof, on the constitutionality of the draft law." [7]

What did Lincoln mean by the expression "or of the judges thereof," as if he were making a distinction between a statement of "the judges" and a decision of the Court? Supreme Court justices in the American system do not give advisory opinions (individually or otherwise), so that could hardly have been the meaning. Justices could have been consulted informally, but that would have been unusual and irregular. All the justices did duty on the circuit as well as on the highest Court, but it is not clear that this is what the President had in mind. There was also the fact that statements which constituted the very essence of the Dred Scott decision were said to be not "judicially decided"—i. e., were not technically before the Court.[8] It will be recalled that Lincoln did not go along with the idea of unquestionable finality attaching to decisions of the Supreme Court. In his first inaugural he had said: ". . . if the policy of the Government upon vital questions, affecting the whole people, is to be irrevocably fixed by decisions of the Supreme Court, the instant they are made, in ordinary litigation . . . , the people will have ceased to be their own rulers, having . . . practically resigned their government into the hands of that eminent tribunal." [9] The Court in 1863 was headed by Taney of Dred Scott fame; it was a close and doubtful matter how the tribunal would have decided on the constitutionality of the conscription act.[10]

---

[7] Nicolay and Hay, *Works*, IX, 60 (Aug. 7, 1863); photographic reproduction, A. Lincoln Assoc.

[8] G. T. Curtis, *Const'l Hist. of U. S.*, II, 268 ff.

[9] The variant versions of this inaugural address include many worksheets in the R. T. Lincoln Collection. In an earlier version, before final revision, Lincoln had used much stronger language concerning the Supreme Court. He had written: "if the policy . . . is to be irrevocably fixed by . . . the Supreme Court, it is plain that the people will have ceased to be their own rulers, having turned their government over to the despotism of the few life-officers composing the Court." R. T. L. Coll., 7743. At the suggestion of Seward the wording was revised and softened as shown in the text quoted above, which is taken from the address as officially printed in *Sen. Exec. Doc. No. 1*, p. 7.

[10] Taney not only opposed the view that the conscription act was constitutionally valid, but actually prepared an (undelivered) opinion denying such validity. *Lincoln the President*, II, 297–298; *Constitutional Problems Under Lincoln* (revised ed., 1951), 274.

## V

Lincoln was acting within the changing American system while state-rights men of the North were unwilling to recognize and accept the changes. Under the impact of war the country was becoming less an aggregation of states and more fully a nation, though by no means a unitary state with all the leading functions consolidated at Washington. In this transitional period, with the nation's assumption of functions not fully realized and vigorously opposed, the President was in a trying position. The enrollment law was consciously intended to make the raising of the army a national function, but that did not mean that people ceased to think in terms of states. While administering this very law the President had to deal with governors all over the country, hearing their complaints when it was felt that burdens, as between states, were unequal.

Lincoln always showed respect for opponents and for men who differed with him. He never assumed the manner of a dictator. It is in this light that one should read his letter of August 7, 1863, in answer to Seymour's of August 3. He began with the heart of the matter. "I cannot consent," he said, "to suspend the draft in New York, as you request . . . ." He explained: "We are contending with an enemy, who, as I understand, drives every ablebodied man he can reach into his ranks, very much as a butcher drives bullocks into a slaughter-pen. No time is wasted, no argument is used. This produces an army which will soon turn upon our now victorious soldiers . . . with a rapidity not to be matched on our side, if we first waste time to reëxperiment with the volunteer system . . . , and then more time to obtain a court decision as to whether a law is constitutional which requires a part of those not now in the service to go to the aid of those who are already in it . . . ." He closed with a reference to his important duty "of maintaining the unity and the free principles of our common country." He signed his name, "Your obedient servant, A. Lincoln." [1]

On the very day that the President was writing this letter stating that the draft would proceed, Seymour, sincere as he was, was making further difficulty. He wrote on August 7 to the President: ". . . I can

---

[1] Nicolay and Hay, *Works*, IX, 58–61.

never forget the honor of my country so far as to spare any effort to
stop proceedings under the draft in this State—and more particularly
in the cities of New York and Brooklyn—which I feel will bring disgrace not only upon your administration but upon the American
name." He stated also that he would send tables to show that "errors,
if . . . not shameless frauds" existed in fixing New York quotas.[2]

On August 8 Seymour wrote in answer to the President's letter of
the 7th (the one, above summarized, in which he refused to suspend
the draft in New York, though making a considerable concession to
correct disparities). The main burden of this August 8 letter from the
governor was a denunciation of the draft in New York and a defense
of his state in its efforts to meet every call with volunteers. Putting
responsibility on Lincoln for the unhappy situation, he wrote: "I
regret your refusal to comply with my request to have the draft in the
State suspended until it can be ascertained if the enrollments are made
in accordance with the laws of Congress or with the principles of
justice." Quoting the President's reference to the enemy's practice of
driving men into the ranks as a butcher drives bullocks to slaughter,
the governor said: ". . . even this . . . is more tolerable than any
scheme which shall fraudulently force a portion of the community
into military service by a dishonest perversion of law." Enclosing a
lengthy report, replete with tables, by his judge advocate general,
Nelson J. Waterbury (comparing quotas by districts) he imputed the
whole difference to partisan motives, and closed by saying: "You cannot and will not fail to right these gross wrongs." [3]

The report by Waterbury, enclosed in Seymour's letter of August 8,
is an example of the voluminous and complicated reading matter
which burdened the President's desk. Supplied with statistics and exceeding four thousand words in length, the report constituted a kind
of argument or brief to prove that the New York draft was unfair to
New York City and especially to the Democratic party. The essence of
the report is contained in the statement that "nine anti-Lincoln
districts [were] required to furnish nearly as many conscripts as the
nineteen Lincoln districts," and in the remark that "The enrollment
is a partisan enrollment . . . ." [4]

To show the light-hearted manner in which one of Lincoln's staff

---

[2] *Offic. Rec.*, 3 ser. III, 636.         [3] *Ibid.*, 639–640.
[4] *Ibid.*, 648–649.

viewed this ponderous report, we have a "private and accidental" note
(August 24, 1863) by John Hay to Fry, the provost marshal general.
"The inevitable Waterbury is again upon us," wrote Hay. "His experience as a political ballot stuffer for twenty years comes up and
troubles his dreams. He is afraid you are stuffing the draft on him.
Read his wail if you don't think life is too short and Lee too near. If
you do, file it. With a firm reliance on Providence and your waste-paper
basket, you cannot fail." The secretary, then headed for the seashore,
signed himself: "Yours, hilariously, John Hay." [5]

With regard to this controversy as to the unfairness of the New York
enrollment, one should notice the following three points:

(1) In order to give every consideration to the Seymour claims, a
commission was appointed with the President's full consent to inquire
into the whole subject.[6] The report of this commission did not blame
the Federal enrollment officers for intentional unfairness, but did
assert that quotas should be adjusted so as to fix the number of drafted
men in proportion to the *entire* population.

(2) Lincoln did not admit the correctness of this formula, since he
considered that quotas should be determined with regard to the number of able-bodied men of military age. The President's view harmo-
nized with the law as passed by Congress.

(3) In spite of this, the President nevertheless brought about a considerable "arbitrary reduction" of the quotas of certain disputed
districts in 1863, following this also with a like reduction in 1864.[7]

Seymour's complaint, stated by his judge advocate general,[8] was that
unjustifiably heavy quotas were demanded of the metropolitan districts (New York City and vicinity) where Democratic voters predomi-
nated, as compared to the rest of the state which had a larger proportion of Republicans. There were, however, so many points in dispute
—both as to the proper proportion for determining quotas, and the
correctness of numerical findings in applying whatever formula was
used—that Lincoln, who was sensitive to the accusation of partisan

5 *Ibid.*, 712.

6 Mitchell, *Seymour*, 346; Nicolay and Hay, *Lincoln*, VII, 40–41. The commission consisted of William F. Allen of New York, a Democrat notably favorable to Seymour;
General John Love of Indiana, a Democrat; and Chauncey Smith of Massachusetts, a
lawyer not strongly committed to either party. It was recognized that Judge Allen domi-
nated the commission.

7 Nicolay and Hay, *Lincoln*, VII, 40–42.

8 *Offic. Rec.*, 3 ser. III, 640–651.

unfairness, considered that it was best, without expecting perfection as to figures or formulas, to make the concession already noted—i.e., to reduce the New York quotas.

This haggling over comparative burdens as between states and groups within states was by no means limited to New York; it was one of the most uninspiring aspects of the conscription controversy. In such a dispute it is futile to look for finality of judgment. It makes the subject no easier to have one formula or finding supported by writers who defend Seymour and another by pro-Lincoln writers. Lincoln himself was not a stickler for the claims made on his supposed "side" of the dispute. There is a certain significance in the carefully balanced statements of the investigating commission (the Allen commission) above mentioned. This commission "acquitt[ed] the [Federal] enrolling officers of intentional unfairness," while on the other hand they made a good deal of the point that quotas should have been adjusted in proportion to the whole population. For New York and Brooklyn the commission found that the quotas were "excessive." [9]

It was on August 11, by way of answering Seymour's communication of the 8th, that the President reported the reduction of New York quotas. He made it clear that he had to get ahead with the job, which would not admit of endless delay. His main principle, he said, was "to proceed with the draft, at the same time employing infallible means to avoid any great wrongs." [10] He was making a practical adjustment, rather than seeking a scientific calculation for quotas of drafted men that would produce precise proportional equality among all districts, remembering that the correct basis of such equality was itself a matter of dispute.

## VI

As the Lincoln administration looked forward to the renewal of the draft in New York City it became necessary to take preventive measures to avoid another riot. Just after the July riot the government

---

[9] Mitchell, *Seymour*, 346. There was nothing in the conscription law that required the determination of district quotas on the basis of total population. The law required an actual enrollment of able-bodied men of military age; this enrollment was the basis of the draft. In section 12 the law authorized the President "to assign to each district the number of men to be furnished by said district. . . ." *U. S. Stat. at Large*, XII, 731–737.

[10] Lincoln to Seymour, Aug. 11, 1863, R. T. L. Coll., 25521.

had sent a high-minded, reliable general, John A. Dix, to command
the Federal forces in the New York area, succeeding the aged General
Wool. Dix was a Democrat with a record for upholding the Union, a
man who knew how to combine discretion with vigor. He had been a
stanch member of Buchanan's cabinet. One can only speculate as to
what would have been the outcome if a man of a different type—e. g.,
a fiery radical Republican—had been given the important New York
assignment. It has been stated by Dix's son and biographer that certain
Republican radicals had been "busily engaged . . . to get General
Benjamin F. Butler sent to command in New York, in view of the
draft." [1] It would be an obvious understatement to say that an orderly
and peaceable situation could not have been anticipated with Butler
in command. Since one of the important functions of an executive is
that of appointment, it is worth while to judge the President's choice
of Dix in contrast to the kind of choice that would have been made
by men of less discretion within the dominant party. In choosing a
Democrat, Lincoln was pointedly avoiding partisanship in this selection. (Butler had been a Democrat, but he was a Republican radical
or extremist in the making. Such extremists were pushing him forward.) The value of Dix was in his well known character, and in recognition of the fact that "he could not be ruled in the interest of any
faction, but occupied a broad, national ground." [2]

In the Dix-Seymour correspondence, which paralleled that of Seymour and Lincoln, one finds two New York Democrats who equally
professed devotion to the national cause, but who differed strongly
in their approach to the problem of the draft and of its enforcement
in state and city. Dix inquired whether state military power would
be used "to enforce the execution of the law in case of forcible resistance." [3] This was in the period when Seymour was assuming that the
New York draft would be "suspended." The governor answered Dix,
if it was an answer, by saying that he had sent Lincoln a letter on
August 3 (it was in this letter that he had requested suspension of the
draft); he thought this would avert the "painful questions growing
out of an armed enforcement of the conscription law in this patriotic
State." [4]

This did not satisfy Dix, who proved an emphatic spokesman for

---

1 Morgan Dix, *Memoirs of J. A. Dix*, II, 85.    2 *Ibid.*
3 *Offic. Rec.*, 3 ser. III, 592.    4 *Ibid.*, 619.

the national side in the controversy. The general made it clear that it was his duty to aid enrolling officers and to put down resistance to the law. He hoped the governor would assist with state troops; otherwise he would have to ask for an adequate Federal force. He regretted that the governor had characterized the law as "the conscription act." [5] This, said Dix, was a foreign phrase. There was danger, thought the general, that the chief executive of New York might "be understood to regard it as an obnoxious law which ought not to be carried into execution," thus throwing his important influence "against the Government in a conflict for its existence." The enemy were making heavy demands on their man power. "Shall not we," asked Dix, "do as much for the preservation of our political institutions as they are . . . to . . . destroy them?" Whatever the defects of the act, Dix urged that "it is the law of the land." He added: "Those, therefore, who array themselves against it, are obnoxious to far severer censure than the ambitious or misguided men [official secessionists] who are striving to subvert the Government," for the latter were acting "by color of sanction" under their legislatures and conventions. Dix concluded by an appeal at this late date (August 8) for the governor's early assurance that the state power would "be employed to enforce the draft." [6]

After a week's delay Seymour answered (August 15) in a manner which convinced the general that he had better look to Washington in making "arrangements for maintaining the law of Congress and keeping the peace in a city which had recently been the theatre of horrible scenes of riot, battle, pillage, and murder." [7] In this letter of August 15 Seymour expressed full confidence that volunteering in New York would adequately serve the need for troops and that no compulsion was necessary. Having said this, the governor added that state authorities could not perform duties "expressly confided to others," nor "relieve others from their . . . responsibilities." Nothing like a riot, however, could occur without infraction of state law; hence state officers would "perform their duties vigorously and thoroughly," if necessary with state military support. The governor, in this letter,

---

[5] Seymour could hardly have been blamed for calling it a "conscription" act. The whole system was so unfortunate in method and emphasis that if its supporters went into details, they were embarrassed in defending it. Under President Wilson, in contrast, the term used was not "conscription" but "selective service."

[6] *Offic. Rec.,* 3 ser. III, 652–654.　　　　[7] Dix, *Memoirs of J. A. Dix,* II, 86.

was standing in a midway position; he was promising action by state authorities to keep order, but was not making it clear that General Dix would have his full coöperation.[8] An indication of Seymour's mood at this time appeared in his letter of August 6 to Samuel J. Tilden. He was satisfied, he said, that the government at Washington "means to go on in a spirit of hostility to this State; that it is governed by a spirit of malice in all things small and great." Under these circumstances, he wrote: "I look for nothing but hostility." It was Seymour's view that conscription would "make the [Lincoln] administration odious and contemptible." [9]

In the uncertain situation in which he found himself, Dix thought it best to apply to Washington for Federal troops to be sent to New York. Stanton replied (August 15) that 10,000 infantry and three batteries of artillery ("picked troops") were being sent. At the same time, Stanton submitted to Dix certain presidential orders, to be issued or not according to the general's discretion. By one order the President called forth the New York militia into national service (of which, of course, the President was commander in chief) in order to suppress "unlawful combinations." By the other order the state major-general of militia (Charles W. Sanford) was directed to "report forthwith to Major-general John A. Dix." [10]

It did not prove necessary to use this double-barreled order from Washington. The large force of Federal troops came, and the state militia was not summoned for the enforcement of the draft, which Seymour and his staff would have resented. Thus another possible misstep in the vexing New York situation was avoided as a matter of Federal policy.

Things were now set for going ahead with the draft. Dix was firmly but unprovocatively in command. Lincoln had made his concessions as to draft reductions. Reënrollment had been ordered, "employing infallible means to avoid any great wrongs." [11] United States troops were in New York by August 17. On that day General Dix issued an address "To the Citizens of New York." He insisted that there must be no resistance to "the law of the land" and earnestly exhorted the

8 *Ibid.*, II, 82.      9 Mitchell, *Seymour*, 344.

10 Dix, *Memoirs of J. A. Dix*, 86–87. These two orders, worded in the manner of formal proclamations, were submitted (for possible issue) over Lincoln's name, but they apparently originated in the war department.

11 Lincoln to Seymour, Aug. 11, 1863, R. T. L. Coll., 25521.

people to preserve the good name of their city, to maintain order, obey the laws, and quietly pursue their accustomed avocations. Should there be renewed disturbance, he clearly warned that violence would be "met by the most prompt and vigorous measures." [12]

When the draft was resumed (August 19) after all this prudent preparation, it proceeded in peaceable fashion.[13] In the long run the main significance of the whole episode was the demonstration that supremacy belongs to regularly constituted authorities when it is known that they are determined to maintain order. The part which Seymour had in this result should not be overlooked. It was Dix's belief that the presence of Federal troops accomplished the purpose, and that without violence; but it should be added that the governor issued a proclamation on August 18 in which he counseled the people to submit to conscription, despite his objection to the system. He admonished officials to enforce the law and preserve order, and declared that "Riotous proceedings must and shall be put down . . . and the lives and property of citizens protected at any and every hazard." [14]

## VII

It would have been an advantage if, in the long-drawn-out New York controversy, a full stop could have been reached, a termination of complaint followed by smooth-working adjustment and absence of friction. Some writers consider the date August 19, the day of the unobstructed resumption of the draft in the state, as the settlement and quieting of the trouble, and in a sense it was. The draft proceeded and there was no further mob disturbance. After August 19, however, there were voluminous queries by the New York governor and his aides as to credits and the like, necessitating time-consuming study and replies by the President and other national officials. It was a high-policy matter, but it was also a tediously involved administrative problem.

There was, for instance, an elaborate letter from Seymour dated

---

12 Dix, *Memoirs of J. A. Dix*, II, 88–91.

13 "There is not the least symptom of disturbance in any part of the city. . . . The militia are all under arms co-operating perfectly." C. A. Dana to Stanton, New York, Aug. 19, 1863, *Offic. Rec.*, 3 ser. III, 693.

14 Wall, *A Sketch of . . . Horatio Seymour*, 51; *Public Record . . . of Horatio Seymour* (campaign document, 1868), 147.

August 21.[1] The governor was unsatisfied as to credits for volunteers; he complained that he had not been informed of the exact dates of coming drafts, and he raised the objection that men in large numbers had been drawn off from New York "into the service of other States." Men enrolled in New York, he said, had been obtained as volunteers and substitutes for adjoining commonwealths. A question was raised as to finality in the determination of the number to be drafted for a district. This was a point that could not be left indefinitely open. Without too much delay there had to be, at some time, a fixing of the quotas and a closing of the books, after which further credits for volunteers could not be made till the next draft.

Lincoln had the Seymour protest studied by the United States provost marshal general, J. B. Fry, who supplied explanatory or refuting comments in the margin. The President then patiently explained to the governor that credits for volunteers would be allowed "up to the last moment which will not produce confusion or delay." [2] He also made it clear that the governor would be notified when the drawing of names was to occur in each district of the state. As he had already explained, he could not give up "a drafted man now" for a volunteer (or the "mere *chance*" of one) later. And, after a draft had actually been made, it would make trouble "to take any drafted man out and put a volunteer in; for how shall it be determined, which drafted man is to have the privilege of thus going out, to the exclusion of all the others?" It would disrupt the system too much "if every time a volunteer is offered the officers must stop and reconstruct the quota." [3]

As to the governor's protest concerning the loss of "credit" owing to a kind of raiding by "agents" of other states, that was one of the numerous headaches of the whole system. It appeared, wrote the provost marshal general, that "the practice complained of, which is general throughout the United States, was especially outraging in New York." A ruling on the subject had been requested of Judge Advocate General Holt, who gave the legal opinion that the state in which a drafted man is enrolled is credited with one soldier whether he serves or furnishes a substitute; if that substitute comes from an-

---

[1] *Offic. Rec.*, 3 ser. III, 703–705.

[2] Lincoln to Seymour, Aug. 16, 1863, photostat, A. Lincoln Assoc. See also Lincoln to Stanton, Aug. 26, 1863, R. T. L. Coll., 25857–8.

[3] Lincoln to Seymour, Aug. 16, 1863, photostat, A. Lincoln Assoc.

other state, that could not be helped; the national government could not be debited with two soldiers when it received but one.[4]

One reason why Lincoln's wish for adjustment of draft difficulties was constantly hampered in New York was, of course, the unending maneuvering between parties. It was hard for partisans to bear the thought that friendly adjustment would have helped the Lincoln administration. It was of course known (though Lincoln was generous toward Democrats) that administration success would be proclaimed in the Republican sense. On October 27, a few days before the New York election of 1863, the subject of the draft was given the main emphasis in a printed circular issued by the Democratic state central committee. Expressing full confidence in success in the coming election, while at the same time urging that faithful and earnest work was required in every election district, the signers of the circular—Dean Richmond and Peter Cagger—made the accusation that the state was "charged . . . for every citizen who has paid the Three Hundred Dollars commutation—receiving no credit whatever therefor." They asserted that "the payment . . . only releases the conscript for the time being, and that the State still owes the Government a man." [5]

This circular was promptly answered by the provost marshal general, who declared the statement "untrue." In refutation of the "misrepresentations," it was pointed out that "every citizen who has paid the $300 commutation . . . is exonerated from military service for the time for which he was drafted, to wit, for three years." [6]

To illustrate another headache in the whole cumbersome administration of the draft, there was the question of where and when troops should be placed for maintaining order where mob disturbance was anticipated. The desired result was to prevent trouble before it started, which meant having soldiers already on hand at each district provost-marshal headquarters at which the need of soldiers was expected. But how could this be done? The suggestion was made that different drafting dates be set up for different districts, so that soldiers could be "moved from point to point as the draft progressed." [7] This was but another example of the awkward procedure of Civil War days. A much better system was used in 1917–18, where, instead of drawing

---

[4] *Offic. Rec.*, 3 ser. III, 729.

[6] *Offic. Rec.*, 3 ser. III, 981.

[5] Printed circular, R. T. L. Coll., 27528.

[7] *Ibid.*, 502.

names at various times by districts within the states, there was "a single national drawing [of serial numbers] for all registrants." [8]

## VIII

The Lincoln-Seymour affair, in its many facets, stands out as a notable case study in wartime administration within a democracy, while it is also a study in personalities. The governor's difference with the President was, to him, a matter of great validity; it was not trumped up. He could not approve a sectional administration at Washington, he detested the war, and he honestly opposed conscription as a method of raising soldiers. He was nevertheless pro-Union and ready to see that New York, without compulsion, would do its part, both in sending troops and in keeping order. As to the preference for volunteering rather than drafting, that was evident even within the conscription system. The poorly devised draft law was itself a considerable factor in putting a stigma and a kind of badge of inferiority upon the drafted man. After the governor's death John F. Seymour remarked that "the only reproachful words he had ever heard his dead brother speak of the President with whom he had felt it was his duty to differ were these: 'Mr. Lincoln was not fair to me.' " [1] As shown earlier in this chapter in his letter to Tilden, Seymour wrote frankly of the "hostility" of men in Washington, but, while constantly expressing opposition to the President's policy, he said in October 1862: ". . . although I am politically opposed to him, never have I allowed myself to utter against him one disrespectful term, nor will I ever allow myself to do so." [2]

Yet Seymour's gentlemanly attitude and the uprightness of his sense of duty were not the whole story. Besides the hard core of the New York situation there was, in association with Seymour, a considerable fringe—a cluster of attendant influences inimical to Lincoln and, as the President believed, calculated to injure the national cause. Lincoln, too, was a gentleman on his side of the controversy. His position was not easy. He had a war to conduct, an army to raise, a whole cause

---

[8] *Second Report of the Provost Marshal General . . . to December 1918* (Washington, 1919), 41.

[1] Mitchell, *Seymour*, 382.

[2] Speech at Brooklyn Academy of Music, Oct. 22, 1862, *Public Record . . . of Horatio Seymour*, 77.

to promote. He had to adjust himself to the bitter problem of administration in a democracy amid powerful divisive forces. On both sides
there were unreasonable partisan maneuvers and tricks. In this complex situation the historian can show that both men were patriotic
and both of them sensible, but patriots differed as to measures. Factors
at work in the crisis were abnormal. Politics was not adjourned during
the war and the blame for that condition rested with both parties. The
Democrats were at a disadvantage. They had reason to resent what a
faction of the Republican party was doing. There were men in both
parties who doubted the wisdom of the contemporary conscription
law, one of the worst of its kind.

In the position in which he found himself, Lincoln played an honorable and a conciliatory, but not a weak, part. To show the President's
lack of personal animosity, there is an interesting parallel between
his attitude toward Seymour in 1863 and toward Douglas in 1858. In
that year of the debate, in the very last speech of the long canvass,
Lincoln had said: "I claim no insensibility to political honors; but
today . . . [if the spread of slavery could be checked], I would . . .
gladly agree, that Judge Douglas should never be *out,* and I never *in,*
an office, so long as we both or either, live." [3]

We even have an indication or hint, in the recollection of Thurlow
Weed, that Lincoln stood ready to support Seymour for the presidency
looking forward to 1864, and that the President wished Weed to
broach this subject to the governor. Not long before Weed's death
(which occurred in November 1882) a New York journalist had, as he
reported, an interview with the aged politician who was then quite
feeble. The interview was at Weed's request. The journalist's account
proceeded:

His purpose in inviting me to call, he said, was to request me to see
Horatio Seymour and extract from him a promise that, when he came to
New York city again, he would give Mr. Weed an opportunity for a long-
sought interview . . . . He said that in the latter portion of Mr. Lincoln's first term that statesman [Weed] became profoundly impressed with
the conviction that the war could never be brought to a successful termination under a Republican President, nor probably under any partisan

[3] Speech, Oct. 30, 1858, photostat of autograph MS. A. Lincoln Assoc.; Oliver R. Barrett
(name not given on title page), *Lincoln's Last Speech in Springfield in the Campaign of
1858,* 14.

President, and that some man must be sought out whose purity of character, statesmanship, exalted abilities and devotion to the Union would be recognized by all parties and all sections, so that he might be carried into the Presidency by acclamation. After long and anxious consideration and discussion, Horatio Seymour was settled upon as the only eligible citizen; that this gentleman was approached and made aware of these views of Mr. Lincoln . . . , and that the negotiations were not at first discouraged or repulsed, but as time passed on the proposed beneficiary of this extraordinary political movement became less inclined to regard the scheme as practicable or desirable . . . , and that the subsequent successes of the Union arms changed Mr. Lincoln's views and purposes, and made him desire and accept a renomination.[4]

There is good evidence that this was Weed's recollection. He mentions the matter in his memoirs and Seymour's biographer writes: "Weed was making use of this story as early as 1864, and in one form or another it has persisted to this day." [5] To contemplate such an "extraordinary political movement" was not unlike Lincoln and there were times in the war when the military and political outlook would have argued the desirability of a President who could have been placed completely above, and aside from, parties. Just who among the leaders of that day could have qualified in that respect is a matter of conjecture, but there are sufficient references to the "story" to indicate that it can be traced to Weed's recollection of what Lincoln said to him.[6]

As to the actual 1863 situation the fact of the President being of one party and the New York governor of another should not be misunderstood. Instead of treating this difference with a party slant as some writers have done, it would be more in keeping with Lincoln's thought to view the subject from a nonpartisan, or unpartisan standpoint. Lincoln felt that he and Seymour had much in agreement in that they had the same stake in keeping the government going. It was

---

4 "Geneva, N. Y. Corr. of the Utica Observer," Washington *Post*, Feb. 4, 1883. The interview was reported as having occurred in the summer of 1882. For calling attention to this article and supplying a copy the author is grateful to David Rankin Barbee of Washington.

5 Stewart Mitchell, *Horatio Seymour*, 273. Mitchell shows (273-274) that Lincoln's proposal to support Seymour as a kind of unpartisan successor was mentioned in such publications as the Albany *Evening Journal* (Weed's paper), the *Atlas and Argus* of Albany (with contemptuous comment), and the New York *Standard and Statesman*.

6 Nicolay and Hay (*Lincoln*, VII, 12-13) mention the story as related in Weed's *Memoirs*.

like saying: We can agree to differ, but let's not allow the government to break down.

The challenge to Lincoln was serious, whether one has in mind his official authority or his capacity for human adjustment. In his management of the affair he succeeded in upholding the national authority while also avoiding a miserable explosion between the Federal government and a leading state. Indeed one of the significant points for the historian in the controversy is to note how a democracy functions when determined and seriously aroused groups are motivated by opposite intentions. Difficulties may become ominous and contention may become warm, but the time usually comes when some kind of working formula, some *modus vivendi*, becomes a necessity. If both sides ultimately realize this, such a realization is an indication that, amid strong diversity, a degree of basic unity is discernible. Such democratic unity was the theme of Lincoln's above-mentioned interview with Governor Seymour's brother. It may be regarded as the key to this chapter, and other chapters, of the Lincoln administration.

# NATIONS UNDER STRESS: UNITED
# STATES AND BRITAIN

IN THE slowness of sea travel and communication in Lincoln's day the Atlantic Ocean might have seemed a vast wall of separation. However natural such an offhand assumption, the true situation was far otherwise. Imperfectly bridged though it was, the ocean was less a factor of isolation than a thoroughfare in which nothing was more certain than the contact of nations and the jostling of international interests. In the *Trent* affair an incident of ocean travel had quickly developed into a menacing crisis. It was only by restraint on both sides and by diplomacy in the valid sense that a war of untold proportions and fearful consequences between the United States and Britain was happily avoided. Statesmen breathed more freely when that severe crisis was passed; but the enveloping ocean was still there, and on its busy ships were laden those questions of commerce, blockade, prestige, international law, economic interest, recognition, and partisan assistance which carried through to the very core of the American conflict.

A small matter might involve the large issue: the repair of a rudder or the detention of a ship was likely to include the whole attitude that a foreign nation might take on the problem of recognizing, perchance of assisting, the forces of secession. Let one step be taken and others would follow. In the construction and fitting out of a single warship to serve against the United States there lurked again the possibility of war between Britain and America. Yet the chance of war has often lurked; in Lincoln's day the avoidance of actual conflict, with no loss of America's true interest, was the significant fact.

To treat the foreign outlook that confronted Lincoln and his administration would be to devote a complicated volume to that phase alone; nothing like an adequate coverage of the subject is possible here. There was Europe and here was the United States: Europe with its reactionary aristocracy, military castes, concepts of legitimate monarchy, predatory nationalism, frontier shibboleths, inflexible groupings, suppressed populations, and rumblings of revolution; the United States, less hampered with inhibitions and burgeoning with impulses of democracy, but threatened with dissolution and racked to its foundations with civil war. Peace on the old continent was inadequately organized. Indeed it was not organized at all. One aggressor might have the nations stymied. In Prussia's assault upon unoffending Denmark statesmen abroad might know well enough what was happening, but Bismarck seemed to have them hypnotized. And the minor Danish War led directly to war on a major scale. The compelling and all possessing impulse in Europe was for unity—unfortunately, however, not helpful human solidarity, but the militant unity of rampant nationalism. In contrast a vast proportion of America was thinking of separation. How could a Cavour, a Bismarck, a Palmerston, or a Gladstone understand what these Americans were about? Political leaders across the ocean might have formulas of peace for America, but they were heading toward wars on their own borders, and desires of certain groups for "mediation" in the American quarrel might bespeak not so much a helping hand as a meddling partisanship. With the fine word peace there went the words independence, freedom, and self government, but these honored words could be bandied about by those who would tear down the very basis of democracy.

## I

Those who had to deal with Anglo-American relations in the days of Lincoln had full need of judgment, skill, and patience. There were pitfalls and danger spots, and at times such elements of instability as to cause statesmen to shudder. As one factor, there was on both sides an unreasonable readiness—among some—to rush into a fight supposedly for "honor" or for an idea, without forethought as to where such a fight would lead or whether the true idea or genuine honor required a fight. To the extent that passions were whipped up, such forethought would be left out of account. Englishmen were unfortunately ignorant of America and Americans of England. There is a record of an M. P. breakfasting with an American visitor in the summer of '63. The M. P. expected to hear next that Lee had entered Philadelphia, Baltimore, and Washington, "& then—a—a—he will just turn round and re-capture New Orleans—New Orleans is about 100 miles from Washington, I think?"[1]

There was always, in the minds of officials, the uncertainty as to what would happen next. What does Seward intend, would be a question in British minds. What about his alleged remark to Newcastle that insulting England was the only sure passport to popular favor in America?[2] Was the Secretary spoiling for a fight? Was Lincoln a boor and a brute? How would the next major battle turn out? Did Americans have aggressive designs upon Canada? What was the meaning of emancipation? Was it to stir up criminal violence against Southern whites?

In America the queries would indicate similar misunderstanding and uncertainty. Would Britain recognize the Confederates? What was the meaning of war preparations, what would Parliament do, how far did Parliament represent the people, why did British investors subscribe to the cotton loan? Sometimes a mere question or doubtful suspicion would become itself a provocative factor. To put a query into words, even though it lacked substance, would arouse distrust and deepen misunderstanding. Through all the speculations much would depend upon the basic good sense of both sides. Waters of diplomacy might be treacherous, but statesmanship might win though if the helmsman at the wheel could keep his bearings. To do so he had to remember that, while war talk was cheap and easy, yet amid popular clamor it was always necessary to keep in view the force of common inheritance, the stability of established relations, and the unquestioned importance of continued peace on both sides.

In Britain there were certain elements whose desire was not so much for "freedom" in America as for defeat and disintegration. It was the common men, the striving British millions, who wished success to the American nation and sensed a common cause with Lincoln. Among those abroad who desired the cracking of the American Union the

---

[1] E. Schuyler to H. W. Bellows, Aug. 3, 1863, Bellows MSS.
[2] C. F. Adams, Sr., to C. F. Adams, Jr., Dec. 20, 1861, W. C. Ford, ed., *Cycle of Adams Letters*, 88.

friends of democracy were few and far between. This is another way of saying that Lincoln's Gettysburg address had validity, and that, however imperfectly they might be fulfilled, the aspirations of democratically minded men were at one with the homely President at Washington.[3]

It was a stage in international relations in which neutrality was both an accepted principle and an imperfectly developed procedure. As a basic concept neutrality signified that if a conflict is alien and foreign, and if the issue of that conflict is not of concern to a nation, participation by that nation is unwise. As to procedures, baffling and difficult issues could arise in matters of reciprocal duties and rights of belligerents and neutrals. In the American struggle the very term "belligerent" was questioned; the rightful belligerency of the Confederate States of America was strenuously disputed by the government of Washington. There was also the inevitable embarrassment of any neutral in a huge and fiercely contested war. It was evident that neither Washington nor Richmond desired Britain to be guided by genuine neutrality. As Earl Russell's biographer put it, referring to the beginning of the conflict when British recognition of the mere belligerency of the Confederacy was resented by both sides: "Thus, even in these early stages of the war, the British Government was ascertaining by experience that strict neutrality in a struggle is never acceptable to either combatant."[4] The United States desired out-and-out denial of Confederate belligerency; this would have rendered pointless all the British emphasis upon the even balance between two conflicting governments in maritime and other matters. Since it was denied at Washington that two governments rightly existed, acceptance of governmental claims of the Confederacy, if only as one of two belligerents toward which Britain would hold an impartial course, was regarded as taking sides.

If one turns to Richmond he finds again that British neutrality was not desired. What President Davis and Secretary Benjamin wanted

---

[3] It is hard to reconcile this concept with actual American developments in the post-Lincoln period with its corruption, predatory exploitation, capitalistic abuse, and unenlightened treatment of the South. The imperfections of American democracy in the period after the Civil War cannot be overlooked, neither can they be explored here. Their significance for the Lincoln theme is obvious: it was the anti-Lincoln element that seized the reins of party and of government in the era of abuse that men have miscalled "reconstruction." And the democratic importance of saving the American nation from dissolution extended far beyond the immediate postwar period.

[4] Spencer Walpole, *The Life of Lord John Russell*, II, 342.

was that Britain should aid and abet their war; they desired unneutral intervention and assistance. The records of Confederate diplomats show that they were most hopeful at those moments when they could report, perhaps by wishful thinking, that Palmerston was about to "shake off his neutrality." [5]

In these trying circumstances it is worth remembering that the friendship of the United States with Great Britain was not in fact broken; on the other hand something equivalent to a breach—if one can speak of a breach where regular diplomatic relations never existed—did occur between England and the Confederacy in the latter part of 1863. Shaken and embarrassed though they were, statesmen at Washington and London did not forget the essential friendliness of nations. They did not overlook the comparative triviality of international disputes when weighed against the colossal disaster of war.

## II

The conduct of international affairs was firmly enough in official hands, but it is surprising to notice how many Americans turned up abroad during Lincoln's administration and tried their hand—some of them semi-officially—at the business of diplomacy or of foreign propaganda. The idea of sending private citizens to serve as agents of good will abroad, occurred to Seward in 1861. After a number of declinations he obtained the services of Thurlow Weed the New York politician; Charles P. McIlvaine, Episcopal bishop of Ohio; and the Most Reverend John Hughes, Catholic Archbishop of New York. The government paid the expenses of Hughes and McIlvaine but not of Weed, whose brand of politics was unpalatable to certain groups, especially those of the antislavery persuasion. Weed was to use his journalistic contacts to combat Confederate propaganda, McIlvaine to make his appeal to the British clergy, Hughes to labor with the Papacy, with Napoleon III, and with other Catholic rulers.

Though somewhat baffled by the British impression that Seward was an ogre, Weed devoted himself to organizing a pro-American campaign in the press.[1] There was something about Weed's lack of enthusiastic fervor, his solidity, and his un-English manner which made

---

[5] *Offic. Rec.* (Nav.), 2 ser., III, 566.

[1] Glyndon G. Van Deusen, *Thurlow Weed: Wizard of the Lobby*, 275-281.

him an effective advocate. He discounted the Newcastle story, created a better attitude toward Seward, kept the secretary informed, and in the winter of 1861–62 played an important part in smoothing over the *Trent* affair. It was not to have been expected that Minister Adams would make the contacts with the English press which the Albany editor could make. Weed did, however, work well with Adams; it was remarked in this connection that politics made strange bedfellows.[2]

Though less was said of McIlvaine than of Weed, the bishop did his quiet work well. Chase thought he was "doing a great work and a good one." [3] Benjamin Moran of the American legation commented on his refinement and his activity in "correcting British opinion on our affairs." [4] As to Hughes, his position as a Catholic prelate caused special reliance to be placed upon his statements. His task was difficult since he encountered much pro-Confederate sentiment, but he refrained from argument with those whose minds were closed and carefully avoided trenching upon the proper domain of Minister Dayton in France. He reported foreign opinion to Seward, presented to Napoleon III the American position on the *Trent* case, and gave pertinent comment on the alleged grievances of the South. His letters to Seward were submitted to and highly appreciated by President Lincoln.[5]

Of importance in financial circles was August Belmont, a Democrat whose opposition to Lincoln did not check his sincere devotion to the Union cause. Visiting abroad in 1861 and 1863, and keeping up an active correspondence with friends in Britain and France, he wielded influence in foreign financial circles and offered timely advice to the Lincoln administration. Belmont was a man of influential family connections, being related to Matthew G. Perry of Japanese fame and to John Slidell. His eminence in finance was illustrated by his serving as American agent of the Rothschilds.

Other representatives of the business world were John Murray Forbes of Boston and William H. Aspinwall of New York, Forbes be-

---

[2] Charles Francis Adams, Jr. to his father, March 11, 1862, *Cycle of Adams Letters*, 118.

[3] Chase to McIlvaine, Feb. 17, 1862, MS., J. P. Morgan Lib. Interesting details concerning Bishop McIlvaine are given by David Rankin Barbee in *Southern Churchman*, Sep. 10, 1932, 12–14.

[4] Sarah A. Wallace and Frances E. Gillespie, eds., *Journal of Benjamin Moran, 1857–1865*, II, 920.

[5] *Cath. Hist. Rev.*, III, 336–339 (Oct. 1917).

ing a power in shipping, Aspinwall in railroad enterprise, and both in finance. Forbes was a man of many public-minded activities, such as helping Governor Andrew in war work, promoting Negro recruiting, and organizing the Loyal Publication Society. His service abroad, on secret mission, was especially valuable in the final adjustment of the affair of the Laird rams. In this enterprise his collaborator, Aspinwall, was respected by mercantile and financial groups and known for disinterested competence. It was specifically the business of Forbes and Aspinwall to undo the work in Britain of Captain James D. Bulloch of the Confederate Navy. Closely associated with this pair was William M. Evarts of New York, a lawyer of uncommon force who used his legal talents to prevent the ironclad rams from reaching the Confederates. It appears that Minister Adams did not relish Evarts's activities, nor did Moran; but the lawyer was of service in unexpected ways, as in making British leaders more familiar with the financial policies of Chase.

One of the most vigorous of the unofficial American advocates in Britain was the fluent preacher-orator Henry Ward Beecher, exuberant antislavery leader and mighty man of the pulpit. His speeches in the industrial city of Manchester and the shipping center of Liverpool were nothing less than sensational. Standing his ground against vociferous and persistent heckling at Liverpool, he felt "like a shipmaster attempting to preach on board a ship through a speaking trumpet with a tornado on the sea and a mutiny among the men." [6] But he did stand his ground, and his Liverpool performance stands out as a memorable feat of endurance against heavy odds. Not confining his talk to religious themes, he enlarged upon the cotton question, the American constitution, proslavery motives of Southerners, and tolerance in America (at least in his Brooklyn church) toward colored people.

Henry's famous sister, Harriet Beecher Stowe, had influential friends in England, having been honored with a remarkable welcome in her visits to that country in the fifties. An active letter writer, she used her pen in personal correspondence for the cause of Union and freedom. An example was an open letter to "many thousands of Women in Great Britain and Ireland." [7] The purpose of this letter was to fasten the guilt of slavery upon the Southern Confederacy and

---

[6] Lyman Abbott, *Henry Ward Beecher*, 256.
[7] *Atlantic Monthly*, XI, 120–133 (Jan., 1863).

to interpret favorably the Union policy of emancipation. In her letter of July 31, 1863, to the Duchess of Argyll she wrote: "Slavery will be sent out by this agony. We are only in the throes and ravings of the exorcism. The roots of the cancer have gone everywhere, but they must die—will." [8]

In a class by himself among Americans abroad was the former secretary of the treasury and governor of Kansas, Robert J. Walker, northerner by birth, Mississippian by residence, and propagandist in Britain for the Union. By his boldness and pranks in England he became one of the wonders of the age as when he rose in a balloon from the Surrey side of the Thames, sailed aloft over London, and descended in Hertfordshire. None of the upholders of the American cause in Britain was more active than this tireless Walker. Knowing quite a bit about finance and having a special relation to Chase, he was listened to with attention. In one of his pamphlets he struck at Confederate financial credit and made it appear, contrary to fact, that Mississippi's repudiation of its state bonds, largely in the hands of British creditors, was the work of Jefferson Davis. He ranged over the whole subject of the war, emphasizing Union victory, exposing Confederate weakness, denouncing Southern slavery as hostile to progress, and linking the Lincoln administration with the liberties of man. By his reports, as in his correspondence with Chase, the British working classes were "all for us," war with Britain was not to be feared, emancipation was enthusiastically hailed by the British people, and "rebel" agents could make but the poorest bargain with British subscribers for their loan. Walker was determined to break their loan, to make them odious, and to ruin their cause both in Britain and on the Continent. In one of his letters to Chase he wrote: "Please say to Mr. Lincoln, that, with steady perseverance in his emancipation policy, & successful results, he will have a higher European reputation than any American since the days of Washington & Franklin, will have exalted our country in the eyes of the world, & given a new & irresistible impulse to free institutions. . . . Please say this to Mr. Lincoln from one, who neither expects nor would accept office or emoluments . . . ." [9]

These men, and a number of others who could be mentioned, may

---

[8] Charles E. Stowe, *Life of Harriet Beecher Stowe*, 370.

[9] Walker to Chase, London, May 8, 1863, Chase MSS., Pa. Hist. Soc. (There are many such letters from Walker to Chase in this series.)

be thought of as Lincoln's unofficial ambassadors of good will. The full effect of their activity may be somewhat a matter of conjecture, but they served with zeal, each in his area of contact, and it may at least be said that good will was for the most part promoted during the time of their various and somewhat miscellaneous missions.[10]

As for diplomacy in the usual sense—international relations on the official level—that was handled by Charles Francis Adams, American minister at London. One could speak of his limitations: his inadequate appreciation of Lincoln's qualities, his imperfect contact with the British people, his failure to give due credit to Dudley at Liverpool, and so on. Yet for performance and results at the assigned task he proved one of the most successful of American servants abroad. British officials recognized in him a man of worth and force. He could play the game, perhaps not always with finesse, but by diligent watching to see that attainable tricks were not lost. To take three Adamses in lineal succession—John, John Quincy, and Charles Francis—and trace their international dealings, is to cover the major chapters in American foreign affairs in the first, and formative, century of American national history. Such a tracing, to give briefest mention of immensely important developments, would include the diplomacy of the Revolution, the treaty of independence, the signing of peace with Britain in December 1814, the formulation of the Monroe doctrine, and the steering of Anglo-American relations under Lincoln.

## III

While in the large the American question abroad might involve the broadest interests, the situation at a given time was reducible to choices between concrete courses of action. So far as it concerned Britain, by far the most important country in American relations, the leading problems were two: (1) the basic issue that came to mind when one mentioned such related words as recognition, armistice, unneutral assistance, mediation, or intervention; and (2) the building of warships for the Confederate States of America. Other matters, such as recruiting in Ireland for Federal service and various forms of financial assistance, might be productive of friction; yet these two

---

10 For a comprehensive treatment of these unofficial diplomats, see August C. Miller, Jr., "Lincoln's Good-Will Ambassadors," *Lincoln Herald*, vol. 50, 17-27 (June, 1948).

main issues contained the core of the difficulty. As to the blockade and the cotton shortage, its serious potentialities were comprised within the ominous word "intervention." Also one might take the question of slavery, but it too was of vital effect chiefly as it bore upon possible intervention or recognition.

It is proper, therefore, to consider mediation and recognition, with its related question of the blockade and its threat of possible intervention, as the central issue, the more so as it occupied enormous space in British, continental, and American newspapers and in the diplomatic correspondence of the time. That Britain never did worse than hover on the brink in this matter when it seemed abroad that the Confederacy was sure to win, was a sufficient indication of the success of Union diplomacy, and of British also. That the imperial government of France made an offer of mediation early in 1863 was a matter of minor importance for several reasons: the offer was indignantly spurned by the United States government without untoward effect; the French government never carried its sympathy for the Confederacy to the point of effective substantial aid; and the mediation gesture from Paris was without British support. What could have made recognition and mediation serious would have been combined action by Britain and France. This was frequently mentioned as a possibility, but, as with many a specter of international trouble, it never materialized.

All nations, especially those newly formed, are sensitive as to international position and prestige. The Confederacy was poignantly eager for recognition. Its diplomats and semi-official emissaries were much in evidence. At the outset of its existence, even before the war, the Confederate government sent three of its hopefuls—William L. Yancey, Pierre A. Rost, and A. Dudley Mann—on a preliminary foreign mission. Later the two aces of cotton diplomacy were sent, James M. Mason to Britain and John Slidell to France. Lesser emissaries tried their hand in approaching foreign governments, including those of Spain, Belgium, the Papal States, Russia, the French-dominated Empire of Mexico, and even dependencies or subdivisions to which diplomats were not usually accredited, such as Ireland, Canada, West Indian colonies, and individual states within Mexico.

In the drive for British recognition the Yancey-Rost-Mann mission of early 1861 got no farther than an "informal interview" with Lord

Russell on May 3, in which his lordship had "little to say." [1] After that, and ultimately, their small degree of luck was shown by the following frigid communication under date of December 7, 1861: "Lord Russell presents his compliments to Mr. Yancey, Mr. Rost, and Mr. Mann. He has had the honor to receive their letters of the 27th and 30th of November, but in the present state of affairs he must decline to enter into any official communication with them." [2]

As early as August 24, 1861, in a letter addressed to Yancey and his colleagues, Russell had mentioned having received a communication from them "on behalf of the so-styled Confederate States of North America." [3] From the Confederate standpoint this was the unpardonable insult. In 1864 Secretary of State Benjamin took the ground that he would refuse to receive any communication in which the Southern government was addressed as "the so-styled 'Confederacy.' " [4] The failure of this preliminary mission to obtain the much desired recognition was definitely indicated in a despatch sent by Yancey and Mann to Richmond on January 27, 1862, when their preliminary mission was about to give way to Mason and Slidell. In this despatch they reported that Russell had informed Charles Francis Adams that such interviews as he had had with the Confederate emissaries were in line with the established British custom of receiving "such persons unofficially" with no implication of recognition, as in the case of "Poles, Hungarians, Italians, etc.," but that "he had no expectation of seeing them any more." [5]

Mason and Slidell did no better as to recognition than the Yancey mission. Mason enjoyed expressions of sympathy from unofficial groups of Englishmen, but Russell's attitude towards him was cold and cautious. Unsuccessful in his efforts to impress the British ministry, rebuffed in curt communications favoring the Washington view as to the effectiveness of the blockade, frustrated in overtures toward treaty relations, and unable even to obtain reception as an accredited diplomat near the British court, Mason announced to Russell as early as September 21, 1863, that he was withdrawing from the country.[6] It would be hard to think of a diplomatic mission that was a more com-

---

1 *Offic. Rec.* (Nav.), 2 ser., III, 214.
2 *Ibid.*, 310.                          3 *Ibid.*, 247.
4 *Ibid.*, 1033. In this connection one may note a Confederate diplomat's reference to "the soi-distant [*sic*] United States." *Ibid.*, 758.
5 *Ibid.*, 320.                          6 *Ibid.*, 904–905; see below, pp. 348–349.

plete failure. Though dealing with a flamboyant monarch given to reckless international ventures, Slidell at Paris did no better than Mason.

## IV

Failing in recognition, the Confederacy failed also in mediation and intervention. Their desire was for the Lincoln government to become embroiled in international war, and to this end they were ready to accept as allies those foreign elements whose hostility to American progress and to the Monroe Doctrine was obvious. For this they would also have sacrificed the American tradition against that type of alliance that was known by the sinister word "entangling." There were times when their hopes were raised. In January 1862, despite official British rebuff, Yancey and Mann reported to Richmond a "prevailing and doubtless correct impression" in London that British and French interference would occur "in some way," there being "indications" that it would go to the extent of demanding an armistice with mediation as to boundaries.[1] This may have been wishful thinking of a sort constantly encouraged by certain British newspapers and private gentlemen, but in the coming months there were slight rumblings in the British Parliament that bore the same tone. In the summer and fall of 1862 the matter came to a head.

In September of that year Lord Palmerston, British prime minister, and Earl Russell, foreign secretary, were cautiously pondering the American question in terms of what seemed imminent Union defeat. Referring to General Pope's "complete smashing" and to the chance that "still greater disasters" were about to occur, with Washington or Baltimore falling into Confederate hands, Palmerston asked Russell: "If this should happen, would it not be time for us to consider whether . . . England and France might not address the contending parties and recommend an arrangement upon the basis of separation?"[2] Cau-

---

[1] *Offic. Rec.* (Nav.), 2 ser., III, 320.

[2] What this amounted to was that in the immediate sequel of Second Bull Run Palmerston and Russell were engaged in deliberation as to whether a change of course might become necessary. In Palmerston's query the key words were: "If this should happen:" If, for instance, the Confederates had taken and held Washington, that "would have" involved a drastic change in American affairs. The fact that in this event the British would have had to consider a reorientation of their attitude is significant as showing that their existing position was far from pro-Confederate.

tious as he was, Russell replied: ". . . I agree with you that the time is come for offering mediation to the United States Government, with a view to the recognition of the independence of the Confederates. I agree further, that, in case of failure, we ought ourselves to recognise the Southern States as an independent State." [3] Clear-cut statements of the United States government, together with instructions to Charles Francis Adams, show that such a proposal, if put into effect, would have been regarded as cause at least for a breach of relations between Washington and London, and that, had Britain sought to implement its mediation and recognition with measures of official assistance to the Confederacy, the result might have been war. Adams had seen to it that on this point the British government was left in no doubt.

In October Russell circulated among his colleagues of the British ministry a confidential memorandum concerning a type of European mediation which, because of its slanting toward Confederate success and victory, would certainly have been regarded by the Lincoln government as unjustifiable interference. Discussion of the matter in cabinet meeting was set for October 23. A dangerous moment indeed had been reached in Anglo-American relations, and the worst might have been expected if the British government had been less deliberate —for example if it had acted on the matter a bit earlier, say in the period just after reception of the news of Pope's defeat. (It will be remembered that an Atlantic cable did not then exist for prompt reporting of that defeat.) As it turned out, the crisis passed with no harm done. International dealing does not consist of what is conjectured at a particular moment in a changing situation or of what is tentatively contemplated, or posed as a question to be decided, in confidential memoranda. Actual decision or dealing is another matter, and in Britain that involved careful and extended consideration in cabinet. Such consideration led to the conclusion that mediation ought to be postponed, and while the British government was still pondering whether to take any steps in the matter it was seen that "the set of the tide was . . . against mediation." [4] This was not merely a failure to reach a decision; the main point was that after due consideration a decision was reached to avoid mediation, as shown by the fact that the

---

[3] For the Palmerston-Russell exchange of views, see Walpole, *Life of Lord John Russell,* II, 349.

[4] *Ibid.,* II, 351.

British government soon took the position of refusing joint mediation with France.

Various contributing factors were responsible for this clearing of the air: the cautious attitude of certain British ministers, the friendliness of the Duke of Newcastle who opposed mediation, the effect abroad of the emancipation proclamation, and the forthright yet skillful diplomacy of Charles Francis Adams. It would seem, however, that the most decisive of all factors was the marked change in the military situation produced by Lee's failure to crush McClellan at Antietam. The chance of his doing so had been the basis of the conditional and confidential Russell-Palmerston deliberations in September. To appreciate the significance of McClellan's contribution one must consider the matter from the London angle. Only if one remembers the possible effect of foreign recognition of the Confederacy and the evident hinging of that issue on military events, can the full measure of Antietam to the Union cause be assessed.

## V

If questions of recognition and mediation were packed with dynamite, no less so was the building and equipping of naval vessels for the Confederacy. This furnishing of ships with the resultant strain on friendly relations, is one of the familiar topics in the diplomacy of Lincoln's day, but precisely because of being so widely "known" this phase of the problem is beclouded with stereotypes and misconceptions. For the avoidance of historical error, two points in particular need to be noted. (1) It is erroneous to suppose that a government policy of unfriendliness to the United States or of deliberate intervention for the Confederacy was involved in the case of the well known (or rather, the oft-mentioned) *Alabama* and those very few other naval ships in which British help to the enemies of the United States was supplied. A correct view of the facts by no means justifies this facile supposition. (2) It is as much to the point to remember Britain's favorable action in detaining ships intended for operation against the United States—e. g., the Laird rams—as to recall those few earlier cases where ships were not detained. Any review of the subject that emphasizes only the *Alabama* is therefore one-sided.

The famous *Alabama,* Confederate cruiser and sea raider extraordinary, began mysteriously, though perhaps with only a superficial mystery, as the "290," or "Enrica," being so designated while building in the Laird yard at Birkenhead opposite Liverpool.[1] There were warnings, protests, and impressive documents of evidence presented by Charles Francis Adams; there was delay while detention of the ship was dilatorily studied by the Queen's law officers; in these circumstances the vessel slipped out to sea.[2] Later it received various kinds of British help:[3] tug, armament, British seamen, and supplies. Off the Azores (on the high seas) the ship was taken into Confederate service as the *Alabama.* From that moment (August 24, 1862) it ranged the seas over vast areas, capturing more than sixty merchant ships of the United States. Needless to say, these noncombatant vessels were not sunk at sight with disregard of human life. Conditions of the Confederacy made it impossible for them to be brought into any port of the capturing government for court adjudication and forfeiture; they were therefore either burned *after the removal of persons on board,* or released on "ransom bond." This meant that the owner was pledged to pay a sum of money "unto the President of the Confederate States of America . . . within thirty days after the conclusion of the present war . . . ."[4] The *Alabama* was a formidable and dangerous raider, bent on damage to the commerce of the United States, but it was not an international outlaw.

The settlement of the *Alabama* case and that of vessels in like situation (the *Shenandoah, Florida, Tallahassee,* and *Georgia*) was deferred until after the war. Ultimately, during the administration of President Grant, the British government gave full satisfaction in terms of a treaty

[1] "I presume that Mr. Dudley [U. S. consul at Liverpool] keeps the Government fully informed of the change of the chrysalis 290 into the butterfly Alabama on a piratical cruise against American shipping." C. F. Adams to Seward, London, Sep. 5, 1862, Diplomatic Despatches (Britain vol. 80), MSS., Department of State, National Archives.
[2] "On Tuesday a . . . screw-steamer, . . . known to the initiated as the 'Enrica,' and to the ignorant as the '290,' built by Messrs. Laird, of Birkenhead, left the Birkenhead Docks, and steamed down the Mersey to sea, as it was understood, on her trial-trip, to test her sailing capabilities." Liverpool *Albion,* Aug. 4, 1862.
[3] In one of his diplomatic documents John Slidell mentioned "the *Alabama* and *Florida,* Confederate cruisers, built and in a great degree fitted out in England, which have been freely admitted in various English ports, have there repaired damages and been supplied with fuel and provisions." *Offic. Rec.* (Nav.), 2 ser., III, 744.
[4] *Ibid.,* 1 ser., I, 782.

of arbitration (involving an expression of "regret" by Her Majesty's government) and financial settlement as fixed by tribunal award.[5] A fact which is abundantly clear in the voluminous and complicated record of this international *cause célèbre,* and which can only be ignored by those unfamiliar with the case, is that the settlement, which was favorable to the United States, was promoted by the very terms of the treaty to which Britain agreed as a matter of negotiation; the whole outcome was a case of friendly adjustment rather than of forced retribution for wrongs committed. It should also be remembered that the British government had taken steps to detain the *Alabama,* but that before such steps could be effective the ship had already departed on its adventures. The ponderousness of lawyers may have been as much a factor in this result as deliberately unfriendly connivance. Lawyers take their time; they must have "proof" (legal evidence) of things that are unmistakably obvious to the layman.

## VI

It is not, however, the *Alabama,* but the *Alexandra* and the Laird rams, that offer the clue to the controlling pattern of British policy in the war. Action at London in the case of these ships was such that no controversy developed and no postwar arbitration was necessary. In these instances the ambitious efforts of the Confederacy to obtain naval assistance from Britain were frustrated. Coming to a head in the spring of 1863, the case of the *Alexandra,* a sea raider being built in England for the Confederate navy, had significance as indicating whether the government of Britain, after letting the *Alabama* and other vessels slip through, would do likewise in other cases, thus making "connivance" at Confederate aid a continuing policy. In this sense it was a test case, and for that reason one should not underestimate the importance of British action in seizing the ship on April 5, 1863,[1] and preventing its ever being delivered into Confederate hands. The legal details of the case, which involved trial, appeal, and final decree by

---

[5] Randall, *Civil War and Reconstruction,* 839–846.

[1] Charles Francis Adams received on April 5, 1863, a note from Russell indicating that orders had been issued for the seizure of the *Alexandra.* Adams wrote: "I rejoice at this . . . disposition to defeat the machinations of those who hope to relieve the rebels by . . . a diversion from this side." Adams to Seward, London, April 7, 1863, *House Exec. Doc. No. 1,* 38 Cong., 1 sess., pt. 1, 228–229.

the House of Lords, may be omitted. The thing that stands out clear
in the episode is the keen disappointment of Southern diplomats and
the evident satisfaction of all who favored the cause of Lincoln. The
Confederate propaganda agent Hotze referred to British official conduct in this case as proving "undoubtedly a strong desire to propitiate
our enemies." [2] Concerning a somewhat similar question Mason wrote
of "the determination of the [British] Government . . . to yield
everything to avoid risk of collision [with the United States]." [3] When,
asserting the doctrine of continuous voyage, the United States seized
the *Peterhoff*, sailing from a British port to Matamoros, on the ground
that its Mexican destination was fraudulent and its cargo intended for
the Confederacy, Adams reported that he had mentioned to Russell
the good effect produced in America by Britain's detention of the
*Alexandra*, as well as of Russell's reply to the owners of the *Peterhoff*.
"On his [Russell's] part," wrote Adams, "he expressed satisfaction at
this as an indication that the . . . hostile spirit to England imputed
to us was not entertained." [4] Essential friendliness toward America in
Britain was promoted in spite of the chilling effect of Anglophobe
sentiment among certain groups in the United States. Whenever a
more amicable sentiment was expressed, its effect at London was both
welcome and officially favorable.

Of like significance as to British attitude, but of even more importance in international relations, was the famous case of the Laird
rams. These two ironclads, constructed by the Laird firm under contract arranged by Captain James Dunwoody Bulloch, Confederate
naval officer and foreign agent, were intended to break the Union
blockade, harass Northern ports, and assault merchant shipping. For
their day they were formidable instruments of war. It was known for
what purpose the ships were building, and as the case dragged on for
anxious months the subject became one of great irritation to all concerned. Contradictory statements as to what Britain would do appeared from time to time, after the manner of diplomatic wishful
thinking. Following months of pressure and controversy, a Confederate agent reported from London that Earl Russell was "said to be
in a state of pitiable perplexity and in a ludicrously ill temper about

the whole affair." [5] It is hardly too much to say that preservation of peace between Britain and the United States depended on the disposition of this question, a fact which Seward and Adams did not fail to impress upon British official minds. Had the ships departed for Confederate service, a breach of relations at the least seemed the certain result; if a breach had occurred, war was considered a probability. This being so, it was an ominous fact that on September 2, 1863, according to testimony taken at Liverpool, one of the rams had her masts in, her rigging completed, her engines and machinery in order, her funnel up, and everything in readiness to slip down the Mersey and out to sea. [6]

It was at this tense moment that Charles Francis Adams wrote his famous note to Russell (September 5, 1863) expressing "profound . . . regret" at developments, reminding the foreign secretary of Confederate threats against New York, Boston, Portland, and other ports, hinting at instructions of an ominous nature from Washington, and reaching a dramatic climax with the statement: "It would be superfluous in me to point out to your lordship that this is war." [7] To a superficial observer it might have seemed a clear instance of cause and effect when by a note under date of September 8 Russell informed Adams that "instructions . . . [had] been issued which . . . [would] prevent the departure of the two iron-clad vessels from Liverpool." [8]

The United States was satisfied and in this way the matter was settled; ultimately the warships were purchased by the British government. The historical error that must be avoided here is a misrepresentation of the episode as one of ultimatum by the United States followed by British surrender under threat. The real situation was far different. Adams and Russell were in fact working toward the same end; it was a mere accident—the absence of Russell from London (at his country home in Scotland)—that gave occasion for Adams's forthright note. As a matter of fact, Russell had decided upon the detention of the rams before Adams's note was written. He had caused the law officers to investigate the case, had been unconvinced by the evidence

---

[5] *Offic. Rec.* (Nav.), 2 ser., III, 915.

[6] Statement of Thomas Sweeney, sworn at Custom House, Liverpool, Sep. 2, 1863, Diplomatic Despatches (Britain, vol. 83), MSS., Dep. of State, Nat. Archives.

[7] *House Exec. Doc. No. 1,* 38 Cong., 1 sess., pt. 1, p. 418.

[8] *Ibid.,* 419.

(bearing the appearance of "legal" evidence) that the ships were intended for a French firm,[9] had given an instruction on September 1 that caused the vessels to be watched against departure,[10] and had actually directed them to be stopped on September 3, two days in advance of the American minister's stern note. On the very day of the note (September 5) he ordered detention; three days later he advised Adams that this had been done.[11]

The awkward thing was that written notes had to be used at all, since they crossed each other in such manner that Adams's statement had already ceased to have significance at the moment of being received. The whole episode illustrates the error of sensationalism in the treatment of historical material. When a public man coins a famous phrase and when superficially the event seems to show that the heroic phrase or gesture turns a trick, the temptation toward sensationalism is too hard for some writers to resist; in this case the overdramatization has passed into stereotyped history. If ever historical revision were needful, it is so here. There was no cause to overawe Russell with an ultimatum. Talking things over was all that was needed. Russell had indeed foreshadowed his friendly policy toward the United States the previous April in connection with the *Alexandra*. His government's amicable dealing with the rams was of a piece with that earlier case. Adams handsomely deserves credit for his persistent, watchful, and sagacious handling of his country's affairs, but in the case of the rams the leaving "no stone unturned" for peaceable adjustment could have been said as truly of Russell as of Adams. The nations that understood each other were the United States and Britain; the party that was checkmated and aggrieved, as the record amply shows, was the Confederacy.

In all this activity to prevent the ironclads from getting into Confederate hands, as in earlier efforts, the tireless work of Thomas H. Dudley, United States consul at Liverpool, was of great importance, and in most accounts the credit given to him has been inadequate. In continual watchfulness, secret investigations, the gathering of affi-

---

[9] Had the British government stood merely on the superficial legal aspects, it could have made out that the ships were not for the Confederacy at all. Bulloch had nominally sold them to a French firm; they were, of course, to be resold to the Confederacy after departure from Britain.

[10] Rhodes, *Hist. of the U. S.*, IV, 381.

[11] *House Exec. Doc. No. 1*, 38 Cong., 1 sess., pt. 1, 419.

davits, and the conveying of information to Adams, his service was of the highest value. This becomes clear when one examines, as the author has, the impressive and voluminous Dudley papers. William M. Evarts wrote to Dudley on September 26, 1863: "The merchants and shipowners of our country owe you a great debt . . . ." "You have had the greatest share of labor . . . in this business, and are entitled to the principal credit . . . for the invaluable result. I left England . . . with entire confidence that the British Government would not suffer these Iron-clads to come out." [12]

## VII

Mention has already been made of the *Peterhoff* case, one of the troublesome questions between the United States and England in 1863. Though it has received inadequate attention, it was very revealing as to Lincoln's handling of international relations. It was significant also as showing how the President was pulled and tugged this way and that by strong disagreements within his cabinet. Though nearly forgotten now, this case was not a minor affair, since it involved talk of possible war with Britain. The *Peterhoff* was a British-owned merchant steamer captured in the West Indies in February 1863. It was on its way to Matamoros, a Mexican port close to the Atlantic Ocean (a little way inland), and across the Rio Grande from Brownsville, Texas. Mexico was a neutral country, but the question arose whether the "neutral" destination was genuine, especially in view of the contraband nature of part of the cargo and the close proximity of Matamoros to the Confederacy. In its supposed hazard of war with England, though war for such a cause was absurd, the case seemed like another *Trent* affair. The analogy was not complete, but the parallel was emphasized by the incidental fact that it was none other than Charles Wilkes of *Trent* fame who made the capture of the *Peterhoff*.

The matter was ultimately settled by freeing the captured ship, releasing the non-contraband cargo, and seizing such of the cargo as consisted of contraband goods. The case became historic because of the principle of "continuous voyage"—i. e., the right of a belligerent

---

[12] Thomas H. Dudley MSS., Huntington Lib.

to seize cargo destined only nominally for a neutral port and plainly intended for an enemy.[1]

The point of interest here is not only the outcome of the case, which was fortunate, but what went on behind the scenes in an affair that offered a real challenge to the President's authority as well as to his skill in personal and official relations. The *Peterhoff* seizure was a bone of contention not only between Britain and the United States, but also between the secretary of the navy and the secretary of state. The President was caught in between, being under pressure from both secretaries though relying especially upon Seward.

The aspect on which Welles was particularly concerned was whether the United States, by a prize court, could legitimately seize the mails on board the captured ship. Emphatically, almost angrily, Welles favored the seizure, showing little regard for consequences, while Seward, giving attention to an adjustment through negotiation with Britain, strongly opposed such a measure.

The President wanted to know the usage as to the right of a belligerent to seize the mails of a captured ship, but all he got was a positive statement from Seward that the precedents did not favor such a "violation," which was flatly contradicted by Welles's statement of the opposite conclusion. The mails having been actually seized and taken into possession by a United States district court in New York, the question arose whether this amounted to lawful possession. Unhappy that Lincoln could not accept his view of the subject, Welles remarked that the "President . . . was a good deal 'obfusticated' in regard to the merits of the question." [2]

For week after week the unsolved problem dragged on, both secretaries continuing their pressure on the President, Welles's aides ransacking the books to get precedents, Welles himself becoming more and more emphatic, and Sumner, chairman of the foreign relations committee of the Senate, favoring the Welles position and making his senatorial views known to Lord Lyons. It angered Welles that Seward "conceded" the main point which Welles thought should have been left with the courts. The secretary of the navy looked on this as an unjustifiable interference, and so did the attorney general, when Seward

---

[1] J. B. Moore, *Hist. and Digest of International Law*, IV, 3838–3843; Peterhoff *vs.* U. S., 5 Wallace 28 (1867); *Offic. Rec.* (Nav.), 1 ser., II, 100 ff.

[2] Welles, *Diary*, I, 280 (April 21, 1863).

directed District Attorney Delafield Smith, an officer under the jurisdiction of the attorney general, to see that the mails were given up,
which was done. It was Welles's view that the President was sincere
and of right intention, but that he had been "imposed upon, hum-
bugged, by a man in whom he confides." Welles added: "the Secretary
of State is daily, and almost hourly, wailing in his ears the calamities
of a war with England which he is striving to prevent. The President
is thus led away from the real question, and will probably decide it,
not on its merits, but on this false issue, raised by the man who is the
author of the difficulty."

Here, as in the *Trent* case, Lincoln's conduct—for, after all, the
President had to decide these things—was determined by the consideration that Britain would not consent to having their mail bags
opened, their seals or locks broken; that war lurked as a possibility;
and that, as Lincoln thought, "we were in no condition to plunge into
a foreign war on a subject of so little importance in comparison with
the terrible consequences which must follow our act." [3] Welles could
see only his side, while the President weighed the great advantage of
a friendly international adjustment against the minor factor of releasing a mail bag.

However Welles might characterize the President as "obfusticated"
or a mere tool of Seward, the Chief saw the case through. He could not
allow such a question between nations to dangle indefinitely in
suspense. As Welles recorded it, Lincoln said to him, "I shall have to
cut this knot." [4]

The case reached its climax on May 15, 1863. On that day the Presi-
dent called on Welles bringing "the basis of a dispatch which Lord
Lyons proposed to send home." [5] Lyons had shown it to Seward;
Seward turned it over to the President; the President was now sub-
mitting it to Welles. The dispatch involved a settlement by which the
United States would give up any effort to hold the mails seized on the
*Peterhoff.* This adjustment had been shaped up in a manner opposite
to Welles's wishes.

Here were strong men of contrary views facing each other in the determination of an issue that had been hanging fire between them for
months. A decision had to be made. Welles wanted the matter to rest

---

[3] *Ibid.,* I, 287 (April 28, 1863).      [4] *Ibid.,* I, 289.
[5] *Ibid.,* 302.

with the courts and be adjudicated according to "law and usage." Seizing on that very point, Lincoln asked: "But have the courts ever opened the mails of a neutral government?" "Always," replied Welles, but with entire vagueness as to cases. "Why, then," said Lincoln, "do you not furnish me with the fact?" Welles made the weak reply that, to his knowledge, the matter had never been questioned, adding that the courts were independent of the departments. Lincoln was not satisfied: "if mails ever are examined," he said, "the fact must be known and recorded." He then pinned the secretary down: "What vessels have we captured, where we have examined the mails?" Welles's answer was again offhand where the President demanded specific citation. "All [vessels], doubtless," said the secretary, "that have had mails on board." The matter went on in this fashion till Welles was stumped. He could recall no actual case and when he sent for one of his staff, Watkins, who had charge of prize matters, that gentleman "could not call to mind anything conclusive." [6]

The President had given his secretary of the navy a respectful hearing, and now his position was all the stronger for having done so. The mails, also the noncontraband cargo, were released and an adjustment satisfactory to Britain, but in no way hurtful to the interest or honor of the United States, was thus arrived at. The President had taken sides with Seward, but the time was to come when Welles himself would come forward in print as one of the strongest defenders of Lincoln as President and statesman in the field of international relations.[7]

As for Wilkes, he was relieved of his West Indies command, where he had not captured the famous *Alabama,* but had repeatedly got his government into serious trouble. He incurred the strong dislike of Welles for negative results in defeating Confederate raiders as well as for insubordination, disobedience to orders, and use of the newspaper press for publicized self-vindication at the expense of superiors. For these offenses he was brought to trial before a naval court martial (1864) charged with insubordination and undue assumption of authority. He was found guilty and sentenced to a public reprimand and suspension from the service for three years.

The matters summarized in this chapter offer glimpses to suggest

---

[6] *Ibid.,* I, 303–304.
[7] Gideon Welles, *Lincoln and Seward* . . . (N. Y., 1874).

the nature of foreign affairs under Lincoln. Here was no dictatorship making decisions by irresponsible order or fiat. Here was a homely President of democratic habits at work in difficult situations. There were buffetings of popular excitement, misrepresentation, cabinet quarreling, and assertions of senatorial opinion. There was the hazard that a small incident might get out of hand and lead to untold consequences. There was the chance that rigid legality might come to the front and obscure the larger factors. Through it all ran the great fundamentals which it was Lincoln's function to keep always foremost. His eye was on the cause of American survival, which he identified with the cause of democracy in the world. While others were legalistic or litigious, he was careful not to be drawn into needless bickering or diverted from the great task as he saw it. He realized that it was not a question of winning a point against Britain (which, if won, might have proved of little value), but rather a matter of mutual interest as between the two nations; the cause of international adjustment was an equal benefit to both. He was shrewd enough to realize that the best victory in international dealing might be in terms of a concession, and that in the family of nations it becomes imperative for statesmen to see more than one narrow point of view. What we have been considering is the challenge of nations under stress; in the next chapter the unfolding pattern becomes steadily more clear in terms of the friendship of nations in a period of great crisis.

# CHAPTER XIV

# FRIENDSHIP OF NATIONS

FOR Britons to understand all that was involved in the American Civil War was not easy. It is therefore unwise to hazard generalizations in this field, as in other complex matters of public opinion and sentiment in international relations. Even at this date, with the records available, it is difficult to get a fully rounded picture of opinion in Britain toward the issue between the governments of Lincoln and of Jefferson Davis. When one points to British sympathy for the Confederacy, he is dealing with a socially prominent, class-conscious, vocal, and assertive element concerning whose activities vast quantities of historical material can be produced; nevertheless only a part of the picture—a minor part—is presented when this phase alone is considered.

## I

British elements which opposed Lincoln were those which thought little of government of, by, and for the people. They were, for the most part, the London clubs, the silk-hatted folk of "society," the enemies of democratic rule, and the men who, from hostility or rivalry, dreaded the rise of the United States as a great and prosperous nation. As a qualification one must of course add that for a long time the Old South had been close to Britain in society and business and that during the war there were many Englishmen whose admiration of Southerners and sympathy for the Confederate cause was genuine. (Others in Britain would have preferred to keep their friendship for Southerners if only that sentiment could have been free from any anti-United-States involvement. If they had an interest in New Orleans friends, it was not by their wish that such an interest was transmuted into hatred of Boston.) Confederate propagandists and diplomats had ready access to social circles and to newspaper columns (some of them) in Britain, and they did not fail to pour out a story that sounded convincing to foreign ears. Lincoln's government was denounced for coercion, shutting off commerce, violating international law, and even, as in the case of an overadvertised and misrepresented order by General Benjamin F. Butler, of crass indecency.

The devil of misunderstanding, aided by a deliberate pro-Confederate effort to magnify it, was illustrated in the minor episode of Butler's "woman order." Having become the most hated Yankee in the South by reason of his administration of Union-occupied New Orleans, Butler had unfortunately issued a military order that any female insulting a Union soldier or officer would "be regarded and held liable to be treated as a woman of the town plying her avocation." The general explained that his action was based on reported insults to his soldiery by women in New Orleans, and that, in exaggerated denunciations, his order was misrepresented as to intent. The most charitable view of Butler was that he had committed a serious blunder. For this and other reasons he was called "Beast Butler" [1] and in the anti-Union propaganda sense in Britain the order was utterly misrepresented as having been directed from Washington and as typical of Northern depravity.[2] Benjamin Moran wrote in his diary on November 5, 1862: "This is Guy Fawkes' day, and at about 11 o'clock a crowd of men and boys brought a gigantic Guy in military dress, with a gallows at its side, past the [American] Legation, labeled 'The Brute Butler.' It was vociferously cheered . . . ."

The resources of the South, its harmony of economic interest with Britain, its military invincibility—all such themes were urged in speeches, editorials, pamphlets, and private conversation. Sometimes the Confederate propaganda theme abroad was the opposite of that at home. Domestically, secession leaders assailed the Lincoln government for its attacks upon slavery as upon Southern rights; abroad they

---

[1] One of Butler's most unjustifiable acts was the military execution of a Southern citizen, Mumford by name, for tearing down a United States flag at New Orleans. The government at Washington was not enforcing the death penalty against participants or adherents of the Confederate cause. Randall, *Constitutional Problems Under Lincoln,* 227, chaps. iv, v.

[2] B. F. Butler, *Private and Official Correspondence,* I, 490; James Parton, *General Butler at New Orleans,* 322–345; C. F. Adams, Jr., *Charles Francis Adams,* 243 ff.; W. Reed West, *Contemporary French Opinion on the American Civil War,* 80–81.

pointed out that slavery versus antislavery was not the issue at all and that the Lincoln government had disclaimed any intention to strike at slavery within the states. As to the blockade, they said both that it was ineffective and that it was a serious menace. In Confederate military historiography one of the familiar themes is the small number of soldiers that were doing battle for Lee, but George N. Sanders, in England on Confederate business, stated in the month of Antietam that the Confederate army east of Petersburg included about 200,000 men and four hundred pieces of field artillery.[3] Henry Hotze handled Confederate publicity abroad, publishing a weekly newspaper, the *Index* (nominally English but actually a Confederate organ) and carrying on a varied activity which included the supplying of articles to British newspapers, the circulating of brochures, and even the coaching of a few members of Parliament and the concealed authorship of a pamphlet entitled *La Question Mexicaine et la Colonization Française*, prepared with the aid of a translator and written "in the hope of its having some bearing on the Mexican debate in the French chamber." [4]

In Britain the Southern cause was served not only by diplomatic and unofficial agents of the Confederacy itself, but by Englishmen who formed the Southern Independence Association of London and other cities. This propagandist group concerned itself with holding public meetings, promoting sympathy for the Confederate cause, combating the arguments of Unionists, and seeking to relieve Southerners from the stigma of slavery by making it appear that slaves had a welcome and significant place in Southern armies. "This association," wrote J. M. Mason in December 1864, "is the largest, as it is the most active . . . of any . . . formed . . . in our behalf." [5] Not only at large gatherings, but more especially at select dinners or banquets, speeches were made which favored the enemies of the United States. British friends of the Confederacy were numerous, vocal, and well organized. In October 1863 Hotze asserted, though with the exaggeration of a propagandist: "Here [in England] there is scarcely a man eminent in letters, in politics, or in society, who dares profess friendship for the

---

[3] Liverpool *Daily Post,* Sep. 3, 1862. In the same issue it was mentioned that Sanders had been United States consul in London and that he had arrived in Liverpool from Richmond incognito "by underground railway."

[4] *Offic. Rec.* (Nav.), 2 ser., III, 1024.          [5] *Ibid.,* 1251.

North." [6] The boasts of Hotze were notorious, but one finds corroboration, at least in part, in a statement made privately by Henry Adams. Writing to his brother Charles Francis early in the war, young Adams indicated that Southerners in London were enthusiastic while Union men there were lukewarm, and that, in general, Americans could expect "no sympathy or assistance in Europe from any Government." [7]

It is unsatisfactory to attempt an enumeration of individual Britons who sought to aid the cause of secession or showed sympathy for it, but among them one would have to include James Spence (Liverpool merchant and author of *The American Union*), A. J. Beresford-Hope, the Marquis of Lothian, the Marquis of Bath, Lord Robert Cecil, Lord Wharncliffe, William S. Lindsay (shipping merchant), and John A. Roebuck. It will be seen on a later page how the parliamentary effort of Lindsay and Roebuck to promote a pro-Confederate movement in the British Parliament broke down completely. So also their somewhat farcical diplomatic contacts with Napoleon III. In fact the cause of the Confederacy in Britain always seemed brighter at dinners of the Southern Independence Association than in dealings with the British government.

Such men as Carlyle and Gladstone could be quoted on the Confederate side. Carlyle epitomized the attitude of a certain type of Britisher when he cynically referred to the American war as the burning out of a dirty chimney which could be regarded only with satisfaction by neighbors.[8] This expressed the view of those in Britain who desired the ruin of both the North and South, thus relieving Canada of an imagined menace and doing away with a cotton competitor of British India. Gladstone, chancellor of the exchequer, came into notoriety for a speech at Newcastle on October 7, 1862, in which he treated Southern military success as certain. He said: ". . . Jefferson Davis and other leaders of the South have made an army; they are making, it appears, a navy; and they have made what is more than either —they have made a nation. . . . We may anticipate with certainty the success of the Southern States so far as regards their separation

---

[6] *Ibid.*, 946.

[7] W. C. Ford, ed., *A Cycle of Adams Letters*, I, 61–62, 66. Henry Adams was writing of opinions in Britain as distinguished from actions. Of the latter he wrote, "There is no danger of any movement from England . . . ." *Ibid.*, 65.

[8] *Offic. Rec.* (Nav.), 2 ser., III, 506.

from the North." [9] This utterance was the more serious because it came at a critical moment of the war so far as British policy was concerned and because at the time Gladstone, being about the age of Lincoln, was a member of the British ministry, though in no sense its approved spokesman. Gladstone fraternized with Hotze, who, after meeting the statesman at dinner, wrote: "He is, of all the members of the cabinet, supposed to be the most friendly to us, and his manner and language . . . so impressed me." A feature of this conversation as reported by Hotze was Gladstone's "emphatic prediction that the war would speedily end in the acknowledged independence of the South." [10]

It is recorded that when Gladstone delivered his famous sentences concerning the success of Jefferson Davis and his Confederacy, his words produced a great sensation in his Newcastle audience. Sensations become events and in this case a momentary utterance became an international incident. In that sense, and in contrast to the whole large view which Gladstone could not then envisage, his phrases, all the more so because of their quotableness, exceeded the bounds of official discretion. Perhaps the main significance of the Newcastle speech was its revelation of the inability of a man so able and so well disposed as Gladstone to look at the contemporary American struggle and see it whole. Gladstone's limitation was simply that he could not foresee Union success at a moment when Confederate armies were riding high.

In a memorandum written in July, 1896, Gladstone stated that his Newcastle declaration "was not due to any . . . partizanship for the South or hostility to the North." It was simply that he thought the struggle was "virtually at an end" and that it was a matter of "friendliness to all America" to recognize the fact. He added that he "was not one of those who on the ground of British interests desired a division of the American Union" but that his view was "distinctly opposite." [11] Looking back from this memorandum to the speech itself, it is significant to read the passage which immediately preceded the sensational

[9] *The Times,* London, Oct. 9, 1862, pp. 7–8; John Morley, *Life of William Ewart Gladstone,* II, 79.

[10] Hotze to Benjamin, London, Aug. 4, 1862, *Offic. Rec.* (Nav.), 2 ser., III, 506.

[11] Morley, *Gladstone,* II, 81.

part; it puts the incident in a somewhat different light, at least to the extent of relieving Gladstone of any animosity toward the North. This part of the speech, hardly ever quoted, was as follows:

. . . I would for a moment make an appeal to you on behalf of the people of the Northern States . . . . Great allowances are to be made for them. . . . let us bear with them all we can; let us maintain toward them a kindly temper; let us not allow ourselves to feel the smallest irritation when we see ourselves adversely criticized on the other side of the water; and let us be very cautious about indulging in adverse criticisms upon them on this side of the water. . . . They are our kin. They were . . . our customers, and we hope they will be our customers again. . . . they entertain warm affections toward England. Whatever momentary irritation may cross the mind of that people, let us not forget their reception of the Prince of Wales. (Hear.) Let every Englishman engrave upon the tablets of his heart the recollection of that memorable day; and, if occasionally he feels tempted to anger by seeing his country misapprehended, or, it may be, misrepresented, let him calm his tendency to excited sentiments by that recollection. (Hear, hear.) [12] It is the more necessary to do this because . . . the people of the Northern States have not yet drunk of . . . the cup which all the rest of the world see they nevertheless must drink of. We may have our own opinions about slavery; we may be for or against the South; but there is no doubt that Jefferson Davis and other leaders of the South have made an army . . . [then followed the sensational passage quoted above.] [13]

To bracket Gladstone with those who wished ill to the United States, therefore, seems hardly correct. It was rather that he was speaking somewhat hastily and out of turn and that, even then, the whole speech was in a different sense than the famous passage so often quoted. Even more does it give a wrong impression to quote outstanding British partisans of the Confederacy and leave the matter there. In so large a subject it is always possible to pick out instances. One therefore needs to be reminded that those in Britain who spoke in a manner inimical to the American Union were giving expression to a sentiment opposite to that which controlled the British government. Despite such statements reflecting the views of certain individuals or groups, the substantial action of the British ministry, supported by the Parliament, remains.

---

[12] In these sections of his speech that urged a friendly attitude toward the North, Gladstone was frequently interrupted by shouts of approval.

[13] *The Times*, London, Oct. 9, 1862, p. 7, c. 6.

## II

Most influential among British newspapers favoring the Confederacy was the *Times* of London. In the summer of 1862 Charles Francis Adams wrote: ". . . I cannot fail to perceive a progressive consolidation of the popular prejudice against America, under the operation of the continuous denunciations of the London Times. The sympathies of the higher classes are decidedly enlisted in the struggle not from any . . . affection for either side, but from a longing to see the political power of the United States permanently impaired." [1] Readers who followed the issues and events of the American war through the pages of the *Times* were given a low opinion of the Lincoln government and of the cause for which it stood. The war was represented as a matter of "mob passions." [2] Methods of war employed by the United States, according to this oracle, were marked by "a cruelty which far surpasses anything that can be laid to . . . England." [3] Southern victories were emphasized even to the point of printing a dressed-up fable that McClellan was capitulating with his entire force.[4] Confronted two months later with the news of Antietam, the *Times* blandly remarked that "had it been the policy of the Confederates to have still held their ground in Maryland, they could have done so notwithstanding this battle." [5] It seemed actually painful to the editors of this impressive paper to record anything but Union defeats.

In its comments on Lincoln the superior tone of the *Times* was particularly evident. The American system was described as "a cheap and simple form of government, having a rural attorney for Sovereign and a city attorney [Seward] for Prime Minister." If, said the *Times*, such a "terrible exposure of incapacity had happened in England we should at the earliest moment possible have sent the incapables about

---

[1] C. F. Adams to Seward, London, July 31, 1862, Diplomatic Despatches (Britain, vol. 80), MSS., Dep. of State, Nat. Archives.

[2] *The Times*, Aug. 14, 1861, p. 8, c. 2.    [3] *Ibid.*, July 5, 1864, p. 11, c. 5.

[4] "Such is the state of opinion here that a despatch incorporating it [the fable of McClellan's surrender] dressed up for the purpose . . . and published in . . . The Times was eagerly caught up and believed . . . ." Adams to Seward, London, July 19, 1862, Diplomatic Despatches (Britain, vol. 80), MSS., Dep. of State, Nat. Archives. The account to which Adams referred was under the heading "Reported Surrender of the Federal Army." It appeared in the *Times* of July 19, 1862, p. 14, c. 1.

[5] *The Times*, Oct. 1, 1862, p. 8, c. 3.

their business, and put ourselves in the hands of better men." [6] Lincoln's emancipation proclamation was misrepresented as the massacre of white women and children: "He will appeal to the black blood of the African; he will whisper of the pleasures of spoil and of the gratification of yet fiercer instincts; and when blood begins to flow . . . Mr. Lincoln will wait till the rising flames tell that all is consummated, and then he will rub his hand and think that revenge is sweet." [7] And again: "Is Lincoln yet a name not known to us as it will be known to posterity, and is it ultimately to be classed among that catalogue of monsters, the wholesale assassins and butchers of their kind? . . . We will attempt . . . to predict nothing as to . . . Lincoln's new [emancipation] policy . . . except that it certainly will not have the effect of restoring the Union. It will not deprive Mr. Lincoln of the . . . affix which he will share with . . . foolish . . . Kings and Emperors, Caliphs and Doges, that of being Lincoln—'the Last.' " [8]

The American President seemed to the *Times* unable to "emancipate himself from the shackles of a merely legal mind." [9] Prophesying (though making no "attempt . . . to predict"!) the effect of a Lincoln victory in the war, the *Times* warned that "the Executive of Washington . . . will, if successful, do what Saracens and Tartars spared to do—will unseat the population generally, and divide their lands among the conquering soldiery." [10] Asserting contrary to fact that Lincoln had "gone through the course of defying and insulting England, which is the traditional way of obtaining the Irish vote," the *Times,* though having no respect for McClellan either, deplored the President's reëlection in 1864, regarding it "as little less than an abdication by the American people of the right of self-government" and "an avowed step toward the foundation of a military despotism." By this time the editor was swinging his pen merrily. He added: "Future historians will probably date from the second presidency of Mr. Lincoln the period when the American Constitution was thoroughly abrogated, and had entered on that transition . . . through which Republics pass on their way from democracy to tyranny." [11]

---

6 *Ibid.,* Nov. 4, 1862, p. 8, c. 6.          7 *Ibid.,* Oct. 7, 1862, p. 8, c. 3.

8 *Ibid.,* Oct. 21, 1862, p. 9, c. 1.          9 *Ibid.,* Mar. 19, 1861, p. 9, c. 1.

10 *Ibid.,* July 5, 1864, p. 11, c. 5. (It is needless to point out that this was completely opposite to Lincoln's intent.)

11 *Ibid.,* Nov. 22, 1864, p. 6, c. 3. The reference to Lincoln "defying and insulting Eng-

By the very oppositeness of its slant, the *Times* went far forward substantiating Lincoln's own contention as to the fundamental cause for which the United States was struggling. That is to say, the *Times*, in revealing its dislike of democracy while assailing Lincoln, was unmistakably associating the opponents of Lincoln with the enemies of the democratic principle. "The real secret of the exultation . . . in the *Times*," wrote John Lothrop Motley, ". . . over our troubles and disasters, is their hatred, not to America, so much as to democracy in England." [12] Though disclaiming any wish to "dogmatize about democracy," the *Times* delivered the obiter dictum that "the form which democracy has taken during the last 30 years [in America] . . . was not unlikely to lead to such consequences"—i. e., secession and civil war.[13] Foreign doubters, had they known it, were offering the most convincing corroboration of Lincoln's argument that his cause was "essentially a people's contest," that it embraced "more than the fate of these United States," that it was a testing of the democratic "experiment," and that success in the experiment would be a "great lesson of peace." [14]

## III

Evidences of unfriendliness to the United States on the part of certain elements in Britain belonged, after all, to the Lost Cause; indeed it was a lost cause in England long before it became so at Appomattox Court House. It is a significant fact that midway in the war, in a manner of speaking, the Confederacy broke with England. It is true that regular diplomatic relations between London and Richmond never existed. There were, however, threads of connection or at least modes of attempted access; it was these which were severed in 1863.

By the latter part of that year Britain had proved receptive to the representations of Charles Francis Adams, had denied recognition to the Confederacy, had remained aloof from James M. Mason, had

---

land"—a complete misrepresentation of the President's attitude, for he did nothing of the sort at any time—is significant only as showing how far the anti-Lincoln press abroad strayed from the path of honesty and truth. It must be added that such straying has been characteristic of the anti-British press in America in our own day.

12 J. L. Motley to his mother, Sep. 22, 1861, cited in E. D. Adams, *Great Britain and the American Civil War*, II, 280–281.

13 *The Times*, Oct. 18, 1861, p. 6, c. 2.

14 Nicolay and Hay, *Works*, VI, 304, 321–322 (July 4, 1861).

avoided a parliamentary resolution favorable to the South, and had detained both the *Alexandra* and the Laird rams. Olympian fulminations of journalists lose somewhat of their terror when one contemplates the rabid utterances of the *Times* in contrast to the habitual and growing aloofness of the British ministry toward secession leaders. Confederate diplomacy had always stopped short of persuasive contact with the British government. It was Seward, Adams, and Lincoln who took the tricks abroad. The Confederate secretary of state admitted Seward's "sagacity," his "penetration" into the "feelings of the British cabinet," and "the success of his policy of intimidation." This being interpreted meant his ability to convince leaders of Britain that the United States was ready, if provoked, to declare war on that country.[1] This should not be understood as a crude threat or a serious expectation that it would actually come to war. Rather it signified a kind of Anglo-American diplomacy that avoided rupture because mutuality, common interest, and statesmanlike intelligence were brought to play on both sides.

One finds in the summer and fall of '63 an increasing note of Southern bitterness toward England. Observing British sympathy bestowed upon Poland, "a people alien to them in every respect except that it belongs . . . to the European sisterhood," Hotze in March 1863 lamented that the Confederacy had not received one tithe of the same earnestness.[2] The previous summer Slidell had commented on the "tortuous, selfish, and time-serving policy" of England.[3] A. Dudley Mann in January 1863 bewailed the lack of courage of the British cabinet.[4] Next month Mason observed that both parties in Britain were "guided . . . by a fixed English purpose to run no risk of a broil, even far less, a war with the United States." [5]

It was but the logical outcome of events when Mason's mission to England was terminated that summer. On August 4, 1863, Secretary Benjamin, noting that "the Government of her Majesty has determined to decline the overtures . . . for . . . treaty . . . relations," instructed Mason that his continued residence in London was not "consistent with the dignity of this Government" and that the Southern President wished him to consider his mission at an end.[6]

---

[1] *Offic. Rec.* (Nav.), 2 ser., III, 817.    [2] *Ibid.,* 712.
[3] *Ibid.,* 485.    [4] *Ibid.,* 658.    [5] *Ibid.,* 687.    [6] *Ibid.,* 852.

On September 30 Mason left London for Paris, having given up his house and removed his archives.[7] The whole story of his effort in Britain was reduced to a nutshell in Secretary Benjamin's remark as early as January 1863 that the highest ranking Confederate diplomat had been "discourteously treated by Earl Russell." [8] Mason himself gave the gist of it by saying that he enjoyed "no intercourse, unofficial or otherwise, with any member of the [British] Government." [9]

Another unmistakable sign of the same breach was seen in the embittered controversy concerning British consuls in Southern cities. The fact of Britain having such consuls within the Confederacy—Moore at Richmond, Fullerton at Savannah, Cridland at Mobile, and Bunch at Charleston—bespoke an anomalous situation between nations that lacked diplomatic relations. They were, of course, merely a carry-over from prewar days when their presence was entirely regular within the pattern of the United States government. Complicating factors arose because these consuls, lacking exequaturs addressed to the Confederate government, took orders from British diplomatic officials accredited to Washington. Offended that Mr. Cridland carried a document signed by Lord Lyons appointing him acting English consul at Mobile,[10] the Confederate government adopted the policy of "prohibiting any direct communication between consuls . . . residing within the Confederacy and the functionaries of their Governments residing amongst our enemies." [11] Under these circumstances the consuls were annoyed and checkmated in their efforts to extend British protection over their nationals in the South. As the months passed, the matter of the consuls became increasingly acute. Finally, coming to the end of his patience in October 1863, President Davis took the decisive step of expelling these British officials from the country.[12] Commenting on these matters, Russell, though probably with no motive other than avoiding any commitment as to recognition, again referred to "the so-styled Confederate States." [13]

---

[7] *Ibid.*, 934.          [8] *Ibid.*, 656.          [9] *Ibid.*, 715.

[10] *Ibid.*, 797. On May 18, 1863, the Richmond *Whig* commented bitterly on the question of the consuls and referred to "the creation . . . of a Lincoln consul at Mobile [Cridland] by the English secretary of foreign affairs." *House Exec. Doc. No. 1*, 38 Cong., 2 sess., part 1, p. 802.

[11] *Offic. Rec.* (Nav.), 2 ser., III, 801.          [12] *Ibid.*, 922.

[13] *Ibid.*, 928.

## IV

An excellent indication of the attitude of the British government toward the American question is seen in the proceedings that were concerned with the parliamentary motion of the pro-Confederate Roe-buck, to which brief allusion has already been made. Roebuck, with his co-worker Lindsay, both being members of Parliament, became conspicuous, not to say notorious, for their efforts in behalf of American disunion. In close touch with the Confederate agent A. Dudley Mann, they sought to promote their object by way of amateur diplomacy and parliamentary maneuver. Napoleon III,[1] with considerable impropriety, had conferred in person with them, after which they posed importantly in Parliament as spokesmen of the Emperor, as if that ruler were avoiding regular diplomatic channels, undercutting the British ministry, and making communications to the House of Commons through these two officious negotiators.

Roebuck's tone may be judged by a speech he made in Sheffield in the summer of 1862. Arguing that a "divided America will be a benefit to England," he declared: "The North will never be our friends. Of the South you can make friends. They are Englishmen; they are not the scum and refuse of Europe." At these words the mayor of Manchester interrupted: "Don't say that; don't say that." [2]

With this background of Confederate collaboration and self-promoted diplomacy, Roebuck argued his motion, that Her Majesty "be graciously pleased to enter into negotiations with the Great Powers of Europe, for the purpose of obtaining their co-operation in the recognition of the independence of the Confederate States of North America." [3] When this effort to commit the British government to the pro-Confederate cause was debated in Parliament, support for it was so slight as to approach the vanishing point. Robert Montagu moved an amendment favoring "impartial neutrality." [4] Then Bright pitched in and showed how small was Roebuck's understanding of the European as well as the British attitude. He "poured out on Roebuck a deluge of weighty ridicule from which he never fully recov-

---

[1] E. D. Adams, *Great Britain and the American Civil War*, II, 167; F. L. Owsley, *King Cotton Diplomacy*, 297 ff.

[2] E. D. Adams, II, 34 n.

[3] *Hansard's Parl. Debates*, 3 ser., vol. CLXXI, p. 1780 (June 30, 1863).

[4] *Ibid.*, p. 1797.

ered." One who heard the debate remarked: "He [Bright] shook him as a terrier shakes a rat." [5] Members of the British ministry sharply criticized Roebuck. Sir George Grey showed how faulty his tactics were,[6] while Lord Palmerston, realizing what a false step had been taken both by the unauthorized Lindsay-Roebuck team and by Napoleon himself, hoped that the debates would include no further mention of this pseudo-diplomatic episode. Fearing an adverse effect upon Anglo-French relations, he wrote to Roebuck: "No good can come of touching again upon this matter, nor from fixing upon the Emperor a mistake which amid the multiplicity of things he has to think of he may be excused for making. . . . Might I ask you to show this note to Mr. Lindsay, your fellow traveller." [7]

Though few persons were taking "Don Roebucco" [8] seriously, it was a relief when his motion faded out of the picture without having come to a vote. This happened on July 13, 1863,[9] when Roebuck withdrew his own motion after debate had shown how overwhelmingly it would have been defeated.

It will be noted that proceedings on the Roebuck motion occurred in the period of Lee's invasion culminating in the Gettysburg campaign, and at a time when some of the British newspapers were predicting that the Confederates would soon take Washington. It is a significant fact, however, that word of Union success at Gettysburg did not reach London until July 16,[10] and that the Roebuck motion had been disposed of three days earlier.

There is a further phase of this parliamentary episode that must not be overlooked: it brought into view the attitude of the opposition— i. e., the Conservative party—in Britain. Leaders of that party by no means associated themselves with the Roebuck type of pro-Confederate maneuver. On this point Lord Derby, the Conservative leader who would presumably have become prime minister if the Palmerston government had been voted down in Parliament, opposed the idea of recognition and mediation, which meant, of course, that he also op-

[5] Trevelyan, *Bright*, 322–323.     [6] E. D. Adams, II, 171.     [7] *Ibid.*, 175.

[8] The member was caricatured by *Punch* as "Don Roebucco, the smallest man 'in the House.'" W. C. Ford, ed., *A Cycle of Adams Letters*, II, facing p. 48.

[9] *Hansard Parl. Debates*, 3 ser., CLXXII, p. 673. E. D. Adams (II, 177) explains that Roebuck "knew that if pressed to a vote it [his motion] would be overwhelmingly defeated."

[10] E. D. Adams, II, 178.

posed any further step which would have led to intervention.[11] Confederate agents were disappointed with Derby. They wrote home that he would not agitate the American question during the period of the Queen's acute grief after Prince Albert's death, that he was careful not to commit himself on this problem, and that during the American war he was by no means anxious to take office. "Lord Derby," wrote the Confederate agent Hotze, "does not come as our ally." [12]

Nor could the Confederates count on Disraeli. That colorful gentleman, high in the leadership of the opposition, was said to have expressed an "interest" in secessionist affairs, yet like Derby he never committed himself to any pro-Confederate move. Few indeed of the opposition leaders showed a disposition to go "so far as to oppose the Government in power" on the American question.[13] In a gloomy letter to Secretary Benjamin on February 10, 1863, A. Dudley Mann wrote: "Many of our friends in England calculated largely . . . upon the opposition for the acknowledgment of our independence. I never for a moment indulged any such expectation. . . . Earl Derby and Mr. Disraeli, regard with the coldest indifference the successful struggles which we have made . . . ." [14] Whatever hopes may have been raised as to Disraeli's attitude, he certainly did not make the Confederate cause his own. Contemplating the prospects as to the opposition members, Hotze wrote on June 6, 1863, when there was much talk of the Roebuck motion: "As a party the Conservatives are inharmonious and cowardly on this question, as on most others." [15] Though it has been suggested that Disraeli thought the United States was breaking up, he kept quiet as to this view. He said not "a word from the front Opposition bench likely to create difficulty with America." [16] His biographers show that he was "determined that Great Britain should preserve neutrality." [17] There had been talk in the Roebuck camp of "turning to the Tories," but this was a total miscalculation. The debate, writes E. D. Adams, showed "a complete misunderstanding of the position of Tory leaders." [18]

What then becomes of the strange popular concept that Britain "sided with the Confederacy" and was unfriendly to the Lincoln gov-

[11] *Ibid.*, II, 51.     [12] *Offic. Rec.* (Nav.), 2 ser., III, 1023.
[13] *Ibid.*, 506.     [14] *Ibid.*, 689.     [15] *Ibid.*, 785.
[16] Monnypenny and Buckle, *Life of Benjamin Disraeli, Earl of Beaconsfield*, IV, 328. This statement is a quotation of the words of John Bright.
[17] *Ibid.*, IV, 329.     [18] E. D. Adams, II, 177.

ernment? Certainly that was not true of the British people, nor of the government (the ministry), nor of the Liberal party, nor of the prime minister, nor of the foreign secretary, nor of Parliament, nor even of the opposition (Conservative) party. One should not speak of the *Times,* of Roebuck and Lindsay, of the Southern Independence Association, and of certain other vocal elements, as if they were the same as Britain. The whole story shows the withholding of British support for the Confederacy, and this fact was nowhere more clearly realized than at Richmond.

## V

This frigidity toward the enemy of the United States was no mere surface manifestation. Deep and underlying forces were working toward friendship between Washington and London. Men in office in Britain were not fire eaters, nor toward America were they international meddlers. At the outset of the war Lord Lyons, British minister at Washington, thought that "excitement" in South Carolina had "carried men . . . beyond the bounds of reason and common sense." [1] When in this same period an "honourable friend" mentioned that "the great Republican bubble in America had burst," the sentiment gave no satisfaction to Lord John Russell. He did not think it seemly to show "exultation at their discord." [2] Midway in the war, addressing the House of Lords on February 5, 1863, Russell spoke as follows: "For my own part, before this contest began, I rejoiced in the progress of the United States of America. The flourishing state of a people descended from the same ancestors as ourselves, and possessing laws of personal liberty similar to our own, was a sight in which Englishmen might rejoice." [3]

After nine months of war Charles Francis Adams noted in London that agitation "against us" did "not find its root deep in the heart of the community." [4] That the influential *Times* was unfriendly should not obscure the fact that other papers such as the *Morning Star* of London gave Lincoln's cause a better press. For example at the time of the congressional election of 1862 the *Morning Star* presented an analysis

---

[1] Walpole, *Russell,* II, 340.        [2] *Ibid.,* II, 338.
[3] Reprinted in *House Exec. Doc. No. 1,* 38 Cong., 1 sess., pt. 1, p. 126.
[4] W. C. Ford, ed., *Cycle of Adams Letters,* I, 107.

to show that the "opposition" had not "won" the contest.[5]

A number of factors were working to create that improvement in the climate of Anglo-American relations which was especially noted from 1863 onward: Confederate defeat, Lincoln's emancipation, the realization in the *Trent* affair that war could be avoided without loss of "honor" on either side, the sympathy of the common people, and the tireless work of John Bright. Emancipation meetings all over England in 1863, treated in a previous volume,[6] being unofficial, spontaneous and genuine, constituted a most impressive demonstration of like feelings between friendly nations. Commenting favorably upon the meeting at Manchester, the London *Daily News* of January 2, 1863, remarked upon the important role of the British working classes in showing Britain's attitude toward the American struggle. This attitude was held to be in keeping with "England's old attachment to the principles of freedom, and its undying hatred to oppression in any form." At this huge meeting, December 31, 1862, the Free Trade Hall, with a capacity of 6,000, was well filled and the address to the American President was adopted "with the greatest enthusiasm and unanimity." It was the sentiment of this meeting that Anglo-American relations "be knit more firmly, and that the people of the two nations may ever be united in the bonds of amity and fraternity."[7] The unemotional Adams was impressed by this meeting. He considered it "in every respect a most remarkable indication of the state of popular sentiment in Great Britain." He believed it would make "a strong impression everywhere" and would do much to promote amicable feeling between the nations.

Lincoln's reply to Manchester[8] combined a sympathy for the British working people with a strong assurance of "reciprocal feelings of friendship among the American people." Similar meetings, with like sentiments, were held at York, London (Exeter Hall), Blackburn, Leeds, Galashiels, Bath, Bromley, South London, Glasgow, Aberdeen, Edinburgh, Bristol, Sheffield, Birmingham, Leicester, Bolton, and many other places. The antislavery leader, George Thompson, wrote to Garrison that these meetings on the American question had been

---

[5] *Morning Star*, London, Jan. 2, 1863.    [6] *Lincoln the President*, II, 176–180.

[7] Abel Haywood, Chairman, to C. F. Adams, Manchester, Jan. 1, 1863 (Britain, vol. 81), MSS., Dept. of State, Nat. Archives.

[8] *Lincoln the President*, II, 178–179.

"densely crowded, sublimely enthusiastic, and all but unanimous." [9]
It would be "impossible," he wrote, "to give you a list of all the meetings which have recently been held [February 1863], for the purpose
of expressing sympathy with the Anti-Slavery movement in the United
States . . . . The men who a few months ago were so bold . . . in
the advocacy . . . of the Southern Rebels, are now silent." [10] It was
felt that these demonstrations showed clearly that the heart of England
was not against the United States.[11] As one Englishman expressed it:
"If our *nation* is consulted, it would rather vote down the House of
Lords . . . than permit war with you." [12] These outpourings of
British feeling kept the staff of the American legation busy. The diary
of Benjamin Moran, one of the staff, in this period frequently mentions emancipation meetings "held very generally in England," addresses pouring in, and visits of numerous delegations. Minister Adams
and his son Henry were kept busy in making suitable personal response.[13]

In the matter of these assemblages a book could be written on Manchester alone. The demonstration there had an effect like a series of
widening circles. Not only did it call for the notable reply from Lincoln. Its sequel appeared in a visit of James William Massie who addressed audiences ranging from New England to the Middle West and
Kentucky, delivering the message of good will committed to his charge
at Manchester. Massie was a British clergyman of Irish birth, friendly
to America and active in free-trade and antislavery agitation. He
wrote: "I have always, everywhere, sought to express . . . an amicable and congenial sentiment, in Americans, toward their English
kindred; giving assurance, that the Lairds, Roebucks, and *Times* are
not England. . . . I can now assure my countrymen, that . . .

9 George Thompson to W. L. Garrison, Feb. 5, 1863, Garrison MSS., Boston Pub. Lib.
10 Thompson to Garrison, Feb. 27, 1863, *ibid.*
11 W. C. Ford, ed., *Cycle of Adams Letters,* I, 107.
12 Francis W. Newman to Epes Sargent, London, April 20, 1863, MS., Boston Pub. Lib.
13 Sarah A. Wallace and Frances E. Gillespie, eds., *Journal of Benjamin Moran,* II,
1107 and *passim.* It was Moran's belief that Minister Adams was "determined to push
his son to the front." Moran felt that the "boy" had "no business" doing such things,
but that he was moved by a "love of distinction." *Ibid.,* II, 1120. In this connection one
may note the unfavorable British reaction to Henry Adams's "Diary of a Visit to Manchester," which was published, not in the *Atlantic* as Henry had hoped, but in the
Boston *Courier* on December 16, 1861. Especially did Englishmen dislike Henry's comparison of "society" in Manchester and in London to the detriment of the latter. See
Arthur W. Silver, in *Am. Hist. Rev.,* LI, 74–89 (Oct. 1945).

there yet remains [among Americans] . . . a partial [i. e., sympathetic] affection for Englishmen and a desire to live in the most cordial terms of international unity with Great Britain." [14]

## VI

It was not merely the antislavery circles, but notably also the labor groups, then inadequately organized, which showed a marked sympathy for Lincoln's cause, as in Trades Unions gatherings in the spring of 1863.[1] If some among the "privileged classes all over Europe" were rejoicing at "the ruin of the great experiment of popular government," [2] it was also evident that the "old revolutionary leaven" was "working steadily in England" and that "the American question . . . [was] organizing a vast mass of the lower orders in direct contact with the wealthy" who were ready to "go our whole platform." [3]

Much could be written on "democratic and socialist" meetings, where Henry Adams noted a refusal to tolerate "interference against us." [4] Sentiment favorable to Lincoln and the Union came naturally to British labor and to socialist groups and there is no need to disclaim it, though as a threat "to the established state of things" agitation by such groups was as "alarming" to some English minds "as a slave insurrection would be in the South." [5] If British labor circles were hopeful toward the American experiment it is not to their discredit that such an attitude was identified with their own uphill struggles for political and economic opportunity at home. It belonged authentically to the history of the time and had its part in those varied manifestations which indicated, from early 1863 on, that popular British opinion was swinging toward Washington.[6]

---

14 James W. Massie to Lincoln, Buffalo, Sept. 21, 1863, R. T. L. Coll. 26467–68.

1 W. C. Ford, ed., *A Cycle of Adams Letters,* I, 296, 298.

2 *Ibid.,* II, 65.

3 *Ibid.,* I, 245. Considerable material on these meetings has been assembled in *House Exec. Doc. No. 1,* 39 Cong., 1 sess., part 1, pp. 59 ff., 141 ff., 214 ff.

4 *Cycle of Adams Letters,* I, 244.

5 *Ibid.*

6 Writing from London in early '63, a Confederate leader noted that "the Radicals, under Bright and others" had the balance of power and that their opposition would be fatal to any ministry in England. He added: "These men are warm partisans of the United States, and have of late made a series of striking demonstrations by public meetings, speeches, etc." L. Q. C. Lamar to J. P. Benjamin, London, Mar. 20, 1863, *Offic. Rec.* (Nav.), 2 ser., III, 716–717.

To make a list of those in Britain who favored the American Union would be unfair to those omitted. Men so disposed were notable for their intellectual ability and human sympathy. One such person was "a curious looking man with a sharp nose, a wen on his forehead and a black cravat, . . . about the ablest man in England," John Stuart Mill. This portrait was drawn by Henry Adams, who referred to Mill as "a mighty weapon of defense for our cause" in England.[7] In *Fraser's Magazine* in February 1862 [8] Mill wrote favorably and convincingly of the Union cause. In his autobiography he records that his "strongest feelings were engaged in this struggle." Dreading what he deemed the "aggressive enterprise of the slave-owners to extend" slave territory "under the  . . . influences of pecuniary interest, domineering temper, and the fanaticism of a class for its class privileges," Mill felt that success of the slave power "would give courage to the enemies of progress and damp the spirits of its friends all over the civilized world, while it would create a formidable military power, grounded on  . . . anti-social  . . . tyranny of men over men  . . . ." [9]

There was also Richard Cobden. Though at first this outstanding British liberal was somewhat affected by Southern support for free trade in contrast to the Northern tariff, and also by his horror of war, he became "an earnest champion of the North," [10] as shown, for example, by his attitude in the *Trent* case.[11] Concerning Cobden's attitude Charles Francis Adams wrote: "In his [Cobden's] opinion,  . . . the moral support of Europe [should have been] so far assured to the Government of the United States as to preclude any hope among the insurgents of possible assistance  . . . ." [12] British friends of America included, of course, the antislavery leaders, notably George Thompson. There were also Prince Albert, the Duke of Argyll, Goldwin Smith, the evangelist Spurgeon, Leslie Stephen, and the journalist Frederick M. Edge, who expressed his passionate interest in the United

7 Henry Adams, in *Cycle of Adams Letters*, I, 253.

8 John Stuart Mill, "The Contest in America," *Fraser's Magazine*, LXV, 258–268 (Feb. 1862).

9 *Autobiography of John Stuart Mill*, 187.

10 Trevelyan, *Bright*, 302.

11 "During the *Trent* affair Lincoln's Government  . . . received from Cobden the same counsels of moderation as from Bright." *Ibid.*, 316. (This was at a time when friends of the Confederacy hoped not for "moderation," but for a breach between America and Britain.)

12 C. F. Adams, to Seward, London, July 3, 1862, Diplomatic Despatches (Britain, vol. 80), MSS., Dept. of State, Nat. Archives.

States and his hope to assist "Americans in working out the . . . re-establishment of the Union's authority." [13]

## VII

Finally, towering above them all, was John Bright. Never did a liberal have a clearer idea of where he was going than this sturdy champion of political and economic rights for the masses of laboring men in Britain. There was consistency in the totality of the causes which he led or sponsored. In addition to the American effort to survive as a whole nation, these causes included relief from the corn laws (that is, from injustices associated with landed privilege and monopoly), free trade, economic liberalism in general, outspoken opposition to the Crimean War, admission of Jews to Parliament, reform in India, and extension of the voting right to British workingmen.

In so busy a life it was a significant thing that Bright found time to devote so great an amount of energy and leadership to advocating the Union cause in Britain. He corresponded with Sumner, urged his thoughts upon Earl Russell, and promoted moderation on both sides in the *Trent* controversy, in which he did much to avert war. He kept at it constantly, exposing the one-sided nature of French "mediation," making vigorous speeches, and laboring successfully for the defeat of Roebuck's motion in Parliament looking toward recognition of the Confederacy. Stressing the cost and tragedy of war between Britain and the United States, the hollowness of British sympathy for secession, the stain of slavery, and the regularity of Lincoln's election,[1] he dwelt with moving eloquence upon the impressive example of American democracy, the effort of the slave power "to break up the most free government in the world," [2] and the unwisdom of recognizing "a new state intending to set itself up [as Bright saw it] on the sole basis of slavery." [3]

Economic interest in the superficial sense might well have caused Bright to favor the Confederacy.[4] Owner of a textile mill in Lanca-

---

[13] Frederick M. Edge to H. W. Bellows, Oct. 9, 1863, Bellows MSS., Mass. Hist. Soc.
[1] John Bright, *Speeches on the American Question*, 107.
[2] *Ibid.*, 27.          [3] *Ibid.*, 113. See also pp. 7, 27.
[4] A bibliography of Anglo-American relations on the economic level cannot be attempted here. One should especially note W. O. Henderson, *Lancashire Cotton Famine, 1861–1865;* L. B. Schmidt, in *Iowa Jour. of Hist. and Pol.*, XVI, 400–439; and J. H. Clap-

shire, he found his business threatened with ruin by the blockade which shut off the supply of Southern cotton. It was precisely this economic dislocation, widespread and disastrous in British manufacturing districts, on which the leaders of secession banked in their drive for foreign intervention. Despite this motive of personal gain, Bright even favored the blockade, because to him the whole Union movement embodied the cause of broad economic opportunity and of political liberalism. Thousands of British laborers were thrown out of work, including employees of Bright, but British and American good will came handsomely to their relief. George Macaulay Trevelyan, biographer of Bright, writes that "all England came to the rescue with abundant generosity"; he adds that three large ships brought American flour as a token of friendship "tangible to eye and hand and mouth." [5]

Bright closely followed every event in the war, cultivated friendly British editors, kept privately in touch with persons in the Government, and expressed satisfaction at symptoms of "break up among the gang at Richmond." He approved a speech of Lord Russell which indicated an improved state of feeling on the state of American affairs, and wrote at one time, "whilst the [American] contest lasts, I seem able to think of nothing else." [6] A keynote to his attitude is to be found in a letter he wrote from Rochdale on July 9, 1863, to Consul Thomas H. Dudley: "I have kept my faith till now [i. e., regarding the outcome in the United States]—& I shall not part with it except as I would part with my life's hope." [7]

Between Lincoln and Bright there grew up a cordiality that was both a matter of personal regard and a factor of solid international import. It was a friendship based on political agreement. Harmony of views was its very essence. Lincoln was in America what Bright was in England. It was a long-range friendship. The two men never met, since Bright never visited America, nor was there direct correspond-

---

ham, *An Economic History of Modern Britain: Free Trade and Steel, 1850–1886.* In a doctoral thesis at the University of Illinois (1937) Martin P. Claussen has presented a careful study of economic factors in Anglo-American relations in the Lincoln period. His monograph is entitled: "The United States and Great Britain, 1861–1865: Peace Factors in International Relations."

[5] Trevelyan, *Bright,* 309.

[6] Letters of Bright to Thomas H. Dudley, Feb. 4, 1864; March 25, 1863; Aug. 27, 1863; Dudley MSS., Huntington Lib.

[7] Dudley MSS.

ence between them. For letters to have passed directly between the President of the United States and a prominent member of the British House of Commons might have seemed out of place. Yet by indirect communications, as through Sumner or Dudley, messages and friendly greetings were exchanged. A photograph of Bright, presented to Lincoln in 1864, was a significant item in these cordial exchanges. The gift is mentioned in a letter of Thomas H. Dudley to Congressman E. B. Washburne (March 14, 1864),[8] and the prominent displaying of the photograph in the White House in Lincoln's day is a matter of well attested record.[9]

A further item in the Lincoln-Bright story was a marble bust of Bright intended as a gift to Lincoln from Thomas G. Blain of Manchester; after Lincoln's assassination it was presented by Blain to the American nation. In a letter from Consul Dudley to President Andrew Johnson, Blain was described as a "warm friend of the United States and a great admirer of John Bright as well as of our late lamented President."[10]

One of Lincoln's many instances of clemency was associated with the Lancashire liberal. A British youth named Alfred Rubery, caught in a privateering escapade which amounted to conspiracy under the law of the United States, was befriended by Lincoln as a favor to Bright. In this rather freakish adventure about twenty men, Rubery among them, were caught in San Francisco Bay operating a schooner under Confederate letters of marque with designs against United States gold-carrying ships and with glittering hopes of private booty. The leader, a Kentuckian named Asbury Harpending, had taken oath as a member of a secret order. There was a dash of melodrama about

---

[8] Washburne MSS., Lib. of Cong.

[9] In the Bright MSS. in the British Museum there is a letter in which a correspondent of Bright named Henry Janney wrote (April 24, 1865) recalling how Lincoln told him of his pleasure in reading Bright's letters. Janney added that Bright's picture hung over the fireplace in one of the rooms of the White House. This is also attested by a letter of Schuyler Colfax under date of May 20, 1866 (Bright MSS., British Museum). Goldwin Smith, describing the ante-room to Lincoln's office, mentioned as a prominent ornament "a large photograph of John Bright." F. Lauriston Bullard, in *Amer. Bar Assoc. Jour.*, XXV, 219 (Mar., 1939).

[10] Information concerning this bust is found in the records of the commissioner of public buildings and in consular dispatches from Liverpool, National Archives, Wash., D.C. For a digest of this material the author is indebted to Dr. P. M. Hamer of the National Archives (P. M. Hamer to the author, Feb. 23, 1943).

the whole affair. The "pirates" were all brought to trial in the United States circuit court at San Francisco, Stephen J. Field being one of the justices, and three of the accused, including the Englishman Rubery, were sentenced to a fine of $10,000 and imprisonment of ten years. Interesting himself in the case as that of a young man of his Birmingham constituency who was adventurous rather than vicious, John Bright brought the matter to Lincoln's attention through Sumner, and Lincoln issued a pardon for Rubery in a formal proclamation, mentioning that in addition to other considerations the act was done "especially as a public mark of the esteem held by the United States . . . for the high character and steady friendship of . . . John Bright." [11]

If the Lincoln-Bright relation, neglected by most of Lincoln's biographers, has been emphasized in these pages, it is because the subject is basic. Regard for Bright was as fundamental with Lincoln as the Gettysburg address. Indeed the theme was the same: it was a question of democracy at large. One cannot write adequately of the American crisis without noting how Bright played his role: doing a man's part in averting war in the *Trent* case, eloquently developing British sympathy for the Union, tying the American cause to that of British liberals, making Lincoln's name a symbol of freedom to workingmen in England. Bright's countrymen by the many thousands realized that their interest and their philosophy was one with that of the rugged American President. If the two causes were of genuine identity, that made the friendship all the stronger. Not only did sympathetic British assemblages express Lincolnian convictions; it is even true that, through Senator Sumner, Lincoln sent to Bright in his own handwriting the draft of a resolution expressing the views which he wished to have adopted in such meetings.[12] In giving his own cue for resolutions of British sympathy, the American President knew well that Bright was the man to whom this cue should be directed. This does not mean that the expressions of sympathy were "inspired" in the propaganda sense; it means rather that the identity of political liberty

---

[11] F. Lauriston Bullard, "Lincoln Pardons Conspirator On Plea of An English Statesman," *Amer. Bar Assoc. Jour.*, XXV, 220 (Mar., 1939); Jay Monaghan, *Diplomat in Carpet Slippers*, 297, 311, 337, 343, 346.

[12] For facsimile see Trevelyan, *Bright*, 303.

with economic opportunity was a subject on which Lincoln and Bright could not be indifferent.[13]

While narrower ideas of gain and profit were voluminously agitated, and while in some quarters international relations were cast in a mold of twisted materialism, it was given to John Bright to assist in averting war, to disprove the economic thesis of "King Cotton," [14] to demonstrate that trade is not all, and to show that trade itself has its liberal and peace-promoting aspects.

Though the Anglo-American situation was at the forefront of Lincoln's international problems, his administration had to deal with nations the world over. In considering the diplomacy of that period —though these wider matters are not treated in the present volume— attention must be given to relations with Napoleon III, the Maximilian venture in Mexico, the Russian attitude toward the American struggle (including friendly visits of two Russian fleets), and complicated dealings in the Far East. A study of these oriental dealings brings into view the Lincoln-Seward policy toward China, and, for Japan, a highly difficult series of incidents in a period of stress, antiforeign feeling, and violence. In addition to all of Lincoln's other problems he and his department of state had to keep in mind the internal confusion of Mikado, Shogun (Tycoon), and feudal daimios. Not only the United States but other nations as well—notably Britain —were seriously embarrassed by the differences, and the challenge of adjustment, between the oriental and occidental mind, in language, background, mores, etiquette, worship, and national (in opposition to imperialistic) interests.[15]

---

[13] This subject is further discussed in "Lincoln and John Bright," Randall, *Lincoln the Liberal Statesman*, chap. vi.

[14] On the Southern economic concept of "King Cotton" in its relation to the Civil War, see F. L. Owsley, *King Cotton Diplomacy, passim* but especially pp. 562–578; Randall, *Civil War and Reconstruction*, 648–654.

[15] The author has prepared two chapters dealing with these further international problems, but their publication is being deferred to a later volume.

# CHAPTER XV

# THE CHATTANOOGA FRONT:
# DEATH OF HELM

WESTERN military operations in the latter part of 1863 form an elaborate and vacillating story. It was a changing situation: temporary Union defeat, serious menace of Confederate advance, decisions to be made as to relative strength in East and West, important shifts of command, and in November —the month of the Gettysburg address—Union triumph. Whether there was defeat or triumph there were always casualties, and to the Lincolns those casualties became close personal tragedy in the battle death of Mrs. Lincoln's brother-in-law. To contemplate the war in disregard of such tragedy, and write only of the movement of divisions and the winning or losing of battles, would be most unrealistic.

## I

In the latter part of 1862, as already noted, there had occurred Bragg's ambitious but futile invasion of Kentucky. When, after the sanguinary battle of Perryville (October 8) the Confederate general pulled his forces back into Tennessee, the situation presented a disheartening anticlimax in Confederate plans. It was hardly to be expected that more than one major army enterprise could be launched in the West in any half-year; yet in the second half of 1862 the army of Bragg had shot its bolt, and the only result to show for it was that the "liberation" of Kentucky was abandoned. It was a cause which had elicited little response from the people of that state. Marching laboriously great distances, fighting indecisively with serious losses, separating and shifting positions—such was the procedure between the contending hosts. On the Union side dissatisfaction with Buell for not dealing more effectively with Bragg coincided with the success of Rosecrans over Price and Van Dorn at Iuka and Corinth. Buell was accordingly superseded by Rosecrans as the commander of the principal army in the West, the Army of the Cumberland.

At the turn of the year (December 31–January 2, 1862–63) there occurred an elaborate engagement between Bragg and Rosecrans at Stone's River (Murfreesboro) in central Tennessee. After this crippling but indecisive battle one heard little of Bragg and Rosecrans while Grant and his Army of the Tennessee were winning their slugging campaign against Vicksburg.

In the strategic planning for 1863 the question arose as to whether Lee should send troops west. Instead of doing so (after Chancellorsville) he spent his great effort in the ambitious but unsuccessful drive into Pennsylvania. There was consequently a great army-and-navy combination under Grant by which—with the surrender of Pemberton at Vicksburg on July 4 and the subsequent operation of Banks at Port Hudson—some of the most important stakes of the whole war were won by the Federals. The Mississippi River came completely within Union hands, western Tennessee was wrested from Confederate control, and the value of Southern trans-Mississippi forces was nullified. As to Vicksburg, three outstanding Confederate leaders—Generals Johnston and Pemberton and President Davis (not to mention Bragg)—had differed as to strategy. Basic orders had not been carried out and the concentration of Southern forces—union of Pemberton and Johnston to defeat Grant—had failed.

Bitter recrimination resulted from that failure, Davis sharply censuring Johnston's conduct and Johnston blaming the President for insufficient support to Pemberton. Looking back from Vicksburg to Perryville and attributing the unfortunate invasion of Kentucky to the Confederate chief executive, Johnston wrote: "If, instead of being sent on the wild expedition into Kentucky, General Bragg had been instructed to avail himself of the dispersed condition of the Federal troops in northern Mississippi and west Tennessee, he might have totally defeated the forces with which General Grant invaded Mississippi three months later. Those troops were distributed in Corinth, Jackson, Memphis, and intermediate points, while his own were united, so that he could have fought them in detail, with as much certainty of success as can be hoped for in war." [1]

## II

After Vicksburg the strategic focus in the West shifted to Chattanooga. This important goal of contending armies was the key to eastern Tennessee and a good deal else, being both a river location and a vital railway point (on the Memphis and Charleston) between East and West. For a time after Murfreesboro it had seemed that the situation between the opposing commanders, Rosecrans and Bragg, had reached a kind of deadlock. There were months of inaction, and in June of 1863 Bragg's force in central Tennessee confronted that of Rosecrans in a confused stalemate. Then things began to happen and Rosecrans won the first round. Putting his divisions into motion on June 23, the Union commander maneuvered Bragg out of central Tennessee into Chattanooga. To maneuver him out of that position was the next task, and by early September this also was accomplished. Yet the great armies still faced each other, and the fate of the Chattanooga area was in the balance.

On September 9, in a despatch to Halleck, with something of a flourish, Rosecrans reported: "Chattanooga is ours without a struggle, and East Tennessee is free!!— Our move on the Enemy's flank and rear progresses while the tail of his retreating column will not escape unmolested. Our troops from this side entered Chattanooga about noon. Those north of the river there are crossing. Messengers go to Burnside tonight urging him to push his cavalry down. No news from him or his Cavalry." [1]

At that stage, while Grant and Sherman were not in the main spotlight (Grant contemplating a far flung movement to Mobile which never came off),[2] the fame of Rosecrans seemed on the point of bringing him to the top among commanders in the West. Iuka, Corinth, Murfreesboro (though a drawn battle), and now Chattanooga, stood

---

1 *Battles and Leaders of the Civil War*, III, 481–482.

1 Rosecrans to Halleck, Camp Near Trenton, Ga., Sept. 9, 1863, 8:30 p.m., R. T. L. Coll., 26166–7.

2 "After the fall of Vicksburg I did incline very much to an immediate move on Mobile. I believed then the place could be taken with but little effort, . . . ." Grant to Lincoln, Cairo, Ill., Aug. 23, 1863, R. T. L. Coll. 25799; see also Grant, *Memoirs*, I, 578; II, 19.

to his credit. As for Bragg, he had withdrawn into nearby Georgia.

As Rosecrans entered Chattanooga, Burnside, heading the Army of the Ohio, moved through Cumberland Gap and took possession of Knoxville, important center of a great mountain region whose inhabitants were predominantly Unionist in sentiment and whose interests were constantly in Lincoln's thought.

At this moment of high promise Rosecrans's luck, or strategic skill, or power of effective command, failed him. In the complicated and elaborate two-day battle of Chickamauga (September 19–20, 1863) a series of factors worked against him. He had not been reënforced by Burnside from Knoxville as Lincoln earnestly wished. On the other hand two corps had been detached from Lee's army on the Rapidan and sent West under Longstreet, whose part in the engagement was of great importance. Rosecrans had been thinking of Bragg as withdrawing deep into Georgia, not expecting that he would take the offensive against him. Bragg's forces were consolidated, while Rosecrans's dispositions were defective and his line weakened by over-extension.

Part of Rosecrans's preparation was a strengthening of the Union left; the result was a weakened right and a weaker center. On the second day of the battle, in a move which effective reconnaissance ought to have foreseen, Longstreet hurled six divisions forward in a powerful assault. Aiming his stroke at the Union right and the center gap, he poured his troops through the Federal line and Rosecrans suffered the "appalling demolition of his right wing." [3] Considering the battle lost, the Federal commander made his way into Rossville and then into Chattanooga to make suitable dispositions of his "disordered and defeated army." Charles A. Dana recalled that he "saw our lines break and melt away like leaves before the wind." He wrote that the whole Union right "had apparently been routed" and that "Everything was in the greatest disorder." [4]

On the Union left, however, it was a different story. In many hours of fierce and terrific fighting, in which the bayonet was used, George H. Thomas held fast, becoming known as the savior of the Union army and winning the sobriquet "Rock of Chickamauga." In addition to other points, the fact that Thomas was a Virginian who adhered to the Union gave him a special distinction. It should be added, of course,

---

[3] *Battles and Leaders*, III, 671.
[4] Dana, *Recollections of the Civil War*, 115.

that it was the building-up of the Union left under Thomas which had weakened the Federal right and center and had allowed Longstreet to rush through. (Considering the terrific punishment inflicted upon Thomas's wing and the dominant part he played, there was nothing unreasonable in the strengthening of his part of the line.)

In a cipher telegram Rosecrans reported the sad result to Halleck: "We have met with a serious disaster. . . . Enemy overwhelmed us. Drove our right, pierced our Center and scattered them. Thomas, who had seven divisions remained intact at last news. . . . Every available reserve was used when the men stampeded. . . . It seems that every available man was thrown against us." [5]

Major General John M. Palmer of Illinois, who commanded a division of Thomas L. Crittenden's corps at Chickamauga, wrote frequent letters in this period to his wife, who was in an agony of suspense as to his safety. On October 2, 1863, with due military restraint, he wrote his summary of Chickamauga: "The Army of the Cumberland has met with a reverse. Not severe relative to that of the enemy. We have had one of those terrific murderous conflicts between two masses of men guided and animated mainly by a mere determination to win and we were beaten by the bad conduct of Generals and the superior numbers of the enemy. Our communications are not safe. I will not therefore be more specific. Our glorious Army is in good spirits and ready to meet the enemy again." [6]

### III

One finds a brief and optimistic comment on Chickamauga in a telegram which the President sent from Washington to Mrs. Lincoln who was then in New York: "We now have a tolerably accurate summing up of the late battle between Rosecrans and Bragg. The result is that we are worsted, if at all, only in the fact that we, after the main fighting was over, yielded the ground, thus leaving considerable of our artillery and wounded to fall into the enemie's [sic] hands, for which we got nothing in turn. We lost, in general officers, one killed and three or four wounded, all Brigadiers, while . . . they lost six

---

[5] Rosecrans to Halleck, telegram in cipher, Chattanooga, Sep. 20, 1863, 5 p.m., R. T. L. Coll. 26404–5.

[6] MS., Ill. State Hist. Lib.

killed and eight wounded. Of the killed one Major Genl. and five Brigadiers, including your brother-in-law, Helm; and of the wounded three Major Generals, and five Brigadiers." [1]

It was thus, almost parenthetically, that Lincoln broke the news to Mary of the death of the Confederate brigadier general, Ben Hardin Helm, husband of Emilie Todd Helm. (The announcement of the fact, in the necessary brevity of this message, was enough; Lincoln was not a man to put his emotions into a telegram.) None of Mary's sisters was closer to her or more beloved than Emilie. Both she and Helm had visited the Lincolns in Springfield and Lincoln had affectionately called her "Little Sister."

Toward this brother-in-law Lincoln at the outset of his presidency had shown a marked friendship. According to the account by Helm's daughter, Katherine, the President sent the young man a cordial invitation to Washington and handed him "a commission as paymaster in the United States Army with rank of major." [2] This was a great opportunity. "The rank of major at his age, thirty, was very exceptional in the army. Nothing had ever touched Helm like this." [3] Here was a fine career opening up for him if he would accept. It seems to have been assumed that, at least for a time, the position would have involved residence in Washington. To Helm the advantage appeared in terms of the rank and the chance to be transferred at an early date to one of the cavalry regiments. To Mary Lincoln, however, in need of having a member of her own family close to her, the great appeal was that her sister could be with her in Washington—a belle on social occasions in the White House, a source of pride, her husband a dignified officer. In this respect Helm had a decision to make that was not unlike that of Robert E. Lee—except, of course, that the great Virginian "went with his State" and the Kentuckian did not. Though grateful to his brother-in-law for the generous offer, Helm declined it. [4] It was a painful choice, and in that choice one may read the difficult problem of those men of the Blue Grass who, though regretting the breaking

---

[1] Lincoln to Mrs. Lincoln, Sep. 24, 1863, MS. Ill. State Hist. Lib.

[2] "Some time ago I requested that Ben. Hardin Helm might be appointed a paymaster, which I still desire." Lincoln to Sec. of War, Exec. Mansion, Apr. 16, 1861, Cameron MSS.

[3] Katherine Helm, *Mary, Wife of Lincoln*, 184.

[4] *Ibid.*, 183–188. See also R. Gerald McMurtry, *Ben Hardin Helm*, 17–24. John Hay made the erroneous statement that Helm "was made a paymaster by the President," implying that the offer was accepted. Dennett, . . . *Diaries* . . . *of John Hay*, 92.

of the Union, cast their lot with the Confederacy.

Commanding a brigade of the division led by his friend and neighbor J. C. Breckinridge (of the Confederate right wing under Lt. Gen. Leonidas Polk),[5] Helm's men had been brought under terrific cross fire from Union breastworks in a "portion of the line [which] proved to be one of the most hotly contested positions of the entire battlefield." [6] Struck while riding toward the enemy's works on the morning of September 20, Helm fell mortally wounded from his horse. He died that night. It was a fearful tragedy in the Todd family and a source of personal sorrow to the Lincolns. We are not speaking here of demonstrations of White House grief. Times were grim and feelings could not always be expressed. One could, of course, weep sincerely for Helm —as one could admire the character of Lee—without favoring the Confederacy. The general had done his Confederate duty. To prominent fellow-Lexingtonians his conduct was as "Kentuckian" as that of Breckinridge and Morgan. The fact that, to the Lincolns, Helm was an enemy had significance not as a matter of hatred between them, but as an added grief, a cause of Emilie's deep resentment, and a bitter, inscrutable token of the unnatural brothers' war. It made it no easier that the Lincolns were in such a position that their genuine grief could find no adequate expression.

The personal agony of war came now to the very White House, but without the sympathy and understanding of friends by which tragedy is customarily softened. Of the genuineness of the President's feeling there can be no doubt. David Davis had never seen him more moved "than when he heard of the death of his young brother-in-law." [7] And what of Mary's feelings? There were thousands of war-bereaved Americans, but the barriers to the expression of feeling made Mary's grief the harder; it was as if she was shut off from the right to feel as a human being and a sister. Devotedly loyal to the Union, she rejoiced in Federal victory, but with a poignant sense of what warfare meant in human terms on both sides. Having brothers in what she herself called the "rebel" army, she utterly disapproved of the cause which they served; yet the rightness of that Union disapproval, which she felt as sincerely as any, was denied her. She became the target of Northern suspicion; "a single tear shed for a dead enemy would bring torrents

5 *Battles and Leaders,* III, 673.   6 McMurtry, *Ben Hardin Helm,* 44.
7 Katherine Helm, 216.

of scorn and bitter abuse on both her husband and herself." That she was a Southerner was true, but that a Southern origin made it necessary to war against the United States she, and many thousands of Kentuckians, denied. Yet Southerners judged her harshly as an enemy and thought of her as having a stony indifference to "the sufferings of her own people." [8] In all, she had four brothers in the Confederate army—George, Samuel, David, and Alexander. Of these only George survived the war. Sam was killed at Shiloh, David at Vicksburg, and Alec in 1862 in the fighting at Baton Rouge. If she wept for these of her kin on the other side, it had to be in secret. One cannot read her story as told by her niece, Katherine Helm, without realizing that there was no one in the land upon whom the unnatural hatreds and distortions of that day bore more relentlessly than upon her.

## IV

Mrs. Helm had attended the last rites for her husband at Atlanta [1] and then stayed for a time in the home of E. M. Bruce in Madison, Georgia. At her request Mr. Bruce wrote to Lincoln reporting the manner of the general's death: "although opposed . . . to your forces, it will . . . be a satisfaction to you to know that he fell at the head of his Brigade—honorably battling for the cause he thought just and righteous—he was *leading* his 'Kentucky Brigade' to a charge which was successful . . . and I know you can but admire him for his deeds, and will regret that he could not have survived the conflict, and shared in the glories of the victory." (The reference here was evidently to the temporary Confederate victory in the battle of Chickamauga.) Mr. Bruce added: "Mrs Helm is crushed by the blow—almost broken hearted—and desires to return to her Mother and friends in Kentucky . . . ." He therefore asked the President to have a pass sent to her to enter the Federal truce boat at City Point: the pass to be sent in triplicate to Mrs. Helm, to William Preston Johnston at Richmond, and to Bruce himself at Madison, Georgia. The letter ended with a personal message from Emilie: "Mrs Helm desires to be affectionately remembered to her sister." [2]

Bound for Kentucky, Emilie made her way by sea to Fort Monroe,

---

[8] *Ibid.*, 217.                    [1] *Ibid.*, 220.
[2] E. M. Bruce to Lincoln, Madison, Ga., Oct. 6, 1863, R. T. L. Coll., 26992-3.

but was informed that she could not proceed further unless she took the loyalty oath to the United States. Though faced with what seemed a helpless situation—in Union hands and "almost penniless"—she refused the oath. The officer in charge, not unfriendly but at a loss what to do, wired the President for instructions. Back came the answering telegram: "Send her to me." [3]

Thus it was that Emilie found herself spending a week at the White House under the affectionate care of her sister Mary and "Brother Lincoln." Yet in her diary she wrote: "Sister and I cannot open our hearts to each other as freely as we would like. This frightful war comes between us like a barrier of granite . . . ." [4] Not by words but by clasped hands of sympathy their griefs were joined—Mary grieving for her lost Willie, Emilie for her husband. Knowing they would hurt each other, they avoided the topic of the war. Emilie wrote of Mary: "Her fine tact and delicacy fill me with admiration." [5]

Emilie's arrival in Washington came shortly after the announcement of the President's broad plan of amnesty, in which an oath of allegiance was prescribed. Lincoln presented her with this oath, which he had prepared for her to sign, [6] but she refused, not with any air of bravado but simply because her loyalty was elsewhere; the Federal oath would have seemed to her and her friends a repudiation of the cause for which her husband had died.

At every stage Lincoln had done what he could. Where it was a matter of sending a pass, [7] facilitating the recovery of property in the South, or extending amnesty, he had given Emilie's situation his personal and considerate care, though always within correct conduct as Union President. He urged her to prolong her stay at the White House, despite the embarrassment that arose from outspoken people who could not understand, and hoped she would spend the summer of 1864 with the presidential family. In a statement in his own hand, "Whom it may concern," he expressed the wish that she might "have protection of person and property, except as to slaves." Back in Kentucky Emilie was again in the Todd fold and the Lexington scene but under poignantly hard times. A tone of bitterness now crept into her letters. On October 30, 1864, she wrote that her half-brother (Mary's

3 Katherine Helm, 221.    4 Ibid., 224.    5 Ibid.
6 Works, IX, 255–256. For the refusal, see McMurtry, Ben Hardin Helm, 54.
7 Works, IX, 169.

brother) Levi Todd was dead "from utter want and destitution." "I would remind you," she wrote the President, "that your *minnie* [*sic*] *bullets* have made us what we are." [8] It is needless to comment on Lincoln's hurt feelings, and Mary's, on reading those stinging and accusing words.

## V

It was characteristic of the war that a "victory" might, in the long run or even in the immediate sequel, signify very little. The situation after Chickamauga was not as favorable to Bragg as would have seemed likely. He had won a battle marked by splendid fighting on the Southern side (indeed on both sides), but he had done so at tremendous cost; then, as his critics declared, he threw away the results. If there had been blunders on Rosecrans's part, the "great blunder of all," wrote D. H. Hill, was that of Bragg in not pursuing the enemy on the 21st. A breathing space was allowed to Rosecrans; he held Chattanooga; days of Confederate opportunity were wasted; it has been remarked that "the *élan* of the Southern soldier was never seen after Chickamauga." The "great battle of the West" as it was called has been described as a "barren victory." [1]

Thus failing to pursue the defeated enemy, Bragg contented himself with instituting a siege of Chattanooga, occupying the overlooking heights of Lookout Mountain and Missionary Ridge, together with Lookout Valley, and seeking, almost successfully, to bag the Union force or make its position untenable.

This siege was of no slight importance. It created a situation where the Union army was said repeatedly to be threatened with starvation. On the Confederate side it was felt that another quick blow close on the heels of Chickamauga would have finished Rosecrans. Since, however, there was no third or fourth day of the battle (such continuous fighting being most unusual in the Civil War), the question as to what "would have" been the result is no part of the actual story.

Both sides now seriously considered a change of commanders. In

---

8 R. T. L. Coll., 37723.

1 *Battles and Leaders*, III, 662. Bragg's failure to pursue was obviously due, at least in part, to his terrific losses at Chickamauga—a total of 18,000 with 2300 killed. (Union losses were about 16,000 with 1600 killed.) To rally Confederate units after such losses, push ahead immediately in pursuit, and fight another terrific battle was not so easy as Hill's words suggested.

that respect, if one accepts the unfavorable view of Rosecrans on which military writers usually agree, the long-range result of Chickamauga was favorable to the Union side: Bragg, the victor, was kept while the defeated Rosecrans was removed, thus setting the stage for later Union success. It was soon to be Grant and Thomas against Bragg instead of Rosecrans against Bragg. Another great campaign and then the Confederates, too late, were to let Bragg go.

On the Confederate side western generals, such as Forrest, Polk, Longstreet, D. H. Hill, Cheatham, and Buckner, so seriously differed with Bragg that some of them were sent off to other fronts, while others petitioned President Davis to find a new commander for the Army of Tennessee. Bragg, however, was a favorite, or pet, of Jefferson Davis, who now made a trip to the western front and by his erratic military intervention eased the problem for the hardly pressed Union army. Bragg was kept in command, and a large force (about 15,000) was sent off under Longstreet to operate without success against Burnside at Knoxville. (These were the troops that had recently been detached from Lee's army.) In the words of E. A. Pollard, Richmond editor and caustic critic of Davis, the Confederate President seems at this time to have contemplated "the visionary project of regaining East Tennessee, and perhaps . . . again penetrating Kentucky, and making the battle-ground of the Confederacy in this impossible country." [2] Davis was sharply criticized by Pollard not only for being "in furious love with the extraordinary design," but for "military conceit" and "vanity" as he boastfully told of Southern plans in public speeches, putting the Union side on its guard.

Lincoln, meanwhile, had been giving careful thought to the situation in terms of strategy, personalities among the generals, and friendliness to the people of Eastern Tennessee where Unionist sentiment (as in West Virginia and eastern Kentucky) was strong. Coördination of military progress with political reconstruction, with sufficient pace to make that reconstruction effective, was continually in his thought. This would have been true in any case, but the men of this region would not let him alone. When in August of 1863 the President was petitioned for greater military aid to eastern Tennessee (in the Knoxville area) he stated that he would do as much for these people as if his

---

2 Pollard, *Lost Cause*, 456. See also *Battles and Leaders*, III, 693.

home and family were in Knoxville, but he stressed the "difficulties of getting a Union army into that region, and of keeping it there." Lines of supply, he explained, could be easily broken, a small force would be of no value because the enemy could match it, a large force would be "very difficult to supply, and [would] ruin us entirely if a great disaster should befall it." [3] It was painful to him to argue thus to a complaining group with whom he genuinely sympathized, since all the time the government was trying to increase its strength in east Tennessee. He alluded to his own efforts "to have a railroad built on purpose to relieve you," and added that Stanton, Halleck, Burnside, and Rosecrans were all at that time engaged in an effort to strengthen the region. After all, Knoxville was not the pivotal point, and the President was constantly receiving requests all over the map to strengthen this or that area for local reasons.

Rosecrans was proving militarily unsatisfactory and personally difficult. In the Union drive against Vicksburg Lincoln had felt that Rosecrans ought either to have attacked Bragg or have sent a force to strengthen Grant. When, however, the general showed that he was hurt by reports of presidential dissatisfaction, Lincoln wrote him a very frank letter stating certain elements of disappointment but assuring the general of his kind feeling. Having indicated that too much should not have been inferred as to any sense of dissatisfaction, the President wrote: "I am sure you, as a reasonable man, would not have been wounded, could you have heard all my words and seen all my thoughts, in regard to you. I have not abated in my kind feeling for and confidence in you." [4] In great anxiety for success on the complicated western front, Lincoln at first wanted Grant strengthened; later (after Vicksburg) he wanted Eastern Tennessee "occupied by us," while impressed with the difficulties involved. In early September he felt easier, since by that time Burnside had Knoxville, Bragg had withdrawn into Georgia, and the President could write: "All Tennessee is now clear of armed insurrectionists." Not a moment should be lost, he said, in reinaugurating a loyal state government; for that there should be "no such word as fail." [5]

[3] Lincoln to J. M. Fleming and R. Morrow, Aug. 9, 1863, R. T. L. Coll., 25468.
[4] Lincoln to Rosecrans, Aug. 10, 1863, R. T. L. Coll., 25486.
[5] Lincoln to Andrew Johnson, Sep. 11, 1863, "Private," photostat, A. Lincoln Assoc.

# CHAPTER XVI

# GRANT VERSUS BRAGG: MISSIONARY RIDGE: END OF 1863

## I

THERE is a tendency to think of the war as forming itself into one grand pattern with strategy under central control in Washington, but for 1863 that would be far from the truth. It is a question how far Stanton had such over-all understanding and direction. Certainly Halleck did not, though that was supposed to be his function.[1] There were times when bad news was deliberately withheld from Lincoln despite his constant visits to the war office. The President carefully pondered eastern and western army problems, weighing them against each other, but he studiously avoided interference in military strategy. In this respect he presented a striking contrast to Jefferson Davis, to whose meddling Confederate failure has been largely attributed. Lincoln by no means considered himself the military genius or master of strategy which some of his eulogists have made him out to be. For one thing, Union armies were not always blessed with the notable success which this appraisal might imply; for another thing, correspondence emanating from Washington did not usually reveal answers as to strategic planning. Often it revealed obscurity in the fog of war and mystification of high command as to what the armies in the field were doing. Again and again it disclosed the

---

[1] Keenly anxious that Meade should pursue Lee after Gettysburg, Lincoln had spoken to Halleck in order to get action, but, according to Welles, the general in chief gave the President "a short and curt reply" and the President said, "I drop the subject." To Welles this seemed Lincoln's error. "His own . . . conclusions are infinitely superior to Halleck's . . . . I look upon Halleck as a pretty good scholarly critic of other men's deeds and acts, but as incapable of originating or directing military operations." Welles, *Diary*, I, 363–364 (July 7, 1863).

President's lack of military conceit. He deliberately kept himself in the strategic background. Repeatedly he wrote that he was not giving orders; field commanders must decide. Sometimes a dispatch from him would be one large question mark, as when he wired General Hurlbut at Memphis: "What news have you? What from Vicksburg? What from Yazoo-Pass? What from Lake Providence? What generally?" [2]

Though the military historian, trying to tell the whole story of the war, would emphasize the Tennessee front in the late summer and fall of 1863, Lincoln, a few days before Chickamauga, was writing, not of Rosecrans and Bragg, but of Meade and Lee. He was deeply concerned—not without reason—as to the chance of Meade getting action in Virginia against the main Confederate army. Recognizing Meade's uncertainty as to what he should do, the President wrote to Halleck (September 15): "My opinion is that he should move upon Lee at once in manner of general attack, leaving to developments whether he will make it a real attack." He thought this would develop Lee's real condition; it would have been something like a reconnaissance in force. He added: "Of course my opinion is not to control you and General Meade." Shortly after this he wrote to Halleck (September 19): "I am not prepared to order, or even advise, an advance in this case, wherein I know so little of particulars, and wherein he, in the field, thinks the risk is so great, and the promise of advantage so small." [3]

Thus in the situation immediately preceding Chickamauga the great problem—or question mark—in Washington was whether Meade should advance. Lincoln really wanted an advance, hoping for a decisive battle. To force the enemy slowly back into his intrenchments at Richmond was what he did not want. In contrast to the attitude of amateur strategists, the President clearly realized that Lee's army, not Richmond, was the "objective point." [4]

While Lincoln was trying to get answers, he had only uncertainty and hesitation from Meade and Halleck. To quote the Richmond Sentinel (as it misquoted Shakespeare): "Meade is making 'I would' wait upon 'I dare not.' " [5] Meade's own words confirm this attitude: "I

---

[2] Lincoln to Hurlbut, telegram in cipher, Mar. 20, 1863, photostat, A. Lincoln Assoc.
[3] Photostats, A. Lincoln Assoc.
[4] Lincoln to Halleck, Sep. 19, 1863, photostat, A. Lincoln Assoc.
[5] Richmond Sentinel, editorial, Sep. 22, 1863, quoted in letter of Meade to Halleck, Sep. 23, 1863, R. T. L. Coll., 26519.

do not feel justified in making a further advance without . . . more positive authority than was contained in your [Halleck's] last letter enclosing one from the President. . . . I am not in condition to follow Lee to Richmond and will be less so after being weakened by a severe battle. . . . I am reluctant to run the risks involved without the positive sanction of the Government." [6] In this difficult phase Lincoln trusted this delaying general (Meade) and was patient with him. He felt earnestly that a strong military move should be made, but he never wished his own judgment to become an embarrassment to a commander so far as a strategic or tactical matter was concerned. (If high policy was involved that was a different matter.) In mid-October the President wrote to Halleck urging that Meade should attack Lee. Then he added that if his suggestion should be adopted, "the honor will be his [Meade's] if he succeeds, and the blame may be mine if he fails." [7]

## II

While the Virginia situation was a matter of uncertainty to Halleck, so also was the western situation. When Union forces had every need to concentrate in the region near Chattanooga, the general in chief was assuming that Rosecrans might occupy Dalton, Georgia, and was showing uncertainty regarding a report by deserters that "a part of Bragg's army is reënforcing Lee." This was September 11, 1863; on the 14th Meade correctly reported his "judgment" that Lee's army had been reduced by Longstreet's corps and perhaps by other troops. Where, however, were these men from Lee's army headed for? In fact they were reënforcing Bragg, but Halleck mentioned "suppositions" that they might attempt to capture Norfolk or to throw Meade off balance by threatening that place. Having mentioned Dalton at the southeast of Chattanooga on the 11th, Halleck sent word on the 13th indicating a possible turn to the west. If the enemy should trouble the Union right through Alabama, Chattanooga was to be turned over to Burnside and Rosecrans's army or a part thereof was to move west to prevent Bragg from entering middle Tennessee. Much of this was contingent planning (or suggestion) in uncertainty as to what the chief contingencies were. Bragg might be planning to pull back into Georgia

6 Meade to Halleck, Sep. 18, 1863, telegram in cipher, *ibid.*, 26359–62.
7 Lincoln to Halleck, Oct. 16, 1863, photostat, A. Lincoln Assoc.

(though probably not very far), or he might turn up in North Caro-lina.[1] Other Confederate forces in the West might push into middle Tennessee. And all the time Lee's army had to be watched. To weaken the front against Lee in order to strengthen Rosecrans might be hazardous, but to fail to do so might be more hazardous.

The Chattanooga story appears but slightly and inadequately in Lincoln's writings. Just after Chickamauga the President was thinking in cautious and defensive terms, cheering Rosecrans with "unabated confidence," advising Halleck that Rosecrans should "hold his posi-tion, at or about Chattanooga," and expressing the hope that Burnside would go to Rosecrans "without a moment's delay" to help him hold, and later to "turn the tide." [2]

It was realized that Rosecrans had been "whipped" but that "Thomas had held his own magnificently," [3] that Confederate losses had been terrifically heavy, that there had been no further Confederate assault, and that the shattered Union army had been able to re-form. The fact that a considerable force had gone from Lee's army to the western front raised a question as to how this could be countered on the Union side. This was the situation on Wednesday night, September 23, when a high-level conference was held at the war department, for which Lincoln was roused from his bed at the Soldiers' Home. Riding out to summon "the Tycoon," Hay took note of the "splendid moon-light"; it is in his diary that one finds brief mention of the conference whose deliberations, if they could be recovered in verbatim report, would be of considerable historical interest.

In addition to the President, the conference was attended by Stanton (who seems to have arranged the meeting), Halleck, Seward, Chase, and a few others. Among those in conference was General D. C. Mc-Callum, superintendent of railroads in the United States. Military transportation would be a vital factor. The consultation ran on till after midnight; Hay's evening ended "with a supper by Stanton at one o'clock, where few ate." What must have been said about Rosecrans, about his subordinates such as Wood and McCook, and about Burn-side for not joining him, can only be surmised. The main business

---

[1] *Offic. Rec.*, 1 ser., XXX, pt. 1, 34–36.

[2] Various telegrams of Lincoln on same day (Sep. 21, 1863) to Rosecrans, Halleck, and Burnside, photostats, A. Lincoln Assoc.; Nicolay and Hay, *Works*, IX, 131–133.

[3] Dennett, ed., . . . *Diaries* . . . *of John Hay*, 92.

of the conference was the important decision to send the 11th and 12th corps west (from Meade) under Hooker's command.[4]

This presented a major enterprise in troop movement in which the importance of engineering was impressively demonstrated. Railroads in the United States were under government control, and though this was a fact which existed chiefly on paper, key railroad officials had governmental status and much of the history of the time was in terms of rail transportation. Able men in the war department were in charge of railroad management—such men as Herman Haupt (till he retired from the army in mid-September 1863), Thomas A. Scott, and D. C. McCallum. Men high in the government were due for a surprise here. As Walter H. Hebert writes: "The 'profound' Halleck protested that it would take forty days [to shift these two corps under Hooker to the western front] and the President agreed with him, but finally Stanton won out when General McCallum . . . said it could be done in a week."[5]

As it turned out it took six days for "the trip." Nicolay and Hay are in error in saying that "the two corps, numbering some twenty thousand men, were brought from the Rapidan to Washington, . . . and carried . . . to the Tennessee . . . with their guns . . . and all their impedimenta . . . in the almost incredible time of eight days."[6] The better statement, detracting not at all from the efficiency of the enterprise, is that of Walter H. Hebert: the whole movement took two weeks (of course the men did not all entrain at once); the roundabout rail "trip" took six days; the total number in the two corps was about 15,000 rather than 20,000. There were several changes of cars because the roads did not all have standard gauge and bridges over the Ohio River were lacking. The project involved the movement of 700 wagons and almost 5000 horses over a distance of nearly 1200 miles. Hebert writes: "This was the most successful movement of so large a body of troops by rail during the entire war."[7] Of course no such thing, nor even any considerable military use of railroads, had happened in any previous war.

This shifting of the two corps from Meade to Rosecrans involved more than transportation. It set off a minor upheaval in the army, and

---

[4] *Ibid.,* 93.    [5] Hebert, *Fighting Joe Hooker,* 250–251.
[6] Nicolay and Hay, *Lincoln,* VIII, 112–113.
[7] Hebert, 251.

showed, as has been seen before, that conduct of war on all levels and especially that of the President is often a matter of human relations. In this case the difficulty as to feelings among generals developed into a hopeless split between Hooker, who was to lead this whole force, and Henry W. Slocum, who was in command of the Twelfth Corps. It was one of those instances when army leaders simply could not, or would not, work together, and when this kind of difficulty arose the appeal always went up to the President who was under the necessity of taking some kind of action, even if no real solution was possible.

Slocum had a considerable record with the Army of the Potomac, having served at Antietam, Chancellorsville, and Gettysburg, but he could not get along with Hooker. When it became known that the Eleventh Corps under Howard and the Twelfth under Slocum were being sent to the Tennessee front, both under Hooker, Slocum wrote a vigorous letter to Lincoln. He had his "opinion" of the general "both as an Officer & a gentleman"; it would be "degrading" to "accept any position under him." He therefore had "the honor" of respectfully tendering his resignation as major general of volunteers.[8] Here, as at other times, was a general quitting, or making a gesture of quitting, in the midst of a war crisis, though in military accounts the word quitting is not used as to generals. The assignment of Hooker to this command had been made and Lincoln did not undo it; neither did he accept Slocum's resignation. Not that the President had full confidence in Hooker either; he had a peculiarly mixed feeling toward this general and wanted always to give him a chance to show his qualities.

Suppressing his disgust at this kind of squabble, Lincoln untied the knot by having Slocum and Hooker detached from each other. He wrote to Rosecrans: "We are sending you two small corps, one under General Howard and one under General Slocum and the whole under General Hooker. Unfortunately the relations between Generals Hooker and Slocum are not such as to promise good, if their present relative positions remain. Therefore let me beg,—almost enjoin upon you—that on their reaching you, you will make a transposition by which Gen. Slocum with his Corps, may pass from under the command of Gen. Hooker . . . ."[9] As for Howard, he also suffered from unpleasant relations with Hooker but without thought of resignation.

---

[8] Slocum to Lincoln, Brandy Station, Va., Sep. 25, 1863, R. T. L. Coll., 26647–8.

[9] Lincoln to Rosecrans, Sep. 28, 1863, photostat A. Lincoln Assoc.

Grant wanted "both Hooker and Slocum removed from his command,
and the Eleventh and Twelfth Corps consolidated under Howard."
Hooker had "behaved badly," he felt, and Slocum had "sent in a very
disorderly communication." All this was reported by Dana, who
added: "He [Grant] would himself order Hooker and Slocum away,
but hesitates because they have just been sent here by the President." [10]
Hooker's position, wrote Grant, was "one that rather embarrasses the
service than benefits it." Though being rid of both men was Grant's
wish, his recommendation was that Hooker be assigned to the command of the Twelfth Corps and Slocum relieved of further duty.[11]
What happened, however, was that Hooker was retained in the command Lincoln had given him, while Slocum, with only part of his
corps, was sent off to an unimportant assignment in a distant section
of Tennessee.

At this conference of September 23 there was no action toward removing Rosecrans. The President was bolstering him and trying to
believe that the army had not been badly worsted.[12] Executive dis-
pleasure was directed chiefly against Burnside to whom Lincoln wrote
the draft of a reproving letter which he did not sign or send. The letter
expressed (for the historian) the President's complete mystification as
to a message Burnside had sent promising assistance to Rosecrans; this
message, thought Lincoln, contrasted strangely with the general's actions. In reading the despatch the President sarcastically doubted
whether he was "awake or dreaming." [13] On Burnside's behalf it may
be said that he was later to be the target of Longstreet's heavy force,
that drawing off Longstreet turned out to be a Union advantage, and
that the Unionists of eastern Tennessee could hardly have borne it to
think of Knoxville being abandoned. "In the name of Christianity
& humanity," they pleaded, "in the name of God and Liberty; . . .
the loyal people of Tennessee appeal to you & implore you not to
abandon them . . . ." [14] Yet in Washington minds anxiety for Ten-

[10] *Offic. Rec.*, 1 ser., XXXI, pt. 1, 73.      [11] *Ibid.*, 740.
[12] Lincoln to Rosecrans, Sep. 21, 1863, photostat, A. Lincoln Assoc.
[13] "Yours of the 23d is just received, and it makes me doubt whether I am awake
or dreaming. I have been struggling for ten days, first through Gen. Halleck, and then
directly, to get you to go to assist Gen. Rosecrans in an extremity, and you have repeatedly declared you would do it, and yet you steadily move the contrary way." Lincoln to Burnside, draft of letter (not sent), Sep. 25, 1863, photostat, A. Lincoln Assoc.
[14] Telegram, John Williams and N. G. Taylor to Lincoln, Knoxville, Tenn., Oct. 15,
1863, R. T. L. Coll., 27282.

nessee required the strengthening of Chattanooga as a place of greater military importance than Knoxville.

### III

In September and October 1863 drastic changes occurred in strategic plans, troop concentrations, and high army command, but it is not easy to pin down a statement as to who, in the last analysis, made these decisions. Who decided to put Grant in chief western command, to remove Rosecrans, to advance Thomas, and to move in full force upon Bragg? Who was it that caused the besieged and defeated Union army near Chattanooga to shake off the threat of starvation, seize the initiative, and win the decisive victory of Missionary Ridge? As to these decisions that set the stage for November victory the passive voice appears in much of the writing. We find it stated that "Grant was assigned" to his important command, that he "acquiesced" in the superseding of Rosecrans, and that Thomas "was made commander" of the Army of the Cumberland.[1] Nicolay and Hay state that "the Government" was convinced that Rosecrans must go, that it was "the intention of the Government" to put Grant in supreme command in the West,[2] and so on.

A writer seeking to give Lincoln credit for it all might be tempted to say that the President made these decisions, but evidence is lacking for that conclusion. Piecing together the information gathered by wading through many pages, it would seem that neither Lincoln nor Halleck was the fully controlling mind, and that the shape of things was brought about largely by Stanton among those in authority in Washington and by Grant in the field. It was Stanton who promoted the conference of September 23; he was in touch with the army before Chattanooga through Charles A. Dana, assistant secretary of war, whose reason for being in the West was to advise the secretary. Lincoln did not at this time "find" Grant, though he felt and expressed high regard for him and found his uncomplaining letters, and his lack of a personal ax to grind, refreshing in contrast to other military leaders. Grant had never been a self-promoting general, he had been the target of newspaper abuse, his performance at Shiloh had been severely de-

[1] J. K. Hosmer, *Outcome of the Civil War,* 43.
[2] Nicolay and Hay, *Lincoln,* VIII, 117, 119.

nounced, and his contacts with Lincoln, even by correspondence, had been slight. Lincoln, as of July 13, 1863, did not remember having ever met Grant, but he congratulated him handsomely on the victory at Vicksburg,[3] and at this time the Illinois warrior, whose career had in 1862 been in serious jeopardy, was advanced to the rank of major general in the regular army. Lincoln referred to him in writing as "a copious worker and fighter," [4] and was quoted as saying: "I can't spare this man; he fights." [5] It cannot be said that Lincoln planned or ordered Grant's November advance against Bragg. The President was thinking principally of "holding" Chattanooga, not of an attack, and was urging Burnside to go to that area, which Burnside did not do.

It would have been difficult to say which capital, Washington or Richmond, was the more troubled in the search for solutions. In reality the Confederacy was about to lose the war in the West, but on the Federal side the situation in October and November was beset with the greatest difficulty and hazard. The country was stunned— "paralyzed," wrote Sherman—by the defeat at Chickamauga, and the army of Rosecrans under siege in Chattanooga seemed to be "in actual danger of starvation." [6] The heights overlooking the city, Lookout Mountain and Missionary Ridge, were strongly held by the Confederates, and the morale of Rosecrans's men was at a low level. The Tennessee River was blocked by Confederate guns, and food—the opening of the "cracker line"—was the first consideration if the army was even to exist within its defensive position.

Then the balance of advantage was rapidly shifted, and in that shifting the trend of events may best be understood by focusing upon Grant. Stanton went west in person; Grant, coming from Cairo, met him at Indianapolis; and the two men rode together to Louisville. On this occasion one of the important bits of business was the decision as to Rosecrans. Stanton handed Grant two orders, saying he could take his choice. Both orders put Grant in broad western command (of the "Military Division of the Mississippi"); in one of the orders Rosecrans was to be retained "while the other relieved Rosecrans and assigned Thomas to his place." Grant laconically wrote in his *Memoirs:* "I ac-

---

3 *Works*, IX, 26.
4 Lincoln to Burnside, July 27, 1863, photostat, A. Lincoln Assoc.
5 McClure, *Lincoln and Men of War-Times*, 196.
6 Sherman, *Memoirs*, I, 346–347.

cepted the latter." [7] When this change was made the work assigned to Rosecrans (the department of the Missouri) was unimportant. The general was removed and the shifting of command was but a softening of the blow. Thus one of the leading generals of the war, who was considered a real strategist and a competent leader, was relieved of command as part of a whole series of significant changes. His good qualities were offset by a tendency to lose control of temper and an obstinate persistence in his own plans. Though proud and sensitive, he took his demotion in good spirit.

## IV

Removing Rosecrans and putting Thomas in his place had not come easy.[1] There were those, according to Noah Brooks, who looked upon him as a "popular idol," a "consummate General," "the hero of . . . Murfreesboro and Corinth." Amid murmurs of discontent, "no man in the nation," wrote Brooks, "was more pained at the necessity of the removal . . . than was the President himself . . . ." Without stating all the reasons for the general's removal—reasons which he declared to be "weighty and all-sufficient" but which could not then be known—Brooks wrote: "It is enough to know that this Administration has never dismissed a valuable public servant or relieved any General of his command without good cause . . . ." Some of the accounts of the time tried to ease the fall by noting that Rosecrans outranked Grant and that it would have been a departure from military etiquette to retain him. "This," wrote Brooks, "is charitable, but it is not the reason . . . ." [2] After Chickamauga it was evident that new leadership was needed and that the team of Grant and Thomas (with Sherman, Hooker, and others) would make a better combina-

---

[7] Grant's command—division of the Mississippi—now included the department of the Ohio (Burnside), the Tennessee (Sherman), the Cumberland (Thomas), "and all the territory from the Alleghanies to the Mississippi River north of Banks's command in the south-west." The various orders making the necessary changes, which were made complete by October 20, were in the President's name. Grant, *Memoirs*, II, 18–19; *Offic. Rec.*, 1 ser., XXXI, pt. 2, 11; 1 ser. XXXI, pt. 1, 669.

[1] "'Old Rosey' has left us, and sorry indeed we all were to have him go, for we 'swear by him'—To be sure he was beaten in his last move, but never, even for a moment has he lost the confidence of his Army." Letter by Dean R. Chester (copy of extract), Oct. 27, 1863, R. T. L. Coll., 27526. This writer goes on to refute the charge of intoxication against the commander as "the *vilest slander.*"

[2] "Castine" (Noah Brooks) letter from Washington, Oct. 24, 1863, in Sacramento *Daily Union*, Nov. 21, 1863.

tion than Grant and Rosecrans. The comments just quoted are of significance because Noah Brooks, more than the usual run of Washington correspondents, was in a confidential relation to the President.

One of the amusing things—if it could be called amusing—in the post-Chickamauga period was the comment of newspapers within the Confederacy. The "new Ulysses" was represented as distinguished in the old army "only for his love of strong drink." As for his victory at Vicksburg, as at Donelson, that was attributed "more to the Confederate Government than to his own genius." He was "a slow motioned General, and as a boaster [a most unusual comment on Grant] fully equal to Hooker or Pope." Thomas, probably because he was a Southerner, was the target of the most scorching sarcasm. He was described as "a fat, beefy man of forty," a "numbskull" in the old army, and such a "rabid and loud-mouthed Secessionist before the war" that Southern officers felt ashamed of themselves; yet he took up arms for the Union. It must have been due to his marrying "a Yankee woman, old enough to be his mother, and whose money has great influence over him." Rosecrans was ridiculed not only for his defeat but for "the art of gaining victories on paper," the reference being to his address to his army after the battle of Chickamauga. Not all the comments on "Rosy" were of this nature, however; the Richmond *Examiner,* now that he was down, characterized him as "the best General the Yankees have." In listing the Union generals who had lost their heads, the *Examiner* noted that Meade was "the only one left, and we predict for him a speedy decapitation." [3]

Accounts agree as to the serious plight of the Union army at the time when Grant took charge. With Confederate forces controlling the area before (i. e., south of) Chattanooga and the Tennessee River below that place, and with mountain roads back of Chattanooga almost impassable, the army was, as Grant wrote, "practically invested." It had been feared that Rosecrans, feeling himself in a trap, would withdraw to the north of the Tennessee River; such a move, thought Grant, would have meant "almost certain annihilation" when pursued as they "unquestionably" would have been. Yet supplies and food were cut off from the army; the "artillery horses and mules had become so reduced

3 Extracts from Southern newspapers of late October, 1863, Sacramento *Daily Union,* Nov. 26, 1863. The papers quoted are the Richmond *Whig,* Memphis *Daily Appeal,* and Richmond *Examiner.*

by starvation that they could not have been relied on for moving any-thing." [4]

Grant arrived at Chattanooga on October 23, and the depressing siege of the Union army was promptly lifted. This vitally important task was accomplished by an operation at Brown's Ferry (October 27–28) on the Tennessee River a few miles below Chattanooga, in which Confederate forces blocking the river were overpowered by surprise attack (troops having been stealthily concentrated and pon-toons thrown into position), so that a regular line of supply was opened. The excellent work of General William Farrar Smith, chief engineer of the Army of the Cumberland, was evident here; but the planning of Rosecrans and Thomas, before Grant's arrival, should not be forgotten. It has been remarked that "Thomas would have made the same move . . . with the same results, had General Grant been in Louisville." [5]

The last word as to the assignment of multiple credit cannot be given here, but the effect on the army was unmistakable. Supplies could now be moved up the river from the rail point of Bridgeport, Alabama; the men had their "cracker-line"; within a week of Grant's arrival, "the troops were receiving full rations." [6] "From being an army in a condition in which it could not retreat, it became an army which . . . [soon] assumed the offensive, and under . . . Grant helped to win the battle of Missionary Ridge, inflicting a mortal blow upon the army under Bragg." [7]

## V

In these weeks when the Chattanooga operation of November was shaping up Lincoln was giving thought to many problems. There was the visit to Gettysburg with its famous dedicatory address. A call for troops—referred to as a new draft because it was a call for 300,000 volunteers with deficiencies to be made up by conscription—had been issued on October 17.[1] Political campaigns of 1863 in the states were raging, with their partisan excess and menace of serious upset to the

4 Offic. Rec., 1 ser., XXXI, pt. 2, 29.
5 Battles and Leaders, III, 717; Offic. Rec., 1 ser. XXXI, pt. 2, 27.
6 Battles and Leaders, III, 689; Offic. Rec., 1 ser., XXXI, pt. 2, 29.
7 Battles and Leaders, III, 714.
1 Nicolay and Hay, Works, IX, 172–174.

administration. This was also the formative period of Lincoln's reconstruction program, with Congress about to meet and a significant statement of broad policy to be formulated by the President. The whole
cause, the great trend of events, was uppermost in his mind. Not that
his published papers gave evidence of this, for in the Nicolay-Hay
edition there is little to be found in the week after November 23 and
up to December 1. This is to be sufficiently explained by Lincoln's
illness following the Gettysburg address and by his preoccupation with
his message to Congress.

During this illness of the President there occurred the three-day
battle (November 23–25, 1863) in which Grant won a victory over
Bragg which was parallel to the July triumph over Pemberton. The
operation was famous for its mountain setting, its distinguished military names (Sherman, Thomas, Hooker, Sheridan, and so on), its de-
cisiveness in the West, and its unusual interest in terms of soldier
conduct.

Sherman's re-entry into the main strategic picture, taking his place
as one of Grant's chief lieutenants at Chattanooga as he had been at
Vicksburg, came at a time of bitter tragedy in his family. Having been
permitted a long lull, a summer of inactivity, following the fall of
Vicksburg, he was ordered to shift with the greatest rapidity to the
Rosecrans front on the Tennessee River. He moved his troops via the
Memphis and Charleston railroad, repairing it as he progressed. Just
before that, traveling on a steamboat from Vicksburg to Memphis, he
was accompanied by his wife and others of his family. When they arrived at Memphis on the second of October the general's son Willie
was ill with typhoid; on the evening of the next day he died. "Of all
my children," wrote Sherman, "he seemed the most precious. . . .
Mrs. Sherman, Minnie, Lizzie, and Tom, were with him at the time,
and we all, helpless and overwhelmed, saw him die."

The general referred to this child who bore his name as one in
whose future he had more confidence than in his own plan of life.
"Child as he was, he had the enthusiasm, the pure love of truth, honor,
and love of country, which should animate all soldiers." He added:
"God only knows why he should die thus young." [2]

Preparations had now been made for the assault upon Bragg. As

---

[2] Sherman, *Memoirs*, I, 347–349.

the Confederates faced Chattanooga, their left wing was at Lookout Mountain and their right wing on and before Missionary Ridge, with Lookout Valley between. In reverse direction, Grant's left was commanded by Sherman, who faced the north end of Missionary Ridge; his center by Thomas, east of Chattanooga and facing the west side of the Ridge; his right by Hooker before Lookout Mountain.

Grant's main plan was to turn Bragg's right, which meant that Sherman's action would be the pivotal part of the battle. Thomas's work in the center, while important, was planned to relieve Sherman. Hooker's assigned part was "the negative task of holding Lookout Valley." It was also expected that Hooker's Eleventh Corps was "to cross the [Tennessee] river and serve as a reserve for the attack on Bragg's right." [3]

Events developed differently from the details of Grant's scheme, though fortunately for the Union side. On the first day of the three-day struggle, November 23, the action was between Chattanooga and the Ridge at Orchard Knob, an outpost hill held by the Confederates. The Knob was taken by sharp fighting and then used as Grant's headquarters.

Now came the Hooker operation, November 24–25, which had been planned by Grant only as a "demonstration" against the enemy left. Hooker's achievement has been known as "the battle above the clouds"; its significance has been questioned but vigorously supported. Grant's postwar remark belittling the battle of Lookout Mountain has been met by answering claims as to the heavy odds, numerous Confederate losses, and "positive gains" of the engagement. As a result of this operation the Confederates abandoned the mountain and Lookout Valley. Hooker's men then swept across the Valley to Rossville (on the west side of Missionary Ridge) and successfully engaged the enemy in the closing phases of the complex battle. [4]

The main operation, however, was that of the center under Thomas; this was the battle of Missionary Ridge. [5] At this position the Confederates had strong entrenchments on the crest, further entrenchments midway down, and a line of rifle-pits at the base. In fierce fighting "like

---

[3] Hebert, *Fighting Joe Hooker*, 262.     [4] *Ibid.*, 265.

[5] A full account of this charge is given in the grand military style by Sheridan, whose divisions were in the thick of the Union ascent. He tells how his men rushed the first line, moved prisoners to the rear, gained the crest, and pushed on in pursuit. That pursuit, however, was not supported. Sheridan, *Personal Memoirs*, I, 308 ff.

another Ætna" [6] the rifle pits were carried. At that point the men had done all that was ordered, having made the "demonstration" in the center that was intended to relieve pressure on the left under Sherman. Then, to the surprise of their officers, the men pushed up to the middle line of works and quickly up to the crest. Large numbers of Bragg's men were captured; "thousands threw away their arms in their flight." [7]

Grant wrote of this charge: "These troops moved forward, drove the enemy from the rifle-pits at the base of the ridge like bees from a hive—stopped but a moment until the whole were in line—and commenced the ascent of the mountain . . . They encountered a fearful volley of grape and canister from . . . the summit . . . . Not a waver, however, was seen in all that long line of brave men. Their progress was steadily onward until the summit was in their possession." He adds, however, that casualties were few probably because in the shock of the charge there was confusion and "purposeless aiming." [8]

The elation and exuberant demonstrations at the moment of triumph have been often described. Though quick in results the victory was not easy. It had been "won against great odds," and was due to Bragg's "grave mistakes." [9] That unfortunate general, a man of fine qualities and a favorite of Jefferson Davis, chagrined by inadequacies which he readily admitted, was now virtually at the end of his military services as he handed over his command to Joseph E. Johnston. Tennessee and the Tennessee River—with control of the West and with the power to drive deep into the heart of the Confederacy—had been won for the Union. In the military annals of 1863 Chattanooga ranked with Gettysburg and Vicksburg.

For the expression of national relief and satisfaction Lincoln was the restrained spokesman. On November 25, the day of Missionary Ridge, he wired Grant: "Well done! Many thanks to all." [10]

## VI

In December 1863 the great dome of the Capitol was finished and its crowning statue—"Armed Freedom" was its warborn name—was

6 *Battles and Leaders*, III, 725.  7 *Ibid.*, III, 706–707.
8 *Offic. Rec.*, 1 ser., XXXI, pt. 2, 34–35.  9 Grant, *Memoirs*, II, 85.
10 Lincoln to Grant, telegram, Nov. 25, 1863, photostat, A. Lincoln Assoc.

fastened in place.[1] It was a heartening symbol of coming triumph of the national cause, just as the jagged spectacle of the long unfinished dome had been a constant reminder of a broken Union. The public unveiling of the statue was to occur the following May, yet the statue was more of a fact than the unveiling and its completion was fittingly associated with the end of the notable year 1863.

The Lincoln administration and the people of the Union, though the war had shaken their democratic process, could have derived great encouragement from the contrast between the end of '63 and that of '62. The accomplishments of those twelve months were evident on virtually every front. So deeply had the President felt the significance of Gettysburg and Vicksburg that he had issued a proclamation for a day of national thanksgiving, setting the date at August 6, and hailing these victories as "reasonable grounds for augmented confidence that the union of these States will be maintained, their Constitution preserved, and their peace and prosperity permanently restored." [2] December of 1862 had been darkened by the gloom and stunning defeat of Burnside at Fredericksburg. In contrast, a year later (December 7, 1863) the President announced Union success in Tennessee, deeming it to be of such "high national consequence" that he again recommended that loyal people "assemble at their places of worship and render special homage and gratitude to almighty God for this great advancement of the national cause." [3] The Mississippi River had been completely opened, the area under enemy control had been reduced, and that diminished area had been "divided into distinct parts, with no practical communication between them." [4] Military discouragement would come again, and come hard, in the summer of '64, but the gains of '63 were never to be undone.

Favorable signs were not wanting in other fields. Politically the year 1863 had seen many a gain for the Lincoln cause. Partisan attacks upon the President had been repulsed in a series of state elections. In foreign relations, as shown in Britain and in the general European attitude toward interference, the situation was vastly improved. This could be measured on the one side by Confederate expulsion of

---

[1] *National Intelligencer*, Dec. 1, 1863, p. 3, c. 3.

[2] Proclamation of July 15, 1863.

[3] Announcement of Union Success in Tennessee, Dec. 7, 1863, photostat, A. Lincoln Assoc.

[4] Annual message, Dec. 8, 1863, Nicolay and Hay, *Works*, IX, 246.

British consuls together with the withdrawal of Mason, and on the other side by Lincoln's statement that the country remained "in peace and friendship with foreign powers" and that international questions "of great intricacy and importance . . . [had] been discussed, and . . . accommodated, in a spirit of frankness, justice, and mutual good-will." [5]

Emancipation had moved forward with Union advance. Not alone had this been achieved by national action; measures had also been taken in the states which clearly indicated their reading of the signs of the times. By the end of '63 it was evident that border states were ready to "declare openly for emancipation." Three years before neither Maryland nor Missouri "would tolerate any restraint upon the extension of slavery into new Territories"; now, wrote Lincoln, they "only dispute . . . as to the best mode of removing it within their own limits." While making real strides, emancipation had come without servile insurrection, had been notably acclaimed abroad, and had produced a situation where "full one hundred thousand" former slaves were in the Union military service. [6]

Under fairer skies and with a nice sense of timing, the President now launched his scheme of reconstruction. He would not dally in the task of restoration nor waste valuable months in quibbling about abstruse theories. While writing of health and increasing prosperity, and of growing good will abroad, he wanted to rebuild at home even as the war progressed. He intended not only to have a plan of restoration and be clear about it; he wanted that plan to be understood, guaranteed, and launched into practical application. He cared more for action than for a volume of words.

That plan of restoration was the main burden of Lincoln's message to Congress of December 8, 1863, and of his simultaneous proclamation declaring on the President's part the terms of pardon, amnesty, resumption of allegiance, and reconstruction of loyal state governments. [7] What Congress would do, and how soon they would do it, was another matter; that would be tardily revealed in subsequent years. One of those long sessions of Congress was beginning; 1864 would be

---

[5] Same message, *ibid.*, IX, 224–225.        [6] *Ibid.*, IX, 246–247.

[7] Treatment of Lincoln's design of reconstruction is deferred to a later volume. The present writer has dealt with the subject in *The Civil War and Reconstruction*, 689 ff.; *Lincoln the Liberal Statesman*, chap. vii; *Lincoln and the South*, 117 ff.

an election year with its tumult, distraction, and obstruction; troubles at home would become intensified as military and international prospects brightened.

Lincoln recognized that the processes of peace are not automatic. His statesmanship was purposeful yet flexible. It was coöperative with Congress if Congress would have it so. "I trust [he wrote in his third annual message] that Congress will omit no fair opportunity of aiding these important steps to a great consummation." Reaching into the future and concerned with making peace a reality, he faced the New Year with confidence as he wrote of "freedom disenthralled, regenerated, enlarged, and perpetuated." [8] The odd-year elections were over, Tennessee was safe, strategy and politics seemed to be working together, and the President, so recently in deep anxiety for his country, was now in hopeful mood.

----

[8] Concluding portion, annual message, Dec. 8, 1863.

## CHAPTER XVII

# "THIS STRANGE, QUAINT, GREAT MAN"

## I

IF ONE seeks to make up a portrait of President Lincoln he will find the color and design endlessly varied, yet broadly consistent, in a wealth of descriptions that have come down to us. First impressions were sometimes disappointing. When A. K. McClure of Pennsylvania turned up in Springfield to confer with the new leader in January 1861, he went directly from the depot to the Lincoln home and rang the bell. Perhaps he was surprised to see the President Elect himself answer the summons and open the door. (Mrs. Lincoln had not been too successful in her efforts to break him of this habit.) "I doubt," wrote McClure, "whether I wholly concealed my disappointment at meeting him. Tall, gaunt, ungainly, ill clad, with a homeliness of manner that was unique . . . , I confess that my heart sank within me as I remembered that this was the man chosen by a great nation to become its ruler in the gravest period of its history. I remember his dress as if it were but yesterday—snuff-colored and slouchy pantaloons; open black vest, held by a few brass buttons; straight or evening dress-coat, with tightly-fitting sleeves to exaggerate his long, bony arms, and all supplemented by an awkwardness that was uncommon among men of intelligence. Such was the picture I met in the person of Abraham Lincoln."

They sat down in the parlor, and, according to McClure, talked without interruption for nearly four hours. (A record of that conversation would be of interest; it probably related to Pennsylvania politics, and especially to Cameron, whose appointment to the cabinet McClure opposed.) McClure continued: ". . . little by little, as his earnestness, sincerity, and candor were developed in conversation, I forgot all the grotesque qualities which so confounded me when I first greeted him. Before half an hour had passed I learned not only to respect, but . . . to reverence the man." [1]

Donn Piatt of Ohio, who, with his friend Robert C. Schenck, enjoyed a supper and a visit far into the night at the Lincoln home late in 1860, wrote: "Mr. Lincoln was the homeliest man I ever saw. His body seemed to me a huge skeleton in clothes. Tall as he was, his hands and feet looked out of proportion, so long and clumsy were they. Every movement was awkward in the extreme. . . . He had a face that defied artistic skill to soften or idealize." There follows a reference to the oft-mentioned contrast of the face in repose and in animation: "It brightened, like a lit lantern, when animated. His dull eyes would fairly sparkle with fun, or express as kindly a look as I ever saw, when moved by some matter of human interest." [2]

Lincoln had been so caricatured and misrepresented in second-hand descriptions that an exaggerated image of crudeness had been created in the public mind. "All sorts of stories had been told and believed about his personal appearance." [3] The face which later became the rugged delight of painters and sculptors was supposed to be coarse, backwoodsy, and boorish. The nickname "Old Abe" might be a title of endearment, but it bore also a connotation of crudity. He had not lived down the impressions of his seedy umbrella, his too-short pantaloons, his rough brogans, and his habit, when carrying books, of wrapping them in a bandanna handkerchief and impaling them on a stick in the manner of a tramp shouldering his baggage.

One returns by a kind of irresistible fascination to Herndon's voluminous descriptions, too long to be fully quoted. In a prodigality of adjectives and phrases, the verbose partner-biographer produced something of a *tour de force*. With his matter-of-fact literalness combined with originality of depiction he had the makings of Lincoln all measured, weighed, taken apart, tagged, and put together again. "Abraham Lincoln [wrote Herndon] was about six feet four inches high, . . . having good health and no gray hairs . . . . He was [a] thin—tall—wirey—sinewy, grisly—raw boned man, . . . standing he leaned forward—was what may be called stoop shouldered, . . . .

---

[1] A. K. McClure, *Abraham Lincoln and Men of War-Times*, 48–49.
[2] Allen Thorndike Rice, ed., *Reminiscences of Abraham Lincoln* . . . , 479–480.
[3] *Ibid.*, 49.

His usual weight was about 160 pounds. [Lincoln himself gave his average weight as 180.[4]] . . . His blood had to run a long distance from the heart to the tips of his frame, and his nerve force . . . had to travel through dry ground a long distance before the muscles & nerves were obedient to his will. His . . . build was loose and leathery. . . . The whole man . . . worked slowly—creakingly, as if it wanted oiling. Physically he was a very—very powerful man, lifting with ease 400—or 600 pounds. . . . When Mr. Lincoln walked he moved cautiously, but firmly, his long arms—his hands on them hanging like giants hands, swung down by his side. He walked with even tread . . . the inner sides of his feet were parallel, if not a little pigeontoed. He did not walk cunningly—Indian like, but cautiously & firmly. In walking Mr. Lincoln put the whole foot flat down on the ground at once, not landing on the heel. He lifted his foot all at once—not lifting himself from the toes, and hence had no spring or snap or get get [sic] up to his walk. He had the economy of fall and lift of foot, though he had spring or apparent ease of motion in his tread. Mr. Lincoln walked undulating up & down, catching and pocketing tire—weariness & pain all up and down his person, . . . . In sitting down on common chairs he was no taller than ordinary men from the chair to the crown of his head. A marble placed on his knee thus sitting would roll hipward, down an inclined plane. His legs & arms were abnormally—unnaturally long, & hence in undue proportion to the balance of his body. It was only when he stood up that he loomed above other men."

Herndon's inventory or bill of particulars, goes on unceasingly from Lincoln's head and brain to the size of his hat, (7⅛) the measure from ear to ear and from front to back, forehead, hair ("almost black and lay floating where the fingers or the winds left it"), cheek bones, jutting brows, heavy jaws, nose ("having the tip glowing in red, and a little awry toward the right eye"), chin, and eye brows ("like a huge rock on the brow of a hill"). "His face was . . . shriveled—wrinkled and dry, having here and there a hair on the surface. . . . His lower lip was thick—material and hanging undercurved while his chin reached for the lip up curved. . . . There was a lone mole on the right cheek and Adam's apple on his throat."

---

[4] Nicolay and Hay, *Works*, V, 288.

By this time Herndon's cataloguing—his curiously pictorial itemization—was well launched. In part his description has been quoted in an earlier volume.[5] He did not consider his hero pretty nor ugly, but "homely looking." He was plain, sad, and weighted with a "terrible gloom," yet "rather humorous by turns." We have already noted how, in Herndon's portrait, Lincoln walked the streets good humoredly, greeting his friends with a "good heart-soul welcome," "stalking and stilting it toward the market house . . . , his old gray shawl . . . around his neck, his little Willie or Tad running along at his fathers heels . . . ." When "lit up by the inward soul" all these features "sprang to organs of beauty . . . ."[6]

## II

In a journalist's description just after the 1860 nomination we have a first-hand composite of Lincoln's physique, manner, and personality. "In walking, his gait . . . is never brisk. He steps slowly and deliberately, almost always with his head inclined forward and his hands clasped behind his back. In matters of dress he is by no means precise. Always clean, he is never fashionable; he is careless but not slovenly. In manner he is remarkably cordial, and, at the same time, simple. . . . At rest, his features . . . are not such as belong to a handsome man; but when his fine dark gray eyes are lighted up by any emotion, and his features begin their play, he would be chosen from among a crowd as one who had . . . the heavier metal of which full grown men and Presidents are made. . . . His head sits well on his shoulders, but beyond that it defies description. It nearer resembles that of Clay than that of Webster; but it is unlike either. . . . A slightly Roman nose, a wide-cut mouth and a dark complexion, with the appearance of having been weather-beaten, complete the description."[1]

The comparison to Clay occurs in a number of contemporary descriptions. William D. Kelley wrote: ". . . as I contemplated his tall, spare figure, I remembered that of Henry Clay, to whom I

[5] *Lincoln the President,* I, 28–29.

[6] "A Lecture [Dec. 12, 1865] by William H. Herndon," *Abr. Lincoln Quar.,* I, 356 ff (Sep. 1941).

[1] Chicago *Press & Tribune* (author unidentified), May 23, 1860, reprinted in *Abr. Lincoln Quar.,* I, 207–209 (Dec. 1940).

noticed a more than passing resemblance; and that of General Jackson, as I had seen him in 1832 . . . ." [2]

Visiting the presidential nominee at his Springfield home in June 1860, a gentleman from Utica, New York, enjoyed the experience and left a glowing account. He found the "modest-looking two story brown frame house, with the name 'A Lincoln' on the door plate." He was impressed with the simple air of refinement in the home; there were flowers on the table; "everything was in its place, . . . [and] ministered to the general effect." He waited in the parlor while a servant carried his note to the master of the house. "Presently I heard footsteps on the stairs, and a tall, arrowy, angular gentleman, with a profusion of wiry hair, 'lying around loose' about his head, and a pair of eyes that seemed to say 'make yourself at home,' and a forehead remarkably broad and capacious, and arms that were somewhat too long and lank for a statue of Apollo, made his appearance."

The portrait continues: "The lips were full of character, the nose strongly aquiline, the cheek bones high and prominent, and the whole face indicative at once of goodness and resoluteness. In repose it had something of rigidity, but when in play, it was one of the most eloquent I have ever seen. None of the pictures do him the slightest justice." The visitor went on to record the effect of the whole personality: "His presence is commanding—his manner winning to a marked degree. After you have been five minutes in his company you cease to think that he is either homely or awkward. You recognize in him a high-toned, unassuming, chivalrous-minded gentleman, fully posted in all the essential amenities of social life, and sustained by the infallible monitor of common sense."

Lincoln took the visitor's hand with a warmhearted greeting, and talked of political topics. His knowledge of details proved surprising; he was "more conversant with some of our party performances in Oneida county than I could have desired, and made some pointed allusions to the great Congressional struggle which resulted in the election of Mr. Conkling in 1858."

Here it appears that the visitor must have changed the subject, asking if the candidate was not "very much bored with calls and correspondence." Lincoln made it clear that he liked to see his friends;

"as to the letters, he took good care not to answer them." (This would be true in general of the great flow of incoming letters.) He went on to say that attempts on his life did not disturb him. His greatest grievance was "with the artists." It was in vain that he tried "to recognize himself in some of the 'Abraham Lincolns' of the pictorials." Summing up, the visitor wrote: "I found him to be one of the most companionable men I have ever met. Frank, hearty and unassuming, one feels irresistibly drawn toward him. In his conversation and bearing he reflects the gentleman." [3]

Cultured men who came from the East with preconceived notions as to Lincoln and the West, were often quite ready to confess that their minds were disabused as to the Illinoisan's crudity. At the time the notification committee from the Republican convention called on him in 1860 we have this record: "A neatly dressed New-Englander remarked . . . : 'I was afraid I should meet a gigantic rail-splitter, with the manners of a flat-boatman, and the ugliest face in creation; and he's a complete gentleman.' " [4]

Another close-up contemporary impression of the Lincoln of 1860 was that of Benjamin Francis Seaver, a business man of New York and Orange, New Jersey, who visited Springfield just after the election of 1860. In a slightly known letter of November 17, 1860, he told of meeting Lincoln. His letter has value as a first-hand record— not a flourish for posterity or a delayed memory, but a home letter written on the very day of his call on the new leader. He wrote: "Last evening we came here [Springfield] to see 'Old Abe' . . . . This too is a beautiful place & this forenoon we [Mr. Seaver and his brother] paid our respects to Mr. Lincoln & sat down & had a brief, but *very,* pleasant talk with him. Everybody goes to see him, at the Capitol, at certain hours of the day. As we entered, he was sitting with an immense pile of letters in his lap & seeing us, he jumped up with 'how do you do, sir' . . . . Altho an awkward looking large man . . . he had a free and easy manner which made us feel at home at once. There were several in the room when we entered, & before we left 3 or 4 real rough looking, half scared 'suckers' . . .

3 Utica *Morning Herald,* June 27, 1860, reprinted in Sacramento *Daily Union,* Aug. 15, 1860. Recent reprint in *Lincoln Herald,* 46:26–27 (Feb. 1944). The writer has been identified as Ellis Henry Roberts, editor of the Utica *Morning Herald.* Rufus Rockwell Wilson, *Intimate Memories of Lincoln,* 299.
4 "Mr. Lincoln and the Official Committee," New York *Daily Tribune,* May 25, 1860.

appeared & he shook hands with all, in the same easy style. Then a fine looking farmer held the door half open, hesitating to enter, when Mr. Lincoln stepped forward & said 'come in friend.' The latter replied 'here are some ladies to see the President elect'—4 or 5 real hale, large . . . corn fed looking country ladies in 'best bib & tucker'; one with a baby in arms!"

It was not a long account nor an important one, but its casualness and directness of record give it value. The ladies were admitted, and the letter continues: "His face is much better than the likenesses make him appear, but such long legs! They stick up in the air, as he sits in an ordinary chair!" There is a word or two describing the house, with broken panes and three broken blinds, then follows a reference to Lincoln's popularity. *"Everybody speaks well of Abe Lincoln* here." [5]

Often we have the adjective "homely" and sometimes "ugly," but a careful student of Lincoln, J. L. McCorison, Jr., who has studied direct descriptions from life, has written: "The stereotyped 'homely' Lincoln is due for revision." Referring to some of the better photographs Mr. McCorison adds: "[They] show a pleasing and personally attractive countenance." [6] If the stock adjectives "homely" and "ugly" are in need of revision, it should be added that the better informed men of that day were often aware of the need. One observer wrote: "The Pres. is not half so ugly as he is generally represented—his nose is rather long but he is rather *long* himself so it is a Necessity to keep the proportion complete." [7] There was, in fact, merit in homeliness so far as it connoted ruggedness.

It was the primal American, the rugged type, that admired Lincoln and described him best. We have, for instance, the description by Walt Whitman: ". . . his unusual and uncouth height, dress of complete black, stovepipe hat pushed back on the head, dark-brown complexion, seamed and wrinkled yet canny-looking face, his black, bushy head of hair, disproportionately long neck, and hands held behind as he stood observing the people." Whitman continued: "four mighty and primal hands will be needed to the complete limning

[5] J. L. McCorison, Jr., "Mr. Lincoln's Broken Blinds," *Lincoln Herald*, 50:43–46 (June 1948).

[6] *Ibid.*, 46, note 18.

[7] F. J. Bellamy to John F. Bellamy, in Pratt, *Concerning Mr. Lincoln*, 88.

of this man's future portrait—the eyes and brains and finger-touch of Plutarch and Aeschylus and Michael Angelo, assisted by Rabelais." [8]

Of Lincoln it was especially true that delineation of the features, in photographic time exposures, in pencil or paint, was inadequate. Frederick Seward wrote "how accurately" the newspapers "had copied his features [this accuracy could have been questioned], and how totally they omitted his careworn look, and his pleasant, kindly smile." [9] It is for this reason that the historian prizes those unstudied vignettes from life which are found in letters of the time, not written for publication. In one such letter (the time and scene being Albany, New York, February 18, 1861) we have this: "Mr. Lincoln looks much wearied & care worn. But his pictures do not do him justice. He is both a smarter & pleasanter looking man than his pictures represent. It was a thrilling scene to see him bowing in his carriage with head uncovered, while the ladies handkerchiefs waived [sic] from every window . . . ." [10]

### III

Since, when he entered upon the presidency, Lincoln was hardly known at all outside the United States, descriptions by foreign observers sounded often like the report of some notable, or curious, discovery. The wholly unusual quality of the man appealed to English journalists, who have forever delighted in detailing to their readers the unusual and unbelievable things in America, and where these journalists had the knack of pictorial reporting the result was striking and memorable. An early account published in England was that of the famous British correspondent, William Howard Russell, of the *Times*. For March 27, 1861, Russell made a more than usually interesting entry in his *Diary*. He turned up at the department of state where Secretary ("Governor") Seward arranged to take him

[8] Newspaper clipping identified as Whitman's, in the Walt Whitman papers, Lib. of Cong. In *Abraham Lincoln and Walt Whitman* by William E. Barton we have a none-too-favorable portrait of Walt, with here and there a *caveat* to the reader as to the reliability of the poet's autobiographical statements.

[9] Frederick W. Seward, *Reminiscences of a War Time Statesman* . . . , 136.

[10] Adoniram J. Blakely to Dan Blakely, Albany, Feb. 18, 1861, in Pratt, *Concerning Mr. Lincoln*, 53.

over a few steps and introduce him to the President in the White House. The minister from the new kingdom of Italy, the Chevalier Bertinatti, entered the mansion at the same time. They were received in "a handsome spacious room, richly and rather gorgeously furnished, and rejoicing in a kind of *'demi-jour,'* which gave increased effect to the gilt chairs and ormolu ornaments." Since this was a set occasion—a formal audience of the President to receive the new diplomat—Seward's son said to Russell: "You are not . . . supposed to be here."

The diary continued: "Soon afterwards there entered, with a shambling, loose, irregular, almost unsteady gait, a tall, lank, lean man, considerably over six feet in height, with stooping shoulders, long pendulous arms, terminating in hands of extraordinary dimensions, which, however, were far exceeded in proportion by his feet. He was dressed in an ill-fitting, wrinkled suit of black, which put one in mind of an undertaker's uniform at a funeral; round his neck a rope of black silk was knotted in a large bulb, with flying ends projecting beyond the collar of his coat; his . . . shirt-collar disclosed a sinewy muscular yellow neck, and above that, nestling in a great black mass of hair, bristling and compact like a ruff of mourning pins, rose the strange quaint face and head, covered with its thatch of wild republican hair, of President Lincoln."

The whole effect was by no means unfavorable upon this urbane Englishman. He continued: "The impression produced by the size of his extremities, and by his flapping . . . ears, may be removed by the appearance of kindliness, sagacity, and the awkward bonhommie of his face; the mouth is absolutely prodigious; the lips, straggling and extending almost from one line of black beard to the other, are only kept in order by two deep furrows from the nostril to the chin; the nose itself—a prominent organ—stands out from the face, with an inquiring, anxious air, as though it were sniffing for some good thing in the wind; the eyes dark, full, and deeply set, are penetrating, but full of an expression which almost amounts to tenderness; and above them projects the shaggy brow, running into the small hard frontal space, the development of which can scarcely be estimated accurately, owing to the irregular flocks of thick hair carelessly brushed across it. One would say that, although the mouth was made to enjoy a joke, it could also utter the severest sentences which the head could dictate, but that Mr. Lincoln would be ever more willing to temper justice with mercy, and to enjoy what he considers the amenities of life, than to take a harsh view of men's nature and of the world, and to estimate things in an ascetic or puritan spirit."

Since coming to the United States Mr. Russell had been supplied with doubting remarks as to whether Lincoln was a "gentleman." "I have heard," he wrote, "more disparaging allusions made by Americans to him on that account than I could have expected among simple republicans, where all should be equals; but . . . it would not be possible for the most indifferent observer to pass him in the street without notice."

The President's western cordiality was brought up short by the stiffness of Seward and the "profound diplomatic bows of the Chevalier Bertinatti." Then Lincoln "suddenly jerked himself back, and stood in front of the two ministers, with his body slightly drooped forward, and his hands behind his back, his knees touching, and his feet apart." When Seward presented the Italian diplomat, "the President made a prodigiously violent demonstration of his body in a bow which had almost the effect of a smack in its rapidity and abruptness." (We have here an impression quite different from Herndon's slow-motion picture.) After the ceremony of diplomacy the President was presented to Russell. "Conversation ensued for some minutes, which the President enlivened by two or three peculiar little sallies, and I left agreeably impressed with his shrewdness, humor, and natural sagacity." [1]

Starting to tell how Lincoln looked, men would glide into comment on his nature or temperament. Those who met him were aware that the man had more than was revealed at first glance, something of depth and at times of mystery. He was described as a man of "deep prudences," [2] a man of contrasts, "retired, contemplative," yet highly sociable, often in gay mood, yet given to a sadness that was impenetrable. The humorist, David R. Locke (Petroleum V. Nasby) wrote: "I never saw so sad a face." [3] Perhaps the briefest vignette

---

[1] W. H. Russell, *My Diary North and South*, 36–39.

[2] "Mr Lincoln was a secretive man—had great ambition—profound policies—deep prudences. . . . Lincoln was about as shrewd a man as this world ever had." Herndon to Ward H. Lamon, March 6, 1870, MS., Huntington Lib.

[3] Rice, *Reminiscences*, 442.

combining the inner and the outer personality is Donn Piatt's: "this strange, quaint, great man." [4]

The contrast between Lincoln's rugged and unfashionable appearance and the sometimes unexpected quality of his inner poise and dignity is well indicated in the following description by an English observer:

"Fancy a man six foot high, and thin *out of* proportion; with long bony arms and legs, which somehow seem to be always in the way; with great rugged furrowed hands, which grasp you like a vise . . . ; with a long, scraggy neck, and a chest too narrow for the arms at its side.

"Add . . . a head . . . covered with rough, uncombed and un-combable hair that stands out in every direction . . . ; a face furrowed, wrinkled and indented, as though it had been scarred by vitriol; a high, narrow forehead, and, sunk deep beneath bushy eyebrows; two bright, somewhat dreamy eyes, that seem to gaze through you without looking at you; a few irregular blotches of black bristly hair, in the place where beard and whiskers ought to grow; a close-set . . . mouth, . . . and a nose and ears which have been taken by mistake from a head of twice the size.

"Clothe this figure, . . . in a . . . badly-fitting suit . . . puckered up at every salient point . . . ; put on large, ill-fitting boots, gloves too long for the long bony fingers, and a fluffy hat, . . . ; and then add to all this an air of strength, physical as well as moral, and a strange look of dignity coupled with all this grotesqueness, and you will have the impression left upon me by Abraham Lincoln." [5]

Still another British description of unusual quality is that of the journalist, George Augustus Sala, who met the Emancipator early in 1864 at a reception in the White House. Steered through the crowd by Senator Sumner, he found himself face to face with the "Tallest Man of All." Next moment his hand was in the "cast-iron grip" of Abraham Lincoln, which made the handshaking painfully memorable. On this occasion the President wore gloves, "a pair of white

---

[4] *Ibid.*, 483. (This pithy and quotable phrase by Donn Piatt is part of a curious, and largely unfavorable, medley of comment on Lincoln.)

[5] *Macmillan's Magazine*, VI, 23 (May 1862).

kids, which the tallest of Barnum's four giants might have envied."
Referring to the cartoon sketches in *Punch*, Sala noted that the artist,
John Tenniel, had "seized upon that lengthy face, those bushy locks,
that shovel beard, that ungainly form, those long, muscular, attenu-
ated limbs, those bony and wide-spread extremities." Lincoln was so
tall, according to this observer, "that, looking up in his face, you
might, did not respect forbid you, ask, 'How cold the weather was up
there.' He is so tall, that a friend who had an interview with him
. . . [said] that when he rose there did not seem the slightest likeli-
hood of his getting up ever coming to an end. He seems to be drawing
himself out like a telescope." These touches might be second-hand,
for we have the same remarks elsewhere.

The Englishman then commented on the President's "dark face,
strongly marked, tanned and crows-footed, and fringed with coarse
and tangled hair, . . . so uncouth . . . that it narrowly escapes
being either terrible or grotesque." He hastened, however, to add that
this impression was obviated "by a peculiarly soft, almost feminine,
expression of melancholy, which . . . seemed to pervade the countenance of this remarkable man." This was the more striking because
our British friend remembered that he was in the presence of "the
great joker of jokes—the Sancho Panza made governor of this Trans-
atlantic Barataria; but there the look was—the regard of a thoughtful,
weary, saddened, overworked being; of one who was desperately striving to do his best, but who woke up every morning to find the wheat
that he had sown growing up as tares; of one who was continually regretting that he did not know more—that he had begun his work
too late, and must lay down his sceptre too early."

In a very brief interview Lincoln remarked upon the unfavorable
impression which foreigners were apt to carry away from a country
when they only saw it in a state of war; he hoped that the Englishman's sojourn would be pleasant. To this visitor the President told
no stories, and talked no politics.

One more impression gained on this occasion is worth recording.
"Mr. Lincoln," wrote Sala, "does not stand straight on his feet, but
sways about with an odd sidelong motion, as though he were continually pumping something from the ground—say Truth from the bot-
tom of her well—or hauling up some invisible kedge anchor. It gave
me the notion of a mariner who had found his sea-legs, and could

toe a line well, but who had to admit that there was a rough sea
running."  [6]

A valuable first-hand record was that of Mrs. Cornelia Perrine
Harvey, who wrote an account of an undated wartime interview with
Lincoln in which they discussed the establishing of military hospitals
in the North. "I had never seen Mr Lincoln before," she wrote. "He
was alone in a medium sized office-like room, no elegance about him,
no elegance in him. He was plainly clad in a suit of black, that illy
fitted him. No fault of his tailor however, such a figure could not be
fitted. He was tall and lean, and as he sat in a folded up sort of a
way in a deep arm chair, one would almost have thought him de-
formed. . . . When I first saw him his head was bent forward, his
chin resting on his breast, & in his hand a letter, which I had just
sent into him. He raised his eyes, saying, Mrs Harvey? I hastened
forward . . . . The President took my hand, hoped I was well, but
there was no smile of welcome on his face. It was rather the stern
look of the judge who had decided against me."

Mrs. Harvey was promoting a plan for Northern hospitalization
of wounded and sick soldiers, urging that Southern swamps were un-
healthy and that the government was responsible for thousands of
soldier graves in the South. Lincoln knew that the military authorities
opposed the plan, and he feared that if the men were sent North they
would never come back. As he spoke, wrote Mrs. Harvey, "a quizzical
smile played over his face at my slight embarrassment." She filled in
with further touches: "He threw himself around in his chair, one
leg over the arm and spoke slowly." "His face was peculiar, bone,
nerve, vein, and muscle were all so plainly seen, deep lines of thought,
and care, were around his mouth, and eyes." [7]

A description of Lincoln by Seward has come down to us in a
record written by Henry Bellows, head of the Sanitary Commission.
In April 1863 Bellows dined with the secretary of state and on the
next day he wrote his wife a full account of the conversation. "Mr.
Seward," wrote Bellows, "had a great deal to say about the President.
He always describes him as the most single-hearted, sincere, affectionate candid of men—patient to a fault—easy to get along with—

---

6 George Augustus Sala, *My Diary in America in the Midst of War*, II, 145–150, quoted
in *Journal*, Ill. State Hist. Soc., XLI, 438–440 (Dec. 1948).

7 MS. of Mrs. Cornelia Perrine Harvey, Ill. State Hist. Lib.

doing ample & generous justice to each & all his ministers. He says his judgment & comprehension are admirable; his right-mindedness infallible. That he has an admirable intellect not invigorated by personal wilfulness, or ambition or intense earnestness—but a little weakened by gentle, mild & candid qualities & affections. That he is afraid of doing injustice, or hurting peoples' feelings. . . . He was most irregular as to his meals & took them *cold* usually—& in a hurry —after breakfast, he was shaved, probably at the time when, & as often as *it was convenient to the barber*—for his sense of justice & kindness made him consult his own comfort & convenience last— then, he rec'd, any & every body, as long as time held out—selecting from the hundreds applying those he thot best entitled to come—and except on Cabinet days Tuesday & Friday, he spent his day morning & evening till 11. in this way. The actual work thrown on him by his ministers was small. He had a notion he was a servant of the people & that he was there to hear their complaints & he spent his time at it." [8]

## IV

It will be well to keep in mind two contrasts: Lincoln's roughhewn exterior contrasted with a dignity that came from some inner source, and the seemingly casual informality of his demeanor as opposed to his exquisite handling of delicate or difficult situations.

The rail-splitter aspect has been overstressed. Lincoln was no stranger to cultured society. He was not ignorant or naïve. There was method in his simplicity, *savoir faire* in his bland unconventionality. This does not mean that his manner was artful in the sense of being affected or assumed. It means rather that he knew his way about. Seemingly artless, his behavior nevertheless amounted to skilled craftsmanship.

People were distressed at his lack of "style." He did not look like a President. He slouched in his chair. He hated gloves and wore them awkwardly. An acquaintance wrote that he had "a habit . . . of passing his right hand slowly around his head and through his unkept hair, when actively engaged in thought. His clothing was in

8 Henry W. Bellows to his wife, Washington, Apr. 23, 1863, Bellows MSS., Mass. Hist. Soc.

hopeless disorder, and I thought him then, and think him now, the most ungainly man that I have ever seen." [1] Gamaliel Bradford, in his delightful but outdated essay on Mrs. Abraham Lincoln, wrote: ". . . it must always be remembered that she had the . . . most undomestic and unparlorable figure of Lincoln to carry with her, which would have been a terrible handicap to any woman." [2] To be *unparlorable* in the Victorian age was indeed a handicap. It was a day of fuss and feathers, of zouaves at home and monarchical trappings abroad.

What must the homespun leader have felt as Siam offered him several pairs of elephants? The offer came in a masterpiece of Siamese-English: "Somdetch Phra Paramendr Maha Mongkut,[3] by the blessing of the highest superagency of the whole universe, the King of Siam, the sovereign of all interior tributary countries adjacent and around in every direction, . . . to his most respected excellent presidency, the President of the United States of America . . . [etc.]."

The King wrote that he was sending a sword and a photographic likeness of himself, holding his daughter in his lap, to the President. He then offered to send several pairs of young elephants to the United States to propagate their kind and to serve as beasts of burden, "since elephants, being animals of great size and strength, can bear burdens and travel through uncleared woods and matted jungles where no carriage and cart roads have yet been made." He would have the United States send ships for the elephants, then added: "At this time we have much pleasure in sending a pair of large elephant's tusks, one of the tusks weighing 52 cents of a picul, the other weighing 48 cents of a picul, and both tusks from the same animal . . . that thereby the glory and renown of Siam may be promoted."

In reply Lincoln assured the King of his appreciation and accepted the gifts to be placed in the government archives as a token of Siam's friendship. As to the elephants, the monarch was informed: "Our political jurisdiction . . . does not reach a latitude so low as to favor the multiplication of the elephant." He also explained that

---

[1] Statement of R. S. Rantoul, *Proceedings*, Mass. Hist. Soc., third series, II, 85.

[2] Gamaliel Bradford, *Wives*, 26.

[3] This was the potentate who appeared in *Anna and the King of Siam*, by Margaret Landon. For the more direct account see Anna Harriette Leonowens, *The English Governess at the Siamese Court: Being Recollections of Six Years in the Royal Palace at Bangkok* (Boston, 1870).

"steam on land, as well as on water, has been our best and most efficient agent of transportation in internal commerce." [4] After contemplating all this oriental magnificence it must have come as a relief to Lincoln to read a letter in which a group of French liberals praised him in earnest and scholarly fashion, addressing him simply as "Citizen Abraham Lincoln."

One may perhaps think of the President's job as legal or official, having to do with executing the laws, sending messages to Congress, serving as Commander in Chief of the army and navy, preserving, protecting, and defending the Constitution. It is all this, but it is much more. Beyond the duty that was official, Lincoln had to remember the adjustment that was personal. In addition to laws, orders, and constitutional matters, he had the constant challenge of human situations.

In his practice of the art of human relations Lincoln regularly and consciously applied that quality known as "tact." That is a way of conveying the idea, but tact is not one thing only. It is a number of qualities working together: insight into the nature of men, sympathy, self control, a knack of inducing self control in others, avoidance of human blundering, readiness to give the immediate situation an understanding mind and a second thought. Tact is not only kindness, but kindness skillfully extended. Charity does not always please, while even a reproof may be tactfully given. Human tact involves *savoir faire,* restraint, patience, ability to reach a person indirectly rather than by frontal attack, approaching a situation in terms of adjustment rather than by way of deadlock or "showdown." Tact requires poise, a potent factor in self control; it constitutes the opposite of brusqueness, clumsiness, or impulsive blurting out of one's feelings.

The finest tact is in terms of the greatest need, or the most intense provocation to be untactful. Lincoln was not only considerate. He was considerate toward Seward, who calmly planned to conduct his administration for him; toward Weed, whose grasping for Warwick-like power in 1861 was a serious embarrassment; toward Chase, who became the center of a radical drive to displace the President; toward Stanton, who was described by men of that day as "mercurial," "dis-

---

[4] *Sen. Exec. Doc. No. 23,* 37 Cong., 2 sess., 7 ff.

courteous," "unreliable," "brusque," "uncivil," "dictatorial," "disrespectful to the President," and almost impossible to deal with. Lincoln kept the most diverse and troublesome men in his cabinet; at least he kept them there so long as that was where they could do the least harm. It has been seen in an earlier volume that Lincoln dealt fairly with Frémont, whose conduct was painfully embarrassing and insubordinate in 1861, and with Mrs. Frémont, whose wrathful self-importance added to the Chief's difficulty in adjusting the Missouri imbroglio.

Lincoln's personal adjustment was suited to the special case. Toward Major Robert Anderson, a Kentuckian, whose duty had placed him at Fort Sumter, the unstable spot where the explosion began, he showed special favors, raising him to the rank of brigadier-general, assigning him to command in his native Kentucky, and later, when Anderson's health had failed, personally arranging for him a kind of nominal army assignment with soft duties at Newport, Rhode Island.

Writing on August 15, 1863, the President explained that he had been "through the War Department" that morning looking up the law in connection with the general's case. He found the current statute very restrictive as to the discretion of the President and other officials, but he concluded that the Newport assignment, while within the law, would serve the purpose—i. e., provide full pay with slight duties; for General Halleck said it would "require substantially no labor, or thought, whatever." Then, sensing that Anderson's spirit was hurt by what he had endured—but without spoiling the subject with too much attention—the President put in a final sentence: "And now, my dear General, allow me to assure you that we here are all your sincere friends." [5] The old warrior, approaching the age of sixty, did not accept the New England post, being placed on the retired list, but until the day of his death in 1871 he carried the mental satisfaction of the President's kindness.

Toward General Meade, Lincoln's kindness showed itself partly in what he refrained from doing; for Lincoln had that priceless wisdom to write a letter—an excellent one, carefully phrased—and then withhold it. At Gettysburg Meade had fought off Lee's invading host, which was a notable triumph, but Lincoln did not think it was

---

[5] Facsimile in New York *Times,* Dec. 26, 1926, p. 2, c. 4.

enough. As mentioned in an earlier volume, the President, with an intensity that must be recaptured if his feeling is to be understood, wanted the whole wretched war ended. For long years it had been a matter of stinging defeat (under McDowell, Pope, Burnside, Hooker) or of hope deferred. Then came Gettysburg with its shining opportunity. The President could hardly bear the realization that the retreating army was not being effectively pursued. He sat down and wrote out a letter to Meade. He used strong words. The letter was bitter because the President felt bitter, but if he had sent that postmortem missive it would have seriously hurt the feelings of a highminded general who had felt sufficient distress, whose services were needed, and who had asked to be relieved of his command. Lincoln thought it over; then he withheld the letter. On the envelope, in his own hand, he wrote: "To Gen. Meade, never sent, or signed." [6]

The President's almost unbearable distress was somewhat relieved by putting his thoughts on paper (a kind of mental therapy); but his wise second thought, as well as his patience and generosity, was shown in sparing Meade the pain of a presidential rebuke. When at a later time, General Sickles bitterly attacked Meade, who asked for a court of inquiry, Lincoln disapproved of such a court because it would have been a footless diversion of effort from the main business.[7] In this connection, however, he took occasion to refer to Meade's "good service." As for Sickles he did not agree with his ugly attitude toward Meade, yet, just after Gettysburg, he had sent him a word of praise for his courage and of deep sympathy for the loss of his leg.

That the management of a war, even on the military side, was more than a matter of recruitment and conscription, of strategy and tactics, of logistics *et cetera,* and that army matters were largely a question of personal relations, becomes evident by even the most cursory examination of the Lincoln record. It was Lincoln's human dealing with his generals that counted. So far was this true that the letters which Lincoln wrote to his chieftains—those highly individual communications which show such unusual distinction—belong together in a kind of series. They show the patient President, over and over,

---

[6] Lincoln to Meade, July 14, 1863, R. T. L. Coll., 24808; *Lincoln the President,* II, 288-289.

[7] *Offic. Rec.,* 1 ser. XXVII, pt. 1, 139.

putting in a word of caution, generous compliment, morale-building encouragement, explanation to avoid misunderstanding, and if necessary, rebuke, until the relation of the Chief Executive to his officers became that of a head of family dealing—by admonition, discipline, advice, and command—with difficult and temperamental children.

Viewed in this light the famous letter to General Hooker, when, after Burnside's failure, he was placed at the head of the Army of the Potomac, no longer stands by itself; it takes its place in a considerable category. To repeat the words of the Hooker letter here is unnecessary, since it has already been considered, but it must belong in any treatment of Lincoln's human relations. It was not a complimentary letter. The President was admonishing and criticising the man whom he was raising to the most important field command in the nation. What gives distinction to the epistle is the fatherly quality of the admonition. The President did not like Hooker's mixing politics with his profession, his attitude toward brother officers, nor his remark about the government needing a dictator. He was "not quite satisfied" with Hooker, yet he was promising him full support. Lincoln had to use such human material as he had. In using Hooker he thought that a little toning down would do no harm. Yet one will search in vain for any phrasing in the whole letter that was sharp or unfriendly.[8]

General Grant, who in the personal sense probably gave Lincoln the least trouble of any of the commanders, was the recipient of more than one gracious letter from the President, who did not reserve his tact for cases of antagonism. After Vicksburg, Lincoln wrote: "My dear General: I do not remember that you and I ever met personally. I write this now as a grateful acknowledgment for the almost inestimable service you have done the country." The President admitted that he had at an earlier time considered some of Grant's strategy defective. He concluded: "I now wish to make the personal acknowledgment that you were right, and I was wrong."[9]

---

[8] *Lincoln the President*, II, 255–256. The letter was dated January 26, 1863. It reads as if Lincoln were thinking out loud.

[9] Lincoln to Grant, July 13, 1863, facsimile in Albert D. Richardson, *A Personal History of Ulysses S. Grant*, 338–339.

## V

Lincoln had often to deal with folks whose malady has recently been given its perfect name, "Injustice Collectors." The phrase is applied to "people who are looking for injustice in a friendly world, because they suffer from a hidden need to feel that this world has wronged them." [1] When Lincoln saw the symptoms of this human ailment, he put in a steadying word. On one occasion he wrote to a complaining general: "I regret to find you denouncing so many persons as liars, scoundrels, fools, thieves, and persecutors of yourself." [2]

When, for some reason that Lincoln knew not, the politician Thurlow Weed seemed offended, Lincoln wrote that he had no unkind thought toward him and concluded: "I am sure if we could meet we would not part with any unpleasant impression on either side." [3] Weed answered in like vein. He was a different sort from Lincoln, and Lincoln had had to watch carefully to see that Weed did not mar his administration; but after that frank exchange it would be unlikely for these two men to feel otherwise than as personal friends.

A prolific source of personal fretting among military men was the bothersome matter of rank and precedence among generals. On one occasion General Benjamin F. Butler's claim for precedence in rank over a number of generals (McClellan, Frémont, Dix, and others) made it necessary for an army board to investigate and report on the controversy. After a careful examination of the law, the facts, and the arguments, they solemnly reported that the other generals "have precedence respectively in point of rank over Major-General B. F. Butler, U. S. V." [4]

When this nursing of a sense of injustice became acute, Lincoln sometimes employed the device of a cooling-off period. General David Hunter, having served in Washington, at first Bull Run, and briefly in Missouri (succeeding Frémont), had been given a command in far off Kansas. He had expected a better assignment. He wrote to the President: "I am very deeply mortified, humiliated, insulted and disgraced. . . . I am sent into banishment with not three thousand

---

1 Louis Auchincloss, *The Injustice Collectors*, foreword.
2 Lincoln to General J. G. Blount, Aug. 18, 1863, photostat, A. Lincoln Assoc.
3 Lincoln to Thurlow Weed, Oct. 14, 1863, photostat, A. Lincoln Assoc.
4 Moore, *Rebellion Record* (Documents), VII, 340, July 1, 1863.

effective men under my command, while one of the Brigadier Generals, Buell, is in command of near one hundred thousand men in Kentucky." [5] It was another occasion to try the President's self control. He wrote to Hunter: "I am constrained to say it is difficult to answer so ugly a letter in good temper." He went into detail to show that he considered Hunter's assignment an honorable and responsible one, and added: "I have been, and am sincerely your friend . . . ."

But the reply of the President was not sent immediately. The Chief kept the letter on his desk for more than a month, and then sent it by a special conveyance, with directions to hand it to the general when he "was in a good humor." The effect was to administer a bit of gentle chiding along with a cordial expression of good will. The letter was signed: "Your friend, as ever, A. Lincoln." [6]

The sensitiveness of General James H. Lane as to the question of rank was equal to that of Hunter, and in the friction between these men Lincoln found one of his thousand difficulties in connection with western command. When in early 1862 an expedition into the southwest (with attention to Indian Territory and Texas) was contemplated—a project which was later abandoned—it was the President's wish "to avail the government of the services of both General Hunter and General Lane, and, so far as possible, to personally oblige both." His problem was comparable to having two prima donnas in an opera. He issued what amounted to an order to settle the issue, but he led up to it by way of suggesting a kind of modus vivendi to keep both generals satisfied. "Gen. Hunter [he wrote in a joint communication to the two men] is the senior officer, and must command when they serve together; though, in so far as he can, consistently with the public service, and his own honor, oblige Gen. Lane, he will also oblige me. If they can not come to an amicable understanding, Gen.

---

[5] Hunter added: "If you thought . . . that there was a political necessity for relieving me from command in Missouri, why should I not have been sent to Kentucky, where there was one hundred thousand men to command, and not to a wilderness [Kansas] with three thousand." Hunter to Lincoln, "Private," Ft. Leavenworth, Kas., Dec. 23, 1861, MS., Huntington Lib.

[6] Lincoln explained that he was losing confidence in Hunter, not from any official act or omission up to the time of his assignment to the Kansas command at Leavenworth, "but from the flood of grumbling despatches and letters I have seen from you since." The President considered the Hunter command "as responsible, and as honorable, as that assigned to Buell." Expressing full friendship for Hunter, he pointedly hinted that the general was "adopting the best possible way to ruin" himself. Lincoln to Hunter, Dec. 31, 1861, original MS., with Hunter endorsement, in Huntington Lib.

Lane must report to Gen. Hunter for duty, according to the rules, or decline the service." [7]

On this subject of rank Lincoln had occasion to write to Rosecrans, who had requested that his commission should have a certain date to give him superiority and precedence. Lincoln wrote that the general was asking for something that was "the right of other men." He gracefully added: "Truth to speak, I do not appreciate this matter of rank on paper as you officers do. The world will not forget that you fought the battle of 'Stone River' [Murfreesboro] and it will never care a fig whether you rank Gen. Grant on paper, or he so ranks you." [8] In this letter it will be noted that Lincoln refused the general's request in such a fashion as to pay him a compliment.

Once Gen. Robert C. Schenck called to see the President but departed without doing so. It was a small matter; Lincoln was ill that day; yet the President did not let it pass. He wrote to Schenck in his own hand to show how mortified he was that the general had left; he explained that he had gone downstairs expecting Schenck to await his return; he wanted it understood that no discourtesy was intended.[9]

While jealousy, recrimination, and answering self-justification among generals created constant and at times almost unbearable difficulties for Lincoln, it became an added cause of bitterness if, of two generals involved in dispute, one was an unprofessional volunteer soldier and another a West Point man. If the untrained officer disregarded the orders or advice of West-Point-trained superiors and, as a result, incurred disaster, the situation would be particularly painful. Such was the case of Major General Robert H. Milroy of Indiana, who had started by raising a volunteer company and had risen to colonel, brigadier-general, and major-general, serving chiefly in the Valley of Virginia. Having been among those luckless Union generals who were hit by Stonewall Jackson in the Valley campaign of 1862, Milroy was most unfortunate in Lee's pre-Gettysburg drive of June 1863, when at Winchester he suffered a serious disaster after having disobeyed orders. His position had not been considered capable of adequate defense, and he had been ordered to evacuate Winchester

---

[7] Lincoln to Major-General Hunter, Feb. 10, 1862, photostat, A. Lincoln Assoc. (same to General Lane).

[8] Lincoln to Rosecrans, Mar. 17, 1863, R. T. L. Coll., 22441–3.

[9] Lincoln to Schenck, July 23, 1863, photostat, A. Lincoln Assoc.

so that Union forces could be better concentrated at Harpers Ferry. Instead of this, he became needlessly engaged with far superior Confederate forces with smashing defeat.

What we are concerned with here for the moment is not so much the failure of Milroy, but the manner in which Lincoln handled it. After the capture of Winchester, while still in the service, Milroy was, as it were, on the shelf, and Lincoln refused to return him to command. The general had annoyed the President by letters he had written, and on June 29, 1863, Lincoln sent him a plain-spoken rebuke. "I have scarcely seen anything from you at any time [wrote the President], that did not contain imputations against your superiors, and a chafing against acting the part they had assigned you. You have constantly urged the idea that you were persecuted because you did not come from West Point, . . . . This, my dear general, is I fear, the rock on which you have split." The President referred to Milroy's disregard of orders calling him in from Winchester to Harpers Ferry, after which he was hopelessly beleaguered at Winchester. Though Milroy hated West Point in general and Halleck in particular, the President added that it had not been Halleck's fault that he was in Winchester against orders at the time of his disaster.[10] The Milroy instance shows that a complaining general whose own performance had been at fault was the kind of case in which Lincoln was disposed to be authoritative rather than too gentle.

## VI

One of the most difficult persons to deal with was the high-minded Carl Schurz. He was forceful, strongly antislavery, tremendously in earnest, ambitious for personal distinction, and disposed to "collect" cases of injustice to himself. In a "Private" letter dated November 20, 1862, he simply tore Lincoln to pieces. The whole emphasis of the letter was that Lincoln was in error fundamentally, did not understand the true situation, and needed Schurz to set him right. The general feared that the Chief had "too favorable a view of the causes of our defeat in the [congressional] elections." He would have the

---

[10] Lincoln to Milroy, June 29, 1863, "Private," photostat, A. Lincoln Assoc. On the previous day Milroy had written to Lincoln a letter full of self-justification and hurt feeling. R. T. L. Coll., 24484–85.

President know that *"the result of the elections was a most serious and severe reproof administered to the Administration."* He admonished Lincoln: "Do not refuse to listen to the voice of the people. Let it not become too true what I have heard said; that of all places in this country it is Washington where public opinion is least heard, and of all places in Washington the White House." He informed the President that the results of the election had "complicated the crisis," so that, "unless things take soon a favorable turn, our troubles may soon involve not only the moral power but the physical existence of the government." "Only relentless determination on your part," he warned, "can turn the tide. You must recognize the confidence of the people at any price, or your Administration is lost."

All this strong language, being interpreted, meant that Schurz wanted a Republican war: "between two Generals of equal military inefficiency [he wrote] I would . . . give a Republican the preference." "What Republican general," he asked, "has ever had a fair chance in this war?" Mentioning the doings of Democratic generals he pointed out: "There was consequently inefficiency, at the very least, in high quarters." Then, with a facility for coining words (a facility shared by his fellow German-American Francis Lieber) Schurz wrote: "it was unfortunate that you sustained them [Democratic officers] in their power and positions with such inexhaustible longanimity after they had been found failing."

With an unconscious egotism which pervaded the whole letter Schurz vindicated his own motives and attitude: "I pray you most earnestly not to attribute the expressions of grief and anxiety coming from devoted friends like myself to a pettish feeling of disappointment for not 'seeing their peculiar views made sufficiently prominent.' When a man's whole heart is in a cause . . . he may be believed not to be governed by small personal pride." With an implied hint that the President did not know, as he did, what war was, the general referred to the brave faces of the thousands whom he commanded. They were entitled to life and happiness "as well as the rest of us." When he saw their faces around the campfires and reflected "that to-morrow they [might] be called upon to die . . . for a cause which . . . is perhaps doomed to fail, and thus to die in vain"—when he thought of these and other things including the "wailings of so many widows and orphans" and realized that all this might "be for nothing," his heart sank within him. The implication of it all was that such serious matters would never occur to Lincoln's mind. He concluded: "I do not know whether you have ever seen a battlefield. I assure you, Mr. President, it is a terrible sight." [1]

It was a busy time for Lincoln (late November 1862), with a serious military situation looming up following the appointment of Burnside as commander of the Army of the Potomac; but the overburdened President had to take time out to read and answer this bitterly personal and partisan complaint from Schurz. He answered it with a reproof. He began by saying that he had received and read the complaining letter, the purport of which was "that we lost the late elections and the administration is failing because the war is unsuccessful, and that I must not flatter myself that I am not justly to blame for it." Touching upon the general's slap as to appointing men who had their "heart in it," Lincoln asked "who is to be the judge of hearts, or of 'heart in it'?" The President then remarked: "If I must discard my own judgment, and take yours, I must also take that of others; and by the time I should reject all I should be advised to reject, I should have none left . . . ." He remembered noble service unto death on the part of Republicans (Baker, Lyon, etc.), but they had done no more than Democrats such as Kearny, Reno, and Mansfield. Having said this, he declined "the ungrateful task of comparing cases of failure." The letter was stiff without being bitter. Lincoln meant it as a refutation and as an indication that unreasonable complaints would not go unanswered. He signed himself: "Very truly Your friend." [2]

One hesitates to report unfavorably on such a man as Schurz, for in the whole course of his changing (or adapting) career he was to bring an invigorating element of liberal thought into American political life. Schurz was more than a man: he was an outstanding representative of a great group—the large foreign-born group whom Lincoln sincerely respected and whose friendship he very much needed and valued. The question "What about Schurz?" usually brought up the corollary: "What about the Germans?" One needs to go back of this November correspondence, and then forward, in order

---

[1] Schurz to Lincoln, Hq., 3d Div., 11 Corps, Centreville, Va., Nov. 20, 1862, R. T. L. Coll., 19638–42.

[2] Lincoln to Schurz, Nov. 24, 1862, photostat, A. Lincoln Assoc.

to understand the relations between Schurz and Lincoln, which on the whole were those of close association, friendship, and almost of confidential intimacy. The distinguished German-American had been one of a committee which notified Lincoln of his nomination, and had campaigned strenuously for his election in 1860. On June 18 of that year Lincoln wrote assuring Schurz that his support of Seward at Chicago in preference to Lincoln was "not even remembered," to which the candidate added: "no man stands nearer my heart than yourself." [3] On July 4, 1860, Schurz was the speaker of the day at a large Republican meeting at Springfield. At that time he was a guest in the Lincoln home and received from the new nominee an autographed copy of the *Debates*.

Under Lincoln's appointment Schurz served briefly as minister to Spain, a diplomatic service which was significant chiefly because of his dispatch (from San Ildefonso, September 14, 1861) urging abolition of slavery for its international importance in placing the war "upon a higher moral basis," a move which he deemed of equal value with military victories. Having resigned his Spanish mission, he was appointed brigadier general and had an important command in a series of major engagements, including Second Bull Run, Chancellorsville, and Gettysburg. If he found himself at odds with the Lincoln administration in November 1862, that was but an episode which he later wished to forget. In his *Reminiscences* he tells what happened after Lincoln's rebuking letter of November 24, 1862 (which, to be sure, was not half so rebuking as Schurz's of November 20). A messenger, he said, brought a note from Lincoln asking that Schurz visit him. There was cordial and friendly talk on that visit, at which Lincoln is reported to have said: "Well, I know that you are a warm anti-slavery man and a good friend to me. Now let me tell you all about it." When they had had their talk Lincoln remarked: "I guess we understand one another now, and it's all right." [4]

Schurz was one of those generals who, while offering superior counsel, constantly tended to carry his advice over into the political sphere. Being the man he was, one could hardly have expected him to keep out of politics. The Lincoln papers are loaded down with his frequent and voluminous letters to the President. Lincoln was to

---

3 Lincoln to Schurz, June 18, 1860, photostat, A. Lincoln Assoc.
4 *Reminiscences of Carl Schurz*, II, 396.

learn in the election year of 1864 that Schurz wanted to leave the military front, to be invited to Washington, and to serve in the coming political canvass, but the President was to reply that it "would be detrimental to the public service." "Allow me to suggest [added the President] that if you wish to remain in the military service, it is very dangerous for you to get temporarily out of it; because, with a Major General once out, it is next to impossible for even the President to get him in again." Becoming more explicit, Lincoln explained: "quite surely speaking in the North, and fighting in the South, at the same time are not possible; nor could I be justified to detail any officer to the political campaign during its continuance and then return him to the army." [5]

That was how Lincoln felt in March 1864, more than two months before his renomination. As it turned out, however, Schurz did engage actively in the political campaign of 1864, making a number of speeches: [6] he was one of those military leaders—of whom the younger Francis P. Blair, Edward D. Baker, Robert C. Schenck, and John A. Logan were examples—whose interests and activities were divided between military duties and participation in politics. That Schurz had also the talents of an orator, author, and editor will indicate something of his vigor and versatility. [7]

It speaks well for both Lincoln and Schurz that they could differ so sharply, each with his own sincere nature, and yet remain good friends. It also speaks well for Lincoln's tactics in human affairs that he realized the value of a face-to-face talk. Schurz knew that the President was generous toward him; Lincoln knew that he could not afford to lose the services of so important a leader. Both men, so different in background and temperament, were devoted to the public service and were in agreement as to ultimate goals while favoring different methods. It was part of the greatness of Lincoln that such differences did not matter and that a personally irritating episode did not cause him, in a mood of resentment, to allow a hopeless breaking of relations with a difficult man whose sacrifice would have been a disadvantage to the nation's cause.

---

5 Letters of Lincoln to Schurz, Mar. 13 and Mar. 23, 1864, photostats, A. Lincoln Assoc.
6 *Reminiscences of Carl Schurz*, III, 106.
7 For new light on Schurz as author, see *Charles Sumner: An Essay by Carl Schurz*, ed. by Arthur Reed Hogue, Univ. of Ill. Press, 1951.

## VII

When one of the governors turned up "bristling with complaints in relation to the number of troops required from his State" the matter was referred from the provost marshal general, General James B. Fry, to the secretary of war, and from that stormy individual to the President. After an interview in which the state executive presented his "ultimatum" to the nation's Chief, "the Governor returned [to see Fry], and said with a pleasant smile that he was going home by the next train," making no reference to the session he had had with the President nor the business in hand. Fry continues the account:

"As soon as I could see Lincoln, I said: 'Mr. President, I am very anxious to learn how you disposed of Governor ———. He went to your office from the War Department in a towering rage. I suppose you found it necessary to make large concessions to him, as he returned from you entirely satisfied.'

" 'Oh, no,' he replied, 'I did not concede anything. *You* know how that Illinois farmer managed the big log that lay in the middle of his field! To the inquiries of his neighbors one Sunday, he announced that he had got rid of the big log. "Got rid of it!" said they, "how did you do it? It was too big to haul out, too knotty to split, and too wet and soggy to burn; what did you do?" "Well, now, boys," replied the farmer, "if you won't divulge the secret, I'll tell you how I got rid of it—*I ploughed around it.*" Now,' said Lincoln, 'don't tell anybody, but that's the way I got rid of Governor ———. *I ploughed around him,* but it took me three mortal hours to do it, and I was afraid every minute he'd see what I was at.' " [1]

Lincoln was tactful even when gently rebuking Governor Beriah Magoffin of Kentucky, though that official's attitude toward the President was that of antagonistic defiance. The governor was urging that the Union military force in Kentucky be removed beyond the limits of the state. Lincoln was not giving in. Though he could not comply with the governor's request, he did take occasion to explain all his reasons for not complying; then he put in a graceful rebuke: "I most cordially sympathize with your Excellency, in the wish to preserve the peace of my own native State, Kentucky; but it is with

---

[1] General James B. Fry, in Rice, 399–400.

regret I search, and cannot find, in your not very short letter, any declaration, or intimation, that you entertain any desire for the preservation of the Federal Union." [2]

This thoughtfulness in human situations was an integral part of Lincoln's technique as President. It is hardly too much to say that it enabled him to keep from being unhorsed. In September, 1862, some of the governors joined in a conference whose purpose, in the exaggerated statement of the New York *Herald,* was to "depose" Lincoln, or to request him to resign. This was after Pope's defeat at Second Bull Run and things were going badly.

The governors had their own meeting, then some of them called on Lincoln.[3] They thought it was their movement. Lincoln calmly associated himself with their patriotic purpose for a better prosecution of the war, clipping their wings and stealing their thunder; but he handled the whole matter so skillfully that the episode, which started as a formidable threat to the President's leadership, ended with a collective gubernatorial endorsement of the nation's Chief.[4]

Again, in December 1862 after Burnside's defeat at Fredericksburg, Lincoln was faced with a concerted attack by Republican senators who met in caucus; according to Senator Browning "enemies" were "doing all in their power to break him down." Lincoln conferred with his cabinet, then smilingly met the senators, never failing for a moment to keep the reins in his hands. Such was Lincoln's adroit planning and exquisite tact in this crisis that the complaining senators, who had planned a remaking of the cabinet, found after they had shot their bolt that the President was still in command, with the cabinet unchanged.[5] Yet all this was done without an explosion, without open hostility, and no one was humiliated. The prairie statesman had met the test.

Preservation of equanimity is usually conceived as a result, or a victory won, but it should rather be viewed as a process or a continuing contest. One does not conquer one's temper once and for all. Self-control is not a knockout, but succession of rounds. Lincoln was at it all the time. Can we see him at it?

---

2 Lincoln to Gov. Magoffin, Aug. 24, 1861, orig. autograph, Ill. State Hist. Lib. Lincoln kept a copy in his own hand; R. T. L. Coll., 11345.

3 *Lincoln the President*, II, 229-232.

4 W. B. Hesseltine, *Lincoln and the War Governors,* 249-272.

5 *Lincoln the President*, II, 238-249.

We can. One of Lincoln's secretaries came in one day to report
that Gov. H. R. Gamble of Missouri had written a very irritable
letter to the President. That letter is in the Lincoln Papers and it is a
sizzler. Gamble accused Lincoln of insulting him and of saying things
"unbecoming your station." [6] It was a moment that called for presidential self-control. In his own handwriting, as we find it in his
papers, Lincoln wrote to Gamble: "My Private Secretary has just
brought me a letter saying it is a very 'cross' one from you, about
mine to Gen. Schofield, recently published in the Democrat. As I am
trying to preserve my own temper, by avoiding irritants, so far as
practicable, I have declined to read the cross letter." Lincoln then
added a few words on the subject-matter of the correspondence. This
need not detain us, except that he said: "I was totally unconscious
of any malice, or disrespect towards you, or of using any expression
which should offend you." [7]

This incident affords almost a ringside view of the President's
continuing struggle to avoid being thrown off balance by bad feeling.
His mail had been screened. The governor's letter had been brought
to him. He declined to read it, yet he answered it. By the very process
of writing out the answer with his own pen he devoted himself deliberately and calmly to the effort for control. He overcame the impetuosity
which, as a kind of involuntary reflex, would have seized and controlled a less disciplined mind. He disposed of the irritating factor in
the incoming letter. Then he told Gamble that in his own feeling
there was no element of malice or disrespect. That task was finished
and the next item could be taken up. But if feelings had been allowed
to boil over, the overburdened Chief could not so successfully have
performed the day's work.

It has already become evident that one of Lincoln's traits was to
give attention when a man's feelings were hurt and if possible to put
in a healing word. This thoughtfulness was so often exhibited as to
constitute a habit. An example was the case of General S. R. Curtis,

---

[6] It is unnecessary to quote at length from Gamble's letter. Here is a sample: "Occupying the position which I reluctantly accepted at the call of my State, animated by
no desire but for the restoration of the Union and the prosperity of my country, I am
obliged to say to you that your insult published over the land was most undeserved,
and in our relations most unbecoming your station." Gamble to Lincoln, St. Louis, July
13, 1863, R. T. L. Coll., 24776–80.

[7] Lincoln to Gamble, July 23, 1863, R. T. L. Coll.. 25067.

who occupied a "delicate position . . . in the Fremont embroglio [*sic*]." Curtis wrote to his brother after the service of Frémont in Missouri was closed, saying he had just received "the most exquisite little note" from the President, which he copied for his brother's perusal. "I snatch a moment," Lincoln had written, "to both thank you, & apologize to you. In all sincerity I thank you for the complete and entirely satisfactory manner in which you executed the trusts I confided to you . . . ." Referring to a general's report in which Curtis had been wronged, Lincoln added: ". . . it never would have been done, if I had had the least suspicion it was to be done." He concluded: "Being done I thought the maxim 'least said soonest mended' applied to the case."

There followed, in Curtis's letter to his brother, a tribute to Lincoln which ought to be better known. "I had always perceived," he wrote, "a cordial friendship was entertained by the President for me and I take this in the hurry and pressure of the times as a gracious legacy, a compensation for many jibes I have received . . . . The purity of our Revolutionary fathers is not universal in these latter days. The President is an exception, his purity is everywhere conspicuous." [8]

Mindful to avoid treading on others, Lincoln was, nevertheless, a man who felt keenly the cruel hurts that were inflicted upon him. When besmirched by men on whom he should have counted he was quoted as saying confidentially to a friend: "I would rather be dead than, as President, thus abused in the house of my friends." [9] Unlike other men, however, he did not make his feelings a matter of complaint.

That the colored people loved Lincoln, indeed the Lincolns, is a matter related not only to the enduring folklore of a people, but in particular to the personal dealing of the man himself. In his meeting with colored friends there was complete absence of condescension or embarrassment. Toward Frederick Douglass, eminent colored orator and antislavery leader, who took a hand in the recruitment of colored troops in Massachusetts, Lincoln showed a marked friendship. The Negro leader, by his own report, met Lincoln a number of

---

[8] S. R. Curtis to his brother, Hq. St. Louis Dist., Dec. 16, 1861, Curtis MSS., Huntington Lib.

[9] Ward H. Lamon, *Recollections of Abraham Lincoln,* ed. by Dorothy Lamon Teillard, 261.

times, once on an invitation to tea at Soldiers' Home. On a social occasion at the White House, amid a "sea of . . . elegance," Lincoln's
face "lighted up" as he caught sight of Douglass. "In all my interviews
with Mr. Lincoln," wrote the colored leader, "I was impressed with
his entire freedom from popular prejudice against the colored race.
He was the first great man that I talked with in the United States
freely, who in no single instance reminded me of the difference between himself and myself, of the difference of color . . . ." [10] This
attitude of the President has significance in race relations. As the two
men conferred about important questions—use of colored troops,
their uniforms, equal treatment with whites, proper respect for them
as prisoners—Douglass was touched and heartened by Lincoln's genuine friendliness.

## VIII

Lincoln had no use for hatreds and personal difficulties. Let "bygones be bygones," he said; "Let past differences as nothing be." [1]
Late in the presidency he said: "For my own part I have striven and
shall strive to avoid placing any obstacle in the way [of a nonpartisan
effort to save "our common country"]. So long as I have been here I
have not willingly planted a thorn in any man's bosom." [2] An opponent of Lincoln's policy wrote: "Mr. Lincoln had no resentments.
He had kind words for men who bitterly assailed him. He joined in
no outcry against men in civil or military life who went astray." [3]
Hay wrote of him: "It seems utterly impossible for the President to
conceive of the possibility of any good resulting from a rigorous
and exemplary course of punishing political dereliction. His favorite
expression is, 'I am in favor of short statutes of limitation in politics.' " [4]

It should not be supposed, however, that Lincoln was always gentle.

---

[10] Frederick Douglass, in Rice, *Reminiscences*, 189–190, 192–193. As an example of
direct contact between Douglass and the President we have the distinguished Negro's
reference to "the interview with . . . your Excellency . . . a few days ago . . . ."
Douglass to Lincoln, Rochester, N. Y., Aug. 29, 1864, R. T. L. Coll., 35652–53.

[1] Speech at Republican banquet, Chicago, Dec. 10, 1856, *Ill. State Jour.*, Dec. 16, 1856.

[2] Post-election response to serenade, Nov. 10, 1864, photostat, A. Lincoln Assoc.

[3] George W. Julian, in Rice, 60–61.

[4] This entry was made on a day of great political gloom for the President and his
party—August 23, 1864. It was on that day that Lincoln wrote a memorandum expressing
doubt of his re-election. Dennett, ed., *Diaries . . . of John Hay*, 239.

If a man's conduct called for reproof, he would let him have it. Some of those who sought to use Lincoln were referred to as "thieves, counterfeiters, blacklegs—the scum and curse of the earth." Lobbyists for special interests crowded the hotel bars and could by no means be kept out of the White House. One of these is pictured by one of Lincoln's secretarial staff as coming out of Lincoln's room propelled by a large foot.[5] Lincoln could not always conceal his irritation when men in responsible civil or military office would get their personal affairs in a snarl and then intrude their quarrels upon the President. On one such occasion he wrote to Senator Pomeroy of Kansas: "I wish you and [General James H.] Lane would make a sincere effort to get out of the mood you are in. I[t] does neither of you any good— it gives you the means of tormenting my life out of me, and nothing else." [6]

The subject of Lincoln's personal thoughtfulness, his tact and gracious dealing, runs on and on. As one goes into it fully, it becomes a significant series of case studies. Lincoln was tactful toward General Patterson, whom he refused to blame after Bull Run, and to whom he spoke, said Patterson, "with a manner so frank, candid, and manly as to secure my respect, confidence, and good-will." [7] He was exquisitely tactful toward the venerable General Scott, easing that veteran's retirement with unusual honors and marks of high respect.[8] McClernand, though an embarrassment to Lincoln, could have testified as to his graciousness. An eminent historian, who had written to the President on Divine Providence, was informed: "I esteem it a high honor to have received a note from Mr. Bancroft." [9] A certain Captain Young, in some difficulty as to his military service, had reason to be grateful to the President for intervening to give him "another chance." [10]

Another captain, J. Madison Cutts, Jr., had the honor—for it was such—of being reprimanded by the President in so exquisite a manner as to be not merely chastened, but personally cheered, uplifted in

5 W. O. Stoddard, *Inside the White House in War Times*, 58.

6 Lincoln to Pomeroy, May 12, 1864, photostat, A. Lincoln Assoc.

7 F. B. Carpenter, *The Inner Life of Abraham Lincoln: Six Months at the White House*, 137.

8 *Lincoln the President*, I, 394.

9 Lincoln to Bancroft, Nov. 18, 1861, copy in Nicolay's hand, A. Lincoln Assoc.

10 Nicolay and Hay, *Works*, VII, 61–62 (Dec. 6, 1861).

morale, and specially favored by the highest official in the land.

Cutts was the brother-in-law and close friend of Stephen A. Douglas. In compliance with Douglas's request, Lincoln had appointed him captain in the regular army; in his dying words (June 1861) Douglas had administered to the young man a special oath of loyalty to the United States. In the course of the war the young captain gave courageous and costly service to the cause and received severe battle wounds, for which in later years he was to be awarded a triple medal of honor. In spite of this, being a spirited and combative person, he had a stormy wartime career. Quarrels and feuds led him into personal difficulties, and in 1863 at Cincinnati he was subjected to court martial for two offenses, one of which was an altercation with a fellow officer, Captain Charles G. Hutton.[11] Cutts was charged with having used insulting words, putting his opponent in the category of "blackguards," "blacklegs," and "bullies." Found guilty, he was given the severe sentence: "To be dismissed the service."

The sentence of dismissal from the army was commuted and it was ordered that Cutts rejoin his regiment after a reprimand by the President. When the Lincoln papers were opened in July 1947 this Lincolnian gem came to light. Fragments from the document had been quoted in various places,[12] but it was not until that opening that the document in full, and in its true character, was known. It is a sheet of paper dimly written in pencil, a draft memorandum of an oral reprimand. It is only by following up the matter in the musty records in the National Archives that the attendant facts (Cutts's court-martial, the sentence, its commutation, Cutts's manuscript account of receiving the oral reprimand from Lincoln, etc.) are given. In the Lincoln memorandum the reprimand was worded as follows:

Although what I am now to say to you is to be, in form, a reprimand, it is not intended to add a pang to what you have already suffered. . . . You have too much of life yet before you, and have shown too much

---

[11] The other offense was that of peering through a transom at a lady undressing in a hotel in Cincinnati. The court-martial proceeding (in the National Archives) has the record. See also Dennett ed., *Diaries . . . of John Hay*, 53 (July 18, 1863).

[12] Nicolay and Hay, *Complete Works*, I, 151–152 (footnote to Lincoln's letter to W. G. Anderson, Oct. 31, 1840); *Abr. Lincoln Quar.*, I, 91; Sandburg, *Prairie Years*, II, 277. For these references the common source is Nicolay and Hay, but they did not indicate what the document was, nor quote more than a fragment, nor mention Cutts. In the real sense the notable Lincoln reprimand was a discovery after the opening of the Lincoln papers in 1947.

of promise as an officer, for your future to be lightly surrendered.
. . . The advice of a father to his son "Beware of entrance to a quarrel,
but being in, bear it that the opposed may beware of thee" is good, and
yet not the best. Quarrel not at all. No man resolved to make the most
of himself can spare time for personal contention. Still less can he afford
to take all the consequences, including the vitiating of his temper, and
the loss of self-control.

Yield larger things to which you can show no more than equal right,
and yield lesser ones, though clearly your own. Better give your path to a
dog than be bitten by him in contesting for the right. Even killing the dog
would not cure the bite.

In the mood indicated deal henceforth with your fellowmen, and especially with your brother officers, and even the unpleasant events you are
passing from will not have been profitless to you.[13]

The patient President facing the young officer and administering
a reprimand that became a gracious interview has been passed by in
Lincoln biography, but this classic comment on quarreling, this
supreme improvement on Polonius, will henceforth be kept in memory. It is so with many another neglected episode. One may take the
more famous things that Lincoln did—the lofty eloquence of the
Gettysburg address, the generous wisdom of his design for peace, the
whole complex of leadership in a fearful crisis—and to all this must
be added that priceless element of human thoughtfulness and personal
understanding.

Such understanding did not come by chance. Like other things with
Lincoln it was the result of planning and study. Where episodes of
personal dealing were "unimportant" in that they touched no great
public policy or well known individual, they nevertheless revealed
much as to the type of man Lincoln was. The very fact that such
dealing was close to earth and part of his everyday job is significant,
for there is inspiration for more people in the thought of Lincoln
working steadily at a hard job day after day than in matters that are
remote and high-flown. Though applied in dealings that seemed
small, his craftsmanship in the human art was one of his greatest
achievements. It was an attribute to freedom and equality, to man's
dignity, to self discipline, to the niceties of courtesy, to successful
living with men—in a word, to democracy itself.

---

13 Autograph document unsigned, R. T. L. Coll., 27496 (Oct. 26, 1863). Lincoln's handwriting, partly rather dim, starts in ink and continues in pencil.

# THE OPENING OF THE LINCOLN PAPERS

IN THE summer of 1947 a new domain was opened in the world of Lincoln research with the release of that vast treasure, the Robert Todd Lincoln Collection of the Papers of Abraham Lincoln. For all the years since Lincoln's death this great body of material had been denied to scholars in general; only Nicolay and Hay had used the documents for a life of Lincoln. Together with a feeling of frustration at this refusal of access to sources that historians needed, there had been added that lure of charm and conjecture that attaches to the unknown. Since, after being opened, the papers were found to constitute a most important and voluminous body of sources the nature of which is still imperfectly known, it is appropriate that some treatment of them be given in these pages.

## I

What had happened to the papers, what were their travels, place of deposit, and guardianship through the years? This story is told with full information and unusual literary charm by David C. Mearns in *The Lincoln Papers* (2 vols., 1948). One must read that book to have the authentic details which can only be given in briefest summary here. Lincoln's home, his Springfield office, the lining of his hat, his pockets, and a rather famous carpetbag in 1861, may be mentioned in passing as temporary archival depositories; but the bulk of the collection during Lincoln's own lifetime reposed in those White House pigeonholes for which Lincoln prepared the labels and to which he often referred. Nor should one suppose that the President was neglectful of his documents or unmindful of their importance.

After Lincoln's death his papers were in the custody of David Davis, administrator of the Lincoln estate, who kept them for a time in a bank in Bloomington, Illinois. Some time in the 1870's John G. Nicolay took charge (though not ownership) of them in his office in the United States Capitol, he being marshal of the Supreme Court of the United States. Nicolay and Hay used them in preparing their ten-volume biography of Lincoln (1890), and in editing his so-called *Complete Works* (2 vols., 1894).

The idea that these "two everlasting angels" (Hay's phrase) had full freedom to use the manuscripts unreservedly is a misconception. The full Collection was open to them, but their work was done by the proprietary authorization of Robert Todd Lincoln and subject to his approval. From the time of Nicolay's resignation as marshal of the Supreme Court in 1887 to his death in 1901 the papers were kept in his home in Washington. Then they found their way to the state department while Hay was secretary of state (1901–1905). The first suggestion that they be deposited in the Library of Congress seems to have come in a letter from the Librarian, Herbert Putnam, to Robert Todd Lincoln, December 31, 1901. This letter, with its suggestion of the most reasonable disposition of the Collection, brought no result. For years after Hay's death in 1905 the papers were kept in Robert Lincoln's office in Chicago while he was president of the Pullman Company. When he resigned from that position in 1911 the Collection went with him, being kept in his residence in Washington (Georgetown), and at Hildene, his summer home at Manchester, Vermont. It was from the Georgetown home that the papers were secretly taken in a wagon to the Library of Congress on May 6, 1919. Eight trunks of them were thus received.

This placing of the papers was only a deposit; full ownership and control was retained by Robert Todd Lincoln. Meanwhile through the years one Lincoln biographer after another was refused access to the Collection, with Robert's brief explanation that the matter of using them had fully been attended to and the information which they contained had been "exhausted" by Nicolay and Hay.

Up to 1919, and from then on until 1923, there was no formal closing of the papers; it was simply that Robert had full command of their use or non-use, and, after Nicolay and Hay, all investigators were denied access. (The case of Katherine Helm, who had a brief peep at the Collection without using it, was the one exception, and this was unimportant.) In the years following 1919 Robert was a frequent visitor to the Library of Congress, where he permitted and watched over the preparation of an index. This project, however, was discontinued after no more than ten percent of the Collection had been covered.

Finally, on January 23, 1923, Robert executed a formal deed of gift, giving the Collection in perpetuity to the United States of America, to be deposited in the Library of Congress for all the people, on condition that the papers were to be put in a sealed vault and withheld from inspection until twenty-one years after the donor's death. He died on July 26, 1926. (On January 16, 1926, Robert had made a modification of his gift to permit his wife to grant permission to see the papers. This, however, was for a limited "special purpose," and it was never effective as a means of opening the papers to any investigator. At this time Robert also formally authorized the making of a complete index.)

Meanwhile, and thereafter, various garbled accounts and uninformed guesses arose to create a sad state of confusion as to the disposition and probable significance of the papers. There were reports that Robert had burned the manuscripts, that he had "purged" them, that they occupied only one trunk, that this was a kind of "mystery trunk," that the closing of the papers was to extend for fifty years, and that this closing was actuated by various alleged motives.

All such accounts were idle conjectures. Perhaps it was these guesses, along with uncomfortable pressure to learn the contents of the Collection, that caused statements to be made tending to play down the importance of the manuscripts and to create the impression that they contained, or were believed to contain, little of significant value.

From 1923 the story of the papers can be quickly told. During the Axis War they were temporarily kept at the University of Virginia at Charlottesville. Then they were brought back to Washington, arranged, repaired, indexed, mounted, bound, and locked up (all with great secrecy) in preparation for the opening in 1947.

## II

What about the picture that has arisen in the popular mind of Robert Todd Lincoln burning his father's papers? Perhaps the obvious answer is simply to go to the Library of Congress and see the immense Collection, bound in 194 handsome volumes, with approximately 200 pieces, well preserved and very much intact, in each volume. One may then inquire: How did the story of the alleged burning get started? There are various versions, one of which is found in *Across the Busy Years* (II, 375–378), by Nicholas Murray Butler. In this book of "Recollections and Reflections" Butler tells of a visit in August 1923 to the home of Robert Lincoln at Manchester, Vermont. The President of Columbia University had just returned from a trip to Europe, and immediately after reaching Manchester, he was told by his and Robert's friend, Horace G. Young, that he must go and see Robert, who was said to be on the point of burning a lot of his father's papers.

According to this account, Butler went the following morning to Robert's home. There he saw "an old-fashioned trunk . . . near one of the bookshelves." Being questioned as to the trunk (as Butler told it), Robert said, "it contains only some family papers which I am going to burn." Continuing his recollection, Butler wrote that he remonstrated with Robert, reminding him that his father belonged to the nation and that these papers were therefore national property. In the strongest terms he admonished him, for heaven's sake, not to destroy the manuscripts. There was "excited and indeed difficult conversation," concluding with Butler's suggestion that the son should deposit the papers in the Library of Congress "and fix a date before which they shall not be opened." "That he did," added Butler.

One does not know fully what really happened at this visit of Butler to Hildene. The plain implication is that the trunk contained the famous collection of the papers of Abraham Lincoln (though this was not made clear), that Robert was about to burn a lot of them, that it was Butler who then and there persuaded the son to make the deposit in the Library of Congress with the time limitation, and that this disposition of the Collection occurred *after* and because of that interview. By this account the credit for placing the papers in the Library was represented as belonging to Dr. Butler.

One need not inquire into the dimming of Butler's recollections between the time of the event and the writing of his memoirs. It is sufficient to note the following facts. The interview, as related in *Across the Busy Years,* occurred just after Butler's return from Europe in August 1923; the date is further confirmed by his statement that he and Robert then had "a chat after a considerable absence abroad, during which time President Harding had died and Calvin Coolidge had succeeded to the presidency." (Harding died on August 2, 1923.) But the clinching fact is that the Lincoln papers had been deposited in the Library of Congress four years before that (1919), and Robert's deed of gift permanently bequeathing them with the twenty-one year limitation had been executed seven months previously (January 23, 1923). We do not know what to believe as to that "old-fashioned trunk" which Butler supposed to contain the papers of Abraham Lincoln. What we do know is that eight trunks of the actual papers had been put safely in the Library of Congress, which has ever since remained their permanent depository.

Butler himself was not sure of his own memories, as is shown by a letter he wrote to Herbert Putnam, Librarian of Congress, on December 18, 1928, asking as to the date when Robert sent to the Library "a box or trunk containing a collection of family papers, with the prescription that they should not be opened for a number of years, I think it was fifty." Butler added that he was "trying to reconstruct" the story of his talk with Robert, and a reminder of the date would help him do so. The facts were promptly transmitted to Butler, who nevertheless published the above-given account in the *Saturday Evening Post* on February 11, 1939. Later he used the same material in *Across the Busy Years.*

The only purpose of giving this summary here is to set the record straight as to the alleged intent to burn and the supposed role of Dr. Butler in the disposition of the Collection. After a careful survey, Mearns writes (*Lincoln Papers,* I, 127: ". . . it has been impossible to adjust that statement [concerning the "one trunk" and the Butler-Lincoln interview of August 1923] to any influence on, or relation with, the delivery of eight trunks [to the Library of Congress] in May 1919."

As to the motive for closing the papers, there is no evidence that it was done because of any family skeleton, which there was not, nor because of revelations of "treason" in the cabinet, however much of a headache Stanton may have been to his Chief. To reconstruct the motive as nearly as is possible, Robert is on record as having thought (contrary to fact) that Nicolay and Hay had made complete use of the papers. In addition—this also is a matter of record—he seems to have feared that some of the documents might give pain to persons yet living, which implies that he was not destroying such documents. Finally, there is no doubt that he was annoyed by incessant requests from investigators, particularly Beveridge, whose friendliness to the Herndon interpretation caused him to be distrusted.

Whatever may be said as to these motives, Robert's ultimate disposition of the Collection, except for the twenty-one year limitation, was admirable. If care had not been taken to guard the Collection and keep it intact, the papers might have become scattered, sold, lost, or mutilated by that miserable practice—all too common—of clipping off signatures of letters. Instead of that, the collection was, with the exception of a very few items, held together by Robert Todd Lincoln. An example of an item given away by Robert—and this was very unusual—was Lincoln's manuscript of the speech he gave from a White House window on the night of November 10, 1864. (The Library of Congress has a copy.) This valuable document was held in the family until April 18, 1916, when Robert presented the original to Congressman John W. Dwight of New York in gratitude for the congressman's service in the establishment of the Lincoln Memorial at Washington. Such instances, however, were very few. What the Library of Congress has is substantially the R. T. Lincoln Collection of his father's papers. In addition, it should be added that the Library has many other Lincoln documents either in originals or in copies.

The Library performed its task well, discreetly suggesting and keeping alive the idea of the Library as depository, fulfilling the terms of the deed of gift, holding the Collection in safe keeping, repairing the papers, mounting them, putting them in chronological order, preparing an "index" (or inventory), and binding them in handsome, permanent volumes. In addition the Library made ready for the opening as an occasion of importance and dignity, prepared many news releases, and served the needs of researchers in the following weeks and months. It is highly appropriate that the papers now occupy a revered place along with the voluminous manuscripts of Washington, Jefferson, and hundreds of other men, North and South, whose record has enduring significance in American history.

## III

When the papers were opened, just after midnight in the earliest moments of July 26, 1947, the event was a mixture of high emotion and bustling excitement. The combinations were twirled and the safes unlocked to the clicking of news cameras. The volumes—194 of them—were brought out. More news pictures were taken as this or that Lincoln student was shown opening and reading some part of the collection. Then followed something rather unique: an all-night session as investigators pursued their searches, going from papers to index and back to papers, gathering in huddles to compare findings, and taking hurried notes for articles to be written or radio talks to be given that very day.

Through the night hours the labor was relieved by the booming laughter of Carl Sandburg. It was by his pen, in an excellent job of spot reporting published on the night of the opening day, that the public got the best immediate account of the occasion itself: the lighter moments at the dinner in the Whittall Pavilion of the Library of Congress, the repetition of last-minute conjectures as to what would be dug up, the battery of cameras, the floodlights, the Librarian's intoning of the deed of gift, the merriment with "a catch in it" as the significance of the occasion was borne in upon those present, the moment of unveiling, the samplings among the scores of volumes, the feeling of satisfaction as the mass of manuscripts came "out of its long hiding . . . into the public domain."

As one of the assembled students expressed it, quoting Keats, "Then felt I like some watcher of the skies, when a new planet swims within his ken." Yet, along with the thrill of the unveiling, there was something in the newspaper coverage of the event that was at least partly unfortunate. The wide public interest and desire for an instant report together with the fact that news writers have to work quickly, led to an over-extension of journalistic lines, with the result that incorrect ideas concerning the papers became well-nigh universal.

It should be remembered that the papers were opened on a Saturday morning—a monumental collection of them—and then one writer after another, writing no later than Saturday or Sunday, gave out sweeping generalizations which, whether intentionally or not, produced the impression that they had seen the whole collection. These premature pronouncements were quite misleading, and overnight, in addition to all the myths attaching to the Lincoln theme, another was added—the myth that the opening was a disappointment and that the Collection contains little of interest. Assuredly no one who has carefully worked with the papers—which requires long sustained labor—would give support to that legend.

For years an attitude had persisted concerning the papers and it was not readily sloughed off. The opening had occurred, but for hurried writers the cogitations that had been accumulated and intensified prior to the opening still lingered. In that long doubtful period a kind of synthetic answer had been supplied, often ignorantly, in efforts to satisfy the human mind in its unwillingness to tolerate a vacuum in any absorbing field of human knowledge. Months before the opening, various writers had been asked what they "expected to find." It was like the burlesque examination question: "Name the undiscovered islands of the Pacific Ocean." A variety of expectations and predictions came forth. Some who expressed themselves wondered if they might find things that no well informed student would have thought of looking for.

It was different, however, with the more serious student. He had maintained a healthy skepticism as to guesses and rumors. Now, as he became absorbed in the actual examination of the papers, all the miscellaneous and often amazing things that had been said as to what they might or might not contain seemed at once outmoded. Reality proved more exciting than any forecast.

And there was another feeling of the researcher—the sense of being a part of that age, living with Lincoln, handling the very papers he handled, sharing his deep concern over events and issues, noting his patience when complaints poured in, hearing a Lincolnian laugh, feeling a cumulative sense of unending presidential burdens and of hope deferred. This feeling that the age of Lincoln had come to life was nothing forced or imaginary; it was a real factor. If this suggests enthusiasm, the researcher must plead guilty to that charge, but it was an enthusiasm that came with that accent on reality that arises from being at the source of things, that realization of authenticity that accompanies the physical handling of original documents whose very penmanship revealed the haste, emotion, or urgency of a momentous period.

## IV

To appraise the Collection would be to write an elaborate work, which would have to be a coöperative enterprise. An initial step toward such appraisal would be to discard certain superficial ideas and misconceptions. One is asked whether there is anything "sensational" in the papers. Certain unfavorable things are revealed as to the conduct of public men other than Lincoln. Would that be called "sensational"? When one asks for the sensational, what does he have in mind? After continued study of the documents in the original the present writer finds this kind of query a bit off key, as if a statesman's record or the inner history of the nation in an era of supreme crisis could be narrowed down to a short order of murder for breakfast or scandal for lunch. What one finds is significance, flavor, human interest, character revelation, grist for the historian's mill, not cheap sensation.

That other question which has become over-familiar—whether there is "anything new" in the papers—may be answered confidently in the affirmative. What we have in this Collection is the very essence of historical data. It is source material a thousand fold. It is the stuff out of which history is formed. It is original, not second-hand or retrospective. It is the impression of the event as it was happening or the thought or feeling as it was struck off or felt. The Collection is notable in that it knows not of the assassination. It knows only the living Lincoln. Despite the fact that Nicolay and Hay made use of the papers in their multi-volume biography, the newness of the Collection is largely unimpaired. Much of it—indeed the more flavorful part—was passed over by those writers. The papers are highly valuable for the kind of book that Nicolay and Hay did not write.

In sheer immensity the Collection is most remarkable. There are over 41,000 pieces, with millions of handwritten words. But the quality of the material is even more worthy of remark than its bulk. To exhibit the Collection illustratively by selection of particular samples is not easy. Many items could be chosen for that purpose, but that is the difficulty. After the culling out of a hundred specimens there would remain further hundreds, as truly typical or representative, that would be equally worthy of emphasis. Mention has been made of the "index," but the *contents* of these letters and documents have not been indexed. There is only an inventory of items by the surnames of those from whom and to whom they were written. The lack of any topical index makes it necessary for the researcher to turn the many pages of the Collection itself (in the original or in microfilm). The inventory just mentioned is highly useful, but there is no short cut—no concordance, calendar, or topical guide—by which one can be told where to look for material on a particular topic of research. For example, the Collection reveals much as to Unionists in the South, but, as with other subjects, the pertinent letters are not listed under that heading. (It should be added that for certain purposes the finding of material is assisted by the chronological arrangement.)

The papers are especially important for the presidency. Only about five per cent of the material belongs to the period before 1860, though the documents in this earlier group are often of special interest, among them a letter from Lincoln's stepbrother, John D. Johnston (May 25, 1849) telling that Thomas Lincoln, in expectation of death, "craves to see you all the time & he wonts you to Come if you ar able to git hure, for you are his only Child that is, of his own flush & blood . . . ." This letter with its backwoods spelling is assuredly of greater historical significance than trashy utterings in which Lincoln's paternity has been ignorantly challenged.

People will have different preferences as to their favorites among the riches of the Collection. The manuscript of Lincoln's farewell address at Springfield, February 11, 1861, would rank high on any list. What home meant to him as he departed "with a task . . . greater than that which rested upon Washington" is poignantly revealed in the jerky strokes of this document as it was written down on the train, partly in Lincoln's hand and partly in Nicolay's. There have been variant versions of this speech, but here we have the text as Lincoln wanted it remembered. High on the list of favorites also would be the draft of Lincoln's letter to Mrs. Gurney, his memorandum in reply to Seward's amazing "Thoughts for the President's consideration" (April 1, 1861), texts of his Mexican War speech, the worksheets of the 1861 inaugural, and the message to the special session of Congress, July 4, 1861. Public affairs, of course, were not all, and one finds special human interest in the letter of Lincoln to his wife (August 8, 1863), giving just the kind of familiar news and comment, including the latest about Tad's "Nanny Goat," which one would expect from an American husband writing to his wife who was away on a visit. And, for another choice item, few would exclude the President's exquisite reprimand to a spirited young captain, J. Madison Cutts, his personal friend and a brother-in-law of Senator Douglas.

One big factor showing the importance of the Collection is that of preliminary drafts which Lincoln made and kept. Even where the finished product has been long available it is of great interest to trace the document through those earlier stages which show Lincoln thinking out what he wrote, considering every word, striking out and inserting, recopying, and coming through with a result to which, not until then, he placed his signature. In this we see Lincoln the lawyer choosing his words for their unmistakable meaning, as well as Lincoln the literary artist seeking to summon forth the utmost rhythm and magic of the English language.

Not only did Lincoln weigh his sentences for their literary effect, which he unfailingly did in important papers as well as in ordinary intercourse; the Collection also shows his courteous effort in a personal situation to seek the utmost in skilled human relations. His letters have at times a classic quality in this respect. It has already been shown in this volume, and it is repeatedly illustrated in the Collection, that if Lincoln had a reproachful letter on his mind he would sometimes work it out with all the care devoted to a finished product, and then, on reconsideration, decide not to send it. He would not impulsively pull the trigger on a letter that was likely to misfire. One can yet read these unsent letters, for they were not thrown away.

An examination of the Collection is valuable for that kind of study which is concerned with the tracing of public speeches and papers to learn their provenance or the manner of their coming into being. By this is meant, not a mere textual investigation to determine the correct final wording, nor literary criticism alone, but, in addition to these, a kind of examination that seeks to bring together the factors that went into the preparation of a public speech, letter, or message. As to the notable first inaugural, for example, along with the literary and the strictly textual aspect, one needs to look into the whole wretched situation facing the country, the manner of Lincoln's approach to adjustment, the prudent consultation with his advisers, the numerous revisions of the address as it went through various handwritten and printed versions, and the ultimate product in which advice was taken and certain parts made over, yet without marring the whole effect of the speech in completed form. One could rewrite the story of secession and the plunge downward into war in terms of this speech of Lincoln's. Such an analysis would bring out Lincoln's emphasis on adjustment, non-provocation, and the utter needlessness of war between North and South.

Of course this inaugural was more than a speech. It was the announcement of a formulated policy, a solemn reminder of the need for second thought as the nation faced a terrible crisis. It was the setting forth of the pattern and design of a new administration taking the reins of government in Washington in an unprecedented threat to the nation's life. One might contrast it with some of the ill considered speeches of that general period—with Southerners in Congress firing off their parting shots, or with Gladstone's Newcastle speech of October 1862. Gladstone's utterance was not a well prepared and matured announcement of policy; Lincoln's inaugural was such an announcement. To re-read that inaugural of March 1861 is to realize anew how unfortunate was the lack of Southern understanding of Lincoln's intentions. It was regrettable that the speech in correct text and with appreciative comment, did not get across to the mind of the South. It is only when one turns the actual pages in its numerous worksheets as found in the Collection that one can properly understand what went on in Lincoln's mind as he phrased this exacting and difficult public declaration. The historian today can appreciate the speech better than the men of 1861.

In pursuing this kind of historical criticism it is well to remember that for every speech there are several versions—the speech as originally planned and (usually) written out in advance; the speech as revised, also in advance; the speech as spoken (for which in our day a sound recording would be necessary for preservation, and there were no phonographs in Lincoln's day); and the speech as reported in newspapers or elsewhere.

As the Collection conclusively shows, Lincoln did not make use of ghost writers. His speeches and letters were his own, unless in perfunctory intercourse a private secretary would produce a letter (by direction) for the President to sign. Sometimes Lincoln himself served as ghost writer for others. He prepared a message for Governor Bissell of Illinois, and in one case he wrote in his own hand a letter which went out over the signature of John Hay.

Of course, in annual messages to Congress—those voluminous documents that supposedly boxed the compass as to governmental problems down the line of departments and bureaus—Lincoln would put together the contributions of various cabinet members, Cameron or Stanton for the war department, Seward for foreign affairs, and so on. Yet even in these messages one can distinguish between those portions that amounted to a kind of catch-all of miscellaneous information and those paragraphs which constituted the President's own recommendations—for example, in December 1862 with respect to compensated emancipation—and which were written by Lincoln. In all these matters the historian can not restrain a feeling of regret that Lincoln did not employ the rather obvious but long unused technique of delivering the message in person before the houses of Congress in joint session. A half century later that governmental resource was used most effectively by Woodrow Wilson; still later by Franklin D. Roosevelt. In Lincoln's case the eloquent message of July 4, 1861, one of his great state papers, was perfunctorily communicated to Congress and unimpressively read by a clerk, while the "inaugural" of that forgotten man, Galusha A. Grow, then entering upon his duties as speaker of the House, was delivered in person.

The Sumter episode was Lincoln's most unhappy problem of state. In his papers we find no confirmation of the accusation that he was purposely provoking the lower South into firing the "first shot." There was no intent to make an attack from Sumter, and there was no element of hostile surprise in the relief expedition which the President sent simply because the alternative would have been the withdrawal of the garrison and evacuation of the fort. Instead of such evidence of intentional provocation we have just the opposite—the mildness of the first inaugural, the numerous concessions (as in the suggestion of offshore collection of duties and the avoidance of unfriendly appointments in the South), and the Chew message to Governor Pickens of South Carolina. This was the message which Lincoln sent for the perusal of the governor, carefully stating in advance what the Washington government was doing in "an attempt . . . to supply Fort Sumter with provisions only." To see that message (which came back to him) in Lincoln's handwriting is to have a new sense of the pressures, dangers, and cautionary measures of those critical days.

This reference to the inaugural and the Sumter problem illustrates a fact that runs through the whole subject—namely, that in studying the "Collection" one is reopening certain phases of American history. This could be further shown in Lincoln's firm but tactful handling of Seward's fools-day aberration as to foreign policy in 1861; in the replies to Greeley, Corning, and Birchard on matters of high policy; in his seeking of cabinet advice on the creation of West Virginia; in his non-provocative handling of the problem of retaliation between the United States and the Confederate States; and so on through hundreds of significant examples. It is thus that Lincoln's statesmanship must be studied and restudied at first hand.

There were abusive letters, expressions of a desire for Lincoln's scalp, and warnings of foul play. It was unhistorically asserted that the only other Whig Presidents—Harrison and Taylor—died in office of poison. (Lincoln, of course, was a former Whig.) Helpful souls offered an assortment of remedies. One writer recommended "a good Presbyterian Druggist, . . . and a good Republican." The President was warned of great danger in Baltimore in 1861 and was told of "a league of ten persons who had sworn that you shall never pass through that city alive." It was considered unsafe for Lincoln as President Elect to stay at a hotel, and Montgomery Blair offered a spare room in his city home, adding that it was "the one Genl Jackson intended to occupy after leaving the White House." (This was an interesting reference to the Blair House as a possible abode for a President.)

Over and over we find misunderstood subjects clarified in the papers. They show, for instance, how utterly untrue is the superficial idea that the British government "sided" with the Confederacy. Relations between the United States and Britain became increasingly friendly as the war progressed, and there are numerous expressions of friendship to Lincoln from Englishmen of the time. There is an unmistakable tone of sincerity in the British and French assurances of enthusiastic support for Lincoln and his cause. There is dignity in an address "To Citizen Abraham Lincoln" by a notable group of French gentlemen extending an enthusiastic greeting to Lincoln and assuring him of genuine support on the part of French liberals. This paper shows that in Lincoln's own day his cause was recognized as the cause of world freedom. These distinguished and thoughtful Frenchmen, intensely interested in liberty at home, realized that Lincoln's cause was theirs; if freedom failed in America, despotism would gain in Europe.

Some of the communications bear a cautionary injunction of secrecy, with such labels as "Private and Confidential" or "Read and Destroy." Now that those papers are available and the secrecy no longer holds, they have for the historian a now-it-can-be-told quality. Much of the information in the Collection was "off the record," such as inside comment on the cabinet or woeful forebodings of Republican defeat in 1864.

## V

The Collection consists mainly of incoming material, but that word "mainly" in so immense a mass of papers leaves a considerable place for Lincoln's own writings, of which there are hundreds of examples. By no means all of these writings by Lincoln have been published, though most of them have. (Where they have been published by Nicolay and Hay, the editing is seldom precise.) Lincoln had a flair for pithy endorsements. Though many of these are in departmental archives as the President referred documents to cabinet secretaries for attention with brief comments, yet a considerable number of the endorsements in the R. T. Lincoln Collection will see the light of print for the first time in the new edition of Lincoln's works soon to be published under the editorship of the Abraham Lincoln Association.

Lincoln is revealed in the Collection in little things as well as great. Nothing seemed too small for his attention. He studied why a captain's commission was delayed, requested a physical examination for a private, dealt personally with innumerable cases of clemency, and in one case refused to consider a man's "excellent work for orphan children" a basis for exemption from the draft. While demands or requests for patronage ran into the thousands the large challenging problems constantly pressed upon him. As one of his correspondents expressed it: ". . . when I think of your Incessant Labours I wonder to myself . . . as you are not Superhuman and cannot any more do without Sleeping Eating and Rest than other men nor cannot extend the day & night Beyond twenty-four hours."

One could make up a composite of American types from the letters that came to Lincoln. Many of them reflected a selfish purpose. One writer reported the death of an office holder with the request that he have the job of the recently deceased. A gentleman of Alton, Illinois (October 10, 1861) gave a list of Federal offices he would "accept," including "Secretary of the Territory of Nebraska," the consulship at Glasgow, congressional librarian, and, lastly, "A Clerkship in Washington—3rd or 4th class preferred." Various successors of Roger B. Taney were offered before that aged Chief Justice passed away.

Many of those who wrote to Lincoln were prominent men—Everett, Bryant, Greeley, Grant, Scott, the Blairs, Beecher, Weed, Archbishop Hughes, Banks, Seward, Stanton, Sumner, Schurz, Frémont, Cassius M. Clay, and so on down a long roster of distinguished names of the time. Men of Congress sent letters to him by the scores, governors by the dozens, generals by the hundreds (over 1200), literary men and editors by more than a hundred. The Collection contains about 1100 letters from members of the cabinet.

Yet these missives from men of fame and high position are perhaps not the most interesting of the documents. The Collection is notable for the descent from the lofty to the lowly. There are family letters, including in-law letters from various Todds in Kentucky, Missouri, and Alabama, and communications from Lincoln's relatives in Coles County, Illinois. With quaint originality of spelling, that unforgettable country cousin, Dennis Hanks, from his backwoods home, tells of the state of health and feelings of Lincoln's stepmother. Another kinsman, John T. Hanks, wrote (July 22, 1860) from Douglas County, Oregon: "Dear unkel: while seting a lone in mi Cabing . . . I . . . write . . . to lete you no thate I was in the lande of the living . . . . it has ben a bout Ten years sense I saw you laste . . . ." "Billy the Barber" (William Florville), who served Lincoln in Springfield days, wrote a long missive (December 27, 1863) as of one neighbor to another. This home-town friend was sure of Lincoln's feeling for the Negro race. "My people," he wrote, "feel grateful to you for it." He went on to offer sympathy for the death of Willie and to inform Taddy "that his and Willy's dog is a live and kicking."

Friends of long ago New Salem days wrote to Lincoln and we have not a few of their letters preserved in the Collection. That backwoods entrepreneur Denton Offutt—now something of an authority on the horse, its treatment in sickness and in health—wrote one of those numerous begging letters asking for an appointment: "I hope you will Give me the Patten office or the office of Agricultural Department or the Commissary for Purchais of Horses Mules Beef for the Army or Mail agent  . . . . I have to be looking out to live  . . . ."

Since the impulse to write to the White House was well nigh universal, the papers reveal the relation of Lincoln to his people. Considering the comparative lack of conscious attention to presidential public relations or of studied contact between the White House and the American fireside, it is remarkable to note how unstintedly and spontaneously Lincoln was addressed as a confidential friend by individuals of all ranks. A deserter who had fought at Chancellorsville and Gettysburg but who had gone home to see wife and children, wrote of his readiness to rejoin his regiment. A prisoner in Castle Thunder, expecting to die, wrote as if putting himself on record before the world. Working people sent friendly appeals from England and America; they were acknowledged in like spirit.

That Lincoln stirred a response in the hearts of the people is shown by the many who requested locks of his hair, or who sent him gifts, from a pair of eagles to a tub of butter or a "Smoking pipe made expressly for you." Lincoln was told that thousands were praying for him. A freedman in the deep South, signing his name "don carlous Butler," wrote asking guidance as to how he should plan for his bit of land and the rebuilding of his house. The lady who wrote the letter for this ex-slave explained: "He, with others of the Freedmen, often expresses a wish to be able to speak to Massa Linkum feeling sure that he will listen to their plea for land & do what is best for them." Without these numerous letters from unfamed beings much of the feeling of the people for Lincoln would be hard to recover. One does not find it in the ponderous pages of the *Congressional Globe*. It existed as something in the air. It was not easily traceable. It spread abroad in the manner of the grapevine telegraph, but these papers show that it was a solid and unmistakable fact.

Recognizing that startling sensationalism is lacking (which is fortunate), one must avoid the mistake of underestimating the Collection. With these papers the portrait is now much fuller, the contemporary scene recreated, not as an album of tintypes but as a throbbing stage of actors who come alive in their own words. From the time the Collection was opened, and more especially after months had been devoted to its study, it became apparent that a new phase in the appreciation of Lincoln was upon us. Little of what was basically known has had to be discarded, but in vividness and glowing detail we have much more of Lincoln and his period than before.

Writers will continue to search, or skim through, these masses of material for divers purposes, though up to now the more careful investigators who have made penetrating and thorough use of the Collection are by no means numerous. The papers could be drawn upon for the lingo and patter of Lincoln's day, for an occasional earthy fable, for evidence of human folly or greed, for bygone excitements that seem stupid in retrospect, for glimpses or self-portraits of Lincoln's contemporaries, and for the psychological, or psychopathic, climate of a day when hate and illogical emotion ran wild and yet below the surface the foundations of sense and sanity remained somehow intact. One cannot easily enumerate the varying purposes for which the papers will yield their valuable product. They hold a mirror to American life.

Abolition, Sumner and, 89; as war aim, 116-117; in Maryland, 286-287.

Abolitionists, disavowal by Republicans, 52 and n.; term inapplicable to Lincoln, 85 n.; denounced by Vallandigham, 213-214; Anna E. Dickinson, 240-242.

Abraham Lincoln Association, edits Lincoln's works, 443.

Adams, Charles Francis (1807-1886), 325, as diplomat, 323; and Laird rams, 332-334; "this is war," 332-333; on British attitude, 353; on friendly meeting at Manchester, 354; on Cobden, 357.

Adams, Charles Francis (1835-1915), correspondence with Henry Adams, 342.

Adams, Henry, quoted, 342; activity in England, 355 and n.; on "democratic and socialist" meetings in Britain, 356.

Adams, Ephraim D., quoted, 352.

Adams, John, mentioned, 56, 323.

Adams, John Quincy, 67-68, 323.

Agnew, David, elected chief justice of Pennsylvania, 275.

Alabama, The, British built Confederate cruiser, 328 ff.

Alabama claims, arbitration, 329-330.

Albany, New York, Democratic meeting and protest, 225-226.

Albert, Prince, 357.

Alexandra, The, sea raider intended for Confederacy but withheld by Britain, 330; mentioned, 348.

American Bastile, 197, 201-203.

American party. See Knownothing party.

Amnesty. See pardon.

Anderson, Robert, commander at Sumter, Lincoln's letter to, 409.

Andrew, John A., governor of Massachusetts, elected 1863, 279; mentioned, 321.

Angle, Paul M., cited, 53 n.

Anglo-American relations. See Great Britain.

Anglo-Saxon principles, 150 ff.

Antislavery. See abolition.

Argyll, Duchess of, and Mrs. Stowe, 322.

Argyll, Duke of, 357.

Arlington (Lee home), seizure, 124 n.

"Armed Freedom," statue on Capitol dome, 389-390.

Army, Lincoln's visits and reviews, 12-15, 17-19; Lincoln's solicitude for, 18; Lincoln condemns army excess, 44-45; traditional American preference for small army, no peacetime compulsion, etc., 150-151, 151 n. See also courts martial, conscription, militia.

Arnold, Isaac N., congressman from Illinois, cited, 53 and n.; intraparty contest with Scripps, 130-131; congressional supporter of Lincoln, 138.

Arrests, arbitrary, of political prisoners, 194 ff.; case histories, 203-205; reasons for, 203-207; public criticism of, 224-226; Lincoln explains, 226-228; congressional debate, 232.

Ashley, James M., congressman from Ohio, and Thaddeus Stevens, 100-101.

Aspinwall, W. H., service abroad, 320-321.

Assassination, Lincoln's attitude toward, 8-10.

Attainder, in relation to confiscation, 120-123.

Baker, Edward D., 93, 133.

Baker, Edward Lewis, 34.

Baker, La Fayette C., under Seward in 1861, 159; secret police service, 199-207 passim.

Baltimore, turbulence in 1861, 158; police commissioners arrested, 208.

Baltimore Exchange, expresses Southern sympathy, 203-204; editor arrested, 203-204.

Bancroft, Frederic, on arrests and prisoners, 194-195, 197-198, 202.

Bancroft, George, 49, 425.

Banks, Nathaniel P., Union general, and

Banks, Nathaniel P. (*Continued*) arrests in Maryland, 159-160; at Port Hudson, 364.

Bass, Mrs. Eugenia P., aided by Lincoln, 43 and n.

Bates, David Homer, on Lincoln's war department visits, 6; on Grant-and-whiskey remark, 62.

Bates, Edward, attorney general, diary cited, 4 n., 32 and n.; and Lincoln on army visits, 17-18; on Henry Winter Davis, 93-94; and confiscation, 120; did not want habeas corpus problem pushed to solution, 167-168; on Supreme Court proceedings in Vallandigham case, 228 n.; supports Lincoln's habeas corpus policy, 232-233.

Bath, Marquis of, 342.

Baxley, Catherine Virginia, Confederate spy, 205.

Bayard, James A., senator from Delaware, on summary military procedures, 224; hostility to Lincoln, 232.

Bayne, Julia Taft, on Lincoln children, 31-32.

Beecher, Henry Ward, speeches in Britain, 321.

Bellows, Henry W., describes Lincoln, 405-406.

Belmont, August, service abroad, 320.

Benjamin, Judah P., Confederate secretary of state, dissatisfied as to Britain, 348-349. See also Confederate diplomacy.

Bennett, James Gordon, 28 and n., 38.

Berdahl, Clarence A., cited, 111 n.

Beresford-Hope, A. J., 342.

Bertinatti, Italian minister, 401-402.

Bickley, G. W. L., founds Knights of the Golden Circle, 188.

Bigelow vs. Forrest (confiscation), 122 n.

Binney, Horace, defends Lincoln's suspension of habeas corpus, 232-233.

Birchard, M., 265. See also Ohio committee.

Bismarck, 316.

Blain, Thomas G., of Manchester, England, and gift of Bright bust, 360.

Blaine, James G., on Roscoe Conkling, 96 n.; on "victim-hunting mania" of congressional war committee, 133; and Maine election of 1863, 280.

Blair family, 282; and cabinet split, 284.

Blair, Francis P., Jr., 93; and Thaddeus Stevens, 100, 101; false charges against, 282-283.

Blair, Montgomery, postmaster general, denounced by radicals, 281; speech at Rockville, Md. (Oct. 3, 1863), 282; counsel for Dred Scott, 283; offers Lincoln room in Blair house, 442.

Blockade, Confederate interpretation, 341. See also Bright, Confederate diplomacy, economic theory, Great Britain, neutrality, Prize Cases.

"Bloody shirt" tradition, 188.

Blow, Henry T., 42.

Booth kidnap plan, 10.

Border states, and use of Negro troops, 60; war aims, 114 ff.

Boyd, Belle, Confederate spy, 205.

Bradford, Augustus W., governor of Maryland, correspondence with Lincoln, 7 and n.; protests against pre-election use of Union army, 284 ff.

Bradford, Gamaliel, quoted, 407.

Bragg, Braxton, Confederate general, and western operations, 363 ff.; invasion of Kentucky (1862), 363; at Stone's River, 364; evacuates Chattanooga, 365; withdraws to Georgia (1863), 366; difficulty after Chickamauga, 372; favorite of Jefferson Davis, 373; defeat of, at Missionary Ridge, 387-389.

Bramlette, Thomas E., and election for governor of Kentucky, 246.

Breckinridge, John C., senator from Kentucky, joins Confederate army, expelled from Senate, 106; at Chickamauga, 369.

Bridgeport, Ala., rail point on "cracker-line," 386.

Bright, Jesse D., of Indiana, expelled from Senate, 107, 250.

Bright, John, and American question, 358-362; attacks Roebuck, 350-351; opposes French "mediation," 358; and Lincoln, 359-362; gifts of his photograph and bust, 360 and n.

Britain. See Great Britain.

Brooks, Noah, 60; accompanies Lincoln on army visit, 17-18; defends Mrs. Lincoln, 38-41; reports Lincoln stories, 64-66; on Henry Wilson, 90; on Wade, 90-91; on Henry Winter Davis, 94; on Rosecrans's removal, 384; and Lincoln, 385.

Brooks, Preston, severe assault upon Sumner, 90.

Brough, John, Union candidate for governor of Ohio, 272-274.

Brown, George William, mayor of Baltimore, 159.

Brown, Mrs. Mary Edwards, cited, 33 n.

Browne, Francis F., cited, 9 and n.; 55-56.

Browne, Charles Farrar. See Ward, Artemus.

Browning, Orville H., 237 n.; cotton trading scheme, 54 and n.; sad interview with Lincoln, 140-141; debate with Sumner on war power, 175; defends Lincoln policies, 232.

Brown's Ferry, operation at, 386.

Bruce, E. M., reports details of Helm's death to Lincoln, 370.

Bryan, Thomas B., and original draft of emancipation proclamation, 53 and n.

Bryant, John H., Lincoln letter to, 52-53.

Buckingham, William A., governor of Connecticut, reëlected in 1863, 240-242.

Buckner, Simon B., Confederate general, 373.

Buell, Don C., Union general, dissatisfaction with, 364.

Bulloch, James D., of the Confederate navy, 321, and Laird rams, 331.

Bunch, Robert, British consul at Charleston, expelled, 349.

Burnside, A. E., Union general, 24, 185, 250, 365, 378; question of relieving, 218; and Vallandigham case, 215-238; criticized by Cutts, 220-221; and suppression of Chicago Times, 233-236; takes Army of the Ohio to Knoxville, 366.

Burr conspiracy, civil guarantees not set aside, 152 n.

Bushnell, Horace, on loyalty, 209.

Butler, Benjamin F., 232, 412; suggested for command in New York (1863), 303; "woman order," 340; execution of Mumford, 340 n.; praised by Anna E. Dickinson, 241; branded as outlaw, 242.

Butler County, Ohio, anti-Vallandigham sentiment in, 214.

Butler, "don carlous," South Carolina freedman, 445.

Butler, Nicholas Murray, and Lincoln Papers, 432-433.

Butterfield, Justin, on "war, pestilence, and famine," 64.

Cabinet, "influence with this administration," 64; unprepared for war, 86; all regretted Vallandigham's arrest, 218, 225; same feeling as to suppression of Chicago Times, 234. See also Bates, Blair (Montgomery), Seward, Stanton, peace movement, Peterhoff.

Cadwalader, George, Union general, and Merryman case, 161.

Cagger, Peter, 310.

California, New Almedan mine, 47; case of W. M. Gwin (Confederate sympathizer), 205. See also Rubery.

Cameron, Simon, secretary of war, at army review, 13; and Maryland crisis of 1861, 159.

Campbell, L. D., on Vallandigham, 237 n.

Campbell, Mrs. Ann Todd, favor requested, 42-43.

Camp Douglas, 233.

Canada, refuge for Vallandigham, 219, 271; fear of aggression against, 317; and Confederate emissaries, 324.

Capitol Building, visited by Lincoln, 15, 26; dome finished (Dec. 1863), 389-390.

Carlile, John S., senator from "restored Virginia," on confiscation, 123.

Carlyle, Thomas, on American question, 324.

Carpenter, F. B. (artist), on Lincoln's strain and anxiety, 50.

Cartwright, Peter, 255 and n.

Cass, Lewis, military service ridiculed by Lincoln, 78.

Castine. See Brooks, Noah.

Cecil, Lord Robert, 342.

Censure (of Lincoln), its avoidance did not lessen hostility of Congress, 137.

Chancellorsville, Lee's situation after, 364.

Chandler, Zachariah, 90-92; belittles Lincoln, 132, 134; member of committee on conduct of war, 134; receives letter from Lincoln on election victories (1863), 291.

Charleston, Ill., 52 n.

Chase, Kate. See Sprague.

Chase, Salmon P., 320, 408; and Lincoln's army visits, 17, 18; disapproves of Lincoln's humor, 69; letter from R. J. Walker, 362.

Chattanooga, falls to Union forces (1863), 365; later operations on Chattanooga front, 363 ff. (esp. 365 ff.).

Cherokee Nation, 48.

Chicago, Ill., and original draft of emancipation proclamation, 53 and n.; Copperhead convention, 256.

Chicago Times, suspension of, 233-236, 263.

Chickamauga, Ga., battle of (Sept. 19-20, 1863), 366; heavy Confederate losses, 378.

China, Lincoln-Seward policy toward (mentioned), 362.

Chronicles of Reuben (Lincoln verses), 59.

Cincinnati, Ohio, 215, 235.

City Point, Va., visited by Lincoln, 17.

Civil government and military authority, Lincoln's views, 44-45. *See also* Anglo-Saxon traditions, habeas corpus, martial law, "military necessity," Milligan case, Vallandigham.

Civil rights, Sumner and, 89; in war time, 97; Anglo-Saxon and American tradition, 150 ff.; Lincoln on, 227; and military authority, 230-231, 234-238.

Civil War, and Constitution (varied interpretations), 108 ff.; "war aims," 113 ff., 116 n.; disloyalty and prisoners of state, 184-211; guerrilla warfare, 191; relation of military to civil authority, 231-238; freedom of speech and press, 231, 233-238. *See also* Confederacy.

Clark, Daniel, senator from New Hampshire, discusses conscription act, 128-129, 128 n.

Clark, John B., congressman from Missouri, joins Confederate army, 106.

Clay, Brutus, 247.

Clay, Cassius M., 9, 247.

Clemens, Samuel L. *See* Twain, Mark.

Clough, Arthur Hugh, 51.

Cobden, Richard, friendly to United States, 357.

Colby, Robert, admonishes Lincoln on reviewing technique, 13-14.

Colfax, Schuyler, 92, 100, 106.

Colleges. *See* land-grant college act.

Colonization, and confiscation, 119.

Colorado, Indian troubles in, 47.

Columbus, Ohio, Democratic state convention (1863), 263.

Committee on conduct of the war (congressional), 132-134; Conkling and, 95; lenient toward military incompetence of favored generals, 133-134; Blaine's comment ("victim-hunting mania"), 133; source of pain to Lincoln, 134.

Confederacy (Confederate States of America), attitude of government at Washington (realistic treatment combined with lack of recognition), 180-183; its government hopeless as agent for reunion, 186; and Vallandigham, 212; and peace movement (1863), 242-245; question of belligerency, 318; and Great Britain, 328, 339; expels British consuls, 349; referred to by Earl Russell as "the so-styled Confederate States," 349.

Confederate diplomacy, 318, 324 ff.; publicity, 341; collapse in Britain, 347 ff.

Confederate vessels and crews, treatment of, 179-180.

Confiscation, military, 44-45; and "war aims," 113, 117-124; in Congress, 117-125; duration of forfeiture, 119-124; and emancipation, 119, 124 and n.; and Supreme Court, 122 ff.; and Federal direct tax in South, 124 n.; financial results, 124 and n.; comment of Fessenden, 141.

Confiscation acts, 117 ff.; Lincoln's veto message, 119, 120-124; explanatory joint resolution, 119-124.

Congress, and Mrs. Lincoln's refurbishing of White House, 20-21; sets Thanksgiving day, 58 n.; in Lincoln's time, 83 ff.; relations with President, 83 ff., 113 ff.; quality, 83-84; inexperienced membership, 1861, 85-86; "rump Congress" of 1861, 85-86; outstanding members, 88-104; wartime procedure and customs, 104-107; expulsion of members who joined Confederacy, 106-107; and Constitution in war time, 108 ff.; "intent" of legislation, 107-108, 117 ff.; and presidential leadership, 111-112; party organization and the presidency, 111 n.; and war aims, 113 ff.; manner of deliberation, 117 ff.; and Negro troops, 125-127; Lincoln's feeling toward, 130; uncoöperative toward Lincoln, 135 ff.; hopeful factors despite war and bickering, 142 ff.; and habeas corpus, 166 ff.; and summary military procedures, 224-225. *See also* committee on the conduct of the war.

Conkling, James C., invites Lincoln to mass meeting, 254.

Conkling, Roscoe, characterized, 94-95 and n.; denounces Vallandigham supporters, 215.

Connecticut, election of 1863, 240-242.

Conscription, and use of Negro troops, 126; act of 1863, repeal of $300 commutation, 127-130. *See also* draft.

Conservative Party (British), attitude on American question, 351-353.

Constitution, varied interpretations, 108 ff.; problem of amendment in war time, 109; debated, 113-114; and confiscation, 118-124; and habeas corpus, 156-166, 223 (*and see* Birchard, Corning).

Continuous voyage, 334-335.

Cony, Samuel, elected governor of Maine (1863), 280.

"Copperheads," 184-211; label misapplied, 186-188; unsubstantial rumors, 249; unsuccessful convention, 256.

Corinth, Miss., battle of, 364, 365.

Corning, Erastus, Lincoln's letter to, 210, 226-228 and 228 n.

Corwin, Thomas, and Mexican War, 267.

Courts (civil), and confiscation, 44-45, 120-124; Lincoln on, 67; relation to military officers, 221 ff.; right to set aside sentence of military commission upheld in Milligan case, 230-231.

Covode, John, 276.

Cowan, Edgar, senator from Pennsylvania, attacked by fellow senators, 104-105; on "war aims," 114-115; on confiscation, 124.

Cox, S. S. ("Sunset"), characterized, 98-99; tactics in Congress, 105; on confiscation, 122; on use of Negro troops, 125; cited, 197; and Vallandigham case, 214-215, 217-218; denounces arbitrary arrests, 224; hostility to Lincoln, 232; mentioned, 253.

"Cracker line" (for Chattanooga), 383.

Craig, Mr. and Mrs. Charles, and Lincoln, 42.

Crenshaw, Ollinger, cited, 184 n., 188.

Cridland, Frederick J., British consul at Mobile, expelled, 349.

Crittenden, John J., on legislative doctrine as to Constitution, 110; on use of Negro troops, 125.

Crittenden resolution (war aims), 113, 116 n.; not supported by Stevens, 104.

Crittenden, Thomas L., Union general, 367.

Cumberland, Army of the, 364, 367.

Cumberland Gap, Va., 366.

Current, Richard Nelson, on Thaddeus Stevens, 102-103.

Curtin, Andrew Gregg, governor of Pennsylvania, 3 n.; and campaign of 1863, 274-278; writes to Lincoln (Sept. 4, 1863) on Pennsylvania election, 275; and Cameron feud, 276; favors McClellan for reinstatement in military command, 276 and n.

Curtis, Benjamin R., befriends William H. Winder, 205; denounces Lincoln, 225.

Curtis, Samuel R., Union general, 43; and Lincoln, 422-423.

Cutts, J. Madison, and Vallandigham case, 220; advises Lincoln to dismiss Burnside, 220-221; Lincoln's reprimand, 425-427, 439.

Dalton, Ga., 377.

Dana, Charles A., assistant secretary of war, 55 n., 366, 381-382.

Davis, David, 369, 430; and Republican disavowal of abolitionists, 52 and n.; opinion in Milligan case, 230-231; demands Hascall's removal, 236.

Davis, Henry Winter (radical), characterized, 93-94; seeks House control of foreign policy, 93 n.; election to Congress in 1863, 287-288. See also Wade-Davis bill and manifesto.

Davis, Jefferson, 104; compared with Lincoln, 50; Jesse Bright's letter to, 107; treason case dropped, 182; denounced by Anna E. Dickinson, 241; proclaims B. F. Butler as "outlaw," 242; and peace movement (1863), 242; wrongly accused by R. J. Walker, 322; and expulsion of British consuls, 349; censures J. E. Johnston, 364; interferes with Confederate army, 375.

Davis, John W., case, Lincoln on, 208.

Dayton, Ohio, 215.

Dayton, William L., minister to France, 320.

Democracy and war power, 149 ff.

Democrats and Democratic party, and Vallandigham, 96 and n., 212-238 (postwar hostility to Vallandigham, 237 n.); "peace Democrats," 96-99 and notes; accuse Lincoln of disregarding Constitution, 108; wartime attitudes, 186-211 (esp. 193), 237; "bloody shirt" tradition, 188; Albany protest, 225-226; and peace movement of 1863, 245; Union Democrats and Peace Democrats in Kentucky, 246; and legislative deadlock in Indiana, 248 ff.; supported the war, 250; wartime difficulties, 312.

Department of the Ohio, and Vallandigham case, 215-238.

Depew, Chauncey M., on Lincoln, 79, 82; elected New York secretary of state, 279.

Derby, Lord, British Conservative leader, attitude on American question, 351-352.

Detroit, hoax concerning ex-President Pierce, 196-197.

Dewey, Thomas E., 111 n.

Dickinson, Anna E., antislavery orator, 17 and n., 240-242.

Direct tax of 1861, and seizure of Arlington, 124 n.
Disloyal societies, 184 ff., 190, 191-192, 193. *See also* Knights of the Golden Circle, Order of American Knights, Sons of Liberty.
Disraeli, Benjamin, British Conservative, and American question, 352.
District of Columbia, 231.
Dix-Hill cartel (prisoner exchange), 242.
Dix, John A., 204; commissioner for political prisoners, 200; and draft in New York, 304 ff. *See also* Dix-Hill cartel.
Dix, Morgan, on New York draft riot, 294.
Dixon, James, senator from Connecticut, on credit for Negro troops, 127; defends Lincoln's policies, 232; on support for Montgomery Blair in Senate, 284 and n.
Dominican Republic, 62-63.
Donald, David, 90 n.
Doolittle, James R., senator from Wisconsin, on crediting of Negro recruits, 126-127; mentioned, 261.
Douglas, Stephen A., loyal-opposition policy, 1; arguments derided by Lincoln, 66-67, 78; great service to Lincoln, 141; mentioned, 213, 312.
Douglass, Frederick, befriended by Lincoln, 423-424.
Draft, enforcement of, 293 ff.; riots, 294; riot in New York City, 294 ff. *See also* conscription, Seymour, Kneedler *vs.* Lane.
Drake, Charles D., and Missouri delegation, 48-49.
Dred Scott case, 229.
Drummond, Judge, and suppression of Chicago *Times*, 234.
Dubois, Jesse K., offended by Lincoln joke, 71.
Dudley, Thomas H., United States consul at Liverpool, 329 n.; and Laird rams, 333-334; and gift of Bright photograph, 360.
Duke, Basil W., cited, 191.
Dwight, John W., 434.

Eastman, Ira A., Democratic candidate for governor in New Hampshire (1863), defeated despite popular majority, 240.
Economic activities (Federal), expansion of, 175.
Economic theory (as to cotton), 358-359, 362. *See also* blockade, Bright, Cobden, Confederate diplomacy.

Edge, Frederick M., British journalist, 357.
Edwards, Mrs. Ninian W., on Lincoln family's grief at Willie's death, 34 and n.
Election of 1862, Republicans in, 86.
Elections in 1863, 239 ff.; in Rhode Island, 239; in New Hampshire, 240; in Connecticut, 240; in Kentucky, 245 ff.; Vallandigham runs for governor of Ohio, 263-274; Pennsylvania, 274 ff.; New York, 278-279; Massachusetts, 279-280; Maine, 280; Maryland, 282-288; effect as to Lincoln, 290-291.
Ellsworth, Elmer E., funeral ceremonies in White House, 16.
Ely, Alfred, 205.
Emancipation, as national cause, 52-53; and war aims, 113, 260; and confiscation, 119, 124 and n. *See also* Negroes.
Emancipation proclamation, 51; history of original draft, 53 and n.; approved by Thaddeus Stevens, 103; condemned, 225.
England. *See* Great Britain.
Europe, and United States, 316.
Evarts, William M., service abroad, 321; and Laird rams, 334.
Everett, Edward, at Gettysburg, 3 and n.; mentioned, 15, 16.
Ewing, Thomas, fears for Lincoln's safety, 10; disapproves Lincoln's emancipation and habeas corpus proclamations, 225.

Fain, W. P., Federal marshal in Kansas Territory, and use of *posse comitatus* as quasi-military force, 162 n.
Falmouth, Va., 17.
Faulkner, Charles J., prisoner of state, 205.
Federal and state relations. *See* state and Federal relations.
Fenton, R. E., on Lincoln serenade, 11 and n.
Fessenden, W. P., of Maine, on use of Negro troops, 126; deplores suspension of habeas corpus privilege, 225.
Field, Richard S., senator from New Jersey, 88.
Field, Stephen J., justice, opinion in Vallandigham case, 229; in Rubery case, 361.
Finck, William E., of Ohio, on war aims, 113-114.
Fithian, William, aided by Lincoln, 43.
*Florida*, The, Confederate warship, 329.
Florville, William ("Billy the Barber"), writes Lincoln, 444-445.
Forbes, John M., service abroad, 320-321.

Foreign relations. *See* international relations.

Forfeiture. *See* confiscation.

Forney, John W., 46.

Forrest, Nathan Bedford, Confederate general, 373.

Fort Fisher, lenient investigation by war committee, 133-144.

Fort Lafayette, 203, 204.

Fort McHenry, 204.

Fort Monroe, visited by Lincoln, 17, 19; mentioned, 204.

Fort Sumter, Lincoln's attitude, 441-442.

Fort Warren, 203, 204, 205, 264.

Foster, John G., 221.

Foster, Lafayette S., senator from Connecticut, 88.

France, proposes mediation, 324.

Franklin, William B., Union general, and Governor Curtin, 277.

Freedmen's bureau bill, irrelevant rider concerning confiscation, 123-124.

Freedom of speech. *See* Speech, freedom of.

Freidel, Frank, cited, 172 n., 173 n.

Frémont, John C., Union general, and military emancipation, 232; praised by Anna E. Dickinson, 241; mentioned, 409.

French, B. B., commissioner of public buildings, and Mrs. Lincoln's refurbishing of White House, 21; and White House social activities, 24.

Fry, General James B., provost marshal general, 303, 309, 420.

Fugitive slave acts, 89.

Fullerton, Allen, British consul at Savannah, expelled, 349.

Gamble, H. R., governor of Missouri, writes "cross" letter to Lincoln, 422.

Garfield, James A., 92-93, 106.

*Georgia,* The, Confederate warship, 329.

Gettysburg address, 3, 363.

Gettysburg, battle of, 15-16, 351.

Gilmore, Joseph A., Republican candidate for governor of New Hampshire (1863), 240.

Gladstone, William Ewart, notorious speech at Newcastle, 342 ff.

*Godey's Lady's Book,* Thanksgiving campaign, 56-57.

Governors, and Thanksgiving day, 56-58; Lincoln's relation to, 420-422. *See also* Bradford, elections, Gamble, Magoffin, Morton, Seymour.

Grant, Ulysses S., Union general, headquarters visited by Lincoln, 17, 18; Lincoln disclaims whiskey story, 62; and Dominican problem, 63; protests military arrests, 224; captures Vicksburg, 364; contemplates drive against Mobile (1863), 365 and n.; opposes Bragg, 375 ff.; and Hooker-Slocum feud, 381; given western command, 383; maligned by Confederate press, 385; arrives at Chattanooga (Oct. 23, 1863), 386; 411; Chattanooga (Missionary Ridge) victory, 387-389.

Gray, Asa, 146.

Gray, Wood, cited, 184 n., 185, 188 n.

Great Britain, relations with United States, 315-362; and building of Confederate warships, 328; friendliness of British people toward United States, 353 ff.; many popular meetings on American question, 354-355; relations clarified in Lincoln Papers, 442. *See also* Conservative party.

Greeley, Horace, target of Lincoln joke, 63; critical of Lincoln, 138; on Pennsylvania election of 1863, 274; mentioned, 237 n., 294.

Greenhow, Rose O'Neal, Confederate spy, 205.

Grey, Sir George, criticises Roebuck, 351.

Grier, Robert C., justice of Supreme Court, delivers opinion in *Prize Cases,* 154; opposes piracy trials, 180; opinion in Vallandigham case, 229.

Grimes, James W., senator from Iowa, 108; on use of Negro troops, 126.

Grimsley, Mrs. Elizabeth Todd, 33-34, 257.

Grinnell, Josiah B., on use of Negro troops, 125-126.

Grow, Galusha A., elected speaker, 1861, 92; mentioned, 100, 441.

Gurley, Phineas D., 34, 35 n.

Gurney, Mrs. Eliza P., Quaker, Lincoln's letter to, 438.

Gurowski, Adam, criticises Lincoln, 70.

Gwin, William M., senator from California, 205.

Habeas corpus, suspension of, not done by Congress till 1863, 152; no general suspension under Wilson or F. D. Roosevelt, 152 and n.; proclamation of April 27, 1861, 157; act of Congress (1863), passage and intent, 108, 166; act not enforced, 169-170; controversy (who has suspending power?), 167; Supreme Court did not

Habeas corpus, (*Continued*)
speak and controversy remained undecided, 167 ff.; in Vallandigham case, 221 ff.; and military power, Judge Leavitt on, 222-223, 229-230; suspension and preventive arrests defended, 226-228, 232. *See also* arrests, Bates, Binney, Burnside, Merryman, Taney, Vallandigham.

Hale, John P., senator from New Hampshire, attacks fellow senator, 104-105; criticizes Lincoln administration, 136; mentioned, 232.

Hale, Sarah Josepha, and Thanksgiving, 56-58.

Halleck, Henry W., general in chief, 6, 19 n., 367; offers resignation, 24; and Lieber code, 172; Rosecrans reports to (Sept. 9, 1863), 365; Lincoln withholds advice, 376.

Hamlin, Hannibal, feared inadequate to succeed Lincoln, 4; request for local favor, 53-54.

Hampton Roads, visited by Lincoln, 17.

Hanks, Dennis, 444.

Hanks, John T., 444.

Hanscom, S. P., *Herald* reporter, on White House invitations, 28.

Harris, Benjamin G., censured by House, 106.

Harris, Ira, senator from New York, on Trumbull's understanding of confiscation bill, 108.

Harrison, John Scott, 185.

Harvey, Mrs. Cornelia Perrine, describes Lincoln, 405.

Hascall, Milo S., and newspaper suppression in Indiana, 235-236.

Hatch, O. M., offended by Lincoln joke, 71.

Haupt, Herman, Union general in charge of railroads, 379.

Hay, John, relations with Lincoln, 5 and n., 6-7; on Lincoln's personality and habits, 6-7; on Lincoln's serenade speeches, 12 and n.; and Mrs. Lincoln, 38-39; diary cited on witticisms, 64-65; on N. J. Waterbury, 303; summons Lincoln for conference Sept. 23, 1863, 378. *See also* Nicolay and Hay.

Hebert, Walter H., quoted, 379.

Helm, Ben Hardin, Confederate general (brother-in-law of Mrs. Lincoln), killed at Chickamauga, 368; had declined Lincoln's offer of commission in army, 368; commanded brigade in Confederate army under Breckinridge, 369; details of death, 369.

Helm, Emilie Todd (Mrs. Ben Hardin Helm) close to the Lincolns, 368; death of her husband, 369; attends his funeral, 370; refuses Union oath, visits White House (Dec. 1863), 371.

Helm, Katherine, quoted, 368.

Henderson, John B., senator from Missouri, votes against repeal of $300 draft exemption, 129-130.

Henry, Dr. A. G., accompanies Lincoln on army visit, 17-18.

Henry, Joseph, 146.

Herndon, William H., Ann Rutledge story refuted by Mrs. Lincoln, 59 n.; mentioned, 21; laboriously explains Lincoln's humor, 71-74; signs call for Springfield mass meeting, 254; describes Lincoln, 394-396.

Hesseltine, William B., quoted, 240, 276.

Hicks, Thomas H., governor of Maryland, services valued by Lincoln, 51-52; apprehensive as to effect of suppressive measures, 158.

Hill, D. H., Confederate general, 372, 373. *See also* Dix-Hill cartel.

Hitchcock, E. A., Union general, and Lieber code, 172-173.

Hoar, George F., on Chandler, 91 and n.

Hogue, Arthur Reed, cited, 90 n.

Holman, William S., representative from Indiana, denounced by Riddle, 105.

Holt, Joseph, judge advocate general, mentioned, 185; on problem of compliance with habeas corpus act, 170; argument in Vallandigham case, 228 and n.; opinion on draft, 309-310.

Homestead act, 145.

Hooker, Joseph, Union general, headquarters visited by Lincoln, 17-18; commands two corps sent west, 379; feud with Slocum, 380; at Lookout Mountain, 388; Lincoln's letter to, 411.

Hopkins, Guy S., and fabrication concerning ex-President Pierce, 196-197.

Hostages, 205.

Hotze, Henry, and Confederate publicity, 341; and Gladstone, 343; dissatisfied in Britain, 348.

Hough, Mrs. Lotty, aided by Lincoln, 43.

House of Representatives, Lincoln's internal improvements speech, 66 and n.; his 1848 speech, 78 and n.; quality assessed, 83-84; as speaking arena, 86-87; leaders in Lincoln's time, 92-104; speakership, 92 and n.; committee on military affairs, and Thaddeus Stevens, 101; only two members defended Lincoln (assertion of Riddle), 138; members denounce arbitrary arrests, 224. *And see* Stevens, Thaddeus.

Howard, F. Key, arrest and imprisonment, 203-204.

Howard, O. O., Union general, 380-381.

Hubbart, H. C., cited, 185 n.

Hughes, James, cotton trading scheme, 54 and n.

Hughes, John, Catholic archbishop of New York, President's appreciation expressed by Seward, 16 and n.; service abroad, 319.

Hunter, David, Union general, 412-413.

Hurlbut, Stephen A., Union general, Lincoln's telegram to (1863), 376.

Illinois, pro-Southern sentiment, 185-186, 192, 193; reaction to Chicago *Times* suppression, 234; political situation in 1863, 250 ff.; unsuccessful constitution of 1862, 252; and exclusion of Negroes, 252; demand for Federal refund, 257. *See also* Springfield, mass meeting at.

Impeachment of Andrew Johnson (reveals attitude of Thaddeus Stevens), 102 and n.

*Index, The*, newspaper for Confederate propaganda, 341.

Indiana, mentioned, 59, 61, 230; Twelfth Regiment serenades Lincoln, 11; receives Lincoln's attention, 46-47; pro-Southern sentiment in, 185-186, 191-193; orders of Hascall for suppression of newspapers, 235-236; politics and breakdown of constitutional government in 1863, 247-250. *See also* Milligan, Morton, Voorhees.

Indianapolis, Hascall episode, 235-236.

Indianapolis *Sentinel*, 250.

Internal improvements, Lincoln on, 66 and n.

International relations, influence of Sumner, 89; resolution of Henry Winter Davis, 93; with Great Britain, 315-362; broader relations (in brief), 362. *See also* Adams (C.F.), Bright (John), Confederate diplomacy, mediation, Seward.

Ireland, 324; Mrs. Stowe's letter to women of, 321.

Iuka, Miss., battle of, 364, 365.

Jackson, Miss., 364.

Japan, Lincoln-Seward policy toward (mentioned), 362.

Johnson, Andrew, in Congress, 85; role played by Thaddeus Stevens in his impeachment, 102 and n.

Johnson, Herschel V. of Georgia, and secession ("sick at heart"), 156.

Johnson, Reverdy, criticizes Sumner, 105; receives letter from Lincoln on Union sentiment in Maryland, 208.

Johnson, Waldo P., senator from Missouri, joins Confederate army, expelled, 106.

Johnston, John D., stepbrother of Lincoln, 438.

Johnston, Joseph E., Confederate general, controversy with Jefferson Davis, 364; replaces Bragg, 389.

Jones, George W., prisoner of state, 205.

Judd, S. Corning, on Sons of Liberty in Illinois, 193 and n.

Julian, George W., opposes Lincoln administration, 136, 137.

Kane, George P., head of Baltimore police, 159.

Kansas, and maintenance of *posse comitatus* as quasi-military force. *See* Fain, W. P.

Keckley, Mrs. Elizabeth, cited, 59 n.

Kelley, William D., on Lincoln story, 70; describes Lincoln, 396-397.

Kemp, *In re*, 168 n.

Kennedy, Anthony, senator from Maryland, 88.

Kentucky, Union loyalty, 115; election of 1863, 245-247; "liberation" abandoned by Bragg (1862), 363.

Kerr, Orpheus C. ("Office Seeker," Robert H. Newell), humor enjoyed by Lincoln, 60.

Kirk, *vs.* Lynd (on confiscation), 122 n.

Kirkwood, Samuel J., governor of Iowa, and enforcement of draft, 299.

Kneedler *vs.* Lane (conscription), (1863), 274.

Knights of the Golden Circle, 188 ff., 190-192; in Michigan, 196 n.; mentioned, 256, 268. *See also* Copperheads.

Knownothing party, in speakership vote, 1860, 92 n.

Knoxville, Tenn., occupied by Burnside, 366; military importance of, 382.

Ku Klux Klan, 188.

Labor, Lincoln's views, 147 and n.

Labor in Britain, and American question, 356.

Laird rams (ironclads intended for Confederacy), withheld by Britain, 331 ff., 348.

Lamon, Ward Hill, and Lincoln's personal safety, 9-10 and 10 n.; accompanies Lincoln on army visit, 17; White House social activities, 24; reports Lincoln story, 80; on relations between Lincoln and Thaddeus Stevens, 103-104; mentioned, 231.

Land-grant college act, 144.

Lane, James H., Union general, guards Lincoln, 9; mentioned, 413-414.

Latham, Milton S., senator from California, condemns arbitrary arrests, 224.

Leavitt, Judge Humphrey H., in Vallandigham case, 221-224, 229-230.

Lee, Robert E., estate seized, 124 n.; foreign effect of failure to crush McClellan, 328; after Chancellorsville, 364; mentioned, 368, 376.

Lee, S. P., United States admiral, and peace movement (1863), 243.

Legal tender act, constitutionality, 108-109.

Liberal Republicans, 95 n.

Library of Congress, receives Lincoln Papers, 431 ff.

Lieber, Francis, career, 172; army code ("General Orders No. 100"), 172-173, 181.

LINCOLN, ABRAHAM, problems in 1863, 1; formula for restoring peace and union, 1; stories, 2, 61 ff.; Gettysburg trip, 3; varioloid, 4 and n., 387; solicitude for Mrs. Lincoln, 4 n., 20, 36; daily presidential routine, 5 ff.; attention to correspondence, 5 and n.; personality and habits described by Hay, 6-7; attitude toward personal safety, 7-10; grief at Willie's death, 10; impromptu speeches, 10-12; appearance on horseback, 12-15; ceremonial duties, 15 ff.; travels, 17-19; the Lincolns (husband, wife, and children in White House days), 20-41; social duties, 22 ff.; his children, 27-28, 31-36; invitations (those invited value prestige, not equality), 30-31; plans change in private secretaries, 38-39; solicitude for personal distress and hardship, 44-45; and "military necessity" (forbids military seizure of property), 44-45; autograph requests, 45; and Indian troubles,

46-47, 48; accessibility, 48-49; endurance and humor under strain, 49-51; and Jefferson Davis, compared, 50; non-war problems, 51; praises Owen Lovejoy, 52-53; and original draft of emancipation proclamation, 53 and n.; and Northern trading within Southern lines, 54-55 and notes; response to attempts at personal exploitation, 54-56; and Thanksgiving, 56-58; laugh described, 59; his humor, 59-82 (in writings, 66 ff.); disclaims Grant-and-whiskey remark, 62; personal influence in his administration, 64; relations with cabinet, 64; on internal improvements, 66 and n.; his own comment on Gettysburg speech, 67 and n.; on his Black Hawk War services, 78; and Mark Twain, compared, 74-77; humor laboriously explained by Herndon, 71-74; personal magnetism, 27, 81-82; disliked title "Honorable," 87; attitude toward Sumner, 88; comment on Roscoe Conkling, 95 and n.; and Thaddeus Stevens, 103-104; and Republican wartime policy, 111-112, 141-142; problem of party leadership, 111-112; and war aims, 114 ff.; leniency, 115; denounced for contradictory reasons, 115.

Opposes long, remorseless struggle, 116-117; intended veto of confiscation bill, 119; slight enforcement of confiscation legislation, 120; and intraparty contests for Congress, 130 ff.; feeling as to Congress, 130; "within one mile of Hell" (the Capitol), 132; pained by war committee, 134; lack of coöperation between Lincoln and Congress, 135 ff.; welcomed recess of Congress, 140; sad interview reported by Browning, 140-141; almost "without a party" (comment of McClure), 141; took over presidential powers, 142; and agriculture, 143 ff.; messages to Congress, 146-148; problem of war power, 149 ff.; made presidency a dominant factor, 150; unusual powers of, 152; stretched constitutional power of executive, 153; emergency acts sustained in Prize Cases, 153 ff.; confers with officials (April 1861) as to moving troops, 159; expansion of executive functions, 171 ff.; and "presidential legislation," 171 ff.; presidential justice, 173-174; vetoes Wade-Davis bill, 175; not eager for arbitrary power, 176; concern as to civil guarantees shown in message of July 4, 1861, 176-177; proclamation against vessels resisting blockade, 179; shrewdness and realism in treating legal problems, 182-183; and Chief Justice Taney (never an open break), 183; directs release of political prisoners, 198-199; suspends habeas corpus privilege, 200 ff.; and arbitrary arrests in Maryland, 1861, 207-208 and n.; instructions on arbitrary arrests, 207-211; lyceum address quoted on need of respect for law, 210; opposes witch hunts, favors full safeguards as to loyalty, 210-211.

Regrets Vallandigham's arrest, 218; commutes Vallandigham's sentence, 218-219; on habeas corpus procedure, 223-224; letter to Corning, 210, 226-228 and 228 n.; and military emancipation, 232; on civil and miltary power, 231-238; policy on freedom of speech, 231; disapproves of newspaper suppression in Indiana, 236; and suppression of Chicago *Times*, 233-238, 269; on freedom of the press, 233-238; and fundamental civil rights, 237-238; and peace movement (1863), 243 ff.; writes to Mrs. Lincoln on Kentucky election, 247; and governmental crisis in Indiana, 248-249; on attitude of legislatures in Indiana and Illinois, 252; and huge mass meeting at Springfield, 254 ff.; and Conkling letter of August 1863, 254 ff.; and emancipation as war aim, 260; position on Mexican War, 266-267; replies to Ohio committee, 266-268; and New York election of 1863, 279; and Montgomery Blair on reconstruction, 283; revokes part of General Schenck's orders in Maryland, 285; proclamation suspending habeas corpus privilege (Sept. 15, 1863), 288; call for 300,000 volunteers (Oct. 17, 1863), 290; political letters of 1863, 290; to Zachariah Chandler (Nov. 20, 1863) on election victories, 291; affected by state elections, 290-291; and Seymour, 292-314; and draft in New Jersey, 299; on Supreme Court, 300; inaugural of 1861, 300 and n., 440; and changing American system (states becoming a nation), 301; reported readiness to support Seymour for presidency, 312-313; summary of relations with Seymour, 314; and foreign relations, 315 ff., 338, 362; deals with difficult *Peterhoff* case, 336-338; not a dictator, 301, 338;

characterized by London *Times*, 345-346; wishes Burnside to reënforce Rosecrans, 366; and Unionists of Knoxville, 366; telegraphs wife results of Chickamauga, 367-368; offers rank of major to Ben Hardin Helm, 368; informs his wife of Helm's death, 368; sorrow at death of Helm, 369; and Mrs. Helm, 370 ff.; petitioned by eastern Tennessee, 373-374; gives assurance to Rosecrans (Aug. 10, 1863), 374; as military strategist, 375-376; telegram to Hurlbut, 376; reluctant to give military advice to Halleck, 376; considers Lee's army chief objective (1863), 376; patient with Meade, 377; urges that Meade attack Lee (Oct. 1863), 377; cheers Rosecrans, 378; attends night conference after Chickamauga, 378; separates Slocum and Hooker, 380-381.

Regard for Grant, 382-383, 389, 411; proclaims days to give thanks for military victories, 390; reports to Congress on favorable international relations, 391; reconstruction program, 387, 391-392; message to Congress, Dec. 8, 1863, 391-392; confidence at end of 1863, 392; numerous descriptions of appearance and personality, 393-427; crudeness exaggerated, 394, 406-407; elephants offered by King of Siam, 407-408; tact and consideration, 408 ff.; letter to General Robert Anderson, 409; letter to General Meade unsent, 409-410; disappointment following Gettysburg, 409-410; human dealing with his generals, 409-419, 422-423; letter to Hooker, 411; tactful letter to Thurlow Weed, 412; answers General Hunter's "ugly" letter, 413; and General Lane, 413-414; writes General Schenck, 414; writes General Rosecrans on army rank, 414; attitude toward General Milroy, 414-415; deals with Carl Schurz, 415-419; relation to governors, 420-422; writes Governor Magoffin, 420-421; attacked by Republican senators (trying to "break him down"), 421; answers "cross letter" of Governor Gamble, 422; writes General S. R. Curtis, 422-423; friendship with colored people, 423; and Frederick Douglass, 423-424; rebukes Senator Pomeroy, 425; tactful reprimand of Captain J. Madison Cutts, 425-427; Mexican War speech, 439; did not use ghost writers, 441; and Sumter ex-

LINCOLN, ABRAHAM (*Continued*)
pedition, 441-442; and French liberals,
442-443.
Lincoln's administration, and Congress,
83 ff., 130 ff.; foreign policy attacked, 93;
and *Trent* affair, 93; and Thaddeus
Stevens, 99-104; remembered for constructive (non-war) achievement, 145 ff.;
"Lincoln's government" (his army, etc.),
150; leniency and tempering of severe
rules, 178; and disloyal societies, 184 ff.;
intelligence system, 191-192; early policy
in arbitrary arrests, 197-198; treatment
of political prisoners, 201-211; and Vallandigham case, 212-238; reported denunciation by Vallandigham, 216-217.
*See also* cabinet.
Lincoln, Mrs. Abraham (Mary Todd Lincoln), worry about Lincoln's safety and
welfare, 8, 36-37; praised by contemporaries, 14, 26-27, 38-41; accompanies
Lincoln on army visits, 17; as First Lady,
20 ff.; refurbishes White House, 20-21;
financial ineptness, 21; physical and
mental health, 21-22, 32-41 *passim;* social graces, 22 ff.; grief at Willie's death,
32 ff.; unjustly persecuted, 36-41; friendliness to Negroes, 37; wartime hospital
services, 37-38; and Lincoln's secretaries,
38-39; defended, 38-41; on Herndon's
Ann Rutledge story, 59 n.; on Lincoln's
laugh, 59 n.; on Lincoln's humor, 81;
learns of Helm's death, 368; loyalty to
Union, 369-370.
Lincoln Papers (Robert Todd Lincoln Collection of the Papers of Abraham Lincoln), 429-446; opening, 435 ff.; appraisal, 437 ff.; letters from prominent
men, 444.
Lincoln, Robert Todd, 31, 35; and Lincoln
Papers, 430-434.
Lincoln, Thomas ("Tad"), son of President, accompanies Lincoln on army
visit, 17-18; closeness to his father, 27-
28, 31-36 *passim;* life in White House,
31 ff.
Lincoln, Thomas, father of President, 438.
Lincoln, William Wallace ("Willie"), son
of President Lincoln, personality, illness,
death, 31 ff.; mentioned, 371.
Lindsay, William S., and Confederate
diplomacy, 342; and Napoleon III, 350.
Liverpool, Beecher in, 321; shipbuilding in
Laird yard, 329.
Lobbying, Lincoln's handling of, 54-56.

Locke, David R. *See* Petroleum V.
Nasby.
London, exhibition in 1862, 147.
London *Daily News*, quoted, 354.
London *Morning Star*, 353-354.
London, *The Times*, and American ques-
tion, 345-347.
Long, Alexander, of Ohio, censured by
House, 106; member Ohio Democratic
committee, 265.
Longstreet, James, Confederate general,
takes two corps from Lee and goes to
Chickamauga, 366; at Chickamauga,
367; sent against Burnside at Knoxville,
373; mentioned, 373.
Lookout Mountain, battle of, 388.
Lothian, Marquis of, 342.
Lovejoy, Owen, Lincoln praises, 52-53.
Loyal Publication Society, 185, 321.
Loyalty, oath, 204, 205; Lincoln favored
full safeguards, 209-211.
Ludlow, Col. W. H., and prisoner ex-
change, 243.
Lyman, Theodore, on politicians, 89.
Lyons, Lord, British minister at Washing-
ton, and *Peterhoff* case, 335, 336.

McCallum, D. C., Union general, superintendent of railroads, 378-379.
McClellan, George Brinton, Union general, headquarters visited by Lincoln,
17; endorses Woodward for governor of
Pennsylvania, 275 and n.; and the situation in Britain, 328.
McClernand, John A., Union general, 257,
425.
McClure, A. K., on Thaddeus Stevens, 101,
103-104; considered Lincoln almost
"without a party," 141; quoted, 277; describes Lincoln, 393-394.
McCorison, J. L., Jr., describes Lincoln,
399.
McDonald, Joseph E., 193.
McDowell, Irvin, Union general, headquarters visited by Lincoln, 17.
McIlvaine, Charles P., Episcopal bishop,
service abroad, 319.
Madison, James, and days of public
thanks, 56.
Magoffin, Beriah, governor of Kentucky,
420-421.
Mails, disposition of, on captured ships,
337.
Maine, new congressmen, 1861, 85; election of 1863, 280.

Mallory, Robert, congressman from Kentucky, mentioned, 101.

Manchester, England, Beecher in, 321; huge meeting in Free Trade Hall (Dec. 1862) and Lincoln's reply, 354, 355.

Mann, A. Dudley, Confederate diplomat, 324, 325, 350.

Mann, Mrs. Horace, Lincoln's letter to, 53.

Marque and reprisal, Confederate letters of, 179.

Marshall, John A., on treatment of political prisoners, 201-203.

Martial law, 151 ff.; overruled in Milligan case, 230-231.

Maryland, turbulent and defiant state of affairs in 1861, 157 ff.; arrest of members of legislature, 159-161, 207-208; civil and military conflict as to fugitive slaves, 231; election of 1863, 280-288; abolition in, 286-287.

Mason, James M., Confederate diplomat, 324; failure of his mission and withdrawal from Britain, 325-326, 348-349; quoted, 341; no intercourse with British government, 349.

Massachusetts, election of 1863, 279-280. See also Andrew, John A.; Sumner, Charles; Wilson, Henry.

Massie, James William, British clergyman, friendliness toward Americans, 355-356.

May, Henry, arrest, 204.

Meade, George Gordon, Union general, headquarters visited by Lincoln, 17; occupies Lincoln's attention before Chickamauga, 376; his uncertainty late in 1863, 376; Lincoln withholds bitter letter to, 409-410.

Mearns, David C., cited, 429, 433.

Mediation, problem of, 324.

Meigs, Montgomery C., quartermaster general, 60.

Memphis, Tenn., 364.

Memphis and Charleston R. R., 365, 387.

Merryman, John (Ex parte Merryman), arbitrary arrest under suspension of habeas corpus, 161 ff.; further history of (beyond law books), 164-165.

Mexico, and Knights of the Golden Circle, 188-189; and Confederate emissaries, 324; Maximilian venture (mentioned), 362.

Michigan, disloyal societies in, 196 and n.

Michigan, University of, 219.

Middle West, "the great body of the republic" (Lincoln's comment), 147; pro-Southern sentiment, 185-186, 191-192, 193; opposition to Lincoln, 251.

Militarism, not traditional American policy, 151.

Military commission, in Vallandigham case, 215-219, 228-230; overruled in Milligan case, 230-231.

"Military necessity," no justification for wanton acts, 151; should be strictly interpreted, 231.

Military operations, western (late 1863), 363.

Military power and civil authority, 221 ff., 231-238; Lincoln's views, 44-45; as to confiscation, 118; subordination of military to civil power, 231; civil significance of President's function as Commander in Chief, 233.

Mill, John Stuart, and American question, 357.

Milligan, Ex parte, in relation to habeas corpus act and release of prisoners, 170; mentioned, 228 n.; quoted as to need for restraining martial law, 231.

Milroy, Robert H., Union general, 414-415.

Milton, George Fort, cited, 184 n.

Milwaukee, 144.

Minnesota, Indian troubles in, 46-47.

Missionary Ridge, battle of, 387-389.

Mississippi River, falls to Union, 364.

Missouri, Drake delegation visits Lincoln, 48-49; and Knights of the Golden Circle, 189; Frémont's action, 232.

Mitchell, Stewart, quoted, 299.

Mobile, Ala., 365.

Monroe Doctrine, 323; Confederate attitude, 326.

Montagu, Robert, Lord, and Confederate cause debated in British Parliament, 350.

Moore, George, British consul at Richmond, expelled, 349.

Moran, Benjamin, on legation staff in London, 320, 321; on British emancipation meetings, 355.

Morgan, John Hunt, Confederate raider, no help from "Copperheads," 191.

Morrill, Justin S., representative from Vermont, 105, 144.

Morton, Oliver P., governor of Indiana, and "Copperheads," 191, 193; asks Hascall's removal, 236 n.; and party situation (1863), 248 ff.; his virtual dictatorship, 248-249; partisan emphasis on his friendliness to soldiers, 250; and loyalty

Morton, Oliver P. (*Continued*)
of southern Indiana (Democratic area),
250.

Motley, John Lothrop, quoted, 347.

Mount Vernon, Ohio, Vallandigham
speech at, 215.

Mumford, William B., executed under
regime of B. F. Butler at New Orleans,
179 n.

Murfreesboro, Tenn., battle of, 365.

Napoleon III, emperor of France, 319; and
Confederate diplomacy, 342; and diplomatic schemes of Roebuck and Lindsay,
350.

Nasby, Petroleum V. (David R. Locke),
and Lincoln's humor, 60-61, 70; describes Lincoln, 402.

National Academy of Sciences, 146.

Negroes, friendliness toward Mrs. Lincoln,
37; equality, suffrage, disavowed by prewar Republicans, 52 and n.; inconsistent
wartime attitudes toward, 60-61; and
Sumner, 89; Illinois constitutional provision to prohibit immigration, 252;
Lincoln's "wish that all men could be
free," 259; in Kentucky, 246; South
Carolina freedman's letter to President,
445.

Negro troops, debated in Congress, 125-
127; and retaliation, 242.

Neutrality, problem of, 318. *And see* international relations.

Nevada, admission to Union, 85.

Nevins, Allan, cited, 58.

Newcastle, England, Gladstone's speech at,
342.

Newcastle, Lord, friendly to the United
States, 328.

Newell, Robert H. *See* Kerr, Orpheus C.

New Hampshire, conscription in, 128-129
and notes; election of 1863, 240.

New Jersey, new congressmen, 1861, 85;
and draft, 299.

Newspapers, report serenade speeches, 12;
criticize summary military arrests, 225;
suppression of, 233-238.

Newton, Isaac, and new department of agriculture, 143.

New York (state), 189th Regiment serenades Lincoln, 11; new congressmen
1861, 85; election of 1863, 278-279; draft
problems in, 295 ff. *See also* Seymour.

New York (city), politics, 1860's, 97; "free

city" proposal, 97; draft riot (July 1863),
294-295.

New York Avenue Presbyterian Church,
Washington, D.C., attended by Lincoln
family, 34, 35 n.

New York *Herald*, varying views of White
House social functions, 28-29; and
Wikoff's intrigues, 38; refutes report of
Lincoln story, 62.

New York *Times*, on Lincoln's trips, 19 and
n.; on Vallandigham case, 230.

New York *Tribune*, 138, 187 and n. *See also*
Greeley, Horace.

Nichols, John W., Lincoln body-guard,
9 and n.

Nicolay, Helen, cited, 5 n., 59 n.

Nicolay, John George, relations with Lincoln, 5, 6-7; on Lincoln's horsemanship,
12-13; on Willie Lincoln's death, 33; and
Mrs. Lincoln, 38-39; envoy of Lincoln to
solve Indian problems, 46-47. *See also*
Nicolay and Hay.

Nicolay and Hay, on "bitter differences"
within Republican party, 291 n.; characterization of Seymour, 296; in error
about troop movement, 379; use of Lincoln Papers, 430, 434, 437, 443.

Nightingale, Florence, 51.

Norfolk, Va., visited by Lincoln, 17, 19.

North, The, factional differences, 113-116;
on use of Negro troops, 125-127; subversive activities, 184-211; division of sentiment in Civil War, 214.

Offutt, Denton, writes Lincoln, 445.

Ohio, pro-Southern sentiment in, 185-186,
191, 192; and Vallandigham case, 213-
238; campaign and election of 1863,
263 ff.

Ohio, Army of the, at Knoxville, 366.

Ohio Committee (Democratic), letter to
Lincoln, 265-266.

Old Capitol Prison, 203, 205-206.

Olin, A. B., representative from New York,
on Constitution in war time, 110.

Order of American Knights, 192; replaced
by Sons of Liberty, 268.

Orth, Godlove S., remarks on duration of
forfeiture (in confiscation debate), 121 n.

Ould, Robert, and prisoner exchange,
242 f.

Owens, Mary, 20.

Paine, Henry W., of Massachusetts, 279
and n.

Palmer, John M., Union general, condemns arbitrary arrests, 224; writes his wife about Chickamauga, 367.

Palmerston, Lord, and Lindsay-Roebuck diplomacy, 351. *And see* Great Britain.

Papal States, and Confederate emissaries, 324.

Pardon, of political prisoners, 198-199.

Parties and partisanship. *See* elections of 1863, and particular parties (Democratic, Knownothing, Republican, Whig). *See also* Union League.

Patterson, Robert, Union general, 425.

Paxson, F. L., cited, 62.

Peace movement in 1863, sponsored by A. H. Stephens, 242-245.

Pemberton, John C., Confederate general, surrender of Vicksburg, 364.

Pendleton, George H., member of Ohio Democratic committee, 265.

Pennington, William, and speakership, 92 and n.

Pennsylvania, election of 1863, 274-278. *See also* Cameron, Curtin, McClure.

Perry, Matthew P., mentioned, 320.

Perryville, Ky., battle of (Oct. 8, 1862), 363.

*Peterhoff*, The (captured British vessel), controversy, 331, 334-338.

*Petrel* (captured Confederate vessel), 179-181.

Piatt, Donn, on Lincoln's stories, 68; describes Lincoln, 394, 403.

Pickens, Francis W., governor of South Carolina, Lincoln's message to, 442.

Pierce, Franklin, letter of condolence to Lincoln on Willie's death, 35-36; target of irresponsible accusation, 195-197 and notes.

Pierrepont, Edwards, on commission to deal with political prisoners, 200.

Pinkerton, Allan, 159, 204.

Pipes, Jeems, humorist, and Lincoln, 61.

Politics, in war time, 1. *And see* elections.

Polk, President James K., target of Lincoln joke, 67; Lincoln's opposition to war policy of, 266.

Polk, Leonidas, Confederate general, 369, 373.

Polk, Trusten, senator from Missouri, expelled, 106.

Pollard, E. A., Richmond editor, quoted, 373.

Pomeroy, Senator Samuel C., 425.

Poore, Ben: Perley, on Lincoln's daily routine, 5; on Mrs. Lincoln, 41; on Wade, 91; on Baker's (Stanton's) secret police, 199.

Pope, John, Union general, deplores summary military arrests, 224-225; international reaction to his defeat, 326; mentioned, 385.

Porter, Fitz-John, Union general, target of war committee, 133.

Porter, G. H., cited, 219 n.

Port Hudson, Miss., 364.

Portland, Maine, as site for prize court, 54.

*Posse comitatus*, not suitable as quasi-military force under Federal marshal to deal with large public disturbance, 162 and n.

Powers, Hiram, statue criticized by Lincoln, 15.

Prescott, Benjamin F., New Hampshire Republican, coaches Miss Dickinson, 241.

President (office, Lincoln in relation to, etc.), Lincoln's personal feeling, 2-4; and Thanksgiving, 56-58; as focus of national unity, 58; question of Lincoln's personal authority, 64; control of his party, 111; problem of presidential leadership, 111-112; relation to Congress, 114, 115, 135 ff.; powers exercised by Lincoln, 142, 152; Lincoln tended to make executive office dominant, 150; constitutional power stretched by Lincoln, 153; extent of executive power, 171 ff.; legislative and judicial functions, 171-174; control of political prisoners, 194-211; as Commander in Chief of army and navy, 232-233; affected by state elections, 290-291.

Press, freedom of, in Civil War, 233-238.

Price, Sterling, Confederate general, 364.

Prisoners, political, arrest of, 194 ff.; control transferred from state to war department, 198-199; number of, 201 and n.; treatment, 201-211; dilemma as to detention or release, 251. *See also* habeas corpus, Vallandigham case.

Prisoners of war, exchange of, and peace movement, 242 ff.

Privateers and privateersmen, treatment of, 154-155.

*Prize Cases* (Lincoln's broad assumption of executive power in 1861), 153 ff.; decided in Lincoln's favor by Supreme Court (including Lincoln's appointees), 154-155.

Prize courts, Welles's comment on sites for, 54.

Property, seizure by provost marshal pre-

Property (Continued) vented by Lincoln, 44-45. See also confiscation.

Provost marshal, Lincoln prevents property seizure by, 44-45.

Pugh, George E., of Ohio, 228; hostility to Lincoln, 232; supporter and running mate of Vallandigham, 264-265.

Putnam, Herbert, 430, 433.

Putnam, Captain, and suppression of Chicago Times, 233-234.

Quakers. See Gurney, Mrs. Eliza P.

Radicals, and Lincoln's policies, 93-94; Roscoe Conkling and, 95 and n.; and war aims, 113 ff.; and dealings in Congress, 141. See also Chandler, committee on conduct of the war, Davis (Henry Winter), Julian, Stevens, Wade.

Railroads, military importance under government control, 379.

Rams (ironclad ships). See Laird rams.

Randall, Ruth Painter, cited, 45 n., 61.

Rapidan River, 366.

Ray, Charles H., cotton trading scheme, 54 and n.

"Rebecca" letters, 76.

Rebellion. See Civil War.

Reconstruction, attitude of Henry Winter Davis, 93; of Roscoe Conkling, 95; Rockville speech of Montgomery Blair (Oct. 3, 1863) in its relation to the President, 282-283. See also Chandler, Julian, radicals, Stevens, Wade, war aims.

Reid, John W., representative from Missouri, joins Confederate army, 106.

Republican party, prewar disavowal of Negro equality and suffrage, 52 and n.; members dislike Lincoln's humor, 60; and Dominican problem, 63; first majority in Congress, 85 ff.; setback in elections of 1862, 86, 225; virtually nonexistent in Kentucky, 246; and Roscoe Conkling, 94-96; role of Thaddeus Stevens, 99-104; and war aims, 113 ff.; wartime policy in relation to Lincoln, 111-112, 141-142; aided by existence of disloyal societies, 193; denounced by Vallandigham, 213-214; managers avoid identification with abolitionists, 214 n.; used Union cause for partisan advantage, 261; adoption of name "Union" party, 273; bitter differences among Republicans, 291 n.; Republican senators attack

Lincoln, 421. See also Congress, elections, radicals.

Retaliation, severe treatment not the purpose of Lincoln government, 179-181; and peace movement, 242 ff.

Reynolds, John, 253.

Reynolds, Joseph J., Union general, letter from Lincoln on unauthorized military seizure of property, 44-45.

Rhode Island, election of 1863, 239.

Richardson, William A., Democrat, senator from Illinois, 232, 253.

Richmond, Dean, 310.

Richmond, Virginia. See Confederacy.

Richmond (Va.) Examiner, comment on Rosecrans, 385.

Richmond (Va.) Sentinel, quoted, 376.

Riddle, Albert G., representative from Ohio, on Congress, 84, 86-87; denounces Holman, 105; predicts end of slavery, 116 n.; his statement that only two men (Isaac Arnold and himself) "openly and everywhere" defended Lincoln, 138; his speech (Feb. 28, 1863) supporting the President, 138-140.

Riot in New York City, 294 ff.

Roberts, Ellis Henry, describes Lincoln and Lincoln home, 397-398.

Robinson, J. F., requires loyalty oath for voters in Kentucky, 246.

Roebuck, John A., and Confederate diplomacy, 342; abortive pro-Confederate motion in British Parliament, 350-351.

Roosevelt, F. D., 152 and n., 441.

Rosecrans, W. S., Union general, and Vallandigham case, 219; success over Price and Van Dorn at Iuka and Corinth, 364; supersedes Buell as head of Army of the Cumberland, 364; at Stone's River, 364; maneuvers and operations near Chattanooga, 365; enters Chattanooga, 366; reports Chickamauga disaster to Halleck, 367; holds Chattanooga (1863), 372; relieved of Chattanooga command, 373, 384; tactful letter from Lincoln, 414.

Rossville, Ga., Rosecrans withdraws to, after Chickamauga, 366.

Rost, Pierre A., Confederate diplomat, 324, 325.

Rothschilds firm, and August Belmont, 320.

Rubery, Alfred, British youth, pardoned by Lincoln, 360-361.

Russell, Earl, British foreign minister, and problem of neutrality, 318; declines communication with Confederate emissaries, 325; and cabinet discussion of American question, 327; and Laird rams, 331 ff.; reported unfriendliness toward James M. Mason, 349; rejoiced in American progress, 353.

Russell, William Howard, describes Lincoln, 400-402.

Russia, and the American struggle, 362.

Sacramento (Calif.) *Union*, 39, 41 n., 66 n.

St. John, Daniel B., opponent of Chauncey Depew in New York election of 1863, 279.

St. Louis *Republican*, on Ohio election of 1863, 273.

Sala, George Augustus, describes Lincoln, 403-405.

Sandburg, Carl, and opening of Lincoln Papers, 435.

Sanders, George N., and Confederate publicity in Britain, 341.

Sanitary Commission (Fair in Chicago) given original of emancipation proclamation, 53 and n.

*Saturday Visiter*, antislavery newspaper, 26.

Schenck, Robert C., Union general, 7 and n., 93; at Baltimore (1863), 280; and election day troubles in Maryland, 284-285; "Order No. 53," 284; Lincoln's courteous letter, 414.

Schurz, Carl, on deterioration of Congress, 84; his unfinished essay on Sumner, 90 n.; relation to Lincoln, 415-419.

Scientists, 146.

Scott, Thomas A., 379.

Scott, Winfield, Union general, advice sought by Lincoln, 17, 19 n.; Lincoln's tactful treatment, 425.

Scripps, John L., embarrasses Lincoln by intraparty contest with Arnold, 130-131.

Seaver, Benjamin Francis, describes Lincoln, 398-399.

Senate, quality assessed, 83-84; leaders in Lincoln's time, 88-92; wartime procedure and customs, 104-107; debate on Negro troops, 125-127; debate on conscription, 127-130.

Seward, Frederick W., describes Lincoln, 400.

Seward, William H., secretary of state, serenade speech, 12; and Lincoln on army visits, 13, 17; and Lincoln's humor, 69, 81; foreign policy opposed by Henry Winter Davis, 93; and Roscoe Conkling,

95; and arbitrary arrests, 194 ff., 203-204; mishandles accusation against ex-President Pierce, 195-197 and notes; current story of his boasting remark as to causing arrests, 197-198; alleged provocative remark to Newcastle, 317, 320; and Laird rams, 332; difficulty with Welles, 243-244, 336; denounced by Anna E. Dickinson, 241; characterized by London *Times*, 345; mentioned, 408, 438-439.

Seymour, Horatio, hostility to Lincoln, 232; and election of 1863 in New York, 278; character and career in brief, 292-293; relations with Lincoln, 292-314; and John A. Dix, 304 ff.; anti-Lincoln associations, 311.

Seymour, John, brother of Horatio, 297-298.

Seymour, Thomas Hart, Democratic candidate for governor of Connecticut (1863), 240.

Shawneetown, Ill., 224.

*Shenandoah*, The, Confederate warship, 329.

Sherman, John, senator from Ohio, 92 n., 94; on conscription act, 128; on President's increase of regular army, 153; on summary arrests, 224.

Sherman, William T., Union general, 99; on effect of Chickamauga, 383; enters fight at Chattanooga, 387; at Missionary Ridge, 388.

Sherman, Mrs. W. T., 387.

Sherman, Willie, son of William T., death of, 387.

Shields, James, Union general, at White House reception, 23-24.

Shutes, Milton H., quoted, 4 n.

Siam, King of, offers elephants to Lincoln, 407-408.

Sickles, Daniel E., Union general, 257, 410.

Silver, David M., cited, 228 n.

Singleton, James W., cotton trading scheme, 54 and n.; hostility to Lincoln, 232.

Slavery, prewar Republican attitude, 52 and n.; Douglas's view (as to territories) derided by Lincoln, 67; and war aims, 113, 116 ff.; as cause of war, 116; Riddle predicts its violent end, 116 n.; Confederate treatment of slavery issue abroad, 340-341. *See also* abolition, fugitive slave acts, Negroes.

Slidell, John, Confederate diplomat, 320,

Slidell, John (*Continued*)
324; disappointing results in France, 326; dissatisfied as to Britain, 348.

Slocum, Henry W., Union general, feud with Hooker, 380-381.

Smith, Goldwin, interview with Lincoln, 69-70; friendship toward United States, 357.

Smith, William Farrar, Union general, 386.

Soldiers, relief of, 53.

Soldiers' Home, 8-9, 378.

Soldier vote, in Ohio (1863), 274.

Sons of Liberty, 192-193.

South, The, potential strength in Congress in 1861, 85 n.; constitutional rights in war time, 109-110; Lincoln's nonvindictive attitude, 114-115; desire for enlightened Southern coöperation, 116; blamed for Civil War, 115; Federal direct tax in, 124 n.

Southern Independence Association of London, 341.

Spain, Lincoln's handling of relations with, 63.

Speech, freedom of, permitted in general under Lincoln (arrests for speech making not the usual procedure), 231. *See also* Vallandingham.

Spence, James, 342.

Spies, Confederate, 187, 198, 205.

Sprague, William, senator from Rhode Island, wedding of, 26.

Sprague, Mrs. William (Kate Chase), 26.

Springfield, Ill., huge mass meeting of September 1863, 253 ff.

Spurgeon, Charles H., British preacher, 357.

Stanton, Edwin M., secretary of war, and schedule for Gettysburg trip, 3; suggestion for Lincoln's protection, 7-8; and Lincoln's army visits, 17, 18; contrasted with Lincoln (as to humor), 69; and question of enforcing habeas corpus act, 170; and arbitrary arrests, 198-211; control of political prisoners, 200-201; and commutation of sentence for Vallandigham, 219; and case of Chicago *Times*, 234, 235; use of troops in New York, 307; and idea of grand military pattern under central control, 375; and military conference of Sept. 23, 1863, 378; favors transfer of two corps to western front, 379; and western strategy, 382; confers with Grant, 383; described as discourteous, uncivil and "disrespectful to the President," 408-409.

State department, resolution of Henry Winter Davis to give House of Representatives control of foreign policy, 93 n.; and arbitrary arrests, 194 ff.

State and Federal relations, and Thanksgiving Day, 56-58; as to conscription, 126-127; in Indiana, 248 ff.

State governors, Lincoln's relations with, 236 and n. *And see* governors.

Stephen, Leslie, 357.

Stephens, Alexander H., sponsors peace movement (1863), 242-245.

Stevens, Thaddeus, representative from Pennsylvania, leadership analyzed, 99-104; personality, role, appearance, 99-104, 106; his part in impeachment of Andrew Johnson, 102 n.; relations with Lincoln, 103-104; and interpretation of Constitution, 110; and war aims, 114; on use of Negro troops, 125; criticizes Lincoln's "hallucination," 136; dictator of caucus, 281.

Stevenson, Robert Louis, quoted, 82.

Stoddard, William O., on Lincoln's mail, 5 and n.; on political and diplomatic phases of White House social functions, 29-31; defends Mrs. Lincoln, 37-38; on persistent visitors, 48; on strange and unnatural wartime atmosphere, 49; on Lincoln's humor, 62.

Stone, Charles P., Union general, guards Lincoln, 8-9; denounced by Roscoe Conkling, 95; victim of committee on conduct of the war, 133.

Stone's River (Murfreesboro), battle of, 364.

Stowe, Harriet Beecher, promotes Union cause, 321.

Stuart, John Todd, requests aid from Lincoln, 42-43; criticizes Lincoln policies, 225.

Substitutes, for army service, 128 ff.

Sumner, Charles, senator from Massachusetts, 84; described and appraised, 88-90; derided by Reverdy Johnson, 105; vote on credit for Negro troops, 127; amendment as to $300 exemption, 127-128; debate with Browning, 175; and *Peterhoff* case, 335; and Lincoln's draft of resolution sent to Bright, 361.

Sumter. *See* Fort Sumter.

Supreme Court, and confiscations acts, 122 ff.; apprehension as to possible decision on habeas corpus suspension, 168-169, 169 n.; Vallandigham case, 228-230; opinion in Milligan case, 230-231.

Swann, Thomas, of Maryland, 281.

Swisshelm, Mrs. Jane Grey (antislavery journalist), impressions of Lincoln family, 26-28.

*Tallahassee,* The, Confederate warship, 329.

Tammany, 97.

Taney, Roger B., Chief Justice of the United States, target of Wade's joke, 65; opinion in Merryman case (suspension of habeas corpus), 161-164; comment by Lincoln, 178; no part in Vallandigham case, 229.

Taylor, Bayard, lecture heard by Lincoln, 17.

Teillard, Dorothy Lamon, cited, 10.

Temple, Wayne C., cited, 66 n.

Tennessee, people aided by Lincoln, 44; Bragg returns to (1862), 363; military operations, 364 ff.; importance of eastern Tennessee in 1863, 365; freed of armed insurrectionists, 374.

Tennessee, Army of the, 364 ff.

Thanksgiving, Lincoln and, 56-58.

Thomas, Benjamin F., representative from Massachusetts, on Constitution in war time, 110; on war aims, 114-115.

Thomas, George H., Union general, "Rock of Chickamauga," 366-367; replaces Rosecrans, 384; at Missionary Ridge, 388.

Thomas, Lorenzo, Union general, 43.

Thompson, George, British antislavery leader, quoted, 354-355.

Tilden, Samuel J., 307.

Todd, Alexander, brother of Mrs. Lincoln, killed, 370.

Todd, David, brother of Mrs. Lincoln, killed, 370.

Todd, Emilie. *See* Helm, Emilie Todd.

Todd, George, brother of Mrs. Lincoln, 370.

Todd, Levi, brother of Mrs. Lincoln, death of, 372.

Todd, Lockwood, cousin of Mrs. Lincoln, guards White House, 9.

Todd, Mary. *See* Lincoln, Mrs. Abraham.

Todd, Samuel, brother of Mrs. Lincoln, killed, 370.

Tories. *See* Conservative party.

Treason and confiscation, 118; and purpose of Lincoln government, 180-183.

Trent affair, 89, 93, 99, 315, 334; part played by Bright, 361.

Trumbull, Lyman, mentioned, 108 n.; and confiscation, 118 ff.

Turner, Jonathan B., and land-grant college act, 144.

Twain, Mark, and Lincoln, compared, 74-77.

Union (cause of), aided by Lincoln's Thanksgiving proclamation, 56-58; as "war aim," 113 ff.; considered indispensable to peace, 245. *See also* Vallandigham.

Union army. *See* army.

Union League, 185, 193, 237, 242, 273; worked for Republican triumph, 261; misleading pledge to support "Administration," 280-281.

Union Pacific Railroad, 47.

United States Military Academy, Lincoln's interest in appointments to, 55.

Vallandigham, Clement L., 97-98, 179, description and career, 212-214; Mt. Vernon speech, 216-217; on Civil War aims, 214, 216-217; tried and sentenced by military commission, 216-218; symbol of civil rights, 218 n.; decision by Supreme Court (*Ex parte* Vallandigham), 228-230; comment on the case, 230-233; runs for governor of Ohio, 219-220, 263 ff.; in postwar period, 237 n.; regrets Lincoln's assassination, 237 n.; and Confederate peace movement of 1863, 245; prisoner of state, 264; supreme commander of Sons of Liberty (1864), 268; escapes and appears in Canada, 271; opposed by "War Democrats" of his own party, 271-272.

Van Dorn, Earl, Confederate general, 364.

Veto, of Wade-Davis bill, 175.

Victoria, Queen, 352.

Virginia, "restored," in Congress, 85, 88; confiscations in, 124 n.

Virginia, Ill., political meeting, 255.

Voorhees, Daniel W., representative from Indiana, characterized, 98; hostility to Lincoln, 232; speaks at Springfield, Ill., 253; supports Vallandigham, 272.

Wade, Benjamin F., senator from Ohio, joke concerning Taney, 65; described and characterized, 90-91; attacks Cowan, 104.

Wade-Davis bill, vetoed, 175.

Wade-Davis manifesto (anti-Lincoln), 136-137.

Wadsworth, James S., Union general, 231.

Walker, Robert J., promotes Union cause abroad, 322.

Wallace, William H. L., of Ottawa, Ill., at White House reception, 22.

War aims (difficulty of using war as instrument of policy, discussion in Congress, attitude of Lincoln), 113 ff.

War department, visited by Lincoln, 6; control of political prisoners, 198-211. See also Stanton.

War power, under American Constitution, 108-110; in a democracy, 149 ff.; Sumner-Browning debate (does Congress or President possess the war power?), 175.

Ward, Artemus (Charles Farrar Browne), humor enjoyed by Lincoln, 61.

Warner, J. R., lecture heard by Lincoln, 17 and n.

Washburne, E. B., congressman from Illinois, 100, 102, 106; and gift of Bright photograph, 360.

Washington, D. C., and Lincoln's safety, 8-10; social life and White House functions, 29-31; inadequate sanitation, 32; unjust criticism of Mrs. Lincoln, 36-41; war emergency and danger in April 1861, 157.

Washington (D.C.) Daily Morning Chronicle, on White House party, 22-23.

Washington, George, attitude toward presidency, 2; and days for public thanks, 56.

Waterbury, Nelson J., and draft in New York, 302 f.

Watt, John, White House gardener, 38.

Wayne, James Moore, of Georgia, Supreme Court justice, Unionist, career and importance in Prize Cases, 155-156; opinion in Vallandigham case, 228-230 and 228 n.

Webster, Daniel, and Mexican War, 267.

Weed, Thurlow, and Lincoln's possible support of Seymour for President (for 1864), 312-313; contacts in Britain, 319; embarrassment to Lincoln, 408; receives tactful letter from Lincoln, 412.

Weik, Jesse W., Herndon's letter to, 73.

Welles, Gideon, secretary of the navy, diary cited, 4 n.; visits to war office, 6; disapproves Lincoln's army visits, 18; criticizes White House social arrangements, 25; and Hamlin request, 53-54; records Lincoln story, 63; his appraisal of Congress,

83; on Henry Winter Davis, 94; complains of congressional treatment of naval legislation, 108; on cabinet discussion of Vallandigham case, 225; and suppression of Chicago Times, 234, 235; on civil and military power, 235; and Stephens peace mission, 243; and Peterhoff case, 335 ff.; criticizes Seward, 336.

Welles, Mrs. Gideon, letter from Mrs. Lincoln, 20.

Welling, J. C., Lincoln's letter to, 5 n.

Wentworth, John, of Chicago, elected to Congress, 131 and n.

West Point. See United States Military Academy.

West Virginia, in Congress, 1861, 85; Union loyalty, 115.

Wharncliffe, Lord, 342.

Whig Party, support sought by Republicans, 52 n.

Whipple, Amiel W., funeral attended by Lincoln, 16.

White House, Lincoln's daily routine in, 4 ff.; Lincoln family life, 20 ff.; social activities, 22 ff.

Whitman, Walt, describes Lincoln, 14-15, 399-400.

Wickliffe, Charles A., and election for governor of Kentucky, 246.

Wikoff, Henry, intrigues against Mrs. Lincoln, 38.

Wilderness campaign, Lincoln's anxiety during, 50.

Wilkes, Charles (of United States navy), and Peterhoff, 334; trial and sentence, 337.

Willey, Waitman T., of West Virginia, blames South for war, 115-116.

Willkie, Philip, cited, 111 n.

Wills, David, 3 n.

Wilson, James F., representative from Iowa, and confiscation legislation, 120-121.

Wilson, Henry, senator from Massachusetts, 9, 101, 104, 232; characterized, 90; dislikes Lincoln's humor, 69-70; on use of Negro troops, 126; unhelpful praise of President, 137-138.

Wilson, Robert, senator from Missouri, 88.

Wilson, Woodrow, and Congress, 135 and n.; mentioned, 152; and habeas corpus (no suspension), 152; messages in person before Congress, 441.

Winder, William H., prisoner of state, 204-205.

Wolfe, James, British general, 62.

Women, Lincoln's concern for working women of Philadelphia, 46; Confederate spies, 205.

Wood, Fernando, appearance and personality, 98; opposition to Lincoln administration, 96-98, 106, 232.

Woodward, George W., chief justice of supreme court of Pennsylvania (had declared conscription law unconstitutional), opposes Curtin as candidate for governor (1863), 274 ff.; endorsed by McClellan; 275 n.

Wright, Hendrick B., representative from Pennsylvania, on interpretation of the Constitution, 109.

Yamashita case, 152 n.

Yancey, William L., Confederate diplomat, 324, 325.

Yates, Richard, governor of Illinois, 71; prorogues anti-Lincoln legislature, 252; signs call for Springfield mass meeting, 254.

Young, Brigham, 47.

Young, James Harvey, cited, 17 n.